THE MEMOIR OF EDNAH SHEPARD THOMAS

PERSPECTIVES ON WRITING
Series Editors, Susan H. McLeod and Rich Rice

The Perspectives on Writing series addresses writing studies in a broad sense. Consistent with the wide ranging approaches characteristic of teaching and scholarship in writing across the curriculum, the series presents works that take divergent perspectives on working as a writer, teaching writing, administering writing programs, and studying writing in its various forms.

The WAC Clearinghouse, Colorado State University Open Press, and University Press of Colorado are collaborating so that these books will be widely available through free digital distribution and low-cost print editions. The publishers and the Series editors are committed to the principle that knowledge should freely circulate. We see the opportunities that new technologies have for further democratizing knowledge. And we see that to share the power of writing is to share the means for all to articulate their needs, interest, and learning into the great experiment of literacy.

Recent Books in the Series

Laura R. Micciche, *Acknowledging Writing Partners* (2017)

Seth Kahn, William B. Lalicker, and Amy Lynch-Biniek (Eds.), *Contingency, Exploitation, and Solidarity: Labor and Action in English Composition* (2017)

Barbara J. D'Angelo, Sandra Jamieson, Barry Maid, and Janice R. Walker (Eds.), *Information Literacy: Research and Collaboration across Disciplines* (2017)

Justin Everett and Cristina Hanganu-Bresch (Eds.), *A Minefield of Dreams: Triumphs and Travails of Independent Writing Programs* (2016)

Chris M. Anson and Jessie L. Moore (Eds.), *Critical Transitions: Writing and the Questions of Transfer* (2016)

Joanne Addison and Sharon James McGee, *Writing and School Reform: Writing Instruction in the Age of Common Core and Standardized Testing* (2016)

Lisa Emerson, *The Forgotten Tribe: Scientists as Writers* (2016)

Jacob S. Blumner and Pamela B. Childers, *WAC Partnerships Between Secondary and Postsecondary Institutions* (2015)

Nathan Shepley, *Placing the History of College Writing: Stories from the Incomplete Archive* (2015)

Asao B. Inoue, *Antiracist Writing Assessment Ecologies: An Approach to Teaching and Assessing Writing for a Socially Just Future* (2015)

Theresa Lillis, Kathy Harrington, Mary R. Lea, and Sally Mitchell (Eds.), *Working with Academic Literacies: Case Studies Towards Transformative Practice* (2015)

THE MEMOIR OF EDNAH SHEPARD THOMAS

Edited by David Stock

The WAC Clearinghouse
wac.colostate.edu
Fort Collins, Colorado

University Press of Colorado
upcolorado.com
Louisville, Colorado

The WAC Clearinghouse, Fort Collins, Colorado 80523–1040

University Press of Colorado, Louisville, Colorado 80027

© 2017 by the family of Ednah Shepard Thomas. This work is licensed under a Creative Commons Attribution-NonCommercial-NoDerivatives 4.0 International.

ISBN: 978-1-64215-009-4 (PDF) | 978-1-64215-010-0 (ePub) | 978-1-60732-863-6 (pbk.)

Library of Congress Cataloging-in-Publication Data

Names: Stock, David, editor.

Title: The memoir of Ednah Shephard Thomas / edited by David Stock.

Description: Fort Collins, Colorado : WAC Clearinghouse ; Boulder, Colorado University Press of Colorado, [2017]

Identifiers: LCCN 2017059423| ISBN 9781607328636 (pbk.) | ISBN 9781642150100 (epub)

Subjects: LCSH: Thomas, Ednah Shepard. | Women educators—Wisconsin—Madison—Biography. | University of Wisconsin. Department of English—History. | University of Wisconsin—Madison—History. | English language—Rhetoric—Study and teaching (Higher)—Wisconsin—Madison—History—20th century. | Report writing—Study and teaching (Higher)—Wisconsin—Madison—History—20th century. | Writing centers—Administration.

Classification: LCC LA2317.T4653 M46 2017 | DDC 371.10092 [B] —dc23 LC record available at https://lccn.loc.gov/2017059423

Copyeditors: David Stock, Susan H. McLeod, and Mike Palmquist
Designer: Mike Palmquist
Series Editors: Susan H. McLeod and Rich Rice

The WAC Clearinghouse supports teachers of writing across the disciplines. Hosted by Colorado State University, and supported by the Colorado State Univeristy Open Press, it brings together scholarly journals and book series as well as resources for teachers who use writing in their courses. This book is available in digital formats for free download at wac.colostate.edu.

Founded in 1965, the University Press of Colorado is a nonprofit cooperative publishing enterprise supported, in part, by Adams State University, Colorado State University, Fort Lewis College, Metropolitan State University of Denver, Regis University, University of Colorado, University of Northern Colorado, Utah State University, and Western State Colorado University. For more information, visit upcolorado.com.

CONTENTS

Acknowledgments vii
Foreword ix
    Susan H. McLeod
Introduction to the Memoir xiii
    David Stock
Biographical Outline 3
Foreword 5
Forebears 11
Harvard Avenue 29
Brookline High School 43
Mount Holyoke 53
Bryn Mawr: September 1923 to June 1924 81
Danielson: September 1924 to June 1925 91
Wisconsin: September 1925 to June 1927 107
New Haven: September 1927 to June 1928 119
Settling Down: 1928 to 1932 127
Domesticity: 1932 to 1943 151
World War II: December 1941 to August 1945 191
Transition: September 1945 to September 1950 251
Construction: 1950–1966 297
Demolition: Sept 1966 to August 1970 385
William Lenehan: A Reminiscence 479
Lunch at the Madison Club: May 12, 1986, Or the King and I 481
Works Cited 487
Afterword 489
    David Fleming

ACKNOWLEDGMENTS

Many people made this publication possible and merit much thanks for their contributions.

First, to Ednah Thomas's children, for their generosity in permitting publication of the memoir: Hannah Morehouse, Tom Thomas, and Bill Thomas. A special thank-you to Bill and his wife, Kathy, for graciously welcoming me into their home (formerly Ednah's) in Madison, Wisconsin and answering questions about Ednah, and to James Thomas, Ednah's grandson, who took time to share his recollections of Ednah with me.

Second, to Ednah's colleagues and friends who generously agreed to share their time and their recollections of Ednah with me: Jim Nelson, Margaret Lacy, and Charles Scott.

Third, to my colleagues: Brad Hughes, for inviting me to join this editorial project, arranging contact with family and friends of Ednah's, and providing kind encouragement; Susan McLeod, for sharing her recollections about Ednah and about the University of Wisconsin-Madison English Department and Freshman English Program, assisting with editing, and constant support and determination in bringing this project to completion; Mike Palmquist, from the WAC Clearinghouse, for showing interest in publishing Ednah's memoir, assisting with digitizing and transcribing the memoir, and providing additional resources and support to see the project through to publication; David Null, Director of University Archives and Records Management at UW-Madison, for providing access to a range of documents and resources needed to provide context for many references in the memoir, securing a copy of the memoir in the university archives, and responding to my continuous requests for additional information or documentation.

Lastly, I gratefully acknowledge financial support provided by the Brigham Young University College of Humanities to assist in conducting research for this project.

—David Stock

FOREWORD

Susan H. McLeod
University of California, Santa Barbara

I am delighted to write a foreword to the Memoir of Ednah Shepard Thomas, for two reasons. First, these pages give us an in-depth look at what it was to be a Writing Program Administrator during the period from after World War II up to the time of the early 1970s, a time for which we have little in the way of documentation for the work of early WPAs. When she took over the job of coordinating Freshman English, it involved little more than arranging TAs teaching schedules so that they did not conflict with their graduate seminars. Although at that time a male faculty member always held the title of Director of Freshman English at the University of Wisconsin (see her reminiscence of William Lenehan, an addendum to the Memoir), it is clear from the description of her duties that Thomas added to her scheduling job much of the work that we now associate with directing a writing program: training and supervising TAs, advising students, working out curriculum, coordinating placement in appropriate writing classes, and working on issues of writing assessment (norming TA's grading of papers, for example). It is also clear from what she writes that she was a pioneer in the teaching of writing: for example, she insisted that individual student papers not be graded, but that the whole of the student's work should be looked at for progress when deciding a grade—an early version of the portfolio system. Her undergraduate degree from Mt. Holyoke was in composition, rather than literature; she had studied classical rhetoric and as she states, she was an avowed Aristotelian; this fact influenced her teaching and her training of teachers. She wrote one of the first handbooks on how to evaluate student themes, a booklet that became a University of Wisconsin Press all-time bestseller (Thomas, 1962). One sentence from that publication rings as true today as it did then when discussing the assessment of writing: "No student should be left without hope and no student should be left without challenge" (v). With her colleague Ed Lacy she wrote a composition textbook, published in 1951. She visited the University of Iowa to learn about the Writing Center there (which started in 1945). She took part in the federally funded Commission on English, leading institutes for teachers. She consulted Paul Diederich of the Educational Testing Service about large-scale assessment for purposes of placement. The work of a WPA at that time, to use David Schwalm's (2002) distinction, was a task rather than a position; as such, it was rarely documented. Because she was in charge of Freshman English

Susan H. McLeod

for such a long period of time, this record of her work and how it changed over the years—as enrollments skyrocketed—is valuable historical information.

The second, more personal reason is that I knew Mrs. Thomas, as I shall always think of her;[1] I was beginning my academic career as she was finishing hers. She was in charge of TA training when I arrived in Madison for doctoral work in 1968, and I (perhaps like many) learned more from her than I realized at that time. (In fact, I was fortunate to be at a school that actually had such a program, since I found that many of my contemporaries doing doctoral work at other universities were simply given a handbook and told to go teach.) We had several days of orientation, as she describes in these pages, as well as a syllabus, and a faculty supervisor, in my case, Joyce Steward, who visited our classes and gave us feedback on our teaching. The new TAs also met weekly with an experienced "Master" TA, a support program I found very helpful.

One memory from that long-ago orientation session she ran stands out: Mrs. Thomas went over the issue of evaluating themes at some length, emphasizing the importance of positive comments and discouraging mere error-hunting and correcting; she ended by showing us an example of a recent phenomenon—the idea that computers could grade papers. It was a paper, as I recall, from Project Essay Grade, or PEG, supported by the College Board and begun in the mid-1960s. It focused only on linguistic elements and as such was, as she pointed out, quite inadequate. She would, I think, enjoy pointing out the inadequacies of the present systems for computer grading. I also remember dinner at her home in Frost Woods with my Master Teaching Assistant and the rest of his group—what must have been one of the last of those gatherings. As she says, her door was always open and we knew she was available to deal with any issue we had; she was no-nonsense in her approach to administration and did not suffer fools gladly, but she was patient with and kind to rookie teachers who wanted to do well in the classroom.

Although she was a pioneer in many ways and was herself was a gifted teacher, the course that she developed, supervised, and finally helped do away with at Wisconsin was what we now call current-traditional, as was then the case in higher education almost universally. The late 1960s and early 1970s was a period of enormous social upheaval, a time of questioning the status quo. It is clear that Mrs. Thomas, at the end of her career, was not happy about questioning what she had

---

1 At the time I was a graduate student at the University of Wisconsin, the faculty members were all known by Mr., Miss, or Mrs., as were the students—I called her Mrs. Thomas, she called me Mrs. McLeod. Unlike the school where I did my undergraduate work, the English Department at Wisconsin made no distinction in title between faculty who had the doctorate and faculty like Mrs. Thomas who did not. It seems quaint now, in these more casual times, but it was an indication of the fact that the department did make an attempt to be egalitarian in terms of nomenclature, for students as well as faculty. As a TA in the department, I was taught to call on my undergraduate students in the same way, which they tolerated but I think must have found amusing at the time.

taken a lifetime to build. Many of the TAs who were my contemporaries questioned everything about the class, but most of those I knew sincerely wanted to improve it. (The Master Teaching Assistant Program that Mrs. Thomas set up had, ironically enough, facilitated the conversations about changing the class to have some input from those of us who taught it.) The entire idea of questioning the authority of the department was not one that the older faculty in the department could stomach; her earlier descriptions of the department as "one happy family" give some insight into how patriarchal it was. Her memoir is therefore an interesting companion piece to David Fleming's (2011) book, *From Form to Meaning: Freshman Composition and the Long Sixties, 1957–1974*, since it gives a privately voiced faculty point of view about why first-year composition was abolished at the University of Wisconsin in the late 1960s. As such, it is at odds with the official version for the abolition given out by the department at the time, and reiterated by some of the faculty later in interviews that are part of the University of Wisconsin Oral History Program: viz., that incoming freshman had sufficient writing skills and no longer needed a universally required course, and that such instruction as they might need was better provided by their departments (Fleming, 2011). Instead, she describes faculty members acting like angry parents disciplining rebellious children by taking away their allowance.

When reading her chapter entitled "Demolition" it is important to remember how chaotic the late 1960s and early 1970s were in Madison. Two books that provide some background about the period are *They Marched Into Sunlight* (Maraniss, 2003) and *Rads* (Bates, 1992). The much-discussed generation gap of the times was evident not only between the tenured members of the department and the TAs, but also between those same tenured members and their younger, more radical colleagues. One of the major reasons for this gap—the opposition to the Viet Nam War and the draft—is mentioned only in passing in her discussion of that time, and I wonder if she really understood that opposition. Her generation's war was a very different one, as her chapter on World War II shows, and it must have been difficult for those who lived through that war to see my generation's opposition to the war in Southeast Asia as anything other than unpatriotic. Her tone in writing about this period is in many places bitter; it must have seemed to her that all she valued in her professional life was being questioned, and also difficult for her to understand that not all TAs under her supervision were part of the rioting mob. Some were quite sincere about solidarity with the working class but amazingly naive: I remember that a few TAs who went out on strike were astonished that they did not get paid for the time they were on the picket lines rather than in class. The addendum to this memoir, "The King and I," is included because it was written at a more mellow time, and also because it shows how highly she was regarded by many of her former students.

It is also important to keep in mind that this memoir was written at a time when the civil rights movement and the women's movement were just beginning to influence the way one thought and wrote about issues of race, class, and gender. We can smile at the reference to the preparation of the English Department's afternoon tea as being "perfectly democratic" because it was prepared by the wives of both faculty and TAs (no one then would have dreamed of telling the male faculty to fix their own tea). It is more difficult to read about the casual anti-Semitism and racism that went unnoticed in the community: that no one (except Mrs. Thomas) was willing to rent a room to a German refugee because he was a Jew, or that her son's elementary school put on a minstrel show for entertainment. She describes herself proudly as a Victorian in some ways; it is useful to keep this description in mind and read her memoir as we would read her favorite author, Dickens, keeping in mind that she, like he, was very much of her own time and place, sharing the opinions and prejudices of many of her contemporaries.

I said that I learned more from her than I knew at the time, since when I was a young doctoral student I had no idea that I would in the future be a writing program administrator. The most important lesson was one she describes in her chapter on Danielson, which she emphasized it talking with all TAs and future high school students: that of respect for the student. The TA training program she designed was founded on that same respect. Some years ago I re-established contact with Joyce Steward, who was working with Mrs. Thomas when I was a TA and who was also a model for me in this regard; I was able to thank her in person for what I learned from her about being an administrator. Writing this introduction has allowed me to express my thanks for, if not to, Mrs. Thomas as well.

REFERENCES

Bates, T. (1992.) *Rads: the 1970 bombing of the Army Math Research Center at the University of Wisconsin and its aftermath.* New York: HarperCollins.

Fleming, D. (2011). *From form to meaning: Freshman composition and the long sixties, 1957–1974.* Pittsburgh, PA: University of Pittsburgh Press.

Lacy, E. & Thomas, E. S. (1951). *Guide to good writing: A composition text for college students.* Harrisburg, PA: Stackpole and Heck.

Maraniss, D. (2003.) *They marched into sunlight: War and peace, Vietnam and America, October 1967.* New York: Simon and Schuster.

Schwalm, D. (2002). The writing program (administrator) in context: Where am i, and can i still behave like a faculty member?" In I. Ward & W. J. Carpenter (Eds.), *The Allyn & Bacon Sourcebook for Writing Program Administrators* (pp. 9–22). New York: Allyn & Bacon.

Thomas, E. S. (1962). *Evaluating student themes.* Madison, WI: University of Wisconsin Press.

INTRODUCTION TO THE MEMOIR

David Stock
Brigham Young University

Ednah Shepard Thomas (1901–1995), a professor of English at the University of Wisconsin-Madison (UW-Madison), was instrumental in developing the department's modern Freshman English Program, from 1945 until its abolishment in 1970. In retirement, Thomas wrote a memoir, addressed to her children but shared with a few former colleagues and close friends, that includes reflections on her New England upbringing and education, her domestic experiences in a small Midwestern village, and her extensive involvement in the English department at UW-Madison. The publication of Thomas's memoir is an effort to memorialize a remarkable individual whose fascinating life story and pioneering contributions to writing instruction and writing program administration merit widespread recognition and respect.

Reflective of her purpose, audience, and genre, Thomas's memoir includes extensive personal recollections that are directed to family and friends, much of which is inflected by significant historical events—two world wars, the Vietnam war, the civil rights movement—which a wider range of readers, particularly younger generations, may find fascinating. For instance, Thomas recounts life as a single mother raising three children in a small town during the ration years of World War II; she shares personal reflections on the memorial services of such iconic leaders as Franklin D. Roosevelt, John F. Kennedy, and Martin Luther King, Jr.; she provides extensive accounts of campus activism and antiwar protests at UW-Madison during the 1960s. Additionally, readers with connections to Brookline, Massachusetts (where Thomas was born and raised), or Monona, Wisconsin (where she raised her family and lived her adult life), or the University of Wisconsin-Madison (where she worked) may enjoy reading references to people, places, or events of local or historical interest. Although Thomas's family was the primary audience, her memoir stands to offer much to a range of readers.

However, the intended audience for this publication of the memoir is those in the discipline of composition-rhetoric, particularly writing program administration. Nearly half of the memoir details Thomas's professional experience as a teacher of writing and an administrator of Freshman English at a historically significant institution during a significant period in American higher education. Thomas's memoir highlights the scope and significance of her contributions to Freshman English and her participation in the emerging profession of composition-rhetoric. At Wisconsin, she was instrumental in expanding the Freshman English Program to accommodate the influx of World War II veterans under the GI Bill in the late 1940s and the influx of graduate teaching assistants (TAs) in the 1950s and 60s. She made substantial and original contributions to curriculum development, student placement and assessment, teaching assistant training, and outreach to high school English faculty in and beyond Wisconsin. She participated in local and national conferences of the National Council of Teachers of English, including the Conference on College Composition and Communication. She participated in initiatives sponsored by the College Entrance Examination Board's Educational Testing Services (ETS), notably the Commission on English, for which she was trained to lead a summer institute for high school English teachers, and she maintained correspondence with ETS's Paul Diederich about large-scale assessment of student writing. She secured grant funding through the National Defense Education Act to organize and conduct a summer institute, similar to that of the Commission on English, held at the UW-Madison campus. Equally important, Thomas's memoir recounts the growing tensions in the UW-Madison English department during the 1960s, increased student activism and protests on campus, escalating tensions among the faculty and between the faculty and teaching assistants, and the events leading to the abolition of Freshman English at UW-Madison.

For a composition-rhetoric audience, Thomas's memoir is significant because it constitutes a narrative of the work of a writing program administrator (WPA) in its pre-professional era, thus answering L'Eplattenier and Mastrangelo's call to expand writing program administrative histories by providing access to "formerly unavailable data and formerly unrecognized figures" (263). While Thomas's account of her work as a teacher and administrator of composition enriches the discipline's awareness of its "complex, multivocal past" (Gold, 2012, p. 17), it has added significance when placed alongside David Fleming's (2011) extensively researched local history of the history, growth, and abolition of Freshman English at UW-Madison. Fleming (2011) acknowledges Thomas's role with program director Ed Lacy in building and maintaining the Freshman English program from 1948–1968, as well as her support of the program's abolishment (pp. 143–144).[1] But there is more to learn about Thomas's contributions to that program, the department, and the profession, than what can feasibly be included in Fleming's history. Although her reasons for abolishing the program resemble those that Fleming's careful history has undermined, Thomas's view

---

1 Joyce Steward, a high school teacher who was hired by the UW-Madison English department, recalls Thomas participating in conversations with Ed Lacy and William Lenehan to discontinue Freshman English and offer "tutorial help of some kind," which resulted in the creation of the Writing Lab at UW-Madison (Hughes, 2017).

of the events—a detailed, first-person, and admittedly biased account from the perspective of an insider—constitutes a compelling and vital counter-narrative that ultimately enriches the contested and inevitably incomplete nature of the "story" of Freshman English at UW-Madison. Hence, recuperating Thomas's counternarrative in her memoir serves an important "additive" function (Gold, 2012, p. 24) in advancing historiography in WPA and in composition-rhetoric.

The genre of the memoir plays a central role in making this scholarly contribution possible because it allows Thomas to speak largely for herself, to share a highly personal account of her professional experiences that is rich in detail, earnest in tone, and unfiltered by a historian's intervention. The memoir also accentuates the inextricable nature of Thomas's personal and professional experiences, the overlap of which is manifest in, for instance, her description of having to deal with home appliance failures on the day she was returning to work as an instructor in Freshman English, or in an account of a student protest involving tear gas in her building followed by her preparations for a child's wedding. While some readers may find that this juxtaposition of personal and professional strains the memoir's coherence, it accurately captures Thomas's lived experience as a WPA, indicating that her professional contributions can't be fully understood or appreciated without the context of her personal life. A more significant illustration of this personal-professional integration is manifest in Thomas's effort to host socials and dinners at her home for faculty and teaching assistants. In the same spirit in which Thomas invited her students to her Frost Woods home at the end of each semester, these regular department gatherings represented Thomas's dedication to fostering a sense of familiarity with, connection among, and respect for all department staff, regardless of rank or status. In this sense, Thomas saw her work as highly personal and individual, even nurturing.[2] Thus, the genre of the memoir is a fitting means of representing Thomas's work holistically, within the context of her lived experience.

WPA NARRATIVES AND DISCIPLINARY HISTORIES

Narratives have played a central role in documenting the history of writing program administration and, thereby, legitimizing its professional and disciplinary status. An accumulation of early WPA narratives has allowed for generalizations about a "typical" WPA profile and experience: a middle-aged woman working in an English department who agrees to work in a position for which she lacks training; who "oversees large, complicated structures and faces adminis-

---

2   Fleming (2011) reports that English faculty member Robert Pooley characterized Thomas's relationship with teaching assistants, prior to around 1967, as "almost maternal" (p. 152).

trative challenges for funding and institutional understanding"; and who finds her administrative work filled with "stresses and successes" that cannot be adequately "quantified," due in part to the promise and perils of such administrative work (Skeffington, Borrowman & Enos, 2008, p. 18). Thomas's experience largely aligns with this narrative: she began her administrative work in her forties; she not only oversaw but also built the structures and processes needed for a functioning writing program; and she found the work stressful and fulfilling in equal measure. But she did not lack training. In fact, her experience moderately resembles a more expansive narrative, captured by a second generation of WPAs "whose graduate careers prepared them to do WPA work in some form, who came to see administration as a core component of their professional and intellectual identities, and who pursued or accepted administrative roles before tenure to satisfy personal or professional needs" (Charlton et al., 2011, p. xi). The consistent attention given to WPA narratives, past and present, affirms the centrality of narrative in legitimizing WPA work by making such work visible and accessible.

The role of narrative in legitimizing WPA work mirrors the role of historical research in legitimizing the discipline of composition-rhetoric. As revisionist historiographers have been illustrating for several years, foundational histories (e.g., Berlin, 1984 & 1987; Connors, 1997) produced grand narratives that legitimized the discipline at the expense of more nuanced, little narratives. In recent decades, the emergence of revisionist histories (e.g., Enoch, 2008; Gold, 2008), local histories (e.g., Donahue and Moon, 2007; Fleming, 2011), and microhistories (e.g., McComiskey, 2016) draw attention to specific and often marginalized individuals and locations that challenge and broaden earlier, foundational histories. In doing so, however, it is easy for scholars and historians to overlook the need to recuperate administrative histories, electing instead to recuperate primarily pedagogical materials or specific individuals at the expense of the managerial dimensions of their work. As Strickland (2011) highlights, the history of composition studies has been equated with composition pedagogy to the exclusion of "the managerial dimensions of writing instruction" (p. 7). Illustrative of this practice is the fact that those who produced foundational histories were themselves administrators but failed to account for the materiality of the pedagogies they recuperated in their research. Because the ubiquity of teaching composition in American higher education has always required that it be managed, Strickland (2011) argues for seeing "the history of the field of composition studies as the history of the increasing importance of managers of the teaching of writing" (p. 17). This makes attending to histories of administration, including those who participate in administration, vital to historical recovery work in composition-rhetoric. L'Eplattenier and Mastrangelo's (2004) collection represents an effort to address this omission, while also honoring those who worked as administrators in an era preceding the 1976 formation of the Council of Writing Program Administrators. The publication of Thomas's memoir aligns with such efforts to recuperate "previously unknown histor[ies]" of individuals who, by today's standards, would be called writing program administrators (L'Eplattenier and Mastrangelo, 2004, p. xvii). It also honors the work of an individual who not only devoted much of her life to helping students and instructors become better writers and teachers of writing but also contributed to the emerging discipline of composition-rhetoric.

UNDERSTANDING EDNAH S. THOMAS

Ednah Shepard Thomas (1901–1995) was an only child born to elderly parents in a comfortable Boston suburb, resulting in a solitary life of relative privilege filled with books, especially those by Charles Dickens. An early twentieth-century Boston Brahmin, Thomas describes herself as Victorian, a natural conformist, a fuddy-duddy, a duty-bound, battle-axe product of New England culture. The UW-Madison faculty memorial resolution for Thomas describes her as having an "Eastern New England speech pattern with its tartness of delivery, a briskness of energy and sharply focused purpose in both work and leisure, a moral rectitude in her interactions with staff and students, a meticulous attention to the conduct of her duties." Faculty who knew Thomas recall her stern personality, her commitment to the Freshman English Program, her extensive knowledge of writing, her widely respected judgment, and her intimidating presence. Faculty and friends also recall her frugality (the temperature in her home rarely exceeded 60 degrees Fahrenheit in the winter), her teetotalism, her environmentalism, her intellectual strengths, and her skill and influence as a teacher and mentor. Jim Nelson, a faculty member and close friend of Thomas, described her as a "towering" faculty member in the UW-Madison English department.[3]

Thomas's background, personality, and education prepared her to be an effective writing teacher, administrator, and mentor. They also explain her rigid response to student and faculty radicalism and her struggle to cope with broader social change. Thomas's grandson, James, remembers his grandmother's formality and propriety; neither he nor his mother, Kathy, would ever drop in unannounced at Thomas's home; they would always call beforehand.[4] He also remembers her inability, or unwillingness, to change with the times. Neither James nor Kathy characterized Thomas as warm or affectionate, yet both spoke

---

3   Jim Nelson, interview by the editor, December 2010.
4   James Thomas, interview by the editor, October 2013.

highly of her incredible depth of feeling and their admiration for her.[5] James recalled his grandmother's kindness and patience as she tutored him in writing during a summer while he was in high school, a formative experience to which he attributes the beginning of his love of writing, and he felt that her personality was central to helping him develop as a writer and thinker.[6] Admittedly, just as Thomas's personality and teaching style weren't universally appreciated by all of her students or the teaching assistants she supervised, her perspective and commentary on matters of social change and unrest will strike some readers as parochial, if not offensive. In such cases, it is important to remember that Thomas was, as Susan McLeod notes in the foreword, a product of a particular time. As with any figure of historical interest, Thomas is a complex character; the fact that she lived during a period of unprecedented educational and social change serves to accentuate both the admirable and the less admirable aspects of her character.

Thomas was uniquely prepared to administer UW-Madison's Freshman English Program. Her appointment as an assistant to faculty member and program director Edgar Lacy was highly unlikely, given Thomas's departure from academia while in graduate school to support a husband and raise a family, followed by an unexpected and, in her words, "crippling" divorce. But in returning to teach and, shortly thereafter, administer composition at UW-Madison, Thomas embarked on what resulted in an unprecedented academic career while successfully fulfilling her domestic responsibilities. This, alone, is an impressive accomplishment, given the social stigma and professional limitations attached to divorced, single mothers in her era. Fortunately for Thomas, and for the hundreds of Freshman English students, instructors, and English department faculty with whom she would work for over twenty years, she found her way back into the classroom and a profession that allowed her to attain "the best of both worlds. I am a full professor (emeritus) of the University of Wisconsin, and the only woman professor to have three children and seven grandchildren." Thomas's memoir is a rich, extensive illustration of a remarkable writing instructor, pioneering WPA, and devoted mother, community member, and friend.

WRITING INSTRUCTION AND PROGRAM ADMINISTRATION IN THE MEMOIR

Several features of the memoir—the length, the blending of personal and professional experiences, the repetition of details, the extensive references to litera-

---

5   Kathy Thomas, interview by the editor, May 2013.

6   James also recalled how, as a student at UW-Madison in the 1990s, his grandmother's reputation was very much alive on campus, and that faculty who knew Thomas had tremendous respect for her and would make time to talk with him because he was her grandson.

ture, places, people, and events—can obscure the portions that are most relevant to a composition-rhetoric audience. This section provides an overview of such content including Thomas's development as a teacher, her contributions to writing program administration, and her account of the decline and abolition of Freshman English at UW-Madison.

TRAINING IN AND TEACHING ENGLISH COMPOSITION

Writing Instruction at Mt. Holyoke

Thomas's interest in English composition was facilitated by the unique status of writing instruction at Mt. Holyoke College, which from its inception had a strong history of rhetoric instruction (Snell, 1942, p. 5). In 1884, after the arrival of Clara Frances Stevens, who received her Ph.D. from the University of Michigan and studied with Fred Newton Scott, rhetoric at Mt. Holyoke was designated departmental status. In 1897, seven years after the rhetoric and literature departments had merged, two separate departments were formed: English and English Literature, a distinction which remained until 1947. Mastrangelo (2012) finds no evidence of antagonism between the two departments, which shared common goals, though some evidence suggests English was more rigorous than English Literature (p. 90). The catalogue description for English Composition in 1919, the year Thomas matriculated, describes a two-semester course focused first on organization in "the whole composition" and at the paragraph level and on reading and outlining expository essays, followed by analysis of literary expression and essays, particularly diction and sentence forms, and practice in various forms of writing (Snell, 1942, p. 2). According to Ada Snell, a faculty member from whom Thomas took several courses, writing instruction at Mt. Holyoke during the early twentieth century was characterized by an emphasis on form and outlining.

Further evidence of the unique status of composition at Mt. Holyoke stems from the college's participation, along with three sister colleges, in an Intercollege conference on English composition. The first meeting was held at Mt. Holyoke in 1919, the year Thomas arrived, and participants from Mt. Holyoke included professors from whom Thomas had taken classes: Stevens, Snell, and Helen Griffith (L'Eplattenier and Mastrangelo, 2004, p. 112). The purpose of the conference was to promote discussion about writing instruction and program administration issues such as entrance exams, class placement, theme writing, and department outreach. This formation of a proto-WPA community among English faculty at Mt Holyoke and neighboring colleges was likely a reflection of the training and commitments that participants brought to the conference: many, like Stevens, were trained at the University of Michigan under Fred

Newton Scott, they viewed writing instruction through the lens of Deweyan progressivism, and, by virtue of seniority in their respective institutions, they assumed a strong institutional presence. Thomas attributes her training in composition at Mt. Holyoke as a primary factor in the UW-Madison English department's decision to invite her to help administer Freshman English. Thomas also notes that the high student-faculty contact at Mt. Holyoke influenced her decision to invite English department teaching assistants at UW-Madison to her home for social gatherings.

Thomas's interest in writing was a primary factor in her decision to pursue graduate school. She chose Bryn Mawr because a graduate course in creative writing was listed in the catalog, but she was extremely disappointed to learn, upon arrival, that the course had been canceled due to low enrollment. Although Bryn Mawr had a history of effective writing instruction (George, 2004), Thomas likely had little exposure to writing instruction, largely because she completed her M.A. degree in one year—the first ever to do so—and spent all her time conducting research on medieval English. Graduate school did, however, help Thomas realize she lacked interest in and aptitude for a life of scholarship. It also introduced her to a graduate student from the University of Minnesota who piqued Thomas's interest in temporarily experiencing the Midwest, which prompted her to apply to Ph.D. programs in Michigan, Minnesota, and Wisconsin. However, she received no offers from these schools, so she sought temporary employment and found a job that profoundly influenced her life.

Teaching English at Killingly High School

Thomas's most transformative and "broadening" experience occurred shortly after completing her M.A. from Bryn Mawr, when she taught English and history at Killingly High School in a rural mill town in northeastern Connecticut. Thomas was clearly out of her element: "I had lived a sheltered life among privileged people, and my experience was very limited and overwhelmingly derived from books." Much of Thomas's broadening experience stemmed from exposure to the realities of education and life in poor, working-class conditions. She also felt inept and unaware as a teacher. But she threw herself "whole-heartedly" into teaching, giving "heart and soul" to her students, who taught her "more than I have ever learned in any other single year before or since." Thomas was invested heavily in her students' learning and lives: she supervised various extracurricular activities, including a writing club and the women's basketball team; she met individually with students, typically those who were indifferent or defiant, after school in what were earnest but often unsuccessful attempts to motivate and help them improve; she even tutored a student at his home on Saturdays when a broken leg interfered with his school attendance.

Thomas felt that most of her efforts were largely wasted on her students, although some expressed thanks before she left and corresponded with her in subsequent years. But Thomas was permanently changed by the experience. Her most profound learning experience, which she later recounted in every section of English 309, a composition course she taught at UW-Madison for prospective teachers of high school English, involved a confrontation with a student, Rukstela, while conferencing about his theme. Thomas disputed Rukstela's claim that a horse weighed a ton, implying he was exaggerating. Rukstela insisted. After a brief struggle, Thomas redirected the conversation to sentence-level issues, where she knew she was right. Later that day, while walking home, Thomas passed a farmyard with a notice for an auction of farm materials, including two horses each weighing 2,100 pounds. After inspecting a horse on the property, Thomas realized she was wrong, that she needed to apologize to Rukstela, and that he was likely better equipped for life than she. Most importantly, she added, "I learned, and never forgot, and never went into class without being conscious of, respect for the student. A teacher should always be aware that given experience many of her own students may beat her at her own game, and that every one of her students is her superior at something anyway." Respect for students would become a hallmark of Thomas's teaching and administration at UW-Madison.

Teaching Composition at Wisconsin

During her one-year tenure at Killingly High School, Thomas sent a second application to the University of Wisconsin. This time she received a response and was offered a teaching assistantship, perhaps in part because one of her instructors from Mt. Holyoke, Kathleen Lynch, was currently a graduate student there. At UW-Madison, Thomas's interest and talent in English composition were clearly apparent, as she was asked to teach extra sections in place of graduate work, which she was happy to do. The course, directed at the time by faculty member Warner Taylor, focused on theme writing and culminated in an autobiography, "standard practice in those days." Thomas's preference for teaching Freshman English was unusual, as was her lack of interest in teaching the sophomore literature survey course, which "everyone else" preferred. Thomas describes her students at Wisconsin as more heterogeneous than she had previously experienced and far more prepared for the practicalities of life than she, which only increased her fascination with and commitment to teaching Freshman English. As an instructor, Thomas continued the practice she started at Killingly of holding individual conferences with students. She feared such individualized assistance conveyed a "high-schoolish" attitude to students by giving them too much individual attention, but she reasoned that it was worthwhile, especially in the post-war years when the student body increased exponentially and had few, if any, opportunities to meet with faculty individually.

After teaching at UW-Madison for two years, Thomas married a fellow graduate student, Wright Thomas, and left the profession, only to return unexpectedly in 1942, in the midst of a divorce, when she began teaching English to servicemen-students via correspondence courses through the United States Armed Forces Institute (USAFI) program, organized that year as Army Institute correspondence and headquartered in Madison, WI. Thomas was very grateful for the opportunity, arranged by English faculty member Helen C. White, as it allowed her to remain at home to care for her young children. Her first course was a basic high school grammar course, where students wrote original sentences to illustrate comprehension of grammatical principles. Eventually Thomas began teaching freshman composition and sophomore literature, which she found more enjoyable. Several students sent her notes of appreciation; their remarks, several of which she included in her memoir, help illustrate the impact of Thomas's work, in particular her written comments on their writing: "'Your kindness in grading my papers as you did and your enthusiasm in my work gave me confidence in myself at a time when it was sorely needed.' . . . 'By bolstering my confidence in my own efforts you removed a psychological block.' 'I want to express my thanks again for your valuable comments on my papers. They were what I needed to put me on a firm scholastic footing and have given me back my self-confidence.'" Thomas felt that these notes validated her approach to commenting, which was characterized by an earnest effort to identify and address both strengths and weaknesses in student writing.

While Thomas was appreciative of the opportunity to interact with servicemen, whom she held in high regard, she admitted that much of the work had been "drudgery," as few students finished the course, making her feel that her efforts were largely wasted. Consequently, she gratefully accepted in 1945 an invitation by the English department chair to teach Freshman English, under the condition that the appointment was a temporary stopgap in response to the influx of World War II veterans on the heels of the GI Bill. She taught two classes and was initially overwhelmed, describing it as "a schizophrenic period" where she had to balance "the professional responsibilities of a man and the domestic ones of a woman." But she was sustained by her love of teaching, described being back in the classroom as "heaven," and admitted having to restrain her desire to plan for her classes so as not to compromise her domestic duties, such as planning meals for her children. By 1946, with the influx of veterans only increasing the demands on Freshman English, Thomas became "a permanent, if humble, member of the department" and continued to teach, this time three sections totaling 95 students, all of whom were veterans, and four of whom were women. Perhaps sensing kindred spirits in terms of discipline, order, and respect, Thomas lauded the veterans as the best and brightest students in the history of American education: mature, prepared, hardworking, resilient—a stark contrast, in her mind, to the permissive, "trashing misfits of the late sixties." Thomas also began teaching an honors version of Freshman English, English 11 (later 181), a one-semester, literature-intensive course conceived by faculty member Ruth Wallerstein. Thomas claimed that students in this honors Freshman Course were the best of any student, freshman or graduate, she had taught or observed at the university.

When assisting in the Freshman English Program required Thomas to be removed from English 11, she was reassigned to English 128 (later 309), a composition course for prospective high school English teachers. She recognized that her high school teaching experience qualified her to teach the course. Aside from her involvement in the Freshman English Program, Thomas's greatest impact on writing instruction at UW-Madison and beyond grew out of teaching English 309. Jim Nelson noted her reputation for preparing strong high school English teachers and characterized English 309 as one of the most important courses offered in the department.[7] Regarding the reputation of English 309 outside UW-Madison, Joyce Steward, a former high school teacher in Madison who joined the English department faculty, worked closely with Thomas, and was instrumental in launching the Writing Lab, recalled that when neighboring high schools were hiring English teachers, they wanted those who had been trained in "Mrs. Thomas's" English 309 class.

The curriculum introduced students to classical rhetoric and consisted of analysis of model essays, regular theme writing in multiple modes on various topics, and a culminating source paper on an English novel. Students conferenced regularly with Thomas. Aristotelian rhetoric was central to the course: "we considered everything we read and everything we wrote from the standpoint of Aristotle's thesis: communication (rhetoric) is a matter of appropriateness and balance among three elements: writer or speaker, audience, situation." While Thomas initially supplied readings and models for the course, she eventually adopted Connolly and Levin's (1968) *The Art of Rhetoric*, a textbook that aimed to incorporate classical and contemporary rhetorical theory with composition pedagogy. Arranged in three sections— (1) the nature of rhetoric, which briefly surveys the classical origins of rhetoric and its development from the middle ages to the eighteenth century; (2) the practice of rhetoric, which consists of selections of essays or speeches organized according to mode (e.g., description and narration, exposition, argument and persuasion, expository narrative, and

---

7   Jim Nelson, interview by the editor, December 2010.

expository argument); and (3) the theory of rhetoric, which includes readings from Plato and Aristotle as well as Richard Weaver, Wayne Booth, and Kenneth Burke—the *Art of Rhetoric* is an intriguing instance of attempting to synthesize and apply contemporary rhetorical theory to composition instruction in its modern (mid-twentieth century current-traditional) form. While the modes frame the organization of the essays, principles of rhetoric and tools of stylistic analysis are present, in the suggested topics for discussion and composition following each reading, and in the glosses of a few of the model essays. While rhetoric was clearly subordinate to composition in the textbook, Thomas's use of it counters Fleming's (2009) suggestion that compositionists in the English department in the 1960s seemed to be "completely innocent of rhetoric, old or new" (p. 43).

Thomas's impact on students in English 309—and likely on her Freshman English students—is conveyed in a letter from a former student, written twenty-six years after taking English 309. After admitting that she thought of Thomas "every year" after taking the class, the student thanked Thomas for teaching her "more about writing and rigorous thinking" than any other professor (at UW-Madison or Swarthmore, where she was an undergraduate), and for being "the first person who thought it was really worth bothering to invest time in teaching me to write." Interestingly but not surprisingly, given Thomas's reputation for sternness, this student admits that Thomas initially "terrified" her, but she learned to appreciate Thomas's high expectations and genuine encouragement. She describes saving all her papers with Thomas's comments and rereading them for inspiration as she practiced responding to her own high school students. She described Thomas's comments as "enter[ing] into the process" and making "[us] compatriots in an intellectual endeavor." She concluded by expressing gratitude for Thomas's "lasting influence."

As an extension of her training in English 309, Thomas regularly conducted workshops for high school teachers as part of the university's summer session, as well as a three-day conference on the teaching of English. Many participants came from the Midwest, but several came from across the nation. With Ed Lacy, Thomas also visited English classrooms at secondary schools and delivered lectures and presentations to high school teachers across the state in order to improve the teaching of writing and better prepare high school students for college composition. Joyce Steward recalls Thomas's profound influence on her and other high school English teachers through these outreach efforts. Such efforts led to Thomas's involvement in the Commission on English, a national committee appointed by the College Entrance Examination Board in 1959 to improve English instruction, curriculum, and training in high schools and colleges nationwide (*Freedom*, 1965, p. i). This experience introduced Thomas to some high-profile individuals in the discipline, including Albert Kitzhaber, who did not leave a very favorable impression on her, and it resulted in her directing at UW-Madison in 1962 one of the Commission's twenty summer institutes. It also led to Thomas's involvement in organizing and directing a similarly focused summer institute for English teachers, which was sponsored by the National Defense Education Act summer institute and also held at UW-Madison, in 1965.[8]

Administering Freshman English at Wisconsin

Thomas's interest in and skill at teaching freshman composition, evident during her two years as a graduate instructor and in her return to the composition classroom in 1945, was unusual among faculty and graduate students and prompted both the department chair and the newly appointed director of Freshman English, Ed Lacy, to invite Thomas to assist with the development of the program. While Thomas would replace the current course scheduler, Charlotte Wood, who was nearing retirement, she was tasked with preparing "a thorough training program" for teaching assistants, who had replaced the full-time faculty as instructors of the course. While Thomas recognized her teaching experiences qualified her for the position, she believed she was asked to assist because she was "genuinely interested in freshman composition and genuinely enthusiastic about it." Thomas acknowledged that the department did not care about Freshman English, that only two men—Warner Taylor and Ed Lacy—took it seriously, and that it was rare to find people "willing to devote themselves to the subject." Part of the reason Thomas cared about Freshman English was that she felt that the first semester of college was an extremely influential learning experience for students.

Just as she had devoted herself fully to her high school students, Thomas fully immersed herself in her administrative work. In 1949, she began advising freshmen and observing teaching assistants in their classrooms. She assumed responsibility for scheduling students and teaching assistants, and scheduling observations of teaching assistants by faculty members, which occurred six weeks into the semester. She assumed a primary role in preparing the pre-semester, four-day orientation meetings for new and experienced teaching assistants. She coordinated student placement and assessment, and she began conducting outreach visits to various high schools and preparatory schools. During the

---

8   This summer institute, held June 28-Aug 6, 1965, included forty secondary teachers of English from across the country and focused on increasing competency in language, literature, and composition. Thomas designed the institute to ensure that participants had multiple opportunities to write about institute topics and conference about their writing.

summer months, she collaborated with Ed Lacy on a composition textbook, *Guide for Good Writing: A Composition Text for College Students*, published in 1951. Of the eleven chapters, Thomas wrote ten, using material from a growing collection of student themes, but she was "not particularly proud of the book." The first chapter, "Approach to Writing Assignments," reveals Thomas's investment in Aristotelian rhetoric as a basis for composition instruction, followed by an outline of a recommended process for writing themes. Subsequent chapters address grammar and usage, sentences, paragraphs, the whole composition, and style. In contrast to *The Art of Rhetoric*, which Thomas used in English 309, *Guide to Good Writing* resembles a generic composition textbook, and it was used for a time in UW-Madison's Freshman English Program (Fleming, 2011, pp. 48).

While Thomas's many program contributions were valuable, two emerge as unique and significant. The first was her 1955 publication of *Evaluating Student Themes*, a forty-page pamphlet consisting of a foreword that highlights an "ideal process" for commenting on student writing, based on conviction that a teacher must aim not to edit but to promote the lifelong development of students' writing skills, to balance criticism and encouragement, and, above all, to show both interest in and respect for students' work as a whole (Thomas, 1955, pp. iv–v). The pamphlet consists of fourteen student themes, arranged according to three levels (unsatisfactory, middle, superior), each with an accompanying terminal comment. Intended for college and high school English teachers, *Evaluating Student Themes* was enormously popular: for a time, it was the all-time bestseller at the University of Wisconsin Press; in Fleming's estimation, it was likely "the most influential and distinctive feature" of the Freshman English Program (2011, p. 49); and as Joyce Steward and other sources indicate, it was highly influential among high school English teachers in and beyond Wisconsin. *Evaluating Student Themes* became the curriculum for weekly staff meetings, which Thomas led, and was the means, along with individual conferences with Thomas, to help teaching assistants "read their freshman themes so that they saw on the paper not what they thought was there or wanted to see there or would have put there themselves, but what actually *was* there." As an extension of responding to rather than correcting student writing, Thomas persuaded Lacy to instigate a minimum grading policy in Freshman English, which consisted of "no grades on individual themes, and only two tentative reports to the students, at six and twelve weeks, before the final grade." Both the pamphlet and the policy illustrated Thomas's emphasis on the role of feedback and revision in students' writing process. The pamphlet in particular reflects an orientation to attitudes and practices in writing instruction that would become central to the writing process movement (Fleming, 2011, p. 50).

Thomas's second significant contribution was the development of the Master Teaching Assistant Program, in which experienced Freshman English teaching assistants were assigned to mentor seven or eight new teaching assistants. The "master" teaching assistants conducted class visits and portions of the weekly training meetings and sought to help new teaching assistants in any way possible (Fleming, 2011, pp. 52–53). Instituted in 1965, the program was an effort to distribute supervisory responsibilities while building trust and collegiality among older and younger faculty. It was also a response to a rapidly growing teaching assistant population. Unlike similar programs at other institutions, Master Teaching Assistants did not evaluate or report on the performance of group members. Thomas maintained contact with Master Teaching Assistants and their cohorts by conferencing regularly with them and by hosting a cohort (teaching assistants and their spouses) and some senior faculty each week at her home for Sunday suppers. This supervisory program can be seen as a culmination of Thomas's efforts since 1947 to develop a robust, supportive training program for teaching assistants, whom she greatly cared about and whom she saw "as much as, if not more than, those [students] actually enrolled in my courses." Thomas attributes the program's success in its first year primarily to mutual goodwill and open communication among faculty and staff. Unfortunately, but perhaps inevitably, the program was short-lived, as the department faculty and staff continued to grow, accompanied by growing tensions and department polarization between the senior faculty and the junior faculty and teaching assistants, which precipitated the abolition of Freshman English (Fleming, 2011, pp. 64–65).

Such significant program contributions validate Fleming's claim that Thomas's approach to writing instruction was "more enlightened than our stereotypes of 1950s composition, or of current-traditional rhetoric in general, allow" (2011, p. 49). Her New England severity notwithstanding, Thomas labeled herself as more liberal than Lacy in her approach toward Freshman Writing: she wanted more than he to involve the teaching assistants "in more or less democratic participation" in course development. She also described herself as more extroverted and accessible to the teaching assistants than Ed, who frequently remained cloistered in his office. Admittedly, the Freshman English Program Thomas supported was a product of its time, and whatever process might have been facilitated with deferred grading, commenting, and individual conferencing was diminished by the product-centered, mode-based, and teacher-controlled nature of the course. (Also, Thomas's praise for the previous program director Warner Taylor's "authoritarian style, with none of this modern nonsense about letting instructors do as they please" admittedly colors her characterization of herself as liberal.) Nonetheless, given Thomas's commitment to Freshman English and her emphasis on respecting students, it is clear that she respected the teaching assistants and wanted to help them succeed. Susan McLeod, recalling her first academic job after graduate school at UW-Madison, explains how much of an anomaly such careful attention and structured support was in English departments: "faculty didn't care about the course, and usually put some junior member in charge who was more concerned about getting tenure than about the course itself. The course was taught by graduate students and hapless lecturers like me; we could order any textbook we wanted to, there was no standard syllabus, and no course objectives. . . . [This] was the case almost universally."[9] Indeed, it is precisely Thomas's extensive commitment to and involvement in Freshman English that makes her decision to support its abolishment so unusual.

ABOLISHING FRESHMAN ENGLISH AT WISCONSIN

Thomas acknowledges her role in seeking to dismantle the Freshman English Program at UW-Madison, admitting that as early as 1966 she had suggested to colleagues that the course be abolished. In October 1969, she wrote to a colleague on leave, notifying him of the plan to propose in a department meeting a vote to abolish Freshman English. She then added, as if to justify such action, "We no longer have any control over the assistants. They won't, or can't, teach composition. They use their students as a captive audience for politicizing. There is no attempt of objectivity of analysis, and certainly no freedom of expression for anyone who doesn't agree—or pretend to agree—with his TA." Thomas then recounted concerns about questionable grading practices among the teaching assistants, apparently as further evidence of their insubordination and justification for the proposed abolition. In a separate, subsequent exchange following the department vote on November 18, 1969 to abolish Freshman English, Thomas wrote with surprising finality, "It is time for the system to end. . . . I feel no more regret over having spent twenty years working in the system than I do over having spent twenty years bringing up my children. The work in both cases was necessary and useful while I was doing it, and when things change so it is no longer necessary and useful you accept the change." But at a later point in the memoir, Thomas reveals a starkly different response, clearly lamenting her lost connection to the teaching assistants: "When I think of the happy years I worked *with* the TA's—all those baby booties and Christmas carol parties! I don't think I can even bear to send them Christmas cards this year. In 1965 I'd walk down the hall on third floor Bascom and be greeted by as many cheerful smiles—"Hi, Mrs. Thomas!" "Hi, Mrs. Thomas!" "Hi, Mrs. Thomas!"—as John F. Kennedy got at the Democratic convention which nominated him for the Presidency. . . .

---

9   Susan McLeod, email to the editor, August 2012.

Now in the same corridor I meet the cut direct, the baleful glare from shadowed eyes that Madame Defarge cast upon little Lucie Darnay." Clearly, Thomas's fallout with the teaching assistants was central to her abolitionist stance, and in her account of Freshman English's "demolition," the teaching assistant system and the teaching assistants themselves play a prominent role.

Thomas described the graduate teaching assistant system as imperfect but satisfactory arrangement to accommodate teaching demands at a growing university, but only when "safeguards and supervision" are in place. In her assessment, Thomas identified two conditions threatening the teaching assistant system's sustainability in the English department: first, the staggering growth in the department's graduate student population, heightened by the faculty's unwillingness to take action that would diminish that growing number; second, the growing feeling of indifference and resentment stemming from requiring all graduate students, who universally disdained Freshman English, to teach in the program. Supervision—from senior faculty and Master Teaching Assistants—was intended to temper such attitudes, but because faculty, as part of a larger pattern of withdrawal from the Freshman English Program, were increasingly unwilling to participate in such supervision, there could be no safeguards. While Thomas acknowledges the faculty's role in weakening the teaching assistant system, she attributes its downfall to the teaching assistants themselves, specifically that they "refused supervision," and insisted on not teaching the prescribed curriculum of Freshman English.[10] And Thomas attributed the permissiveness and antagonism of the teaching assistants to another teaching assistant system: the Teaching Assistants' Association (TAA), which in her mind institutionalized the adversarial relationship between the teaching assistants and faculty.[11] Given her personal and professional efforts, year after year, to reach out to new teaching assistants and new faculty, to help them feel welcome in a department with hundreds of faculty and staff, to prepare them to teach Freshman English effectively, and to entertain them in her home—in short, to treat them as colleagues, with

---

10 Thomas's perceptions of teaching assistant insubordination were certainly influenced by the outcome of a teaching assistant staff meeting in October 1969 with department chair Tim Heninger and Bill Lenehan, who had replaced Ed Lacy as director of Freshman English—a meeting which Fleming (2011) describes as a "watershed moment" in the history of Freshman English. In Fleming's account, this meeting gave rise to faculty perceptions that teaching assistants were seeking to take over Freshman English (pp. 135–138), a perception which expedited the faculty's decision to abolish the program.

11 The Teaching Assistants Association (TAA), organized by a small group of teaching assistants in late June 1966, is the oldest graduate student union in the US. Faculty member Charles Scott recalls that many senior faculty in the department did not view the TAA favorably, particularly given their adversarial posturing and aggressive bargaining tactics (interview with the editor, June 2016).

respect—she must have felt a sense of betrayal, and she despised the organization that, in her estimation, "turned our co-workers into antagonists."[12] And as campus conditions in the late 1960s continued to deteriorate, with student protests, strikes, and violence increasingly directed toward the university itself and undermining any last sense of community or respect, Thomas's criticism and resentment of the teaching assistants likewise increased. Indeed, it seems that what Thomas perceived as a lack of respect in the teaching assistants—for her, for the department faculty, for students in Freshman English, for the university, and even for the project of higher education itself—is what most troubled her and what triggered her visceral abolitionist response.

For such a thoroughly principled, New England Victorian, a woman who had dedicated her life to education, living through as disruptive a period as the late 1960s at UW-Madison must have been thoroughly disorienting and understandably embittering. Thomas described the campus and department as consumed "in the most heated political atmosphere you can imagine. I feel as if I had lived through every war in history, and I understand much more how wars are conducted than I ever did from history books, with everything neatly analyzed by hindsight. The reality is not two neat sides, but positions sliding all the way from extreme right to extreme left, people shifting back and forth, traitors on your own side, no one you can trust, lies and rumors and fantasies everywhere." Thomas's grandson James surmised that Thomas simply couldn't comprehend why students would want to destroy the university, to "Shut it down!" Thomas's own recollections suggest as much: "All this [protesting] is striking at the concepts of discipline, loyalty, impartiality, which is what distresses . . . me. The academic community should stand for the humanities, for reason, for the continuation of education, which is its business, not for any single cause."[13]

---

12 Fleming (2011) notes that in the latter part of the 1960s, "[t]here was disrespect, even rudeness, shown toward Ednah Thomas and Joyce Steward by some of the TA" (p. 57)—a far cry from the days in the 1920s when the department was, as Thomas recalls, "one happy family."

13 Gunner's (2004) observation about the ideological function of WPA work helps illuminate Thomas's struggles. When recuperating WPA histories, Gunner notes the necessity of accounting for how contexts shape the nature of and discourse about administrative work, which in turn shape the formation of writing instruction and its accompanying administrative practices. WPAs like Thomas have been "historically unable to grapple with political cultural realities" (p. 270) because, historically, the WPA "has no clear social agenda, and so the prevailing construct and practices of the WPA are inevitably and primarily conservative" (p. 274). In addition to her New England proclivities and personality, Thomas's "administrative discursive heritage" and desire for professionalization prevented her from even considering an engagment in social or political issues, at least to the degree that the radical teaching assistants were seeking. However, in fairness to Thomas, she does demonstrate openness to teaching assistant experimentation in Freshman English by signing off on what Fleming (2011) characterizes as a basic writing course for struggling students (pp. 87–89).

What was true for Thomas was also true for senior faculty, who were nominal leftists but "opposed to what they saw as the reduction of intellectual and cultural problems to ideological positions," especially when doing so threatened the safe space of the classroom (Fleming, 2011, p. 105). For Thomas, as with nearly all senior faculty in the department, politics and education were separate spheres of activity, and politicizing education and the university countered Thomas's perception of both as rational, disinterested enterprises. In her mind, the singular focus of her career—"to foster precision of language as a reflection of precision of thought"—was private and apolitical.

As politics infiltrated the department, it likely triggered Thomas's rigid moral indignation that, at times, was even directed against senior faculty. For instance, when Thomas had a student who refused to revise a theme despite Thomas's annotations and recommendations, she approached Ed Lacy, who advised her not to make an issue of it, but to let the student choose. Thomas commented indignantly, "This was against my principles. To me it was not only silly but morally indefensible to have in my class a student who refused to learn anything from the instructor." On another occasion, during the Dow riot, when a few teaching assistants went on strike and a few others volunteered to cover their classes, Thomas enthusiastically sought approval from Lacy, who declined the latter teaching assistants' offer. At this point, Thomas compared Lacy to Jewish rabbis who led their congregations to the concentration camps. Later, Thomas wrote, "I'm open to the charge of rigidity, of lack of realism, of youthful naiveté (despite my chronological age)." But she felt it necessary "to act in accordance with what we Victorians call our duty." For Thomas, this required voting to abolish Freshman English.

Thomas's assessment of teaching assistant behavior and her arguments for abolishing Freshman English, which were shared by her senior faculty colleagues, have been called into question by Fleming's careful reconstruction of the story. Rather than blaming the teaching assistants for the abolition of Freshman English, Fleming blames the senior faculty, ultimately arguing that, when faced with teaching assistants' efforts to exercise greater control over the content and instruction of Freshman English, and amid both a department climate of intense polarization and a campus climate of increasing student unrest, the faculty "exaggerated the incompetence and insubordination of their TAs," abolished the program as a means of retribution, and offered specious arguments about the improved writing skills of incoming students and the benefits of writing instruction offered in specific departments as post-hoc justification for their premeditated, unilateral decision (Fleming, 2011, pp. 161, 151). It is admittedly difficult to reconcile the compelling nature of Fleming's argument, which is strongly supported by extensive archival research and interviews with former faculty and teaching assistants who experienced this turbulent period, with the certainty of Thomas's account. But given the nature of history, and especially the contested nature of the abolition of Freshman English at UW-Madison, clearly one version of the events cannot provide the final, uncontested account of why Freshman English was abolished, for there will be as many accounts as there were participants. As Fleming acknowledges, it is difficult to find definitive answers to questions about teaching assistant and faculty behavior during this volatile period, "given the number of individuals involved and the time elapsed" (p. 154). Hence, just as Fleming's goal was to provide "a wider range of voices than could be accessed previously" (p. 154), publishing Thomas's memoir provides an additional, invaluable voice, a first-hand witness conveyed with all the passion and partiality implied by that word. As a counternarrative to Fleming's account, Thomas's memoir prompts questions that invite additional lines of inquiry, such as the impact of Thomas's outreach to high schools on the writing skills of incoming students from Wisconsin to the UW-Madison Freshman English Program. Incorporating Thomas's narrative into this unfolding conversation—hearing her voice, so to speak—allows us to pay our respects to her and enriches our understanding of a historical event at UW-Madison that, as Fleming has demonstrated, has implications for the discipline of composition-rhetoric and for the project of general education.

CONCLUSION

Early in the memoir, Thomas suggests that she was "born out of my generation." While Thomas is referring to her early years as a child, when she was almost exclusively in the company of adults, and as a youth, when she was, physically, a late bloomer among her peers, this observation can be applied to her academic and professional life. For instance, had Thomas been born in the 1990s, she would have been an ideal candidate for a college or university with a writing major and an MA or Ph.D. program in composition-rhetoric; had she directed a writing program in the 1980s, she would have benefited from the professional support available through the Council of Writing Program Administrators (CWPA); had she continued teaching through the 1970s, she would have seen a hallmark of her pedagogy (responding to student writing) and its rationale (respecting students' voices) become enshrined in the process movement. Perhaps this latter scenario, in particular, would have led to experiences or optimism that could have tempered the pain and bitterness she felt at the conclusion of her otherwise distinguished career. Yet, Fleming's (2009) argument about the role of the process movement in the disciplinary emergence of composition-rhetoric provides a different perspective.

Fleming (2009) argues that the "process revolution" gave full disciplinary standing to composition-rhetoric, but the discipline's emergence required a firm break with its past. Despite disciplinary gains made through professionalization and research during the 1940s, 50s, and 60s, it was "the turbulent years of 1967–1970" that functioned as a metaphorical wall which the emerging discipline of composition-rhetoric "could not surmount" (p. 45). While current-traditional rhetoric was invalidated during this period, "there was nothing pedagogically or institutionally powerful enough to take its place," until the emergence of the process paradigm in 1971 (Fleming, 2009, pp. 44–45). The years that comprise this metaphorical wall, this liminal space between current-traditionalism and process, are precisely the years that mark the most turbulent period of Thomas's career. Her retirement and the emergence of process occurred almost simultaneously. Given what Thomas's memoir reveals about her Victorian–New England convictions and her ideological grounding in current-traditionalism, she likely would have resisted the process paradigm, with its emphasis on displacing traditional teacherly authority. However, she certainly would have endorsed its underlying motivation to "treat each student as a unique and whole person who needs time and support to find his or her voice" (Fleming, 2009, p. 47). Thomas's commitment to students and their writing, before such was the professional norm, further attests to the pioneering nature of her work as a writing instructor and WPA.

Fortunately, despite the turbulent end to her career, Thomas found personal fulfillment in retirement by volunteer tutoring at UW-Madison's Writing Lab and especially by providing English tutoring to the spouses of international graduate and post-doctoral science students who were living in the university's student housing. As she did with her students and teaching assistants in the English department, Thomas regularly invited these women to her home for Sunday dinners, and she maintained written correspondence with many of them long after they had left the university, a witness to Thomas's profound and lasting impact on their lives. And, unsurprisingly, Thomas's continued efforts to support individual students and community members in their efforts to communicate more clearly foreshadowed the process movement's emphasis on the whole person and on promoting the development of that person's unique voice.

Fleming's account of the emergence of composition-rhetoric suggests that the growing pains preceding the emergence of composition-rhetoric as a full-fledged discipline were analogous to the turmoil evident in the UW-Madison English department during the late 1960s. In both cases, the tensions facilitated growth and change, but not without costs. So although these events coincided with, and partially contributed to, the end of Thomas's career, they were historically significant—for the discipline of composition-rhetoric, for general education, for U.S. higher education. It seems fitting to treat Thomas's memoir as a memorial to that highly volatile but highly generative period.

Ultimately, however, the publication of Thomas's memoir functions as a memorial to Thomas herself, to her dedicated and far-reaching service as a writing instructor and writing program administrator that influenced countless students, teaching assistants, high school teachers in and beyond Wisconsin, and members of the English department, the University of Wisconsin, and the discipline of composition-rhetoric. While publishing her memoir probably wouldn't replicate the gratification Thomas enjoyed by being publicly honored on the UW-Madison campus by television actor Daniel J. Travanti, her former Freshman English student,[14] it will at least introduce her to a new audience of scholars and teachers who will benefit from hearing and learning from the perspective and achievements, both personal and professional, of a unique and remarkable teacher and mentor, whose underlying focus in writing instruction—to treat students with respect—remains highly relevant to our work and central to our discipline.

EDITOR'S NOTE

As Fleming acknowledges in the afterword, the memoir lacks extensive editing because my goal was to preserve it largely as it was written. Further, the memoir is replete with references—to literary figures and works, friends and neighbors, faculty and staff at UW-Madison, places and events of local and national significance—that will be familiar to some readers but unfamiliar to many others, especially younger generations. Given these factors, I've focused my editorial work on contextualizing the memoir by providing a variety of explanatory footnotes for a range of references that I hope will make the memoir accessible to a range of readers. When an individual (e.g., faculty member) who has been introduced earlier in the memoir makes an appearance in a later chapter, I generally repeat the explanatory footnote for that individual in order to facilitate clarity.

For a composition-rhetoric audience, I've made extensive efforts to corroborate Thomas's account of student unrest at UW-Madison in the 1960s and the abolition of Freshman English with content from the university's multi-volume institutional history and Fleming's book *From Form to Meaning: Freshman*

---

14 Kathy, Thomas's daughter-in-law, described this experience as having profound significance for Thomas. Receiving official acknowledgement from a former student (and a famous actor, no less) that Thomas had made a difference in his life, that her life's work mattered and was worth the effort, was enough validation to last a lifetime. As Kathy recalled, even so proper a Victorian New Englander as Thomas couldn't help manifesting a tinge of "shy pride" at receiving such prominent recognition for having positively influenced such a prominent, and kind, person.

Composition and the Long Sixties, 1957–1974. These footnotes attempt to situate Thomas's individual account within a larger scholarly context, add depth and complexity to that account, and affirm its centrality in contributing to the "multivocal past" (Gold, 2012, p. 17) of historical research on teaching and administering first-year writing in twentieth-century American higher education. Ideally, the memoir and footnotes will model a kind of dialogic exchange about the historical events under consideration that will advance inquiry and understanding.

REFERENCES

Berlin, J. A. (1987). *Rhetoric and Reality: Writing Instruction in American Colleges, 1900–1985.* Carbondale: Southern Illinois University Press.

Berlin, J. A. (1984). *Writing Instruction in Nineteenth-Century American Colleges.* Carbondale: Southern Illinois University Press.

Charlton, C., Charlton, J., Graban, T. S., Ryan, K. J. & Stolley, A. F. (2011). *GenAdmin: Theorizing WPA Identities in the Twenty-First Century.* Anderson, SC: Parlor Press.

Connolly, F. & Levin, G. H. (1968). *The Art of Rhetoric.* New York: Harcourt, Brace & World.

Connors, R. (1997). *Composition-Rhetoric: Backgrounds, Theory, and Pedagogy.* Pittsburgh: University of Pittsburgh Press.

Donahue, P. & Moon, G. F. (Eds.). (2007). *Local Histories: Reading the Archives of Composition.* Pittsburgh: University of Pittsburgh Press.

Enoch, J. (2008). *Refiguring Rhetorical Education: Women Teaching African American, Native American, and Chicano/a Students, 1865–1911.* Carbondale: Southern Illinois University Press.

Enos, T. & Borrowman, S. (Eds.). (2008). *The Promise and Perils of Writing Program Administration.* West Lafayette. IN: Parlor Press.

Fleming, D. (2011). *From Form to Meaning: Freshman Composition and the Long Sixties, 1957–1974.* Pittsburgh: University of Pittsburgh Press.

Fleming, D. (2009). "Rhetorical Revival or Process Revolution? Revisiting the Emergence of Composition-Rhetoric as a Discipline." In *Renewing Rhetoric's Relation to Composition: Essays in Honor of Theresa Jarnagin Enos.* Borrowman, S., Brown, S. & Miller, T. (Eds.). New York: Routledge.

Freedom and Discipline in English: Report of the Commission on English. (1965). New York: College Entrance Examination Board.

George, D. (2004). "'Replacing Nice, Thin Bryn Mawr Miss Crandall with Fat, Harvard Savage': WPAs at Bryn Mawr College, 1902 to 1923." In L'Eplattenier, B. & Mastrangelo, L. (Eds.)., *Historical Studies of Writing Program Administration: Individuals, Communities, and the Formation of a Discipline.* West Lafayette, IN: Parlor Press.

Gold, D. (2008). *Rhetoric at the Margins. Revising the History of Writing Instruction in American Colleges, 1873–1947*. Carbondale: Southern Illinois University Press.

Gold, D. (2012). "Remapping Revisionist Historiography." *College Composition and Communication 64*(1), 15–34.

Gunner, J. (2004). "Doomed to Repeat It?: A Needed Space for Critique in Historical Recovery." In L'Eplattenier, B. & Mastrangelo, L. (Eds.)., *Historical Studies of Writing Program Administration: Individuals, Communities, and the Formation of a Discipline*. West Lafayette, IN: Parlor Press.

Hughes, B. T. (2017). *An Interview with Joyce Steward*. Edited by Susan H. McLeod. Fort Collins, Colorado: The WAC Clearinghouse and University Press of Colorado. Available at https://wac.colostate.edu/books/thomas-steward/.

Lacy, E. W. & Thomas, E. S. (1951). *Guide for Good Writing: A Composition Text For College Students*. Harrisburg, PA: The Telegraph Press.

L'Eplattenier, B. & Mastrangelo, L. (Eds.). (2004). *Historical Studies of Writing Program Administration: Individuals, Communities, and the Formation of a Discipline*. West Lafayette, IN: Parlor Press.

Mastrangelo, L. (2012). *Writing a Progressive Past: Women Teaching and Writing in the Progressive Era*. Anderson, SC: Parlor Press.

Skeffington, J., Borrowman, S. & Enos, T. (2008). "Living in the Spaces Between: Profiling the Writing Program Administrator." In Enos, T. & Borrowman, S. (Eds.)., *The Promise and Perils of Writing Program Administration*. West Lafayette. IN: Parlor Press.

Snell, A. F. (1942). "History of English Studies in Mount Holyoke Seminary and College." Unpublished manuscript. English Department Records. Mount Holyoke Archives and Special Collections, South Hadley, MA.

Strickland, D. (2011). *The Managerial Unconscious in the History of Composition Studies*. Carbondale: Southern Illinois University Press.

Thomas, E. S. (1954). "Devices for Training Graduate Assistants." In "The Graduate Assistant and the Freshman English Student: A Panel Discussion." T. J. Kallsen. (Rec.) *College Composition and Communication 5*(1), 35–36.

Thomas, E. S. (1955). *Evaluating Student Themes*. Madison: University of Wisconsin Press.

THE MEMOIR OF
EDNAH SHEPARD THOMAS

BIOGRAPHICAL OUTLINE

1901	June 14: Born in Brookline, Massachusetts
1919	June 20: Graduated from Brookline High School
1923	Graduated from Mt. Holyoke College (major in English composition, minor in literature)
1924	Graduated from Bryn Mawr (M.A. in English)
1924	Taught English and history at Killingly High School in Danielson, CT
1925	Enrolled in English Ph.D. program at University of Wisconsin and taught Freshman English
1927	Sept 1: Married Charles Wright Thomas (known as Wright), fellow Ph.D. student at UW-Madison, and moved to New Haven, CT
1928	Wright hired by UW-Madison English department
1931	Moved to home in Frost Woods (Monona, WI)
1938	Wright denied tenure
1941	Oct 21: Wright asks for a divorce, moves to Washington, DC on Dec 6
1942	June: Thomas begins teaching correspondence courses in the United States Armed Forces Institute (USAFI) program
1943	July 14: Divorce finalized
1945	Invited to teach Freshman English at UW-Madison as part-time teaching assistant
1947	Appointed as Instructor and invited to help administer Freshman English
1951	*Guide for Good Writing*, co-authored with Ed Lacy, published; Promoted to Assistant Professor
1955	*Evaluating Student Themes* published by University of Wisconsin Press
1959	Promoted to Associate Professor
1962	Directed Commission on English summer institute at UW-Madison

Biographical Outline

1965   Directed National Defense Education Act (NDEA) summer institute at UW-Madison; Master Teaching Assistants Program implemented

1966   June: Promoted to Full Professor

1971   Retired; Volunteer tutored in the UW-Madison Writing Lab and in the community

1986   Invited to lunch with Daniel J. Travanti at the Madison Club, hosted by the Alumni Association

1995   May 25: Honored by Daniel J. Travanti at the UW-Milwaukee School of Education's 10th Annual Gala Tribute to Teaching

1995   Oct 27: Died in her sleep in her Frost Woods home at age 94

FOREWORD

For some little time I've played with the idea of writing an autobiography when I retired. "I have often thought," says Dr. Johnson in his noble way, "that there has rarely passed a life of which a judicious and faithful narrative would not be useful. For, not only every man has, in the mighty mass of the world, great numbers in the same condition with himself, to whom his mistakes and miscarriages, escapes and expedients, would be of immediate and apparent use; but there is such an uniformity in the state of man, considered apart from adventitious and separable decorations and disguises, that there is scarce any possibility of good or ill but is common to human kind. . . . We are all prompted by the same motives, all deceived by the same fallacies, all animated by hope, obstructed by danger, entangled by desire, and seduced by pleasure."[1] But the real reason is probably just that I like to write, especially to an elite and appreciative audience like you.[2] When I was in college, I thought vaguely that I would spend my life "writing." That I haven't is no evidence of any sacrifice. I've taught because I wanted to (and I think I've been a better teacher than I would have been writer, for whatever value that may have). But now what better way for me to fill the time on my hands?

As Peter[3] pointed out, I should have a theme, a focus, a center, and I said certainly I had one. My first idea was that I wanted to leave you evidence that I had enjoyed my life. I don't remember my mother as happy in her last years, and I wish that you could remember me as happy. She became increasingly anxious over increasingly infinitesimal things, and since I can see that happening to me already, I'd like to counteract the effect on you while I still can.

As a matter of fact, I doubt if anybody's last years can be particularly happy. "Her last years were not happy but she had her memories" seems a note often struck in biography. Memories are not much comfort, I think. As Dante observed (and I get this *not* from the original but from George Eliot's use of it in *Daniel Deronda*), "This is truth the poet sings/ That a sorrow's crown of sorrow/ Is remembering happier things."[4] No one can enjoy recognizing that his powers,

---

1 Samuel Johnson (1709–1784), English writer and critic, published "Biography" in *The Rambler* on October 13, 1750. The essay was reprinted in Connolly's (1968) composition textbook *The Art of Rhetoric*, which Thomas used in English 309: Composition for English Teachers at UW-Madison.
2 Thomas is addressing her three children: Hannah, Tom, and Bill.
3 Thomas's son-in-law.
4 These lines appear in chapter 12 of Eliot's 1876 novel, where they are attributed to Alfred, Lord Tennyson (1809–1892), specifically his 1835 poem "Locksley Hall."

physical and mental, are failing. Even now it is an annoyance to me, repeated a number of times every day, that when I get up from a sitting position I move stiffly and awkwardly for a dozen steps before I walk easily. If you have had a busy life and believed it to be a useful one, it is particularly painful to recognize you are no longer of real use. My mother, I believe, on the whole did have a happy life. She was the youngest of a large family and had three older brothers who were very fond of her and took great care of her, so she certainly had a happy childhood. From my own observation I know she had a supremely happy marriage. When I was no longer living at home but coming back for visits, there was never a time my father and I were alone together that he didn't say, "Your mother is the most wonderful woman in the world." It used to bore me then but I like to think of it now. He never came home without looking for her and was never contented unless he knew where she was; and although she was much the stronger of the two, the love between them was equal and infinite. This is certainly one of the greatest happinesses which can come to any woman. She had the pleasure of motherhood, though she bore one child only, and she had pleasure from her grandchildren, though it was limited by distance and the age gap. The older I grow, the less I think of her last years and the more I think of the middle ones which I knew—as you will probably do for me, since it seems to be one of Nature's many kind provisions. But I can help by putting down here enjoyments you from first-hand observation couldn't know anything about.

But this won't quite do, alone, for a theme. To adopt the sundial motto and count only the hours that shine would certainly be lacking in depth for a life which has included two world wars, the dropping of the bomb on Hiroshima, the Great Depression, the pollution of the environment to an extent which may be irreversible, Lewis Mumford's megamachine technology,[5] and what may turn out to be a complete world revolution.

My second idea came to me suddenly, a couple of years ago, when it occurred to me for the first time that my first remembrance gave the key to my whole character: lack of initiative. In a three-year-old child, the incident revealed the way I was going to live my whole life. So here surely is a second theme.

The great fictional autobiographies make keen use of the first remembrance. The happy little David Copperfield remembers his mother, "with her pretty hair and youthful shape," and Peggotty—"these two at a little distance apart, dwarfed to my sight by stooping down or kneeling on the floor, and I going unsteadily from the one to the other. I have an impression on my mind which I cannot distinguish from actual remembrance, of the touch of Peggotty's forefinger as she used

---

5   Lewis Mumford (1895–1990), American historian and philosopher, coined this term in his two-volume treatise, *The Myth of the Machine* (1967, 1970), on modern technology.

to hold it out to me, and of its being roughened by needlework, like a pocket nutmeg-grater." He remembers the yard, "a very preserve of butterflies, where the fruit clusters on the trees, riper and richer than fruit has ever been since, in any other garden" and "the red light at sunrise shining on the sun-dial." For the sad little Pip,

> my first vivid and broad impression of the identity of things, seems to have been gained on a memorable raw afternoon towards evening. At such a time I found out for certain, that this bleak place overgrown with nettles was the churchyard; and that the dark flat wilderness beyond the churchyard was the marshes; and that the low leaden line beyond was the river; and that the distant savage lair from which the wind was rushing, was the sea; and that the small bundle of shivers growing afraid of it all and beginning to cry, was Pip.

The incident which is my first remembrance became a family story, of course, told and retold, but I am convinced from one detail, like David's memory of Peggotty's roughened forefinger, that I remember it myself apart from hearing it repeated. It happened the latter part of a calm summer afternoon at South Yarmouth, on the Cape. Your Aunt Hannah, who was always very good to me, had taken me out for a row. She brought us back, took the oars out of the boat and laid them on the pier, and then stepped out herself; the little push of her getting out gave the untied boat enough impetus to send it out of her reach. She ran up to the house to get help. The boat drifted away and I sat perfectly still. It drifted under a long pier stretching out into the water on which some boys were playing, and they reached down and lifted me up. I don't remember being pulled out, or the boys, or waiting for my mother; but I do remember the rough feel against my cheek of the golf cape she was wearing when she carried me home, no doubt because at three I was past the stage of being carried, ordinarily.

In this case I owed my survival and you owe your existence to the fact that I sat still and did nothing. And I see now as I look back over my life that, with one single exception, I have never taken the initiative. That exception was my decision to come to a Middle Western university—just for one year. And to that decision of course also you owe your existence. Do you remember Huxley's account of the player on the other side, who plays against us, hidden from us, whose moves are always fair, just, patient, but who never makes a mistake? He rewards us generously if we make the right move; if we make the wrong one, he checkmates, without haste but without remorse.[6] I have been very generously

---

6   Thomas Henry Huxley (1825–1895), an English evolutionary biologist. This analogy appears in Huxley's "A Liberal Education; and Where to Find it," a lecture delivered in 1868 at the South London Working Men's College.

rewarded with a full rich life—and three children—for that one act. And it was so decisive that I never again showed initiative. Here surely is something of a second theme.

The older I grow and the more I look back, the more insistently a third theme seems to present itself—and considerably to my reluctance. For one thing, it is hardly consistent with my first purpose. It is derived less from my private than from my public life—which hasn't been very public at that, but which after all has been spent in public service. And thought I agree with Thoreau that if you read one newspaper you need never bother to read another,[7] and though I'm proud to say that no tree has ever been cut down to furnish *me* with newsprint, still I am an American citizen and I can hardly have lived over seventy years, more than forty of them in such a politically aware community as Madison, without being to some degree conscious of what was going on in my society.

This theme is stated in an essay by Sir James Jeans,[8] which I encountered in an anthology Somerset Maugham brought out in the thirties. Jeans, of course, is a bona fide scientist, a member of the Royal Academy, not a science fiction writer, but he dealt here with a popular science fiction theme, the end of the world, which was to be destroyed by contact with a piece which would break off from the moon. Astronomers were able to predict the event with so much time to spare that man had time to prepare for it: "Men will die but man will live forever." The preparation took the form of breeding a new race of men who could colonize another planet, and not just move around on it in space suits as our astronauts are now doing on the moon, but live in it freely, adapted to its physical conditions. The colonization came off successfully and the human race survived. But the new world, as necessitated by the enormity of the physical obstacles to be overcome, was so highly organized that no personality or individuality was left. Human society was conducted inflexibly under orders from a central control, like ant society. The interesting point to me when I first read the essay, and the relevant one here, is Jeans' discussion of the objection which he felt might be raised, that the creation of such a society is hardly more tolerable to us than the destruction of humanity would have been. Pointing out that the Pilgrims were much happier in the England of King James, which they left to

---

7   A reference to remarks in American transcendentalist Henry David Thoreau's *Walden* (1854) about the frivolous content of news: "I am sure that I never read any memorable news in a newspaper. If we read of one man robbed, or murdered, or killed by accident, or one house burned, or one vessel wrecked, or one steamboat blown up, or one cow run over on the Western Railroad, or one mad dog killed, or one lot of grasshoppers in the winter—we never need read of another. One is enough."

8   Sir James Jeans (1877–1946), an English physicist, astronomer, mathematician and co-founder of British cosmology.

build a new world, than they could be in the world which has resulted from their efforts, he said: "The future will not be as we would have it."

In the forty years since I first read that statement, and increasingly in the last ten, it has become more and more impressive to me. Education is the field in which I have had my experience. I think of the ideal of the Founding Fathers that in the new country education should be available to all to could profit by it. I look at education today: students ignorant and arrogant; respect for the wisdom of the elders buried in the grave with Helen White,[9] and perhaps rightly so; faculty self-centered and self-seeking on the right, or flaming demagogues on the left bent on blowing up—literally—the ivory tower. "The best lack all conviction," in the words of the later Yeats, "while the worst are full of passionate intensity."[10] I hear the roar of almost universal public condemnation of the results of the American dedication to education. And Jeans' statement takes on a bitter truth. It will have to play some part here if I am going to make any approach to giving you a true view of my life.

I don't know that this will be a true view of my life. I won't say anything that isn't true, but like Jane Fairfax in *Emma*, I may leave some truths untold. It doesn't do children any harm, perhaps, to think more highly of their mother than she deserves. I don't know that it is possible for anyone to give a true view of his life. Oliver Wendell Holmes speaks of the three Johns: one known only to his Maker, one known to himself, one known to whoever is speaking to him or thinking of him or remembering him.[11] Remember me kindly.

---

9   Helen Constance White (1896–1967) earned a Ph.D. in English from the University of Wisconsin-Madison in 1924 and remained there throughout her distinguished career as a specialist in British literature. She became the first female full professor in the university's history in 1936 and served as chair of the English department between 1955–1958 and 1961–1965. She was also active professionally, serving as president of the University of Wisconsin Teachers Union, as the national president of the American Association of University Women, and as a U.S. delegate to UNESCO meetings (Hoeveler).
10 An excerpt from Irish poet William Butler Yeats's "The Second Coming" (1920), a modernist poem about post-war Europe.
11 A reference to American physician and writer Oliver Wendell Homes Sr.'s (1809–1894) collection of essays, *The Autocrat of the Breakfast-Table* (1858).

FOREBEARS

> "All these things have worked together to make me what I am."
> – Charles Dickens[12]

My father was Lindsley Horace Shepard, born in 1863. It is from him that you derive whatever blue blood flows in your veins. His mother was Hannah Bartlett Spooner of Plymouth; and while the Spooners did not come on the first voyage of the Mayflower they arrived shortly after, and a Spooner son married a daughter of John and Priscilla Alden. The Spooner house in Plymouth is now a museum, left to the community by the last owner, my father's childless Cousin Ruth.[13] I remember going as a child to the house, full of all sorts of treasures brought back from all over the globe by sea captains, and we have a picture of the doll Williamina which William Lloyd Garrison gave to Cousin Ruth when she was a little girl. Hannah Bartlett Morehouse[14] is the twelfth in succession to bear the name.

The Shepards were in the lumber business. A psychoanalyst might say that it is from this fact that I derive my phobia about cutting down trees. I can't recall any conscious feelings of guilt but I don't know about my subconscious. The firm of Shepard Morse was very prosperous and still has a big plant on Route 128. My grandfather, Horace, worked for the firm as bookkeeper, sitting behind a high desk like that of Mr. Fezziwig, as did his son Morris, Pauline [Shepard] Blood's older brother, after him—though by then at a modern desk. Horace was an employee and not a partner and therefore not one of the very opulent Shepards. My father as a boy went to the famous Boston Latin School, the first public school in the country, where Hancock, Samuel Adams, Benjamin Franklin, Emerson, and other famous men had preceded him, and did well there, but was not able to go to college, for financial reasons.[15] I think my father worked briefly for the firm, but as far back as I can remember he was running his own much smaller business.

---

12   An excerpt from the first of a three-volume biography, *The Life of Charles Dickens* (1847), by English biographer and critic John Forster (1812–1876).
13   The Spooner House was built circa 1749, converted to a historical museum in 1954, and renovated in 2011 by the Plymouth Antiquarian Society.
14   Thomas's daughter.
15   The Boston Latin school, founded in April 1635, predates Harvard, making it "the oldest school in America."

Horace Shepard served in the Civil War. When I married it seemed romantic to me that my grandfather and Wright's[16] father had both been soldiers, Yankee and Johnny Reb respectively, and that therefore you would be living symbols of peace and union. The story goes that Horace and his intended wife with her parents were guests at a New Hampshire summer hotel when war was declared, that they were married at once on the hotel piazza along with another couple, and that both bridegrooms left immediately to enlist. Horace returned home safely, and I know no details of his service. I have a very dim memory of him as a handsome old man with a white beard, and his wife died long before I was born. They had four children, of whom only my father lived to maturity. About the time my father married his first wife, my grandfather married his second, an English girl about my father's age, known to and loved by us as "Aunt Annie." I don't know how they met. She had some locutions strange to me ("git" for "get," "wash my hairs") but what locale they represented I still don't know. She was a tall handsome woman with large dark eyes, and her three children, Morris, Pauline [later Pauline Blood], and Arthur, were all tall and handsome. My father was not particularly tall, perhaps five feet eight, but in general the Shepard men are all tall and handsome, a tradition I'm delighted to have been able to carry on with my sons. These three children were born within a five-year span during which my father and his first wife had two, Hannah and Clarence. So these five children were very close in age and had a wonderful time together, regardless of the fact that Pauline and Arthur were younger than their niece Hannah and nephew Clarence, and Morris, oldest of the group, only a trifle older. Horace and his family lived on a farm in Sharon, Massachusetts, about half way between Boston and Providence. Lindsley and his family went there often, driving out by horse and buggy, and my brother and sister hunted for eggs, slid in the hay mow, drank milk fresh from the cow, and did all the other farm things I wish I could have shared. Aunt Annie, incidentally, was a wonderful cook. By the time I was old enough to remember going to Sharon, my grandfather had died, and his widow had moved to a small house in a small yard near the center of town. Her children had left home or were finishing college.

My father's first wife died in childbirth with her second child—according to family report because she objected to being examined by a doctor until too late. (We certainly differ from the Victorians in our attitude to the medical profession. You remember that Richard Feverel, on his fourteenth birthday, was asked by his father—in advance of his time in this respect—to submit to a medical examination "like a boor enlisting for a soldier" and Richard "was in great wrath.") She was Grace Whittaker, but I know almost nothing about the Whittakers except

---

16 Charles Wright Thomas, Thomas's husband from 1927 to 1943.

that they came from North Adams, in far Western Massachusetts. Hannah Davis[17] has a charming picture of her, wearing a big hat, sitting in a carriage with her husband and father-in-law, and once when Hannah and I were going over family pictures she told me something which threw light on difficulties I've observed adopted children often have. When she was a little girl, Hannah said, her father used to try to tell her about her mother, but since by that time she looked upon her stepmother, my mother, as her real mother, it seemed a sort of disloyalty to her to listen, so she knew almost nothing about her blood mother; but now, so many years later, she was sorry she hadn't listened. It was very interesting to me to see how strong the blood bond was, for no relationship could have been happier than that between my mother and her stepdaughter. That Hannah and I are so different in every respect—we've only been able to come up with one similarity, that we both have a knack for finding four-leaf clovers—I suppose is due largely to her Whittaker and my Goodwin blood.

My father married his second wife about two years after the death of his first (a Whittaker cousin had kept house for him in the meantime, an elderly woman not well fitted for the care of small children), but I was not born for eight years after that. I was the only child of rather elderly parents (they were both in their thirty-ninth year), and the result for me was a very solitary childhood and much more reading than real life. Hannah and Clarence were both very fond of me and very good to me when I was a baby, but by the time I can remember much they were away from home. I've always been very thankful for you that there were three of you and that the neighborhood had children of about the same age. Hannah as for some time the only girl was less lucky than the boys, perhaps, but she always had her brothers.

Horace Shepard was one of twelve children, and my father had well over forty first cousins, most of whom I never knew. The oldest son of the founder of the firm, Otis, his two brothers, and his sister, Cousin Emily, all lived in Brookline,[18] in big estates on or near Rawson Road. Cousin Emily, following a pattern common in her generation, never married, but stayed in her father's house to care for her widowed mother. The house was very large, cared for by plenty of servants, and the grounds included the coach house where the horses were kept. Again according to the proper Bostonian tradition, when it became clear that the automobile was inevitably superseding the horse, the family coachman, Joseph Brady, was taught to drive a car and became the family chauffeur, a position he continued to hold until Cousin Emily's death in her ninety-sixth year. No better example ever existed of the devoted family servant. One of his

---

17 Thomas's half-sister, mentioned in the preceding paragraph.
18 A Boston suburb in Northfolk County, Massachusetts, where Thomas was raised and attended high school.

grandchildren, incidentally, was born on the same day as Anne Morehouse. I spent Easter once at Hannah's while Tom was at BU,[19] and he took me to the service at the First Unitarian Church in Brookline, where I had gone as a child and with Cousin Emily attended all her life. The neighborhood was surprisingly little changed; we arrived early and walked around a little to look at the big houses and their gardens, and got back to the church just in time to see Joseph driving Cousin Emily to the door, helping her and her companion carefully out and taking them up the steps, and then driving away again. "Why doesn't Joseph go to church *with* her?" said Tom democratically. "Joseph will go to his own church and certainly doesn't want to go to ours," said I. This was after Al Smith's[20] defeat for President and before John Kennedy's election smashed forever the taboo against a Catholic president. As I write, Muskie[21] is the leading contender for the Democratic nomination for the election of '72, and I doubt if one comment out of a thousand on him refers to his religion. We saw a good deal of Cousin Emily, who was very fond of my mother, but of the other Brookline Shepards I saw little or nothing. The children went to private schools, I to public. I do remember one Christmas—perhaps I was twelve or thirteen—when Otis had a big family party and asked all the relatives. But most of my second cousins were young married people, the ages of Hannah and Clarence, and their children were babies or toddlers, so I was out of it from both ends.

Several of my great aunts made marriages which connected us with interesting and even well-known people. One married the publisher George Haven Putnam. Their daughter Bertha[22] was a distinguished pioneer in the field of women's education, an early Bryn Mawr Ph.D., the first woman to receive a research fellowship from Harvard, and a professor of history at Mount Holyoke, where she was very kind to me. Her sister Corinna married Joseph Lindon Smith,[23] an artist and archeologist. In the early excavation of Egyptian tombs, objects crumbled to dust on being exposed to air and light, and the only known method of preservation was to draw them in situ. Much of his work of this sort is now in the Boston Museum of Fine Arts. He and Corinna belonged to

---

19   Boston University, a private research university established in Boston, M.A. in 1839.
20   Alfred Emanuel "Al" Smith (1873–1944), the three-time governor of New York and Democratic U.S. presidential candidate in 1928, was the first nominee for President who was Roman Catholic.
21   Edmund Muskie (1914–1996), Governor of Maine, U.S. senator, Democratic nominee for Vice President in 1968, candidate for the Democratic nomination for President in 1972, and Secretary of State under Jimmy Carter.
22   Thomas describes Bertha Putnam's impact on her in the "Mount Holyoke" chapter.
23   Joseph Lindon Smith (1863–1950), American painter and founding member of the Dublin Art Colony.

the circle dominated by the famous Mrs. Jack Gardiner,[24] and both of them appeared in the biography of her I read a few years ago. Another great aunt married Rafael Pumpelli,[25] the distinguished geologist and explorer of the west, the friend of Clarence King.[26] I remember also the Fishers; one of my father's cousins married a wealthy Chicago businessman, and devoted much of her life to the development of the voice of her oldest daughter Bernice. Bernice studied abroad, became a member of the Boston Opera Company, and sang Gretel one Christmas in "Hansel and Gretel" there, among other roles, of course, but I was taken to see that performance. She made a wealthy marriage herself not long after, and left the opera stage.

If you want to picture my father physically, you have only to look at Bill.[27] He did not have red hair, but brown, about the color of mine, and it never turned gray; but with that exception, physically and temperamentally, the two are almost uncannily alike. It is interesting to see the genes at work in trivial things. My father was always complaining that his food was too hot, and I can remember how he disconcerted restaurant waitresses by putting ice from his water glass into the coffee they had tried hard to bring him piping hot. I can also remember time after time when the four of us were having soup, say, for lunch, and Hannah, Tom, and I would have emptied our plates while Bill was still complaining that his was too hot to touch. Our explanation that if he would eat around the edges instead of dipping his spoon into the center he'd have no trouble had no more effect on him than it would have had on my father.

One of my favorite passages in literature is in *Emma* because in it my father appears to the life. Isabella Woodhouse and her family are visiting her father at Christmas, and he urges her to go to bed early because she must be tired from the journey. "'And I recommend a little gruel to you before you go. You and I will have a nice basin of gruel together. My dear Emma, suppose we all have a little gruel.' Emma could not suppose any such thing, knowing, as she did, that both the Mr. Knightleys were as unpersuadable on that article as herself, and two basins only were ordered." Mr. Woodhouse indulges in "a little more discourse in praise of gruel, with some wondering at its not being taken every evening, by everybody . . . ." I never read that without hearing my father say, as he did every

---

24 Isabella Stewart Gardner (1840–1924), an art collector and philanthropist who founded the Isabella Stewart Gardner Museum (known as Fenway Court during her lifetime) in Boston in 1903.

25 Raphael Pumpelly (1837–1923), an American geologist and explorer and professor of mining science at Harvard.

26 Clarence King (1842–1901), an American geologist, mountaineer, author, and first director of the United States Geological Survey (1879–1881).

27 Thomas's son.

morning on every visit I made my parents after I had left home, "Won't you have some oatmeal this morning, Ednah? Your mother makes it so nicely." He was incapable of understanding that I was "unpersuadable" when it came to enjoying something he so much enjoyed and so generously wanted to share. I also think of him when I read in *David Copperfield* of men who possess "a certain freshness, and gentleness, and capacity of being pleased, an inheritance they have preserved from their childhood." I want to choose my words carefully because this is a matter of semantics. To call a man "childish" is by no means a compliment; to call him "childlike" may be. Either perhaps carries with it today a connotation of naïveté. You couldn't call my father sophisticated, nor me either, and I have lived my life in the academic atmosphere where "naïve" is about the most devastating adjective you can apply.

My father was personally neat to the point of fastidiousness. He wore a mustache which gave him a strong resemblance to Teddy Roosevelt, a bit unfortunate because he considered Teddy's action in bolting the Republican Party an act of great treachery and never had any use for him after that. I can remember him wearing a top hat and carrying a gold-headed cane, taking me as a little girl for a Sunday walk on the Charles River Esplanade.[28] I also remember Sunday drives. He was very fond of horses and very good with them, not as a rider but as a driver. In my babyhood he kept his own horses and we had a coachman. Later he gave them up but continued to rent an equipage from the livery stable and take us to ride. At this time, the automobile was making advances, but slowly, and none of us had any idea of the extent of the changes it was to bring about. For quite a time automobile traffic was prohibited in the Arnold Arboretum,[29] and my father knew a number of private roads where it was also forbidden, so we could get in as extensive and pleasant a drive behind the clop-clop of the hoofs as you would wish for on a spring day. He tried later to learn to drive a car but never succeeded in mastering the art and finally at my mother's urgent request gave up the effort.

A very great debt I owe my father is my passion for Dickens. It was the strongest bond we had in common, and it has been a source of enormous pleasure to me all my life. Our family was a small one, actually, but the hundreds of Dickens characters who looked down on us from the dining room walls in the two steel engravings which are today among my most cherished possessions, enriched and expanded it, and their phrases were part of our family language: "the beer being served up in its native pewter," "don't know what the good of minding it would

---

28 This state-owned park, originally the Boston Embankment, is located near the Back Bay area of Boston.

29 An arboretum of Harvard University designed by American landscape architect Fredrick Law Olmsted (1822–1903).

be," "and on they went as merrily as before," and so on indefinitely. All my life I have controlled troubling details by translating them into allusions to Dickens. If I drive into Madison on a nasty sleety day, I think, "This is just the day for Lady Dedlock to be found dead on her lover's grave." I never put a turkey in the oven at Thanksgiving or Christmas without encouraging myself by Ruth Pinch's comment on her first beefsteak pudding, which may turn out to be a stew or something else: "the meat must come out of the saucepan at last, somehow or other, you know. We can't cook it into nothing at all; that's a great comfort." The only year in my life I spent Christmas vacation alone without any one of you here, I read chronologically through the whole canon of the fourteen novels and never felt lonely for a minute. My passion has been the means of many pleasant contacts with others, including many students and the members of the Dickens Fellowship.[30] My only regret is that although I think I have made a number of converts, particularly Sam Blount,[31] I never succeeded in inspiring any one of you. I won't give up hope, though; before I die perhaps I may see my father reincarnated in this respect in one of my grandchildren.

I think the essence of my father's character—and Bill has this quality too—was geniality. His courtly manners, rare if not extinct in this degenerate day and age, were the outer manifestation of an inner warmth, a sincere cordiality, a genuine liking for and reaching out to anyone with whom he came in contact. I have yet to see the man, woman, or child, of any age, from any quarter of the globe, who does not instantly respond to this quality in Bill, and I think no one ever failed to respond to it in my father. My mother told me that as a young man he was in great demand because he assured the success of any party he ever went to. Wright, who called on my parents the first Christmas vacation after we met, when I was in Minneapolis, was much more attracted to my father than to my mother and wrote me of his kindness "with a cold vainly tugging at his good disposition." I suppose this quality contained something of a wish to be liked; but it contained much more of liking. In this respect he was so much like the early Dickens as to go far toward explaining why Dickens was so great a part of his life, and I could take passage after passage that Dickens himself wrote and feel that it showed what my father was like as well as it showed his idol. I'll close with just one, from Dickens' own (third-person) preface to *The Pickwick Papers*:

---

30   The Dickens Fellowship was founded in London in 1902, a branch of which was established in Madison in 1927 and remains active.
31   Nathan Sam Blount (1929–1989) taught high school in Miami before earning his doctorate in education at Florida State in 1963, after which he was hired by the UW-Madison English department. He held a joint appointment in English and in Education.

Forebears

> If any of his imperfect descriptions, while they afford amusement in the perusal, should induce only one reader to think better of his fellow men, and to look upon the brighter and more kindly side of human nature, he would indeed be proud and happy to have led to such a result.[32]

I never found my mother in Dickens or Jane Austen, but she had much in common with some of the women in Sarah Orne Jewett or Mary Ellen Chase,[33] those New Englanders whose combination of strength and sweetness would be unbelievable if you hadn't known it in real life in Mrs. Wing.[34] But she was unique. She was far more complex and mature than my father, and I was so much more deeply attached to her than to him that it is much harder for me to get the detachment the portrayer in writing should have. I deeply distrust my power to make her come alive for you, but I have to try.

My mother was Florence Annabelle Goodwin, born in Haverhill, Massachusetts, the same year as my father. Her parents were James and Martha Goodwin, who had seven children over a period of twenty years or so. The oldest was Jane; then three sons, Charles, George, and James; then two boys who died in infancy; then my mother, the baby. Brought up by three older brothers who were very fond of her and took great care of her, she had an enviable childhood, and it gave her an enjoyment of men so that she would have preferred a boy to a girl for her own child, I think, though no one could have been loved more tenderly than I was. Perhaps the most important thing about my mother was her power of giving love.

James and Martha both lived well into their nineties, along with James' twin brother, whom I do not remember. My mother was their youngest child and she was nearly forty when I was born; so the gap between them and me was over eighty years and too great for bridging. I have a visual memory of them, rather New England Gothic. Haverhill is only thirty miles from Boston, and was then about an hour's ride by train. Mother could easily go up to spend the day and often took me with her. I also have a picture very far back in my mind of one time when they must have come to Brookline: a small child playing in the front yard and a very old man walking slowly and stiffly out to speak to her: but she was too shy to respond. According to family legend, he gave me my first compliment the first time he saw me: he said I was "worth raising."

---

32 This excerpt appears in the preface to the first (1837) edition.
33 Sarah Orne Jewett (1849–1909), an American novelist and short story writer; Mary Ellen Chase (1887–1973), an American scholar and author who earned a Ph.D. in English from the University of Minnesota and taught there and at Smith College.
34 An acquaintance from the Isle of Springs.

According to family legend also, when James and Martha married each brought an equal amount of money to the union—not much. I'd like to think that Martha was one of the factory girls Dickens approved so on his first American visit, because they had their own piano, published their own magazine, wore modest finery, and altogether were possessed of amenities the English victims of the Industrial Revolution were not, and which many English men and women of the time believed quite improper for factory workers. Dickens of course did not share that view. But I'm afraid this is only romanticizing on my part. I don't really know anything about it. My grandfather had a small farm. I remember the farmhouse very well, at the top of an extremely steep hill known as Mount Washington, in the typical New England pattern; you went from the kitchen to the pantry, from the pantry to the shed, from the shed to the barn, so that you could care for the animals in the snowy winters without having to go outdoors. By the time I went there, of course, James was far too old to care for animals and the barn was empty. Some of the furnishings of the Island cottage,[35] notably the worn red and yellow carpeting, came from that Haverhill house, and there three little girls, Florence Goodwin, Ednah McClure, and Katherine Gage, played together, sometimes with the miniature cast-iron stove and wooden village that ornament our house in Frost Woods[36] every Christmas.

The oldest daughter, whom we called Aunt Jennie, was a very able and unusual woman, possessed to a high degree of the quality of initiative I lack. Since she was so much older than my mother I saw her rarely, when my mother took me with her on visits. Aunt Jennie was then an invalid confined to a wheel chair living in a private home in or near Haverhill. (This arrangement seems to me infinitely preferable to the modern nursing home. You had your own room and while you had your own infirmities, you were surrounded by people in ordinary health, not by those whose infirmities are much worse than yours and therefore extremely depressing.) But though I have an impression of a good keen alert mind—as we say in New England she had all her buttons—again the gap was too great for bridging. But I have heard a good deal about her and have always felt a great interest in her. By her own efforts she put herself through normal school and became a teacher, and saved enough money to take a trip abroad alone—an unheard-of show of independence for the period. She spent some time in Germany and made friends there with whom she continued to correspond, in German, until her death. At that time, one of them sent a note of condolence to my mother written in English, and I remember Mother's regretting

---

35 A reference to Isle of Springs, an island community located in BoothBay Harbor, Maine, where the family spent summer vacations.
36 A community in Monona, WI, where Thomas lived and regularly hosted neighborhood and department gatherings.

that she could not return the courtesy by acknowledging it in German. If I had had a fourth child and it had been a girl, I intended to name her Jane Goodwin.

Uncle George and Uncle Charles lived into middle age; both married and both had children, so that I had five first cousins on the Goodwin side. But they died before their mates, and I don't remember them. Aunt Frances, Uncle George's widow, for many summers shared the present Potts cottage with Aunt Ednah and Mrs. Cox (née Katherine Gage). She was what Dickens called "a comely matron,"[37] with beautiful snow-white hair and a figure not artificially constrained by our modern notions of dieting. She lived in the winters with her son Harold, who was very prosperous and built for his family (he had four children) a very large and luxurious house, where I used to visit for a few days during spring vacations, when I was old enough to travel alone. It was good of Mary, Harold's wife, to have me, since as usual I was out of step—ten or twelve years younger than the parents and a lot older than the children, and not the type to coo over the current baby. Aunt Frances had her own suite of bedroom and bathroom and large sitting room, and was very comfortable. It is characteristic of my mother that when I once spoke of how much more luxuriously Aunt Frances was living than Aunt Annie, alone in her very small and modest house, she said Aunt Annie's independence was infinitely to be preferred to Aunt Frances' position as a guest in her son's house, good son though he undoubtedly was. Uncle Charles and Aunt Dora had three children, of whom we saw much of only one, Helen, whom Hannah at least will remember. She lived in our Brookline house while she was taking nurses' training at a Boston hospital, and after she had followed her profession for some time she left it to marry an old childhood sweetheart who was then a widower with three children. They lived in Brookline, and we saw a good deal of each other. Helen's husband was a CPA and of great help to my parents professionally in their old age. Helen was a typical Goodwin, very active and very long-lived. Her stepchildren, who were all devoted to her, called her "the lively lady." She drove her own car many more years than you would think possible, traveled extensively, and only died a couple of years ago (in her nineties, of course). Like Flora Finching,[38] she never stopped talking from the time she set eyes on you till the time you had gotten out of hearing, and I asked my mother how her husband (his last name was Tompson, and we called him Tommy) could stand it. But she said that Helen could make a man very comfortable (he was diabetic, and her nurses' training was useful), and I'm sure it was a very happy marriage. Only about a year before her death she turned up at the Island unexpectedly, with a friend who was staying at Sprucewood with her

---

37 An excerpt from Dickens's novella, *A Christmas Carol in Prose, Being a Ghost-Story of Christmas* (1834).

38 A character in Dickens's serial novel *Little Dorrit* (1857), a satire of British society.

and the friend's son, and luckily found me in the cottage. We took a brisk walk around the Island and they took the next ferry across. The last thing she said to me was "Your mother was always my favorite aunt."

James, who never married, played a very large part in my life up to his death when I was in college. In fact, I loved and admired him much more than I did my father. Like many New Englanders, he was a very complex character indeed, a man of great ability and certainly some eccentricity. When my mother considered naming me, there were two possibilities: Martha, for her mother (which incidentally I think I would have preferred); Ednah, for her lifelong friend who at the time she believed would be her sister-in-law. That never happened. James Goodwin and Ednah McClure must have loved each other; neither married anyone else; they saw a great deal of each other throughout their lives; but they never married. In those days—and in New England—people's private feelings were their own business and were not discussed. But I did once ask my mother why Uncle James and Aunt Ednah had never married, and she said that as far as she could make out they never both wanted to at the same time.

Uncle James had an excellent mind and a forward-looking one. In contrast to my father, who still kept on driving horses long after it was clear the automobile was here to say (it would probably be more accurate now for me to say "to stay until the fourth quarter of the twentieth century"), he was interested in all technological developments. He bought one of the first radios on the market and though he never drove a car himself, extremely early in the development of the automobile he would rent a car and a driver and come and take my mother and me out for trips. I remember breakdowns when the driver would have to walk to the nearest farmhouse and negotiate for a team of horses to come and tow us back to a garage. Uncle James had worked his way by his own unaided efforts first through Harvard itself and then through Harvard Law School. I still have his Phi Beta Kappa key, and I hope some one among my grandchildren will be entitled to wear it. He accumulated an excellent library, and many of my books were his. While of course the Dickens set was my father's, my white-and-gold Austen was Uncle James's, as well as the Meredith, the Balzac, Smollett, Boswell, Cooper, Emerson, *The Decline and Fall of the Roman Empire*, *The Rise of the Dutch Republic*, and almost all of the rest of my history, and the New England poets, which I take out of a winter to re-read "Snowbound" to myself or "Paul Revere's Ride" to the Monona Friendship Group of International Wives, and many many others. If I had had a fourth child and it had been a boy, I intended to name him James Goodwin. Ideally, after Bill I would have had twins: James Goodwin and Jane Goodwin. But now that I am a septuagenarian, the thought of these two strangers in our lives is a little frightening, and I am glad to call them up for a moment and then dismiss them forever into the shades where Betsey Trotwood Copperfield lives.

Forebears

Uncle James furnished a very stimulating element of the unexpected in my young life. As the fancy took him, he would turn up unannounced with a car and a driver and take my mother and me off for the day. Sometimes we spent the night with him. He lived at the Phillips Inn in Andover, Massachusetts, from which he commuted easily every day to his law office in Haverhill. He had a suite of rooms with fireplace in both bedroom and living room and was very comfortable, eating in the Inn dining room. So it was easy for him to get a room for my mother and me at any time. The Inn in those days had all the comfort and warmth in real life Dickens is able to create in his novels. I know of no creature comfort pleasanter than falling asleep as the firelight plays on your bedroom walls, and waking in the morning when the housemaid comes in to lay and light the new fire, and staying in your warm bed until the temperature of the room gradually becomes ideal to get up and dress in. The only contribution I made in our Frost Woods house, which Wright and Ham[39] had such a good time designing, was that I thought it would be nice to have a fireplace in the master bedroom. Alas, we overlooked the fact that the housemaid could not be built in. The next day we would usually come back on the train. I remember once Mother had been in such a hurry when we left (Uncle James was not a patient man and as usual had given her no advance notice) that she had picked up her season train ticket between Boston and Haverhill but realized on the train when she offered it to the conductor that she had no money at all with her to get us home from the station. The conductor—oh, those simple, sweet days!—put his hand in his pocket, pulled it out full of coins, and held it out to her for her to take whatever she wanted. One trip with Uncle James became a habitual thing; he would drive us down to the Island at the beginning of the summer. We arrived in Wiscasset [Maine] after the Winter Harbor had left on its last trip to the Harbor, so we always spent the night at the Wiscasset Inn and took the steamer down on its first trip next morning—a day and a half for what is now a little over three hours. But in general the expeditions were unplanned. I wonder now if my mother felt any difficulty in reconciling the claims made on her

---

39   Hamilton (Ham) Beatty, son of English faculty member Arthur Beatty (1869–1943), studied English at UW-Madison and architecture at London's Bartlett School of Architecture. In 1935, Ham and Allen Strang, who studied engineering at UW-Madison and architecture at the University of Pennsylvania, founded the Beatty and Strang architectural firm in Madison, WI. Initially, the firm specialized in residential International Style architecture, and several of its unornamented block homes in the Madison area have historic landmark status. The firm's first commission was in Frost Woods, then a village in Monona, just outside Madison, WI, and included Thomas's home. Ham and his wife, Gwen, were neighbors and lifelong friends of the Thomas family. After the Beattys moved, Thomas and Gwen corresponded regularly for more than thirty years. Thomas later borrowed and used her letters to Gwen as source material for portions of the memoir.

by her husband and brother respectively. I think my father's essential kindness, coupled with his knowledge that no one could be loved more devotedly than he was by his wife, probably prevented any strain. At least I was never conscious of any, and I enjoyed every outing to the hilt. Uncle James was also in the habit of arriving unexpectedly at the Island whenever the fancy took him, almost always preceded by a big hamper of fruit sent down from Boston, which was a great treat since, as always, provisioning was a problem. He would stay two or three days and leave as suddenly as he had come. The summer I was sent to a girls' camp in New Hampshire he turned up one day without warning, took all the girls in my cabin out to dinner, and left to their enthusiastic cheer: "One, two, three, four! Who are we for? Ednah's uncle!"

In his latter years he did what many men do—developed an interest in his forebears and tried to find out as much as he could about them. The Goodwins came from northern Massachusetts, near the New Hampshire line. He took a good many trips, looking at old graveyards and the like, and Mother and I often went with him. He discovered and bought the site of the original Goodwin farmhouse, where the only trace of occupation was a row of lilacs along the road, beautiful in spring, but planted in a fit of orneriness by the husband to keep his wife from looking out of her kitchen at passersby and therefore neglecting her work. (I heard recently an ornery story which I can't resist quoting, though it doesn't belong to our family, because it is so characteristic. On an icy day a man carrying an old pitcher slipped in the yard and fell. His wife, in alarm but not for him, called out, "Did you break Grandmother's pitcher?" he answered, "No, my dear, I didn't, but I will now." And he did.) This ornery streak is marked in New England men, though not in my experience in New England women, and I think Uncle James was not free of it though he never showed it to me. It may have been the consciousness of this that made Mother once express a doubt to me as to whether Uncle James would have made Aunt Ednah happy if they had married. On this family site Uncle James built a very handsome summer cabin, a huge living room with a beautiful fireplace, complete with old cranes and pots and oven, and bunks for sleeping. Mother and I quite often spent the night there spring and fall, and I remember how brilliant the red cardinal flowers were along the nearby brook. Harold Goodwin took it over after Uncle James's death.

Uncle James was a handsome man, with prematurely white hair (like my mother), as long as he did not open his mouth. But his teeth were decayed and he did not have courage enough to go to a dentist. He never learned to shave himself, and while this was no problem to him when he was living at home and had his regular barber, at the Island he had to make a special trip to the Harbor every day. He never went unshaven. He was not a well-balanced man, perhaps, but he was never dull. He was not a happy man; but he received a great deal of enjoyment in his life, and he gave a great deal, especially to me. As I said, he died while I was at college. I got the news in the morning and it never for a moment occurred to me that I should go home or would be of any help or comfort to my mother if I did. I went to the library stacks, and stayed there all day, without coming out for lunch or dinner, until the library closed that night. Then I went back to the dormitory and the next day I went to classes as usual.

To come back to my mother. I haven't spoken of her appearance. Her friends with good reason used to condole with me on not having inherited her coloring, which was striking and unusual. Her eyes were bright brown and her hair had turned white prematurely, while she was still in school. With this pure white hair and the high color she had as a young woman, she made you realize why at certain periods of history, women have powdered their hair to achieve the contrast. Since Hannah Davis remembers her as a younger woman than I can, she knows this better than I.

Mother had the unfaltering New England conscience and sense of duty, redeemed from sternness by the spontaneous warmth of her love for those to whom she owed it. In her time your obligation was personal rather than social. She married a man who had already a four-year-old daughter and a two-year-old son, and while there had been nothing like cruelty or real neglect of the children, certainly their situation after their mother's death had not been ideal. Mother had to bring up two children not her own, whom therefore she could not understand with the familiarity that comes of knowing family background, and repair mistakes already made but not of her making. As I have already said, with Hannah the relation was a very happy one. Unfortunately Clarence turned out to be the family black sheep (de mortuis nil nisi[40] notwithstanding). According to modern standards, when an adolescent in the best family becomes a junkie and pusher at the drop of a hat, he wasn't a very deep-dyed black, but he was far from satisfactory. In spite of all his parents' efforts he never did well in school, he never settled down to anything, he never was able to earn much of a living, and he was always getting into various difficulties. At the point in their lives when parents reasonably expect children to take care of themselves, or if anything even to help them, my father and mother, up to Clarence's death, were never free from repeated demands to help him out of some trouble or other, usually financial. Clarence was a good-natured man, like his father, without an ounce of malice and unfortunately also without an ounce of reliability. I'm not sure that without my mother my father would have been strong and patient enough to bear this burden so long; but there was never a doubt in her mind of their joint

---

40   An abbreviated version of the Latin phrase *De mortuis nihil nisi bonum* ("Of the dead, nothing unless good")—an admonition to "Speak no ill of the dead."

responsibility and she never faltered in trying to meet each new demand to the best of her ability, always trying to build self-respect and responsibility in the recipient. I'm not very proud, as I look back now, on the part I played myself in this family problem, which was just nothing at all. I can rationalize that I was younger, and that I gave my parents no anxiety on my own account; I had a brilliant college record and with scholarships and a year's teaching was practically self-supporting from the time I graduated from Holyoke to my marriage. Still if I had had as much sense of responsibility as my mother and applied it to my parents, I think I could have done a good deal better than I did.

She showed this bravery and steadiness in small things as well as great. She married a man who could, I think, be called wealthy, and the establishment he took her to had three resident servants, a cook, a housemaid, and a coachman. But I think my father lost a good deal of money when I was about three, because there were a good many retrenchments. Most of the time I remember Mother did the housework alone, with a weekly cleaning woman, and always with perfect cheerfulness and competence, although she didn't really enjoy cooking (as I do). At a time when most people were throwing all the vitamins from their fresh vegetables down the kitchen sink, she was saving the water for soups. She was thrifty and had clear common sense. I remember once we got an ad for having your photograph taken at a great saving, which I pointed out to her; she said, "If you don't want your photograph taken at all, there wouldn't be *any* saving." Doctor and dentist expenditures without question came before anything else. Good nutrition came before luxury food, though she always celebrated my father's birthday at the end of March by the first asparagus on the market, his favorite vegetable, and took endless pains to keep him supplied with the fresh fruit he loved all through the year. In the days before frozen food, incidentally, the first asparagus or strawberries in season had the relish which can come only from a preliminary period of doing without. She never, as I now am ashamed to find myself doing, evaded anything. Once when I was back on a visit when I was married and had children of my own I found that she regularly read in the newspaper a column conducted by Angelo Patri on how to bring up your children, and I asked her why, since she no longer had to do it. "I'd like to understand my mistakes," she said.[41]

She was very generous and one of her greatest pleasures was to give presents. I have said I think perhaps her most significant quality was her power of loving. She especially loved little children, and to the end of her life kept a toy or so in the house so any who came to see her would have something to play with. I wish

---

41 Angelo Patri (1876–1965), surname Petraglia, an Italian-American author and educator who hosted a radio show and wrote a syndicated newspaper column, "Our Children," on child psychology.

we had lived nearer so that she could have had more enjoyment from you three; but I'm glad to think she did have some. She kept an album of all the pictures of you I sent her, and in one respect at least I feel I was a reasonably good daughter; I wrote her regularly twice a week. (She showed her common sense again in this correspondence. When I went to college, I asked how often she would write to me. "I'll write to you as often as you write to me," she answered.) The age gap again was unfortunate in addition to the distance. I wish she had been a younger grandmother so that she could have known more of your development, which in you all would have given her great pleasure. I wish even she could have been a great-grandmother. No one would have enjoyed that more.

After my father's death in my mother's last years her mind was affected and she lost her powers of memory and association to some extent. It was a profound comfort to me then to see that her humor and her consideration for others, the two things which were the essence of her being, never failed. Of all qualities, humor is the hardest to capture and set down in words. (Over the dinner table, when a story fell flat, we had a family phrase, "Well, it was funny at school.") My mother was bright. I don't use the word in the sense of intelligence alone, though she was certainly a very intelligent woman, though not educated beyond the normal school necessary for her training as a kindergarten teacher. But "brightness" is the best word to describe the impression she made, her aura, say. What she said was funny, unexpected, original, unpredictable. The humor wasn't obvious: in fact, dull-witted persons would sometimes take her literally and then she would be embarrassed (as has sometimes happened to me also). And unlike my father, who sweet and generous as he was, like Mr. Woodhouse could only extend the generosity on his own terms, she had the power of entering into the other person's mind and feelings.

The dark thread which perhaps runs through some of the Goodwins appeared in her in apprehension; she was a worrier, and this quality grew as she grew older. The worries seemed to me sometimes so trivial and so poorly based that I was not always as patient as I should have been. I have felt this quality, tiresome to oneself and annoying to others, growing in me of late years: but a good deal to my surprise and relief, retirement does not seem, as yet, to have accentuated it as much as I feared.

I felt very deep pity for Marie Sharp on one occasion when she told me she saw herself growing more and more like her mother as she grew older and resented it, because she did not want to be like her.[42] Marie may have had some

---

42   In the Settling Down chapter, Thomas introduces Marie and Robert (Bob) Sharp, who moved to Madison in 1927, when Bob was hired to teach in the English department while completing his Ph.D. at Harvard. Marie had an assistantship in the history department. Like the Beattys, the Sharps became lifelong friends of Thomas.

justification; Mrs. Barstow was a rather limited and tiresome and complaining woman in my rather casual contacts with her. It must be one of the worst destinies imaginable to feel yourself growing into something you resent. On the contrary it is one of the happiest to feel so grateful for the qualities of your mother that you are thankful for the least sign of them you can detect in yourself. I wish I could detect more. I do not look like my mother, and in character there is certainly a very large amount of my father in me. But I am grateful for whatever of my mother there is. I loved and admired my mother with all my heart as far back as I have any memory at all, and I could wish you that I had told her so more often—but you know how new Englanders are. It was in college, when it seemed highly unlikely to everyone that I would ever marry, that I consciously expressed to myself the wish that I could, since I was the only possible means of transmitting my mother's genes to posterity so that they would not be lost. I don't say that is the best motive for marriage, or that it was my main motive when I did marry; but at least it expresses how I felt about my mother. In some respects, I think, Hannah is like her, and though we can hardly say that Grace Coleman's judgment is infallible, I was glad to have her say—one of the few living people who have known both—that she thought so too.

I was the child of an ideal marriage. The love between these two was perfect and never failing. Perhaps I can descend from the sublime to the homely in order to give you a concrete image of it. My father's favorite year-round vegetable was onions, and we had them every Sunday dinner. (One thing I learned, with mild surprise, the first year of my marriage, was that onions were not universally regarded as a company vegetable.) My mother suffered, as I do, from dry skin in the winter, and if she kept getting her hands too often wet she would have painful cracks in her fingers. So my father himself peeled the onions every Sunday morning before he went in town to his club, and left them in a bowl of water on the kitchen table. I can see that symbol now.

HARVARD AVENUE

When Hannah and I drove down Harvard Avenue in June, 1971, in our low-comedy quest for the suitcase the young man who drove my car from Madison had casually walked off with, it was a pretty blighted place: high rise apartments, stumps of elm trees, a big barren playground covering the lower quarter on one side, and only a few of the old houses, set in cruelly cropped grounds, to suggest what the street had been when I was a little girl and walked up it on a pleasant spring day, probably coming home from the Brookline Public Library only a block or so away, careful not to step on the cracks of the pavement and careful to crunch underfoot the cherry stones some young passerby had cheerfully let fall as he ate the cherries. It was a very pleasant shady street when I was young, set on both sides with big houses in wide and deep grounds. When my father took his bride there, it was about a block over from the end of the streetcar line from Boston, then a horse car line.[43] That's before my time, although on a trip to New York when I was very small my father made a point of taking me to ride on a horse car line there of a few blocks, kept as a tourist attraction, so I could tell my grandchildren I had ridden on one. I remember myself the streetlamps which a Stevenson "Leerie" lamplighter[44] came around every evening to tend, carrying a long pole which swung open the glass door of the lamp and then lighted the gas jet inside. Our house was lighted by gas. Harvard Avenue was a spacious place; the big estates were further out and one of them could have taken up our whole street; but we had plenty of room to breathe, inside and out.

Harvard Avenue was based on the existence of a servant class which could be counted on to do the work necessary to keep the houses clean and hospitable and the yards green and flowery; and it was built on the confidence that this class would always exist. Boston was in the full flow of Irish immigration, and many immigrants came to a position ready for them because a relative or friend had preceded them. We had three resident servants: Maggie, the cook; Joseph, the coachman; Mary Ann, the housemaid. Mary Ann was Maggie's cousin; on Maggie's recommendation my father sent her the money for her passage, and she came over on the next boat and joined our family. She later married Thomas, but for years after they were no longer living with us she came back to help my mother. Samuel Eliot Morison, whose account of his Boston boyhood covers the period of my sister's childhood rather than mine, speaks of the enrichment

---

43   A horsecar or horse-drawn tram is an animal-powered streetcar.
44   A reference to Robert Louis Stevenson's (1850–1894) poem "The Lamplighter," from *A Child's Garden of Verses and Underwoods* (1913). The term "Leerie" refers to the lamplighter.

Harvard Avenue

of the world of the children of his day, compared to the limitations of the world of today's children, who know only their parents' friends.[45] The children of his period spent a lot of time in the kitchen, talking familiarly with Irish servants and Irish policemen. Our policeman on Harvard Avenue was Irish, Mr. Sullivan. He and his wife were childless and they adored children; and every child in the neighborhood adored him. It's a mercy he can't know what the synonym for "policeman" has been since about 1968.[46] Our gardener, or rather yardman, Owen, however, was not Irish but Welsh. He is the only actually illiterate person I have known in the course of my life, as far as I am aware. This is not to say that he was unintelligent. He was very intelligent indeed, and had the illiterate's power of observation which is sometimes atrophied in the educated; he just never had had the chance to go to school. He had a good-sized family of eight or nine children: they all went to American schools and all did very well, getting good white-collar jobs, for example, in the post office. (I hope the term "white-collar" will still be understood; a recent *New Yorker* points out that *nobody* wears a white collar any more and we'll have to get a new term.) The wave of Italian immigration had begun by my childhood, and I remember handsome sinister dark women like Madame Defarge wearing bright bandanna kerchiefs over their hair and carrying bright knives with which they dug up dandelions from the Harvard Avenue lawns to take back with them to their homes in South Boston for greens or wine. Euell Gibbons is a throwback, not a pioneer.[47] No one ever objected to their trespassing since they never spoke to anyone and then as now everyone wanted to get rid of the dandelions. My father, as a matter of fact, was fond of dandelions himself and we quite often ate them. Do you remember the O. Henry story where a young man is able to find his sweetheart in New York because a restaurant serves dandelions for spring greens?[48] There were plenty of dandelions for everyone, but the knives were a little frightening in the eyes of a timid small girl.

The Harvard Avenue lots were not only wide but deep. Perhaps the typical amount of land was about what we have here for the Frost Woods house, though some had rather more or less. Our house, and the one next it, the Cases', were both built about halfway down the lots, so that the front yards were about the

---

45   Samuel Eliot Morison (1887–1976), a Pulitzer Prize-winning American historian and U.S Naval officer.
46   The synonym is "pig."
47   Euell Gibbons (1911–1975), an American outdoorsman and writer who promoted natural diets.
48   William Sydney Porter (1862–1910), penname O. Henry, was an American short story writer. The story is "Springtime a la Carte," published in a collection called *The Four Million*, published in 1906.

same size as the back, which was unusual. A semicircular drive gave access to both houses, the double front lawn being bisected by a privet hedge. The drive was bordered by flowering shrubs, forsythia, syringa, weigela, and the like. Old lilac trees, not bushes, where I could climb and sit, flowered across our drive on the other side, next to the Burdetts'. Many of the yards had fruit trees. The Cases had a big secks pear tree and they would certainly have shared the fruit with us if the squirrels hadn't gotten most of it before either family could. This offended my mother's sense of thrift very much, because the squirrels didn't eat *all* the pears; they just nibbled out the seeds, leaving the rest useless. Both of us had Concord Grape arbors. That our back yard was less deep than most of the others didn't make any difference to the pleasantness of my mother's view when she changed her dress in the afternoon and sat by the bedroom window sewing, for she looked out into the Chandlers' place, which backed onto ours in part, and theirs really was extensive enough to be called an estate; it had a brook and lots of beautiful big trees, and all kinds of wild flowers grew there in spring. There were no fences between neighbors and the Lewises never minded if I took the short cut across their yard to the library instead of going down Harvard Avenue and walking around the block. But the Goths were at the gate, though we hardly realized it. A rather slummy neighborhood was spreading up from Brookline Village, and we walked in that direction less and less. I remember getting off the trolley at Harvard Avenue on Harvard Street once, with two or three roses someone I had been to call on must have given me. A little girl about my own age came up to me out of an alley and asked for one. I gave it to her, and she asked for another, but I said I wanted to keep that myself. She ran off without protest and I certainly hadn't enough imagination to follow her in my mind to her home. But her descendants have inherited the earth—literally. That bare ugly playground Hannah and I saw in June of 1971 was in my day a big expanse of green grass and tall trees, the yard of Mrs. Fegan, a wealthy childless widow. For years the town wanted that land for a school playground, for it was just across the street from a school which had been built in this slummy area. They had to wait for it a long time, but at her death they moved in.

Our house was number 48. I don't know who built it, or when. Grace Coleman has a romantic story which I do *not* believe that it was a station on the Underground Railway. It was built on sloping ground, like the Frost Woods house, so that it was a story higher at the back than at the front. Walking down the drive and passing the blushrose bushes, you entered the front door at the short end of an L-shaped piazza, where woodbine grew up the pillars and in summer you could swing in the hammock. From the small vestibule you went directly into a good-sized hall with a curving staircase, lit by a hanging lamp in Turkish style, jewel-like vari-colored pieces of glass, and a niche at the bend. All the rooms had comfortably high ceilings. On your right was the dining-room, facing west: the food came up from the basement kitchen on a dumb-waiter, and there was a small pantry with a sink for washing the dishes. To your left was the parlor at the front of the house and the living room or library behind it, both good-sized oblong rooms. The parlor was not shut up, as was sometimes the case, particularly in the country, but we spent most of our time in the library. We always had the Christmas tree in the parlor, and the piano stood there; I did my practicing conscientiously before breakfast every morning. The room was a good distance from the bedrooms, and I disturbed nobody. Another piece of parlor furniture was the love seat, like half a figure 8, so that the two people sitting in it were facing different ways. The Franklin stove was in the library, and much used, and that room had a number of glass-fronted bookshelves, which contained in addition to books bound volumes of *Harpers* and the like from the end of the preceding century. I read everything voraciously—as Hannah seems to have done in the Frost Woods house. In my own house, I didn't like the idea of locking up books and I wanted them on open shelves, but when I see what this has done to the bindings I understand the reason for protection. Of various oil paintings in the library, I remember clearly one: a man is coming home at dusk through snowy woods to a solitary house; and there is no light in the house. The thought still gives me a pleasant shiver of melancholy. At the end of the hall was the guest room, which Aunt Ednah used to occupy every year for a month or so, when she came north for the summer to escape the heat of Washington, where she had moved to keep house for an uncle, and made leisurely visits to family and friends as well as spending two months at the Island.[49]

Upstairs if you went straight ahead through the hall to the front of the house you went into a small room which was my playroom when I was little and which later my father used for an office when his business had declined. On the way you passed on your right two large bedrooms, over parlor and library, my mother's and father's respectively. Each had a big double bed. If I was sick, Mother would bring me into one of the big beds during the daytime, and I remember how cool and pleasant the sheets felt and how nice it was to have so much space to move around in. Across the hall was an extensive wing stretching to the back of the house. The first room, mine, was small and narrow with one window looking out on the street and one facing west. Nowadays I sometimes wake up in that room and have to struggle in the dark a moment before I can orient myself to the place of the windows in the room I have slept in for forty years. In this room I tried the experiment of sleeping on the floor because Maggie Tulliver had

---

49 A reference to Isle of Springs, an island community located in BoothBay Harbor, Maine, where the family spent summer vacations.

done it, but I didn't try it very long.[50] Along the hall were three other bedrooms and a bathroom. Could we have had only one bathroom? I guess so. But later we rented the downstairs bedroom to Mr. Case (no relation to our neighbors), an elderly widower who taught math at Brookline High School, and he occupied it a number of years. I think a bathroom for his separate use must have been put in then, if not before. According to custom, the coachman's quarters were in the upper story of the barn.

The kitchen, as I have said, was in the basement, a big comfortable room looking out on the back yard. Delivery men came around the house to leave their groceries or whatever at the back door. The big black stove burned coal. With it is connected one of our favorite family stories. As a little girl, I always wanted a cat. Mother, who didn't really care for pets, had for years done her duty by providing her stepchildren with pets, which were sick on the hall carpet or howled all through company dinners because they were shut up in the basement, and so on, and she said she thought it was only fair that the next pet should be her choice before we got round to mine. Since allegedly the pet she wanted was a giraffe, somehow we never got it, and I never got my cat. For a very brief time, however, I think because we had mice, we did have a kitten which Mary Ann brought us. He was black with white feet and white shirt front, and his name was Tommy Tucker because he sang for his supper. Before he came Mother carefully provided him with a nice soft bed in a little basket in the kitchen. When she came down stairs the next morning, he was lying on the more remote of the two plate-warming shelves with which the stove was equipped, with a singularly happy expression on his face. He got sick, I think, and lasted only a short time. When my mother was doing the housework alone, we stopped using the upstairs dining room, and ate in a former storage room underneath it, across from the kitchen. The windows came down nearly to the ground (rather like our rumpus room in Frost Woods) so that it was light and pleasant, especially at the evening meal. The house was completed by a subterranean coal cellar.

Here I was born on June 14, 1901. In these days you were born in your own house, not in a hospital, and your mother had a nurse who stayed as long as was desirable. I didn't make a very good impression on my mother's nurse, who refused to show me off because she didn't want the neighbors to see that Mrs. Shepard had such a homely baby. But that didn't bother me at the time, and it doesn't now.

Without question I was tenderly loved by all around me, and according to modern psychology this is all you need; this fortifies you for life, whatever it may bring you. Certainly my childhood was not unhappy. But it was lonely.

---

50 A character in George Eliot's *The Mill on the Floss* (1860).

Harvard Avenue

I spent most of my time with books or with adults, and very little of it with other children of my own age. As is often the case, the neighborhood had been full of children when Hannah and Clarence were small, but by the time I can remember, these children, like Hannah and Clarence themselves, had grown up and gone away from home, and the next generation had not come along to take their place. My parents, with what today you'd call snobbishness, innocently compounded the deficiency by sending me to the Lawrence Grammar School, where Hannah and Clarence had gone and where it seemed natural to them to have me go. But in the meantime a school had been built a good deal nearer to Harvard Avenue, the one of which I have already spoken in our slummy area, and today of course the town would require me to attend that. When I got to Brookline High School, one girl from there, Iris Woodman, was in the college preparatory course, and we were good friends, as we might have been all along. But she was the only one from there I ever knew, since no other were destined for college, and therefore took the general or commercial course. I think now it would have enlarged my experience if I had gone there. Not that there was anything snobbish or elitist about the Lawrence School. The most dedicated member of our class, who much to my surprise turned up in Newcastle, Maine, a few years ago, organizing our fiftieth reunion, spent his life in the Brookline Fire Department. He and his wife and I now exchange visits every summer, to our mutual pleasure. It was just that it was too far away for me to drop in on my classmates, whom generally I didn't see from the time school let out in the afternoon until we were in our seats next morning. I saw enough of two girls to be still exchanging Christmas cards with them more than fifty years later. One, Margaret Spaulding, married Rudoph Berle, brother of Adolph Berle, who played a big part under FDR in the New Deal.[51] She lives in Scarsdale and carries on a very popular program of story telling to children and adult audiences, gathering material for it in out-of-the way places in Europe summers. The other, Beatrice [Bee] Chambers, lively and gay, was a favorite of my mother, who liked me to play with her because she thought Bee—certainly no intellectual—would be a good antidote to my bookishness. My mother didn't like to see me carrying an open book with me everywhere I went, while I was dressing, walking up and down stairs, and so on, but she never succeeded in breaking me of the habit, which I still possess, though she did enforce the rule of no reading at meals. Bee and I didn't influence each other, but we had fun. I remember once we got into such a silly giggling streak we couldn't stop, and Bee finally started home, coming back after she had gone a little way to look in at the parlor window and

---

51   Adolf Augustus Berle, Jr. (1895–1971), professor of corporate law at Columbial Law School, was a member of President Franklin D. Roosevelt's original "Brain Trust," a policy advisory group.

show me she was still laughing. Poor Bee has had, it seems to me, a poor and thin life compared to my own, the life of the New England spinster to which so many of my contemporaries were destined. Of course with more initiative and self-confidence I could have gone to see my classmates. The distance wasn't that great. But it was too much for my shyness, and most of the time I played alone. I would have been willing to read non-stop, but when my mother very properly chivvied me outdoors there wasn't much of anything to do except wander around the yard, looking at the little maple seedlings or kneeling on the wooden planking put down in the winter for the delivery men beside the house, enlarging the miniature spring brooks that came down the slope as the snow melted.

I had pleasant adult contacts. Sometimes on Saturday for a treat my father would take me in to his office in Boston, which was on an upper story of a building in Post Office Square, into which streets led at all four corners and which was a busy place. We would go to the window and look down on the apparent maelstrom, and my father would say, "Look for the white horses," and at once a pattern would begin to appear. I've done the same thing today with white cars, looking down from a high rise. His stenographer would be typing—it was long before offices were closed on Saturday mornings—and I thought I was very smart to be able to read the clear letters which instantaneously appeared on the empty paper under her hands. Then he would take me to lunch at Young's Hotel, in the big Victorian dining room with thick carpeting and massive mahogany furniture. Young's was a time-honored Boston institution, where my father had been taken as a little boy by his father, so that he had been known for years by the genial colored waiters (this was fifty years before the term "Black" came into use and it would have been thought as much of an insult as "Nigger"), who were always delighted to see him, and me, since the clientele was predominantly businessmen and children were almost unknown there. We always had the same menu: mock turtle and tomato soup (it's years since I tasted it, but how good it was), roast beef, and pistachio ice cream. It is hardly the conventional menu for a child's lunch, but I enjoyed every bite and I have never suffered from indigestion in my life.

Among my mother's friends, three spinsters lived on Harvard Avenue—the salt of the earth like the typical New England spinster of the period. Miss Kate Adams, like many daughters of her generation, never married and spent her whole life caring for a cantankerous old father. She was a Mount Holyoke graduate of the seminary days and took a special interest in me when it was later decided that was to be my college, but she was always kind to me. Her niece Harriet, just my age, occasionally visited her, and then we played together, usually card games. Miss Adams drove an electric automobile; no better vehicle has ever been devised for a town car, and of course it was completely pollution-free. Two or three years ago there was an attempt to revive it, but this came to nothing. She sometimes took me to ride in hers. The other two ladies, Miss Sabine and Miss Dana, were cousins who lived together in the big house next to Mrs. Fegan's. Like my uncle they were interested in the emerging automobile, and, being very comfortably off, they had a standing arrangement by which they rented a car and a driver afternoons, and out of the goodness of their hearts often took along friends who didn't have cars. In 1971 when official surveys of the Holland Tunnel and the Los Angeles Freeways, not to mention my own unofficial survey of the rush hour beltline traffic when I was waiting to take the left hand turn onto Bridge Road, show that ninety per cent of the cars on the road are occupied by one person, I can hear my mother observing sixty years ago with her solid common sense what a pity it seemed to see so many cars with one person only in them going in town in the morning and back again at night. They often took Mother and me, and we would get fresh vegetables at road-side stands. Once they took us to afternoon tea with cinnamon toast at the famous Wayside Inn in Sudbury of which Longfellow wrote, later burned to the ground.[52] The New England spinster was the salt of the earth, and there were a good many of these admirable women in my young life. But I don't think destiny even then gave her a fair chance of fulfilling her potential, far less now. Almost all my childhood friends at the Island, like Bee Chambers, were fated to this lot. It seems to me a miracle that I escaped it.

At the Lawrence School, as you can easily imagine, I was a very good little girl and teacher's pet. I didn't do well in drawing or in sewing. I remember one occasion when we were supposed to draw an accurate square without a ruler, and as soon as a child had succeeded, he stood at the front of side of the room holding the evidence of his success to encourage the others. The room was completely lined with children while I still sat at my desk getting hotter and hotter and dirtier and dirtier as I rubbed out the false lines and tried to do better. The same thing was true in sewing, where I had no skill at all. (They taught sewing differently then, starting out with basic stitches which must be done perfectly on a piece of cloth, the descendant of the sampler, before you could make anything interesting—quite unlike Wisconsin High were Tom[53] made a Hawaiian shirt that dazzled you in sewing required of boys, who it was felt should have the home-making skills of girls—not a bad idea in these times of the development of the unisex and the blending of the roles of father and mother.) I also remember one awful day—and that's just the word—when the superintendent of schools

---

52 In 1863, inspired by a visit to Howe's Tavern, Henry Wadsworth Longfellow published a series of poems as *Tales of a Wayside Inn*. In 1892, the inn was renamed Longfellow's Wayside Inn. According to the Inn's website, it is "the oldest operating inn in the country," but there is no mention of the inn burning to the ground.

53 Thomas's son.

of Brookline visited our classroom to enquire how many children could swim. All hands went up except mine. "Little girl," said the superintendent who in appearance and majesty of demeanor was indistinguishable from Jehovah or from any of the bearded New England poets whose pictures in the early part of this century were standard schoolroom equipment, "Little girl, *why* can't you swim?" I suppose the reason these old wounds never healed is that usually school life was so halcyon—just as Benvenuto Cellini's first memory is that of his father's striking him, not in anger or in punishment but to impress upon the child the sight of a salamander sporting in the flames, a marvel he wanted his little son to remember.[54] One year my teacher boarded in the next block to the school, and ten minutes before the recess bell she would send me over to the house to get her lunch and bring it back to her. It's hard for me now to describe the feeling this privilege—which was really what it was—gave me, though it is perfectly vivid in me still: the feeling of being out on the street, presumably free (though of course I went right there and came right back) when everyone else was shut up in school.

It's a pity I don't remember any of the individual teachers. They were all competent and the school system was excellent. At that time it provided nine grades, not eight, before the four years of high school, which was unusual and was later discontinued, so that although I had started in kindergarten a year younger than usual (this was one of the retrenchments I spoke of when my father lost some money and Mary Ann had less time to devote to me), I graduated from college no younger than anyone else. In this extra year I started Latin, so that I was already well grounded in it when I got to high school. Also during this time my mother arranged for me to have private lessons in conversational French, so that I went into high school with some command of two languages.

I had music lessons from a very early age. My mother was very musical, and hoped I would be too. I was no genius, but I enjoyed the lessons and the practicing, and the ability to play, though far from brilliantly, has been a pleasure all my life. Wright was glad I could play when we married, and it was his idea to buy the piano, the only article I ever owned paid for on the installment system instead of in one lump sum. In the old days in Frost Woods the piano was the basis for the neighborhood carol parties, and it was also useful for rhythm games for you and the other children in our informal nursery school. I hope it may be again for Jimmy and Lisa.[55] It has also been a pleasure to play hymns at the Island, at the Sunday services or even more to go up to the Casino on a rainy day and play through the book.[56] I'm glad I could play at Hannah's wedding, and

---

54 Benvenuto Cellini (1500–1571), an Italian goldsmith and artist, recounted this in The Autobiography of Benvenuto Cellini, translated into English and published in 1910.
55 Thomas's grandchildren.
56 The Casino, built in 1892, was for a time the only public resort on the Isle of Springs.

every Christmas I have two happy evenings, one at the Lacy's, one here, when I play for the Lacys to sing.[57]

I went to dancing school at Coolidge Corner. This is did not enjoy at all, though one of the mild regrets I have of things missed in my life is that I never had enough dancing, especially square dancing, which I could have done forever when we did a little in the early Frost Woods days. The reason, of course, was that none of the boys ever willingly asked me to dance. It wasn't that I was clumsy. I completely lacked S.A.[58] (as we used to call it) and hadn't then developed any small talk. The class was coeducational, and, according to the New England pattern, there were plenty of superfluous females, I among them. However, I learned the steps, I did get some practice in dancing, and if I had gone to dances I would not have been uncomfortable because I didn't know anything about the art.

I walked to all these engagements, by the way. It was growing more difficult to get servants and technology had not developed all the skillful mechanical robots a housewife has today; but at least she didn't have to spend her time driving her children hither and yon. I walked to our dentist, who had an office in a business block at Coolidge Corner, and—think of it—if you needed to see a doctor he came to see *you*. Church was about a mile away. The First Unitarian Church was a very handsome building, and the rather sparse congregation were in general very wealthy people. My way there took me past Brookline High School, which I later attended, and across Boylston Street, one of the main arteries out from Boston, though at that time, particularly on a Sunday, traffic was not a menace. It was for this reason, of course, that I walked to so many places and went in and out of Boston freely comparatively young. I'm sure you think of me as a country mouse, but I took the street car and the Boston subway and was at home in the heart of the city quite early. There were two convenient ways of getting in town from our house, through Coolidge Corner and through Brookline Village, and both lines were within easy walking distance. At Boylston Street there was a shoe repair shop which had hanging in the window two little miniature shoes, miracles of handicraft. The shop of course was shut Sunday and I never went in but I always looked at the pair of little shoes. Perhaps the proprietor was like the German craftsman Galsworthy describes in his sad short story of the man

---

57   Edgar W. Lacy (1914–1981) earned his Ph.D. from the University of Illinois (1939) and served in the U.S. Army prior to being hired in 1946 as assistant professor in the UW-Madison English department. In 1948, he became director of Freshman English and invited Thomas to assist him (Fleming, 2011, p. 46). His wife, Margaret (1923–2014), met and married Ed while pursuing her Ph.D. in English literature at UW-Madison. Margaret and Thomas were lifelong friends.

58   An abbreviation for sex appeal.

who lost his custom and starved to death because his shoes never wore out.[59] The other side of Boylston Street I was in the region of big estates; the Brookline Reservoir extended to my right, and sometimes in vacation or weekends I would walk around it. Amy Lowell's estate, where she kept her famous dogs, fronted on it at the other end.[60] Along the path to the church tiny sweet white violets blossomed in spring, and there were beautiful gardens to look in at through the opening in the gates, for they were walled. About the church itself I remember that the very last lingering winter snow stayed in one north corner when it had long ago melted everywhere else—very much like our Frost Woods driveway. As I said, the members of the congregation were generally wealthy, and they sent their children to the famous Boston private schools, like Miss Wheelock's, instead of to the Brookline public schools, excellent though the latter were. So my Sunday school experiences here provided me with no companionship except that of sitting through the same service with children I didn't see again until the next Sunday. One great benefit I derived from this Sunday school though was the acquisition of a very large number of passages from the Bible, particularly the psalms and the parables. Our superintendent believed in memorizing, and included in the service unison reciting (not reading) of a variety of passages, for which I've always been glad. It goes without saying that we used the King James Version.

About twice a year, my mother and I would go in town Saturday morning to buy me shoes. We went to Thayer McNeil's on Tremont Street, the only store where a proper Bostonian would think of buying shoes, and we always waited for Mr. Pretto to be at liberty to attend to us. Since he was popular, we sometimes had to wait quite a while, which annoyed me since I was never noted for patience, but Mother would not have dreamed of letting a stranger wait on us. The proper Bostonian store par excellence of course was S. S. Pierce, of which we used the Coolidge Corner branch.[61] S. S. Pierce was held in the same regard as the Boston *Transcript,* of which the story is told that the maid of a family where something newsworthy had befallen told her mistress, "There are three reporters downstairs, ma'am, and a gentleman from the *Transcript.*" When I heard this year that S. S. Pierce had gone out of business, it was like hearing of the death of George Washington. The old world and all that it stood for has certainly gone from the earth forever.

---

59   A reference to the short story "Quality" (1912) by John Galsworthy (1867–1933), a Nobel Prize–winning English novelist and playwright.
60   Amy Lowell (1874–1925), an imagist American poet who posthumously won a Pulitzer Prize, was born in Brookline.
61   Samuel Stillman Pierce (1801–1881), a Boston grocer, established the S.S. Pierce company. This Tudor-style building is now designated as a significant historical landmark.

Harvard Avenue

We didn't shop for clothes, since this was before the era of ready-made clothing and was the time of the home dressmaker. Ours was Miss Atkinson, who came regularly for three or four days or perhaps a week, every spring and fall, and spent the day, of course joining us for lunch, in my mother's bedroom, where the sewing machine stood, making new dresses and doing over old ones from whatever female members of the family were living at home. I'm very sorry for her now when I think how trying I must have been. I didn't like to stand still and I didn't like to be touched, and I must have been a very difficult subject for fittings. As ready-made clothes began to come on the market, the home dressmaker was destined to disappear. But I'm glad to report that Miss Atkinson at least was not a victim of technological unemployment. She married the owner of a chicken farm near Concord, in the country, and I went there with my mother to pay her the wedding visit.

I should not leave this time and the Lawrence School without telling of my first—and for many years only—encounter with the problem of race, which occupies so large a share of public and private attention today.[62] I was startled once to meet in the hall a tall, handsome and very black man who asked me to direct him to his son's home room—startled as perhaps Jimmy was at the appearance of Kwame Okoampa-Ahoofe of Ghana, Anthony Mogbama of Nigeria, and A. M. Ishaq of Ceylon [Sri Lanka] when those three dark men came to dinner at Thanksgiving time this past year. The man was Mr. Ridley, a Brookline lawyer, who had married a white girl. They had a large family of mulatto children, of whom the oldest had been in school with Hannah and Clarence, and the youngest, Archie, was a year ahead of me. He therefore graduated from high school the year before I did. He was able and very popular—class president, if I remember rightly, and went on to Harvard with most of his classmates. I remember hearing vaguely that it was at college, when dating became serious and might lead to marriage, that he encountered his first difficulties. How serious they were, or what happened to him and his siblings I don't know.

I should not leave this period, either, without speaking of some fears and phobias from which I suffered. One was that of fire. When I was small, there had been a disastrous fire in Charlestown, where the Fire Departments had been unable to control a blaze which swept through flimsy wooden buildings for blocks and caused much loss and suffering. Many insurance companies went bankrupt. I had heard about this and it lingered in my mind, though our neighborhood was not so built as to be subject to the same sort of thing. At that time, the Brookline Fire Department operated by a system of bells: they were rung in a certain pattern as soon as an alarm was turned in to indicate where the fire was,

---

62 Thomas is referring to the civil rights movement.

and two slow bells, "All Out," were rung when it was brought under control. These bells woke me from the soundest sleep, and I could never go back to sleep again until the "All Out" rang, and sometimes not then. I remember one nightmare I had in which our house burned. My mother consulted our doctor about my phobia (not that we used the word then) and he good-naturedly told me not to worry about fire; that was the business of the Fire Department, not mine. This well-meant advice obviously did no good, for exactly what I was worrying about was that the Fire Department wouldn't be up to its job. I came to think later, as I have told Hannah, that if my parents had said to me, "Yes, it's possible, though unlikely, that we may have a fire in our house; but if we do, we'll repair the house or build a new one," that would have cured me. At least now, at seventy, I think this is the answer. No one can know what misfortune, great or small, will come to him, but human nature fortunately possesses a very deep-rooted characteristic, the instinct to meet the emergency, to rise to the occasion, to deal with the misfortune, to clean up and go on. I've observed this in history, in literature, and in life, and I ask my descendants to trust to it, believing that they may do so safely.

On Harvard Avenue, before I was in my teens I had my first, and I think my only, contact with high tragedy. The whole thing was truly Greek: "whom the gods love die young." You remember the myth of the woman whose two sons yoked themselves to her chariot, when they had no oxen, so they could draw her to the shrine of Hera, where she wished to worship. She prayed Hera to give these good sons the best gift in the goddess's power, and Hera struck them dead.

I have already spoken of our next door neighbors, the Cases. The family consisted of a couple ten or a dozen years older than my parents, and their only child Arvin, eight years older than I. Arvin Case had every gift the gods could give. We would say today he had charisma. We said then that everyone liked him, of any age, any type, any relationship. He was good-looking. He was a top high school athlete (track, not football). He played the violin. He was class president; he was class valedictorian; he was kind and thoughtful to everyone, even to a little kid next door whom most boys his age would barely have noticed. In all my life I have never come across a young man of more promise. The summer after his first year at Harvard he was drowned at the camp where he was a counselor. He had slightly strained his heart in the high school athletics, which contributed to the accident, for he was a first class swimmer. A boy had been left by mistake on the opposite shore of the lake, Arvin volunteered to paddle over and bring him back; he ran down to the canoe in a hurry, started paddling, the canoe overturned, and he was dead when they pulled him out, probably as the combined result of drowning and a slight heart attack brought on by the over-exertion.

It was the supreme gift of the gods all right. He died in his glory before any touch of shadow dimmed the brightness. And the gods may have known what they were doing. In another year he might have left college (like Paul Fulcher) to go to France, and he might have died a sordid and agonizing death in the trenches.[63] Of course no one can know. But high tragedy does not confine itself to the hero alone. I wonder how many years Hera's worshipper lived by herself with the results of the granting of her prayer. Arvin's parents were completely broken. He was their only child, no son could have shown more promise, and they were totally bound up in him and his future. Their reason for being was shattered, and they were too old to find any other. And they lived on. They did not die.

As you can imagine, this had a profound effect on me. I idolized Arvin as any small girl might idolize such a young man. His study faced the west window of my bedroom, and we did not draw our shades. Often as I fell asleep the last thing I saw was a white marble half-moon Diana on the wall above the desk where he sat studying. He played the violin and I the piano, and he good-naturedly let me play his accompaniments sometimes. We played together the Beethoven Minuet in G, the only piece I could now, nearly sixty years later, play from memory. It happened that the morning of his death he had written and mailed to me a postcard from camp. When it arrived he was dead. It is very poignant to see something tangible and trivial which survives after spirit and life have gone, like old photographs. I kept the card for years, and when I set myself to the business of clearing out my drawers I may even find it again. As time has gone by, I have thought more and more in this connection of a poem in which a traveler comes across an old wrinkled woman mourning by the grave of a man who died young. He condoles with her on the loss of her son. "I was not his mother," she says. "I was his wife."

The death of the darling of the gods in his undimmed youth and strength has been observed by many people I have met in the course of my life. Some of my students have had the experience of seeing it. But perhaps the strangest chance was that at the end of 1971 the Indonesian girl I'm tutoring, Tien Anggerodi, sat down at my piano and played first an Indonesian air and then the Minuet in G.[64] I told my guests the story I have just told you, and the man from Ceylon not only recognized the experience but also recognized the poem. Harvard Avenue was sheltered, but no man escapes his destiny. High tragedy as well of many of the more prosaic and sordid aspects of life is universal.

---

63 Paul Fulcher (1895–1958) joined the English department in 1925 and taught literature and creative writing. During World War I, he volunteered as an ambulance driver with the American Field Service in France.

64 After retiring from the English department in 1971, Thomas spent several years befriending and tutoring women who were living in university student housing while their husbands were pursuing graduate degrees at the university. These women were often isolated from the university and the community. Thomas refers to this volunteer experience throughout the memoir.

BROOKLINE HIGH SCHOOL

When I went from Lawrence Grammar to Brookline High School in September, 1915, my experience was enlarged, though perhaps not as much as might be expected. Intellectually I was precocious; socially—using the word in either the narrow or the broad sense—I was a very late bloomer indeed. I pause to philosophize on the question of timing, which has influenced my life as it has that of most other people. Already I have dwelt almost ad nauseam on the effect on me of having been born out of my generation. As I look back now, it seems to me that I have had in my life practically all the experiences for a full and rich life (though I never drank bathtub gin at any time), but I haven't had them at the usual times and so my development has been uneven. I tend to agree with George Eliot and Novalis that character is destiny.[65] But I'm not sure I can completely reconcile that belief with the influence of timing, which is external and fortuitous. For example, five years ago, very inferior Wisconsin Ph.D.'s in English were getting topnotch jobs; today topnotch people are getting no jobs at all. Perhaps I am too strictly limiting my interpretation of destiny, and perhaps things eventually even up anyway. The good people may eventually get good jobs, and I know for a fact that some of the weak sisters are being non-retained (to use the graceful and elegant phrasing of Academe). Once in my life timing was wonderfully lucky for me and for you too, in 1946 when the returning veterans flooded the university and I was offered the chance to come back to the [English] Department just the fall that Bill went into first grade at Nichols School, which served a hot lunch, so that I was free from eight to three. To return to Brookline High School, when I entered the pattern was already set, and I continued to develop academically at high speed with far less than usual social growth. There was however some, as I shall presently show.

The school was actually nearer to my house than Lawrence, and I had passed it countless times. It was a large school for the period, with a number of academic divisions: college preparatory, general, commercial, and some others. All students enrolled in college preparatory were placed together from the beginning, even in a universally required subject like English, so that I had no academic contacts with students in other fields who might have given me other points of view. Class officers of course were elected regardless of academic classification, but the college preparatory section furnished a good share. There were all-school activities, athletic and otherwise, and by my senior year I was doing my share,

---

65 Novalis is a pseudonym for Georg Philipp Friedrich Freiherr von Hardenberg (1772–1801), author and philosopher of early German Romanticism.

but it took some time for me to become at all involved. Bee Chambers took the general course and I saw less of her. Some of the Lawrence School students were in college preparatory, and there were many new people.

To one particular group I owe a great advantage. The students from Devotion Grammar School were by and large the most intelligent in the class, the most public-spirited, and the natural leaders, compared with the group from any other grammar school. They were all Jewish. The section of Brookline from which they came is now so overwhelmingly Jewish that the Orthodox Israeli who spent his first night in Madison at my house and could not eat my salt would be as much at home there as in his native Israel, and though the ethnic group was not so total then it was already established. As a result, my first contacts with Jews were with the best of the race and in the environment most favorable to them, an intellectual one. The parents of my classmates honored and revered learning and had brought up their children in this tradition. Far from having any contact which might give me any excuse for anti-Semitism, I had only such as developed respect and admiration for Jews. For most of my teaching at the university, too, my contacts with Jewish students (who were extremely well represented in Freshman Honor Composition) were with those who came from the same tradition, and my admiration for the race was continually reinforced. I hope you will all remember Ruth Wallerstein well enough to realize how brilliantly she contributed to it.[66] It has only been in the last few bad years that many a young Jew who had cut himself off from the traditions of his race and therefore was as unhappy and restless as any person must be who has severed his roots, became a professional troublemaker in academic circles and elsewhere if you look at it from the viewpoint of the conservative, a professional reformer of existing abuses if you look at it from the viewpoint of the liberal, a professional revolutionary, perhaps, from any point of view.[67] Up to the very recent time all Jews that I knew were content to work within the system, very likely for change, but for change and growth from within.[68]

---

66   Ruth Wallerstein (1893–1958), educated at Bryn Mawr and University of Pennsylvania, joined the English department in 1920 and taught English literature until her untimely death in an automobile accident in England while on research leave.

67   Thomas is likely referring to Ira Shor, professor of rhetoric and composition and New York native who received M.A. and Ph.D. degrees in English from UW-Madison in 1968 and 1971, respectively. Shor was actively involved in the creation of the Teaching Assistants' Association, the first graduate student employee union in the nation, at UW-Madison. According to Susan McLeod, Shor was considered by many English professors to be a trouble maker.

68   UW-Madison institutional history helps contextualize Thomas's comments: "Wisconsin's well-publicized commitment to free speech and association, as well as its non-discriminatory open admissions policy, began attracting sizable numbers of Jewish students from the Eastern seaboard in the 1920s, who experienced quotas and other barriers at colleges and universities in

Brookline was one of the top ten high schools in the country then, along with its main rival Newton, and I imagine both schools probably rank as high today. Newton has had an advantage, it seems to me, in that it was able to split its high school like an amoeba into Newton North and Newton South, each on a separate campus, whereas Brookline was trapped on its old site. I can see from the suburban train that it has expanded enormously, but I don't think this solution is so good. Modern American education has its critics, including me, and this may not be the place for my no doubt biased remarks. As Paul Fulcher used to say, I'm just an old fuddy-duddy. By coincidence, however, I read Silberman's massive four-year study of crisis in American education while I was working on this chapter, and discussed it with Sam Blount.[69] Silberman and I differ as to what is wrong, but agree that plenty is. An example to my mind was a student I had from New Trier,[70] as prestigious in this part of the country as Brookline or Newton in theirs, to whom I gave a D in my advanced composition course,[71] almost an unheard of grade for an English major who had been admitted to the School of Education, but quite rightly so, since he could talk the hind leg off a donkey but no one at New Trier had ever bothered to discipline him to do any writing for fear of destroying his free spirit; he couldn't write a decent English sentence. The D incidentally was compensated for by A's given him by staff members beginning to turn in all-A grade sheets to show their contempt for the grading system, or by others. As Abraham Lincoln observed, you can fool some of the people all of the time. Sam Blount, who is nobody's fool, in his gently acid way would say from time to time that Jesse Goodman had been in again;[72] Sam had suggested he go into the business of his father, a very prosperous ladies' garment manufacturer in Chicago, where Jesse, Sam thought, would be a great success with the customers, instead of going out to get American education into more trouble than it's in already—but with no success. It is unfortunately obvious what ethnic group this young man belongs to. But I digress.

---

their own region" (Cronon & Jenkins, 1999, p. 4). Many of these students held more liberal-to-radical views than most students at UW-Madison and were disproportionately active in campus politics, including in organizing the anti-war movement in the late sixties (p. 450).

69   Nathan Sam Blount (1929–1989) taught high school in Miami before earning his doctorate in education at Florida State in 1963, after which he was hired by the UW English department. He held a joint appointment in English and in Education. Charles Eliot Silberman (1925–2011), an American journalist, criticized the American educational system in *Crisis in the Classroom: The Remaking of American Education* (1970).

70   Likely a reference to New Trier High School, located in Cook County, Illinois.

71   English 309, Composition for English Teachers, which Thomas taught at UW-Madison.

72   Jesse H. Goodman, now professor emeritus of Education at Indiana University-Bloomington, earned a BS in English Education from UW-Madison in 1970, the year before Thomas retired, followed by his MS and Ph.D.

In my day Brookline High School was first rate, and so were all teachers with whom I had any contact. While unfortunately I don't remember the teachers at Lawrence, I do have clear memories of those at Brookline High, for one reason because I worked under some of them for three or four years. Perhaps the most distinguished was Dr. Roberts, head of the Latin Department. The title was not a courtesy one; he had a Ph.D. Even in those days it is unusual to find a man with a doctorate in a high school. I have never anywhere in my life encountered a better teacher. We did a great deal of sight reading, and it was his theory that if we knew one single word in a Latin passage we should be able to figure out the meaning of the whole text. We were of course well grounded in declensions and conjugations and so on, and when Hannah was taking Latin in high school I could read her assignments without difficulty; the language was a permanent possession. At the end of senior year we were required to write a paper on some relevant topic of our choosing. Half the class *voluntarily* wrote it in Latin instead of English and some of us voluntarily wrote Latin poetry rather than Latin prose. It is clear that Dr. Roberts did not preside over any rote or mechanical learning. He made us want to work.

My French teacher, Miss Henry, was not a Frenchwoman by birth. As a matter of fact, her older sister had been a friend of my sister Hannah. But she was well trained, had lived a considerable amount of time in France, and went back there every summer. Under her chaperonage, we took advantage of some of the resources offered by a big city. We went over to MIT to hear lectures from visiting French professors. We went down to the Charlestown Navy Yard to visit a small French ship where one of the officers, a friend of hers, showed us around. It was here for the first time that I realized that animals understand, if they don't exactly speak, a given language; the ship's dog understood French, not English. We went to the theater to see a French play. I am ashamed to confess that the only thing I remember is the entrance of a character leading a real horse, Lulu: but animals always steal the show, don't they? Remember *Aida* with elephants. I tried out for and got a part in a French play we put on at school. (Bee appeared in the Spanish one.) I wrote a French poem for Miss Henry, which pleased her so much that she submitted it to a French magazine, but it wasn't accepted—not surprisingly, I think, for the idea was hardly original; it was merely based on the old saying that every man has two countries, his own and France.

We had Miss Sawyer for Freshman English, and then Miss Spaulding, the department head, for the other three years. She too took advantage of an opportunity in Boston which transformed our work. An English repertory company, the [Henry] Jewett Players, came to Boston, and put on in the Opera House all of Shakespeare, comedies, and tragedies, a different play each week, through one season; and we went to them all.[73] The next year they established themselves in a small theater in Copley Square, and put on Galsworthy, Shaw, and Barrie, Pinero, Maugham, and Robertson, the whole sequence of the development of the modern British theater, again a new play every week. Miss Spaulding turned our English course into a history of drama, and many of our class discussions and papers were based on the current offerings. There was no fuss and bother about expenses or transportation. All of us came from families in comfortable if not wealthy circumstances, and our parents thoroughly approved of our going to the theater. We all knew our way around Boston and could take care of ourselves; generally we went to the Saturday afternoon matinees. When I graduated from high school, then, I had seen all of Shakespeare and most of Shaw, as well as every important play in the development of the modern British theater. The productions were probably not distinguished, but they were adequate, and they familiarized us with the plays. You can see how taken aback I was when in my early teaching at Wisconsin a freshman wrote a theme on the thesis that you could get more out of a play if you saw it acted than if you just read it. That anyone could question such a truism—that the idea could even arise that it needed defense—was incomprehensible to me. The student probably came from a small Wisconsin town where he had perhaps seen a Christmas pageant and nothing more until he got to Madison and went to see the Wisconsin Players—in Bascom, before the Memorial Union was built.[74]

Mr. Case, later our lodger, head of the Math department, was a very ugly man and very reserved, but unquestionably at the top of his field. I got my usual A's in algebra and geometry and remember not one thing about either. We were required to take one year of science, and I took physics, leaving chemistry for college. I do remember about that taking a telephone apart to see how it worked, but that's all. One summer in Wisconsin I went to a symposium on science where I heard it argued that knowledge of the physical sciences is essential today when we are all completely dependent on machines. Intellectually, I sympathize with this view and applaud it; but practically I have gotten on very well while totally dependent on my car without knowing one single thing that goes on under the hood, and I am not conscious of any psychological phobia; I just take

---

73   Henry Jewett (1861–1930), an Australian-born performer, established the Henry Jewett Players (also known as the Repertory Theatre) in Boston. The troupe was active roughly between 1910 and 1930.

74   Bascom Hall, named after university president John Bascom (1827–1911), housed the English Department until 1971, when the department moved to the newly-built Helen C. White Hall. The Memorial Union, the campus student center, was built in 1928 and includes the Terrace, an outdoor space situated on the shore of Lake Mendota. The Union has historically been a hub for student activity, especially in the 1960s, and was recently added to the U.S. National Register of Historic Places.

it for regular check-ups. Tom and Bill don't get their mathematical and computer ability from me. We also were required to take ancient history, of which I do remember a fair amount. Part of my knowledge comes from literature, no doubt, but Alcibiades, Cato, Hannibal, and a good many other real men mean something to me and fit, if rather vaguely, into a time scheme.

Most people who are bookish, like me, can point to one period in their lives when—to use the recent phrase—the aptitude exploded. For most I think this happens in college; for me it was in high school. I read all the time. I read everything. All sorts of new possibilities turned up, particularly poetry, fiction, and drama. One item in my diary is "Quiet and peaceful and full of books." At this time I was conscientiously reading Henry James, but commented truthfully, "I don't really like him." Much of my literary company was not so high. I did like Archibald Marshall,[75] a very minor writer of the first of the century rather in the tradition of Trollope,[76] whom I think no one reads now. I liked the Irish dramatists and poets, Synge, Dunsany, Padraic Colum. I began to buy books on my own. I liked Percy Mackaye and Alfred Noyes, and bought their works, still in my library.

For the first time in this autobiography, I have another source to turn to beside memory alone. On January 1, 1919, I started keeping a five-year Line-a-Day diary, wanting a record of college and thinking it would be a good idea to begin with the last semester of high school. I kept a line-a-day for twenty-five years, and then stopped, thinking nothing interesting enough to be worthwhile putting down would ever happen to me again—obviously a great mistake. I began again on January 1, 1969, and devoutly wish I had a record of the sixties, the most exciting time of my life. But we'll use what we have. As I go through the items for my last semester of high school, I am struck by how dead the pages are. The entries have recalled to me a good many things I had forgotten, and they must be factually true: but they're not alive. I don't re-live them, as I've been able to re-live what I remember. But they give a fuller picture of what I was doing.

By the last semester of my senior year, I was one of three girls who made up the girls' Interscholastic Debate Team: the others were Iris Woodman and Margaret Spaulding, both of whom I have mentioned. I was also Exchange editor of the school magazine, a member of the Class Day Committee, a member of the school Honor Society, and the class poet. The magazine was named the *Sagamore*, from the first written reference extent to Brookline: "there being sag-

---

75   The pen name for Arthur Hammond Marshall (1866–1934), an English author, publisher, and journalist.

76   Anthony Trollope (1815–1882), a highly successful and prolific English novelist during the Victorian Era.

amores and many Indians at Muddy River." The class poem has disappeared, as far as I know, fortunately, no doubt, but I have a sneaking feeling that my class book, which must contain it, will turn up somewhere; if it does my picture will be in it, since one notation was on going to have it taken for the purpose. The Honor Society, I now recall with this prodding, you were admitted to when you attained a certain number of points, which had to include a minimum in both scholarship and extra-curricular activities. I must have depended heavily on the former for my total, but I had enough of the latter to make it. Those are cooperative activities, you notice. Day after day the notation occurs of working at the library with Iris and Margaret on debate. We debated a number of neighboring high school girls' teams, sometimes winning, sometimes losing, and we gave an exhibition debate with Newton High before the Women's City Club of Boston. One of the few flashes of individuality—and a regrettable individuality too—is "congratulations from all the old hens" on that occasion. (It's fair to say the Line-a Day format doesn't encourage literary creativity, since it hasn't room for much but bare fact.) I went repeatedly to school athletic events, hockey and baseball games this semester, always with other girls, but with a variety of them. My location was now an advantage, since I was near high school and others lived further away (this was long before school busing), so fairly often a girl came to lunch with me, to dinner, or even to spend the night. I had no dates. The boys crowded around my desk every morning, all right, to get the translation they hadn't been able to work out or the right math answer, but my social contacts stopped right there. Still I made candy for and sold it at a "social," which I think must have been a fund-raiser for Class Day. I was on the Class Day committee, which met repeatedly with the advising teacher all through the spring. We wore crepe paper costumes, including hollyhock batons, and I put in a lot of time with my friends working on these. The word "lonely" appears only twice in the diary in these six months. During spring vacation, I took a couple of five mile walks and commented "I'm getting to be quite a pedestrian, but it's lonely." The other was Class Day itself. For some unnamed ailment I had to stay home just before Class Day missing the only day of school I missed all year, and on the day itself, which occurred during a heat wave, I had to stay inside the building during the outside festivities on the big town playground, and I "wandered lonely as a cloud" there. But I did get to sit on the platform at the indoor part of the celebration and I recited the class poem.

This semester gave me my first teaching experience. Early in January the principal asked me if I would tutor one "Annette" in math, meeting her twice a week and being paid a dollar and fifty cents for each two meetings. She paid me three dollars after the first two weeks. This must have been the first money I ever earned, and I "felt proud." For someone destined to spend her life in teaching

I show a very undesirable attitude. Generally, I just record the meetings, but once in a while I say Annette is "stupidity personified" or make some other very unprofessional comment. Once I needed for some reason to change our appointment and had to walk three miles to her house to do so because the telephone operators were out on strike. This brought home to me the convenience of modern inventions and the inconveniences of modern labor struggles, which have certainly not decreased in fifty years. Not that I minded the walk as such; the automobile had not yet developed to the point of depriving Americans in general of the use of their legs. The meetings with Annette lasted all semester and I can only hope the poor girl got something out of them. Occasionally one of the teachers, who might have a cold and be unable to talk, would ask me to take the class, but this doesn't seem to have made much impression on me either.

I was not entirely untouched by outward events. Of course we debated current issues, and I went sometimes with my mother to a series of lectures given on these, particularly the League of Nations, by a woman speaker. Before TV and before radio you didn't get your daily five-minute dose from Eric Sevareid.[77] Armistice Day had occurred on November 11, 1918. The town authorities rather hastily organized a parade to keep the high school students in Brookline for fear they might get into trouble in the Boston crowds, and like a good girl I stayed home in that pretty flat one while most of my friends went in town and saw life. But I "got a good view of Wilson" when he came to Boston in the winter of 1919. While her husband was overseas, Pauline [Blood] had spent most of the time at our house, so she could attend the Boston Conservatory of Music more conveniently than by commuting from Sharon every day. This had been a great pleasure to me; I played her accompaniments for her singing, we went to concerts together, and we went to my first opera, *Aida*. On April 6, 1919 she brought Robert to call; he was "complete with overseas cap, Sam Browne, YD, and looking plump and very well."[78] The famous Yankee Divisions, the 26th, to which he belonged, paraded in Boston the end of that month, and he kindly got seats for Mother and me to see the parade as well as for Pauline. Mrs. Hutchinson's brother George Mellon was also back from overseas, and once Mother and I went out to Newton Highlands by invitation "to hear him talk"—which must have been about his war experiences, but I don't remember what he said.

Towards the end of the semester day after day was devoted to studying for College Boards. It was the first year these were required for college admission:

---

77   Eric Sevareid (1912–1992), a CBS news journalist from 1937 to 1977, was a protégé of Edward R. Murrow.

78   The Sam Browne belt, part of military uniform, is a wide leather belt supported by a strap over the right shoulder. The Yankee Division (YD), a World War I infantry division of the U.S. Army, was created in 1917 and consisted of units from the New England area.

up to then this had been granted on high school record alone. My friends and I went in to Boston ("like lambs to the slaughter"—I blush at the cliché) for three successive days to take these the middle of June. We had worked very hard for this ordeal, afternoon after afternoon, evening after evening, and certainly with our school background we had no reason to fear it—though of course I did. (I got the notice of my acceptance at Mount Holyoke early in July.) We graduated from Brookline High School on June 20, 1919. By the end of my high school career I was a functioning member of a community and was well known enough to receive a respectable number of votes for Class Sphinx. I had made a lot of girlfriends. I must have been sorry to have this time come to an end—but this is an inference rather than a true memory.

I am indebted to Brookline High School for some social development and for an excellent academic education. No one anywhere in the country could have gone to college with better preparation. A phrase Silberman is much given to is "happy and engaged"; he finds students invariable "happy and engaged" in informal schools (though he admits sometimes they aren't learning much) and invariable unhappy and disengaged in formal schools. But "happy and engaged" exactly fits our attitude at this formal school, and we learned a great deal. Above all, Brookline High School gave me the one thing, and the only thing, which in my view education needs to give, and the lack of which makes American education today in my view a good deal of a failure: a sense of the joy of work.

MOUNT HOLYOKE

In the fall of 1919 I went to Mount Holyoke, thinking even less of the pain and emptiness my absence must cause my mother than does the average teen-ager, I suppose, and was immediately overcome by a severe attack of homesickness. Like polio and diphtheria, this disease has entirely vanished in modern society—which opens up interesting speculations and value judgments on the home which I won't go into here. It was inevitable that a girl as sheltered as I should have a very bad case indeed.

My first real absence from home belongs earlier chronologically but here logically, I think. The summer of 1917 my parents sent me to a summer camp in New Hampshire, Camp Winnetaska on Lake Winnipesaukee. Since I was completely happy at the Island[79] and had no desire to go anywhere else, and since it was ideal in every respect except that of putting me on my own I am sure my mother sent me for this experience. I was homesick every day of the eight weeks; I woke up early every morning while the other girls in the cabin and the counselor were still asleep, and lay until it was time to get up in utter misery at the thought of the day before me; and that morning misery was nearly as profound at the end of the eight weeks as at the beginning, except that it was easier to bear as the end approached. Camp counselors in that day would have told you that homesickness was not at all uncommon; in my case the unusual thing was the passive endurance. Most homesick girls either got over it or wrote their parents to come and take them away. I did neither. I stayed and suffered.

Of course the summer had its compensations. I have learned that always the day offers some respite in its activities to the early morning waking when you feel it will be impossible to live through—as was true during the greatest suffering of my life. At camp I learned to swim well enough to pass the swimming test; Maine water is too cold to be a good place to learn in, and I was always glad that Sally Marshall taught you all to swim in Frost Woods so early, for when you went to Maine you were all good swimmers, and then cold water is stimulating.[80] The coldest water I ever immersed myself in was a mountain brook melted from year-round mountain snow, on an overnight camping trip that summer up in the White Mountains.[81] I wrote a lyric which was accepted for a camp song, and this gained me a note of music to put on my headband. We all

---

79 A reference to Isle of Springs, an island community located in BoothBay Harbor, Maine, where the family spent summer vacations.
80 Sally Marshall was a neighbor of the Thomas family in Frost Woods, WI.
81 A New Hampshire mountain range considered the most rugged in New England.

wore green headbands, Alice in Wonderland style, with our green uniforms, and each achievement or proficiency had a symbol stenciled on it on acquisition, for passing the swimming or diving test, recognizing a certain number of flowers or birds and so on. The best experience of the summer, perhaps, was walking thirty miles in a day. Quite a few Madison teen-agers nowadays, including Martha Lacy, have done that in the past few years in "Walk for Development," which raises money for some social project. Just before construction started on Bill's house, the walkers passed by here, and Kathy and I were hypnotized for an hour watching them.[82] My walk had no social purpose. A fifteen-mile hike had been scheduled, and the camp director had buses at the end of it to take us back to camp; but it was a beautiful cool day, we were in good training, and three other girls and I felt so fresh and ambitious we begged him to let us walk home too, and good-naturedly he did, coming along with us. We got to camp after dark to a hero's welcome. I can still remember moving automatically the last few miles with the feeling that if I stopped I could never start again. I've always been mildly proud of this physical feat, which was characteristic of me, wasn't it? No initiative, no daring, no bravery, just endurance.

This endurance came into play again at college. My freshman dormitory was at the edge of the campus, next to a farm, and every morning I woke up early and heard the hens clucking in the barnyard. That comfortable farm sound—you'd be hard put to hear it these days—will always to me be associated with misery. It's not unpleasant in itself, like a power saw; it just expresses having to live through the day. I had sense enough to know that the best thing to do was to go everywhere I was supposed to, so I did—in tears. The spectacle of a freshman crying unobtrusively but steadily all over campus naturally attracted some attention, not of a very favorable kind. One of my instructors, I remember, kindly suggested it might help me to go home for the weekend; if I actually saw things weren't as they used to be and my friends were all away at their colleges, I would come back happier, she said. I saw no point in going home to see something I already knew perfectly well, and in time I wore the Heimwehr out.[83] I don't know how long it took. I made no notation of it anywhere in my line-a-day and I'm sure I didn't mention it in my letters home any more than I had in my letters home from camp. Mother came up to see me about the middle of October, and I think I must have worn it out by then. She did not come to college with me to settle me in as many mothers did because I wanted to face it alone.

---

82   Thomas's son Bill and his wife, Kathy, built a home across the street from Thomas's home in Frost Woods.

83   Heimwehr ("Home Guard"), a nationalist paramilitary group formed during the 1920s and 1930s to defend Austria's borders.

My parents had chosen Holyoke for various reasons. It went without saying that I would go to one of the four dominant women's colleges: Wellesley, Smith, Vassar, or Mount Holyoke. Academically they were all first rank. (Once in Frost Woods when I wasn't home Tom and Dick Ragsdale rummaged through the secretary and found my report cards, and Tom told Dick Holyoke couldn't have been much of a place if I never got any academic mark below A there in all four years. I never knew this story till years later.)[84] Two of my high school friends were going to Vassar, and I think I would have liked to go with them; but I'm sure Mother thought it would be better for me to be on my own. Another friend went to Smith, but I hadn't any particular desire to go there. The campus was less beautiful because much more crowded than that of Holyoke. I always liked Wellesley, but that was only minutes away by commuter train—too close to home. Though it would not seem so now, Holyoke was at a real distance then. Once the brother of one of my roommates drove us back after spring vacation, and we left at 9:30 in the morning and arrived at 4:30 in the afternoon—seven hours for about ninety miles. On the other hand, it was near enough for me to come home Thanksgiving; Vassar would not have been. By an arrangement which seems odd now, we had Thursday and Friday as holidays in Thanksgiving week, but went back to college Friday night for Saturday morning classes. One of my father's cousins (whom I had not met) was on the faculty at Mount Holyoke. Pauline was a loyal and enthusiastic Holyoke alumna, which may have had some bearing.

After the first few weeks I had a very good time at college. Above all I enjoyed contemporary companionship. Lack of this was the great deficiency of my early life, in spite of all the blessings, and now when I hear Harry Harlow of the University of Wisconsin Primate Lab state his thesis of the essential value for young monkeys of play with their contemporaries if they are to develop into normal adults, I'm tempted to use this lack as an alibi for all my adult shortcomings.[85] I had begun to get some of this valuable experience in high school, but I had much more of it in college; whenever you wanted a girl to walk or talk with, she'd be down the corridor or around the corner. Dormitory life is very pleasant, though like many things it palls after a time. I noticed at Holyoke that the girls who had been away to boarding school before coming to college—and there were a good many of them—were getting tired of it. But it was new to me

---

84   Richard Ragsdale (1935–2004), a school friend of Thomas's son Tom, was the physician who opened the Northern Illinois Women's Center in Rockford, also known as the Rockford Abortion Clinic, in 1973, after the Roe v. Wade U.S. Supreme Court ruling.
85   Harry F. Harlow (1905–1981), an American comparative psychologist who joined the UW-Madison faculty in 1930 and conducted landmark but controversial research on rhesus monkeys, using maternal deprivation, surrogate mothering, and isolation to study social and cognitive development.

Mount Holyoke

and I loved it. I was never at the heart of any special group, but I had plenty of friends, and a variety of friends; I would sometimes wonder why A and Z, who had nothing in common and never spoke to each other, both seemed pleased to see me.

    Holyoke was a country college, with a beautiful campus, surrounded by beautiful unspoiled country, set in the Connecticut Valley at the beginning of the mountain ranges of Western Massachusetts. There was nothing but open country between the Tom Range and the eastern exposure of the campus.[86] I lived my sophomore year in Mountain View, which was just what the name says. The most beautiful season in New England, especially the hilly parts, is fall, when the leaves turn. One October day every fall, with no advance warning, we would go to chapel as usual and hear Miss Woolley[87] announce that it was Mountain Day, which meant all classes were cancelled, and we'd hurry back to the dormitory kitchens where sandwich makings were spread out to put up our lunches and get off to tramp the Tom or Holyoke Range or climb Sugarloaf. Most of the trees were hard maples, which seem to hold the sun even on a gray day, and on our sunny Mountain Day we walked for miles held in that sunlight. In winter there was plenty of snow, and I used to snowshoe—we didn't ski much—over foothills where the shadows of the snow were blue and rose and lavender and purple. In the spring we picked bunches of wild flowers in the woods, including big bunches of trailing arbutus; that the arbutus would disappear was as unthinkable then as that the stars will disappear is now. I still remember a spicy-sweet scent in the spring woods which I never identified—from a shrub, I think, not a flower. We had a lake of our own at the bottom of the Pageant Field, and the Connecticut River was within walking distance. The only connection of this pastoral with the industrial city of Holyoke was a single track which came up the main street, which had the campus on one side and a few modest scattered houses and small farms on the other, making up the village of South Hadley. Up this track a trolley car came once an hour, if I remember rightly, turned around and went back. When I was a senior, our class presented a pageant of the Odyssey in the Pageant Field, and I had the awe-inspiring title of Chairman of Animals. Since the director, very wisely I'm sure, decided to do the changing of Ulysses' men into swine by Circe symbolically instead of actually—a lingerer looked in the door and was overcome by horror at what he saw within—my duties were confined to managing a team of oxen, a calm anachronistic pair who had left agriculture for dramatic life and were accustomed to

---

86   A reference to Mount Tom Range, located in the Connecticut River Valley of Massachusetts.

87   Mary Emma Woolley (1863–1947), an American educator, served as the eleventh president of Mount Holyoke College from 1901–1937.

public appearances, usually in historic performances of Pilgrim days. My committee—one girl—and I had to drive them at the proper time to meet Nausicaa across the street from the farm where they spent the night. The motorman of the trolley which arrived just at the crucial moment, courteously stopped the car until we had crossed, and the passengers, much interested, leaned out of the windows and cheered us.

There was no doubt in those days that a college stood in loco parentis.[88] No one dreamed of questioning it. Holyoke was very advanced in having student government and being on the honor system. We enforced our own regulations, which were freely discussed between student officers and faculty advisors. To my mind, both then and now, the regulations were completely benevolent and in our best interests. As a natural conformist, I was never bothered and I can't remember that my friends were. The rules gave a pattern and propriety to life. We used to laugh at the old seminary rules—the one, for instance that at ten o'clock each young lady must be in bed "horizontally between the sheets." The current sloppiness of our language and its debasement by social science jargon make me more inclined to cry now at our loss of precision of language. This week I heard on the radio a panel report of a national commission studying the effect of television on children. "There's a lot of wobbling in the statement," said one of the speakers honestly; and he was right. It was actually impossible to tell whether they were saying yea or nay. When Mary Lyon founded Mount Holyoke, she knew her own mind and she made it clear.[89] The regulations in effect in 1919 were reasonable and no one objected. Lights were put out at 10 p.m., but you could take a certain number of "sit-ups" a semester, including one all-night one, if you signed in the hall book and went to a room kept for the purpose so your roommate's sleep was not interfered with. (I remember that late at night the dormitory was still as death, except for the tiny noise of a mouse rustling in the wastebasket. In all the dormitories big cartons of "cow crackers," plain soda crackers stamped with the print of a cow, were kept in the dining rooms for girls to help themselves whenever they wanted; as a result, the dormitories were full of crumbs; and as a result of that, full of mice.) Quiet hours were in effect for the bulk of the morning, afternoon, and evening so we could study—in other words, fulfill our purpose in being at college. I never understood in the ten years or so I served on the Residence Halls Faculty Committee [at UW-Madison] why it was impossible, as apparently it was, for dormitory students here to police

---

88   Latin for "in the place of a parent," a legal doctrine in which an institution (e.g., a school and its teachers) assumes certain parental rights and obligations on behalf of student welfare.
89   Mary Lyon (1797–1849), an American pioneer in women's education, established the Wheaton Female Seminary and the Mount Holyoke Female Seminary (now both colleges) in Massachusetts.

themselves so they could study. Another regulation for our own benefit, a health one this time, was that we were required to put in so many hours of physical outdoor exercise a week. Any sport counted, but walking was perfectly acceptable, and I used to meet most of my required hours that way, sometimes alone, more often with one friend or another. It was ideal country for walking.

A regulation for our spiritual welfare was compulsory morning chapel and Sunday church. Chapel seemed to me then, and still seems to me, an excellent way to start the day. We sat by classes: seniors in the main part of the chapel, juniors behind them, sophomores and freshmen in the balconies. Seniors wore cap and gown; it was an impressive ceremony when they "came out," that is, wore cap and gown for the first time, early in the fall. In double file, led by president and vice-president, and thereafter arranged by height, shortest girls first, they came down the center aisle and took their seats on each side of it, row by row. Generally, a plain white pique collar was worn over the gown, but on this occasion and special times like Founder's Day and Commencement, the net-boned choker was worn which you see in Edwardian pictures; it makes the wearer hold her head high and look very proud and elegant. The academic gown always seemed romantic to me. It's convenient and becoming; I used to think something surprising and significant would happen to me when I was wearing mine, but nothing ever did. "Best looking in cap and gown" is one of the first awards that we voted for in the list that came out in the class yearbook. When Miss Woolley was on campus, she conducted chapel; when she was away, some senior faculty member. She was gone for about six months during my time on a trip to China, Japan, and Korea as a member of a commission appointed by the President of the United States to study conditions there, and we were proud of that honor. Each Sunday there was a different guest minister, all WASPS, of course: we must have heard most of the best-known preachers of the day in New England.[90] The visitor ate Sunday dinner after church in a dormitory, and the one masculine voice would make itself clearly heard under the many high feminine ones. I'm sure we had a certain number of allowed cuts, which we were honor bound to sign up for in the hall book, but it was an integral part of life to go to church and chapel, and a part of life enjoyed and not resented.

Another significant manifestation of the honor system was academic. I never took an examination in the four years with any proctor in the room. The professor brought us the test, handed out the books, announced where she would be during the period in case anyone wanted to come to ask her any question, and left until it was time to come back and collect the books. To the best of my

---

90   WASP is an acronym for White Anglo-Saxon Protestant, an informal term referring to privileged elites.

knowledge and belief there was not a single violation of this honor code during the four years I spent at Mount Holyoke.

There were plenty of faculty contacts, for many of the younger women lived in the dormitories, in a room with bath, and ate in the dormitory dining room. Some lived in Faculty House, just off the campus looking out at the Tom range. I went there often, since the two women who influenced me most, my father's cousin Bertha Putnam and Miss Snell, head of the English Department, both lived there.[91] Each had one of the best apartments, with a mountain view, consisting of living room with fireplace, two bedrooms, a bathroom, and a kitchenette. Some were smaller. Miss Ball, a close friend of Bertha's, had no guestroom but shared the use of hers.[92] Meals were regularly served in the dining room, where guests could be entertained. Since my day a number of faculty have built their own houses in the village, obviously necessary for married men. Then the college was like Cranford, a community of Amazons.[93] As a matter of fact, I went through my four years without a single male instructor. This was unusual, though. There were some men on the faculty, among whom Mr. Warbecke, a tall thin professor of philosophy who had received his doctorate at Bonn, made a gorgeous spectacle in academic processions in flowing robes of royal purple, looking at least ten feet tall. Since everyone lived within a few minutes of everyone else, there was a great deal of student-faculty contact. It was most uncommon if the professor did not ask the class to tea or supper or some kind of social gathering during the semester. It was this experience at Holyoke which has made me consistently ask my students to the Frost Woods house every semester, in spite of the transportation problem here, though I suppose out of thousands of faculty at Wisconsin the number who do this (graduate seminars excepted) could be counted on the fingers of one hand.

Holyoke was originally organized as a cooperative college. It was financially the poorest of the four [sister colleges], and a high proportion of the early students were daughters of missionaries, who are not a wealthy class. So each student, with no exceptions, gave a certain number of hours a week to work in the halls, which reduced costs. Pauline was at Holyoke under this system. But it was changed in 1912, on the theory that it was tending to make the student body

---

91   Bertha Haven Putnam (1872–1960), an American historian, taught at Mount Holyoke from 1908 to 1937. Ada Laura Fonda Snell (1870–1972), a graduate from Mt. Holyoke who studied under Fred Newton Scott in the Rhetoric department at the University of Michigan, returned to Mt. Holyoke in 1900 as an English professor (see Mastrangelo, 2012). Later in this chapter, Thomas describes Miss Snell's formative influence.
92   Margaret Ball (1878–1952), taught English at Mt. Holyoke from 1901–1945.
93   A reference to *Cranford*, by British novelist Elizabeth Gaskell (1810–1865), which was first published serially in 1851 in a magazine edited by Charles Dickens.

too uniform—an admirable type perhaps but still too much of a type. In my day, at Holyoke as at the other colleges, there were only a couple of cooperative dormitories where all girls did some housework and board was therefore reduced. In any dormitory a girl could earn extra money by waiting on table and washing dishes. We all made our own beds and cleaned our own rooms—which was not the case at Bryn Mawr.

The day in the dormitory began with the informal meal of breakfast, which late risers skipped and to which we came when we liked within a certain time range and sat wherever we wanted to eat our orange, oatmeal and/or slabs of toast, each piece buttered by a woman in the kitchen as it came from the grill and piled up on another to keep warm and moist. At lunch and dinner, though, we had assigned places, changed every six weeks. Change is so hard for me to meet that even this mild fruit-basket-upset always upset me. Each table held fourteen seats; a faculty member had the middle place on one side, a "senior opposite" sat across from her, and they kept the conversation going and included everyone. The faculty member carved the roast or chicken or whatever, and the senior served the dessert. This was very trying on Tuesday and Sunday, when it was invariable a large rectangle of vanilla ice cream. Fourteen is of all numbers, I think, the worst divisor; you can cut a slab into halves, but it's very difficult to divide each half into sevens. When I was senior opposite I'm sure I never got anything like my fair share, I was so intimidated by twelve pairs of hungry eyes from well-fed girls staring at me like so many Oliver Twists to see if I was favoring myself.

Holyoke, like the other colleges, had sister classes: junior-freshman, senior-sophomore. An entering freshman was assigned to a "Big Sister" junior, and the bond between the classes was strong. The junior class serenaded the freshmen, and gave them a party. Later the younger class returned the courtesy. At Commencement time sophomores stayed over after their exams to pick big bunches of wild forget-me-nots from the brook for the seniors to carry. At both Holyoke and Wellesley, the authorities were confronted with the same problem, which they solved in different ways. The campus dormitories would accommodate only three classes, and the fourth had to live off-campus, though in college-owned houses. At Wellesley all freshmen lived together in houses in the village, each with a "Village Senior," an outstanding member of the senior class, a position which carried a great deal of prestige. Frances Sturgis was one. At Holyoke the campus dormitories held seniors, juniors, and freshmen, and the sophomores, who had learned their way around the first year, were the off class, without any upper classman.

Every spring, juniors, sophomores and freshmen went through the ordeal of room-choosing for the next year. The system kept us in turmoil for weeks, and as I look back now it seems to have caused as much heart burning and bitterness as you find now only among the followers of Malcolm X and Angela Davis.[94] Each girl drew a number, and made her choice according to it, beginning with 1. Of two prospective roommates, the girl with the lower number could choose a double for both; but often in order for friends to get together in the dormitory they wanted, new pairings had to be made. The spaces for seniors and juniors in each dormitory were limited. Entering freshmen of course took what was left over.

Room choosing kept everyone unhappy for weeks. There was a lot of Machiavellian plotting, which would often backfire. Our class was particularly badly served by this. Freshman year a group of girls who were the natural leaders found each other and decided they wanted to be together as sophomores. They chose one of the undesirable sophomore houses, and let it be known they hoped everyone else would keep out. There was a tremendous backlash. They were thought snobbish and selfish and anti-social, and they got scattered all over campus not only their sophomore year but also their junior. It wasn't until we were seniors that their leadership potential was acknowledged and they got together again, and the class got its best officers, which it had gotten along without for the rest of the time. The agony of suspense before room choosing was only equaled by the agony of knowledge after it. Fortunately, the summer intervened, and by fall the human instinct to make the best of things, which is surely one of our greatest blessings, was in operation. Shaw's comment on democracy, I think, might well apply to our room-choosing system; it's a terrible system but no one has ever come up with a better. At least, what with one thing and another, everybody on campus knew everybody else. I think we had about five hundred girls at Holyoke in my day, perhaps a hundred and fifty in the senior class. My experience at Wisconsin convinces me that you do not have a larger acquaintance in a larger place, but the reverse. Even in our comparatively small days before we got up to 35,000, it was clearly impossible to know everyone on campus, and students took refuge in a much smaller group than would be the case on a small campus, and never went outside it at all.

Next to the beauty of the countryside one of the nicest things about Mount Holyoke was music. In my day the head of the Music Department was Mr. Hammond, an excellent organist and choir director, a dedicated teacher, and much beloved.[95] Under him our college music was distinguished, and I missed

---

94 Angela Davis (b. 1944), a political activist and professor, became a prominent radical activist in the 1960s through her association with the civil rights movement, the Black Panther Party, and the communist party.
95 William Churchill Hammond (1860–1949), organist and professor of music at Mt. Holyoke from 1899 to 1937. He was a founder of the American Guild of Organists (1896) and wrote an arrangement of "White's Air"—an 1850s folksong—for organ, which was played at the end

Mount Holyoke

music very much when I went to Bryn Mawr, where, because of the Quaker origin of the college, there was little or none. Under Mr. Hammond the choir gave Christmas concerts in Boston, New York, Philadelphia, and Washington. These were particularly beautiful. Pauline with her fine voice had been one of Mr. Hammond's best students, and she hoped I might enjoy that aspect of college as much as she had done. She told me to tell Mr. Hammond that I was her relative and that I could sight-read "very well." This was true. But unfortunately I was like the primates Emily Hahn reports on in the *New Yorker*;[96] they have the intelligence to master symbolic concepts and can converse in the deaf-and-dumb system, but they haven't the physical configuration of mouth and throat necessary for talking. My voice wasn't good enough for me to make choir when I tried out, so I could only listen after that. But there was much pleasure in listening. With thousands of other Holyoke alumnae, I remember Mr. Hammond's kindly custom of playing the organ during the vesper hour every day during both midyear and final exams, for any students who wished to drop in and rest and relax. He ended every performance he ever gave with the signature "White's Air," which any alumna during his long tenure at college would recognize with pleasure to the day of her death.

In the halls we all sang. There was a music director among the house officers, and any dormitory could have been called a nest of singing birds, in the pretty phrase someone (Dr. Johnson?) applied to Wright's college at Oxford, Pembroke.[97] We generally sang together after dinner, in good weather on the outdoor hall steps. The Music Department gave out two or three songs for all dormitories to practice, and the hall which rendered them best was proud of the honor. We also sang by classes, and the class which won this annual competition was recorded in the senior yearbook.

Another mild competition between the halls was building snow statues. As I look back I am impressed by the fact that we had so many innocent pleasures, and that the involvement in them was practically one hundred per cent. I shudder at what seems to me today the curse of TV on the young: not that its violence fosters violence in them, which the social scientists seem unable to decide one way or another, but that it fosters complete passivity. I was horrified at Frances Curti's seven-year-old granddaughter—admittedly a problem

---

of each Vesper Service at Mt. Holyoke.
96   Emily Hahn (1905–1997), an American journalist and author, graduated from the University of Wisconsin in 1926 with a degree in Mining Engineering. The *New Yorker* articles referenced are from the April 10 and 17, 1971 issues.
97   Samuel Johnson's phrase "Sir, we are a nest of singing birds"—a reference to the number of poets produced at Pembroke College—is recorded by James Boswell in the first volume of *The Life of Samuel Johnson*.

child from an unhappy home situation, who is a TV addict and has no interest whatever in anything else, in anything at all I'd consider normal at her age.[98] At Holyoke it was impossible for any gift to go unnoticed—though I've always thought it was only too possible here at Wisconsin. One of the biggest events of the year, for instance, was Junior Show, a musical put on by the junior class which in some capacity or other had to involve every single class member. Our class was lucky in this connection, since one of our members, Polly Barnes, had had an unusual amount of training in dance; she was chairman of dancing for ours, and it was particularly good. But what do you think it could have been about? I remember appearing as a lettuce leaf, in a pale green crepe paper costume, in a number having to do with the items in a mixed salad. Polly, incidentally, was from Chicago, one of the few Midwesterners in college, and for a number of years after I had gone to Madison, I would have lunch with her when I crossed Chicago. In those days you had to take a Parmalee bus from one Chicago station to another on every trip, and it was bitterly said that a hog going from west to east didn't have to change trains but every person did. Another big event was Senior Pageant, which again involved every girl in the class, and I have already referred to ours. I'll tell another story about those oxen because it was one of the few times I consciously practiced duplicity, though Ed Lacy certainly taught me a lot of tact when I started working under him. At dress rehearsal some girl—and not anyone in authority, which would have called for a different response altogether—said to me, "Ednah, don't you think those oxen would look much better if they were washed?" The fee for the oxen at the farm covered room and board, so to speak, but not washing, and I had no confidence in my ability to do anything about it, so I said noncommittally, "Well, that's an idea," and did nothing. After the pageant the same girl came up to me beaming with pleasure and said, "How *much* nicer those oxen look after being washed, don't they?" I smiled at her.

Overall participation was encouraged by a point system, on which every extra-curricular activity and office was ranked. No girl could get more than a given number of points. A major office like Chairman of Judiciary or Editor-in-Chief of the *Round Table*, the literary magazine, was ranked so high that a girl could not hold anything else at the same time. Small offices which required less time were ranked accordingly, and several varied ones could be held together. This obviously prevented letting anyone load herself too heavily on the one hand, and encouraged as many people as possible to have some share in college life. A freshman could hold no office at all her first semester; she had to keep

---

98   Frances Curti, wife of Merle Curti (1897–1997), the Pulitzer Prize-winning American historian who taught at Wisconsin from 1942–1968.

free from extra-curricular demands until she knew how much of her time would be required for satisfactory academic performance. We never were allowed to forget our main purpose in coming to college. My chief interest was literary, and as soon as I could I tried out for a position on the literary magazine board, getting instead the job of reporter on the college newspaper, which I didn't want. I learned a useful lesson from it, however; if you have to write something up and think you can't do it, you put a sheet of paper in the typewriter and start the sentence, and then somehow you will finish it, and the article. I made the literary board as a sophomore and ended as editor-in-chief. One of the significant experiences of college is, as a senior, filling the shoes of the person you most looked up to as a freshman, and then wondering if like yours her feet were also of clay. I submitted a number of contributions to the magazine and was early made a member of the literary society, Blackstick (after the fairy in Thackeray's *The Rose and the Ring*). At the end of my sophomore year I was awarded the Florence Purington Prize,[99] specified for the sophomore who made most progress during the year; mine must have been extra-curricular. As a junior I was an intercollegiate debater in the system involving Holyoke, Smith, Wellesley and Vassar.[100] From the squad of volunteer debaters each college chose two three-member teams, affirmative and negative, of which one went to another college and one stayed home, to debate the same overall topic. Each debate was judged by three judges, a visiting faculty member, a visiting student, a local person not connected with the home college such as a lawyer. As a senior I could not continue debating, since I was editor-in-chief of the magazine, but I went to Vassar as student judge. All of these activities included both success and failure. It was success to work up to editor-in-chief, but when I represented Mount Holyoke at a four-college meeting at Smith to put out an intercollegiate issue, I lacked proper aggressiveness to push my own wares, and Holyoke was not as well represented in the issue as it should have been. It was success to get on the debating team at all. The coach told me I talked so softly I could not be heard, and therefore had no chance, and with a devoted friend sitting in the last row of the auditorium I spent all of the next two days, except for classes, before the final try-outs, talking on the stage until my friend could hear me perfectly. It was success to receive the college prize for the best debater on either Holyoke team. But we lost our debate to Wellesley, a bludgeoning blow. We were hostesses to the Wellesley team, of course, and I remember what it cost to be cordial and cheery with them the

---

99   According to Mt. Holyoke archival records, this prize, awarded to one of the top five freshmen in the fall after their first year, was established in 1919 by the Sigma Theta Chi Alumnae Committee. Thomas must be referring to a different award.

100   These are the four "sister" colleges that participated in a series of intercollege conferences on English composition between 1919 and 1924 (see Mastrangelo and L'Eplattenier, 2004).

next day until they left, after what I think was my first sleepless night. I forced myself to recite poetry to forget my trouble, but as soon as I began to drift off into unconsciousness and there lost control of my will, the defeat would rise to the surface and jerk me awake. I'm glad to say I was popular enough in my dormitory to be elected hall representative to Student Council, but I couldn't serve because I was already holding a major office. I made Phi Beta Kappa as the first of three juniors only. I did go to my own Junior Prom under the urging of one of my roommates, who pressed her brother on me for escort, but my first real date was to come in Wisconsin. There was not so much dating in women's colleges in those days, when the automobile was only beginning to change our lives, and a girl's effect on men was not a particularly important criterion for a successful college career.

As I have said, I had a great many friends, and a great variety of friends. One was Sydney Mclean, a sophomore when I was a freshman, introvert, brilliant, clumsy, overweight to the point of obesity, destined to write an excellent life of Emily Dickinson, another brilliant Holyoke introvert, and to spend her life on the English Department of Mount Holyoke.[101] (If you had asked me to guess how I'd be spending mine when I was an undergraduate, I'd have given that answer for myself.) At the other extreme was Marion Lewis, our senior class president, voted "best looking in cap and gown," handsome, attractive, popular, destined to marry (I think) a corporation lawyer and live a prosperous socially prominent life in Scarsdale or the equivalent—destined also to have her son marry a Maori girl in Australia when he was bumming his way around the world. Those I saw most were those who shared my literary interests, and this included Elizabeth MacKinnon and Kathleen Moore, Peter's[102] mother, freshmen when I was a sophomore. They were both on the *Round Table* board with me and also in Miss Marks' play-writing class.[103]

The girl to whom I was most attracted, however, and the only one with whom I am still on intimate terms, was Rebecca Smaltz, who majored in Economics (an extremely strong department at Holyoke), who was in the same dormitory

---

101 Sydney R McLean's contribution to scholarship on Emily Dickenson are highlighted in Richard Benson Sewall's *The Life of Emily Dickenson* (1974, p. 360, footnote 18).

102 Thomas's son-in-law.

103 Jeannette Augustus Marks (1875–1964), graduated from Wellesley College (1900), where she met Mary Emma Woolley, who, after her inauguration as President of Mt. Holyoke in 1901, appointed Marks as an instructor in the English department. During her 40-year tenure at Mt. Holyoke, Marks initiated a Play and Poetry Short Talks lecture series and the Laboratory Theatre, and she eventually chaired the English Literature department, which was separate from the English (composition) department. She was also politically active in the National Women's Party and a supporter of national socialist causes during the 1920s. Thomas describes her experience with and perception of Marks later in this chapter.

Mount Holyoke

I was as a freshman. In a completely different environment, it strikes me she's much like Biddy in *Great Expectations*. In the class awards, she was voted the best sport and the most all-round, and her life has borne that out (which is not always the case with class awards: I was voted most scholastic). She was Chairman of Judiciary as a senior, perhaps the most important office for any student. She is one of the best-balanced, broad-minded, and altogether admirable persons I have ever known. She and her roommate Davy (Frances David) were Philadelphians, and graduates of the famous Germantown Friends School, though not themselves Quakers. The bond between them came from earliest childhood and was so close that no third could have much chance of developing as strong a one with either. Davy died of cancer years ago, comparatively young. I have been lucky in actual contacts with Becky over the years; without some the strongest friendship in time weakens to an annual Christmas card, which you're always glad to get but which you don't think much about for the next three hundred and sixty days or so. Becky's older (and much prettier) sister Eleanor married a medical student at the University of Pennsylvania, and his first practice was in Green Bay, Wisconsin. The family bought land near Sister Bay[104] and put up a summer cottage used for family meetings for years after Eleanor and her family had moved to California. I've visited Becky there and seen her when I was at Tom's or on my way to Milford, and never without feeling refreshed and stimulated by contact with someone whose experiences are very different from and much broader than mine. The family was wealthy, but not thereby immune from trouble. Mr. Smaltz had a retarded aunt, who was lovingly cared for at home all her long life. Becky's parents took this responsibility until their death, but then she accepted it and gave up a career of her own to do so. When Frances Perkins[105] was secretary of labor (another of our most distinguished Holyoke graduates), Becky worked under her, after getting her master's from Bryn Mawr the year I got mine, on surveys of conditions in industries employing women and children, a job which required much traveling. When she came home to live, she took the aunt every summer to Door County, but for the rest of the year spent her time in important and admirable volunteer activities; I couldn't list them all, but she has spent a great deal of time on alumnae work for Mount Holyoke and served for some years as President of the Philadelphia City YWCA. (I wonder what her reaction will be to a fascinating item I heard here the other day: the Madison YWCA is sponsoring a weekend seminar on Lesbianism, appealing to Gay Mothers among others.) Becky has always found time for private kindnesses; for instance, when Hannah was at Swarthmore she

---

104 A village in Door County, Wisconsin.
105 Frances Perkins (1880–1965) graduated from Mt. Holyoke in 1902 and was U.S. Secretary of Labor under Roosevelt from 1933–1945.

took her out every year for the day on a trip to Valley Forge or some other place of interest, and Hannah told me these expeditions were one of her nicest memories of college. When her great aunt died, Becky moved from the family house into a house in Germantown where her parents used to visit, now made over into apartments, of which she has one on the ground floor looking out into a lovely yard with fruit trees and flowers. Though the other renters are white, the neighborhood is now almost entirely black, and she has been burglarized three times. The spring of 1971 when I was pondering on retirement she drove down to Milford to take me back to spend the night with her before I flew back to Madison the next day. "Have you read Muriel Sparks' *Memento Mori?*" I said. "Have you read that book by Marya Mannes where they put everyone over sixty-five in a concentration camp and don't let them hear from their families or read any newspapers and then give them euthanasia at seventy?"[106] "No," said Becky, driving through the Philadelphia rush hour traffic with ease and grace. "I haven't read any of those things!" You can see why I feel she always does me a great deal of good.

The girl I saw most of in college is still a mystery to me. This was Marjorie Cook, from Fall River, [Massachusetts] my freshman roommate and my senior one. She was an English major like me and we were in a lot of classes together. One incident connected with her took on particular significance for me after I became a teacher because it presented an ethical problem. We were assigned a long source paper on a topic of our own choosing, which was to be the main piece of work of the course and the main determining factor of our grade. The date due was announced weeks ahead. I can't remember my topic, but I worked hard, put a lot of time into the paper, and had it ready well before the deadline. Marjorie couldn't find a subject she liked and the day before the paper was due still had nothing. She went to see Miss Snell, who suggested she should look at a new exhibit of pictures in the Art Building and write a criticism on them, which she could do in an afternoon. Marjorie did. We both got A's. I can see that this presented Miss Snell with an ethical problem, and a problem in itself implies varying possibilities of solution. I can see that Miss Snell didn't want to give a punitive grade to a brilliant student which would not represent her ability. I don't know how I would have handled the problem myself, but I didn't think Miss Snell's solution was fair then, and I don't now, though I didn't say anything about it to anyone, least of all Marjorie. Perhaps fairness is not the only thing a teacher should consider?

Marjorie and I were closest during our junior year, though owing to trouble with the room-choosing system we were not roommates. Looking back a long

---

106 Marya Mannes (1904–1990), American author and critic, published sharply critical essays and books on American society. The book Thomas refers to is *They* (1968).

time ago on what I didn't really understand even then, I think it was because she wanted to make Phi Beta Kappa as a junior, as I inevitably was going to do. She was very kind to me all through the strain of my intercollegiate debating, and she insisted on appointing me assistant chairman of Junior Show—she had been elected chairman and it was a good choice—just to give me some status. But she didn't make Phi Beta Kappa. (The Junior Show chairmanship had nothing to do with it, since it was only grades through first semester which were considered.) We had already chosen our rooms for next year, and she and I were sharing a single suite (two separate rooms with an inner connecting door) in Rockefeller. When we came back she had changed. Two of the very few personal entries I made in my line-a-day during college were "worried about strained relations with Marjorie" on one occasion and "looking for Marjorie all over college" on another. There was no quarrel, nothing to quarrel about. I interpret it now that she had tried to be the kind of person I was because she wanted a certain reward and when she didn't get it she turned against the concept and against me. In this connection, it was fortunate that our dormitory burned to the ground the morning of Christmas vacation, so that we were no longer living under the same roof. I wasn't in touch with her after college, but heard through mutual friends that she became what today we'd call a hippie, that she married unhappily and unsuitably, and that she died shortly after.

I'll digress here to tell the story of the fire, one of the few exciting episodes in my life, where I ran true to form. It was the morning of Christmas vacation, I had a ride home at noon, after morning classes, and I was all ready, with my suitcase packed and my purse lying on the chair beside it. I went to chapel and on to my first class. "Don't you live in Rocky, Ednah?" somebody said. "It's on fire. Don't you want to go see it?" My first instinct was to stay in class, but my second was to go, and I got there before any cordon had been drawn around the dormitory. My suitcase held a few clothes and a lot of manuscripts submitted to the *Round Table*, which I was taking home to read over vacation, and I felt keenly my responsibility for these. "Is it all right to go in?" I said to some girl nearby. "I guess so," said she, knowing no more about it than I did. So I went in, up the stairs and down the corridor to my room which, as I found out later, was directly over the part of the building in which the fire had started. I picked up the suitcase and the purse and got out again into the hall, where the smoke was so bad that for the first time I realized my stupidity and the urgency of getting out. I dropped the purse and with the first gleam of sense I had shown that morning decided it would not be a good idea to stop and look for it, and I made it outdoors into the fresh air. If I had been sixty seconds slower I would not be writing this now. In the years since if I have heard of people trapped in a burning building this experience has always given me some comfort because

I think they would have lost consciousness from smoke inhalation before they could suffer.

Holyoke has a very bad fire record, partly because they kept gas long after it was obvious that electricity was a better and safer method of lighting (when the Wellesley debate team was at college I went over to see the girl who was my particular charge and found her in the dark because she was afraid to turn on the gas jet) and partly because the fire-fighting resources of South Hadley were meager. Rockefeller was a total loss, but luckily it was named for a plutocrat, not, like most of the other dormitories, for early spinsters of noble character and no money who left no descendants to earn any. The current Rockefeller gave the college money for a "new Rocky" to replace the old. The timing also was lucky, for the authorities had Christmas vacation to arrange some housing. Trustees coming over from Holyoke saw that all girls who had lost their money got home safely. The solution was ingenious: they set up booths on the main floor of the gym, like those at a county fair, with four little singles, one in each corner of the running track in the balcony. These accommodated seniors and freshmen; juniors were put up in the guest rooms of the different dormitories all over campus. Bertha Putnam at once offered me her guest room, so I slept in Faculty House the rest of the year. The big overhead light was turned off at 10, and each cubicle had its own desk lights. Of course the building was already equipped with showers, though not tubs; it was a common sight all the rest of the year to see a girl carrying a bath towel going over to take a tub bath at some friend's. We all ate together in the basement of SAH (Student Alumnae Hall), the equivalent of the Memorial Union, which was equipped with kitchen facilities for banquets and the like and now was used daily. The fire at least solved my own personal problem about Marjorie.

I should speak here of another friend, Brenda Glass, voted our "class genius," "most temperamental," and "most absent-minded." This story again deals with a teacher's ethical problem, solved this time by justice rather than mercy. Brenda was in Miss Marks' play-writing class, as I was, and she spent so much time on the class yearbook that she didn't turn in her work to Miss Marks, who told her she must flunk the course. This meant Brenda could not graduate with her class—not much in these days of drop-outs and stop-cuts and the blurring of class lines by summer school credits and so on, but a real disgrace then. The class chose me as spokesman to try to plead with Miss Marks to let Brenda graduate, but she wouldn't budge. "It would not be fair to you and the others if I let Brenda pass," she said. "I've seen you come to class all semester and turn in your work no matter how tired you were as your parched lips showed. It would not be right for the rest of you if I passed Brenda." "Oh, we wouldn't mind," I said. "We *want* you to—" completely of course missing the point that this was a matter of principle. I was still childish as to the ethics of my future profession.

Mount Holyoke

The first real experience of it I remember took place at Holyoke, and I have told the story often to teaching assistants at Wisconsin to introduce the light touch and to encourage them about our training system here. It was in a course in English literature conducted by a visitor, the wife of an Amherst professor, a large imposing woman whose name I have forgotten. Coming to class one day with an attack of laryngitis, she said to me, "You come up here and take the class." I came. "Will you sit or stand?" said she, but before I could answer she answered for me, settling herself comfortably in the desk chair. "Stand—it's always better to stand in front of a class. Now begin." I started on whatever occurred to me about the assignment for the day and was just off and away when she said suddenly, "Stop. You aren't giving them enough time to write down what you're saying. Watch their pens. All right now. Go on." And I went through the hour under this stop-go direction, a sink-or-swim introduction to my life profession.

Mary Emma Woolley was inaugurated as President of Mount Holyoke in 1901, a position she held for thirty-seven years, so that she was at the height of her career when I was at Holyoke, and the college was at its height as the expression of her ideals. The connection was to have a tragic ending some fifteen years later. I say tragic, rather than merely sad, for I think Miss Woolley was a great woman, worthy of greatness to be the heroine of classical tragedy, and fitted for it by the possession of the tragic flaw. Since I started working on this chapter I have re-read Jeannette Marks' biography of her, which serves her very badly indeed.[107] Miss Marks loved and admired Miss Woolley after her fashion, and they shared a companionship of fifty-two years; but she was no Boswell. She completely lacked the self-effacement which alone can make a biographer great, and she was a woman of many flaws, including a curious lack of taste and a subconscious jealousy of her subject—all revealed in her writing. (Writing reveals the flaws of a writer as pitilessly as an X-ray, and I wonder at my own temerity.)

In 1930 the *Good Housekeeping Magazine* Board of distinguished judges (whoever they were) voted the following for the twelve foremost women in America: Grace Abbott, Jane Addams, Cecilia Beaux, Martha Berry, Willa Cather, Carrie Chapman Catt, Grace Coolidge, Minnie Maddern Fiske, Helen Keller, Florence Sabin, Ernestine Schumann-Heink, and Mary Emma Woolley. It might be an interesting research project for my grandchildren, if they ever read this, to look up the reasons why these women were so distinguished; or for that matter, for you: or even for me. Miss Woolley deserves to survive—whether she has done so or not—for her services to women, particularly women's education, and to world peace. In addition to the trip to China, she went to Geneva in

---

107 *The Life and Letters of Mary Emma Woolley* (1955).

1931 as the first woman delegate ever appointed by a United States President (Hoover) to a Disarmament Conference. Until her long, sad last illness, she worked devotedly all her life for both causes.

The relationship between Miss Woolley and Miss Marks is, it occurs to me, not unlike that between two gifted women I knew as a personal friend, Helen White and Ruth Wallerstein.[108] Miss Woolley and Helen were both great; Miss Marks and Ruth were brilliant, but lacking in the patience and stability essential for greatness. Helen was much more fortunate in the friendship than Miss Woolley: she must have had much pleasure in hers and no harm, for she was not in a position technically superior to her friend's which might interfere with intimacy. But Miss Woolley was president of a college, and it was unwise of her to take a member of her faculty as a housemate. She did not deceive herself when she felt she was doing a service to Holyoke in recruiting Miss Marks for the faculty. (They had met at Wellesley, when Miss Woolley was a young instructor in Bible, and Miss Marks her not much younger student.) Miss Marks was a stimulating teacher, as I know from personal experience. She was also a poet, though I doubt if her poems survive, and a personal friend of most of the contemporary poets, who came to talk to us at college as a personal favor to her. But Miss Woolley did deceive herself when she failed to see that it was improper to put any member of her faculty in a position of privilege and favoritism, particularly such a person as Miss Marks, who inspired strong dislikes and great antagonism. Miss Woolley was betrayed, I think, by the tragic flaw of her feminine need to give and receive love—and I'm *not* talking about Lesbianism, for heaven's sake.[109] Subconsciously, I suspect, she felt Miss Marks' need of her, for as the stronger she would have had the more to give, and she certainly would have felt it disloyal to admit there was any justification for the attacks Miss Marks' militancy increasingly gave rise to. I'm sure Miss Marks was right, but she was in advance of her time, and we had a conservative board of trustees. She spoke before the College Forum on behalf of the political prisoners at Fort Leavenworth for one thing, for instance. It was our regular joke in the play-writing class that the girl whose play was being read and criticized should sit in a special seat, called "the electric chair." When I saw Miss Marks on coming back to college for my first reunion and referred to this old joke, she rebuked me sharply; in the interim

---

108 Ruth Wallerstein (1893–1958), educated at Bryn Mawr and University of Pennsylvania, joined the English department in 1920 and taught English literature until her untimely death in an automobile accident in England while on research leave.
109 The dismissal of lesbianism between Woolley and Marks was criticized by Blanche Wiesen Cook (1979) in "The Historical Denial of Lesbianism," a critical review of Anna Mary Wells's book, *Miss Marks and Miss Wooley: The Portrait of a Lifelong Relationship between Two Prominent and Independent Women* (1978), which denies Woolley and Marks' lesbianism.

Sacco and Vanzetti had been executed.[110] It was of course quite proper for Miss Woolley to protect the freedom of speech of her faculty, and a wild-eyed revolutionary would not have mattered if she had not been living in the President's house and therefore involving the official head of the college. This isn't the place to go into the complicated business of the trustees' replacement of Miss Woolley by a man. It was her tragedy, and it broke her physically as well as spiritually, for it was not only personal but the downfall of a cause, and a not ignoble one. We have never had another woman president since, and like many alumnae of my generation, I have never felt the same about my college.

When I was there, however, it was the hopeful dawn of the freedom of women. In these shrill and strident seventies, it's interesting for me to think about those faculty women who seem to me the true women's liberators. The faculty were distinguished and dedicated; my father's cousin Bertha Putnam was typical. She had been an undergraduate at Bryn Mawr, the most exacting women's college in the country and the first to give the Ph.D., but had received her own doctorate from Columbia. She was as well known in England as in America, a Fellow of the Royal Historical Society, among many other honors. Our yearbook among "Impossibilities" lists "that Miss Putnam should fail to state an authority." She was a scholar, and perfectly fulfilled in scholarship and teaching, as was Emma Carr in Chemistry, Amy Hewes in Economics, and many others. And they weren't grabby. Today it seems to me the typical Woman's Libber, with no effort or work on her part, expects as her right to have a doting husband and children (like those phonies in the "incredible" Geritol commercial, which I whole-heartedly nominate, in the teeth of tremendous competition, for the award of most obnoxious commercial in America),[111] a rating as a beauty queen, a seat on the Stock Exchange, and the presidency of IBM or the United States. The reason there are so few women in absolutely first class top positions today is not male chauvinism, I think. (In a recent *New Yorker* squib, a woman asked a bookstore clerk why they had the novels of Alec Waugh but not of Evelyn. "Because the owners are male chauvinistic pigs," he answered.) The reason, I believe, is that only a small minority of women (or of men) are qualified to fill such positions; and that all of this small minority of women only a small minority are willing to pay the price which such positions demand: single-minded devotion to the end. I am a case in point. I have had the best of both worlds. I am a full professor (emeritus) of the University of Wisconsin, and the only woman full professor to have three children and seven grandchildren.

---

110 Ferdinando Nicola Sacco and Bartolomeo Vanzetti, two Italian immigrants accused of murder during an armed robbery, were executed by electric chair in 1927.
111 The commercial for this dietary supplement, which first aired in 1973 during the Women's Liberation Movement, concluded with the tag line, "My wife—I think I'll keep her."

But no one would dream of ranking me as a first-rate scholar, like Helen White, Ruth Wallerstein, and Madeleine Doran,[112] whom the *Publications of the Modern Language Association* called "the distinguished triumfeminate of the University of Wisconsin English Department."[113] They all died unmarried, as did all the faculty I knew at Mount Holyoke, after happy, rich, fulfilled scholarly lives. Those women were perfectly realistic. They knew what they wanted and they were glad of the opportunity to pay the price for it. It was the great good fortune of many generations of Holyoke students that such women formed the faculty.

I went to college with topflight preparation and rather inclined to major in Latin or French, since I had had my best teaching in those subjects. I changed my mind freshman year. Dr. Roberts had over-prepared me for Holyoke in Latin, and I wasted my first year waiting for the rest of the class to get where I was at the beginning. I regret in a mild way that I didn't start Greek instead of going on with Latin, though I'm probably fooling myself when I think that if I had I might have gone on with it on my own. The teacher was competent, an elderly New Englander with the interesting locution of "for tomorrow I want that you should" … which though it sounds like a literal Latin translation was not, I think, but provincial new England speech derived from the strong classical emphasis in the New England seminaries. The French teacher was incompetent, one of the very few poor teachers I had at college, and probably she didn't last. She didn't even conduct class in French, and I was completely turned off. But I had Freshman English with Ada Laura Fonda Snell, Head of the Department, and this determined my professional life.[114] Behind every dedicated woman teacher—I'm not so sure about men—I think there stands another teacher whose influence has lasted for life. I have said this at various meetings of Wisconsin high school teachers, and it has always struck a chord. The *New Yorker* once printed an interesting profile on a woman whose name I have forgotten, a professor of Middle English, a subject with very little popular appeal. She did not have many Ph.D. candidates, but the ones she did so venerated her that "all the rest of their lives they would stand up if she entered the room." Miss Snell was this person for me.

---

112 Madeleine K. Doran (1905–1996) was an American literary critic and poet who earned her Ph.D. at Stanford (1927) and taught at UW-Madison for four decades (1935–1975).

113 The source for this citation has not been identified.

114 As Thomas explains in the following paragraph, writing and literature were taught in separate departments. Mt. Holyoke had a long tradition of teaching rhetoric. In 1897, following a seven-year period where rhetoric and literature were taught in a single department, the two separated into the English department (formerly rhetoric, with an emphasis on composition) and the English Literature Department (Mastrangelo, 2012, pp. 74–75). However, contrary to Thomas's account, Mastrangelo finds evidence that the two departments co-existed peacefully, with writing assigned in literature classes and literature being read in writing classes (p. 89).

Mount Holyoke

Holyoke had separate departments of English Composition and English Literature, for the reason, as I learned later, that no one could get along with Miss Marks, who headed the latter. This arrangement is unusual, but I still think logical. It was a very lucky one for me. Usually it is hard for an English major to get in much advanced composition, but I built up the bulk of my work in it and was therefore particularly well prepared for my work in Wisconsin. I had a course with Miss Snell almost every semester, since you could repeat your own writing indefinitely. Our Freshman English certainly wasn't "creative" writing; I can't imagine now what we did with Huxley's "[On] A Piece of Chalk"[115] day after day, but according to my line-a-day we stayed with it for weeks. I was never able consciously to analyze Miss Snell's methods anyway. When I started at Danielson with no preparation for teaching whatever, I used to try to remember what she did and how she did it, and I never could. I only knew that I always came out of her classroom walking on air.

She was very kind to me, not the less I suppose because I was the cousin of her friend Bertha Putnam. Bertha was also very kind to me, partly because she had a strong sense of family but also perhaps because she saw in me, naïve as I was, some intellectual potential. She was away on leave of absence my first semester, which was probably just as well in view of my early homesickness. Her close friend Miss [Margaret] Ball invited me down to meet her when she came back, and I brought a friend. I was innocently surprised that she recognized me, not the other girl, as her cousin; it had never occurred to me that there is such a thing as "a family look." I was also naively surprised one day when as I said good night she said she must prepare her lecture for the next day. I thought professors knew so much they just went into class and let the spirit move them, like so many Quakers bearing testimony. My first visit was the beginning of many, and eventually it was a habit every Sunday evening when I had done my preparations for the coming week. She and Cousin Emily were close friends all their lives, and Cousin Emily not infrequently spent a week or so in her guest room, and I also met her sisters there, Corinna Lindon-Smith and Ethel (who never married). Usually of course she was alone. I would run down the hill in the cold winter night and slip in the back door instead of going all around the building to enter as I ought through the front. Faculty House faced the Tom Range, and the front apartments had beautiful views, but a very cold wind blew across on the unsheltered side. Bertha thought it was not proper to come in the back door, so like Mr. Knightley and Emma we did not speak much about it. The fire would be burning in her room, which was crowded with books, pictures, tomb rubbings, and treasures of various sorts she

---

115 A reference to English Biologist Thomas Huxley (1825–1895), whose essay, published in Macmillan's Magazine in London in 1868, uses a single object (chalk) to create a geological history of Britain.

collected in her annual visits to England. I had one course with her, Renaissance and Reformation, though I would have preferred to avoid my relative; but the course offered me the broadest period of history for my single elective in the field, and she was an excellent teacher. At the end of the first semester she read my exam aloud to the class; I think she too would have preferred to avoid this, but if my examination was the best in the class there was no reason not to let the class profit by an excellent example. Generally, we talked about ideas. Her mind, it occurs to me now, was very much like Ruth Wallerstein's in its power of illumination, and like Ruth she was a woman of great culture and breadth of background. She spoke to me as to an equal. I can remember my shock on hearing her say, "Of course I don't believe in personal immortality." When I thought about it, I guess I didn't either, but I would never have dared to make such a forthright statement. Bertha said just what she thought, and she thought on the basis of a width of experience of philosophy, literature, and art as well as history, as well as extensive European travel. Mark Hopkins on one end of a log and the student on the other parallel Bertha and me sitting before her fire.[116] Mount Holyoke gave me much more, but she alone would have been worth my going there.

There were several other faculty I should speak of. One was Miss Charlotte D'Evelyn,[117] fresh from Bryn Mawr (it was very heavily represented on the Holyoke faculty) where she had received her Ph.D. from Carleton Brown, under whom I got my own M.A.[118] She was very shy and very scholarly. I had two years of Anglo-Saxon with her, in a class of only three students, so I had pretty good grounding in the early part of English literature before I went on to graduate school. Another young woman was Miss Kathleen Lynch, with whom Becky and I took a survey of English Literature course. We both admired and called on her together, and we pitied her for being under the domination of a rather forbidding old mother. It is through her that I came to Wisconsin. She had been an undergraduate at Mount Holyoke and had gone to Wisconsin to start her doctorate under Karl Young.[119] The year we knew her she had come back to

---

116 The phrase is attributed to James Garfield and is the title of American education historian Frederick Rudolph's *Mark Hopkins and the Log: Williams College, 1836–1872* (1956).
117 Charlotte D'Evelyn (1889–1977), English literature professor at Mt. Holyoke from 1917–1954.
118 Carleton Brown (1869–1941), a prominent medievalist trained at Harvard.
119 Karl Young (1879–1943), who studied at the University of Michigan and at Harvard under G. L. Kittredge, taught in the UW-Madison English department from 1908–1923, then taught at University of Michigan before becoming chair of English at Yale and president of the MLA in 1940. Young published several textbooks for use in Freshman English while at Wisconsin, but his later publications, and his move to Michigan, indicate a shift in career interests. According to Brereton (1995), Young was one of several "promising rhetoricians who taught and published in rhetoric while young and migrated to literature when older" (p. 25).

Holyoke temporarily with the understanding that she would come back permanently after receiving the degree. Some sort of similar arrangement might have been in the cards for me, but it didn't work out. Karl Young moved to Michigan and she followed him there, so she left Wisconsin in June the year I arrived in September. But she spoke to Miss [Helen] White about me, and engaged a room for me at the Women's College Club so that I had a place to come when I arrived a stranger in Madison.

I was a member of the elitist play-writing course given by the formidable Miss Marks, which met in the president's house. She was a stimulating teacher, but fifty years later I am still smarting under what I think was a case of injustice on a stage direction of mine: "Enter Helen in a last year's suit." Miss Marks said that was ridiculous; I might as well have said "Enter Helen having had a cup of tea." Well, I admit I don't know how an actress could convey the effect of just having had a cup of tea, but I deny the analogy; it seems to me the easiest thing in the world whenever the play might be produced, to dress the actress in a suit just behind the current fashion, whatever it may be. But I had to give in. The printed direction (the play was published in the *Round Table* as well as produced at college) is "Enter Helen dressed for traveling." We produced a couple of our own plays that semester, the beginning of what developed into a very well-equipped workshop for future students. We did scenery, costumes, acting all ourselves, which of course was a lot of fun. I have said that Miss Marks was responsible for friction with other faculty members. I'm afraid I contributed to it rather innocently myself, since by an odd stroke of fate I was living in Faculty House when I was taking the play-writing course, and therefore going back and forth regularly between two places generally not much frequented by students. I don't think I made as much noise as a mouse when I slipped out of Faculty House at dawn to go paint scenery, but the conventional ladies there were probably not best pleased; they could hardly feel their students would be getting up like so many larks to do extra work for them. It seems rather remarkable now that I was able to hold a middle course, for in general there were no two ways about it for Miss Marks: you were a devotee or an enemy. But I did manage to enjoy the work with her and yet in general submit to the influence of the other faction, to which both Miss Snell and Miss Putnam belonged.

The question came up what I was to do after graduation. Miss Snell, Bertha, and several of the English professors encouraged me to apply to Bryn Mawr for a scholarship and become a candidate for the master's there. One of them, Miss Griffith, wanted me to submit a scholarly paper on Ben Jonson with the application, though this was not essential. I spent all Christmas vacation reading and working out when I showed her the paper she thought it would not help my application, and advised me not to send it—a clear indication, if we'd realized,

Mount Holyoke

that I wasn't really cut out for scholarship. I got the scholarship anyway, and a larger one awarded by Mount Holyoke itself to a senior going on to graduate school. Miss Marks "feared the cloistered effect of another woman's college on Ednah," and wanted me to go to Yale instead of Bryn Mawr. She also came up with a most original proposal for a teaching job a year later, when I had left Bryn Mawr, which I shall speak of later. But everyone else, including my cousin, threw their weight in the Bryn Mawr scales, and I went to Bryn Mawr. Nor have I ever been sorry. Bryn Mawr was cloistered, true; but I found it out for myself, and Bryn Mawr led directly to Danielson, where I had the most valuable single year of my whole education. And the year after that Bryn Mawr led directly to Wisconsin, for it was through my contact with a University of Minnesota graduate there that I realized life at a Midwest university was quite unlike life at an Eastern woman's college, and formed the desire to see for myself—just for one year—what it was like. And the rest you know.

I'm very much indebted to Mount Holyoke, and I'm not quite free from a sense of guilt at not having paid my debt, which I can't rationalize away even by what I believe to be the great betrayal of the cause of women. One of our college songs puts rather euphemistically the steady appeal for funds: "And when soft in a whisper thou callest / For the treasures unlocked by thy key," and goes on idealistically "Our achievements, our hopes, and our glorious faith / Shall answer, Mount Holyoke, to thee." (That was written in a period considerably earlier than my own, even; I wonder if they still sing it.) The actual physical distance has been a barrier. After my first reunion, I never went back to another, because I was in Wisconsin, where Commencement always came a week or two later than at Mount Holyoke. One summer I drove over from Pauline's to see Bertha in her last illness, with nurses around the clock. Miss Snell visited the Frost Woods house the first year it was built, when Modern Language Association met here, and one of the few fires ever lighted in the upstairs bedroom burned for her. Gradually I lost touch with one person after another, and inevitably my interests and energies were spent on Wisconsin. From time to time an alumna has arrived in Madison and tried to organize an association; but each time the group has been so heterogeneous, ranging from an elderly Seminary graduate to a student or student's wife only out a year that we had no common ground at all but a name, which said something radically different to each of us, and we wouldn't meet again.

The two reunions you make a particular effort to attend are twenty-fifth and fiftieth. The twenty-fifth came at an unhappy time for me. I had not been divorced long, and the program committee had come up with a particularly disconcerting idea, dividing the class into married and unmarried, each to be responsible for its own share of the program. With no husband but three chil-

Ednah Shephard Thomas. The typewritten note on the back states: "Mt. Holyoke Selects Its 'Mostest' Seniors. The Mt. Holyoke University, Mass., has elected its seniors who carry out the superlatives of the best qualities. Those selected range from 'most innocent' to the 'cutest' and all the way back again. Here is Ednah G. Shepard of Brookline, Mass. selected as the 'most scholastic' girl in the senior class. She was snapped at one of her most studious moments." Source: Bill Thomas.

dren, I hardly fitted into either. The preliminary material had a column for your achievements and honors; here I was starting in again at Wisconsin as a teaching assistant, having spent in a completely different world the best twenty years of any professional life, these from twenty-five to forty-five. So I didn't go. In July there was a bulky envelope in my mail box, and when I opened it there was a picture of a lot of middle-aged women in white uniforms, all singularly unattractive, who somehow suggested to me the idea of a convention of dietitians, and I wondered why it had been sent to me. Then it suddenly came over me: My God, that's the class of 1923.

But as time went on I began to think I'd go back to the fiftieth. All my friends who had gone to theirs had enjoyed it. I was mellowing. There would be plenty of time, since I'd be retired. If you survive to your fiftieth, you don't need any achievement but survival. I was quite looking forward to a good euphoric trip into nostalgia. Then came the educational revolution of the late sixties, and Holyoke, as well as I could judge by the *Alumnae Quarterly*, was just as insane as anywhere else. I lived through the madness myself at one of the worst places in the country, and I was worn out. Being a good alumna is like anything else; you have to work at it, as Becky Smaltz has done. I was out of touch. When the time actually came, it was only a couple of months after Aunt Hannah's death, and the preceding months were so uncertain I could hardly have committed myself anyway. But before that I had decided not to go. I do not regret the decision, and, as was true of the twenty-fifth, the class material I received after the event made me feel it was a wise one. The last straw was a story Pauline told me a couple of years ago. The oldest living graduate of Mount Holyoke, it seems, lives in Concord, New Hampshire, and went back for Commencement. Everyone was very nice to her and she enjoyed herself very much the first day. The next morning she went into the bathroom and found a young man there brushing his teeth. Perhaps I haven't paid my debt to Mount Holyoke, though sometimes you pay a debt to others than the debtor and I may have paid something in my thirty-one years of service at Wisconsin. Anyhow I didn't go. I accept the fact that life means change; I accept the fact that my Mount Holyoke does not, and could not, exist any longer. But that doesn't mean I had to meet that young man in what physically remains of it.

BRYN MAWR: SEPTEMBER 1923 TO JUNE 1924

Bryn Mawr, I think, is the most distinguished women's college in America. Though not as old as Mount Holyoke (it was founded in 1880), it was a pioneer in women's graduate education and the first to give the Ph.D. The formidable M. Carey Thomas refused to apply for a chapter of Phi Beta Kappa on the grounds that all her students would be eligible, and I believe she was right.[120] (She is also credited with the statement, in answer to the charge that higher education would make women unfeminine, that 50% of Bryn Mawr graduates marry and 75% have children: and with saying "When my beautiful seniors present their crude parents to me, I am amazed at how much we do for our students.") She had a particular gift for identifying promising young men and getting them on her faculty for a time before they went on to greater things: example, Woodrow Wilson. The entrance examinations were exacting and the college was highly selective. In my day I think there were about a hundred girls in each of the four undergraduate classes, and in the graduate school. The English influence was very strong. The campus buildings were all in that day consistent in style, gray stone, copies of Oxford colleges, and there was a real cloister with a fountain. All students, not just seniors as had been the case at Mount Holyoke, wore cap and gown to the all-college meeting which started each day (there was no music because of the Quaker origin of Bryn Mawr). The campus was very beautiful, and the Main Line suburbs of Philadelphia are the most beautiful I know.

I was too late for Miss Thomas. The president in my time, Miss Park, had a personal interview with every graduate student, and expressed herself as particularly pleased that my high school background was a public, not a private, school;[121] she wanted to attract more public school girls. The Bryn Mawr undergraduates were overwhelmingly the product of excellent, expensive private schools and wealthy families. All but three members of the graduating class of June, 1923, received European trips from their parents as graduation presents—which meant considerably more financial outlay than in these days of cheap student tours and hostels. Being born to wealth and privilege in those days gave you self-confidence; the Bryn Martyrs were an elite before "elitist" became a dirty word. Could you call them snobs? Miss Park might want to leaven the

---

120   Martha Carey Thomas (1857–1935), American educator and suffragist, was Bryn Mawr's second president, from 1894–1922.
121   Marion Edwards Park (1875–1960), who earned a Ph.D. from Bryn Mawr, was the college's third president, from 1922–1942.

mass, but the undergraduates never even saw us graduates when they passed us in the hall—unless, of course, we had graduated from Bryn Mawr itself, as was the case with a few. My degree from Bryn Mawr has been very useful to me professionally, but I never had any feeling of belonging to the place and therefore none of responsibility to it—as I tried unsuccessfully to explain to the president of the Bryn Mawr Midwest Alumnae Association when she wrote me appealing for reasons why I, and other graduate alumnae, did not contribute. The college was extremely advanced in many ways: the first workers' education summer schools were held there in summer.[122] But the undergraduates personally did not seem to share the official attitude, and the atmosphere was far from democratic. Holyoke had been a very friendly place and we always tried to make strangers feel at home, so I was innocently surprised at my first meal when I tried to start a conversation with the undergraduate on my right, and then the one on my left, and was completely cold-shouldered by each as soon as I said I came from Holyoke. When I was at Bryn Mawr, a wing in each hall was set aside for graduates, though I'm told that not long after all graduates were housed together in one segregated hall. After routine was established, the classes were segregated at meals: freshmen at one table, sophomores at another, juniors, seniors, graduates.

At dinner the seniors presided; that is, there was a pleasant custom of singing between courses, and the seniors would sing one of their class songs if they felt like it or call on any other class to sing: "1925, song!" or the song might be specified. Very occasionally they would call, "Graduates, song!" I bravely soloed once for the honor of Mount Holyoke with "I wish I were a hicinorarius," and was kindly applauded. Of course we had no songs in common. The singing is a pleasant memory. One was set to the Londonderry Air, and the only time I have heard it rendered more movingly was by a street quartet of World War I veterans I heard in London. Democratically, the graduates were included in the Big May Day, of which I shall speak later, and practice of Elizabethan songs began very early in the fall.

The food was excellent. Coming from Holyoke, notable for plain living and high thinking, I found myself among the fleshpots. Sunday night suppers were particularly good; we had such delicacies that sometimes I couldn't even identify them. Almost every night we had the most delicious salad I have ever tasted anywhere in my life, served as a separate course: a great silver bowl of crisp lettuce, with some kind of Thousand Island dressing I've never been able to

---

122 Initiated by Cary Thomas and part of the wider labor education movement, the Summer School for Women Workers in Industry was first held at Bryn Mawr in 1921 and continued until 1938. It was meant to increase younger working women's influence in the industrial world by providing access to higher education. For detailed treatment of the summer school from a composition and rhetoric perspective, see Hollis (2004).

duplicate. A representative of each class, including the graduates, served on a committee to meet weekly with the housemother; the purpose, as far as I could see, was to complain of the food, because they never did anything else. I never opened my mouth, waiting hopefully for lightning to strike them while a senior observed that the soup had not been sufficiently hot one night or a sophomore that the scrambled eggs had been insufficiently moist one morning. At Holyoke we never saw an egg in four years. At Holyoke also we had made our own beds and cleaned our own rooms, but at Bryn Mawr as well as colored waitresses there were colored maids to do this. During World War I there had been some difficulty in getting labor, and it was proposed that the girls might do this chore themselves. Miss Thomas proclaimed that the doors of Bryn Mawr would close before any girl had to make her own bed. (She must now be turning in her grave.) The rationale was that a Bryn Mawr student should be devoting all her time to studies—with proper provision for exercise, of course, again according to the English model—and not waste any of it on housework.

My dormitory was Radnor, one of the smallest, and there were only six graduates. Charlotte Keyes was a tall, striking sexy girl from the University of Minnesota, who, like Becky, was in Economics. Miss Marks had been afraid of the "cloistered effect" of another women's college on me, and Bryn Mawr was certainly cloistered, literally and figuratively. But it was meeting Charlotte there which was responsible for the one action in my whole life in which I have showed initiative. The more I saw of her, the more convinced I became that life in a big Midwestern university was quite unlike life in an Eastern women's college, and the more curious I grew to experience it—just for one year, no more. Charlotte had some beaux (the then term for "boyfriends") in graduate schools in the East, particularly one in Harvard Medical School, and she came home with me for Christmas vacation so she could see them. Daytimes she and I went to the historic sights of Boston I'd never bothered to go to alone, and nights she went out with them. One interesting detail on this transitional period between horse and car: the medic had a car but it had no windshield wipers, and since it was a very snowy season Charlotte sensibly gave him a pair as her Christmas present. My first year at Wisconsin I spent Christmas vacation with her in Minneapolis, my first experience of the intense subzero cold which actually feels balmy when you first step out into it, and my first experience of outdoor lighted Christmas trees. She married a Minnesota man. The next winter five of them went tobogganing, and three suffered broken necks, including Charlotte. When she visited me in Frost Woods a couple of years later, she had completely recovered except that she had to lie on her back and raise her legs in the air to put on her stockings. The Minnesota climate became too severe for her husband and they moved to Carmel, California, where they still live. We still exchange Christmas cards.

Bryn Mawr

The third of our group was a Russian, Maria Stadnichenko, a political refugee, a plain girl still suffering from what she had undergone during the revolution and her escape. Sometimes as she sat at meals her hand trembled so she could not lift the spoon to her mouth. She never took any initiative and never opened a conversation, and none of us succeeded in establishing any contact with her. But she spent her Sundays with us. The fourth was a Scotswoman, rather older than the rest of us, Margaret Steele, with that calm self-assurance that seems to mark most Britons and Scots I have met and that I envy them. The rest of us were Americans. Laura, whose last name I can't remember, was a Jewish girl from Barnard. I saw most of Irene Chrisman, whose family must have been what Ruth Wallerstein[123] (a Bryn Martyr herself, you remember), used to call "quite simple people." She had gone to a municipal university in her home town, Cleveland, and was at Bryn Mawr (geology) on a scholarship. Two men were in love with her and wanted to marry her: one, the son of a minister, was all for having her go on in graduate work and raise her status; the other, a garage mechanic, naturally enough was not. She told me near the end of the year that she hoped a man I didn't care for would fall in love with me first, and then one I did—a penetrating statement and one I was lucky enough to fulfill. She decided to go home and marry the garage mechanic. I sent her a toaster for a wedding present and she wrote how much they used and enjoyed it: breakfast was their best meal, the equivalent of dinner for most people, because he was on the night shift, and when he came home they were happy together at the end of his working day before he went off to put in his necessary hours of sleep. But I suspect it didn't work out. She stopped writing to me, and after a long time in which I wrote steadily to her without response—I don't let go as soon as I should, I'm afraid, when the other person may want to—I finally decided she didn't want to hear from me anymore and stopped too. I think if she had been happy and contented she would have kept on writing, especially since the next year I was in Danielson, not Bryn Mawr; but of course I can be wrong and she just got tired of writing.

We were, as you see, a very varied group—if not ill-assorted—but we were thrown very much upon one another for company since no one else knew we were alive. Becky was enrolled as a graduate student in Economics but living at home. I saw something of her and of Davy, of course, and I went to Davy's for Thanksgiving dinner. Her mother had been a widow for some years, but it was a big family. Davy was much the youngest; she had an older sister and three older brothers, all married, all with children. I can remember today, with the same feeling of admiration tinged with envy, sitting in the living room after

---

123 Ruth Wallerstein (1893–1958) joined the English department in 1920 and taught English literature until her untimely death in an automobile accident in England while on research leave.

dinner, the adults discussing this and that and the children playing on the floor in the center of the room; every so often a child would come to show its mother something and then go back to the other children, like a little ripple washing up on the shore and then returning to the pool. But since Becky and Davy both had their home obligations and engagements, and lived at a fair distance from the campus, the other Radnor graduates were the ones with whom I spent most of my free time. This was generally Sunday, and Sunday only. All of us were working very intensively in our respective graduate courses, but we took Sunday off and spent it together as a group. In good weather—and that's a mild climate with a short winter—we would take our mending outdoors and find a pleasant nook on the campus to sit in while someone read aloud. We took walks around the town and the estates with their beautiful flowering shrubs—my first view of dogwood, which at that time you didn't see in New England. We went together to church services of various denominations, from a Catholic mass to its opposite pole, a Friends' meeting.[124] And, as I've said, Sunday night suppers were the best meal of the week. Sundays were very pleasant days.

This is probably the place to speak of two other interesting foreigners, two Czechoslovakian girls. One, a medical student, nearly died of shock the first time she visited an American hospital and saw temperature recorded in Fahrenheit instead of Centigrade; she didn't see how the patients could be alive. I didn't see much of her, but the other, Maria Isakoviscova, was a humanist, studying philosophy with one English seminar on the side where I got to know her well. She was full of interesting theories on esthetics, politics, everything, and like the stereotype of a philosopher, very impractical. A young girl in Czechoslovakia in those days was even more sheltered than I had been. A big girl with a big peasant build, Mitzi didn't wear a bra and someone persuaded her to buy one for the President's Reception. Her married sister had always bought all her underwear for her, so being fitted was an ordeal for her she must have skimped, for she came back from the reception in tears: "I slipped out of it." The first time it was her turn to serve tea (another English custom where the graduates took turns being hostesses) she gave us dog biscuits, having gone to the grocery and pointed at random to a box on the shelf because she didn't know what to ask for in English. She saved the *Saturday Evening Post* all through the year because she thought they were the best representation of American culture to take home (in which she was no doubt right), and tragedy was barely averted the last day when a maid naturally thought they were to be thrown away and took them down to the furnace. She then packed them inside her suitcase for safe conduct and strapped

---

124   A reference to Quakers, now part of a group of religions known as the Religious Society of Friends.

her dresses to the outside. She married a master at Eton of all places, and Wright and I spent the day with them there when we were in England. She and the students in Radnor were my first real contact with foreign students, and it was a valuable experience for me. I am finding my work for the Madison Friends of International Students my greatest pleasure in retirement.[125]

The first academic hurdle of the year for me was the language exams. I succeeded in receiving an M.A. from Bryn Mawr at the end of one year of graduate work, and no one, not a Bryn Martyr had ever achieved this before. The reason was the stringency of the language requirements: you had to pass an exam certifying reading competency in both French and German at the beginning of the academic year in which you hoped to receive the degree, on the grounds that you needed this competence to perform the work satisfactorily. The Bryn Mawr undergraduate curriculum made it easy to get a good knowledge of two languages, but few other college curricula did. I had a good command of French, but only one semester of German at college (if I remember correctly), which I took when I decided to go to Bryn Mawr and knew the requirement. So I had to read German by myself at the Island that summer.[126] The Island is not a good place for serious study. Too much else is going on. I struggled through the books I brought with me, including Goethe's *Faust*, but I hadn't a glimpse of the greatness of the work and little comprehension of it on any level. I did, however, pass both language exams at Bryn Mawr in September, with the aid of a few German lessons from a tutor in the village who had had a good deal of experience in getting people through. When Bill came back from Europe, I rather hoped he and I could read German together, but it didn't work out and today I really know only a few words. I can still get the sense of a French passage—by eye, not by ear.

One of my main reasons for choosing Bryn Mawr was that the catalog listed a graduate creative writing course. I was considerably disappointed when I arrived and found it would not be given because there were not enough students to take it. (I have seen these things from the other side now.) The substitute they offered was a course in biography, where I presume I wrote some papers, but I don't remember much about it. I spent most of my waking hours in the Middle Ages, with Carleton Brown.

Perhaps the most distinguished medievalist in the country, he had come to academic life late and was probably in his sixties when I knew him. His first profession was the ministry. He had been a Unitarian minister in a parish in rural Minnesota where the winters were so long and (pre-car) driving so bad

---

125 This organization, now a non-profit, aims to connect international college students in the Madison area with local residents to promote cultural exchange and global friendships.
126 A reference to Isle of Springs, an island community located in BoothBay Harbor, Maine, where the family spent summer vacations.

that he had a lot of leisure time. To pass it, he began to read about the Middle Ages, was fascinated (hooked, we'd say today), and stayed in them the rest of his life. About ten years earlier he had married a young graduate student, with the idea, according to gossip, that she would be a first-rate research secretary. Instead she produced three little girls, who took up most of her time, which was considered a joke on him. Both he and I were handicapped, he told me once, because we had been brought up as Unitarians and therefore had none of the firsthand knowledge of saints and holy days and Church procedures that a cradle Catholic would have drunk in with mother's milk. One such cradle Catholic was in the seminar: Mary Isabelle O'Sullivan, whose home was in Philadelphia. I have never encountered anyone else so out of touch with her own time. She wished she had been born in the Middle Ages and did the best she could to compensate for her nineteenth century birth (she must have been forty when I knew her) by living in them spiritually. A born spinster, she pulled her thin light hair back in a little pug, wore dowdy clothes, and spent a lot of time washing her hands, which as a result were always red and chapped—a neurotic symptom a kindergartner would probably recognize now. Once when we were both working in the seminar room, she fidgeted a good deal and finally went out, returning after about half an hour; she explained she couldn't stand the feeling on her wrist of the ribbon on her wrist watch, which she had just gotten back from a colored repairman, and had had to go out and put on a fresh one he hadn't handled. She told me I reminded her of herself at my age—a relationship expressed in Hardy's poem. A man gives a boy a gift of apples because the boy makes him think of his young self; the boy takes the gift with thanks but "is filled with dread / Lest I should grow like him the years ahead."[127] In this case, life was much kinder to me than to Mary Isabelle and my dread was not fulfilled. We exchanged Christmas cards until her death, which came comparatively young, and she spent her life in a rather unremarkable teaching position in or near Philadelphia.

The deepest, most persistent, most characteristic memory of the year is that of sitting in seminar meetings in the late afternoons, my eyes on the sky outside the window deepening to the blue which is the blue of the Madonna's robe before the brightening lights inside the room made it black and invisible.

Carleton Brown was mildly opposed to the institution of the M.A. If students took the time to stop and take it, sometimes they never went on to the Ph.D. Since it was only a pausing point on the way to the goal, he thought it not worth bothering with. He was right in my case; my work was satisfactory

---

[127] This poem was actually authored by Alfred Edgar Coppard (1878–1957) and appeared in the *New Republic* in December 1925.

enough for him to recommend me for the Master's, and I never got all the way. I spent the year working on a photostat of Harley 2253, and made a true original discovery:[128] I dated the Battle of Bannockburn from a reference in the manuscript, which was conclusive evidence.[129] Though Carleton Brown himself had not known it, it turned out afterwards that someone else had figured out the same thing earlier. I grew less and less dedicated to scholarship and less and less convinced I had any aptitude for it or desire to spend my life in it. Like Arabella Allen, I may not have known what I did like but I did know what I didn't like, and I was sure I did not want to come back to Bryn Mawr, at least the next year.[130] It took me a long time to get this idea across to Carleton Brown, however, who was completely convinced that all his students lived only for their Ph.D.'s, and it wasn't until Bertha Putnam made a visit to her Alma Mater in the spring and talked with him that he believed it. He recommended me for a fellowship, and the college offered me the job of warden (social hostess in one of the halls, rather like a dormitory fellow here), but I refused it. Carleton Brown suggested that I should teach in California for a year substituting for one of this students who wanted to come back to Bryn Mawr for a year's research, and I was in the mood to like the idea very much, but for some reason she changed her mind. On my own initiative I wrote to four universities at random, Wisconsin, Minnesota, Michigan, and California, but Wisconsin and one of the others didn't even acknowledge my letter and the other two had nothing to offer me. So I left Bryn Mawr at a loose end.

Before Commencement I had the pleasant experience of the Big May Day. Each year there was a Little May Day when a Maypole was set up for each class and the graduates to dance around, braiding our streamers. It was interesting to see that winding the Maypole, which must have been done perfectly for centuries by the entire illiterate peasantry of Europe, was done pretty well by Bryn Mawr freshmen, not so well by sophomores, and very badly indeed by graduates, most of whom were quite incapable of taking first one step to the right and then the next to the left. The Maypoles, of course, stood as visible evidence. Big May Day came only once every four years, so that everyone might have the experience during her college career, and I was very lucky to hit upon it the single year I was there. The campus was a perfect setting, and the procedures lasted for two days, including a crowning of the May Queen, a team of white oxen bringing in the Maypole, morris dancing, country dancing, tumbling, wrestling and other Old

---

128 Harley MS 2253, a manuscript dated around 1340 and housed in the British Library, contains a collection of Middle English, Middle French, and Latin lyrics, called the Harley Lyrics.

129 The Battle of Bannockburn (1314), a significant battle in the First War of Scottish Independence.

130 Arabella Allen is a character in Charles Dickens' *The Pickwick Papers* (1837).

English sports, gentle dancing, English plays—Shakespeare, Lilly, Greene, St. George and the Dragon, Alexander and Campaspe, masques, all sorts of things presented all over the campus. We did not move to our audiences like miracle and morality players; the audience came to us. We repeated our performance each hour at an assigned station, and the guests, guided by programs, went where they chose. Everyone in college was involved, including graduates, and no other extra-curricular activities were permitted that year so that all energies and time could be devoted to this. My friends and I were "gentlemen and gentlewomen," dancing on the green to "Gathering Peascods" and the like with steps carefully learned, and dressed in authentic costumes from the handsome collection built up over the years. I wore the most beautiful dress I have ever put on in my life, green and lavender with a gold stomacher, copied from a Holbein print. Hannah came up from Milford to see the festivity.

The last week of college I worked so hard preparing for exams that I had had almost no sleep, subsisting on coffee alone for a week or two, and when commencement was over and I had moved the tassel on my cap to the side which showed I had the M.A., I spent a day or two with Becky and Davy before I went to Brookline and fell asleep in the hammock on the porch that evening. No doubt physical fatigue intensified my grief at saying goodbye to the friends I had made that year. I remember how hard I cried and also that I realized clearly at the time that the keenness of my regret at parting with them would be dulled in the natural course of events; and I cried even harder then because it seemed to me sorrow's depth of sorrow to realize that your sorrows and sufferings would be healed by time. I would rather *not* have realized that nothing, not even friendship, endured forever. I was young.

My Bryn Mawr degree has been very valuable to me. I could not have received any permanent appointment here at all, without it; generous as they were about my lack of the doctorate, they couldn't have gone that far. No M.A. in the country carries more prestige than that from Bryn Mawr. In the early days of my work with Ed Lacy,[131] "the Bryn Mawr line," as we called it, was very useful with staff members who came from snob places like Harvard. When a man (or woman) was having trouble concealing his superiority to the Middle Westerners, Ed would send him in to talk to me. "I know just how you feel," I would coo. "When I first came here from Bryn Mawr . . ." and he would go away eating out of my hand. In those days we had a good many graduates from topflight places. Apart from these purely pragmatic consideration, my immersion in the Middle Ages and things English gave me a number of things in

---

131 Edgar W. Lacy (1914–1981), English professor and director of Freshman English at UW-Madison who worked closely with Thomas for over twenty years. Thomas describes her administrative experience and working relationship with Lacy in the Transition chapter.

common with Wright, fresh from his three years at Oxford as a Rhodes Scholar. Though it seems like a completely separate part of my life now, I am glad to have had the experience. But also I have never been anything but glad that I left, and did not go back.

DANIELSON: SEPTEMBER 1924 TO JUNE 1925

On September 10, 1924, I came out at Coolidge Corner from keeping a dentist's appointment with the realization that thenceforth there was absolutely no reason for me to be in any special place at any special time; and I still remember what a desolate feeling this was. It was this keen memory which made me apprehensive about retirement. But I didn't realize before retirement that a tree in spring with the sap rising in it trunk and branches feels different from the same tree in fall with its leaves fallen and its sap sinking back down to its roots.

There had been a couple of nibbles during the summer. I went up from the Island, spending the night with Elizabeth Mackinnon in Brunswick, to interview in a Portland hotel the head of a private girls' school near New York, who had gotten my name from Bryn Mawr. She offered me a position in her English department at a very good salary; ironically, what she considered (and rightly so) a great asset, that she gave her staff regular weekends off so they could go into New York and profit by the opportunities there, merely put me off, in my timidity. I rationalized this by saying to myself you ought to be so dedicated to your job you didn't want to take time off from it. So I politely refused. A week later at the Island I got a letter from her repeating the offer at a higher salary. Since money was not a factor anyway, again I politely refused. Kay Burlingame and I were sitting in one of our favorite spots on the east shore, then beautifully wooded, when the *Winter Harbor* went by to the wharf and picked up the mail sack with my letter. I'm glad I refused. The girls at the school would have been the same type of privileged wealthy people I had already had sufficient experience with at Bryn Mawr.

Then I got a letter from a school superintendent in up-state New York saying they were looking for a teacher and asking for my qualifications. Completely out of touch with reality, I wrote back a detailed and careful account of my academic career, specifying all my Bryn Mawr seminars. The answer to this was that the superintendent had worked on Miss Marks' summer cottage and she said I was all right and that was good enough for him and I could have the job. The building was a very good one, but I'd have to light the fire in the stove myself every morning because they didn't have a janitor. Miss Marks was right in there trying to counteract the Bryn Mawr cloisters, and the job would surely have done so. A more adventurous girl would have taken the dare, but again I was timid, and I wrote another polite refusal. Laura Ingalls Wilder didn't even begin her writing till the thirties,[132] and I had no romantic prototype to imitate. Again, the event was fortunate. Danielson was completely uncloistered, and as a mill town it gave me much more relevant experience than a backwoods rural community could have done.

I registered with an ordinary commercial teachers' agency in Boston, and on September 13 I was called in to interview the principal of the Killingly High School of Danielson, Connecticut, and the superintendent of schools of the district. They asked me various questions, among them whether or not I had bobbed my hair (I was wearing a hat).[133] I hadn't and had no desire to, and whether for that or other reasons, they telephoned me forty-eight hours later giving me the job and asking me to come down the next day. School had already been in session a couple of weeks. Danielson was a mill town, and beginning to feel the shadow of the oncoming Great Depression. The first employees to be laid off were naturally the last ones hired, the boys just out of school. Many of them were still of school age, and with nothing else to do they had come back to school, so that enrollment was much larger than expected, and another teacher of English and History was needed. How much I educated my students I don't know. But without question if I consider my own education after the fashion of Henry Adams, this year went far and away beyond any other of my whole life in educating me.

It was a completely new world, as far away from Bryn Mawr as Mars. Danielson is near the eastern border of Connecticut, close to Providence, and I went over by bus once or twice to see Kay Burlingame. I also saw something of the Ellingly Commercial teacher, a newcomer like me. With her instruction, I learned to touch-type, practicing in her room after school, which has been a great practical advantage to me in my teaching. But for the most part I was very much alone, with no one to talk to.

Danielson had some beautiful old New England houses, and one of the lovely white churches whose spire points up to God which are one of the most characteristic features of New England. The streets were lined with fine old elms. One of the most impressive estates was now owned by Polish bootleggers. The people included some decaying Americans, who didn't get along very well with the Jaworskis, Kivistos, Lagues, Rukstelas, Samberskis, Savareses, Tetreaults, Dubucs, Miejadliks, Hellstens, Elfgrens, Giambattistas, Gundersens, and the like, who had come to work in the mills. One theme I got describing Danielson

---

132 Laura Ingalls Wilder (1867–1957), the American writer who published the *Little House on the Prairie* children's novels in the 1930s and 1940s, was born in Wisconsin and spent her childhood in the Midwest.

133 For an examination of the rhetoric of bobbed hair in the U.S. in the 1920s, see Gold (2015).

observed that there were a good many factory houses which were very dirty, owing to the foreigners. The mills were mainly textile mills, and around each a little village had grown up: "Quebec, for instance, a terrible double row of little dog kennels, all just alike." Each of these had its own grammar school, but the town had only one high school, to which, in addition to the mill children, farm children, mostly Americans, were bused in from the surrounding countryside. It was customary for school teachers to board with one of the decaying Americans, an elderly widow, but she would have no vacancy for some weeks, so I took an attic room, unheated except for the warm air that came up through a hole from the kitchen underneath, at the small neat house of the Dysons, on the edge of town, about a mile from the school, to and from which I walked each day. This lodging contributed much more to my education than one would have in the conventional place, where I would only have seen a phase very common then in small New England towns (and I was reminded of it later when I went to La Grange), clinging to the past and ignoring the present.

The Dysons were a middle-aged English couple who had come to Canada some thirty years before to seek their fortune. They crossed the ocean, got on a train in the East coast, rode for four days, and got off to find that the pioneer prairie town to which they were accredited had burned to the ground while they were on their way to it. Somehow or other they had come down into the States and settled in Danielson, though I think they never really made many friends or fitted in. Mr. Dyson worked a ten-hour day in one of the mills, and for months of the year never saw the sun, because he went to and came back from work in the dark. Mrs. Dyson worked very hard—it impressed me that she had herself papered the rooms in the house, for this was long before the facilities of the do-it-yourself era—but every morning her husband brought her a cup of tea in bed before she got up. They had one son, Ernest, about my age, who had a foreman's job in Providence, and they were very proud of him. He came home occasionally weekends—he had a girl in Providence, Maud, whom he married the next summer—and on one of these visits was seized with acute appendicitis and was taken to the hospital for an emergency operation. His father went with him, and I sat with Mrs. Dyson all that afternoon, marveling that an educated person like me who knew so much English literature and composition could find no words at all to give comfort. To the Dysons, you went to the hospital to die, a point of view I had never dreamed of. But they had lost Ernest's little sister, Dorothy, some years before, which may have been one reason for it. When Ernest was convalescing, I went over with his parents one Sunday afternoon to see him in the hospital, and he asked them, "What do you come to see me every day for? Do you think I ain't going to get well?" I remember a man in his ward with a broken jaw, who had a bandage on tied with a coquettish gauze bow on the top of his head. The afternoon of the operation Mrs. Dyson said only one thing, David's lament for Absalom, over and over: "If I could only bear it for him. If I could only bear it for him."

I saw little of Mr. Dyson; who had an Englishman's love of privacy and didn't care much for strangers in his house, though no doubt my modest rent came in handy. Mrs. Dyson gave me my dinner at night by myself before he came home from his ten-hour day, and he had gone to it before I had breakfast in the morning. I think she was rather lonely for woman-talk. She gave me some revealing family glimpses: "Ernest asked where his baby sister came from and the doctor said he brought her in a box. Then one of his friends saw a calf born and told him about it, and Ernest said, 'Ma, you didn't tell me the truth about Dorothy.' I felt kind of cheap." When Ernest wore his first long pants, "Oh, dear, it was funny. I used to watch him going down the street looking at his legs." In the cemetery where the daughter was buried, "our little lot is in a new part under some pines and just now it's a blue carpet of violets. We always get some when we go up. Ernest picked some for Maud and put them in a little box. I don't know whether they'll live or not, but they're in wet moss. He didn't want his father to know. He didn't mind me, but when his father asked what it was he said, 'Oh, just a box.' But he asked me what I thought would be best to keep them. I don't think they like another man to know. I said, 'Your father used to bring me my flowers under his hat.' 'Under his hat!' He thought that was terrible. 'Well,' I said, 'you didn't want him to bring them in his hand in the train, did you?'" She and her husband, who was a little deaf, once went to hear an evangelist. "Mr. Dyson wanted to hear so we sat down front, and all the time he wasn't pointing at me; he was pointing at him. I sweat, I did."

In addition to family glimpses, Mrs. Dyson gave me town glimpses, such as this newspaper clipping: "Mrs. John A. Melton and her four children were found lying on the kitchen floor with their throats cut by Mr. John A. Melton on returning from work. All were dead." I had of course made visits to Milford, but I had never lived continuously in a small town. One village tragedy which had made a deep local impression was that of the leading citizen, a banker, very much respected, very generous, president of the YMCA, who was found to have abused his trust and stolen money from the bank. When he was found out, he tried to commit suicide and succeeded only in blinding himself; he was tended in the hospital by the doctors and nurses who had lost their savings through him. Mrs. Dyson felt this would affect his young daughter all her life. Perhaps she'll go to some other place where people won't know, I suggested; oh, everybody will know everywhere, said Mrs. Dyson. A picturesque item was that of the man who was carrying home a load of chickens and was killed in a railroad accident. His car was smashed and white feathers were all over the track.

I was fond of Mrs. Dyson, and the tomato-and-cheese sandwiches she often gave me for the lunch I carried to school were such a good combination I often gave them to you for your school lunches. Except for her and Iva Bryant, I really had no one to talk to. Since I was living at a mill worker's, the town elite ignored me, and no one made any advances to me at the Congregational Church, where I went regularly every Sunday. The minister often mispronounced his words, and in my Bryn Mawr snobbishness I looked down on him for it. A few years later I ran across the statement that this, on the contrary, is a sign of intelligence, for it marks a man who keeps better company in what he reads, which he can control, than he does in his actual social contacts, which he cannot. After five years of college, I did miss people to talk with who spoke my own language. But I felt all along that this single year was to be an isolated period in my life, and the great bulk of my time I was involved heart and soul with my students, which was the best thing that could have happened to me.

My courses were freshman and sophomore English, and freshman and sophomore History. Though I had had plenty of work in composition and literature, I had had only a single year course in history, though luckily a broad one, Bertha Putnam's Renaissance and Reformation. The Killingly freshman history text was entitled "From Prehistoric Times to 1800," and the sophomore "From 1800 to the Present Day." By an easy exercise in simple arithmetic, I figured out that we should cover six pages in each text daily to finish by the end of the year, and I went into class each day as innocent as my students of what would happen on the seventh. If the students got interested and asked ahead, I'd have to tell them to wait till tomorrow for a surprise—which of course never fooled anyone. When I was teaching English 309, I told this story year after year at the first class meeting to explain to those prospective high school teachers why I was willing and anxious to put in as much time with each of them individually as they needed so that they wouldn't have to undergo the worst humiliation a teacher can suffer—inability to answer legitimate questions.[134]

When *Up the Down Staircase* came out it reminded me very keenly of my own Danielson days.[135] My Line-a-Day shows plenty of material for a similar novel. "Grimm [epileptic] had a fit in Algebra—luckily not in English." "Yesterday I was full of love for them all—today the blues." "I knew they couldn't behave so badly two days running." I might say at one that I had had no practice teaching and no Education courses of any kind, and absolutely no idea what to do in a classroom.

---

134 English 309, Composition for English Teachers, was the advanced composition course for English education students at UW-Madison.

135 American teacher and author Bella "Bel" Kaufman's (1911–2014) epistolary novel *Up the Down Staircase* (1964), explores an idealistic English teacher's experiences teaching literature in an inner-city high school.

Nor did I have anyone to whom I could go for advice. Iva Bryant had much more trouble with discipline than I did, and the other two English teachers were at least forty years older than I and completely living in the past. The principal had no backbone. Discipline was supposedly maintained by a system of demerits: any teacher at any time could assign as many demerits as she chose for any offence—two for coming late to class, three for being unprepared, or whatever. Once a student had accumulated a given number—I think two hundred—he was automatically expelled. Shortly before I came, a student had reached the number and had *not* been expelled. As a result, the place was chaos. The boys who had been let go from the mills were really men, in that they had once, they believed, finished with school, and in that they had actually earned money; they resented being back and [were] not about to be cooperative. I was young and looked younger. Once I tried to stare down one of these young men, failed, and had to confess my failure by looking away with what composure I could. Once I kept a boy after school for something or other, and on a suggestion of Iva Bryant's told him he could go as soon as he had memorized Keats's "In a Drear-Nighted December."[136] He was a bright boy and I knew he could get it in five minutes. Unfortunately for me, he was proud; staying after school was an accepted penalty, but memorizing a poem was a cruel and unusual punishment, and he refused to try to do it. Time moved ever more slowly on, each of us was wondering if his stamina would outlast the other's, until my proposal that he should learn the first verse only struck us both as a chance to save face. He did it in ninety seconds flat, and with the resilience of youth came in next day to ask, "Are we going to learn another pretty poem today?" It took me longer to recover but at least I learned never to try that method of discipline again. I had been given a temporary state license to teach in the public schools, since I had no Education credits, which was to be made permanent if I passed a state examination in the spring. I duly took the exam and I duly passed. The only question I couldn't answer was "List the Education publications you have read for this examination"; not only had I read none, but I didn't know that any existed. If I could pass an examination simply on common sense, without opening a single book or periodical or even knowing that there were books or periodicals to open, it was hard not to acquire a contempt for the whole field of Education with the capital E. Knowing some able people in the field at Wisconsin has not really freed me from it. Someone who agrees with me is Mortimer Smith.[137] In "Planned Mediocrity in the Public Schools" he

---

136 English Romantic poet John Keats's (1795–1821) poem was written in 1817 and published in 1829.

137 American writer Mortimer B. Smith (1906–1981) co-founded in 1956 the Council for Basic Education, a private organization aimed at improving K-12 education by emphasizing basic skills. Smith edited the council's bulletin (1958–1974) and served as executive director (1961–1974).

cites the figures of the Educational Testing Service, who in 1951 tested 97,800 college freshmen and found those in Schools of Education by far the lowest of any college, with only 27% passing.[138] Seniors tested about the same. Smith cites authority after authority to the same effect; "Our most poorly educated college graduates are our teachers," and adds: "If anyone wants to maintain that one of the worst things that ever happened to American education was the formation of Teachers College, Columbia University, I am willing to go along with him."[139]

Back to my Line-a-Day. "Whithy: 'You teach better when you're angry.'" "History I-c is trying to be good." "Hanson wants to learn to typewrite—very gentle and sweet. I wonder what's up his sleeve." "I wish I was a teacher—just one week. I'd give you forty-nine demerits." "Jaworski tells me socialism is a capitalist movement." Jaworski was a beautiful young Pole, a stunning athlete, with perfect coordination (like Bill) on the basketball floor. He (unlike Bill) had never heard of the Gettysburg Address, and we worked together on it after school every afternoon for a week. "Tibbetts hovering around: 'Oh boy' as a conversationalist." "Traver after school, much upset at my dumbness over football." "Jaworski tells me popular sovereignty is government by a king with all the powers." "Deborah looking and acting like a dishrag." "Yound and Savarese after school to complain of demerits," ending by telling me ghost and murder stories in the friendliest vein." "'Why did the bell have to ring?'" "Tillinghast's theme: 'I looked in the cabin and they were all seasick.'" "Conklin sleeping sweetly in History—poor little brat." "Derivations in English 1, which raised the roof." "Triumph: quiet when I read 'The Revenge.'" "Debate on capital punishment." "Debate on England's treatment of India. That class is good, especially Pike." "Debate on whether a man is justified in cutting the rope if Alpine climbing." "Teaching Miss Chollar's girls marching. They like that." "Nash unbearable in History, angelic in English." "Tillinghast lighting matches in class." "Kimball's and Grantista's outlines alike." "Phosphorous set off in the hall." "Nelson *so* good." "Nice little freshman oral themes on Washington Irving." "Almost cried in sophomore English, they were so dumb." "I should say everyone had adopted Jaworski's theory: 'I never do nothing over the weekend.'"

I was involved in a great many extra-curricular activities. There was an Outing Club, and we went sledding in the winter and took hikes in the spring. "Sun coming out and going in all afternoon, lovely brown lights in the water, and vistas of trees and rocks and ferns. Lovely cloud effects on hills—pale bright green, then black purple." I might add a note of my own description of a win-

---

138 From *The Diminished Mind: A Study of Planned Mediocrity in Our Public Schools*. Chicago: Henry Regnery, 1954. Reprinted in *American Conservative Thought in the Twentieth Century*. William F. Buckley, Jr., ed. New Brunswick, NJ: Transaction Publishers, 2011: pp. 318–337)
139 Ibid, p. 334

ter landscape, and balance it with a student's. Mine: "walk alone—mild, blue shadows on the snow, pink, mauve, yellow, very clear tree tracery like palmetto fans against the horizon. No sound except the humming of wires. A dog who rushes out plowing through the snow at each farm-house, barking. The houses very desolate, mostly only partly inhabited, blinds closed. A brook partly choked with ice, the dark water running underneath and coming out on top, over ice cakes with grimed dirt patterns. Very still and permanent. Danielson down in the valley. The roar of the train and its smoke. Potter: "It was winter in the North Woods. The ground was all covered with snow and 3 feet deep. All the trees around gave the appearance of fairy land. Some of the animals such as squirrels were scampering around leaving their tracks. Others were digging for food, while the biggest part of them were asleep under the ground. Now and then a deer would be heard going to his den. The birds that could stand the snow and cold were singing. From now until spring the land would be enclosed by snows."

There was a Writers' Club. There was a school play. I chaperoned the girls' basketball team whenever they went away for games, which was whenever the boys' team did, for it was the custom for the girls' teams to play between halves. Once I was unexpectedly called on to be umpire and rushed around the floor in a pair of borrowed sneakers four times too large for me while my hair fell down my back like Pleasant Riderhood's, but usually I just sat with the girls at the game, and rode the bus, which was fun, especially on the way home after our team had won, when we all felt good and sang the current popular songs, like "All Alone."[140] Once in class at some allusion to Washington I said as a joke, "Come in after school and I'll tell you about the city," and I was flabbergasted to find my room full of senior boys and girls who had taken me seriously, and had to improvise a travelogue as well as I could. As spring came on the students brought me daffodils, tulips, lilacs, even lady slippers. The last day of school with no preparation for the next there was "nothing to do in the afternoon—funny feeling." At the graduation rehearsal, the singing was "horrible" but at the ceremony itself "everything was serene." I was "overcome and weeping" when I said good-bye, and my first day back in Brookline was "another tearful day; I miss Danielson." Two days later a letter came from another tearful female, Ethel Wells, who was "crying herself sick" because I had gone: "'I prayed every night all spring to be like you.'" It must have been many years since there had been a young teacher at Killingly High School, and youth called to youth. "Wore my new yellow dress. Students all excited." But I think the real reason for whatever affection I roused and success I had was that I was deeply and genuinely involved

---

140 Pleasant Riderhood is a character in Charles Dickens' final novel, *Our Mutual Friend* (1865).

with my students, all of them. (Years later here a girl was to say to me, regrettable in Educationese rather than English, "I never saw a teacher relate to her students as you do.") And I always have been, even in the last sad bad years you will read of in the "Demolition" chapter, with all who would let me be. About this, students are never fooled. I think it made up for all my many mistakes.

During this year, student after student contributed to my education. I learned, for example, from Savarese, the son of a Negro Pullman porter who abandoned his Italian wife soon after the marriage and a girl who died shortly after he was born. (Now that life has robbed me of my innocence it occurs to me now that I have no evidence of marriage, as far as that goes, and "Savarese" is surely an Italian name.) Savarese lived with his maternal grandmother. It occurred to me he was a problem and it might help if I could talk with his grandmother. This was long before the days of ITA's.[141] I asked the principal about it. "Not unless you speak Italian," said he. "She doesn't talk English." (This indifference was typical, but I think it's fair to say he was growing old and was getting worn out in a struggle where he had too much against him.) Savarese had big brutal hands, but was the essence of mildness; in fact, I now suspect he may have been a little retarded. He never spoke in class and showed no interest whatever in the discussion. So I kept him after school every afternoon for two weeks patiently going over the lesson for the next day with him, trying to rouse his interest. It never entered my head that his grandmother might need him at home or that he might have been earning a little money by odd jobs. A spark began to glow dimly, brightened, and one day he actually volunteered in class. I felt as if I had scaled Everest, and stopped the afternoon sessions, confident he would on his own maintain his ground. Of course I was wrong. He relapsed into the former complete indifference. I used to think that he would be a perfect tool for any criminal. He was so passive he would do just what you told him to do as long as you were exerting pressure on him, and he had absolutely no power of judgment or decision to do anything, good or bad, on his own. And I thought that his chance of falling into good hands was infinitesimal compared to that of falling into bad.

I also learned from Nash. He stood out on the very first day, small among the hulking farmer boys, with clear fine features and bright eyes, his short little trousers of a different material from his coat and unmended holes in both, because he sat directly in front of the teacher's desk and gave me the right answer every time I called on him, when the others were stupid or blank. When the principal kindly inquired how I had gotten through my first day, I was delighted to report

---

141 Apparently a reference to an individualized form of instruction, perhaps akin to today's Individualized Education Program (IEP).

I had one very intelligent student—Nash. "Nash?" said the principal with some reserve. "Oh yes, he's intelligent enough." Next day in the middle of the period he put his head down on his arms and apparently went to sleep. The next day I noticed a very disconcerting echo of the tones of my voice after every statement I made. The class of course noticed it too, and laughed themselves sick. Nash, intelligent and alert, looked shocked at their behavior, and it was some time before I was sure who was responsible. We then entered into a contest for the leadership of the class, in which I was hopelessly outclassed. When I tried sending him out of the room, he would wander around the corridor in view of the class, on whom I didn't dare turn my back, making faces or worse. When I went to the principal he was not at all surprised. "I thought you'd have trouble with him," he said. "Everyone does. It's too bad, because he has lots of brains. Well, if you must, just send him out for a week."

Nash was one of eleven children. Each one, on his fourteenth birthday—"his birthday present," said the principal grimly—had been yanked out of school and put into the mill. It was from Mrs. Dyson, who did not sympathize with the point of view but had practical understanding of why it existed, that I learned many parents felt their children were not blessings but economic liabilities, and that they only chance they had of getting back any monetary return from them was to put them in the mill on the first legal date. As they grew older, of course, they would spend their money on themselves and their own families. Nash's oldest brother had been a school leader and had passionately wanted just to finish high school; I don't suppose college even occurred to him. The principal had appealed to the father without success; he had appealed again for two other brothers without success; and now he had given up trying. Once when Nash had kept the class in an uproar and I kept him after school, trying with all my college debater's experience to appeal to any motive I could think of, I asked, "Why won't you study?" "Why should I?" said Nash. I had no answer to that. His behavior fluctuated from time to time, but I never got through to him. I thought he was perhaps trying to goad me into giving him so many demerits he would be expelled and have a few days or weeks of freedom to himself before he went to the mill. I didn't, but perhaps I should have. He went into the mill on his fourteenth birthday, and Saturday of that week I noted in my diary, "Stayed in bed till 8. Heard the factory bells and thought of Nash." Of all the students, I think he had the most potential and his fate was the saddest. I used to fantasize that he would become a revolutionary leader and sack my house someday, but I think probably he just vanished into a life of quiet desperation. I never heard any news of him after I left Danielson. We live today in deeply troubled times, but at least Nash's children and grandchildren have a better chance than he did.

I learned from Salmon, one of the farm boys, who broke his leg. I went out to work with him sometimes on Saturdays to keep him from falling too far behind, and got a glimpse of rural loneliness. His house was on a back road where there was so little passing that I automatically jumped up and ran to the window when once a wagon went by. He missed school, of course, and wrote themes going through the day as he thought of it at home: "12:00 Now for the English class. What will they be doing today? Oh, Friday, "Lady of the Lake." Probably Nash or Young or Proulx is either getting sent out of the room or getting some glaring looks from the teacher." Incidentally, I kept quite a few synopses of Scott's poem, and everyone was struck, understandably, by the harebell. "As Ellen stepped on the tiny flowers, her elastic footing was so light that the small flowers rose their heads again when she stepped off of them."

I learned from Bowen, a Puckish boy with bad teeth (another sophomore got a complete set of false teeth while I was there), who was not my own student, but who used to spend every afternoon in the commercial room until Iva Bryant and I went home. What his own home situation may have been we can guess from the facts that he once told us he had gone to the movies in the evening, fallen asleep, slept in the theater all night, and was never missed. He was my longest-lived correspondent from Danielson (the only person I have any contact with now is Iva Bryant, with whom I still exchange Christmas cards, and whom I once called on in Muscongus, Maine, where she retired) and even called on me in New Haven after I was married. He wrote to me for a number of years. He had a very clever knack at drawing, and sent me letters in envelopes I was afraid the postman would complain about, for the address would be written perfectly but minutely in a space about the size of a postage stamp while all the rest of the envelope would be covered with elaborate pictures of cupids or fairies or landscapes. I wish I had kept some of them.

But the most valuable lesson of all I learned from Rukstela. He was a farm boy (Central European?) whom I kept after school afternoon after afternoon, completely oblivious of the fact that he might be needed for work on the farm, for his knowledge of what in Wisconsin Freshman English we called "minimum essentials" was very scanty. Once we were going over a theme he had written about his horse, which, he said, weighed a ton. I didn't know anything about horses, but I knew that a ton was two thousand pounds, and I knew a man who weighed two hundred pounds was an unusually heavy man, and I didn't think a horse would weigh ten times as much as a man, so I demurred—following perhaps a proper syllogism but operating on a false proposition. "Oh yes," Rukstela said. "He weighs a ton. He ain't one of them little riding animals. He's a work horse." I pressed him, but he knew he was right and he wouldn't yield, so we discussed "ain't" and "them horses," where at least I knew what I was talking about according to standard English, though how much Rukstela needed standard English I wouldn't want to be dogmatic about now. On my way home I went past a farmyard where the notice of a farm effects auction was posted on the gate. I stopped to look at it and saw that it listed two horses, 2100 pounds apiece. I went in and looked around the barnyard till I saw the two horses close to, and realized that a horse is made differently from a man, with an enormous amount of bone in its legs; and I knew that Rukstela was right and I was wrong and that I owed him an apology the next day. I also realized that he was far better equipped than I for survival. If we should be ship-wrecked on adjacent Pacific islands the rescue ship would find that Rukstela had cultivated a fine breadfruit grove and raised a nice harvest to bring back to civilization, while like the Babes in the Wood I would have been buried under leaves by the local equivalent of pitying robins. And I learned, and never forgot, and never went into class without being conscious of, respect for the student. A teacher should always be aware that given experience many of her own students may beat her at her own game, and that every one of her students is her superior at something anyway. I told this story year after year at the last meeting of English 309, marveling at how far the little candle cast its beams, in that Rukstela year after year was teaching a lesson to prospective teachers in Wisconsin, a state of which I doubt he ever heard. The last years the need for the lesson seemed to have passed, with the rise of the ridiculous theory that students know better than their teachers to begin with, and then I said goodbye to my classes in another way. But I needed that lesson when I learned it, and the next year at Wisconsin I felt more than once that it would have been well if some of the bright young men in the department had had a chance, like me, to learn it too. And all through my association with the Freshman English work, the respect for the student that Rukstela taught me was a basic tenet of our course.

I think I have never had so strong a sense of the joyous coming of spring as I did in Danielson. The town was rather dingy, but there seemed to be an apple tree in full bloom in every little yard, and I remember the sense of the whole world bursting into bloom. I used to stop to recite Housman every day on my way to school before one particularly heavenly crabapple tree.[142] And I was very happy because I had been given a teaching assistantship at Wisconsin. Kathleen Lynch, of Mount Holyoke, was there as a graduate student under Karl Young (she moved with him to Michigan the next year), which perhaps is why this time the department answered my application. I was strongly pressed to stay in high school work and come back to Danielson by the superintendent of schools. He

---

142 Alfred Edward Housman (1859–1936), an English poet and classical scholar, is best known for his collection of poems, *A Shropshire Lad* (1896).

had visited my classroom and had been much impressed by my performance, as well he might have been, for I was reproducing one of Bertha Putnam's brilliant lectures on what makes a nation. Fortunately for me as a disciplinarian, he arrived in class before I did, and the students were so much in awe of him that they behaved perfectly. But I had known all along I was here only for a year. I didn't then have any idea that the rest of my life would be lived in Wisconsin, but I did know it wouldn't be lived in Danielson. I was sorry to say goodbye to my students and I was glad so many were sorry to see me go, but I was glad to go.

Perhaps I should speak of a unique experience in my life which took place in Danielson, though it really did not contribute very greatly to my education. This was a total eclipse of the sun. It took place in the middle of the morning, and we all went up on the roof of the school to see it. Mark Twain in *A Connecticut Yankee* greatly exaggerates the effect of a total eclipse. The sky does not become completely dark, but it does darken enough for you to see clearly several stars shining. What I remember as most noticeable was the distinct drop in the temperature. As one of the students observed (I fear deficient in the sense of wonder), "It was all right but I don't want to freeze my feet to see another." I never have had another chance, though I have seen a total eclipse of the moon here and an over 90% eclipse of the sun at the Island.

Like any teacher, I made a collection of boners. "The early pioneers went through so many hardships that they got hardened to it, making them very bold and peculiar." Among these hardships, "some were eaten by the cannibals." "The nobles persecuted the common people by stringing them up on telephone wires." They threw the martyr "into the lions." "Moving pictures have a mortal." "We came to a gate with a few large fur trees." "It happened just in the neck of time." "The family curdled around the fire." "The whole cabin was developed in flame." "He dispersed to his cottage." "The house was old-fashioned with its large pillows." "The moon discovered the sun." "Coleridge and Southey fell into chumship." "They are no longer burdened with bungly clothing." "It did not comfort but only further engrouched him." "The picture threw the ball over the plate." At Christmas "in each window hung a reef with a red bow on it." "Napoleon was able to place a throne on Josephine's head." "The river overflew its banks." "Jaques was the duke's singster." "I saw some light flittering in the mirror." Fourth of July is "a national holler day."

On a more significant level, it is impossible to over-estimate the importance of my nine months in Danielson. At the time it might have seemed a complete waste of time, a useless interruption of my career, a going off on a total tangent. But it was of the very greatest value to my career. When Bob Pooley became chairman of Integrated Liberal Studies and the [English] Department had to find someone to take over the advanced composition course for English majors working for the University Teaching Certificate, I was the only member who had ever been in a secondary school classroom as a teacher, and accordingly it was given to me.[143] Professionally I have divided my time between administrative work and staff training in Freshman English, where I was working under Ed Lacy,[144] and English 309, where I was on my own. As a matter of fact, the two aspects worked very well together. The more contacts we had with high schools the better we could do in Freshman English for their products. As my students began to go out into Wisconsin schools, my contacts increased, and my association with the Wisconsin Council of Teachers of English and my summer workshops for re-training high school teachers all were enriched by 309 and in turn enriched it. And another very great advantage of Danielson was that it enabled me to hit just the right pitch for teaching university freshmen at Wisconsin. The leap from the academic arcana of Bryn Mawr to the industrial reality of Danielson was a dizzying one. After that it was not hard to swing back a little, and hold the right balance here when I first taught, and, later when I was involved in administration, to help other cloistered graduate students without the advantage of Danielson to do better with their freshmen.

The first year of teaching is like first love. You have something to give you can never give again. You make a lot of mistakes which experience saves you from repeating, just as later love may be wiser, stronger, more mature; but virginity can be given only once, and perhaps something about the gift compensates to some degree for the lack of experience and wisdom. I made all kinds of mistakes, and I was often very stupidly unaware of what I was doing. But I did throw myself whole-heartedly into my work, and the Danielson boys and girls responded and taught me more than I have ever learned in any other single year before or since. The first year is significant for any teacher (the reason why, I have heard, twenty-five percent of beginning teachers leave the profession after it). Mine was especially valuable for me. Not often can it be such a sink-

---

143 Robert C. Pooley (1898–1978) taught English and Education courses at UW-Madison from 1931–1968 and conducted pioneering research in English usage alongside fellow faculty member Sterling Andrus Leonard (1888–1931). Pooley was president of the National Council of Teachers of English (NCTE) and founder and past president of the Wisconsin Council of Teachers of English. In light of his education background, Pooley was asked to direct Freshman English after Warner Taylor's retirement in 1945. However, in 1948 Pooley was asked to direct the newly created Integrated Liberal Studies Program (ILS). Inspired by philosopher and education reformer Alexander Meiklejohn's (1872–1964) Experimental College, a residence-based liberal arts college that operated at UW-Madison from 1927–1932, ILS was established in 1948 and is one of the oldest continuous interdisciplinary programs in the United States.

144 Edgar W. Lacy (1914–1981) earned his Ph.D. from the University of Illinois (1939) and served in the U.S. Army prior to being hired in 1946 as assistant professor in the UW-Madison English department. In 1948, he became director of Freshman English and invited Thomas to assist him (Fleming, 2011, p. 46). Lacy worked closely with Thomas for more than twenty years.

or-swim experience. In no other year of my whole life have I been so much on my own.

Finally, this year was the most broadening of my life. It is almost entirely responsible for whatever little openness of mind I can claim. I had lived a sheltered life among privileged people, and my experience was very limited and overwhelmingly derived from books. This year was a revelation. The great maturing experience of my life was not to come for fifteen years. I was still naïve, still childish, still unaware of the implications of what I saw. But in Danielson I did see that real life for many people was different from anything I had ever dreamed of.

WISCONSIN: SEPTEMBER 1925 TO JUNE 1927

When I took the Wolverine from Boston to Chicago I had never been on a train overnight before. As dusk fell I grew a little melancholy, but when the porter made up my berth and I saw what an ingenious little room it made for me to sleep in ("a darling cubbyhole") I cheered up and lay all night happily in bed wondering what a wolverine was, and imagining it some fast, tireless Western animal, steadily racing west, west, beside the train to the rhythm of the wheels. Polly Barnes met me in Chicago, where I had a stopover of three or four hours, and took me to tea. It was dark as soon as I got into Wisconsin, which I thought of as being practically a Pacific state, not as middle west at all. In the Madison station where crowds of students were meeting and being met by friends, I felt a little lonely again, but not very, for I was excited in new experience.

Kathleen Lynch had left Madison to follow her thesis director to Ann Arbor, but she had engaged a room for me at the Women's College Club, so I had a place to go. She had told Helen White about me, and I had called on her in Roslindale [Massachusetts], the only contact I had had with anyone I was to meet in Wisconsin. Both Helen and Ruth [Wallerstein] showed me great kindness, but I was pretty much on my own in a larger world than Danielson.

The College Women's Club, on what the old-timers called "Aristocracy Hill," at the corner of Gilman and Wisconsin Avenue, near the then governor's mansion, was one of the show places of Madison, and many Madisonians today regret its demolition in the fifties as an irreparable loss to the city.[145] It had been built by Vilas, a robber baron who had made a great fortune exploiting the timber of the state, and four presidents had slept in it, including General Grant. If he took a bath, which is perhaps not certain, he took it in the same bathtub I used, an enormous one, at least seven feet long, where I could lie down without touching either end. There were flowered china knobs on the bedroom doors, a magnificent paneled dining room, and an impressive library with a huge plate glass window overlooking the lake. (That Christmas vacation I was to sit there looking out at the lake where the search was going on to recover the body of a young man in the department who had gone out when the ice was too thin—one of the victims predicted by Black Hawk, who according to legend said when

---

145 · The College Women's Club, the Madison chapter of the American Association of University Women (AAUW), provided room and board and allowed female faculty members and faculty wives to socialize and collaborate on work-related projects (Cronon & Jenkins, 1994, p. 518).

he and his people were driven out of the region that Mendota in revenge would take toll of one white life each year.[146] Black Hawk hadn't enough vision to foresee the population explosion when one life would be a grain of sand among thirty-five thousand students and as little regarded. Last semester a teaching assistant in our department turned in a passing grade for a student killed in an automobile accident in October, and her parents, justly incensed, wrote to our chairman complaining bitterly.) The house was often used for AAUW functions, meetings of the Madison Literary Society, or the like, and was ideally suited for them until practically all members had moved out into the suburbs and it was impossible to park within walking distance any longer.[147] It was not without disadvantages for those of us who lived there. We ate in a rather cheerless basement, not the official dining room on the first floor, and we had no sitting room except the library, so if that was taken we had no place to entertain callers. Worse yet, the house was impossible to heat, and in my bedroom the water leaking from the radiator in steam would freeze on the floor. The big bedrooms had been divided up into small ones by beaver board partitions, so that you could hear everything going on in the rooms around you. Since I took my meals there, I walked to and from the university twice a day, four miles in all, and in winter with the wind blowing straight off the lake it was a frigid walk. The way lay along Langdon Street, and the first time I took it and realized I was seeing the famous Wisconsin fraternity and sorority houses I was impressed at their exotic flavor as if I had been walking through a bazaar in Constantinople, never of course dreaming that a son of mine would be living in one of them for three years.

My roommate was Martha Kohl, a medical student, from a small town in northern Wisconsin, a girl of great force of character. We didn't have a great deal in common but we got on well enough, and she asked me to be one of her bridesmaids when she married the next summer; but I had gone back East before the wedding. She had set her heart on becoming a doctor, and was engaged to a young man from her home town, whom she had promised to marry for the sole reason, as far as I ever discovered, that on that condition he would support

---

146 Black Hawk (1767–1838), a war leader of the Sauk American Indian tribe in what is now the Midwest, dictated what became the first Native American autobiography published in the US, in 1833.

147 The Madison Literary Society, originally Club, was founded in 1877 by Joseph Hobbins (1816–1894), a physician who belonged to a similar club while working in Brookline, MA. One of a few "town-gown" clubs that sought to link the university with the wider Madison community (Cronon & Jenkins, 1994, pp. 517–518), the Madison Literary Club was organized to promote literary discussion and social interaction among individuals "'of acknowledged literary taste'" (Thwaites, 1904, p. 27).. In its infancy, club membership was limited to 50 men and women. Meetings, which would last several hours, consisted of individual presentation of papers, followed by lengthy discussion, refreshments, music, and socializing (pp. 30–31).

her through medical school. She got the MD, went home, had a baby, left it with her mother, and went to California where she took a position in a hospital exclusively devoted to the care of women and children. There was a nice little girl from Alaska, Leota—Madison being her furthest point east and mine west—but she had various troubles, including financial ones, and went home after Christmas. The other residents were mainly older women, Madison high school teachers in near-by Central High.

The first thing that happened was assignment committee duty Saturday morning, which for so many years I was to manage myself. Then it was Charlotte Wood's job,[148] and it was held in the old red Men's Gym, still standing in spite of an abortive bombing several years ago.[149] From the beginning I avowed myself an advocate of plain speech for I noted that Mr. Rogers, next to me, told each student "Retain this and present it to the instructor" to my "Keep this and give it." Sunday I unpacked my trunk, and Monday registered myself in the morning and came back to assignment committee in the afternoon, where I sat between Mr. Thomas and Mr. Silverman: I noted "supported by Mr. Thomas—Texas charm."[150] Mr. Silverman took me out for my first date the next Sunday, and when he called up I hoped it would be Mr. Thomas calling. And then it very often was. Letoa came in to say "Someone to see you with a little mustache," and when I went downstairs there was Mr. Thomas: "Will you go out tonight?" I wrote Mother that he was "interesting to talk to," and she told me later that when she read that she knew. The English Department had a group of attractive, confident, able, interesting, well-groomed new young instructors living at the University Club that year,[151] and Wright was the most attractive of all, with youthful exuberance and gaiety. There was a special amount of glamour about him because he was a Rhodes Scholar and fresh from Oxford, where he had picked up sophisticated customs like wearing a tuxedo to go to a play at the University Theater (then in 272 Bascom, since the Union was not built). He had his picture taken (to give to me) and the photographer put it in his window on State Street. He teased me the first time we met by telling me he had a BS from Texas A and M, which was of course quite true but hardly seemed to me just the proper preparation for being an English instructor

---

148 Charlotte Wood (1878–1966) began working as an instructor and scheduler in Freshman English in 1924.

149 For an account of the Old Red Gym arson attack, committed by Karl Armstrong in 1970, see Bates (1992, pp. 170–172) and Cronon and Jenkins (1998, pp. 490–491).

150 Charles Wright Thomas, Thomas's soon-to-be husband.

151 The University Club opened in 1908 in response to President Charles Van Hise's (1857–1918) call for a faculty club that would build community across departments and disciplines. Initially, the club served social and residential purposes, but its popularity resulted in the club being used for official university business as well. The club became "a symbol of faculty unity and center of campus fellowship" (p. 532).

Wisconsin

at Wisconsin, without mentioning the subsequent three years at Oxford studying English literature. That fall I overheard myself described as "that sweet little English girl that Mr. Thomas likes." There were obvious factual errors in this (as in the case of the Holy Roman Empire), but I think it is significant that I was immediately dependent on him for the impression I made on others, and I was in his shadow until he left me. While those years were rich, and I am thankful for them, I can see now that not until after he had done so was I aware of myself as a personality in my own right.

It was a very happy courtship. At twenty-five, I had never had a real date, and with the exception of Harold Blanchard, no man had ever shown any sign of being attracted to me. Now I was like a nurse in the South Pacific, the *only* young woman in a group of extremely attractive young men, sharing a common interest and a common profession with them but with no sense of competition. I did not wear my Phi Beta Kappa key. Though I think Wright must have made it clear to his friends that he was very serious with me and they gradually dropped off, I had enough attention from a number of men to give me some self-confidence and a lot of enjoyment. And it became clear that I was sought by the most brilliant and promising of all. He fell into the habit of walking home with me down Langdon Street in the pleasant fall late afternoons. Day after day the entry read "Texan walked home with me," and only occasionally was there a sad "Didn't see the Texan all day." Rather strangely, in view of the fact that no one could be less like the stereotype of a Texan than Wright after he had been to Oxford—he had completely divested himself of his Southern accent in England—I always thought of him as "the Texan," and it was a full year before I called him "Wright" in my diary. His friends here in general called him Tommy. He took me to plays, to dinner dances at the University Club, to football games, the next spring out canoeing, but it was Sunday night which established itself as our regular date night, according to the Madison custom. If you paid board, you paid for twenty meals a week, and the twenty-first was Sunday night when couples went out to tea rooms, of which there were then a good many. After we had eaten we'd come back to the College Club library if it was not occupied, and the matron could get undressed and be ready to slip at once into bed after she had turned out the hall light when he left, since she could trust me to send him home punctually at the appointed time (10:30). He and I had our little misunderstandings and reconciliations but we came steadily closer and closer together. The schoolteachers looked kindly on and teased me about "the Texan." At the house Christmas party, when we exchanged little jokes, I got a pink celluloid napkin ring with a verse:

> One day a Texan shopping went
> And many dollar bills he spent.
> Oh tell me, did he candy buy,
> Or did he pause for a reply
> Before he bought a fairer thing?
> Ask Ednah if it was a ring.

Because of the distance and expense of the journey I did not go home at Christmas but instead spent the heart of it with Charlotte Keyes in Minneapolis, where I had my first experience of the dangerous sub-zero Middle Western cold that actually feels so deceptively balmy, and of lighted out-door Christmas trees, then an innovation. Wright went to New York, and from there to Boston to call on my parents. I was so anxious to get Mother's letter about him! On January 27, between semesters, on a cold snowy night, I stood in the hall window upstairs at the College Club watching him come up the street, cross under the street light, and come up the path to the heavy front door with its beautiful ironwork. When my bell rang and I went down into the library which I can see as clearly as if it had not vanished from the earth, I knew I would not be the same person when I went up the stairs again. Up to then I had loved to talk about him and hear him talked about; after that night I never initiated a conversation about him to anyone. I believed that from then on, all the rest of my life, Wright and I would be on one side of a line, and all the rest of the world, friends, parents, children (not that I was thinking of children) would be on the other.

The undreamed-of blackness of the Great Depression of 1929 was hovering over our innocent heads as the undreamed-of blackness of World War I had hovered over so many innocent heads in 1912. The great difference between the first quarter of this century and the last, as I see it, is that now we *know* that we are living under the sword of Damocles.[152] No disaster of whatever magnitude, right up to the total destruction of the planet with either a bang or a whimper, will surprise us if it comes. In Barzun's phrase, we are schooled in apprehension. This was not true then. Personally, Wright and I were extremely and exceptionally lucky. Oil had been discovered on Thomas land in Texas, which made life easy for Mr. Thomas, who was in a mood to be generous to his son. We were not formally engaged until the next September, when Wright came to the Island[153] and brought me a ring he had bought abroad, and we did not announce

---

152   The sword of Damocles refers to a moral anecdote that illustrates the imminent peril faced by those in positions of power. The allusion typically denotes experiencing a sense of foreboding in the face of uncertain circumstances.
153   A reference to Isle of Springs, an island community located in BoothBay Harbor, Maine,

the engagement for another year, after Wright had gone to Texas for Christmas vacation and his father promised to give him two thousand dollars (plenty for a couple to live on in those days) so that he could take the next year at Yale and complete his doctorate. But we both knew what would happen, and Wright honorably informed Mr. Lathrop,[154] then Department Chairman, that we were planning to marry. Mr. Lathrop kindly said his only regret was the loss to the profession of my leaving it. If I had been a Women's Libber, avid for my degree, I could have had a grievance—and over the years I think we must say in honesty that various teaching assistants in various departments did have a grievance—in that I had both semesters been asked to teach extra sections of Freshman English and reduce my graduate work accordingly. As a matter of fact, I was only too glad of the chance. I loved the teaching, but I had realized at Bryn Mawr that I was not temperamentally a scholar. (By the way, I had completely forgotten until I looked at my Line-a-Day recently that in 1927 Bryn Mawr offered me the post of instructor in the English Department.)

The coup de grace to my scholarly career was furnished by six weeks of illness second semester. I went to the University Infirmary with a bad attack of sinus, and they must have mismanaged the case, for they dismissed me too soon, so that I had to come back, much more seriously ill, a couple of days later, and my stay there was extended two extra weeks in quarantine for German measles, to which I was exposed there. When I finally got out I dropped the only graduate course I was taking, a seminar in Shakespearean manuscript writing, given by an eminent English visitor, Mr. [C. J.] Sisson.[155] My advisor had forced me into it against my will—and I was such a rabbit I didn't put up much of a fight—because no one wanted to take it and most of the other graduate students had a better sense of self-preservation than I. (I have now seen these things from both points of view.) The only notation I ever made on it in my diary was "Going blind." I was delighted to leave it and I've never done any scholarly work since. As for the sinus, oddly enough—but happily—after that very bad first winter I have never had any trouble at all in the Wisconsin climate.

While I was quarantined I had a nice undergraduate roommate who told me a lot of lurid stories about life on Langdon Street—this was the twenties, remember. And I received a postcard signed by virtually every member of the

---

where the family spent summer vacations.
154 Henry Burrowes Lathrop (1867–1936), a scholar of the Elizabethans and the novel, published a freshman English textbook, *Freshman Composition*, in 1920.
155 Charles Jasper (C.J.) Sisson (1885–1966), scholar of Elizabethan drama from the University of London.

department—Mr. Lathrop, Mr. Cairns,[156] William Ellery Leonard,[157] Arthur Beatty,[158] Paul Fulcher, Warner Taylor,[159] Helen White, Ruth Wallerstein,[160] Charlotte Wood, and so on. Wright must have taken it around to get the signatures himself, I'm sure, but that all the senior as well as the junior members would sign it, and that one postcard had room on the back to hold all the signatures, testifies to a golden age that will never come again. I have given the relic to Charles Scott, our present chairman.[161] It seems to me now, looking back, that the department really was one happy family, though I know the past is always bathed in rose-colored mists. We certainly had one pleasant custom: afternoon tea served in 361 Bascom for so long that the room was still known as the tearoom long after World War II had ended the custom and no beverage but coffee had been poured there for years. Every afternoon a woman, teaching assistant or professor's wife—the system was perfectly democratic—was hostess, bringing cookies or sandwiches she had made herself, boiling the water for the tea on a very feeble electric plate, and using the sugar, lemon, and cream it was the duty of a committee to provide. I served on that committee second semester and used to wonder what sort of diet the grocer thought I was on since I never bought

---

156   William B. Cairns (1867–1932), a pioneering scholar of American literature, published textbooks on composition early in his career, including *The Forms of Discourse*, with an Introductory Chapter on Style (1896) and *Introduction to Rhetoric* (1899). Cairns's scholarly trajectory seems to resemble that of Karl Young and other "promising rhetoricians who taught and published in rhetoric while young and migrated to literature when older" (Brereton, 1995, p. 25).
157   William Ellery Leonard, (1876–1944), an Old English scholar, translator, and American poet, taught in the English department from 1906–1947.
158   Arthur Beatty (1869–1943), a graduate of Columbia University who specialized in Wordsworth, taught in the English department from 1897–1939. His son, Hamilton (Ham) Beatty, and Allen Strang founded the Beatty and Strang architectural firm in Madison, WI, in 1935. The firm specialized in residential International Style architecture; its first commission was in Frost Woods, WI, and included Thomas's home. Ham and his wife, Gwen, were neighbors and lifelong friends of the Thomas family.
159   Warner Taylor (1880–1958), earned BA and M.A. degrees from Columbia and taught there for six years before teaching at UW-Madison from 1911–1947, where, beginning in 1921, he directed the Freshman English Program (Clark, 1966, pp. 5–6; Fleming, 2011, p. 38).
160   Ruth Wallerstein (1893–1958), educated at Bryn Mawr and University of Pennsylvania, joined the English department in 1920 and taught English literature until her untimely death in an automobile accident in England while on research leave.
161   Charles Scott (b. 1932), a professor of English as a Second Language at UW-Madison from 1963–2000, was hired by the English department to direct the ESL program. Scott was a prolific scholar, achieving full professor in 1968 and becoming department chair in 1970, shortly after Freshman English was abolished.. At the urging of former department chair Walter Ridcout, Scott agreed to be nominated for department chair because he would be seen as a reasonable compromise candidate between the older and the younger faculty. Thomas describes Scott's influence as chair in the Demolition chapter.

anything but those three items. The first time I was hostess I didn't allow enough time for the water to come to the boil, and I still quake at the remembrance of all the full professors coming in looking for their tea when it wasn't ready. "I'm so sorry," I said. "I just can't hurry it." *"Don't try,"* "said William Ellery in his Jove-like way. There is a story that once when he tasted the tea and realized it hadn't been made with truly boiling water he threw the pot out of the window; but there were a lot of stories about him, and most of them were apocryphal. It's hard to think what crime today is comparable to making tea with water not boiling, then. Anyhow the custom was very pleasant, and very friendly.

This semester I got an anonymous letter, fortunately the only one of my life. I am quite sure it came from one of the women at the College Club who was too unhappy herself to bear the sight of my happiness. It accused me of bad behavior at the Club, of negligence with my students at the university, and ended by urging me to leave the Club because the women there were "not my friends." I took it to Mr. Lathrop, who thought it might be from a student with a grudge, and assured me the department was more than satisfied with my work; and then to the College Club matron, who also assured me she was more than satisfied with my behavior, and was indeed particularly grateful because, as I have said, Wright always left so punctually that she could get ready for bed beforehand rather than having to stay dressed and come in to suggest it was time for him to go. I think she suspected who might have written it, for she wanted to take the letter to check the handwriting. But I was far too happy to want to punish anyone, and I wasn't coming back to the College Club next year anyway, since I was to share an apartment on Gorham Street with Ruth Wallerstein and Julia Grace Wales, where I could have kitchen privileges. So instead of giving it to her I just tore it up.

I haven't said anything about my teaching. I loved it, and continued to learn here as I had begun to learn in Danielson. In the fall I had bought a magnifying glass at a jeweler's shop for use in Mr. Sisson's seminar, and he had accidentally overcharged me. When he found out his mistake, he asked another member of the seminar, who came in for the same thing, who I was so that he could refund the money, describing me as "a nice little girl with high color so shy she could hardly speak." I wasn't shy with my students, nor have I ever been at any time in my life. As I had done in Danielson, I held conferences until the "office looked like the subway in rush hour." I was teaching Freshman English, a composition course where most of the theme material was drawn from the students' own experience—the main piece of work for the first semester was an autobiography, standard practice in those days—and I found it fascinating. In fact, the next year when I was given literature to teach, the sophomore survey course which everyone else preferred, I enjoyed it less. One of my students then wrote "The Prioress was a great beast who lived with her son as outcasts," which seems to show some confusion both in literature *and* in composition.

Warner Taylor was director of Freshman English and ran a tight ship. He was a well-read prose stylist, and the course was excellent in its authoritarian style, with none of this modern nonsense about letting instructors do as they please. We had weekly staff meetings at which Mr. Taylor analyzed the essays to be studied: these were for new staff only, but everybody in the department, full professors and all, had one section of Freshman Composition,[162] and each semester a committee distributed ten themes to be graded by everyone teaching the course, and a total staff meeting was held at which Mr. Taylor gave up beautiful graphs he had made of the grade distribution. As soon as you grasped the simple fact that of ten themes, two would A, two B, two C, two D, and two F, of course you had no trouble in turning in a nice middle-of-the-road evaluation. But the meetings were always interesting because some of the full professors were highly idiosyncratic and of course felt no bashfulness at presenting their individual points of view. I'll always remember one theme my first year in which the writer referred to Wisconsin as "this broad cheese country"; isn't that a good description of your native state? The second year I was on the committee to select the themes, and we included one I had received in my own class, a theme so good some of the rather cynical older men refused to believe it was bona fide student work; and I was not too shy to defend its authenticity before the whole department with as much vigor as Cicero used defending Archias.[163]

During my first semester Mr. Taylor visited me in class, according to standard department procedure, and I told the story year after year to our teaching assistants who were to be visited themselves, to show them I had survived and to promise more consideration than I had had. Mr. Taylor telephoned me one noon when I was eating lunch at the College Club to say, "Miss Shepard, would it bore you if I visited your 1:20 class today?" "Oh, no, Mr. Taylor," said I truthfully. "It wouldn't bore me at all." When I arrived at the class, however, Mr. Taylor was not there, and he didn't come until about fifteen minutes after class had started, when he opened the door, walked in, and sat down. The class were a little surprised, but nobly sprang to my defense and volunteered so fervently—

---

162 Thomas's observation that everyone, including senior faculty, taught Freshman English would be valid for only a few more years. In his national survey of Freshman English (reprinted in Brereton, 1995, pp. 545–562), Taylor notes that when he joined the UW-Madison faculty in 1911, department policy dictated that everyone taught one section of Freshman English; however, by 1929, Taylor notes, "I am the only person instructing in the regular course" (quoted in Brereton, 1995, p. 556). But it is true that the economic realities of the 1930s caused many senior faculty to resume more direct involvement in the course (Fleming, 2011, pp. 40–41).

163 A reference to Cicero's oration, *Pro Archia Poeta*, a published form of Cicero's defense of a poet, Archias, accused of not being a Roman citizen.

if not particularly intelligently—that I was as much surprised as disconcerted when Mr. Taylor got up after about fifteen minutes and walked out. After a day or two in which he made no sign, I finally went to his office and asked him if he could give me any suggestions as to improving my teaching. "Well, Miss Shepard," said he, "it was a very interesting hour." I realized at once that he might not give me any suggestions for improving my teaching, but that he had presented me with an all-purpose word which I could make use of all the rest of my life on practically any occasion. And I assure you it has come in very handy, again and again.[164]

Wisconsin was a larger world than Danielson, and I learned more and more. As I do from Danielson, I remember certain individuals: for example, Mr. Hagerty, whom I always thought of as "Susan," because of his theme describing a baby calf to which he had given that name; he had raised it on bran mash and a number of specific foods I've forgotten now, and he ended triumphantly, "That baby calf is now the mother of eight Jersey cows, on which I am going through college"—evoking an image of Ben Hur and the chariot race. I had one little Jewish girl who was so desperately homesick she cried at every conference and almost all the rest of the time for the first month or two, just as I had done as a freshman at college myself: Sylvia Friedman. She brought her parents to call on me at the College Club one weekend, and her father, an antique and furniture dealer in Chicago, was overwhelmed at the impressiveness of the woodwork and the furnishings. But most of my students were mature, far more so than I. I was more sophisticated in reading; they knew very little of books. But in practical experience, social and financial, in the details of making a living, holding a job, spending money, contact with the world, the practical side of life, I was very childish compared to them. I began to do a little generalizing, which I had not done in Danielson. When I passed Abraham Lincoln, sitting patiently in his chair, I regretted that industry and ambition, which one of my students had in his measure, would not be enough for that boy to get very far without brains, which my student did not possess.[165] One young man came up with a theme I had just handed back (they gave me a sub-freshman section the first semester) and said, "I am the father of a six months old son, and I am not at all satisfied with the grade you have given me on this paper." While it was hard not to feel guilty of injuring generations barely born, I still was unconvinced

---

164 An illustrative example of this is found in Fleming (2011), when Ira Shor asked Thomas about the role of social issues, such as civil rights, in Freshman English. Shor described Thomas's response as, "'Well, those are interesting questions, Mr. Shor, but they're not really appropriate for this teaching session'" (p. 106).

165 A memorial of Abraham Lincoln is situated to the east of Bascom Hall, where the English department was housed until it moved to the newly constructed Helen C. White Hall in 1971.

that there was any logical connection between the two parts of his statement. I had never, of course, been in contact with any student body so heterogeneous in sex, age, background, interests, amount of money, and experiences, and the variety made teaching fascinating. Physically at that time the student body were very attractive. Long before the New York influx, the majority of them showed clearly their Scandinavian and German ancestry, and I used to look out the window and think they were like young Norse gods and goddesses walking up and down the hill. If I choose one single tangible detail from that year, perhaps the most significant was the sign "Hog-Breeders Banquet" I saw on the Ag campus; there had never been anything like that in any ivory tower where I'd ever been. The main difference between Holyoke and Wisconsin, I thought, was that Holyoke was like a potted tree completely separate from its society while the roots of Wisconsin spread wide and deep all over the state. It seemed to me that American education was sound and healthy as long as it comprised these two completely different types.

The second year at Wisconsin was as happy as the first, but in a different way, serene instead of exciting. We were secure. I was living with Miss Wallerstein and Miss Wales, who of course knew of the engagement, so we could count on privacy and I usually cooked the Sunday night supper myself. We tried to restrict ourselves to the weekly date so that we could both do justice to our work, though perhaps we made some exceptions. Wright wrote me notes and mailed them in the department brown paper envelopes, so that they looked official on my desk; but they weren't. He had left the University Club this year, and was a resident house fellow in the first-built group of Residence Halls by the lake shore (of whom, in later years, serving on the Residence Halls committee, I was to interview so many); and through the lovely Indian summer, which is the best season in Wisconsin, I would walk over from Bascom and we would meet for the noon hour. It was quiet and beautiful by the lake, the campus just beginning to be built up and still practically unspoilt. It was so still there in the sun that when a leaf fell from the tree it sounded like a little note of music as it struck the water. Candles on a birthday cake; red and blue and green and silver balls on a Christmas tree; sunny Indian summer noons: I see them all shining as I look back over my life. In all my life, for pure felicity these fall moments are the clearest, the most delicate and beautiful—sitting beside the lake, alone with Wright, in the sunshine, while, from time to time, a falling leaf struck the water with a sound like a note of music.

NEW HAVEN: SEPTEMBER 1927 TO JUNE 1928

This is my lost year. A pendant to Danielson, the most significant learning year of my life, this was the least. From no other year did I bring away so little. Nearly fifty years after Danielson, I am still exchanging Christmas cards with the commercial teacher of Killingly High School; but in New Haven, where my husband was a graduate student at one of the leading universities in the country, where presumably the city was overflowing with people with whom we had social and academic interests in common, I made not a single personal contact which lasted beyond the day we left. It is, as I look back now, both sad and significant that this year was the first year of my marriage.

With my usual lack of initiative, I left the selection of our apartment to Wright, and did not see it until we arrived. Obviously I have no right to complain of his choice. But it wasn't a very happy one. The apartment (reminiscent of the house Arnold Bennett says was designed by an architect in a drunken stupor)[166] had a very small kitchen, a small living room, and beyond that a small bathroom and a small bedroom, adjacent. Since there was no door in the wall between the bedroom and the bathroom, if I had gone to bed and Wright had a caller, I was trapped. The whole place was very dark, because it was on the first floor, on the back of the building, giving on a paved alley and overshadowed by the fire escape. The building, however, was across the street from a city park where I spent a good deal of time. I fed the squirrels, and one, I remember, was tame enough to take a nut from my hand; once he missed his aim and sunk his teeth deep into my thumb. Nowadays you would die for fear of tetanus, but in those happy days we didn't know anything about such things and consequently didn't worry about them. My thumb rapidly healed. (Robert Blood says cheerfully that doctors never catch anything because they're not afraid of germs.)[167] I loved being in the park all fall, a good deal of the winter, and all spring, though by then, since I knew we were leaving New Haven for good in June, my ingrained sense of the cycle of nature made me feel something not right in seeing the opening leaves and the flowers when I wouldn't see the falling leaves and the fruit.

---

166   Arnold Bennett (1867–1931), an English writer.
167   Likely a reference to Dr. Robert Blood, who was governor of New Hampshire and married to Pauline Shephard, mentioned in the Forebears chapter. Thomas knew Pauline as a child, and would stay with the Bloods when she went East en route to the Isle of Springs. From 1944 to 1960, Blood was the New Hampshire delegate to the Republican National Convention.

New Haven

Unfortunately, the apartment was on the wrong side of the tracks—the east side, completely across the city from Yale. This effectually cut me off from forming any neighborly contacts with young women with whom I might have had something in common. A woman with more initiative would not have been defeated, but in my shyness I was unable to cope. I did go two or three times to the university organization for wives of graduate students, but the second time I saw no one I had seen the first, and the third no one I had seen the second, and I gave up.

Bertha Putnam had given me excellent advice, which would be standard procedure today, but which I was then too stupid and old-fashioned to take. She pointed out that it was a perfect opportunity for me to go on and get my Ph.D. at the same time Wright got his, and she was quite right. As a matter of fact, our preparation was almost exactly equal; my Master's from Bryn Mawr was the equivalent of his Second Class from Oxford. But I had gotten my bellyful of scholarship at Bryn Mawr, and I'm not by temperament a scholar and never was. If I had been aiming at a career in college teaching, for which, we hear, the Ph.D. is the union card, I would have forced myself to go through the discipline, arid as it might seem, and I think I could have done it successfully. But when I married I gave up any such ambition, and I put my energy into working to help Wright get ready for his Ph.D. oral: reading materials, making synopses, formulating sample questions, and the like. I also had the silly idea that I should devote my first year of married life to learning to cook—silly because even then cooking wasn't that difficult and it has been getting progressively easier until today all you need to know is how to turn on the oven and put a TV dinner in, and how to heat water for powdered coffee. I made the usual bridal mistakes. Although I wasn't quite as ignorant as the bride who called Home Economics to ask what brand of soap you should use to wash the lettuce, I remember putting hot red peppers into a salad under the illusion that they were pimentos. I also remember making a Lady Baltimore cake for Wright's birthday, the traditional birthday cake in my family. Since according to Fanny Farmer's recipe one egg white was left over, which of course I didn't want to waste, I put it in the frosting with the result that the frosting never hardened, but slid off the cake as fast as I put it on and had to be eaten with a spoon.[168] I spent time on cooking, I spent time on making notes for Wright, I spent time in the park, and I was very lonely. One thing I had had all my life was the companionship of women. This year I had almost none, and I missed

---

168 Fannie Farmer (1857–1915), an American culinary expert whose *The Boston Cooking-School Cook Book* (1896), later known as the *Fannie Farmer Cookbook*, introduced the concept of standardized measurements in recipes. The cookbook was extremely popular and remains in print.

it very much. Wright sometimes brought other graduate students home to dinner, and I liked that, but they were men—bachelors.

In the same apartment house lived the only couple with whom we had any contact. I've forgotten their surname; the wife's Christian name was Constance. She was pregnant; she had had several miscarriages, and had been told she might bring a baby to full term if she stayed in bed the whole nine months. I used to go up and get her lunches while her husband and Wright were at the university. We didn't have a great deal in common, but under the circumstances we enjoyed seeing each other. I marveled at the difference in our conception of the duties of a wife. Constance never wrote to her mother-in-law because she felt the mother would rather hear from her own son than from the girl he had married. Since the son never wrote, the mother never heard anything at all. Wright and I came to a very good arrangement on this point: he would write one week, I the next. On my week I wrote Sunday. On his I'd say on Sunday, "Remember this is your week to write to your mother," and he'd say, "Yes, of course." On Monday I'd say, "Have you written to your mother?" and he'd say, "Not yet but I will." On Tuesday I'd say, "Have you written to your mother?" and he'd say, "Stop nagging." After a few weeks, I settled down to writing Mrs. Thomas every week, and this was no hardship to me. As you all know, it's easy and pleasant for me to write letters.

On the other hand, Constance managed their finances completely, and once when she went away for a few days (toward the end of the pregnancy when things were obviously going well and the baby well developed the strictness of the regime was somewhat relaxed) her husband had to eat all his meals with us because she hadn't left him any money at all. In June, when they moved, he went away and Constance conducted all the business; when we moved, I went to Brookline and Wright did it all. As they say, it takes all kinds to make a world. As a wife, I had many deficiencies. As a daughter-in-law, I did give pleasure to Mrs. Thomas by my letters, which of course I continued up to her death. Mary Simons once told me I had written my way right into her mother's heart. Constance bore her child successfully, but they never had another, because she was understandably reluctant to pay the price of nine more months in bed. I don't know what happened to them.

Though I made not a single personal contact which survived the year, I did have one very important experience—important because I had a great deal of influence on me and on my behavior for many years in Madison, first as a faculty wife and then as a faculty member myself. Tucker Brooke, the distinguished Shakespearean scholar, was then on the Yale faculty, and Wright had a seminar with him.¹⁶⁹ Once Wright took me with him and asked Mr. Brooke if I might visit, and he kindly said yes. There are a few experiences in my long life in academe—de Selincourt's lecture on Dorothy Wordsworth here at Wisconsin,¹⁷⁰ Paul Fulcher's birthday tribute to George Bernard Shaw, and a few others, perhaps not too many to be counted on the fingers of one hand—which are outstanding; and this seminar meeting of Tucker Brooke's is one of these. He was dealing with *Hamlet*, and did so by taking the minor characters Rosenkrantz and Guildenstern, and opening out the play from them. (A few years ago a modern playwright used the same approach, in a play named for the two men.¹⁷¹ I remembered Tucker Brooke when I read it. I thought it fell far short of his performance, but perhaps by then I was too old and set to appreciate merit.) When we spoke to Mr. Brooke in his office, just before the seminar, I noticed his hands were shaking, and it seemed very strange to me that a man at the top of his profession, with years of experience behind him, should be nervous before a class meeting. In my humble way, I understand it now. I have never heard the bell ring before a class and gone to the door to close it that I didn't wish I could go out the door, close it behind me, and walk away from the class instead of back into it. It only lasts a minute, this sinking feeling, and as soon as I actually started the class I was as happy as a clam at high water. But I never failed to feel it. I think it is the mark of the professional who must never become inured to what he is doing; for if he did, he would be no good. I read once of a case where experienced surgeons condemned a young man who had operated with great skill because "he didn't sweat."

The important experience, however, was not the seminar visit but something else. Tucker Brooke had been one of the first Rhodes Scholars ever appointed, and therefore took an interest in Wright, in any other Rhodes Scholars at Yale, and in things English. One night Wright came home and said Tucker Brooke had invited us to dinner. Of course I was pleased and excited, but I was also worried about what to wear. In those days in academic circles people still often, though not invariably, dressed for dinner. If Mrs. Brooke had telephoned me to deliver the invitation herself, I think I might have had courage enough to ask her if they dressed. Since it came from her husband by way of mine, I certainly was not brave enough to call her. I finally wore as dressy an outfit as I had that wasn't long, Wright wore a dark suit with a white shirt, and we set off hoping for the best.

---

169   C.F. Tucker Brooke (1883–1946), an American academic specializing in English literature and drama, taught at Yale from 1909–1946.
170   Ernest de Selincourt (1870–1943), British literary scholar and critic best known as an editor for William Wordsworth and Dorothy Wordsworth.
171   Tom Stoppard (b. 1937), a knighted British playwright who wrote *Rosencrantz and Guildenstern Are Dead* (1966).

The Brookes did dress. Tucker Brooke was wearing a tuxedo and Mrs. Brooke a long dress, as was Mrs. Pottle, the only other woman guest, wife of Yale's new and very promising assistant professor. There were half a dozen extra men or so, all bachelors, several of them Commonwealth Scholars here from England. The bond was obviously English connections, which Mr. Brooke must have felt outweighed the difference between those who had the Ph.D. and those who were seeking it; but it should be remembered that in those days Ph.D. candidates were a very small and elite group compared to the hordes who walk the halls of Bascom today. The Englishmen, kindly adapting themselves to the customs of the savages, wore business suits and colored shirts, and several of the Americans were dressed like Wright, so he wasn't conspicuous. I was a little taken aback, but I cheered myself up by remembering a recent article on Russia I'd seen where the reporter was describing living conditions (this was after the Revolution when very little information was coming out) and illustrated the shortage of clothing by saying that at a concert he had sat next to a man wearing a bathing suit. And I got through the dinner reasonably well. I was on Tucker Brooke's left—Mrs. Pottle of course on his right—and the conversation was general enough so that I could hold up my share. He was a courteous host, and after all, wasn't I an M.A., from Bryn Mawr? There was a lot of deference to Mrs. Pottle because she was a bride. (Dear old Mr. Woodhouse: "A bride, you know, my dear, is always the first in company, let the others be who they may.")[172] She had been married in June, I in September, but no one asked or cared when my wedding had been, and I really didn't see any reason why anyone should. This was Pottle's first year at Yale, and he was their white-headed boy; and they had made an excellent choice in selecting him, for he has been for many years one of the most distinguished researchers and teachers in the country. His wife certainly rated attention.

After dinner the women, according to the old English custom, retired to another room and left the men at table. The three of us were a very long time alone, since all the men had a great deal in common, both in English literature and experiences in England itself, where they had all lived, at least for substantial amounts of time; in fact, they spent the bulk of the evening in the dining room and the party broke up almost as soon as they joined us. During the whole time Mrs. Brooke did not once address a single remark to me or bring up any topic of general conversation in which I could join. Her guest followed her lead, and the two women talked exclusively of people whom I had never seen or heard of and department and local matters which I could know nothing about. To all intents and purposes I wasn't there; the two of them were alone. Of course there was no real reason why Mrs. Brooke should put herself out for a graduate student's

---

172 A character in English novelist Jane Austen's *Emma* (1815).

wife whom she'd never see again—none except common courtesy and humanity. After all, I was an invited guest in her house.

Someone gave us a lift home, and it was all I could do to keep from crying until we got into the apartment; and then I cried and cried and cried. Poor Wright. He'd had a very enjoyable evening. This quite unimportant incident made a deep impression on me. I vowed that no guest in my house, when I had one, should ever feel as Mrs. Brooke had made me feel; and when I did have a house of my own, I did a great deal of entertaining, year after year, which involved the teaching assistants' wives. For years I called on all of them. When Dick Quintana was chairman, I used often to go with Janet when she called on instructors' wives.[173] I went alone to call on the wives of the teaching assistants. This was before the university built Eagle Heights to provide housing for graduate students, and the poor things lived all over, in substandard housing on the wrong side of the tracks, and were delighted to see *anybody*.[174] And for years every baby born into the department, whether to full time faculty or teaching assistants, got a pair of booties I had knitted—even twins.

A few years after we had come back to Madison, Tucker Brooke was visiting professor for a summer session, of which Wright was chairman. I entertained for him, at a lovely garden party in Frost Woods with plenty of ripe strawberries—a nice English touch, I thought. I don't know where Mrs. Brooke was that summer. She didn't come with him.

At that time Yale gave an oral for the general Ph.D. examination (unlike the written sequence here). Wright took his at the end of May. He had decided, rather to my distress, that he wouldn't be able to spare the time to take me to Texas in spring vacation to present me to his family, as had been the plan when none of them came north for the wedding. (We went the next Christmas.) I spent the time he was away at the examination on my hands and knees scrubbing floors. Never in my life when the outcome of an event was in doubt have I swung so rapidly and repeatedly from one extreme to the other. One moment it seemed completely unthinkable that he shouldn't pass; the next, that he should; and this alternation kept up like a pendulum until he got back. He did pass, and we had looked forward to the event for so long that it seemed now our whole lives would be completely placid and no problem or difficulty of any sort could ever arise again. It took two or three days to get back to reality.

---

173 Ricardo B. Quintana (1898–1987), a Harvard graduate, taught English at UW-Madison from 1927–1969. His wife, Janet, graduated from UW-Madison in 1925..

174 Eagle Heights, a high promontory on the south shore of Lake Mendota, is part of UW-Madison's Lakeshore Nature Preserve. The name now refers to a student apartment complex, built in the 1960s and surrounded by Preserve lands, which houses a culturally diverse group of international and American students and their families.

We had left Wisconsin with no particular idea of coming back. We planned to stay at Yale until Wright had finished his course work and his dissertation and had his degree, and then see what offered. But, owing I'm sure to Mr. Beatty, who always had a very high opinion of Wright, the Department of English at Wisconsin now offered him an assistant professorship beginning in the fall of 1928, with the promise of a semester off the next academic year so he could go to England and do the research for his dissertation. Yale ended early, and we went to the Island for the month of June, the earliest I've ever been there, with lilacs and apple blossoms in bloom. We spent the summer at my parents' apartment in Brookline while they were at the Island,[175] and Wright worked at Widener.[176] So we left New Haven. I've never been back.

---

175 A reference to Isle of Springs, an island community located in BoothBay Harbor, Maine, where the family spent summer vacations.
176 A reference to the Harry Elkins Widener Memorial Library, at Harvard University.

SETTLING DOWN: 1928 TO 1932

In September, 1928, we came to Hawthorne Court for two years. When we left Madison in June, 1927, we had no particular idea that we would be back after Wright had finished up his course work for the doctorate at Yale, which he could do in two semesters. He was certain to get a first-class job somewhere. And so he did. But many men with equal reason for confidence (Bob Sharp among them) through no fault of their own were victims of timing. It was pure luck that Mr. Thomas gave Wright a year's support so that he had his job when so many were desperately looking for one. The same sequence of academic sellers' and buyers' market is repeating itself as I write. The appointment was that of assistant professor, with the understanding of a leave of absence the first semester of 29–30 so Wright could go to England and collect the material for his dissertation on Erasmus Darwin.[177]

Hawthorne Court today is as grim an example of urban blight as you want to see, with the huge Lake Street parking ramp walling off the whole west side, but then it was very pleasant. Our apartment house was newly built and did not add to the beauty, but the apartment itself was much more livable than the one we had had in New Haven: a rectangle where you entered a large living room with a fireplace and windows along the opposite side, passed through a small kitchen with a window on your left and an inside bathroom on your right, and went into a square bedroom on the street with cross ventilation. Pets were allowed, and I had the pleasure of my first cat, Euphues. The Paynes, a couple of whom we had seen a good deal before we married (Wilfred was in Philosophy, Helen in my office in English; they went to the municipal university in Omaha, and Helen is now in a California nursing home, showing indomitable courage after a series of strokes), owned a beautiful honey-colored cat, Melissa, and had offered us a kitten for a wedding present whenever we were in a position to accept it. The name (in case you've forgotten your sixteenth-century English literature) means Golden Legacy, because we had had to wait a year for him.[178] The Quintanas[179] and Sharps both lived in the next apartment, an older one. The opposite side of the street was still private houses. One had belonged to the famous Babcock,

---

177 Erasmus Darwin (1731–1802), grandfather of English naturalist Charles Darwin, was a physician, natural philosopher, and poet.
178 Euphues actually means graceful or witty. Thomas is likely referring to Thomas Lodge's (1558–1625) pastoral romance novel *Rosalynde, Euphues' Golden Legacy* (1590), the probable source for Shakespeare's pastoral comedy "As You Like It."
179 Ricardo B. Quintana (1898–1987), a Harvard graduate, taught English at UW-Madison from 1927- 1969. His wife, Janet, graduated from UW-Madison in 1925.

Settling Down

who had left it as a cooperative for Ag students, and the yard was beautiful in summer with the many vari-colored hollyhocks which had been a hobby of his.[180] The next house stood in a good-sized green yard with oak trees, and when we looked out from the Sharps' second-story window at the proper season of the year we could see the little squirrels playing like kittens in the branches. (I have always been fond of the German word *eichkatschen*.[181]) The location was ideal, within easy walking distance of grocery stores on University Avenue, book stores on State Street, Lake Mendota, where in hot weather we used to swim at night—and that was a novel experience for a girl used to Maine water, I can tell you—and best of all, the campus. Some years after its disfigurement had begun, to culminate in what the *New Yorker* aptly calls the New Brutality,[182] I once met a woman walking down the hill behind Bascom looking unhappily about her. "What is this building?" "Commerce." "What is that?" "Social Science." And so on. "When I was here," she said sadly, "these were all green slopes." In 1928 the campus was all green slopes, and we spent a lot of time there very happily.

We were glad to come back to Madison where we had already many friends and were to make four more: Dick and Janet Quintana, Bob and Marie Sharp, two couples who had joined the English Department the year before. All six of us were congenial. Dick was a little older than the other men and during this year was promoted to tenure, which made a little difference though not much. With the possible exception of Marie, whom you may not remember, I think you've seen enough of them to know them yourselves and can easily imagine what fun we must have had when we were all young. By coincidence the Sharps' wedding ceremony was being performed in Springfield at just the time ours was at the Island, four in the afternoon on September 1, 1927. We invited the Sharps to the Island[183] the next summer, and it turned out so well that we did cooperative housekeeping there for several summers, until they bought the cottage they have kept ever since and became an integral part of the Island for many years when I myself never got back. When we were there together, we had a double celebration of the anniversary—going over to the Pemaquid pound for

---

180 Stephen Babcock (1843–1931), American agricultural chemist who conducted pioneering research in nutrition, taught at UW-Madison from 1888–1913. In 1951, the university constructed Babcock Hall, which houses food science labs and the dairy plant, which produces the highly popular Babcock Dairy ice cream.

181 German for "squirrel."

182 A reference to Brutalist architecture, or brutalism, an outgrowth of early twentieth-century modernist architecture, which flourished in the 1950s-1970s and is characterized by massive concrete structures. The term derives from Swiss-French archtect Le Crobusier's (1887–1965) description of the material: *béton brut* (raw concrete).

183 A reference to Isle of Springs, an island community located in BoothBay Harbor, Maine, where the family spent summer vacations.

lobster or having at the cottage any fancy meal with a Frenchified menu Marie and I could concoct. It can be an extremely pleasant relationship when the four members of two couples are all congenial. I am very fortunate in having had it twice, first with the Sharps and then with the Beattys.[184] Marie was a classmate of Marion Wing's[185] at Smith, and like all Smith women I've known, very capable; and she was a much better housekeeper than I, having been thoroughly trained by a German mother. She had an assistantship in History, and she and Bob had planned, very reasonably, to live on her salary and save his until they had enough for him to devote full time to his getting his doctorate at Harvard. Unluckily, as I have said, they were victims of timing. When he did get his degree he had no job at all the first year, and a poor one at a technical college in New York state the second, though he then went to Wheaton, where he eventually became Department Chairman. Marie, who was not only capable but also good-looking, well-dressed, and sophisticated, got a highly paid job as dean at Katharine Gibbs in Boston,[186] where those qualities were important, and kept it through the second year, when they had to commute to be together weekends, and all the rest of her life. In the Hawthorne Court days, the four of us often played just one rubber of contract [bridge] at the beginning of the evening before the men settled down to their work, and this was only one of a lot of pleasant activities.

The pleasure of coming back to Madison and of all the companionship there was marred by one disappointment. Since I had taught successfully, I had hoped to get a section or two of Freshman English to teach, but since I was now married to an assistant professor and the department had a rule against nepotism, this was impossible. I hoped I might do some work in the English Extension, but they were jealous of their position as part of the "real" department and rather indignantly told me the same principle applied. For a couple of months in the late spring of 1929 I did fill in there and enjoyed it very much, but I must have been filling only a temporary emergency. This brings up the whole question of what today is known as "Women's Lib," and a highly complex question it is. At that time, I simply felt aggrieved; if I had taught successfully before marriage, why couldn't I after it? This very much over-simplified the problem, as I can see now. The English Department has always subsidized its graduate students by giving them teaching assistantships—and this is not an ideal system, as I shall say when I try to analyze it in a later chapter. However, even assuming some other method of financing graduate students, teaching by wives, who are here today and gone

---

184 A reference to Hamilton (Ham) and Gwen Beatty, neighbors and lifelong friends of the Thomas family.
185 An acquaintance from the Isle of Springs (ME).
186 Katharine Gibbs College, a for-profit college system founded in 1911 to provide career education for women.

tomorrow and who have divided loyalties, would present even more difficulties. I have seen a good many problem couples among the assistants, when the gray mare was the better horse,[187] enough to make me feel that on the whole the principle was justified, though it may seem old-fashioned today. The basic problem, I think, is the psychological relationship between husband and wife; and such a combination as Joan Sutherland and Richard Bonynge is as rare as it is ideal.[188]

In this connection I'm going to insert a rather long quotation from Rebecca West's *Black Lamb and Gray Falcon*, written in 1940, since I think it a very provocative statement of an almost impossibly difficult problem.[189] I wouldn't for a moment agree that it is reasonable to weep when a girl is born, for by her sex a woman has potentialities of joy that a man does not: she can bear children. But I think that in her account of the women of the Skopska Tserna Gora in Macedonia, though she offers no solution, Rebecca West does throw light on a problem which the years between 1940 and 1973 haven't done much for in spite of the increased interest in it—a problem which must appear in multitudinous forms, since every couple is individually different from every other couple.

> Men must be reassured, hour by hour, day by day. They must snatch every aid they can in their lifelong fight against seen and unseen adversaries. It would comfort them enormously if they knew that they were stronger than others. But what others? It would seem obvious to answer, their enemies. But little comfort can be derived from them, for sooner or later comes the battle, to settle the value, never satisfactorily; for an enemy that defeats in plainly superior, in some sense, and an enemy that is defeated appears so contemptible that it is no comfort to be above him. There are, however, exquisitely convenient, all women. It need only be pretended that men's physical superiority is the outward sign of a universal superiority, and at a stroke they can say of half the world's population, "I am better than that." This declaration is the more exalting because that half includes the people on whom the

---

187 A proverb referring to a situation when the wife rules, or is more competent than the husband.

188 Dame Joan Alston Sutherland (1926–2010), a renowned opera singer, was married to Richard Bonynge (b. 1930), who conducted nearly all of Sutherland's performances during her nearly thirty-year career.

189 Dame Rebecca West (1892–1983) was a decorated British author, journalist, critic, and travel writer. *Black Lamb and Grey Falcon: A Journey Through Yugoslavia*, published in two volumes in 1941, is an ethnographic account of West's six-week visit along with a history of the Balkans.

man who makes it had been the most dependent, even the person through whom he received his life.

If the community is threatened by any real danger, and only a few fortunate communities are not, women will be fools if they do not accept that declaration without dispute. For the physical superiority of men and their freedom from maternity makes them the natural defenders of the community, and if they can derive strength from belief in the inferiority of women, it is better to let them have it. The trouble is that too often the strength so derived proves inadequate for the task in hand. The women in the Skopska Tserna Gora were repaid for their subordination by a certain mitigation of their lot, which is proved real enough when it is compared with the darker misery of the women on the plains below, who suffered far worse at the hands of the Turks, but which was far from giving them security in any ordinary sense of the word. Intense and lifelong discomfort seems an excessive price to pay for this; and they might easily have gone on working out this inequitable contract till doomsday, since their menfolk were never able to liberate their community from the Turks until they were aided by the Serbians, who were outside their sexual transaction. In far worse case were the Turkish women in Macedonia, who received nothing in return for their subordination except the destruction of their community.

Even when the men of the community derive an adequate amount of strength from the suppression of their women, the situation is ultimately unsatisfactory; for it undoes itself, to the confusion of both parties. When men are successful in defending their community they engender a condition of general peace, in which people attempt to live by reason. Then women use their full capacities of mind and body, not because they want to prove their equality with men, for that is a point in which it is difficult to feel interest for more than a minute or two unless one has an unusually competitive mind, but because in such use lies pleasure. In such a world the young woman and the young man dash together out of adolescence into adult life like a couple of colts. But presently the woman looks round and sees that the man is not with her. He is some considerable distance behind her, not feeling very well. There has been drained from him the strength which his forefathers derived from the subjection of women; and the woman is amazed, because tradition has taught her that to be a man is to be strong. There is no known remedy for this disharmony. As yet it seems that no present she can make him out of her liberty can compensate him for his loss of what he gained from her slavery. The disagreeable consequences of this are without end, and perhaps it may be counted the worst that there never can be a society where men are men and women are women, that humanity never reveals the whole of itself at one time. Until there is achieved a settled condition of world peace hard to foresee anywhere nearer than the distant future it will always be more necessary that the revelation should be made. Therefore, it will perhaps be reasonable till the end of all time within imaginable scope, to follow the ancient custom and rejoice when a boy is born and to weep for a girl. But there are degrees in the female tragedy. It is our tendency nowadays to deplore as worse than all others the woes of the woman whom modern capitalism allows to earn her own living but deprives of a husband and children, since the wage-slave is an uneager lover and a worse provider. But nowhere have I seen such settled and hopeless despair, such resentment doubled by its knowledge that it might not express itself, as on the faces of the women of the Skopska Tserna Gora.

When I was doing the first draft of this chapter, I heard a news item of a woman, incidentally a professor at Emory, Georgia, who was about to sue the man who registered voters because he refused to register her while she refused to declare herself "Mrs" or "Miss" on the standard blank; she thought "Ms." should do. As I do the final draft, "Ms." is very generally used, and, I must say, often very convenient particularly in business or professional contexts where you don't know the woman's marital status. But the registrar in the Georgia incident perhaps did have a point when he said, "I don't think the Lord made a mistake when he created two sexes."

Back in 1928 I was unconscious of the scope of the problem, and I was just unhappy because I didn't have enough to do. The small apartment required little housework, especially with my sloppy habit of cleaning with a lick and a promise. There were details in those days, though, of which a modern housekeeper doesn't dream. Once when both Wright and I had colds, one day I "boiled about a million handkerchiefs" and the next day "ironed thirty-seven handkerchiefs." This kind of labor might give pause to the modern beneficiary of disposable

Kleenex who is idealistically anxious for us to stop choking ourselves with our own waste—an unsolved contemporary problem. I did a lot of cooking of the sort that no one bothers with now: "made little cakes and put pink flowers and green leaves on bitter chocolate frosting." I made my own mushroom soup and I made my own mayonnaise. I did some jobs for Wright, particularly galley and page proof for a collection of essays he published with Stuart Gerry Brown.[190] My best time-use was manuscript editing for Mr. Vasiliev.[191] But I needed more outlet for my energies than I had, and I'm afraid I often behaved badly to Wright.

A. A. Vasiliev was Professor of Byzantine History at the University of Wisconsin, and one of the two top scholars in the field in the United States. Even now, when the emergence of Russia as one of the two leading world powers has contributed to increased interest, I don't think the field is over-crowded. A great linguist, he could read twelve languages, but he didn't have idiomatic command of English. The first volume of his monumental two-volume *History of the Byzantine Empire* had been published as translated by a woman who knew both Russian and English, but neither the publishers nor the Department of History were satisfied with the translation, and it was thought another method might be better: revision of Vasiliev's own English by a qualified person. Mr. Lathrop, chairman of the English Department before we married, had the kindly thought that I might be glad to occupy myself with editing since I couldn't teach.

The relationship was a great success. It is characteristic of me, I think, that my most successful relationships with men have been those that were work partnerships. Mr. Vasiliev was a White Russian who had escaped during the Revolution, and I wish I knew more about his life. Years later he started an autobiography, but he wrote only a chapter or two, and I learned nothing from it except that as a boy he used to go out gathering mushrooms, which all characters in Russian novels seem to do. I don't know whether he ever married or had any children. He seemed a typical bachelor. He lived alone all his life in Madison, first at the University Club[192] and then when that was taken over for officers' quarters during World War II in a room he rented in an apartment on Gorham Street. He was an absolutely delightful man with a great zest for life, much energy, and a

---

190   Stuart Gerry Brown (1912–1991), who taught at Syracuse University and founded the American Studies department at the University of Hawaii, published two edited collections with Wright Thomas: *Reading Poems: An Introduction to Critical Study* (1941) and *Reading Prose: An Introduction to Critical Study* (1952).

191   Alexander A. Vasiliev (1867–1953), whose history of the Byzantine Empire was published in English in 1928–29 by the University of Wisconsin Press, acknowledged Thomas's "remarkable conscientiousness" in revising the manuscript and correcting his "inadequacies" in English (iv).

192   The University Club, which opened in 1908 and served social, residential, and university business purposes, became "a symbol of faculty unity and center of campus fellowship" (Cronon & Jenkins, 1994, p. 532).

wide range of interests. One summer he took a Mississippi paddlewheel steamer down the river to recapture the feeling of Mark Twain's days, and another year he went to Alaska. He was very knowledgeable in music and extremely popular in Madison society. He was a prolific scholar, and after we finished the second volume of the *History* he continued indefatigably to produce shorter works and articles, all of which I worked on, even a few after he had retired from the university and gone to live at Dumbarton Oaks in Washington, a haven for elite scholars. Most of the time we had regular meetings at which we discussed together any passage where I wasn't completely certain of his meaning or he of my revision, and after each of these I typed up the material for the printer. It was hard typing, for sometimes he'd have four or five lines of text to all the rest of the page in footnotes, and he was always adding insertions on strips of paper neatly pasted at the proper place on the original sheet; but his handwriting was beautifully clear, and the conferences were always a joy.

The relationship continued practically to his death, long after I was more than busy with other things. I wrote Gwen in 1974 that I was going to do a book for him.[193]

> You hear them say that the Russians are impractical, but I never knew anyone so meticulous about time as he is. He wrote me last week, "I shall arrive in Madison on June 4, and I shall telephone you the evening of June 4 or possibly the morning of June 5 if the telephones are running."
>
> The University Press decided to bring out a new edition of his chef d'oeuvre, and I am to revise the whole thing. I have no business doing it, but I did feel so sorry for the poor man. Besides, he can't understand English—at least when I say "no" he can't. At his age it is hard to get used to anybody new, and it is such specialized work I know he would have a very difficult time finding anyone anyway. I told him I was too busy. "But such interesting work!" said he. "It will be so interesting for you!" I explained that I was not primarily a scholar but a mother. "But this is interesting for a mother!" said he. I then explained that I was doing a full time job in addition to being a mother, and he looked as if I'd taken away his candy bar. I finally broke down and agreed to do it, since we had no fixed deadline to meet.

---

193 After Gwen and Ham Beatty moved from Frost Woods, WI, Thomas and Gwen corresponded regularly for over thirty years. Thomas later borrowed and used her letters to Gwen as source material for portions of the memoir.

Mr. Vasiliev was a scholar in the German tradition, an immensely conscientious and thorough collector of facts, down to the minutest detail discoverable. The work was completely factual and thoroughly documented, and unspoiled by interpretation or opinion. It was very interesting to me to find that one or two such scholars in his field—not more—existed in practically every country in the world, even in the unlikely continent of South America. And this was before Russia was a great power. And all these scholars, oblivious of the twentieth century and of World War II, were continuing to live and work in the Byzantine Empire. After the war, as communications were resumed, from time to time Mr. Vasiliev would tell me with the greatest pleasure of receiving a new article from Czecho-Slovakia or Egypt or Brazil or wherever, written by a man who, like himself, had spent the intervening years going to the library day after day, faithfully and patiently following his gleam. Perhaps the library wasn't heated, and perhaps it was only open a few hours a day, but the man had been there whenever it was, and now all of them were getting in touch with each other again. This seems to me a very limited kind of scholarship; but it is absolutely pure. My work for Vasiliev is perhaps the only thing in my life which is absolutely pure. Certainly there can be far richer and more fruitful human relationships, and I have had my share; but about them all, like a speck on a peach, there will be some kind of imperfection, some emotional taint, something small to regret even if the regret is heavily outweighed by the values. My contribution to Vasiliev's scholarship was limited, only typist's work; still it was necessary, and without it he could not have fulfilled himself as a scholar. My own limited work was applied to his greater work, also limited; but I think it is the one contribution I have made in my whole life which is complete and perfect of its kind.

Though when this work started in 1928 I enjoyed it very much, it still was not enough to absorb all my energies. This winter was memorable for our visit to Texas at Christmas for my introduction to the Thomases. I am ashamed now as I think how badly I must have behaved, especially when I contrast it with Hannah's first Christmas with her in-laws, when she rose so nobly to the occasion. I was shy, and everything was strange to me, including the fried chicken and hot biscuit with which they hospitably plied me until I longed for a plain lettuce leaf and a piece of what they nastily called "cold bread." Mrs. Thomas deserves great credit for her tolerance; she had written Wright that she never expected a son of hers to marry a Yankee, but "time changes all things." She was already resigned, I think, to the fact that he had grown away from her and her world—she was devoted to the Methodist church and had hoped he would be a Methodist minister, she was the local president of the Daughters of the Confederacy which decorated the veterans' graves on the Southern Memorial Day (much earlier than ours), and so on. She told me Wright was completely changed when he came back from Oxford; he had been very social, friendly, and popular as a boy, but then he was very quiet and didn't care to see people any more. Those Oxford years undoubtedly changed him very much, and of course I belonged more to the new life than to the old; since she had already accepted the change, I don't think she felt any particular resentment against me. I am thankful that if I didn't behave very well on this visit—and what could I say when she told me about the old mammy she had had when Wright was a baby who always slept on the floor outside her room? The most I was capable of was saying nothing at all—I did write to her dutifully and regularly, and Mary Simons told me I had written my way "straight into Mamma's heart." It was certainly much easier for me to be a good daughter-in-law at a distance of fifteen hundred miles or so.

Mr. Thomas was twenty or thirty years older than his wife; he had been a friend and war comrade, I think, of her father's, and she always called him "Mr. Thomas." He was very old by this time—you remember he had been a boy soldier in the Civil War—and I was far too shy to speak to him, except to thank him for saving a cotton boll for me to see. He was obviously a man of great force of character and independence of mind, though not of education or breadth of experience. Mary Simons said there was always an enigmatic quality about him that she, his daughter, never fully understood; far less I. I think this may be the mystical strain sometimes attributed to the Welsh: Tom may have a touch of it. The oldest son, Lyttleton, twenty years older than Wright, was a doctor living in Oklahoma, an able and interesting man, married to Nelle, a very sweet and friendly girl with some Indian blood. They had two daughters, one of whom (also Nelle but called Bill) was the most beautiful girl I ever saw in my life when she and her sister came up here from boarding school in St. Louis to spend spring vacation the year before Hannah was born. Lyttleton and Nelle are now both dead, but they lived to celebrate their golden wedding anniversary, and I have always appreciated very much the fact that they sent me an invitation. Mary, next in age to Lyttleton, has had a very tragic life. She is one of the most admirable human beings I have ever known—in a class with Mrs. Wing,[194] Helen White, and Grace Hughes.[195] There was a gap (two children had died young) before Will Clint, who took care of all the business details for all the family. He was destined, poor man, to a horribly drawn-out last illness, from which he has now been released. His wife Elva was an elementary school teacher. They lived in Houston, and were childless. I had noticed that Wright was not talkative at home, unlike my father, and when I saw the Thomas family I understood why. All the men were taciturn (except possibly when they were together,

---

194 An acquaintance from the Isle of Springs.
195 Wife of Merritt Y. Hughes (1893–1971), a Milton specialist trained at Harvard who taught at UW-Madison from 1936–1963.

about which I wouldn't know), and the women talked steadily. Mrs. Thomas had two unmarried sisters who lived around the corner in the old Moore house (she had the nice maiden Irish name of Mollie Moore) and they came over every day to sit with her, all three talking steadily and never listening to anything any of the others said. This confused me a good deal at first, but I realized that it was simply their way of enjoying being together. The purpose was sociability, not exchange of information.

We went over to Galveston [Texas], where Mary was then living, where for the first time I saw palms growing. The great masses of wild flowers I think of as one of the most beautiful sights of my life I saw on later visits, when you were along, and we went in spring vacation. Childless then, I had no idea whatever of what was involved in bringing up lively children, and I was horrified at Mary's housekeeping because her sons had washed their hands and wiped them on the guest towels she put out in the bathroom for us. I later apologized to Mary mentally again and again when my own children showed me what life was like and never bothered to wash their hands at all. We also spent a day or so at Texas A&M, with Wright's cousin, head of the English Department, who was responsible for getting him interested in English literature and therefore for the Rhodes Scholarship and all that followed. He was William Henry Thomas, named for Wright's father, and of course that's where Bill's name comes from. One thing which I hope pleased Mrs. Thomas was that I initiated giving the boys Thomas family names. My sons were the only males to carry on the name; so Wright Moore is named for his father and his father's mother's family, and Bill is named for his grandfather. William's wife was also christened William, according to a not uncommon practice in the South, but was called Bill. I liked them both very much and felt at home with them; academic people are the same wherever you find them. I do remember, though, a strange note struck at the dinner party Mrs. Bill gave for me that night: one of the guests had been down to the jail that morning to bail out her cook, who had carved up another woman to whom her husband was paying attention, and everybody took this as one of the minor inconveniences of life, much like getting stuck in your driveway in the winter in Wisconsin. Mrs. Thomas visited us here when Hannah was a baby, Lyttleton and Nelle's daughters the spring before Hannah was born, as I have said, and Mary one summer when you might have been about nine, twelve, and fifteen respectively. I correspond pretty regularly with Mary now, and Elva and I exchange a remembrance at Christmas, as Nelle and I did until her death.

The second semester of this year was an ordeal for Wright, for I developed purpura hemorrhagica, something like the hemophilia which Queen Victoria's descendants transmitted all over the royal houses of Europe, a disease where great purple bruises come out all over you and your blood doesn't clot. At that time very little was known about it, and the treatment for a woman's extended monthly periods was simply bed rest, which of all types I was least well equipped to make the best of. As my condition grew worse, I had to go to the hospital and have a series of blood transfusions—rather primitive in those days, with actual contact with the donor. The disease was rare, and I was an object of great curiosity to the entire medical profession of Madison. Finally, it was decided to resort to what was heroic surgery at that time, the removal of the spleen, an operation performed for this purpose for the first time only a few years before; a surgeon came up from Chicago to do it since no one in Madison was equipped to. Mother, making what I know was a great sacrifice in leaving my father, came out and stayed for a couple of months. Not only did it take more time forty years ago to recover from operations, but over months of continuous loss of blood I had become extremely anemic. But the operation was a complete success. I gradually improved, and in June I saw the famous Dr. Minot in Boston, who was awarded the Nobel Prize in 1934 for his work in anemia.[196] He told me to eat half a pound of liver every day; they were sure that would cure the condition but they were not yet sure of the potency of the extracts they were working on, which makes life much easier for sufferers today. Again, Wright was very fortunate in having a father able and willing to pay my hospital and doctor bills; medical costs were not as inflated as they are now, of course, but mine had been very high. It's a bad time to think of, and I know I made it a bad time for Wright too. But when by the end of the second year I had completely recovered, I've been strong as a horse ever since. This is another example of lucky timing. If I had been born a few years earlier the curative operation would have been unknown. In the same way, the very recent development of brain surgery was lucky timing for Kathy. All this put off our having children, and none of the doctors then thought I would be able to have any of my own without bleeding to death. But they were wrong, and here you all are.

This also postponed our trip abroad by six weeks or so. We waited until midsummer instead of leaving as soon as the university was out in June. We sailed from Boston on the *Laconia*, a small Cunarder. Your Aunt Hannah saw us off, and I recollect her saying, "Now, Ednah, this is a *pleasure* trip." I wish I had made it so for Wright, but again I remember with remorse, futile now, that a good deal of the time I must have been a very disagreeable companion. He of course knew both England and the Continent well from his time as a Rhodes scholar.

We went tourist third, of course, but since we were off season all the academic

---

196 George R. Minot (1885–1950), an American surgeon trained at Harvard and Johns Hopkins, shared the 1934 Nobel Prize in Physiology or Medicine with George Hoyt Whipple and William Parry Murphy "for their discoveries concerning liver therapy in cases of anemia" (Nobelprize.org).

crowd, which usually made the crossing one of the best parts of a European trip, had already gone. The ship was full of coal miners and their families from Pennsylvania going to a Welsh Eisteddfod [festival] who all knew one another and weren't paying any attention to outsiders. So the crossing wasn't particularly exciting, but at least it was calm, and Wright, who is not a good sailor, didn't miss a meal. A picture which remains with me as one of the most striking examples of lack of communication I have ever seen is that of the last meal in the dining saloon: all the Americans at the next table getting up to go, shaking hands individually all around with their waiter, thanking him cordially for his services on a pleasant trip, and then leaving while he looked unbelievingly and in vain under all the dishes left on the table for the tips they never realized they were supposed to give.

We made our landfall August 6 at Ireland, a pleasure whose every minute was savored, a pleasure which modern aviation has made obsolete.

> We saw the Irish hills about four Sunday afternoon. The sun was bright and the waves fresh. The gulls came flying out in twos, in tens, in hundreds, to join the one or two who had been with us for several days, and like a long line of cloud the Irish hills showed faint and gray against the white horizon. All the way in the gulls flew around the ship, below us and above, still in the wind, swooping straight down to the water, the wind blowing their bodies up and their legs out, coming up with their beaks shining wet, white bodies shining in the sun, heads turning slightly this way and that, the continuous broad gray band that marked their wings and back beautifully defined.
>
> The Irish hills grew nearer, and showed as gray cliffs. We passed Fastnet Light, a heavy solid building on a gaunt pillar of rock. The cliffs began to lose their grayness, and changed to slopes of green hills, the lines of the fenced-off fields showing plainly. The sun was setting as came into Queenstown Harbor. We passed the *Celtic*,[197] rotting on the rocks, when the harbor fortifications, a barracks on a hill, like a castle out of Grimm's fairy tales, mouths of guns showing in the green hillside. Inside were mere marked fields, one with a herd of cows grazing, "red like hens," a woman said. The harbor widened; the boat moved more slowly; the gulls' circling was calmer; in the sunset, journey's end and peace.

---
197 The ocean liner RMS Celtic (1901) ran aground in December 1928.

Settling Down

> It was still light enough to read the name on the tender which came out for the passengers to debark. First the stewards went in single file down a double gangplank, each carrying a bag of mail on his shoulders, going back like ants. A man with a cornet stood aft on the tender and played Irish and American songs ("The Wearing of the Green") and people threw down money. The lights came out around the harbor. The stevedores were sliding trunks and big cases down the gangway, the stewards went down again with hand luggage, and finally the Irish passengers filed off. It was dark and cold, but the lights were on in the town, and the ship quiet in the circle of harbor with its single opening out to the sea.

The next day we had a slow trip down to Liverpool in sight of land, for by some accident or other only one engine was running. We disembarked at Liverpool with practically all the Boy Scouts in the world, for they were celebrating a World Jamboree, and we saw scouts in every imaginable costume, with turbans around their heads and in other exotic dresses, and the bare-legged English Scout Masters. Wright had been at Oxford when Baden-Powell received his honorary degree, striding up the aisle with his crimson doctor's robe swinging back from his knee pants and bare legs. Most of the Scouts, a thousand or so, seemed to be on the train we took down to Oxford, which gave me my first view of the justly famous English countryside.

We spent the first night at the Mitre Inn, where I had my first encounter with the well-trained, impersonal English servant, and with my American ideas found her inhuman. I was rather worn out from the trip—you remember I was still a convalescent—and went to bed instead of going down to the dining room, and the chambermaid came to take my dinner order. There is a story of a Boston aristocrat who went to Durgin-Park and was insulted when the waitress cheerfully asked her, "What'll it be, sister?"[198] But that wouldn't have bothered my plebian soul while the total absence of any human recognition did. The next day we found lodgings rented during term to an Indian student but available to us for the rest of the summer and later for the long Christmas vacation. The landlady and her daughter were very friendly in spite of class differences. I was automatically a "lady" because my husband was an M.A. from Oxford and therefore a "gentleman," and it surprised them that I washed out my own stockings. But they were much interested in America, and we had nice talks. In a moment of nostalgia I bought a *Saturday Evening Post* and gave it to them, and

---

198 Durgin-Park, a venerable Boston restaurant and landmark that has served traditional New England-style foods since 1742.

they were amazed that in the States it cost only five cents. "The adverts alone are worth the money." The house was very dark, one of the typical English row type, with windows only in the narrow back and front, and a little back garden. Mrs. Morris had a black cat which in the kindness of her heart she had allowed to go on producing kittens indefinitely, and you couldn't put your foot down anywhere without stepping on a black kitten. Nothing could have pleased me more, particularly when a new family arrived and I looked forward to seeing it grow up. Unfortunately, Mrs. Morris did feel that one was too much of a good thing and one day while we were gone the whole litter disappeared.

Before it tried to emulate Detroit as a producer of motor-cars Oxford could well claim to be one of the most beautiful cities in the world, if not the most beautiful. The college gardens were at their best: sweet peas espaliered on the gray stone walls like big bushes of pink or red or white roses; the American roadside weeds of goldenrod and asters in gorgeous clumps, the flowers bigger and brighter than here. To some extent the brightness of color appears in Maine flowers too, and for the same reason, the sea air. Of course I worked with Wright in the Bodleian[199] copying, as much as I could, and we fell into the habit of working through tea time without a break and then taking country walks after early supper in the long lingering northern mid-summer evenings, when it was still light at nine. We would pass cottages where the walls were a mass of flowers, those in the window boxes falling down to meet those in the beds below; climb the hills where we could look down on the colored fields in crazy pavement patterns; and sit in the stillness until we could almost feel the world turning slowly under us on its axis. Once when we had lost our way and asked a man in a field to direct us, his dialect was so strong we couldn't understand him; and it struck me that for this to happen within walking distance of one of the great centers of culture of the world made an accusation against British society that could never have been made against American. Once when we were coming back on a bus, a man got on who had a sackfull of things that moved—poor little Peter Rabbits. Once we had dinner at an inn, a delicious fricassee of chicken; it wasn't, fortunately for my appetite, until I had eaten all my helping that I realized the bones on my plate had never come from a chicken. We took weekend trips, to Blenheim, to Cambridge, to the Washington home, to Stratford, of course. We went punting on the river,[200] a skill Wright had mastered in his student days. We took a river steamer down the Thames to London, and I was entranced by its little smoke stack which folded neatly down when we went under a bridge.

---

199 The Bodleian Library is the main research library of the University of Oxford and one of the oldest in Europe.
200 Punting refers to boating in a punt, a flat-bottomed, square-shaped boat used in shallow water and propelled by a person using a pole.

Settling Down

Recent visitors to Oxford have told me it is ruined. Like W. H. Hudson I can only be thankful that I shall never revisit a place where beauty has vanished from the earth.[201]

I was sorry to leave Oxford but we had to work at the British Museum, and we treated ourselves to two weeks on the Continent the first of October; and Wright with his knowledge of Europe made the best of our time and money. We crossed to Holland, took the trip up the Rhine and spent the night at Bonn, had a few days in Switzerland at Berne, went through the Simplon to Florence and spent a few days there, and then back to England via Paris. Wright was knowledgeable in both architecture and art; I regret that I was a good deal of a barbarian, like Mark Twain's innocents abroad, and like Landor I have always given priority to nature over art.[202] So I liked Switzerland best and it's the only part of Europe I've felt a desire—mild and easily controlled—to revisit. In my provincial way I said it was like Maine—which meant that I thought it was as beautiful as any place in the world could be and that I would love to spend a long, long time there. We arrived at Berne at night, and when I went out on our balcony the next morning I looked up in the sky and saw great clouds floating overhead—and they were mountains! We went up the Jungfrau in a cable car, looking down on white clouds floating below us—a commonplace in these days of air travel but a thrilling experience then before technology killed the sense of wonder. We took a lake trip on a little steamer where passengers rode on the upper deck and cows on the lower. I loved the sound of the cowbells, and would have liked to do some hiking—I had no aspiration to mountain climbing—when the fields were green. At this time of year they were covered with a little heath-like plant which had turned red; I have only seen pictures of the Alpine spring flowers. There were far too many art treasures in Florence for me to take in, but I saw some, and we took an expedition to Siena. By the time we got back to Paris it was late in the season, cold and rainy, and I didn't enjoy the City of Light. Wright said it would be pleasant to get back to an English-speaking country, almost like coming home, and he was right. A very badly behaved American woman, however, created an embarrassing scene on landing because she was expected to disembark through a door marked "Aliens." "I'm not an alien," she screamed. "I'm an American citizen, and I won't go through that door!" I told this story many times later in my teaching when we were discussing word connotation.

November is not a good month in London. We were paying for the lovely long light summer evenings by short dark days—about five hours of daylight,

---

201 William Henry Hudson (1841–1922), an English naturalist and author.
202 Walter Savage Landor (1775–1864), an English writer and poet.

it seems to me, shortened by rain, soot, fog, and smoke. ("Smog" had not yet been coined.) We stayed in a Bloomsbury boarding house with all the stereotype characters and props—the waiter with the dress coat green and shiny with age, the slaveys, the retired Indian civil servants who spent all their time doing crossword puzzles and sending in coupons for advertising contests. I did some work in the British Museum and saw plenty of the characters for which it is famous; the one I remember most clearly sat next to me in the famous Reading Room all one morning busily taking notes with no ink in his pen. Of course he might have been using invisible ink. But I had a good deal of time to myself when Wright was busy, and I found it a little dreary exploring London alone. I used to wish I had a child with me because there were so many things I had read of—Kensington Gardens, the changing of the Guards—that I would have loved to show a child. November is a good month for the theater, of course, and I've never at any other time approached such a number of performances. We heard Chaliapine in the Albert Hall, and saw Gilbert and Sullivan at the Savoy, Sean O'Casey's "The Silver Tassie," Shaw's "The Apple Cart," and "Journey's End," the latter on the night the Prince of Wales had a box and entertained all the surviving winners of the Victoria Cross in World War I. Owing partly to the British habit of smoking in the theater but mainly to my sentimentality, I was weeping uncontrollably by the time we left the theater, and we had walked every step of the way home to the boarding house before my tears dried up. We had veal and kidney pie at the George and Vulture, where Mr. Pickwick was suspended, with a fellow Rhodes scholar of Wright's and his wife, and played cards with them (for money, which completely paralyzed me) several times, but she and I were not congenial. Out of all the London stay my most vivid memory is being in Trafalgar Square on Armistice Day. Traffic was excluded and the Square was solid with people and murmurous with the sounds crowds always make; then I *heard* the silence, heard it rolling across the great space while the pigeons, startled by the cessation of ordinary sound, flew up in a great flock into the sky. November 1929 was the month in which the Great Depression struck America, but it made no impression on me, though Wright must have been aware. Until the sixties I succeeded in insulating myself from my society.

During this month we went to Nottingham to spend four or five days with the Darwins, and this brief experience of country house life is clear in my mind. Wright's thesis subject was Erasmus Darwin, grandfather of the much more famous Charles, and Mrs. Darwin, then head of the family, kindly gave him permission to look through family letters. You may be surprised, but I slipped right into the lap of luxury and service like a fish slipping into water—morning tea in bed (the family commented on the fancy the cat took to me, not knowing I gave him milk from my tea every morning), clothes laid out on the bed for you to dress for dinner, your tub run ready to step into, and all the rest of it. I particularly remember that just the moment *before* it occurred to you the afternoon was growing dark the butler came in to draw the shades and light the lamps. We had six meals a day: early morning tea, breakfast, lunch, afternoon tea, dinner, and a tray of beverages such as barley water before we went to bed. This never lifting a finger for yourself had not in any sense made Mrs. Darwin lazy or effete; she expended all the energy her easy life saved her in worthy causes. As an analysis of a World War I British Army captain said of him, she was not democratic; she was the justification of aristocracy. Since we were there to work, she did not have to worry about filling our time, though she took us to see Lincoln Cathedral, and took me to the village school. We met various guests at lunch or dinner, including "a sketching lady from Jamaica." That I should have felt so happy in a way of life you'd think totally alien to me is a tribute to her hospitality and to the quality of the life itself. The return was as great a shock as Cinderella's when the clock struck twelve. The chauffeur left us at Nottingham station, we got into a third class carriage for London, and the dream was over.

We had some pleasant final weeks in Oxford, for luckily we finished at the British Museum and our lodgings were free again for the long Christmas vacation. We had "lunch baskets on the train, cold chicken and salad, so cute," greeted Mrs. Morris, and settled down to a "cosy evening" with the kittens, of whom of course there was a new supply. I now experienced the English winter and learned that the English must drink afternoon tea in order to survive in their climate. The thermometer registered about the same inside and out, say 45. Our only heat was a coal fire in the sitting room where our meals were served, and I'd pick up my plate and rush it to the fire before the food congealed. American ladies were cold, Mrs. Morris truly said, because they didn't wear any underclothes, and I bought long red flannel underwear. Baths were extra in our lodgings, and well they may have been, since Mrs. Morris had to heat teakettles full of water in the kitchen and carry them up three flights of stairs. They barely took the chill off the tin tub, and we weren't brave enough to indulge very often. One of my best memories is going to bed every night, easing my shrinking body gingerly down into sheets apparently freshly wrung out in ice water. Way at the bottom there would be a tiny spot or warmth: a hot water bottle. When my toes touched it, it emitted a glow which gradually spread and spread until I fell asleep in perfect bliss. I couldn't imagine why all my life I had been missing this great pleasure, and I resolved to buy a hot water bottle as soon as I got home. When I did, of course, and used it in a warm room, I realized the pleasure had only come from contrast—the secret of true enjoyment. This is confirmed by my diary entry for January 3: "Such a pleasant evening: fire, kitten, *Unnatural Death*." We discovered Dorothy Sayers and went through everything she had written to date, bringing her back to America long before most people had heard of her. Both in London and in Oxford, I had a Mudie's subscription,[203] tailor-made for me: you paid a month's fee and took out as many books as you wanted, one at a time. I took out a new one every day, including, oddly enough, a mystery where the murder took place in North Hall on the University of Wisconsin campus in Madison, Wisconsin, unmistakably written by someone who knew the locale though I can't remember his name.

There was fog in Oxford, just as there had been in London, but it was white, not black, and I thought the city as lovely in winter as in summer, perhaps even lovelier since with the leaves off the trees the beauty of line of the buildings was even more apparent. There were days of beautiful hoar frost by the river where I walked in the parks, enjoying the green grass, the holly bushes with red berries and green leaves, and the bright small brisk English robins. We had a happy Christmas—the only one I have ever spent outside my own country. *The Oxford Book of Carols* was published that year, and besides carol singing in the streets there were a number of special concerts to celebrate it: one at the town hall where the mayor presided with his chain of office around his neck, another at St. Michael's of the North Gate under a man knighted for his work in community singing during World War I. We went to the traditional Christmas pantomime, *Babes in the Wood*. We bought our own little tree, and an eccentric aged don, Darwin of Denstone, whom we had met in the Bodleian and who came to see us from time to time as he might Iroquois, was much surprised that we had given presents to each other. He had certainly preserved into old age the sense of wonder. The first time we went to tea at his lodgings he showed us his cat with great pride, observing that he knew we would hardly believe that she was already a grandmother, and he never could get over the fact that we had traveled on land *one thousand miles* before we even could get on the ship that brought us to England. It was now that I bought the little wooden figures you remember from each Christmas, the lantern bearers, St. George and the princess and the dragon, Robin Hood and his men, the Canterbury Pilgrims, at the Alley Gift Shop around the corner from our lodgings. Wright was smoking American cigarettes, which were very expensive in England, and he agreed when I suggested I should have the same amount of money to buy things to bring home. Christmas Day itself we went to the service at Christ Church Cathedral, following down the street a don robed in his crimson gown and carrying an umbrella, had noon turkey and plum pudding kindness of Mrs. Morris, and evening turkey and plum pudding kindness of the Wylies, Sir Francis Wylie being the Oxford don

---

203 Charles Edward Mudie (1818–1890), an English publisher whose lending and subscription libraries revolutionized the circulating library movement.

in charge of all the Rhodes scholars. It was a very nice party, with other foreign guests like ourselves, from Germany, Arkansas, and Australia, and in the pudding I got the little money charm, which I carried in my purse for years. It suddenly occurs to me at this writing that now I am Aunt Hannah's legatee—it told the truth!

We sailed for home early in January on the *Aquitania*, having seen Stonehenge as the last sight before sailing. Unlike the midsummer crossing, this was a rough one. "'Nasty lurch that sends everyone back to bed,' says the bath steward, and boat goes all ways at once—seems to stand on its hind legs and wave its front paws in air." She made four to five hundred miles a day. By good luck we came into New York about dusk, which gave me one of the most memorable sights of my life. All the buildings were lighted, every window, for the offices had not yet been closed for the day. Nowhere in Europe had I seen, and nowhere in the world is there to be seen, I think, anything to touch the sight of lighted New York from the water—the buildings are so tall, so strong, and yet so delicate and light. Since then I have several times seen New York from the air, under smog increasing each year, and found it far less impressive. So back to Madison—where our steam-heated apartment and all the other houses too seemed stifling to me not only all the rest of that winter but all the next winter too.

We settled down again, and I particularly settled down to eating half a pound of liver a day, according to Dr. Minot's directions, which I had not always been able to do in England where I wasn't keeping house. This was a very trying diet, as you can imagine. I was given recipes to provide variety, but since I was doing the cooking as well as the eating, the extra time fussing with it in the kitchen seemed more trouble than it was worth, and I stuck to plain broiling. I had a few discouraging set-backs this year and had to go back to the hospital again, though not for very long. Wright brought Euphues to see me once in a basket, and when I was home again Euphues was a great comfort during the tedious times I had to stay immobile in bed. It was easier to get help then, and a student came in and cleaned the apartment once a week. Gradually I improved and increased my activities. Cashing in on our English stay, we sometimes entertained by English breakfasts on Sunday morning: broiled lamb chops, bacon, mushrooms, tomatoes, sausages. As our friends were more and more kept at home by small children, that time for entertaining became unsuitable, but we had some pleasant meals that year, with such people as the Agards, for instance.[204]

In October of 1930 Mr. Thomas died. He left some of his money directly to his children, so that Wright could hereafter count on some income in addition

---

204 Walter R. Agard (1894–1978), a Classics professor at UW-Madison from 1927–1946, taught in the Experimental College (1927–1932) and in the Integrated Liberal Arts (ILS) Studies Program.

to his salary, and he decided to build a house, with the addition of some of mine, which my parents had saved for me and had made over to me when I married. (My father told me with simple frankness that they had never thought anyone would want to marry me so that they had felt it was their responsibility to try to provide for me as well as they could.) If it had been left to me, I probably would have looked for a house in the Heights, where the Quintanas and Grace Hughes and the Curtis and many of my Madison friends live, since that section is the equivalent in Madison of the part of Brookline where I had been brought up. But Wright was much more adventurous, and it is owing to him that you were brought up in what Josephine Tey calls "a beautiful calf country," one of the best gifts a child can have. By several other lucky bits of timing—extending the electric power line to Frost Woods so that it was possible to build a year-round house there, and Ham Beatty's return from his work in Paris with Le Corbusier,[205] anxious for a chance to show what he could do—we built the Frost Woods house where you were all born (figuratively speaking) and where I should like to die.

You know the Beattys well enough so I don't have to describe them, and you can well imagine what a lot of pleasure was ahead of me in the nearly ten years we were next door neighbors. I know no one who produces more euphoria than Ham in any human being he has the most casual contact with, and Gwen and I, Wright said, were cut out of the same cloth. I've always thought of her as Emma thought of Mrs. Weston: "There was not a creature in the world to whom she spoke with such unreserve . . . not any one, to whom she related with such conviction of being listened to and understood, of being always interesting and always intelligible, the little affairs, arrangements, perplexities, and pleasures of her father and herself. . . . Half an hour's uninterrupted communication of all those little matters on which the daily happiness of private life depends, was one of the first gratifications of each."[206] So deep an intimacy can hardly survive thirty years of living apart, but Gwen and I correspond regularly still, and see each other from time to time, and the Beattys contributed to making the first years in Frost Woods one of the happiest times in my life. The friendship was strongly based on Ham's building our house—his first.

Wright showed more courage than I not only in buying land in an unsettled region way out in the country as it then was, but also in giving Ham free rein in building a modern house. If not the very first, it was certainly one of the first of

---

205 Charles-Edouard Jenneret-Gris, known as Le Corbusier (1887–1965), was a Swiss-French architect and urban planner who pioneered in modern architecture. Ham Beatty, Thomas's neighbor and son of English department faculty member Arthur Beatty, studied under Le Corbusier and, with Allen Strang, founded the Beatty and Strang architectural firm and built several modernist homes in the Madison, Wisconsin area.
206 Mrs. Weston is a character in Jane Austen's novel *Emma* (1815).

the type to be built in this part of the country, and it was still several years before most people were to get their first sight of one at the Chicago World's Fair. A lot of TLC went into it. Ham oriented it so it would get the maximum sunlight in winter and minimum in summer by asking the university astronomer, Joel Stebbins, to site it;[207] Mr. Stebbins said he had often been asked to do this for pigpens, but never before for a human dwelling. The window space is thirty-three and a third per cent of the floor space, the requirement then for a model factory but undreamed of for houses. Madison residents, experienced in snow on the roof and icicles in the eaves, were most dubious about the flat roof, which has worked perfectly. It is not completely flat, but slopes slightly to an opening in the center, so that the snow, melting from beneath in contact with the roof, runs off through the house, where it doesn't freeze, through a pipe concealed in the linen closet upstairs and the broom closet downstairs. Ham made one serious mistake from lack of experience, the driveway; but he put into his first house what you put into first love or first teaching, something you never have to give again. The house is light, livable, restful, spacious. The living room is so beautifully proportioned that it looks wonderful when completely empty. I always come into it with a sense of gratitude, and hardly a stranger enters it without expressing interest and admiration. The house has worn well, and is remarkably flexible. When I'm alone in it, I don't rattle around, but it expanded comfortably for my students, for Hannah's wedding, for the Sunday night supper parties for the teaching assistants, even for some years for the reception for the whole Department of English. Because it was a novelty when it was built, it created a lot of interest and people would drive out on good weekends to look at it, their dogs barking from the back seat, and would even get out and peek in the windows. An Art History professor came out to take pictures of it. For a long time I had to keep every room in what with me passes for apple-pie order because our friends wanted to go over all of it—but of course that's true of every new house. Hamilton built his own next door at the same time; it was then very small, and if someone stopped to ask if it were ours, Ham took great pleasure in saying, "The master lives over in the big house, sir," pointing across the lawn. All through the spring we kept driving out to see progress, and each time the sky, the lake, the trees looked more beautiful as the house grew. As warm weather came and Ham took to shorts, he looked about fourteen. I went East before Wright, and we believed that when we came back together the first of September our new home would be ready.

Well, of course it wasn't, and in the course of a long life I have yet to hear of any that does come up to schedule. This was one of the summers the Sharps

---

207 Joel Stebbins (1878–1966), an American astronomer who pioneered in photoelectric photometry, worked at UW-Madison from 1922–1948.

and we were keeping house together at the Island, and since Marie didn't have to start at Katharine Gibbs till the first of October the idea was raised that she and I might stay at the Island together through September. As it turned out, I'm sorry my New England conscience didn't allow me to do it. But I felt I couldn't possibly let Wright go back alone to settle into a new house, so back we came to find that not a bit of mill work—no closets, shelves, book shelves, drawers, cupboards of any kind and in a house with a very unusually large proportion of built-in stuff at that—had been installed. You have no idea how bare a house is under those circumstances. Wright would have been much more comfortable without me, taking a room in town, say! As it was, we moved in and the carpenters knocked together a couple of sticks, on one of which I hung our towels and the other our clothes. We lived in one room while the men worked in another, and then moved into that, cooking meals meanwhile over the fireplace. We're not the first who in desperation moved into a house which was a-building to live with the workmen until they got tired of the owners and moved out. Slowly we made some progress. On October 26 there was something freshly painted for Euphues to step on. Finally the men re-did the floors, which had been finished once but had been ruined by the putting in of the mill work when it finally came, and that night we ate in town, climbed a ladder to our bedroom, and by morning were able to walk down the stairs and cross the living room floor. By the middle of November we were settled enough for Mother to come out for a visit, and she stayed through our first Thanksgiving.

We enjoyed our first entertaining. Carrying on the Beacon Hill Christmas Eve tradition of my girlhood, I gave the first Christmas Eve party for the neighbors with white candles in every window and carols. That year Modern Language Association met at Wisconsin, and we entertained a lot of friends: Miss Snell (as a house guest) and Miss D'Evelyn from Holyoke, Tucker Brooke from Yale, the Craigies (of the great *Oxford Dictionary*),[208] and a number of others. That winter I reached the high point of my social career when we were asked to dinner at President Frank's.[209] I noted the guests were "the governor, two chief justices, the richest man in Wisconsin, the dean, full professors—why were we asked?" We were asked, of course, because Glenn Frank thought Wright one of the most promising young men on his faculty. But Frank's connection with the university ended, and his life ended in tragedy. He was running for governor

---

208 Sir William Alexander Craigie (1867–1957), a prolific Scottish philologist and lexicographer, was a co-editor of the *New English Dictionary* (later retitled *Oxford English Dictionary*) and editor of the *Dictionary of American English*.
209 Glenn Frank (1887–1940), editor of *The Century Magazine*, was president of the University of Wisconsin from 1925–1937 and was instrumental in launching the university's Experimental College (1927–1932).

The Thomas home in Frost Woods, taken in 2013. Source: David Stock.

of Wisconsin, and with a friend, and his only son and only child, was driving Saturday before election to keep a speaking engagement. At ninety miles an hour the car ran into a big pile of sand by the roadside, and Frank and his son were both instantly killed.[210] Poor Mary Frank had been misplaced in Madison all along. She brought her butler with her from New York, who received a good deal of sympathy here on the score of loneliness, since he was the only one in the whole city. On this occasion she called me "just a doll," thirty-five years before the phrase was popular. I don't remember who my dinner partner was—certainly not the governor, for I must have been way below the salt—but I do remember that the dinner was an interminable affair of course after course until I was exhausted doing my best to keep up some conversation with him. I was much happier the next night in my lovely new house in Frost Woods, when we had "stew for dinner" and then went next door to play cards with the Beattys.

---

210 Frank was running for the U.S. senate seat held by Robert La Follette (Cronon & Jenkins, 1994, p. 317).

DOMESTICITY: 1932 TO 1943

The year Tom was at Orlando a hurricane struck the Florida coast and the power was off for four days. Tom wrote, "Everyone else was griping, but I said it was just like the good old days in Frost Woods." The storm went on up the seaboard to Boston and the power was off for two days. Hannah wrote, "Everyone else was griping, but I said it was just like the good old days in Frost Woods." You remembered various adventures, climaxed by a four-day stretch one sweltering August when we cooked all our meals outdoors and carried all our water up from the lake. I was delighted with your letters, since in these days of rapid technological change few parents are able to prepare their children to meet the breakdown of civilization as enjoyably as the Ingalls family made camp for the night.[211] The old days in Frost Woods were good days.

The name simply comes from the Frost family, who originally (that is, after the Indians) owned the land, but we always thought it lucky that it has such attractive connotations. The neighborhood was small and intimate, going back to a much earlier American tradition than the nineteen-thirties. Walter Lionel George ascribes real hospitality, real sociability to the American, defending us from the charge of fraudulent mercantile geniality. "I am not deceived by the reasons for this: the pioneer had not a warmer heart than anybody else; he gave hospitality because in pioneer days he had to give hospitality so as to enjoy it himself when in need. That taught all men hospitality, and much of the tradition stays in the American spirit."[212] When I had to go East suddenly at Mother's death, Hannah stayed at the Maikens and the boys at the Pooleys.[213] When Dick Fredrickson's mother had an operation, he spent two weeks with us. No mother ever knew how exactly how many children would be sitting down to a meal. Tom might stay to dinner with Don Schmitt or Dick Ragsdale, and Alice Stomp spend the night with Hannah. On Hallowe'en the big children had a party at the Ragsdales, the medium ones at the Marshalls, and the little ones here

---

211   A reference to the family in the *Little House on the Prairie* children's novels by Laura Ingalls Wilder (1867–1957), who was born in Wisconsin and spent her childhood in the Midwest.

212   Walter Lionel George (1882–1926) was an English writer known for his popular fiction, wrote a six-part series titled "Hail, Columbia!" for *Harper's Magazine*, volume 142 (December 1920-May 1921); the quotation above is taken from the February issue ("The American Scene," pp. 300–314).

213   Robert C. Pooley (1898–1978) taught English and Education courses at UW-Madison from 1931–1968 and conducted pioneering research in English usage alongside fellow faculty member Sterling Andrus Leonard (1888–1931).

Domesticity

with Setzie [Pooley] and me. Ruth Wallerstein,[214] coming out for the night with me, would get a ride out with Ham Beatty and a ride back with E. A. Thomas (the Wrong Thomases, since we were the Wright ones). If a car wouldn't start, a neighbor drove its owner in or out, as the case might be. We had car pools for Sunday school while you children were going to day school at Nichols, which was walking distance, and for Wisconsin High later when you went there. In our isolation we could hardly have managed without this interchange, but those of us who came here to live were temperamentally inclined to find it congenial.

When we first came to Frost Woods, the Owens' was the only house here.[215] For twenty years they had had a summer cottage which they used from spring vacation to Thanksgiving, taking an apartment in Madison for the winter. But when the electric power line was extended, year-round houses became possible. It was very good luck that we were looking for a place to build (Wright's share of his father's estate had just come in) at the same time that Ham Beatty came back from his year with Le Corbusier looking for a client brave enough to let him put his then revolutionary ideas, such as a flat roof, into effect. The Winspears were the first to build and got into their house in the spring of '31;[216] the Wheelers built next to them but within a few years moved back to Canada and sold the house to Colonel Garey. Neither of these houses was Ham's. In the summer, though, he built our house and his; and gradually during the decade the E. A. Thomases, the Pooleys, the Fulchers, Miss Cronin and Miss Meyer, the Ragsdales, and Miss Heath became his clients and our neighbors. We all had our own wells and our own septic tanks. A stock entry in my diary was "burned up the garbage"—very difficult for such things as cauliflower stalks and melon rinds—which never ceased to prey on my mind, since it had been so easy and pleasant at the Island[217] to throw it to the gulls—another delightful old custom now unhappily obsolete. Wright's first idea on garbage was to give it to near-by farmers for their pigs, as had been done in Texas, but these Wisconsin pigs were on a scientifically weighted and measured diet and turned up their noses at

---

214 Ruth Wallerstein (1893–1958), educated at Bryn Mawr and University of Pennsylvania, joined the English department in 1920 and taught English literature until her untimely death in an automobile accident in England while on research leave.

215 Ray Sprague Owen (1878–1967) earned a degree in civil engineering from UW-Madison (1904), served in WWI, and returned to UW-Madison as a professor of Topographical Engineering. He surveyed much of the land outside Madison.

216 Alban Dewes Winspear (1899–1973), a Rhodes Scholar at Oxford (1926), was a Classics professor at UW-Madison (1927–1942). He resigned from Wisconsin to direct the Abraham Lincoln School for Workers, a labor institute in Chicago. He later founded and taught in the Classics department at the University of Calgary (1957–1970).

217 A reference to Isle of Springs, an island community located in BoothBay Harbor, Maine, where the family spent summer vacations.

it. We dug a garbage pit across the street, and the top caved in. I wish we had known about the compost heap.

"Where we walk to school each day/ Indian children used to play." Ray Owen was fond of saying that Hannah was the first white child born in Frost Woods. He had seen a new-born Indian baby in a tent in what is now the park strip between our house and the Marshalls, whose father told him they had come back so the child could be born here on tribal land, where he himself, his father, and his father's father had been born before him. But that baby never came back to have his son born here. I am sure you will remember all the Indian mounds in the woods, though we had none on our land, and I still have arrowheads we found when we started plowing up the garden. You may not remember the all-neighborhood pot-latch on the Island, where Mrs. Brown, who was an expert, told us Indian legends, but you may remember the Whitehorse children at the Nichols school.[218]

The village of Monona (now a city) then had a population of a little over a thousand and was in process of changing from farms to suburb. I used to worry about your walking to school in the hunting season since there were so many cornfields on the way where hunters still, though illegally, appeared. One day a man shot at Cellophane [the cat], thinking she was a fox, and she rushed home with her tail as big as a fox's. Before going to bed, sometimes at dusk you and I would all take a brisk run up Owen Road, across the top, and down Frost Woods Road, without seeing a house but our own and the Beattys. This was before the roads were named, I think. The first time we came out to look at the land the side road was so muddy we got stuck and Ray Owen had to push us out. Our mail box was way at the end of Winnequah, on Bridge Road, so I didn't see the mail till Wright brought it when he came home at night. In this small community we took our civic responsibilities very seriously, went to all village and school meetings, ran for office, and served as PTA officers and Girl Scout leaders. I was very pleased to be elected PTA secretary, particularly since I was nominated not by a Frost Woods neighbor, but by Mrs. Griffiths, a native who lived down beyond the Black Bridge.

Frost Woods from the beginning had its own sewing circle, which met weekly. Everyone came every time she could (if she wasn't having a baby or if some of the children weren't sick) and we talked "woman talk." I used to fancy the meetings were like those of the Roman women to worship the Bona Dea, meetings from which men were excluded on pain of death. The hostess baked her own refreshments in those pre-mix and pretty much pre-diet days ("very busy

---

218 Potlatch, a term used by many indigenous peoples, refers to gift-giving feast held to honor major events. In the "World War II" chapter, Thomas mentions the term used for gatherings in the Frost Woods community.

baking for Sewing Circle; not very successful angel cake, hermits" or nut bread or casserole fruit cake or whatever), and the tipple was tea. Afternoon teas were a very common mode of entertainment in those days (the cocktail party fortunately not yet having been invented), particularly for visiting mothers, of whom in our experience there were a good many: Mrs. Wallerstein, Mrs. McQueary (Janet's [Quintana's] mother), Mrs. Quintana, mine, and many others. Frost Woods was predominantly English in the early days anyway. Gwen, Canadian born, had gone to live permanently in England at three. The older Beattys had come from Canada. The Winspears were English and the Wheelers Canadian. Mary Winspear kindly indulged the American neighbors in their quaint habit of taking lemon in tea as long as they didn't waste any by leaving cut-up bits on the lemon plate, and I indulged her by eating them all up and taking hot lemonade rather than tea, the way I prefer it anyhow. With the national self-confidence, the English women no more gave in to the local custom of calling a spring flower a primrose when it wasn't an English primrose than the traditional Empire-builder dressing for dinner each night in the wilds of the African jungle ever gave in to the weakness of adapting himself to the society he was living in. Through these years I went in regularly to take my turn serving at the English Department daily afternoon teas in 361 Bascom.

At first there were only a handful of houses, and lots and lots of woods to roam in, and even as the neighborhood grew, it grew so slowly that new neighbors at once became old friends. In fact we were too woodsy for Mrs. Norg, the wife of the Executive Director of the Boy Scouts of Madison, who came here from Chicago with their two daughters, near Hannah's age. They rented the Strang house a couple of blocks up from Winnequah in the woods and it seemed so lonely to the poor city-bred woman that she drew all her curtains at night against the trees (where she probably imagined wild Indians were lurking) and they moved in town next fall. Of course I loved the woods, and spent a lot of time in them first while I was alone, and then with you as you all came along. The fall of '31 was the time of finishing up the house, the spring of '32 the landscaping of the grounds (which sounds highly pretentious). Apr 21: "Nice and warm. Everyone out gardening, even to Richard and Euphues." We put grass in the front yard and watched it devotedly. (Once reason we bought these lots was that the front space was already cleared, so we didn't have to cut down any trees. The red maples we planted ourselves.) Apr. 30: "first sight of grass, barely visible at eye level." May 2: "watered spring grass." May 3: "rainy; grass improving hourly." Ham and Wright moved small elms across the road and spaced them around Bill's present land, unconscious of the Dutch elm disease to come, to which the two elms Ham put close to his house have already fallen victim. Mr. Beatty [Sr.] knew so much about trees that he could identify them in the winter, before the leaves were out, by their bark, which impressed me. He helped the men put in the lilac hedge. We left the back yard pretty much of a jungle, because we wanted to go through a whole year to see what was already growing wild. The present park-like effect is the result of the installation of the Madison Metropolitan Water and Sewage system through all the yards along the lake, in the forties. In the early days we had a rough and ready tennis court where the black-top parking lot is now. Wright was neighborhood champion, beating Alban Winspear for the title, and we all got in some games, the women often doubles during the day while the children watched. But since the court faced due west it was bad in the evening, and it was gradually abandoned as the men turned more and more to vegetable gardens, most of them on our land across the street, virgin soil and open all day to sun, which we had plowed and harrowed by a farmer every spring. As Ham Beatty said, he understood now why so few farmers installed tennis courts.

You and I were outdoors as much as possible all through the beautiful changing cycle of the year. We'd ride down early with Wright as far as I could push the baby carriage back or as far as you could walk back. ("Hannah very good but would take off her mittens.") She and I would ride over with Gwen to get Richard when he went to nursery school in Maple Bluff. But most of the time we ranged the neighborhood on foot. On a cold winter day ("Tommy says, 'There's frosting on the windows'—I seem to have recorded very few bright sayings from your childhoods but at least there's one") we'd walk down beyond the island to see the men cutting ice on the lake, and except for the main road no wheels or feet had left prints to spoil "little squirrel, rabbit, bird prints in snow." After spectacular ice storms when "you could skate on the driveway, the lawn, the road," it was too dangerous to walk on the road, but we could slide down the Pooley's hill on boxes and see the flashing jeweled trees. The hoar frost was as lovely but quieter: the smallest dried umbrella made visible in its shape and the trees like great grey bouquets against the sky. We watched for the breaking up of the ice in the bay on the first fresh spring days that make the long Wisconsin winter worth living through; for the gulls on their way north, "flying and crying like the Island"; for the robins ("snowing heavily; saw poor robin on branch like Christmas card") until there were so many we no longer bothered to count them; for the springing of the bright yellow color in the raining-down branches of the willows, as sunny as forsythia; for the green spangles shining on the crabapples in the light spring rains. Robins nested on the window sills, where in domestic comfort inside we had a perfect view of the whole process: building the nest, lining it with mud, shaping it by sitting down and turning the rump round and round, taking a full day's vacation—who could blame the mother for the breather?—, and then the laying of one blue egg each day for four days. Do you remember the day which was certainly the most suspenseful of my whole life? A pair of robins had built on the sill in the boys' room in the addition and successfully hatched three baby birds (we never knew what happened to the fourth egg). They had been hopping up and down a little outside the nest, and we knew they would fly soon. One morning early first one little bird and then another left the nest for the last time, but the third was timid. Time and again the parents patiently flew by, swooping down to show him how easy it was; he seemed ready to go any minute, and we all were fixed to the spot to see him; but still he couldn't go. I rushed to the kitchen to improvise lunch and rushed it back to you afraid I had missed the flight. But not until nearly five did he finally grow up and fly into the world. Turtles came up from the lake to lay their eggs in the freshly spaded flower bed; once I held an umbrella over Hannah in a spring shower for thirty minutes so she could see the whole process of the turtle digging the hole, laying the eggs, and plastering them over with mud. When the little turtles hatched, they were ideal presents for a sick child who had to be kept quiet in bed. The Baltimore oriole sang by day and the whippoorwill moaned by night. Wild flowers came up in the woods: bloodroot, the round fairy rings of mayapple, whose tiny water-lily-like flowers I floated in a shallow bowl (the only exception I know to the general rule that flowers look best in arrangements with their own leaves), trillium, shooting stars, wild phlox, wild geraniums. Oddly enough, at first we had no trout lilies at all; but to my great pleasure they made a steady peaceful takeover of our land from the Beattys' and are now moving beyond me into the park. Wright, who had had plenty of actual gardening experience, put in flowers and vegetables, and by June I was picking sweet peas. Never before had I had the enjoyment of having both garden and wild flowers to pick and arrange. The yard was at its best in May, with apple trees, pink wild crabs, yellow roses, white and purple lilacs; and since the living room calls for big vase arrangements this was its best time too, with pink and lavender and yellow tulips added to the big sprays of the shrubs. As the new maples grew, I had their bronze leaves and yellow honey-sweet flowers. In the summer Sally Marshall taught you all to swim, and on hot nights you could run down for a last dip before you came back straight to your beds.[219] Gwen and I cut up fruit together for midsummer jam. We picked and preserved raspberries, currants, and grapes (some of the latter still survive as Bill knows) on the fruits we put in across the road, and elderberries and wild grapes took thirty-five years before Euell Gibbons.[220] We gathered the hickory nuts which are so much

---

219 Sally Owen Marshall, daughter of Ray Owen, was one of three students who in 1931 helped form the Wisconsin Hoofers, a group of outdoor recreational clubs operated by the Wisconsin Union Directorate at UW-Madison.

220 Euell Gibbons (1911–1975), an American outdoorsman and writer who promoted natural diets.

more fun to pick up outdoors than to crack. Almost every day through Indian summer Gwen and her children and you and I ate our lunch in the back yard, soaking in every ray of the serene sun which was moving inexorably south. The leaves fell, and the men raked and burned them—another enjoyable custom now obsolete. No longer can we say with Stevenson "Sing a song of seasons/ Something bright in all./ Flowers in the summer/ Fires in the fall."[221] The bay skimmed over; then it froze over, and everyone went skating. It was cosy indoors and the fireplaces burned through the long winter evenings. The neighbors began to drop in for singing, and before long we were practicing the carols we would sing on Christmas Eve, when I lighted the house with white candles, bringing to my home in the Midwest the custom from Beacon Hill which had given me some of my loveliest memories. We were rather short on women singers, but had good "lusty men's voices." I can still hear John Marshall trolling "Wassail, wassail" (rather ironically since the mulled cider wasn't spiked)[222] and Ham caroling his favorite "Eia, eia."[223] If we were lucky, the snow lay deep and white outside and a moon drew the black stripes of tree trunks across it. As you grew older, we marked the cycle of the year with all the holiday accompaniments: dyeing Easter eggs and hunting for them out of doors (when possible; once "Bill brought in a dead mouse"); making Valentines; picking the first green leaves—it was often too early for flowers—and hanging May baskets; making the family mass-production Christmas card; making Christmas favors and presents and cookies. December 24 was the neighborhood delivery day for presents.

All of you were born during this time: October 1932, June 1935, October 1938. No mother ever wanted children more than I did or was happier when she discovered she was pregnant. I'm not an intuitive mother like Margaret Lacy,[224] and I never was particularly drawn to small children, like Frances Sturgis, who always had a baby in her arms at the Island. Your Aunt Hannah loves little children. Once when she was visiting and Hannah was about a year old, the two were playing outdoors with an acorn, rolling it across our picnic table, which has a hole in the center; it would fall through the hole, of course, Aunt Hannah would pick it up, and both Hannahs would laugh and laugh. Perhaps three times would have been my limit, but they both seemed happy for hours. I know

---

221 A reference to Robert Louis Stevenson's "Autumn Fires," from the collection *A Child's Garden of Verses* (1885).
222 John Marshall is Sally Owen Marshall's husband.
223 The name of this early German carol is "From Heaven High, O Angels, Come."
224 Margaret Swanson Lacy (1923–2014) married UW-Madison English professor and Freshman English director Ed Lacy in 1952, whom she met while enrolled in the UW-Madison English Ph.D. program. She earned the Ph.D. in 1956, raised three children, and taught at UW-Madison following her husband's untimely death in 1981.

how sweet the small baby can be, and I loved my babies (when I got home after Bill was born, I noted "Seems lovely to have a little baby again"). But I never wanted to prolong babyhood for any of you, and I was always glad as you grew. This may be all for the best, since the four of us seem to be having a good many years together as adults. I intensely wanted children. Dr. Harris had tried to reconcile me to the idea that I could never bear my own, and had suggested adoption. But we decided to wait another year or two before taking that step, and it proved unnecessary.

No one can tell how a woman will feel during pregnancy. Some people—I think the majority of my friends, very strikingly Janet, who never looked so beautiful, and Gwen feel at their best throughout. I had what Dr. Harris called an ordinary pregnancy: three months when I felt nauseated and generally miserable, three months when I felt wonderful ("You'll have more energy than you'll know what to do with," he said), and three months when I felt heavy and awkward. Since I have always had poor teeth, pregnancy of course put a particular strain on them, and I spent a disproportionate amount of time in the dentist's chair. But my first pregnancy was for me a remarkable emotional experience, especially because it had been put off for so long and because I had feared I could never have it at all. As I began to get over the nausea of the first three months, spring was at its best; and I shall never forget the beatitude of lying outdoors, basking in the sun, feeling that I was protecting and nourishing life within me. Planned parenthood seems to me thoroughly admirable; but the strident shrieks of Women's Lib against motherhood seem to me to deny physiological fact. There can be no other example of fulfillment as complete as a pregnant woman; she can feel that every act conscious or unconscious, every breath she draws, every bit of food she eats, everything, is creating; body and soul together the woman can be fully absorbed in the business of creating, and I was always aware of it. Physically, for anyone with my past medical history, pregnancy, fulfilling the physical function I as a woman was made for, was a tremendous benefit; emotionally it was an equal benefit. Instead of having whims and fancies and maladjustments, which used to appear in rather dubious fiction, I had never felt so peaceful and happy. I thought at the time that even if I lost the baby, I should feel grateful to have had the experience of the pregnancy. I told Dr. Harris if there were any question of saving my life or the baby's, it should be the baby's. (Could I have been reading *The Forsyte Saga*?)[225] With his sterling common sense he pointed out that the baby couldn't get along without me anyway for the first seven months so we'd better not worry about it. As with Dr. Weston, I was very

---

225 *The Forsyte Saga*, a series of novels published between 1906 and 1921 by John Galsworthy (1867–1933), a Nobel Prize-winning British author.

Domesticity

lucky with Dr. Harris. He inspired confidence. Every month I'd make out a list of things to ask him about; then at the appointment he'd tell me about delivering a baby on a train with nothing but a red string from a candy box to tie off the umbilical cord; or what happened to a cousin of his who learned to drive while pregnant, wrapped her car around a telephone pole, and walked away without a scratch and no harm to the baby; and it never seemed worthwhile even to bring my problems up. With my previous blood history, I was his second most interesting patient, he told me; the first was a woman who had combined pregnancy with psittacosis. Highly distinguished in his profession—he came here from Johns Hopkins to head the OB Department at Wisconsin General—he was not just overweight, but obese. The last time I saw him before Bill was born, I dropped my car keys; he and I looked at each other, it being equally difficult for either of us to get down on the floor and pick them up. As a woman, however, I had the experience no man ever has of regaining the youth and agility I had lost. In those days it was also a pleasure to get back to ordinary clothes; nowadays maternity clothes are so pretty that no prospective mother minds, but then they were hideous. The only place in Madison which carried maternity clothes was Manchester's, and they were hidden in an obscure corner of the basement as if the store was ashamed of them, as well it might have been.[226] The only thing I could get was a wraparound dress of a particularly repulsive shade of dirty green, which would have rendered unattractive a raving beauty, which I never was.

There's a little story about the birthday of each one of you. Hannah was a little football baby (which really would have been more appropriate for Bill). I went to the hospital the morning of the first game of the season, and heard the band go past up University Avenue while I was waiting, and hoped that when it came back I would know whether the baby would play football or be taken to watch the games. When Tom was born, I went to the hospital in the morning but the pains decreased and Dr. Harris sent me home. Gary Cooper, an actor I have always admired and a physical type I've always had a predilection for, was playing in *Lives of a Bengal Lancer*. It didn't look as if I'd have much time for movies in the near future, so Wright and I went in to see it that evening, and as the torture scenes progressed my labor pains returned, and we went to the hospital from the theater (after the end of the movie, of course) without going home. On Tom's nineteenth birthday he took me to see Gary Cooper in *High Noon*; and Cooper was as attractive as he'd been nineteen years before—or as Tom was by my side. For Bill I went to the hospital on Columbus Day; the intern suggested that if I would wait over till the next morning the baby could be born on

---

226 Manchester's Department Store, located in downtown Madison on Capitol Square, operated from the 1920s to the 1970s and was known for its tea room and white-gloved elevator operators.

the anniversary of the first use of general anesthetic at Massachusetts General. But I said that would be very nice of course if the child turned out to be a doctor, but we couldn't be sure, and Columbus Day would be a good birthday for any profession. But you can't be sure of anything, and now through the rewriting of history to create Monday holidays, Bill's birthday and Columbus Day will only occasionally coincide.

All through my first pregnancy I wondered what giving birth would be like. I looked at all the women I knew who had had children, and they looked just as they always had. How could they pass through such an experience without showing it? Well, if they could, probably I could too. Dr. Harris told me childbirth is the greatest pain a woman experiences and the one she forgets most quickly. He was right. The morning of Hannah's first day of life I told Wright I was quite ready to do it over again. Some women may take a little longer than that to forget—say a week. Before she was born I sometimes was afraid I might think of her as an extension of myself instead of a person in her own right. But the moment I looked at her I knew that was just silly. She was unmistakably herself.

Though "if" is always futile, it would have been easier if Tom had been the first child; he was better equipped than Hannah to be learned on, so to speak. Hannah was three weeks early, weighed only six pounds, and had infant eczema so badly she was smeared with coal tar most of her first year "like a nigger baby or a coal miner." She was a feeding problem and had crying fits at night. All these problems I intensified by my inexperience and worry. Wright was marvelously patient and sweet with her always. Tommy was full-term, weight eight pounds, and slept and ate like the model in a book for mothers. I had enough milk for some months to give him all his food; with both Hannah and Bill I had to use supplementary feedings, which combined the disadvantages of both systems but which I continued a long time because I didn't want to give up the nursing myself. June is a good birthday month with summer coming up. Jan Marshall had been born six months earlier, and John Hamel three. Sally was taking care of both babies while Merle finished the work for her MD, and she would bring them over and we would give the three babies sunbaths together on the front lawn, their heads in the shade of the tall hollyhocks.[227] Tom turned over phenomenally early, and as a baby was perfection. I remembered his first year as the happiest of my life. I had completely forgotten until I read my diary that two weeks after we came home from the hospital I ran a temperature of 106, was delirious, and had to go back with him for two more weeks—which doesn't sound like a happy interlude. I had also nearly forgotten the bad attacks of croup he had his first couple years, though now I remember clearly springing out of

---

227 Merle Owen Hamel (1910–1966), daughter of Ray Owen. John Hamel was her son.

bed at the sound of his first labored breath and carrying him to the bathroom to turn on the hot shower, and the repeated times of keeping him in a steam tent, once for sixty hours straight. On the worst attack he had to go to the hospital, and Wright had to spend the night there, to be on hand to give permission if an emergency operation was required. One of the nurses on that floor had nursed me after my operation, and could not at first believe he was my own child. The most painful thing of all was that I couldn't see him, since it upset him too much to have me go away, so that Wright had to take me in at night to look in the door at him after he was asleep. It is remarkable what you forget. God's—or Nature's—kindest gift to man, I think, is that we remember the pleasures and forget the pains of the past. Perhaps my memory is really truer than the factual truth. On the whole, Tom and Bill unquestionably were strong healthy children, and of course my experience with Hannah profited her brothers.

This may be the forgetfulness I've just spoken of, but I'm not aware of any jealousy on Hannah's part when Tom came, or on Tom's when Bill did. As I said, Jan Marshall and John Hamel were born before Tom, and Hannah and I had gone over various times in the spring to see them have their baths and their bottles. I think Hannah was very pleased to have a baby of her own in her own house. At that time there was a big porch on the front of Wisconsin General, shaded by magnificent elms, so that in good weather mothers could be wheeled out there, and the older children could come to visit. Hannah came, "much pleased with big balloon," and had a lot of fun pushing my wheel chair. The nurses warned me not to be disappointed if my child didn't recognize me, which they said often happened, but she was too bright not to know her own mother. When I came home, she stood by while Tom had his bath, ready to put her doll in the bath water as soon as I took her baby brother out. And I'm sure both children were delighted with Bill and his distinctive red hair. It is the first child who revolutionizes the parents' lives; after that each addition to the family circle is taken in stride. My mother told me if I had one child it would take all my time, and if I had six children it would take all my time. As usual she was right.

The fall of '35 Hannah was enrolled at the University Nursery School. Its main purpose was to furnish an observation laboratory for students, who watched the children through one-way glass, came to their homes to interview parents, and prepared the lunches.[228] (Of all the cases of sheer nerve I've known in my life, the sheerest is the girl who said "Isn't it lucky *you* got it?" when I lifted to my lips the glass she had just poured and a thumbtack fell out. Of course she meant it was lucky I got it instead of a child who might have swallowed it, but I

---

228 This experimental program, which included nursery and elementary school, became known in 1937 as the Laboratory School and was regarded as highly successful (Cronon & Jenkins, 1994, p. 766).

must say my own impulse would have been apology rather than congratulation.) In addition, however, it was an attempt to educate parents in taking the first faltering steps to the permissiveness that Dr. Spock has achieved in seven-league boots.[229] Parents were required to go to two evening meetings every month, and each mother had to work all morning at the school seven days a semester. This was very inconvenient for those who had younger children at home, and I found it pretty trying. The teachers, Miss Newsome and Miss Roberts, were very nice girls and especially good to Hannah, who was shy. I had them out to dinner a number of times, sometimes combining this with their speaking at the Nichols PTA, of which I was now program chairman. But I never completely got over a feeling of resentment at their calm certainty when it seemed to me they had little sense of reality when it came to family life. At 5 p.m. they were through with work for the day and probably taking a relaxing bath in preparation for dressing for a date. Even with all that forgetfulness does for me, I still don't like to think about the hour from 5 to 6 during this period. The baby would be yelling (we were still following fixed feeding schedules), Hannah and Tommy would be fighting, Hannah complaining I spoiled Tommy because he was younger, Tommy that I spoiled Hannah because she was older. Wright would arrive after a hard day at the office. And there was still the baby to feed and get to bed, and dinner to get, and get through. (I've always been in the habit of saying that I did have one qualification for motherhood, which was that I was by nature an early riser; but it occurs to me now that unlike Edna St. Vincent Millay I was unable to burn the candle at both ends and wasn't at my best by late afternoon.) Even today there seems to be an element of artificiality about nursery school, since the children are about the same age, and a chronologically homogeneous group is a far cry from a real-life family, where almost all the problems—and all the continued accusations of unfairness—arise from the different interests and abilities of differing ages. In my own childhood, I had been a quiet, precocious child of elderly parents, with my nose always in a book, and it had given me no preparation at all for the real thing. Even at the worst, though, I was conscious that being an only child had been a great disadvantage to me and that the fact that there were three of you was the best thing in the world for you. The Reading Group was a great comfort to me since we were all young mothers and shared the same problems, and an even greater comfort in the next decade as the problems, so to speak, grew up. We were also very fortunate in our family

---

229 Benjamin McLane Spock (1903–1998), known as Dr. Spock, is an American pediatrician and political activist whose enormously popular *The Common Sense Book of Baby and Child Care* (1946) advocated a non-mainstream approach to parenting (e.g., encouraging increased flexibility with and affection for children) that has been criticized as promoting permissiveness and instant gratification.

doctor, Dr. Weston (good old), who had six children of his own and therefore had firsthand acquaintance already with anything any of you could possibly come up with. A realist if there ever was one, and a man of sound values, when he found Katrina on the bed with Tom he knew she was being a comfort and no fussy idea of dogs carrying fleas or germs even entered his mind. During this period of development of miracle drugs, he held the very sound view—verified over and over again today—that you should let Nature take its course and use as few drugs as possible. How many times something like this telephone conversation took place! "I think Hannah is coming down with bubonic plague, Dr. Weston," I would say. "Well," he would say. "I'll tell you. Let her ride and call me in the morning." Hannah would get a good night's sleep because there was nothing wrong with her; I would get a good night's sleep because I had relieved my conscience; Dr. Weston would get a good night's sleep (though I'm grateful to him for a lot of house calls he did make when there was reason to); and I didn't bother to telephone in the morning.

I might digress here for a paragraph on pets, of whom we had a series. As a cat-lover myself, I started my married life in Hawthorne Court with Euphues, the "golden legacy" the Paynes had given us from the lineage of their honey-colored Melissa. In Frost Woods we had a series of dogs and cats, and I'd recommend the cat-dog combination to any family. Our pairs always enjoyed each other, though an incumbent dog welcomed a new kitten more quickly than an incumbent cat welcomed a new puppy. Tony Weller, Euphues' successor, loved to sit on the arm of the davenport and play with the waving tail of the police dog Sam. (I don't think there was much appropriateness about those names; they were just Dickensian.) In a letter to Gwen in the hospital, I wrote that Fatima has just come in "with her tail as big as her waist measure" from playing outdoors with Sam, so she was the second cat while we had him. I think the name was because she was smoke-colored, from a World War I song which went "Ashes to ashes and dust to dust, If the Camels don't get you, the Fatimas must"[230] which now seems remarkably prophetic. After Sam was shot we had a series of cockers, all very agreeable if not very bright, and the main incumbent cat was the beautiful Cellophane, whom I'm sure you do remember. All the cats hastily learned where "sanctuary" was—the ledge between dining room and living room, and not only enjoyed looking down on us haughtily but knew as well as you that they were untouchable there. My most beautiful cat was Charis (named for the Ben Jonson poem, "Oh how white, oh how soft, oh how sweet is she"), a lovely white cat showing her Persian blood, with smutches of black and

---

230 This ragtime song, called "Good Morning Mr. Zip-Zip-Zip!," was popular among U.S. soldiers during World War I.

Domesticity

yellow.[231] I've forgotten which one used to go upstairs every night to sit on the edge of the bathtub, knowing I would come up and run the tub and get in, so she could dabble her paw in it and play with the water. My longest-lived cat and the companion of my declining years is Mewa (Polish for seagull because of the seagull's mewing cry), who is going on sixteen.

In 1938 I felt the urge to write, which I am now indulging at leisure, and started an autobiography addressed to Hannah with the avowed purpose of bridging what we hadn't then learned to call the generation gap, which I didn't have time to finish until 1940. Since some of it now sounds pretty phony and embarrassingly suggestive of the letters Christina addresses to her children for posthumous reading in *The Way of all Flesh*, I shall tear it up, but it has been very useful for this version.[232] At the end of the long gray winter of '71–72, Kathy says all her friends are depressed, complaining, and overworked. At least in the American culture, the children's early years seem to be a hectic period for the young mother at any period you want to name. I'll take without censorship two long paragraphs from my 1940 version.

> I have always worked hard. Yesterday, for example, chosen purely at random, Bill woke up at 5 a.m. From 5 to 8 I dovetailed doing the week's washing and getting it out on the line with getting breakfast, seeing that you children get up and dressed (this is the time you have a broken arm so I have to dress you too), and seeing that you ate breakfast and that everyone got smoothly off to school. From 8 to 9 I made the beds and washed the dishes and cleaned out the dining room cupboard. At 9 I took you in town to the hospital to have the cast taken off your arm, and when I got you back to school it was time to get Tommy's lunch and read to him before he went to kindergarten. I then got Bill to bed (he had been at nursery school in the morning) and, I confess, lay down myself for half an hour. I then got up, took in and folded up the washing, washed the spinach for dinner, got the other things in the oven, and it was time to pick up Bill, get you and Tommy from school, and take you in town to see the orthodontist. We got home in time to get dinner on the table; after dinner I gave the boys their baths and put them to bed, did the same

---

231   The poem is "A Celebration of Charis: IV. Her Triumph" (1640), and the actual line is "Oh so white! Oh so soft! Oh so sweet is she!"

232   *The Way of All Flesh* (1903), a semi-autobiographical novel by Samuel Butler (1835–1902) attacking Victorian-era hypocrisy.

for you, and spent the evening at the Nursery School meeting to which mothers are required to go and which, with my third child in school, has long lost any novelty for me. I got to bed about 10:30, a nineteen-hour working day, and a strenuous one at that. You may say that there were extra things, and so there were: of course you don't have the cast taken off your arm every day; but there are always extra things of one kind or another. I started this autobiography, you may notice, over two years ago, and I honestly have not had enough sustained time to finish it until the spring. Alice—you may wonder what she does do—works two afternoons a week and Saturday mornings, and does the dishes at night;[233] that gives me a chance to go in town to the dentist for myself and my shopping and my friends and so on. There is always a good deal of work; when babies are little there is formula, sterilizing, feedings every four hours, washing every day; when the children are at the run-about stage it is impossible to do anything while they are around but keep them from getting into mischief; for a long time I got up at 5 to do the washing because before Bill was up was the only time I could get anything done. Now that he is in nursery school, I have mornings free, except when Tommy's friends come here to play (Tommy was at kindergarten at Nichols, an afternoon one); but the rest of you are getting along so that I do the washing and cooking for a family of six[234]—you are eating like an adult now, I should rather say two or three adults, and Tommy not far behind—and at that I send out sheets and shirts! If I did what Tommy wanted, I would read to him twelve hours a day—you read to yourself now, and Bill is too little for reading, but a year or so ago you were just as greedy for reading as Tommy is, and Bill will be in another year, I have no doubt. The broken nights are the worst. I like to sleep, I like to go to bed early, and have a long night; but for years I have barely had an uninterrupted night; I could literally count them on the fingers of one hand. You have very largely outgrown your crying fits, which were one of the great distresses of my life; but for months and years whenever I went to bed I knew that I would be waked out of

---

233 Alice Case Ream, a nursing student who lived with the Thomas family during the war years.
234 This number includes Alice as part of the family.

sleep one, two, as many as five times by your crying and that I would have to get up and do the best I could—sometimes entirely unavailingly—to soothe you. Bill often wakes at 4:30, though thank heaven he is outgrowing that now. Then there are no night or early morning feedings, there is training, and you either have to get up out of sound sleep or sit up till the proper time to pick up the child and take him to the bathroom. I have said nothing about illness, which is hardest of all for me. Some women are "born nurses"; I am not. My own hospital experience fortunately has given me a lot of experience as a patient, with the double advantage of teaching me sympathy and some tricks of making people comfortable—making a bed with the patient in it, hospital bath, and so on. But my weakest point as a mother is that I am a poor nurse. And any mother has a lot of calls on her nursing ability. This year, for instance, from the time that you came home from school with chicken pox in Thanksgiving to the middle of May when you are still wearing your arm in a sling we have had only one week when everyone was well. That is, of course, unusual; but every winter means a streak of colds and flu, in spite of our vitamins and capsules and Irradol.[235] Tommy has frightful attacks of croup and it takes time to pass things around in a family of six. Perhaps you will remember this past Christmas when Wright—who had chicken pox in his youth—left for Boston for the Modern Language Association meeting at 8:30, on Christmas morning, leaving behind him three members of the family in quarantine, of whom one was myself. This has again been an unusual year because Wright has been working so very hard on his book,[236] which the Oxford University Press brings out this spring, that he has given literally no time to the family at all, and he has usually worked every evening, into the small hours of the morning, in town at his office.

I'll come back to this paragraph later, which I have chosen for another reason beside the piling up of household detail. (Did you notice that in those days spinach didn't come pre-washed? And of course frozen vegetables had not been

---

235 Irradol-A was a molasses-like vitamin syrup given to children in the 1930s and 1940s.
236 *Reading Poems: An Introduction to Critical Study*, published by Oxford University Press in 1941, was co-authored by Wright Thomas and Stuart Gerry Brown.

invented.) The chicken pox episode was the one that convinced me how valuable it was to get childish diseases over in childhood—which very fortunately I had done for everything else. We all four had it, but you quite lightly (though Bill had six soda baths in one day to reduce the itching); but I was very sick and "loathsomely spotted." I lay all night unable to sleep in a soda bath reading *For Whom the Bell Tolls,* which I noted was "a great mistake as a bedside book." On December 31, I went out of the house for the first time in twenty-three days, to go to the dentist.

The second paragraph is "a little chat on traveling with children."

> This is a field with great tragic possibilities in literature, a field unexplored, as far as I know, barely scratched by Robert Benchley.[237] He describes traveling once from Philadelphia to Boston with a man who started with three tiny tots; at New York there were two tiny tots; at Springfield one; at Boston none. But, says Benchley, nobody asked him what had become of them. It seemed kinder to say nothing. Since my family lives in Boston and Wright's in Texas and we in Wisconsin, I have certainly had more than my share of dragging children over the continent; and never have I been on a train with any one of you that other women have not looked at me with sympathetic comprehension in their eyes and come up to me and said they never could forget taking little Susie to California when she was nine months, or going to Alaska when the three boys were little, or traveling from Honolulu when Betty came down with the measles. We look into each other's eyes and for the moment we are sisters. Whether the time we drove to Maine when you were nine months, and I developed an attack of bursitis the first day out, and we kept on driving for four days, I having to lift you and take care of you all the time, and Wright thought it was just my normal disposition, and the Boston doctor, to my great gratification, said any of his patients would have been screaming for morphine by the time he saw me; or the time I was on the train alone with Tommy, and the Pullman porter didn't pin the snuggle ducky properly, and woke me up in the night to say he thought something was wrong with the baby, and I looked up in the berth above me and saw Tommy, perfectly naked,

---

237 Robert Charles Benchley (1889–1945), an American actor and humorist who wrote for *Vanity Fair* and *The New Yorker*.

Domesticity

swinging gently with the motion of the train, hanging by his neck; or all three of you going to Texas, and Bill, at eighteen months, so tired and cross from the strange surroundings, and your grandmother, who belongs to the old school, being very annoyed because he cried whenever she tried to hold him (perfectly naturally, I thought), and writing me afterwards that I ought to take Bill to the doctor because it wasn't right for a child to be so cross, he ought to be happy all the time—well, I could keep on with this sort of thing all day.

I went on to say it was all right with me if I never met my grandchildren until they were old enough to come to college. But of course you mellow. I am frank to admit I've always been a bad traveler. When I started writing this autobiography, I thought the experience of traveling by train was as obsolete as traveling by covered wagon anyway, and the only chance my grandchildren would have to experience it would probably be in the Railway Museum between Boothbay and Wiscasset. But Tom will be taking his family to Florida by AMTRAK this spring.

Of course many of the activities I thoroughly enjoyed. One of the happiest occupations in my life as a young mother was reading aloud, and as things turned out, my only regret now is that Bill was too active to care for it as much as his brother and sister had done. We went through the Pa and Ma books as they came out, and the first and best belong to this period.[238] I'm using them as rather unorthodox texts for the Japanese wives I talk English with once a week, and their charm never palls.[239] Reading aloud was largely a winter pleasure, but it must be confessed that the Wisconsin winter isn't for weaklings, in the immortal phrase of Rodney, the Bascom Hall janitor. Every bit of winter is a pleasure up through Christmas; but January, February, March, a good deal of April—these are the times that try men's souls, especially with colds and flu jumping from one member of the family to another like fleas from dog to dog (another immortal phrase of a young man in the department to whom we gave a lift, seeing him standing on the corner with his dog. After he got in, he said he was taking the dog to the vet's to have him de-flead—"but don't worry," he added, seeing my

---

238 A reference to the *Little House on the Prairie* series by Wisconsin-born American writer Laura Ingalls Wilder (1867–1957). The "first and best" Thomas refers to is *Little House in the Big Woods*.

239 As an extension of her memoir, Thomas wrote about her extensive involvement in retirement with English tutoring for spouses of international graduate and post-doctoral science students who were living in university student housing. In addition to meeting these women in their homes, Thomas regularly hosted Sunday dinners in her home, and she maintained written correspondence with many long after they had left the university.

face, "they only jump from dog to dog.") But there are a lot of good months in spring, summer, and fall, and a lot of enjoyment. Wright put in a big garden, we ate vegetables literally garden-fresh, and I did a lot of canning. I've already spoken of my pleasure from our flowers; we all got a lot from the fresh vegetables, and so did our friends. A garden is either a feast or a famine; the birds get the peas before you do, or you have more cucumbers than the city of Madison can eat. ("Did I ever spread sweetness and light. Took flowers to Stallmans, string beans to Eccles, flowers to Cassidys, summer squash to Quintanas.") We could follow the good old New England recipe for sweet corn: have the water boiling, fully boiling; pick the corn; *run* (don't walk) back to the stove with it, and put it in. We ate a lot of meals outdoors, the bulk of the time, I really think, only breakfast inside, and often roasted the corn. I loved putting up fruits and vegetables for two reasons. First, it gratified my New England thrift. (How pleasing to find in your seventies that all your life you have simply been well ahead of your time.) Second, it is almost the only thing where a housewife can see results. In general she keeps on running to stay in the same place. I never got a washing out on the line that more dirty clothes didn't at once begin to collect (and I didn't have an automatic washer and dryer until you had all left home); never got a room clean but a child or dog tracked in mud (cats never do, but they sometimes throw up—as do dogs and children for that matter; remember the cough-up pan?); never got a meal cooked but the family immediately began to get hungry again. I complained of this to Mother the first year I was married. "I spend so much time cooking for Wright," I said, "and he looks just the same." "Well," said Mother, "if you didn't, you'd see pretty fast that he'd begin to look different." With a baby, who doubles its weight in the first six months and triples it in a year, and with home canning where you see your shelves filling up with lovely colored jars, you can see you are accomplishing something. I sew badly, and I never felt much enthusiasm for cleaning. When Mother sent me down to open the Island cottage I felt I'd done it when I got a bunch of daisies in the blue-and-white pitcher, and a centerpiece of mosses in the old yellow baking dish; I always feel my preparations for guests are done when I've made the flower arrangements. But I always liked to cook, and I liked to can. This, of course, was the time of glass jars in steam baths; by the time freezing had come in I no longer had a family to make the work worthwhile. The canning of course was done in the summer but we let some of the legumes ripen for fall picking and drying: "filled interstices of day with shelling black-eyed peas." One of our favorite winter meals was homemade black bean soup.

That the Beattys were our next-door neighbors was one of the greatest sources of pleasure in these years. This contact was even pleasanter than that with the Sharps, since it was an all-year one, and not a matter of two congenial couples

Domesticity

only but two congenial families—even to the cats, who had the same coloring, as it happened. The Beattys' was named Juliana, Princess of Orange, but she/he later turned out to be Julian. Richard was eighteen months older than Hannah, Hannah than Bobby, Bobby than Tommy; the sequence was broken there since Bill is older than Arthur. Once I was waiting at the curb with the first four children while Gwen went back in the house for something she had forgotten, and a woman stopped her car to ask me "Are these all yours?" On December 2, 1932, instigated no doubt by his mother, Richard brought Hannah flowers for her second birthday—monthbirthday, should I say? In the first years Ham had quite a bit of free time, since he was only beginning to establish himself as an architect and any client of his had to have more than the ordinary amount of the spirit of adventure—which really extended to some of his contractors, particularly the plumber, as you shall see. The four of us had a continuing bridge tournament, Wright and Gwen against Ham and me. We kept a running score, and every six months or so wiped the slate clean with a dinner given by the losers to the winners. I think we usually lost, and I was cook while Ham made a magnificent butler. I noted that he was "a bad but very cheerful player." During the thirties we were certainly very much aware of the state of the world, though I haven't tried to reproduce it here. There are plenty of good histories for you to read. It was a thrilling experience at Roosevelt's March 4, 1933 inauguration, when by noon all forty-eight states had gone on the bank holiday he decreed, to hear him over the radio—then a novelty. On March 31 we went over to the Beattys and "talked about condition of world but grew cheerful"—as well we might when Ham was of the party. Le Corbusier came to Madison to lecture in 1934 and dropped in to see our house—certainly our most famous visitor. The Beattys, "including Julian," came yearly to celebrate Wright's birthday, for which the traditional meal was steak, mushrooms, fried potatoes, spring salad, and banana cream pie—Wright's favorite dessert for years, which must have been a carryover from his La Grange days, since certainly it wasn't in my tradition. The four of us went down on the train to Chicago for the day once to hear the famous D'Oyley Carte Company[240] in *Yeoman of the Guards*, eating dinner on the diner on the way back. I can't begin to tell you all the things we did together, but what I've said of our general neighborhood life will give you a pretty good idea.

When the Beattys left, Gwen and I agreed to write each other regularly once a month, an agreement we have faithfully carried out for over thirty years. Also, Gwen saved all my letters, and loaned them back to me when in 1972 I visited them at Heritage Village, a brief immersion in luxury American style compara-

---

240 The D'Oyly Carte Opera Company, a professional light (comic) opera company that performed Gilbert and Sullivan's Savoy operas in the UK, Europe, and North America from the 1870s-1982.

ble to our visit to the Darwins in England. She also kept the letters I wrote to her in the hospital when Bobby was born (1934) and in those days you spent two weeks there for childbirth, real periods of rest for young mothers, and I wrote her a letter every day, as well as the letters I wrote Ham when he had an appendectomy a couple of years later—at least a ten-day business then—and the Fulchers returned expecting to get into their new house, which of course wasn't done. Nothing evokes the exuberance of the early days in Frost Woods like these letters—admittedly written to entertain convalescents.

> To Ham: The Fulchers, you will be glad to hear, are in town. They blew in yesterday evening, as happy as clams at the prospect of sleeping under their own roof. I started to condole with Polly: "Why, is anything wrong?" said the poor innocent, and I had to break the news to her. [In a later letter I reported the Bronzells, their contractors, asked the Fulchers when they intended to move in. "As if it depended on us," said Polly.] Well, they had supper here, and we saw the dog. Paul appeared with his mother on one arm, and carrying in the other, wrapped in a blanket, much more carefully than I carry my baby, the little dog. The first thing we did was to heat water for the dog's supper, measure out his formula, mix it with water, and watch him eat. The animal not being housebroken, I suggested the rumpus room, and in glancing carelessly into it this morning, I can see a good half hour's work ahead of me cleaning it up. Then Polly thought we could leave him, if he could have a drink of water. I inquired if it should be boiled, but she said it wasn't necessary. So the animal stayed downstairs, emitting those blood-curdling moans that a lonely dog does emit while we were eating, and driving my poor mother frantic because she couldn't be sure the dog was making all the noise, and was afraid some of the echoes came from Hannah or the baby. Of course, I immediately followed up my report on the house with a description of your bed of pain, and the sharpest thing Polly said was that she "wondered" why everything wasn't finished. So I am sure it will be safe for you to get out of the hospital.
>
> I suppose Gwen told you Wright is going to have his tonsils out tomorrow. I don't know what is wrong with the air of Frost Woods. It resembles to Montenegrin village in *The Native's Return* which was a village entirely of women, the

men all having left to make a living somewhere else.²⁴¹ The men come home for two weeks every summer, and then next spring all the babies are born together in a space of two weeks. To return to Wright's tonsils. In the last eight years he has had one slight attack of flu and one cold, so I can't feel his tonsils are doing him any harm. But then, he wants to have an operation too.

Polly took the car in town for an overhauling which was to take seven hours, and she occupied the time in reading Irish history at the library to find a suitable hero for whom to name the dog, who is still as far as I know anonymous. The name most favorably considered up to yesterday was Brian Boruma, but she may have found something better.

I'm sure you can hardly wait to see the dog. Gwen said she had her first sight of him yesterday. He seems to have filled my life so completely for the past week that I can't imagine how she could have put it off so long. He is really awfully good at night, only wakes up two or three times and whimpers a little, and then they change him, I suppose, and he goes back to sleep again.

I have chatted so much about the Fulchers that your pat speech when you come out will be "I'm so glad to meet you, I've heard so much about you." But I must tell you about the dog's diet. He is fed five times a day. The foundation is a prepared dog food that looks on the order of Pablum. You know, things ground together.²⁴² This is dissolved in hot water, not cold, it must be hot, and to it is added one-half teaspoon cottage cheese, and one half-teaspoon ground raw beef. The cereal part, I forgot to say, is also measured—an amount equal to the size of one egg. They are just now very much distressed because he ought to have also mixed with the above one tablespoonful of Page's Evaporated Vitamin D Irradiated mild, canned. But they are unable to find it anywhere in Madison, so Rennebohm's is trying to order it

---

241 Louis Adamic (1898–1951), a Slovene-American author, translator, and Guggenheim Fellowship recipient (1932), whose *The Native's Return* (1934), about King Alexander's rule in Yugoslavia, informed many Americans about the Balkans.

242 Pablum ("foodstuff"), a processed, fortified cereal created to alleviate infant malnutrition.

for them.[243] And then people say that young children are hard work.

Speaking of children, we took the baby to Dr. Weston Monday, and had a very characteristic visit. Everything was fine and nothing should be changed. I inquired if the sun were valuable enough now (September) to keep on with sun baths. "Well, they're a chore, aren't they," said Dr. Weston. "I wouldn't bother." We mentioned Hannah's unfortunate habit of waking and screaming in the night. "Well, some of mine do that," said the doctor. He always speaks as if he had a regiment of children, and so he has. "I had to give my oldest a night light. I hated to do it but I'll do anything rather than get up myself at night." He certainly is one to make life as easy as possible. I'm sure he must be cheering you up like anything.

When you consider that the time Dr. Weston was giving this permissive advice was the time when the Federal Bulletin, *Infant Care,* and authorities in general were being as rigid as Communists following the party line on toilet training as early as the child could life its head and feedings when the clock struck and not one second before, you could more deeply recognize your good luck, as well as mine, in having him.

Back to my letters to Ham:

> Ruth Wallerstein says when she thinks of our living room she always thinks of music, the simplicity and clarity of eighteenth century music, particularly Mozart. Isn't that a pretty compliment?
>
> I am driven to fill up space, as the columnists say, by a poetic description. You may have three guesses as to what is described. New York? No. Constantinople? No. Frost Woods? Well, aren't you clever.
>
> Squirrels gather acorns in the leafy trees,
>
> Diapers are drying in the soft September breeze.
>
> In the dusk of evening the sly mosquito roams.

---

243 Oscar Rennebohm (1889–1968), an American pharmacist, graduate of UW-Madison, and governor of Wisconsin (1947–1951), owned and operated several drugstores, the first of which opened in 1924 near the University. "Rennie's" soda fountain, with its shakes, floats, grilled Danishes, and weekly fish fry, became a popular gathering place for students, faculty, and locals.

Domesticity

> Rubberneckers stare at those funny looking homes.
> Quantities of canines trotting down the street,
> Haughty Hedge, and Simple Sam, and Bungle's sturdy feet,
> Siren Bella, spaniel pups, the champion in state
> Who eats a balanced diet from a boiled and sterile plate.
> How our friends do envy all our little toys!
> Pulling weeds and shoveling snow and other sylvan joys!
> Oh, your lovely garden! Oh, horizons wide!
> Oh, the peace and quiet of the countryside!
> Soft I sink to slumber. Can I hear aright?
> Robert, Jan, or Hannah, John, or little Wright?
> Morpheus reluctantly wings his way afar.
> Undoubtedly some cherub is yelling for his Ma.
> Peake is in the bathroom, playing with his tools.
> Meek is in the bedroom, plashing paint in pools.
> Bronzells energetically rush from room to room.
> Are we ever sharing in the building boom!

This is the place for a thumbnail sketch of Peake, to whom I have already referred as a key factor in the spirit of adventure Ham's business enterprises seemed to involve. Ham remembers him affectionately forty years later as the plumber whose greasy finger marks were invariably found in the second floor bathroom when he came into the house to work in the basement and never left it. He was a Seventh Day Adventist, a great asset in his profession because of course your plumbing always goes out of order on Sunday because it knows your plumber won't come then, and he fooled it. Since he is also distinguished for connecting the hot water instead of the cold with the toilets in one house so that to flush the toilet was to reproduce Old Faithful, it's not clear that his visits on any day were unmixed blessings.

Dogs played a very large part in the early days in Frost Woods, and my letters to Ham ended with this effusion.

> The Bronzells work in the shade of the trees,
> The sunflowers bloom in the sun,
> But the Fulchers are crying and moaning, "Please,
> When will our house be done?
> When will our homeless, wandering dog

Be able to lay his head
Down on his pillow, eat from his dish,
Sleep in his own little bed?"
Peake has installed another pipe.
The sunflowers bask in the sun.
The hearts of the Fulchers with joy are ripe
Waiting for Hamiltun (sic).
"Hamilton comes from his bed of pain
And we shall nevermore roam.
The water is running, dry is the stain,
And the puppy is quite at home."

Gwen's hospital stay with Bobby coincided with the time the Winspears' dog Bella was in heat, so some of her letters too were taken up with canine affairs. I did make one courteous allusion to the baby: "Does Robert yawn? I think that's the cutest thing with new babies—they look so grown up when they do it." The dogs in the neighborhood got there first, of course, but every dog in Dane County eventually made it. First I described Ray Owen's rushing Hodge, bleeding profusely to the vet's, and said I was going to be a neutral observer in the neighborhood feuds which obviously would develop; but just after that Sam got badly bitten, and I came down heavily on the Owen side.

> Wright said the Winspear yard looked like a shambles, like a Roman arena after the Christian corpses had been carried off. Blood goes a long way on the snow, of course. Well, by all means you must remain in your present dogless condition, so there'll be one family in Frost Woods who can speak to all the others.
>
> P.S. I reopen this, in the style of Mr. Micawber,[244] to say that Ray Owen has just driven by with Hodge in the back seat; and you can hear the baying of dogs like lions in the zoo at feeding time. I should say circumstantial evidence points to Hodge's rushing in to the doctor again. What an Easter Frost Woods is having.
>
> Among the neighbors were four Physical Education teachers from the university, of whom you will remember Miss Cronin and Miss Meyer, who still live here. When Hannah was a

---

244 Wilkins Micawber is a character in Charles Dickens's novel *David Copperfield* (1850).

> baby and she and I were out walking in the morning we'd see the four cars go in one after another like a procession, one woman in each, going to the same destination, Lathrop.[245]
>
> One last repercussion from l'affaire Bella. We saw Miss Meyer Saturday night and she said that they kept Dinny shut up all week, and he howled all week, day and night so they couldn't get any sleep. They tried to arrange things so they could take naps in the daytime in at Lathrop, and at night each of them would take turn holding Dinny's paw so the others could sleep. With someone holding his hand it seemed he only sobbed pitifully instead of wailing loudly, and the sobbing was not audible beyond the room he was in, so the others could snatch a few winks. So I don't know but what the Phy Eds were the greatest sufferers after all, for I will say for Sam that he slept all night and allowed us to do so. Sam, incidentally, thinks you and I have had a feud. When I go out with Hannah he turns down your driveway and is quite grieved that I don't come, and I have seen him several times going over to your house by himself to look around.

I had a couple of experiences with guests while Gwen was in the hospital that I passed on to her. The Morrisons must have been English friends of Wright's, but I don't remember anything about them.

> I vow here and now upon a stack of Bibles that I have no more tea parties until Hannah is ten. *Especially* people who are fond of children. People who don't like children and ignore them may come in the house, but people who think there is something about themselves irresistibly fascinating to all children, and who roar "hello, hello" and chirp "tweet, tweet" whenever they see a child shall enter this house only over my dead body. You infer that Mr. Morrison père belongs to this class. He kept setting Hannah into one fit as soon as she got over the one before. Also he was one of those trying guests who refuse all food as if it were poison. I don't know whether he has dyspepsia or dislikes American cooking. Altogether it was the world's least successful tea-party!

---

245 Lathrop Hall, on the UW-Madison campus, originally served as a social and recreational center for women at the university (1910). These social functions were moved to the Memorial Union in 1927. The building was added to the U.S. National Register of Historic Places in 1985.

The other guest, however, was internationally famous, or notorious, according to your point of view. This was the anarchist Emma Goldman, with whom Wright had become very friendly in his Rhodes Scholar days, in America on a lecture tour.[246] I think the moment we set eyes on each other we recognized we were *not* soul mates. While I was putting lunch on the table I heard Wright offer her a cigarette and heard her answer, "No, thank you. I realized very young I would be spending most of my time in prison and it wouldn't be a good idea to get the habit." What my father would have thought of my luncheon guest! I laughed to myself in the kitchen, and fortunately was not called on for very extensive efforts as hostess.

I had to make very little effort at conversation because the talk was between her and Wright of political refugees and other members of the criminal classes they had known in England. In fact, when I finally inquired if Miss Goldman would have some more to eat, she was quite startled to find I was in the room. Thus recalled to my presence, she turned to me and said, "So you have a daughter." "Yes," I answered proudly. "She looks just like Wright." At that scintillating remark Miss Goldman smiled vaguely and then turned back to Wright and began to tell him about a new edition of her autobiography. The only other interchange we had was when I said "Will you have coffee?" and she said "Yes, please." She didn't stay very long after lunch because she had a number of people to see in town, so you might say everything passed off very well.

I don't know that Gwen wrote to me every day when the next year Tom was born, but my stay included my own birthday, and I do remember that she brought me in a beautiful big basket full of presents from all the neighbors.

An enrichment of our friendship with the Beattys was that it brought us into a good deal of contact with the elder Beattys, with whom lived Miss Carlotta McCutcheon, Mrs. Beattys' sister. Mr. Beatty was the essence of geniality, exactly like his son, who resembles him almost uncannily in both physique and temperament. He was a distinguished Wordsworth scholar. Mrs. Beatty was a highly intelligent woman and a conscientious citizen. She took her undergraduate work at the University of Wisconsin after she was married and received her degree here—an amazingly advanced procedure for the time. She refused to join the League of Women Voters because she didn't believe in voters as men *or* as women, just as voters, which seems in these days of splinter groups an even more intelligent statement now than it did when I first heard her say it. She belonged to the Civic Club, which still exists, and which held monthly luncheon meetings with big name speakers, and she often included me in her invitations to Gwen.

---

246 Emma Goldman (1869–1940) contributed significantly to anarchist political philosophy in North America and Europe. Her first visit to UW-Madison, which generated controversy, occurred in January 1910 (Curti & Carstensen, 1949, 2: pp. 63–66).

Domesticity

She was incidentally a charter member of the Madison Dickens Fellowship.[247] Since your grandparents were so far away, it was very fortunate for you to have this substitute, for we were included in many of the three-generation activities: trips to the zoo (a characteristic story is told of Ham as a boy when his parents took him to London and he told the retired Indian civil servants at the Bloomsbury boarding house that the roaring of the lions often kept him awake at home in Madison, Wisconsin—the Beatty house was on Vilas, only a block from the zoo),[248] to the university barns to see the little pigs and lambs in spring, to picnics, to university band twilight concerts on the peaceful Lincoln Terrace, and many others. Once the elder Beattys, Gwen, Richard and Robert, Hannah, Tom and I all started out to take the boat trip around Lake Mendota. We got half way and the guide had just announced that we were over the deepest part of the lake (as if you could drown more easily in sixty feet of water than in sixteen) when the engine failed and they couldn't get it started; so we waited, rocking gently, until the competing boat, which went around the lake in the opposite direction, arrived, and towed us ignominiously home over the water we had already covered.

An even greater enrichment of my life which I owe to Gwen is Reading Group. This started the year Tom was born. Virginia Bowman was the originator. Frank Bowman, Dick Ela and Ham Beatty (college friends) belonged to a poker club, and their wives decided to have a club themselves, each asking one friend to join. I was Gwen's selection, and she said there would be no problem about transportation (it was before I learned to drive) because she would always take me. The six charter members were Virginia Bowman, Dorothy Ela, Gwen Beatty, Eleanor Miles, Sally Reynolds, and I.

Our numbers have fluctuated over the years; we've usually been eight. If a congenial friend moved to Madison, a member would suggest her; or if a member moved away, someone would suggest a Madison replacement. Our policy is not to meet if fewer than four people are able to come, and we do miss a few meetings during the year, but not many. The others were very forgiving about my unavoidable absences the first two or three weeks of every semester. There's a minimum of red tape: no officers, no dues, no records. We meet in rotation at the homes of the members, for lunch and reading. The rotation has now settled down, much to the gratification of Patty Stedman and me, both of whom have

---

247 The Madison branch of the Dickens Fellowship, a worldwide association founded in London in 1902, was established in 1927 and remains active.
248 The Henry Vilas Zoo opened in 1911 on a portion of land donated to the city by William Vilas (1840–1908), a U.S. senator and law professor at UW-Madison, who stipulated that the land be used for an admission-free public park. The zoo is free and receives over 750,000 visitors annually.

been pressing this for years, to alphabetical order. For a while it was geographical, harder to remember. We're flexible anyway; if it's inconvenient when it's your turn, someone else steps in. I wish we had kept a list of books read; it would have been interesting. The book is usually chosen because someone owns it, and some choices are more successful than others. But the main purpose is not reading; it's companionship.

The membership has been a pretty good mingling of town and gown. Sally Reynolds brought in, at different times, Sally McGinnis, Katherine Post, and Marion Sarles. Sally knew the McGinnises at Beloit, where her mother, Mrs. Chickering, was a sorority house mother and John McGinnis was in the psychology department. Both McGinnises, incidentally, had Ph.D.'s in psychology, and Sally was at Holyoke just after me. For some years John held a position here as industrial psychologist at Oscar Mayer's,[249] and then they moved to Natick [Massachusetts], where I usually see Sally when I visit Hannah. Gaines Post, like Bob Reynolds, was a professor of history. Katherine was much interested in amateur theatricals. The Posts were both Texans, and after a few years at the Humanities Institute at Princeton when Gaines retired, returned to their native state. Bill Sarles, Marion's husband, was head of the Biochemistry Department here, served as chairman of the University Committee for several years, and was national president of the American Association of Biochemists, in which capacity, at a world conference at Moscow, he behaved, under provocation, with the good temper and wisdom that would put the whole world in a lot better shape than it is today if more people possessed these qualities.[250] Virginia Bowman, at different times, brought in Betty Patterson, wife of the minister of Grace Episcopal church; they later moved to Rome and ran a school there; Patty Stedman, whose husband is in the Law School and has spent a great deal of time in Washington; and Helen Thompson, whose husband came here to the Medical School remarkably late in his career, after working with Cushing in Boston and then holding a commercial position. She is a very enthusiastic, warm-hearted, cultured person, and it was a personal disappointment to me that they moved to New York just when I thought my retirement was going to give me more time to spend with her. Our only unmarried member is Ellen Ela, Dorothy Ela's sister-in-law, who spends half the year in Florida, where she ran a bookstore for some years and still owns a house. Dorothy also brought in Teddy Kubly, whose

---

249 The Oscar Mayer Company, an American meat company made famous by its touring Wienermobile, was headquartered in Madison from 1919 until 2015, when owner Kraft Heinz announced its relocation to Chicago.

250 William B. Sarles was hired by the Bacteriology department in 1932. In 1966, Sales was editor of the *Journal of Microbiology*, and in 1967, he was president of the American Society for Microbiology (ASM).

husband has just retired from the School of Business. Eleanor Miles I think you all know. While everyone is interested in ecology and nature, Eleanor is our most knowledgeable naturalist and knows a great deal about birds. She made the bird map at the Island cottage. We have an annual Christmas party, and many of the decorations I preserve for the Christmas tree each year come from this source. Each member is given a birthday party.

The group is notable for civic responsibility. Most of the members were born or married into Madison First Families, and they belong to Attic Angels (the Madison social equivalent of the New York Junior League).[251] This organization (the nineteenth century aura of the name shows it belongs to the same vintage as the Ladies Improvement Association of the Island) identifies a community need, sets up an organization to meet it, and then moves on to another. It was responsible, for instance, for the Madison Visiting Nurses' Organization, and for the Attic Angel Home, the best of its kind in Madison, where Theo Owen is now living. Most of the members are Episcopalians, and spend a good deal of time in church service. I'm the only member who does not have a long list of volunteer services to her credit, but also the only member who held a full-time job, which must be my excuse.

It is a privileged group financially. I think everyone is in easy circumstances, and a number are really wealthy. With this in mind, it is sobering to consider the sorrows that have come to us. Two of us are divorced; two of us have seen one or more children divorced, which I sometimes think would be even more painful; one of us has borne an abnormal child, which fortunately died before it was two. Two of us have spent very substantial amounts of time, months and even years, in institutions for the mentally ill. Two have died of cancer, one after an illness of six months, the other after one of many years, including many operations. Sally Reynolds, our first loss by death, died of emphysema. She suffered not only herself but in her care of her husband. Bob Reynolds had a very difficult heart operation the year Hannah was married; Sally didn't come to the wedding, because he was in the hospital at the time in a crucial situation. He survived, and lived ten or twelve years after, also surviving Sally. I thought of him recently when I heard a talk on "heroic surgery" on WHA:[252] the speaker, a doctor, raised the point of the best use of medical achievements from the social standpoint. A heart transplant, he said, receives a great deal of publicity as a success, while the real effect on the patient, doomed to an abnormal kind of life which may impose unbearable strain on those around him, is never given. The precariousness of

---

251 The Attic Angel Association, formed in 1889, is a not-for-profit organization providing health and human service needs for children and the elderly.

252 WHA, a non-commercial AM band radio station, now the flagship for Wisconsin Public Radio, was started at UW-Madison in 1922.

Bob's life was brought home to me once at Reading Group when Sally complained of the lack of manners of university faculty who did not erase the board when they left the room; Bob, she said, simply didn't have the strength to do it himself. While I think it's bad manners not to erase the board, it never would have occurred to me that the next teacher would be physically unable to do it. Once I got to Reading Group at Sally's early, and was there when Bob came back from his university class in a taxi. It drew up just outside the door, and he walked perhaps six feet, on the level (no steps), came in the door, and stood resting for an appreciable time, two or three minutes, before he had the energy to cross the floor and go to his room. This went on for ten or twelve years, and when Sally died she left him as an irritable, unhappy, insoluble problem to the only one of the children who lived in Madison, and to his sister Marion. When I think of what has happened to this exceptionally fortunate group, it would make me fear for you—except that you, and I for you, must accept the human condition with what grace and courage we may.

The great gift Reading Group has given me is contemporary companionship. Though Urie Felsenbrenner may say there is too little companionship between generations in America,[253] contact with your own is important and I know I have suffered all my life because I lacked it as a child. That was why I was so glad that you all had it. I am the oldest in this group, but not by much; Eleanor is only a year younger than I, and the spread down to the youngest is gradual. We supported each other when our children were babies, and continued to do so through conferring with teachers, serving as Den Mothers and Girl Scout leaders, selecting colleges, going through the teen age years (before drugs! How easy), becoming mothers-in-law, becoming grandmothers. We went through it all together and were supported by the realization that our problems were not unique. I got comfort from listening to *Henry Aldrich* and reading *Penny*, but more from talking with my friends.[254] The perspective was particularly valuable for me because so much of the time I was a single parent; and on occasion I realized that being so, however difficult, protected me from having the problem of divided loyalty, say between father and son, which I saw happen.

Also, as I grew more and more immersed in my work in the English Department, this was almost the only contact I had with people outside it—indeed the only regular such contact. And it was more and more valuable to me, as my work grew more and more important, to have a steady contact with peo-

---

253   Urie Bronfenbrenner (1917–2005), a Russian-born American developmental psychologist who conducted groundbreaking research on the impact of environmental and social forces on child development.

254   *The Aldrich Family* was a popular radio show in the 1930s-1950s; *Penny* was a popular comic strip in the 1940s-1970. Both were about teenagers.

ple who cared no more for it than mere politeness required and we had interests outside it.

When Max Beerbohm wrote his last review, he took leave of his readers in a passage I've been in the habit of bringing to my classes for analysis: partly because it was an example of brilliant sentence handling, partly because it presented an interesting view of the feelings of the writer, and partly because of this sentence: "Thursday, the day chosen by me (as being the latest possible one) for writing my article, has for twelve years been regarded by me as the least pleasant day of the week."[255] My students, whose weekly theme was due Friday, never failed to have a fellow feeling. To Reading Group I owe it that for forty years Thursday has been regarded by me as the most pleasant day of the week. I am deeply indebted to Gwen for this pleasure.

It was a great personal loss for me when in 1940 the Beattys moved to Detroit. Of course we were together as much as we could be through the summer, but on August 10 the movers appeared, the family had lunch with us, and then went in town to spend their last night with the elder Beattys, Ham and Gwen coming out in the evening to say goodbye. Aug 11: "Miserable day, thinking of Gwen driving further and further away all day."

Of course the Beattys, though our closest friends, were not our only ones, and through these years on the whole we had a good deal of social life. The English Department, like the neighborhood, was small and intimate according to present standards, and we saw a lot of many of its members. The novelty of the house attracted people, who enjoyed taking a little trip out to the country, as it seemed then. Helen White, Ruth Wallerstein, and Leslie Spence came out frequently; the latter more than once skated across the lake. Some of the younger people, including Mark Schorer, fairly often bicycled out.[256] The wife of the Department Chairman had a department tea in her house early each fall, and I would pour, as a personal friend first of Janet's and then of Grace Hughes's.[257] Ruth Wallerstein got the first Phi Beta Kappa award for a book of distinguished scholarship (on Donne), Janet gave a tea in her honor, and I decorated a little Christmas tree with symbols from the book, one of which still remains in our Christmas tree box. Wright was summer school chairman, and I heaped coals of fire on the head of Tucker Brooke, a visiting professor, by giving a tea with strawberries, English fashion: "45 people. Hollyhocks at their best."[258] The Hugheses gave a

---

255 Sir Henry Maximilian "Max" Beerbohm (1872–1956), an English essayist, caricaturist, and drama critic for the *Saturday Review*.

256 Mark Schorer (1908–1977) earned his Ph.D. from UW-Madison in 1936 and spent most of his career at UC-Berkeley.

257 Wife of Merritt Y. Hughes (1893–1971), a Milton specialist trained at Harvard.

258 In the New Haven chapter, Thomas recounts an unpleasant experience with Mrs. Brooke.

department party for Sinclair Lewis, who had invited himself to teach here but stayed, if I remember correctly, only a few weeks.[259] We entertained eight people for dinner fairly often, to be followed by contract [bridge], English Singer records (of which Wright was very fond), play reading, or conversation, and we went to many such dinners. All these were popular ways of spending the evening. The favorite neighborhood game was Guggenheim (a word game where each player suggested one category and you filled in blanks according to the initial letters of a given word) and later charades. Our social contacts were not confined to department and neighborhood only. Bertha Putnam visited us, and Mrs. Slaughter, her Bryn Mawr classmate and at the very apex of old Madison society, gave a dinner for her, at which I noted I talked with Lloyd Garrison, dean of the Law School.[260] We went as guests to the famous Madison Literary Society (Mad Lit),[261] I think the most continuous and successful town and gown organization in the country. Many of our personal friends belonged and would invite us if they were giving a paper; once Helen White gave one, and we went on after it to a reception at the Clarks' for the Irish poet James Stephens.[262] As time went on, Wright more often went alone, sometimes as one of the three critics who always commented on the papers. In this period started the monthly play reading group you will remember because Frances Becker always had a Christmas carol party for the families: Agards, Beckers, Hugheses, Twaddells, Zawackis, Thomases. Sometimes we went to the movies: Fred Astaire and Ginger Rogers in "Springtime," certainly the most pleasure-giving couple ever to appear on stage or screen; "Midsummer Night's Dream," where the Mendelssohn music is always associated in my mind with one of the heaviest and loveliest snowfalls I ever saw, to which we came out as we left the theater; "Grand Illusion," the movie which seems to me to justify Francophilism, to which in general I haven't been much addicted. In October of 1939 the Union Theater, superlatively well equipped for the time, opened with a performance of the Lunts in *The Taming of the Shrew.* Wisconsin residents, this famous theatrical pair were very generous about giving opening performances

---

259 Sinclair Lewis (1885–1951), a Nobel Prize-winning American novelist, visited Madison in the fall of 1940, impulsively volunteered as a visiting instructor in the English department, and taught one class until early November, when he abruptly left without explanation (Cronon & Jenkins, 1994, pp. 293–495).
260 Lloyd K. Garrison (1897–1991), dean of the UW-Madison Law School from 1929–1942, was also appointed chairman of FDR's National Labor Relations Board (1934), received a Guggenheim Fellowship (1938), and served on the National War Labor Board during World War II.
261 The Madison Literary Society, originally Club, was founded in 1877 to promote literary discussion and social interaction among individuals "'of acknowledged literary taste'" (Thwaites, 1904, p. 27). Thomas mentions this club in the Wisconsin chapter.
262 James Stephens (1880–1950), Irish poet and novelist, contributed to the Irish literary revival at the turn of the twentieth century.

Domesticity

here so that we often saw what was in a year or two to be a smash Broadway hit before New York had heard of it. Later we saw them in *There Will Be No Night*— by that time heart-breaking in view of European conditions. Wright had his students out every semester, a custom with which I was thoroughly in sympathy: and "how they eat!" They might come for a wienie roast outdoors, and then sing and talk through the evening in the house.

We always gave the neighborhood Christmas carol party. I remembered as a girl going in town on Christmas Eve to walk around Beacon Hill. It was then the custom to burn real white candles in the windows, and curtains were never drawn, so some of the most beautiful old houses in Boston were on display. In one window there might be a great illustrated Bible perhaps brought back from Florence; before another door a huge flaming torch. Fires burned in the fireplaces, and Florentine fruit wreaths were hung. Bell ringers (like *The Nine Tailors*)[263] went around and rang their carols in Louisburg Square. Once in a while we would be lucky enough to have a soft light glinting snow, like the one that fell the night of Hannah and Peter's wedding. And everywhere you saw the flames of the white candles. The first year I had a house of my own I lighted it with white candles on Christmas Eve, and invited the neighbors. This party went on for many years, though at the request of the neighbors, who had their children to think of, I changed it from December 24 to December 21 or 22. It was the only thing in our early Frost Woods days where the children were *not* included, and therefore it became a great thing for the children as they grew old enough to come. At first, in the early leisurely days, we used to meet every week through December to practice—part singing in "Lo how a rose," for instance. Two or three years we went up to the tubercular sanitorium on the hill to sing to the patients and put a little cheer into their lives. But one particularly nasty Christmas, when it was abnormally warm and therefore foggy and muggy, when the group had trudged a long way to a special cottage whose inmate refused to turn off the radio because she'd rather hear Schumann-Heink than us, we gave up that idea and after that did all our singing indoors.[264] At first when the neighborhood was small I had a little joke and a personal rhyme on the tree for everyone; as it grew larger, I gave a little present: a red net bag of pine cones from the Island, a red candle in a cork float (that was the year a whole supply of them had washed upon the beach); during the war a little package of coffee, saved from my ration, so everyone could have an extra cup on Christmas Day. They were jolly parties. I can hear Ham singing "eia, eia" now and John Marshall and Alban Winspear coming in strong on "No-o-ell." One year the Fulchers gave "Twelfth

---

263 *The Nine Taylors* (1934), a mystery novel by British writer Dorothy Sayers (1893–1957).
264 Ernestine Schumann-Heink (1861–1936), a German-born American operatic singer.

Night Revels," a great success. We all did scenes from *Twelfth Night*. Paul made a brilliant Sir Andrew Aguecheek (few people so well cast physically for the part would have been brave enough to do it), and I played Olivia in a dress I know Hannah remembers, a floor-length black velvet with a little white gold-tipped frill at the neck, in which I had the happy illusion I looked like Mary Queen of Scots, with silver tinsel from the tree in my hair. After the holidays we settled down again to the weekly Sewing Circle, and in addition the women would not infrequently get up a bridge four in the evenings, since a good many of us played—not only Gwen and I but also Alice Strang, Faye Nagdegall, Marie Ragsdale, Irene Thomas, so that it was no problem to get up a four. So all in all we had our diversions.

Out of this period I can find a record of only two trips which Wright and I took together. We celebrated our tenth wedding anniversary by driving up to Door County for the weekend, staying in Ephraim. One of my former students was working there (the anniversary was September 1, a convenient time for anyone in academic life), and as we drove away the whole staff gave us a send-off by banging cheerfully on dishpans, like an old-fashioned chivaree. The other trip was in August of '39. It "wrung my heart to leave Bill" (this is always the way with the baby, who is the one who will hardly notice whether you have gone or not) but we had a beautiful trip, going up the Mississippi on the Wisconsin side, which has been compared to the Rhine, stopping from time to time to climb a bluff or explore Pepin, "sacred to Laura and Mary."[265] We crossed at Red Wing, where we spent the night, and climbed the town bluff after dinner. The next day we drove back on the Minnesota side, stopped at Richland Center to see Robert Donat in "Goodbye, Mr. Chips," had dinner at the Farm Kitchen in Baraboo, and so home. I had such happy memories of the weekend that one of my most cherished ambitions in the forties was for the four of us to take the trip together, but by then you had reached the state of developing separate and sacred peer interests, and it never worked out.

Without doubt, the days in Frost Woods were good old days. But as I look back now I see that like everything else good they had to be paid for. The remoteness established two related problems. The first was transportation. When we moved out, it was thought we would have bus service before long. Even forty years later, it's in a rudimentary stage. Wright, who told me early in our acquaintance that he "teethed on a steering wheel," twice started to teach me to drive, but I didn't get my license until 1937, when I asked him to hire a mechanic from the garage to do it. I don't know how we managed before that, though some of the girls we had as "help" could drive. That year Tommy went to the university

---

265 A reference to characters in Wilder's *Little House in the Big Woods* children's novels.

Domesticity

nursery school and Hannah to kindergarten at Randall, for the Nichol kindergarten was not started until the next year. I drove regularly for them every day. But I didn't enjoy it, and it was not until I had been back in university teaching for some time that I felt at all at ease with a car. Even now I don't like to park near anyone else. Look over in the remotest corner of a shopping center, far away from any other car and a health-giving constitutional from any store, and there will be my car. And as I grow older, I find myself more and more reluctant to drive. The best of drivers are hardly completely at ease every day of a Wisconsin winter, and it was much worse in those days, before snow or stud tires. People used chains, but those were beyond a woman's strength to put on and they couldn't be kept on all winter because they were a menace once the roads were cleared. The process of street clearing, too, has enormously improved since the thirties. And our driveway—the price we paid for Ham's maiden house—has gotten better drivers than I into trouble, and I think now all our friends have learned never to enter it from November to May. In the snowy winters of '41 and '42, when I was alone and the boys too young to shovel, I would be so angry I felt as if I could pick up the car in my hands and carry it to the street—a delusion. There were neighborly arrangements, but they were tried to the utmost.

The other problem was help. In the early days, we thought the university would always supply seasonal labor, and Wright often brought boys out for raking leaves or the like, sometimes his own students, sometimes not, and this was fun. They liked my cooking and were interesting to talk with. But over the years students came to refuse any job not on a regular semester basis, and labor troubles at the Memorial Union have nearly killed that institution dead. After Hannah came, I needed inside help. But no girl we ever found before Alice Case Ream, pleasant though most of the contacts were, ever stayed with us when she could get any job in town. My worst problem was illness, particularly illness where one child had to be isolated. I envied Sally Marshall, who would take her sick child across the street to her mother and deal in peace with the well ones, or vice versa. You and I just passed things around. "Alone all day with three children, each of whom must be kept separate from the other two, and each yelling for me"; that was a skin infection, flu, and a stomach upset, and the incumbent help, Arlyn, was home for the weekend. Arlyn and Norna at different times went to the Island with us for a summer and enjoyed the trip; but neither stayed on. I'd always rather do something myself than ask someone else to do it (my weakness later as an administrator) and like Oliver Alden's mother I shrank from servants.[266] I didn't really want in the family someone who didn't belong

---

266 A reference to a character in George Santayana's *The Last Puritan: A Memoir in the Form of a Novel* (1935).

to the family, especially as they kept changing. Wayland Wood, a university student who later served in various countries in the State Department, solved the problem for the Beattys, and a nice university girl, Helen Ward, came to us for a year, leaving us affectionately but gladly—and understandably enough—to take a job at Pres House in town the next year.[267] A university student, who was working for room and board, of course gave only a limited amount of time anyway, though that was a help and gave parents some freedom to get out evenings. Alice, who did not come until September, 1940, was the only one who made any real impact on the family and became permanently one of us.

This period, of course, was marked by growing disasters in Europe, and growing threats to America. I have plenty of notations in my diary on them, always balanced by private concerns: Sept 3 (1939): "England and France declared war. King George's broadcasts and Roosevelt's. Took mother (her last visit to us) and children out to ride in morning, finished canning peas. Bill weighed 20-2"; May 15 (1940): "Holland surrendered. Made outline of *Moby Dick* for Wright." May 30, 1940 is the date of Dunkirk, but I was personally concerned with Hannah, whose bad case of measles forced me to postpone my trip East to see Mother until she was up, though still in dark glasses. Mother's mind by then was failing and it was a terrible problem (of which Hannah Davis bore the brunt) to provide her with a proper companion. I ended 1938 with the theatrical statement: "We are all prepared for the crash of the world." Even today in 1974, when we know man's stupidity makes this quite literally possible, we don't think it will happen quite so suddenly. But though I had no suspicion of it, my own world, the one Wright made for me to live in that snowy night he came to the College Club, was suddenly to crash, leaving me in as great a state of shock as if I had seen the sun fall out of the sky, and in as thick and confused a darkness.

In May 1938, the Executive Committee of the English Department voted not to promote Wright to associate professor and tenure. I have never heard a word from any of the people concerned in the decision, many of them my closest personal friends, as to the reasons.[268] To my own knowledge, the department has over the years made many mistakes in judgment, and failed to keep a number of brilliant young men. This included Mark Schorer, who has had a distinguished career

---

267 The University Presbyterian Church and Student Center, or Pres House, was established in 1907 and, by 1931, was housed in a newly constructed church that is now listed on the National Register of Historic Places.

268 Minutes of the Department Executive Committee meeting, dated March 8, 1938, indicate that the decision against promotion , which was nearly split (5 to 3), was determined by Wright's "failure to give evidence by some form of publication—either in formal scholarship, literary criticism, creative writing, or educational discussion—of his ability to establish his reputation among scholars."

Domesticity

both in literature and scholarship at UCLA,[269] and who received an honorary degree from the University of Wisconsin when he brought out his definitive biography of Sinclair Lewis; Lionel Trilling, probably our most outstanding literary critic today;[270] Francis Steegmuller[271] and Wallace Stegner,[272] noted authors and consistent *New Yorker* contributors. Wright may have been one of these mistakes. There may have been a political factor. He had allied himself with a very active group of liberals in the department, very much like the group we have just had in the late sixties, now called anti-establishment. In his day they were Young-Men-in-a-Hurry, the title of a dinner club he belonged to. The one of these who has attracted most national notice was Hayakawa, who in the course of his life has moved from far left to far right and became nationally famous or notorious, whichever way you want to look at it, as president of San Jose State College in the late sixties.[273] The Agards, both strong liberals, came out to pay us a sympathy call a few days after the Executive Committee action. Wright never discussed his alliance with me and I had not intruded. When I wrote in these pages of our first visit to Texas, I said I thought his mother felt he had changed radically at Oxford, had cut himself off from his old life, and that I belonged to the new life rather than to the old. I wonder now if I didn't really belong more to the old life, Northern college woman that I was, than any of the three of us knew. Was he perhaps drawn to me because he felt subconsciously that this girl who spoke his academic language embodied the values his mother had, from which he had not entirely withdrawn? However this may be, those values were not reconcilable with those in him which attracted him to Emma Goldman, say. If Mrs. Thomas had met Emma Goldman when I did, I think her instinc-

---

269 Mark Schorer, referred to earlier in this chapter, spent most of his career at UC-Berkeley, not UCLA.

270 Lionel M. Trilling (1905–1975), an American literary critic associated with the "New York Intellectuals," taught at UW-Madison in the late 1920s before returning to Columbia University, where he earned a Ph.D. in 1938 and spent his distinguished career.

271 Francis Steegmuller (1877–1979) , American writer and Flaubert scholar, taught English at UW-Madison after earning his master's degree from Columbia University in 1927. He was affiliated with the UW-Madison's Experimental College, a residence-based liberal education program founded in 1927 by philosopher and education reformer Alexander Meiklejohn (1872–1964).

272 Wallace Stegner (1909–1993), a Pulitzer Prize-winning novelist, was hired in 1937 as a temporary instructor and was "unwisely" let go in 1939 to pursue his career at Harvard and later Stanford (Cronon & Jenkins, 1994, p. 493). Archived correspondence between Stegner and the English department chair indicates that the department wanted to retain Stegner but was unable to match Harvard's offer.

273 Samuel Ichiye Hayakawa (1906–1992), an English professor who popularized the study of semantics and would later become a U.S. Senator in California, graduated from UW-Madison in 1935, taught there until 1939, and was president of San Francisco State College, not San Jose State College, from 1968 to 1973.

tive reaction would have been the same as mine: "this is no soul mate for me" though she wouldn't have put it the same way. Wright and I both enjoyed singing Elizabethan part songs. Did he mistake a similarity in taste and experience for a similarity in something deeper—what today you'll probably call basic lifestyle? Of course he told me of the Executive Committee action, and of course I was very much upset, as was he. For the next two years, he was on the lookout for another job, and he had a number of nibbles, going as far as taking trips to North Carolina and to Grinnell for interviews, but he got no offer. Of course, I would have gone anywhere he wanted—as a matter of fact I was rather hoping something might come of Cornell, which was mooted temporarily—in spite of the fact that I had put down roots and it would have been painful for me to tear them up. . . .[274]

---

274 At this point in the memoir, Thomas recounts the event and aftermath of Wright asking for a divorce in October 1941, which was finalized in July 1943. Reflecting on this difficult period in her life, Thomas writes poignantly about her "insensitivity to my husband's unhappiness," her shock and suffering "on a tragic scale," her efforts to live so that this "irreparable" loss would have minimal impact on her children, and her sincere gratitude for her fourteen years of marriage. Thomas's humanity and grace are acutely illustrated in this portion of the chapter; however, out of respect for Thomas's privacy, and at the request of her children, this account has been omitted.

WORLD WAR II: DECEMBER 1941 TO AUGUST 1945

This chapter would be more exciting if I had been in a different age group, or if, like so many even in my own, we had left home. Marion Wing,[275] for instance, rose to the highest position possible in the Women's Marine Corps, subordinate only to Olveta Cuppy, who was appointed by the President, and spent most of the war in Hawaii. (During this time, incidentally, Mrs. Cuppy came to Boston and got in touch with Mrs. Wing. The paper reported, much to Mrs. Wing's annoyance, that she was so excited she went right in to Mrs. Cuppy's hotel without making her bed. "I never left my house in my life without making my bed," she said, and I'm sure she never did.) If this were a novel instead of an autobiography, of course I would put the heroine in her twenties. As it was, my friends and I had little first-hand contact with the front-line adventure of war or the agony of suspense of women whose men were having it. DeWitt Bowman, Frank Bowman's much younger brother, was a fighter pilot in Britain, and was first reported missing and then killed in action over Germany. His widow was left with a baby girl, for whom, I noted, she must have been very thankful, and remarried not long after. The Agards' only child, Walter, fought in the Battle of the Bulge, but received not even a scratch. Jack Maiken[276] was a Navy lieutenant in the pacific; among our letters to him I quote Tommy's Christmas poem: "I send you Christmas wishes/ And lots of fishes." Chuck,[277] trained as a meteorologist, also saw service in the Pacific. But even with them, so much time proportionately was spent in training and America's entrance into the war was proportionately so late, that the actual combat period was fairly brief. In general, among my friends the husbands were too old and the sons much too young to be subject to military service, although the great majority of the men were involved in essential industries, such as war housing construction, or war work in federal administration. Bob Pooley made repeated trips to Washington on curriculum planning for the induction course for drafted men. Wright's[278] first job was assisting Fred Winant, brother of the ambassador to Britain,[279] as liaison officer between the State Department and

---

275 An acquaintance from the Isle of Springs.
276 Jack and Grace Maiken, next-door neighbors to the Thomases, first rented and then purchased Ham and Gwen Beatty's home.
277 Chuck Ream, Alice's husband.
278 Wright Thomas, Ednah's husband from 1927–1943.
279 John Gilbert Winant (1889–1947), who was also Governor of New Hampshire (1941–1946).

the Lend-Lease Administration on the one hand, and the representatives of the foreign governments getting Lend-Lease aid on the other, a position he owed to the good offices of Charles Bunn of the law School.[280] "It is a marvelous job, right in the center of things—as one of his friends told him, he had better look out for beautiful women spies who would undoubtedly be sicked on him—and every man he knows envies him." In September 1942 he changed to the "Board of Economic Warfare instead of the State Department. I don't understand any of it except that he has two telephones on his desk, just like the movies." At all ages and on all levels, there was a great deal of disruption. For instance, Bob Reynolds had "a rather hush-hush job—something to do with aliens, I think," and Sally, "spunky and serene," took the children to Washington to be with him as long as possible. She wrote "all about starting housekeeping with three orange crates for a dining room table, the floor for chairs, and everyone's clothes in piles around the room. But they had a silver coffee pot even if they had to dry their dishes with bath towels." When Bob went to England, Sally and her mother and the children went to New Hampshire, the original family site, where they had no hot water for the first two weeks, and "the coolth of the bathroom discouraged bathing." They spent several years there, but came back to Madison when Toby entered high school because the schools there were not good. But you and I stayed right here for the duration. Travel except on official business was discouraged, and was difficult. I left home only on very occasional visits to my mother, in her last years, and I don't think you were out of Frost Woods during the war.

No one was taken by surprise by World War II, though everyone was shocked by Pearl Harbor. Everything I've read about World War I emphasizes total astonishment at its outbreak, but we saw this one coming. Everyone I knew had strong British sympathies, of course. There were in Wisconsin a large number of citizens of German descent, in those days a much greater proportion of the population than now, when there have been big immigrations of Polish-Americans and Blacks, but we had no contact with them. It's not the only time I've felt the university did not necessarily represent the state as a whole. Not that I'm impugning the patriotism of the German-Americans. The country was solidly behind the President. One of the most interesting experiences of writing this autobiography is re-living the forties, when the war united us all, and contrasting them with the sixties, when the Vietnam War seemed almost as completely divisive as the Civil War. Nor do I remember any pacifists. Merritt Hughes,[281]

---

280   Charles Bunn was the principal draftsperson of the *Uniform Commercial Code*, a body of laws governing commercial transactions in the US that was eventually adopted nationwide.
281   Merritt Hughes (1893–1971), a Milton specialist trained at Harvard (1921), was hired as a full professor from the University of California. He taught at UW-Madison from 1936–1963. Hughes served as a field historian with General George Patton's headquarters in Europe.

a life-long and dedicated Friend and far over the age of military service, volunteered, and spent the war in the European theater, with the rank of colonel, as a military historian. Of course this was not a combat position, but as far as I know he had no compunctions about his son's service in the ranks. You remember that Elspeth Hughes spent three months with us, because her father and brother were both in the Army, and her mother in Philadelphia caring for an elderly relative for whom they could get no reliable help. I don't think Merritt questioned his own and his son's response to patriotic duty any more than he questioned his wife's to family duty. Even now (though I am of course aware of the current view that the seeds of World War II were contained the Treaty of Versailles) I don't see what else we could have done then. (I was surprised to read the other day that the statement "There never was a good war or a bad peace" was made by a contemporary of Henry VIII.) Certainly our horror of the Nazis was confirmed by the reality of the concentration camps. No one questioned the justice of our cause. Combatants went to war without delusion of romance, but with a sense of necessity, and their wives and mothers concurred.

The neighborhood was strongly pro-British, and as a matter of fact in some cases actually British. Gwen didn't become an American citizen for many years after this, when her sons were grown, and Mary Winspear's parents, like Gwen's relatives, were living in England. All through the thirties our atmosphere was very British. We had tea parties, not coffees, and all read *Punch*.[282] Wright's Rhodes scholarship had influenced him strongly, and both we and the Fulchers applied to take a British child for the duration. (Paul had been an ambulance driver with the French during World War I, and had received the Croix de Guerre. You'd never have thought it to look at him, would you?) Paul characteristically told a reporter they were asking for a boy twelve or fourteen so he could be useful in the yard. It's a mistake to be funny with the press. The reporter took him literally and faithfully reproduced the statement in the paper. Anyway, it came to nothing. The British were more reluctant to send their children away than some Americans had thought, partly no doubt for fear the ships might be torpedoed in crossing, but largely, I suspect, because they didn't want their children in impressionable years to live in other than an English environment. So they sent their children to the country—as you can read in Angela Thirkell's[283] novels—but no further. It was all for the best for me, since I had my hands full, but the neighbors rather regretted that the childless Fulchers did not have a broadening experience (you note, I'm sure, that my accounts of their devotion to their dog are hardly free from malice). The Haugens, the first tenants of the

---

282 *Punch*, or the *London Charivari*, was a British weekly satirical magazine established in 1841; its circulation peaked in the 1940s.
283 Angela Thirkell (1890–1961), an English and Australian novelist.

Beatty house, took "for an indefinite time a little Norwegian refugee, Siri, a girl of three and a half, who escaped with her parents across Siberia. They have been traveling practically a year, without being settled anywhere, and the child is terribly nervous. She looks very white. . . . All the children in the neighborhood are very interested in her." But this came from personal connections; Einar Haugen, Chairman of Scandinavian Languages, must have friends and relatives in Norway. In the end we didn't see much of her, since the Haugens bought a house in Shorewood and left Frost Woods.

Wright left for Washington only two days before Pearl Harbor. I think the state or personal shock in which I had been living since October is reflected in my letter to Gwen. "I went in town last Sunday night and the newsboys were shouting 'Extra! Extra! Japan declares war on U S!' on every street corner, and I thought, 'This is just a scene from *Cavalcade*.[284] Twenty, thirty years from now they will be re-enacting this, sound effects and all, on the screen to whoever survives.'" I was on my way to our monthly play reading group. The men, particularly Bob Reynolds and Howard Becker (later to enter OSS),[285] were very knowledgeable about what the loss of our fleet would mean, and I listened to everything they said, but it didn't really reach me. I had whined to Gwen in November: "The weather is very depressing, and to think of six months of short dark days, of driving with frosted windows on slippery or snowy roads, of shivering all the time, having to put on layers and layers of stuff to go out, of the children playing in the house all the time and getting too restless to stand it—Alice enquired the other morning in a nasty way what was that herd of buffalo tramping over the house when she was trying to sleep—and of their sniffing and coughing continuously—when I think of that for the next six months I don't seem to have the courage to face up to it. Also I have mice in the house. They keep knocking over my jam jars in the garage. Cello is no earthly good. She is decorative but not functional." We did some real shivering when fuel oil rationing came in.

I wrote Gwen again after Christmas. "I had a very exclusive carol party this year—asked just the Strangs, the Fulchers, and the Pooleys. After we got through singing, we sat around talking of the war, prospects of bombing and air raids and shelters and so on, and it was exactly like the first act of a play. Act I, Christmas Eve 1941: living room of the Thomases. And the mind couldn't avoid sketching out Act II, Christmas Eve 1943: air raid shelter of the Thomases; Act III, Christmas Eve 1945: hole in the ground filled with rubble which once

---

284 *Cavalcade*, a 1933 award-winning American film on English life from the perspective of wealthy London residents during several historical events in the early twentieth century.

285 The Office of Strategic Services (OSS), a U.S. wartime intelligence agency during World War II and predecessor of the Central Intelligence Agency (CIA).

formed the Thomas house; a few heavily bandaged survivors sitting among the ruins till the curtain falls with the final bomb." But the future, of course, wasn't to be like that at all.

On February 20, 1942, I started "a war journal from the standpoint of the consumer, particularly the housewife" and kept it through April 1943, and much of the material of this chapter comes from that as well as from my letters to Gwen. I put in various ads and pictures, which show that the Madison Avenue boys (if Madison Avenue existed then) were quick to mine the vein of patriotism which, to the best of my belief, existed throughout the country. Schenlye's Royal Reserve, the World's Best Whiskey, shows a distinguished elderly gentleman elegantly dressed in a tuxedo on a bicycle with bottles in the basket, "Riding Home to Toast America with a Drink of the Best—America Makes the Best of Everything." The Aetna Fire Group, with the slogan "Protection and Plenty of It," shows a housewife walking home clasping to her bosom a jar marked "coffee," escorted by the family dog, by her small son on one side with a sling-shot and her husband on the other with a rifle. The same concern urged "War Damage Insurance" with a picture of a woman getting a suit of red flannel underwear out of a chest, labeled "something you can't afford to be without these days." The Hotel Pennsylvania ran a whole series featuring two businessmen with briefcases; the second is always giving the refrain "And now we'll still reach the Hotel Pennsylvania in time for dinner and a grand night's sleep." Once they are behind a dog team of terrier, whippet, bull dog, sheep dog, and Great Dane, while the first man says, "What with the transportation problem, it wasn't very patriotic of Fred to refuse us the use of his dachshund"; again, on a giraffe (one briefcase tied to his tail), while the first says, "The keeper at the Zoo was very cooperative when I explained our transportation problem to him"; again, on a flying carpet: "I couldn't get reservations on anything, and then he walked in with *this* under his arm." The fine print always begins: "There's no denying that the *first* job of the transportation people is to see that Uncle Sam's official business gets through on schedule. Which means that, for many of us, traveling isn't as carefree and certain as it used to be" or an equivalent. Gluyas Williams ran a series called "Wartime Readjustments." In #2 a portly couple are riding a tandem bicycle, with two small children in a basket on the handlebars, a boy between the, and a girl at the rear, pulling a toy wagon piled with packages. Caption: "The Gibsons get around rubber rationing—and get around." In #7 the mother is counting on her fingers, the father punching an adding machine, Sis crossing out sums on the wall, and Junior fiddling with an abacus on the floor, table and floor littered with crossed-out papers. Caption: "Before Mother goes marketing, the McArgles always call a kitchen conference to figure coupon points." There

World War II

must have been people who cheated and black marketed and griped, I suppose, but I don't remember any.

March 1942. I saw Mary Winspear the other day. Her mother's house had been bombed twice, the second time so badly she just moved out to live with Mary's sister, and left it without trying to repair it. The city fixed it up, converted it into four flats, which are now rented, and Mary's mother gets the rent. She said they could get just about what they wanted, in spite of all the stories—the mother felt a craving for a lemon, and got one—price one shilling.

Did you hear Churchill? Everything is pretty grim, isn't it? Well, it's just a question of taking it for a while; we'll win eventually; and it will all provide stories to tell our grandchildren.

What a ghastly idea daylight saving is! It couldn't be any blacker than it is in the morning, and at night I don't like the light—it seems sinister. Alice says to sit down to dinner without a light you look out expecting to see apple blossoms, and get a sleet storm instead.

April 9, 1942. The neighborhood is quite seething with excitement these days. In the first place, the Fulchers' dog is in the hospital with convulsions. The vet keeps him under an opiate all day, allows him to wake up for his dinner with added calcium—for although the animal has had a quart of milk daily since birth he attributes this attack to a calcium deficiency—and then puts him under to insure a night's rest. I do not wish to be unsympathetic, but considering the state of the world, isn't there a little, leetle something out of proportion in their solicitude? Sally Marshall is going to offer to be a blood donor for the dog, and I am about to send him flowers.

We are organizing Civilian Defense.[286] Mr. Simon has been appointed Commander for the village by Ace Fisher, but his general attitude being "I don't know what it's all about," Bob Pooley is being the power behind the throne and pushing gently when necessary. A First Aid Course starts Monday at the school: a Nutrition Course Tuesday. The latter is my baby. Setzie [Pooley] is now Red Cross Chairman for the township

---

286 The Office of Civilian Defense, a US federal emergency war agency established to coordinate and ensure civilian protection, operated from 1941–1945.

of Blooming Grove and the village of Monona; she asked me to be Nutrition Chairman, tactfully saying she couldn't get anyone else; so I am. The Nutrition Course will be followed by a Canteen Course. And I am having a garden. Worse than that, the Girl Scouts are having a garden. I think it will be a hard summer.

Ednah Thomas working in her victory garden, 1940s. Source: William Thomas

World War II

My sources are unfortunately silent on the Nutrition course, and I don't remember much about it. I do remember a meeting of all state nutrition chairmen held in Ag Hall, where we were addressed by various university faculty, and I never admired anyone more than the doctor who responded with perfect calm and perfect courtesy to a woman's question if drinking milk made black spots come out on your teeth: "I know of no evidence of any sort which supports that view." A great effort was made to promote soybeans, which nutritionally are as good as steak, which of course had disappeared. Our Red Cross Nutrition consultants had recipes for everything imaginable made with soybeans, including chocolate chip cookies, but ours confessed to me that she had never eaten anything made with soybeans that she thought wouldn't have tasted better if it hadn't. I bought a lot of seed (I can still see the man's face at Old's Seed Company when I told him they were just as good as steak), planted them, and they did well. One and only one soybean product was really palatable: Salty Soys, like salted peanuts, and I'm rather sorry this went off the market. But in general, nutrition or no nutrition, war or no war, people just wouldn't eat soybeans, and I guess that now the acres and acres of them annually planted all go into steering wheels and other plastics.

> You should see the campus—the fleet's in! Three hundred sailors have already arrived, three hundred more come the first of each month till a total of twelve hundred is reached, and that will be maintained, for a four months' special course in radio.[287] It is very picturesque to see them going to and from classes, fifty or so in a group, walking two by two like an English girls' school crocodile. They are very nice-looking boys, and terribly, terribly young. There are some repercussions on campus, but no doubt they will all settle in. The present ones are in the Short Course dormitories over on the Ag Campus.[288] They have only one night out, Saturday, so we hope the Union and the various social organizations ought to give them a little fun then.

Once when Bill and I, who walked the streets or went to the Zoo while Hannah and Tommy were at the First Congregational Sunday School, met a group, one boy saw Bill's gorgeous hair, swept off his own cap, and bowed to us to show us that his was the same bright color. Grace Maiken found the offi-

---

287 The Navy Radio School, which began on April 1, 1942, was the first university-based military training unit in the country (Cronon & Jenkins, 1999, p. 414).
288 The Farm Short Course, a twelve-week training program for future farmers, was established in 1885 as part of the newly created College of Agriculture and played a significant role in shifting Wisconsin's agricultural production from wheat to dairy (Cronon & Jenkins, 1999, p. 768).

cers something of an embarrassment when she took Tony in town, because he insisted on addressing every one of them as "Daddy." Jack was away in training, and Tony was too little to remember anything about him but the uniform.

> April 30, 1942. It is so lovely here now, just the best time of year, as you know. All the little pink leaves on the oaks are the size of a mouse's ear, and the lilacs are just coming out. The big hickory buds are just in the act of unfolding like magnolias. I wish it were possible to hold everything just as it is for another month.
>
> We are gardening for Victory. And the great neighborhood excitement is watching Paddo Bloodgood, who has taken part of Ruth Wallerstein's land.[289] Did I write you all this—how he came out to look at it accompanied by a federal agricultural expert, and then each time afterwards brought a friend who did the work while Paddo stood around communing with nature? Yesterday was one of those sudden hot spring days, with a blazing sun, and in the afternoon Paddo turned up and began to work. I saw Jane in the car, so I asked her in where it was cooler because I was afraid if she sat in the unshaded car she would die of heat prostration and I wouldn't remember the right First Aid treatment for it. She came in and I gave her some iced tea, while Paddo kept on working, stripped to the waist—a fine figure of a man. I forgot to say she had been reading a book called *Faith Under Fire*; it must be wonderful to be spiritual like that. She said they had only a few minutes to work, so I handed Paddo a glass of iced tea on the wing, so to speak, and they drove away. Just then I heard someone calling me, and it was Mr. Pond, the federal agricultural agent, whom I had previously met. "Mrs. Thomas," said he, "I am worried about Paddo's tomato plants." And when I found Paddo had put them out on the blazing day without a drop of water or a bit of covering, so was I. Mr. Pond borrowed a pail and watered them, and when he came back I gave him some iced tea and cake. I didn't give the Bloodgoods any cake because they are both exceptionally well-nourished, but if ever a man deserved it, Mr. Pond did. He said Paddo was a

---

289 Ruth Wallerstein (1893–1958), educated at Bryn Mawr and University of Pennsylvania, joined the English department in 1920 and taught English literature until her untimely death in an automobile accident in England while on research leave.

wonderful man and did a lot of good, but he thought he was a little too much in the habit of delegating authority. . . . This morning is overcast and showery, and the tomato plants are standing up straight as soldiers. It is ideal weather for them. Could God have spoken more plainly? I am humbled. He is certainly looking out for His own. I hope Paddo prays for Mr. Pond. Mr. Pond deserves it, and Paddo must have God's ear.

Early in May the Girl Scouts had "got about half of their garden planted, and God, looking out for it as He did for Paddo's, watered it with a heavy shower. As a matter of fact, I'm afraid He overdid it because there was such a downpour it must have washed away the carrot seeds." A week or so later Paddo "abandoned his garden. He can't get tires after all, being classed as a city minister, so he has just gone away and left the tomato plants. A summer of entertainment snatched away from me, but I ought to be so busy working in my own I won't have time to regret the loss."

The end of July I went to see Mother, leaving the children with Alice. Here is Hannah's letter, which I submit is perfect evidence for both parts of Peter's classic utterance: "I love Hannah dearly, but she cannot spell."

July 28, 1942

Dear Mother,

When we went to the zoo there was the cutst little deer and monkys. You must see them when you come back.

We are having the first summer sqaush for supper. The green peas are almost ready. We gave some cucumbers to the Owns and Marshalals. By the time you get back there will be anofe tomatos to can. We have pulled up all the onines.

I am reading *Rewards and Fairies*. My eye is much better. I have read *Puck of Pooks Hill*.

Miss Roberts called up and said she was going to be in town off and on. She will call you when you come home.

It rained early in the day but it has carled off.

We are all well. Bill is just have one off his temper spells but ullsy he is a good boy. Alice's cooking is just fine.

Jan is coming ofter to spend the night.

Love,

Hannah

So far food, except for almonds, pineapple, and sugar, was obtainable about as usual, though prices were steadily going up. I naively recorded, "I'll get advertisements from the papers once a month to clip in, to have some accurate record of food prices." But living today in inflation, you'd just laugh at how ridiculously small the prices were anyway, and I won't bother with them. By March "children now perfectly accustomed to Karo on oatmeal and waffles. I have used five pounds of sugar in a month, which is only about one third of the ration—60 ounces a week for a family of five. There is no use saving it up because they say you must declare what you have got on hand before you get any more; and some people feel so badly they threaten to destroy hidden supplies rather than be known as hoarders. I hope more will be available in canning time."

(The summer of 1941) Women in general went frantic because it was said there would be no silk stockings available, and there were terrific scenes in stores. I hadn't been wearing silk for some time—I went into lisle as a protest, boycotting Japanese silk at the announcement of the Sino-Japanese War. When nylon first came out (midwinter of 40–41 if I remember correctly), I tried that, and was delighted—even better than silk in appearance and much better for wearing qualities—one pair lasts six months. So I have on hand three pairs of nylons, and I expect those to last a long time. Otherwise I am not buying cotton for everyday—Woolworth's 29 cents. I wear anklets all summer.

(February 24, 1942) I wore nylon stockings because I was going to University League tea at Mrs. Dykstra's.[290] It seems very odd to wear them. With formal dress on a formal occasion I do, but for everything else, including Reading Group or something like that, it is always cotton.

February 20, 1942. The worst shortage to date is rubber. The Japanese by December 14 had invaded or occupied areas which produce 50% of our crude rubber, and menaced regions which account for 43% more. Civilian consumption is cut down to 10,000 tons per month—80% below the recent

---

290   The wife of Clarence Addison Dykstra (1883–1950), who was president of UW-Madison from 1937–1945 and, during World War II, directed the Selective Service System (1940–1941) and chaired the Defense Mediation Board.

> monthly rate. Retail sales of tires were prohibited till January 4. A quota is eventually to be established, handled by local defense boards. Tires rationed to 1) vehicles necessary for public health and safety—doctors, police cars, ambulances, public nurses, veterinarians, etc. 2) buses 3) essential trucks. No provision is made at all for people in our position who need cars to get to work. Less than 1/10 the normal number of tires are assigned for January.
>
> The American automobile industry, employing 10 times as many people as are employed in any other, is stopped completely; on February 1, manufacture of trucks and cars for civilians stopped. The sale of the cars on hand roughly is on the same lines as tires.

The radio program *Information Please*[291] which many of us remember so fondly had a pertinent answer in an April program: asked to use in a quotation "some commodity which is imported and getting scarce," Franklin P. Adams responded, "And all our pomp of yesterday/ Is one with Ninevah and Tyre."

> All rubber articles are supposed to be difficult to get. I wonder if the children will have overshoes next year. All rubber and all metals are scarce. Wool will be rationed probably, but cottons are plentiful. Cans will presumably be replaced as largely as possible by glass. Paper is getting scarce. Stores are reluctant to wrap packages. At the A& P they have begun to sell big paper bags for a penny instead of giving them to you.

In March it was announced that there would be no re-treading of tires till after the war and tires not used for defense might be confiscated; also typewriters were to be rationed and all rented ones turned in by April 1. I made my first soap this month, which wasn't bad, and I got only one slight burn from the lye; but I was rather relieved later when the housewife was urged not to make her own soap but to save the fat and turn it in for mass production. I also bought a bicycle (they were frozen in April) and strained my ankle trying to learn to ride it, but "fortunately owing to the First Aid course, I knew the right bandage to put on." By April I could ride as far as the Fulchers and back without falling, but my legs were "very spectacularly colored and Alice talks about gas gangrene and tetanus." I would have had to ride a long way to get groceries, you realize; there are now three or four stores within walking distance, but then there were none.

---

291 *Information Please*, an award-winning American radio quiz show and an early example of a panel game genre, aired from 1938 to 1951.

I never really did get comfortable on the bicycle, but it was a very fortunate purchase because you all used it a lot, and it was a very long time before bicycles were available again. In February I baked a big batch of bread.

> I have done it six or eight times, but in small quantities. Now I am going into it in a big way, wholesale—so much so that like a bride I had everything in the house overflowing. But I shall get onto the proper amounts soon. I have just used up a 25-pound sack of flour. The next time I shall buy fifty pounds.

In the spring of '42 a test drive for metal was held in two counties, our own Dane of Wisconsin and one in Virginia, and in the summer a nation-wide one.

> All available scrap iron people could spare, pots, pans, everything we could get along without. All metals are supposed to be scarce. Toothpaste tubes, which are pure tin, have to be returned before you can buy a new one, but not shaving cream tubes, which are pure lead.
>
> May 5, 1942. Sugar rationing week. This had been put off for a time because of the complications of the business.
>
> No sugar sold anywhere in the United States for a week preceding this, then registration the first four days of this week at the school houses. You have to give your age, height, weight, color of eyes and hair and declare the amount of sugar you have on hand, including brown, loaf, powdered or syrup (from sugar, not corn). You are allowed two pounds per person per family; if you have six pounds per person you can keep it, but the first four stamps are torn out of your book. Anything above that is hoarding. This is to serve as basis for all future rationing, which is why so many details are given. I registered tonight at the school and got four books: mine 353527–163; Hannah's 353528–163; Tommy's 353529–163; and Bill's 353526–163. Alice got her own at the university. I use her coupons as long as she lives here with us.
>
> On June 19 I went to register for extra sugar for canning.
>
> People in the city are allowed 6 pounds per person, in the country 10 pounds per person, and everyone allowed 1 pound per person for jams, etc., which are discouraged. Canning of fruits is to be encouraged. I am allowed 40 pounds. They want

> me to take it in two 20 pound lots, one now, one August 1, because it is too heavy a load on the grocers to get it all now. Everyone in the county registers in Madison, over the police station. Quite a sight—all of us buxom farm women seeking sugar. The woman ahead of me had never got her original ration book, so she had to answer all those questions. When the registrar asked her her weight she lowered her voice and leaned forward and whispered—very softly—something beginning with two hundred. All the women were scared to death they would be put in jail if they didn't answer everything accurately to the last inch. "How much did you can last year?" "Well, about a hundred quarts. *About*. I can't be exactly sure." "How much have you left?" "Oh, nothing. That is, three or four. Well, there might be four. I can't be exactly sure."

The Middle West, at its reassuring distance from both oceans, was much less apprehensive about attack than either east or west coasts. A correspondent in California, a Frost Woods neighbor in the thirties, wrote at Christmas 1941 that they were substituting "Happy black-out!" for "Happy New Year!" but here we had neither black-out or dim-out. I do remember one test, when for some reason I can't now imagine I was standing on the steps of the University Club—I might have been in town and waiting there for a neighbor who was going to pick me up and take me home—and saw all lights in the city of Madison extinguished for a few minutes, but I remember no other. It was quite different in Boston, where I went to see Mother, taking advantage of Alice's being here to keep house for you.

> August 3, 1942. Back from a trip to Boston. Traveling daycoach sitting up all night while the Army and Navy in boyish spirits sang lustily and horseplayed. Traveling is not rationed and my trains were all on time; but conditions not luxurious. All trains very crowded.
>
> Boston had no beef whatever of any sort. Meat shortage non-existent in middle west but true in east. Gas rationing in force. The original scheme didn't work and now the cards are like the sugar cards; they have to turn in the stamps to get new supplies. Hansom cabs in Boston again, but still more or less of a fad. They ply around Copley Square but you don't see them downtown. Very odd feeling when I got in at 9 p.m. to see the dim-out lights—all street lights painted dark gray over the top two-thirds—and hear the clop-clop of horses' hooves.

(I remembered how fond my father had been of horses and how he had regretted their disappearance, and wished he could have lived to see them come into their own again.) The city traffic doesn't seem much diminished but the highway traffic is practically non-existent. The subways in Boston are jammed.

I saw the Sharps on this visit. Bob was in the Navy, with a desk job at the Charleston Navy Yard, and he and Marie sat out the war very comfortably in an attractive apartment on Beacon Street overlooking the Charles River. They reported that at the Island[292] "all the cars are sitting in their garages on Sawyers[293] while people save up enough gas to go home on. The Reeds have had their boat out only twice. The only way to get to the Harbor is to make reservations ahead with Paul Abbott, go in his car to Southport for the mail at 11, take the *Richard II* to Boothbay, and reverse the process at 3." On the way back I stopped over twenty-four hours with the Beattys in Detroit, and noted that there "the traffic hadn't let up one bit. Apparently no one will conserve rubber until he is forced to." Another drive in August for old records, "to be sold for scrap, the proceeds to go to USO[294] to buy new records for soldiers, and to get shellac to make new records."

Through this time I was very busy showing the Beatty house to a succession of officers from Truax.[295]

> No day without a visitor and this morning a regular traffic jam, one prospect barging in before the other one had gone. Don't any of them write to you? I give them all Ham's address, and tell them all the same thing, that he wants $70 a month, hoping neither he nor I will be put in jail for wanting. One couple I bet you won't hear from—Major Bond and his wife. They came Thursday, and I liked them very much. All the Army wives, as a bunch, seem to compare favorably with the Duchess of Windsor in the time, thought, and money

---

292 A reference to Isle of Springs, an island community located in BoothBay Harbor, Maine, where the family spent summer vacations.
293 A reference to Sawyer Island near Boothbay, Maine.
294 The United Service Organizations, established in 1941, is a nonprofit organization that provides programming and entertainment to US service members.
295 Truax Field, formerly the Madison airport, was commandeered by the army in 1942 and converted into a complex for military training. In 1946, the War Department transferred portions of the Truax facilitates to UW-Madison to create temporary housing for the influx of veterans attending the university on the GI Bill (Cronon & Jenkins, 1994, pp. 33–38).

they spend on their clothes and appearance, but Mrs. Bond was the pick of the bunch. She looked so much like Myrna Loy she could have gone into any picture without anyone's noticing the difference.[296] They were the pleasantest and most attractive couple who have been here, and have a little boy Bill's age, and of course they liked the house very much. As we emerged onto the lawn, Robin, Tommy, and Bill all bore down upon us, each child holding a live, squirming snake in assorted sizes. I endeavored to fend them off, saying that perhaps Mrs. Bond didn't care for snakes. "As a matter of fact," said she, "I don't." Just at that moment another snake passed rapidly across the lawn under Mrs. Bond's feet. She let out a yell and leaped two feet up in the air. The Major then assisted her into the car, and they drove away—out of my life forever, I believe. Of course really it is not snakes, but transportation, that keeps people from writing to you—if they don't write. Everyone says the same thing. In all other respects the place is perfect, but "It's so far out."

Ham succeeded in renting it this month to the Maikens, who afterwards bought it, a very fortunate circumstance for me, since Grace was a very good neighbor to me. Later, while Jack was in his Navy training program at Harvard, I continued for them my role as real estate agent.

In August, Alice and Chuck suddenly decided to get married, and the wedding was held here. Chuck, who was in an officers' training corps at the university, was allowed the next year to finish college, so they were reasonably sure of one year together, and Alice was resolved to marry, whether or not it meant she must leave Nursing School. As a matter of fact, it didn't, since in response to the times the authorities canceled the provision in force up to then that students could not be married. "Alice is terribly excited and exhilarated. The children are very pleased." Alice's relations with her own mother were not happy, and the only member of her family at the wedding was her younger sister Caryl, a university student. I decorated with a big bold-color vegetable arrangement, tomatoes, summer squash, corn, which pleased Chuck very much. They were appropriate to the season and to his profession, and free for the gathering (generally the motive behind my esthetic creations). I lent Alice the string of seed pearls which Hannah also wore at her wedding. There were perhaps twenty guests, young university friends and a few of the closest neighbors like the Pooleys. The

---

296 Myrna Loy (1905–1993), an American film, television, and stage actress who served in the Red Cross during World War II.

day was memorable for one of the concomitants of life in Frost Woods in the good old days—the electricity went off in the night and didn't come on till three p.m., the wedding being set for four. The worst thing about this always was no water; it was before the Metropolitan Water and Sewage system was extended around the lake, and we had our own septic tank and well, operated by electricity. We sat around all morning waiting for the current to come on any minute, unable either to clean, cook, or wash. Luckily I had made the cake the day before, but I hadn't made the frosting, and the punch was warming up as the ice chest defrosted itself. Chuck arrived from town with ice cubes, showing the calm competence that always marks him, and the electricity came on just in time to allow one bath, which by common consent we awarded to the bride. I wiped the children—and myself—off with a damp cloth, and hoped for the best, and they behaved very well, though Bill insisted on laying flat on his stomach, gradually inching out farther and farther into the room during the ceremony. An historic family incident which has provided an oft-told tale occurred in September.

> A week ago I heard a noise outside, but you so often hear noises I paid no attention; but it grew louder and before I knew what had happened my house was full of boys, all yelling at the top of their lungs, escorting Bill, who was spattered from head to foot with blood and roaring like a lion. Robin Pooley has certainly missed his vocation. He should have been one of those messengers in Greek drama who come in to announce deaths and murders and catastrophes of all sorts. With great relish he announced that Bill had fallen thirty feet out of a tree and landed head first on some rusty nails. (I found out later, by visiting the scene of the crime, that it was fifteen feet onto a pile of iron pipe and old boards, just over the edge of the park line onto Ray Owen's land—bad enough, of course.) I tried to calm Bill, which was like calming a calliope, and undressed him to see if there were any other injuries beside a very obvious scalp wound. While I was doing that, Tommy came to the door and said, "Is he very badly hurt?" "I don't know yet," I said. "We're cleaning a sunfish," said Tommy. "Could you cook it for us?" "Not now, dear," I said, and called Dr. Tenney, and at his direction took Bill in to the hospital where someone took five stitches in his scalp. He looks very funny now with a little shaved place and white dressing like a cap right on the crown of his head like a tonsure, but the cut is healing all right and I am to take this last dressing off myself in a couple of days.

The boys' fish catches were to come in very handy when the meat shortage spread to the Middle West, and I was to be very grateful for everything I grew and canned, though in this same letter I wrote to Gwen, "I am harvesting carrots. How I wish I hadn't put in such a large garden. Shall I send you some soybeans for Christmas?"

As time went on, of course, scarcities increased. Bananas and chocolate disappeared. One of our favorite Reading Group topics of conversation was the substitutes we produced for our children's birthday cakes. In October, Franks, the grocery store on University Avenue where I had shopped for years, stopped delivering. I shopped once a week, on the only regular weekly trip I made in town, to Reading Group. At the A&P, a customer was limited to two cans meat, two cans fish, one can salmon; there were restrictions on canned fruits and vegetables but not such stringent ones. Of course we had our own. "No metal lunch boxes left, so I could only get a composition one for Tommy— 'all right as long as you don't get it wet.' No half pint thermos bottles left and none being manufactured, no chewing gum left in a big chain drug store." There was another nation-wide scrap drive in the fall, and the fraternities and dormitories had a contest collecting scrap instead of decorating in the usual way for Homecoming. Alice asked me to give mine to the Nurses' Dormitory, which had a big pile, as tastefully arranged as possible, with "Beat Ohio" spelled out in big letters formed by the tops of tin cans. These drives continued all through the war. At Nichols School, the children got to be called "Corporal," "Sergeant," "Lieutenant," "Captain," and so forth for a day, according to the extent of the contribution they brought in. One of the bravest actions I ever performed for my children, considering how easy it is for me to feel guilty without reason, was picking up a carton of tin cans put out on a Madison street for collection, putting it in the car, and carrying it home as if it were the Mona Lisa. When the Beattys moved to Cleveland the next spring, I consoled Gwen for the trouble of moving again with "No doubt in your clearing-out you can find donations for scrap metal and rubber drives."

Hannah now developed allergies. "The dermatologists has taken her off eggs, tomatoes, all citrus fruits, pineapple (that doesn't worry me—no one has seen any since Pearl Harbor), feather pillows, and soap. It's hard to cook without eggs or tomatoes, two articles of food I seem to put into everything. Think of the eight dozen jars of tomatoes in the basement that she can't eat." When she had the full series of tests, it turned out she was very allergic to cats, and we had to get rid of Cello—a great grief to us all. We loved her so much, and she contributed so much; Bill would take a nap every day as long as she lay down with him. The poor cat had as much trouble as a war refugee in finding a home.

When I first asked Virginia if she'd like Cello she was so cordial I felt very comforted, and when I asked after her from time to time everything was as rosy as a sunrise. So it was rather a shock when she called up and said she wanted the New Year by being perfectly frank, and Frank didn't like cats, and Edith, the maid, didn't like cats, and she'd like me to give Cello to someone else. Of course if Virginia clings to the quaint old-world custom of keeping a maid, I can see she'd honor her prejudices, but I don't know why she didn't tell me that in the first place. I have now placed Cello at the Eccleses, feeling rather like a social worker trying to place a problem child for adoption.

Unfortunately she stayed there less than a year.

> Cello has moved on *again*. Elizabeth Eccles called up and said she was so sorry, they were all devoted to her (or "him" as they insist on calling her, I can't think why, although of course it's true), but Cynthia has asthma, and Dr. Ganz was very severe about the cat. It seems as if poor Cello were like Typhoid Mary and carried disease wherever she went.

Katherine Post took her for a little, but then returned her also.

> Hannah's hands were getting much worse, and I realized all at once that since the cold weather Cello spends a lot of time in her room, which she keeps warmest in the house. So I took her to the vet's for euthanasia. Of course there is no hesitation in a choice between a cat and your child's welfare, but I felt like Judas, and I miss Cello terribly; she was the one living thing in the house that never caused me trouble, and she was always without exception nice to me.

But I had the satisfaction that Hannah improved very much, and by January was "back on a fairly Christian diet—no egg yolks and no oil or shortening other than butter—of all times to choose that—but otherwise pretty normal." That she couldn't eat eggs, though, was a difficulty all through the war, since owing to our bountiful supply of vegetables the boys and I could get on well a great deal of the time with eggs instead of meat. Do you remember the black bean home-grown, home-made soup?

At the end of October, I filled out my application for fuel oil. "Measured all rooms to be heated, submitted measurements, number of people in house,

World War II

appended certificate from Co-op of number of gallons bought last year, size of storage tanks." This shortage was for us the greatest hardship. In November there was "a great flurry over coffee, which is to be rationed the end of the month" (when gas rationing also started here)—one pound per person for five weeks, one cup a day. "Everyone I know honeying up to me to give them my extra coffee since I rarely drink it myself. All stores absolutely cleaned out now in preparation—none at all available. Waiting in a drug store yesterday for a prescription I saw customer after customer come in and ask for a cup of coffee and be refused because the store couldn't get any." For the favor-present at the Christmas party this year, I gave "little paper cupfuls of coffee, done up with a sprig of evergreen and a red holly berry, so everyone could have an extra cup of coffee on Christmas. A great success." I gradually did begin to drink coffee in the next few years, but as you know I have never smoked, and I enjoyed an entirely spurious popularity through the cigarette shortage because I could give mine away, a shortage which of course was perhaps the hardest of all for addicts. It was particularly hard for Grace Maiken during the time she was under the strain of having her husband in the Pacific.

The neighborhood—and the Fredricksons—were mildly enlivened by Dicky's breaking out in spots on Christmas morning: German measles. "Opening at random a book given to Hannah for Christmas, I came upon this sentence. 'There was the yellow couch on which she had had German measles every Good Friday and Easter for three years in succession.' The incubation period is fourteen to twenty-one days so we may expect a source of interest and suspense for the rest of the winter." Faye Nagdegaal, the former neighbor, reported on her work in California. "She is assistant to the Field Director of the Red Cross in the San Jose area, and serves as liaison officer between the soldier and his family back home. 'We are sometimes known as the Wailing Wall.' They have lately been dealing with the problem of bringing out to the post a number of girl friends who needed to get married after the boys had been home on furlough." This Christmas Bill "got a piece of construction paper and punched holes in it and made me run a string through to make a sort of envelope, and put some Kleenexes in, all his own idea, and hung it in the kitchen. He did it, he said, because Santa Claus might come, and he might be sniffing, and he would look around and find the Kleenexes." It's as futile to choose any period in family life as the best as to choose any years of your whole life as the best, but I do think that time ranks very high when the youngest child still believes in Santa Claus and the older ones do not, but cooperate with the parents to preserve that belief.

This was an unusually cold winter. We had three sub-zero spells before the middle of December. I was allowed 1800 gallons of oil for a house that had used 3097 the year before. I shut off the addition, and it was fortunate that Alice was married and was no longer living with us, and that, although I had registered the addition to rent at the University Housing Bureau, no one had even come out to look at it. I observed that the children could have a chance to enjoy the pioneer conditions Laura Ingalls Wilder's books had always made them envy.[297] "Thermostat at 60 for duration. Children and I eating dinner with coats on over sweaters. Shut off bedrooms, which are therefore about 30 all the time. Brought cotton sheeting—outing flannel blankets to use as sheets." This was a *very* great help; they are infinitely warmer.

> We have a wonderful hot water bottle system. It's like the traveler who, overtaken by darkness, went into a peasant's hut in the forest and asked for a night's lodging. The good woman welcomed him, but the traveler was a little perplexed, because there were a dozen children and only one bed. After supper the mother put the baby in the bed, and it went off to sleep. Then she lifted it out onto the floor, put the next child in, and so on till the oldest child had gone to sleep. Then she lifted him out and indicated to the traveler that his bed was ready. He demurred, but she insisted, saying the children were used to it. So he went comfortably off to sleep, and woke up in the morning to find himself on the floor among the children and the woman and her husband in the bed. Well, to return to our hot water bottles. Tommy and Bill go to sleep with them, then I steal them out for Hannah and me. In the morning when I get up I return mine to each boy in turn on successive mornings so they can have a warm one to play with in bed the first few minutes in the morning.

This is, I must admit, pretty effete compared with Pa and Ma. Why didn't I buy a hot water bottle for everyone? No rubber goods of any sort available. Why didn't we have electric heating pads? They hadn't (I think) been invented. In January I congratulated Gwen on having coal.

> My father was always reminiscing about the great winter of '88, and I'm getting all ready to tell my grandchildren about '43. Do you remember the year the snow was so deep it was piled up higher than a car on the sides of the road by Hollywood? We're in the running for that this year. Our driveway is

---

[297] Laura Ingalls Wilder (1867–1957), an American writer who published the *Little House on the Prairie* children's novels in the 1930s and 1940s, was born in Wisconsin and spend her childhood in the Midwest.

> already so high that I can't throw the snow to the sides, it being above my head; so I have to carry every shovelful either to the top or the bottom. It's an awfully pretty winter. The snow never has a chance to get dirty, even in town, and of course out here it looks like a rabbit was sitting right in the middle of the path, just as still.
>
> The neighborhood is going in for square dancing; and is it ever fun. It's the best exercise I've had for twenty years, since I used to play tennis with the men in Maine, and guaranteed to warm you up no matter how cold the house. Perfect entertainment for this winter, for the guests furnish their own heat.

I have had a very full and rich and fortunate life, and I have few or no unfulfilled wishes. But I *could* wish I had had more chance to do square dancing; I never enjoyed any other recreation so much. I've spent a good deal of my life as an extra woman in a society of extra women—true of New England in general and the Island in particular; and by now it was certainly true in Frost Woods.

On December 27 "Wickard and Davis broadcast to the nation, announcing the rationing of all canned, dried, and frozen fruits and vegetables to take effect in February, and announced—without explaining—the Point System."[298] The winter dragged on. Mr. Beatty died in February, my mother in March. "The driving has been worse than any year I ever knew here—ice on the roads all the time." After the beginning of 1943, my entries in the consumer notebook get shorter (the Army Institute papers, of which I shall speak separately, were piling up heavily, and perhaps I had no time to keep it), and they stop altogether on April 21 with "new potatoes ten cents a pound."

> Jan 28. All sliced bread out for the duration. Squibs in the papers and magazines about how awful for the housewife, who has no bread knives to cut with. But I've been baking my bread for some times, and have always had a serrated bread knife since I was married.
>
> All pleasure driving—concerts, theaters, etc.—in the East banned entirely. Fuel oil situation serious there. In Providence, all stores, offices, and schools closed on Mondays to save fuel.
>
> Feb 7. Announcement over the radio that shoes are to be rationed. No shoes sold tomorrow then on Tuesday stamp 18 (of coffee and sugar book) is good—one pair until June

---

298 Claude Wickard (1893–1967), Secretary of Agriculture from 1940 to 1945. Elmer Davis (1890–1958), Director of the U.S. Office of War Information during World War II.

> 15, three pairs a year, but a family can pool its tickets. Manufacture of patent leather, evening shoes, two-tone, etc. to be stopped. No ration on repair work.
>
> Feb 10. All sales of canned meat and fish frozen.
>
> Feb 20. At midnight all sales of canned fruit and vegetables frozen for a week. Registration for Ration Book 2 next week.
>
> Mar 20. Frank's, the largest delivery grocery store in a city of 70,000, has for meat at 8 a.m. Saturday morning various kinds of bulk sausage, wienies, some of the pre-cooked veal-loaf delicatessen meats, and several frozen beef kidneys. No poultry, beef, veal, pork, or lamb of any kind.

I have no reference to it in my journal, but I remember well that mutton was not rationed, and was often available, and we liked it very much indeed. I simmered it in the thrift cooker, cooled the liquid to solidify the fat and get rid of that, and then reheated meat and broth with vegetables in as good a dish as Brillat-Savarin himself could want.[299] I wish I could get some now.

> Cocoa, chocolate, cocoanut, dried apricots have all entirely disappeared.
>
> Mar 24. Went in town with my ration books. Girl laughing about a man who brought 196 points worth of goods to be checked yesterday with 8 points to pay for them. (By this time, you never thought about money; if you had the points, you had the money.) Meat counter full of sausages, pig's tails—very odd looking—and pork rib bones, skeletons with their layers of fat and meat. I asked the clerk about cooking them. She seemed depressed and said she had no idea how it was done. Quite a time counting up my cans and points. The total was never the same twice.
>
> Mar 27. Getting very tired of vegetable soup and cheese.
>
> Mar 29. Point rationing of fats, meat, salad oil, cheese.
>
> Apr 11. No poultry. Red stamps seem to be holding out fairly well, but blue stamps not. Shark meat for sale at A&P fish counter.

In March I had flu. "That's what I've been afraid of all winter, of course, my being sick, but we did pretty well. Hannah got the meals and Tommy washed

---

299   Jean Anthelme Brillat-Savarin (1755–1826), a famous French epicure and gastronome.

the dishes; I could hear them fighting, which was no more soothing to an invalid's nerves than Bill's bouncing on my bed like a springboard, but no bones or dishes were broken, and I think Hannah did well. She has quite a sense of responsibility. Heavens, who invented the month of March? Everyone sniffing and coughing, and 'mud, mud, mud' (to quote Kipling)."[300] But "I have seen two robins and there are water patches showing through the dead ice on the lake." Alice came back to stay "indefinitely. She's given up the nursing school for a year because of health; she can't do any work. If Chuck were stationed permanently anywhere she would join him, but until he is she will probably stay here. It is a great help to have her, even though she can't do any work, because she is another adult. It's still too cold here to plough."

Perhaps this is the place to insert that one great difficulty for me in much of this period was lack of contemporary (i.e. adult) companionship. If you have a monopoly of contemporary companionship, as has been the case in the last few decades, as in housing developments where everyone is twenty-five to thirty or in homes for the elderly, that can be as bad as lack of it; but I do think a reasonable amount throughout life is a requisite for the good life. I suffered from this lack as a child, and I suffered to some extent again during this time. I can never be sufficiently grateful to the neighbors; but Setzie, as is always true of a particularly efficient person, was overloaded with war activities, and Grace was away much of the time, and all of us were very much confined to our own houses by our small children, especially during the bad months from November to April. Since everyone was on gas rationing, no one came to see me; of course the Reading Group was a life-saver, but it was only once a week, when I could make it. Your brain deteriorates without some contact with maturity. One of many reasons I was grateful for the Army Institute work was that the students were adults. Of course I could read, but sometimes when you read you want to share. In Denis Brogan's analysis of the British character, he discusses the British Tommy, who had a reputation for picking up anything not nailed down.[301] Once when the British Army was stationed in Palestine on Christmas Eve, someone commented, "I'll bet the shepherds watched their flocks *that* night." I wanted to share that with someone. There's nothing dirty or immoral about it, but it wasn't for children; only an adult could think it funny, and at the same time be able to succumb completely to the magic of the beautiful words when Christmas came again.

At the end of April, "This is the most reluctant spring I ever knew. I still haven't got my garden in. It has been ploughed, but not dragged. I shall be

---

300 A reference to a line from "A Song of Winter Weather," a poem by the British-Canadian writer Robert W. Service's (1874–1958), who was nicknamed "the Canadian Kipling."

301 Sir Denis William Brogan (1900–1974) was a Scottish author, historian, and professor of political science known for his broadcast radio talks, primarily on historical themes.

so thankful when I can get out of my house into the garden all the nasty little seedlings I have there; they are all 'leggy' in the extreme. Mr. Balde, the school janitor, is supposed to do the ploughing and dragging. The furnace blew up there the other day, so no doubt he has been otherwise occupied." The Strangs left for Glen Ellyn, [Illinois,] where Allen had a war housing job, and rented the house to the new executive secretary of the Madison Council of Boy Scouts. "He has two daughters, nine and twelve respectively, which is very very nice for Hannah, especially since Jan leaves this summer." But his wife was a city type, and the change from a Chicago apartment to Frost Woods was too much for her. The first night she was here she pulled down all the shades either from fear of wolves or Indians, and they moved in town as soon as he was able to find a house. (You remember this was the Strangs' first house, up in the woods, not the one in Wennequah.)

> Patty Stedman up for a last fling before her maid left, visiting Virginia. She was telling us horror stories about the Washington hospitals. A woman came in at 1:30 to have her baby, had it on a stretcher in the hall with no assistance of any kind, there was no place to put the baby so they put it back on the stretcher beside her, and by 4:30 she was back in her own house. Once might just as well be a pioneer woman and stay right in one's own log cabin.
>
> I have just read a very good book—*And Keep Your Powder Dry: An Anthropologist Looks at America*, by Margaret Mead. I'm urging it upon the Reading Group. It is very interesting for a parent, I think. Of course it leaves me baffled—what complexes one's child will develop and ought to develop are very confusing. As Katherine Post said, it was lucky the psychiatrist and educator usually had no children, because after you once had them you didn't dare speak with authority any more.
>
> I have ordered new rugs for the living room. The old ones all went at once. After you have been in a house just about this long everything falls to pieces at once, like the One Hoss Shay—a singularly awkward time, too. The new ones are Kleanflax, not wool, for patriotic and economic reasons.

In May we came into the happiest period of the year. We were all healthy, outdoors as much of the time as we could possibly be, gardens in and growing, lilacs coming into blossom, and everything easier.

May 8. Tell Ham Mr. Morgan is having a field day digging up my back yard. The actual digging is done by an old gentleman who can't be a day over seventy-five. It is a little appalling to see the old men who are working these days. The man at the Co-op filling station now is so frail he looks as if a breath would blow him away and he shakes with palsy when he moves like somebody in Keats' "Eve of St. Agnes." But he is very cheerful. I am sure really they are very happy to be working and to feel they are useful.

Tommy Thomas has joined the Navy. Alice Strang writes that the pink sofa, which is among the furniture Allen rented with the house, is having the worst possible effect on her nerves. We've all got our gardens in. My rows would break a snake's back. Bill earned twenty-five cents in one morning! Five cents from Mrs. Fredrickson for picking up dandelions, and a dime each from Paddo Bloodgood and Ruth Wallerstein for putting in their onion sets. This is certainly an employees' market nowadays.

I read your account of Mrs. Beattys' arrival to the Reading Group and they all enjoyed it immensely. As Hannah said, after listening to the *Henry Aldrich* programs,[302] when Henry was kicked by a horse and his father was put in jail and Mary came down with the measles for Mother's Day, "it was just like any family."

Bill had his tonsils out the first of June, and I remember this as the hardest thing I ever had to do as the mother of young children. Dr. Tenney had been "cautious about taking them out" because Bill was so little, but he had had a number of bad attacks of tonsillitis, once with a temperature of 105.2, when his body felt as if it were on fire. It was terrible, though, to take a *well* child to the hospital, knowing it is going to make him sick, whatever your reason told you, and it was a terrible problem to prepare him. I didn't want to scare him to death, but on the other hand I didn't want him to be hurt without preparation, because then he would never trust me again. Dr. Nesbit was very kind. He gave Bill a general anesthetic because he was so little, and he let me stay with him until it took effect. He told me tonsillectomy was often the first experience a child had with a hospital, and if it could be done without trauma the person would be able to go to the hospital all his life without difficulty, so it was very important. Bill

---

302 *The Aldrich Family* was a popular radio show in the 1930s-1950s.

came out the anesthetic just plain *mad*. I was kneeling by his bed, and he threw out his arm—he's always been very strong—right across my throat like a karate chop. The nurse said, "I see he's got what goes with the red hair." Of course it was a great relief to have it over with. When Tom and Hannah had their tonsils out a year or two later, they went in together, and they were old enough to understand what was involved, so the whole thing was much easier. And it is still easier to be the mother of young children than of adolescent ones. The problems with young children tend to be physical, and you can be confident that it is right to do what your doctor says. Since we are all human, of course he can be wrong, but it is right for you to obey him, however hard it may be for you. But adolescent problems are so complicated that neither you nor anyone else—relative, minister, guidance counselor (*particularly* guidance counselor, I may observe, showing my prejudice)—can have confidence that you are doing the right thing.

Polly Fulcher gave a big tea this month, a hundred people or so, for Paul's niece, who was here as an ensign with the WAVES.[303]

> All the neighbors cursed having to go because we had the first shower for a long time in the morning and everyone wanted to be out cultivating her garden. But it does you good to be dressed up—occasionally. If you had seen me at 3:15, pushing a hand plow in a play suit so full of holes it was held on my shoulders only by a miracle, and then at 4:15 in the best dress I have pouring punch at Polly's tea, you would have felt it couldn't be real—it must be a movie, pictures taken at two different times and then spliced together.
>
> I wish you had been here for my birthday, for the neighbors gave me a surprise party—Setzie, Grace, Polly, Mrs. Owen, Sally, Marie—and Sally did the cutest decoration on the cake I have ever seen—little pipe cleaner figures for Hannah reading, Tommy in swimming, Bill climbing on my back like a monkey, I with a rake in one hand and Army Institute papers in the other, a Victory Garden, and a clothes line strung between two candles all complete. She is so clever.

She certainly was, and a great boon to the neighborhood, for besides her skill in arts and crafts (she was the manager of the Union Craft Shop for a number of years), she was an athlete, the first woman (and almost the only one) ever to go down the ski jump that they used to have on the campus, above where

---

303 Women Accepted for Volunteer Emergency Service (WAVES), the women's branch of the U.S. Naval Reserve established during World War II.

World War II

Helen White Hall is now, and she taught all the neighborhood children to swim. "Yesterday afternoon there were fourteen children swimming at the beach, and they're all getting so good they are practically amphibious." The mothers took turns serving as lifeguard. In July [1943] I was divorced, while Hannah, the only one of you old enough really to be concerned, was at Girl Scout camp. "She had a very good time at camp, and is very glad to be back, both of which things please me. She said she was so happy to get back to my cooking—think of a compliment like that from your own child!" Frost Woods was "a wonderful place for children."

The smallness of the neighborhood and the privacy of our beach was some protection against the fear of polio, which all through this period cast a shadow over the best time of the year. You will never be sufficiently thankful for your freedom from this fear, because you will not remember living under it. But all through this time I and every other mother never forgot it, and every time you said "I'm tired" or "My throat hurts," we'd say cheerily, "Oh, you'll be all right in the morning," and then lie awake half the night, getting up from time to time to go in and feel your forehead to see if you were sleeping quietly or developing fever. The medical profession knew nothing about cause, treatment, or cure, and in this respect I can enter into the feelings of the Middle Ages, when men suffered the plague, suffered the Black Death, and could give no more reason for it than the superstition that God was punishing them for their sins. The most inept example of public relations I ever heard was a talk broadcast over the university station by a member of the University Medical School. He told us that research was going on, that eventually a cure would be found and the disease would be controlled and eliminated, but that for the time being they had no idea where it came from, how it spread, or what to do about it. "But if your child comes down with it, bring him to us at once." As a reasonable woman, I could understand that research can't be expected to meet a timetable, and of course I didn't blame the doctors for their ignorance. But if that was all they could say in a talk whose aim was to reassure the public, they would have done far better not to go on the air at all. As often happens, there was a public conflict between the orthodox and an unorthodox treatment. The Australian nurse Sister Kenney instituted as much exercise as possible for limbs which were atrophying, and of course had better results than came from the standard treatment of immobilizing patients in plaster casts.[304] This division was no help to the ordinary mother. I'm very thankful that none of you ever had to go through anything like this, and in Frost Woods we were fortunate. Kit Steele

---

304 Elizabeth Kenny (1880–1952), an unaccredited Australian nurse whose approach to muscle rehabilitation, which countered conventional medical wisdom, was the forerunner to physical therapy.

came over for the summer with his grandparents because there was an outbreak in Milwaukee, where his family was then living. The most famous victim of polio, of course, was President Roosevelt, and there can be no doubt that the undeniable personal courage he showed as a lifelong cripple was a strong factor in the feeling he inspired. Even those who most strongly resented his political liberalism—and I've heard statements which in their savagery recall the unbelievably savage contemporary attacks on Lincoln ("The first happy day I'll have will be the one when Jimmy Roosevelt is assassinated coming back from his father's funeral") —could not deny him that.

In September Ham sold the house to the Maikens. They were certainly as good as I could ever have hoped for for second choice, but the actual sale was still a blow to me, though I knew it was inevitable; as long as the Beattys still owned the house there was a tie, now broken. Grace and Jack went to Chicago for the weekend to celebrate, leaving Jack's mother and aunt in charge of the house and the children.

> Mrs. Maiken is one of the best looking women I have ever seen, and particularly soignée, never a hair out of place. I was therefore slightly surprised to see her appearing at my door carrying two pails—they seemed like a somewhat incongruous appendage. She said the pump wouldn't work and they would like to "borrow some water to flush their toilets— surely an innocent request. The pump was out of order *all* three days *all* the time. The plumber came out once, started it, and left. Mrs. Maiken, when I called to inquire how the little invalid was (i.e., the pump) the next morning, said that it was off again. She had felt dirty the night before—as well she might, you know it was a terribly sticky weekend—and had "inadvertently" taken a bath, and that had been too much for the feeble constitution of the pump, which had at once succumbed. That day the plumber had not come at all. I leave you of your experience to imagine their troubles with the baby. On Sunday I had no hot water myself because my heater had gone off, as it does periodically. On Monday when I got it fixed, I urged them to come over and have baths, but they refused—too proud, I suppose. When Jack got back, *he* started the pump with a turn of the wrist. I should say plumbing lost a good man when he went into the Navy. In addition Pete was sick all the time his parents were gone. Mrs. Maiken said Monday he had had a better night than the night

before—he had slept from half past one to four. Before he hadn't slept at all; he had terrific paroxysms of coughing. So in addition to no water by day they had no sleep by night. They leave today, this being the end of their vacation—both of them have jobs.

The payment for a good action that they got is only equaled by poor Bob Pooley. Alice asked him for yesterday's paper, because it had in it the picture of a friend of hers who had just gotten married. He couldn't find it then, but appeared in the morning with it and this story. He had said to Robin after supper, "Take this paper over to Alice and come right back and do your practicing." Twenty-five minutes later Robin returned. Bob asked why it had taken so long to go over to the Thomases, and he said, "Oh, I took the paper up to the Strangs." To do so, he had walked in bare feet—or in shoes, it makes no difference—over a newly tarred road, and then come back and covered Setzie's precious blue rug all over with tar. Bob says the entire surface is black. And Setzie, who was away, on the train at the moment, drawing nearer and nearer and nearer to her home. It just shows you.

You were speaking a propos of Phyllida, of the difficulty of writing letters when you don't see someone over a period of years. And I know that is true, and it concerns me especially now that you have sold your house. But in our case we always have one great advantage. Just as Dr. Weston was ideally qualified for his profession, because at least one of his children must have had anything any of his patients could have had, so you and I have enough children to make each letter a catalogue of childish illnesses, which will be breathlessly read by the other, because if her children haven't already had them, they undoubtedly will soon.

Arthur, like Bill, was to have a lot of trouble with his tonsils, and when he finally had them out I regretted I couldn't send him one of the little twenty-five-cent-size turtles that in Frost Woods kept coming up from the lake.

They make the ideal present for tonsillectomies, quiet, yet with enough motion to keep the child happy. I gave Sally Reynolds' child one when he had the mumps, and she said it was wonderful.

More and more men were leaving for service. Jack Maiken reported to Hollywood, Florida, for training, on October 15. Grace was left here, with a small baby, and without a car, since the one he used belonged to his company.

> I don't know that mine does me much good now, with so little gas, but I like to think I have it. Alice brought her husband here for a week. He had a week's furlough just before she went back in to the Nurses' Dormitory, so they spent it here. I was glad they could have the time together, and glad the children could remember a soldier in uniform spending a furlough here, but it was certainly a strain to produce company meals for a man three times a day for a week. I did more cooking in that week than I did in the whole summer. Chuck is professedly an admirer of home-baked bread, and what with hot rolls and whipped cream desserts and potatoes and hearty meals in general I don't know about Chuck but I think I put on five pounds right around the waist. It was rather a comfort to come back to tomatoes and milk for supper.

Also in October the Marshalls left for Texas. Jan was a great loss to Hannah, but at least she was here for Hannah's birthday.

> I made crepe paper cooks' aprons and caps in red, white, and blue, organized and partly pre-cooked a meal, and made out a stack of little cards so that each girl—there were seven—would have five or six things to do about getting and serving the meal. Jan said what a good idea of mine, then I didn't have to do any work. Three of the girls came out from town, so they are spending the night, and I'll take them back when I take the children to Sunday school.
>
> The woods are getting lovely. The hickories are all yellow and the sumac is at its best. We are having those lovely warm hours where you can sit outdoors and drink in the sun all over.
>
> Bill has to go to kindergarten alone, and that mile walk for a five-year-old is rather forbidding. I'm not going to have gas to take him, so I don't want to start doing it. I walk with him usually up past the Blaneys, but he says good-bye to me so bravely and pathetically it tears your heart strings, and he keeps on calling back, "Good-bye. See you this afternoon. Good-bye. See you this afternoon" over and over. He comes home feeling chipper enough. I'm sure next year when he goes

in the morning with the big children it will be all right. It's unfortunate he should be the only one in the neighborhood in kindergarten. There were three last year and will be three again next.

Alan Pooley and Bill are only a month apart in age, and had of course done a lot of playing together. But since Bill's birthday is in October and Alan's in November, Bill started school a whole year ahead of Alan. With only three years difference between Bill and his older brother—there was a gap of eight years between Alan and his—and his splendid coordination and liking for games, Bill had pretty much forced himself into the older group of boys and been accepted as one of them.

We agreed, when Grace read the Sewing Circle the details of Jack's basic training program, that it was very strenuous, and that the physical part of it would be far easier for a housewife, who is already pretty much in training, than for a man. "Eleanor's maid has left; like the buffalo or the Indian, Virginia has the only specimen still extant of the vanishing race." The bus, which had run for about a year, stopped, a terrible blow. It ran infrequently and not at all weekends, but it was something to fall back on. On the other hand, I looked forward to an easier winter as far as heating was concerned. Hannah had a persistent cough, and Dr. Tenney told me to keep the house warmer for her sake and promised to write a note to the ration board if I ran short. We got a puppy named Trouble Thanksgiving Thomas—a name which is self-explanatory. I didn't really want a dog. "Whereas a cat is a center of peace in a house and perfectly self-reliant, this puppy is restless and wants more attention than a baby. However, she is loving, and since we can't have a cat, she's something. I think it's good for the children to have a dog. No matter how much they fight each other, they are always all of them sweet to the puppy, and if there is any sweetness in your children's natures, the parent has a definite obligation to provide an outlet so it can come out, I think." We only had Trouble about six months, because Hannah's allergies started again and we realized we couldn't have any animal. Trouble went to the Ragsdales, where she lived long and happily but—very strikingly—came back here to die. While we had her, Hannah went in town to spend the night with Carol Miles. "She was gone just twenty-four hours and when she came back was so glad to see Trouble. Trouble was mildly pleased, but having been at home with the rest of the family, and receiving her meals, hadn't really noticed much difference. Hannah said, "Mother, you know those stories where the dog dies because she misses her master? Well, I don't believe they're true." But within twenty-four hours of Trouble's death from old age, I happened to go down into the garage and to my great surprise found her in the darkest corner. Dave came and carried her home when I telephoned him, and she died the next day.

> Robin Pooley contributed another story to entertain Gwen.
> Robin wears a retainer—a contraption to keep his teeth from sliding back—not bands, but on the order of a plate. He will have to wear it for ten years. Fancy. When he loses his teeth as an old man, the plate will be no novelty to him. Well, he came home from school and told his mother he had lost it. He remembered taking it out at lunch—which he isn't supposed to do—and then presumably everything went black. So Setzie went up to school and couldn't find it, so they looked through all the school garbage, thinking it might have been cleared off his dish there. One of the cooks takes garbage home for her animals, so when they didn't find it at school, Setzie went from pillar to post after that cook, finally tracked her down, and searched *her* garbage. No soap (which no doubt she needed by then). So she came home and went to bed. At 10:30 Robin came out of his room and said he had been thinking it over and remembered he had put it in his vest pocket—and there it was. Setzie said she could have killed him when he lost it and even more when he found it—and I am sure no feeling is more natural than that in any mother, under those circumstances.

Grace Maiken, who was lonely and sociable, kept asking the neighbors in for afternoon coffee parties, and I developed a taste for it. I was dreading the winter driving, now there was no bus to fall back on to get to Reading Group on icy days, but was cheered because she offered me her garage to spare me my impossible driveway. Jack was transferred from Florida to Cambridge, where he was to be for five months, so Grace decided to join him.

> Everyone says the housing situation is frightful, but she is going just the same. She has her reservations for Saturday, and now that the government has taken over the railroads she can probably get there. She has rented the house to a Captain Tandy, who has a wife and a three-months-old baby, for two months. He is here at the university taking a training course for officers who are to do occupation work. Then she hopes someone in the next batch will take it for the next two months.

World War II

She didn't leave till December 30th, but the Owens went to Betsy's for Christmas, since the Marshalls were gone, and let the Tandys move into Bungalowen on the 24th; and they were so impressed with the hospitality of the neighborhood that I am still exchanging Christmas cards with them thirty years later. They had less than a month here, for the occupation training course was dropped at two days' notice and Captain Tandy sent overseas, leaving his wife to drive the three-months-old baby back to California alone. "They had counted on six more weeks together, and it was heart-rending to see them." I also felt very badly for Grace, because if she couldn't re-rent the house she'd have to leave Jack and come back here. "But she wired asking me to re-rent the house for her, and after a somewhat complicated week I got it rented to an Army lieutenant who is a doctor at Truax, and I only hope the Army will leave him where he is till Grace gets back the first of June. They have an eight-months-old baby. They are taking care of Raven, the Maiken dog, which takes five dollars off the rent; I'm glad to get rid of feeding her."

> The people who rented the Marshall house are a middle-aged couple named Williams with one child, a daughter who is a sophomore at the university. She was in love with a young flier in California, but her parents thought she was too young to marry—only nineteen. They let her go out to California to visit him for Christmas, and spent their first Christmas alone; she had promised them she would not marry when she got there. And just as soon as she got there, she did marry, and now they don't even know where she is. They are terribly upset; at best it means she will lose a semester's work here, at worst that she'll never finish college at all. She will undoubtedly stay with her husband till he is sent over-seas, which will probably be soon. I could thank Heaven on my knees that my children, both girl and boys, are too young now to be affected by the war. The age group from eighteen to twenty-two seems to me to be the worst. It must be bad enough to see your children grow up in normal times and break away from you, and let them go with a good grace and let them make their own mistakes; but to have them do it now, when everything is so abnormal and hectic—I'm glad you and I are both spared that.

The neighborhood was growing increasingly intimate. "We are just one big happy family. Grace started the fashion for coffee in the afternoon, and the Sewing Circle was never livelier." I had planned of course to have the Christmas party, and had meant to ask all the women to dress up and wear long skirts for morale. But you all three had whooping cough, and I had to rescind the invitation. "Hannah had quite a case. Tommy never did get it, and the doctor and health officer said he could be released from quarantine now with her, since the incubation period is long over. They are both just out. Bill had a very light case. The shots worked for Tommy, you see, and to a very large degree for Bill. I had school all through December, every morning, just like rural school, three grades in a room. Setzie and I traded off, since their boys had it too, which helped." It also helped very much that we could share the holiday, according to custom. The Pooleys came here Christmas Eve, and we went there Christmas Day. Bob very kindly put one of their cars in my garage in dead storage and let me use the space in his; Grace's garage of course was now being used by her tenants. At year's end I sat "writing and listening to the needles dropping off the Christmas tree, like the dying embers in a melancholy poem. A friend once said of his financial condition that it was just a race between him and the capitalist system, and that's what I think of my tree. I wonder if it will hold out till I clean house on Saturday."

Ham was deferred from service for six months because he was in an essential war industry, construction, and I wrote Gwen in March, "Since nobody knows where he's going to be from one day to the next, six months is a long and lucky period for you to count on."

> The children and I have all been sick, and since unfortunately I had to take care of them when I was sickest I had a relapse, and have now been in bed for two weeks—quite a long time, I'll tell you, to be at the mercy of your three small children, though they have really been very good. Still, you can easily imagine that the household is disorganized. The doctor said I mustn't even get out of bed to go to the bathroom, which obviously presented a problem. Hannah has very little Florence Nightingale blood—and I can't say I have much myself—and I really don't blame a child of eleven for not wanting to empty bedpans. You'll pardon my calling a spade a spade. Fortunately Katherine Post brought out some lemon drops for the children, so I said anyone who emptied the bedpan could have one. Hannah's fastidiousness was proof against bribery, but it was different with the boys, who are now fighting for the privilege. If you could see Bill emptying it, you'd never forget it. The neighbors have been wonderful, especially Setzie, and have had the children out for meals and brought in food and so on, and I had a Visiting Nurse out a couple of times. But

it has been rather a bad pull. I expect to get up tomorrow for the first time. The doctor said that I would be weak, and I guess I will, for I have enough sulfa in me to kill a horse; but now I've finally got rid of my temperature I ought to snap back all right.

April 1, 1944. Children are exhausting and irritating and coarsening, but people with children never wonder what it's all about. They know. They have a purpose. Emerson perhaps puts it more elegantly when he says that we all crave for reality even at the cost of pain.

Since our real spree the children have had off and on a sort of bug which seems to be going round, and what we frankly call "the cough-up pan" has been by one or another bed constantly.

The captain that Grace Maiken rented your house to first sent me a V-mail letter from England the other day.[305] He was much impressed at the clean-up job done in the English cities, and said the children all asked him for "American gohm." He didn't know why they wanted it but he hadn't any anyway. (His child is only six months old now. In a few years he'll know a lot of things he doesn't know now, but, as Sam Weller says, whether it's worth going through so much to learn so little is a question of taste. See my first paragraph.) Helen White's brother is also in England. Helen is afraid Anglo-American relations will not be improved by all the Americans there—not that she is casting aspersions on her brother, of course, who as a matter of fact is exceptionally mild, not to say timid, so that his efficiency as a soldier seems to me rather doubtful—but because there are just so many of them. Did you see in *Time*, I think, some American saying that when we got out of England the inhabitants would be just dizzy with *lebensraum*.[306]

The neighborhood is very cordial. Someone throws a coffee party in the afternoon whenever it's anyone's birthday, and

---

305 V-mail (Victory Mail), based on the British Airgraph, was a secure, economical method for corresponding with soldiers stationed abroad and entailed small letter sheets being censored, photographed, captured in thumbnail-sized negatives on microfilm, and mailed. Upon arrival, the negatives were blown up, printed, and delivered.
306 Lebensraum ("living space"), which refers to territory claimed by a nation or state as necessary for survival, was a policy central to Nazi Germany.

we all bring little presents. I have given away all my pre-war chocolate.

It was a late spring, and there were no flowers for the May Day baskets, so we stuck gumdrops on twigs and filled in with a few currant and gooseberry leaves. In May Elspeth Hughes came to live with us while her mother was in Philadelphia, which was very nice for Hannah, the only girl in the neighborhood now that she had lost Jan. When Grace Hughes came back to Madison the end of July, she kept house for my family while I went East, and during that visit Hannah Davis and I made the only war-time trip to the Island. "July 21. The garden is wonderful; every conceivable vegetable is there in abundance, except tomatoes, which in general are not yet ripe, though we had one this noon from Bill's garden. The neighbors canned twenty-four quarts of beans for me while I was gone, and if they haven't hearts of gold I don't know who has. Schmutzy Cronin bit Susy Ragsdale very severely about the head and neck. Luckily the bites were in back."

By the terms of the divorce, Wright had to wait a year before re-marrying, and by a truly Hardyean stroke of irony his letter announcing his marriage arrived the day before a pathetic farcical proposal of marriage to me from one of my USAFI students. And this brings me to the Army Institute work, which occupied a great many of my waking hours during the war, starting with a trickle and mounting until one typical week of fifty-three hours by actual count, when I kept track of the time out of curiosity.

The United States Armed Forces Institute (USAFI) had been established soon after the beginning of the war, and offered correspondence courses in all fields on high school and college level to men and women in any branch of the service.[307] I owe my involvement in it to Helen White. I was very grateful for the work. I felt I should do nothing which would take me away from home, with Bill so little. This of course was the beginning of the working mother, a movement which has spread enormously, and which still presents various problems. I had written

---

307 In March 1942, the War Department, recognizing UW-Madison's Extension Division's pioneering work in correspondence study, designated UW-Madison as the headquarters for a new U.S. Army Institute correspondence study program, which provided college-level work to servicemen-students. Popular subjects included English grammar (Cronon & Jenkins, 1994, p. 414). Signaling a desire to reach a broader military audience, in early 1943 the Army Institute title was changed to the U.S. Armed Forces Institute (USAFI); by mid-1943, enrollment in correspondence courses had surpassed 30,000 (p. 430) and continued to grow after World War II (see Palmer, 1955).

to Gwen, "I know how you feel about getting a job. But after all, mothers with young children are supposed to look after them. I hear on the radio authorities are very concerned about the problem—not just children of pre-school age, but adolescents. Juvenile delinquency is going up horribly." Not only could I not leave home, but I couldn't undertake anything there which required sustained and continuous mental effort (like this autobiography). The correspondence lessons, where I could do an individual one at a time whenever I could spare it and which were not continuous anyway, since in one day a scattering of lessons might come in at all points of the courses I was teaching, was the ideal solution. The headquarters of the Institute were in Madison. You may just dimly remember having some of the officers out for Thanksgiving—mainly WACS.[308] The papers were mailed to me, but returned through the kindness of a neighbor whose office was in the same building as USAFI, so that I got them back promptly. One of you would take up the day's batch to him every night. They had started by June, 1942, and at first there was a mere trickle. By January, 1943,

> I have a lot more soldiers to handle by correspondence now.
> The number is increasing all the time. I notice that quite
> a number have taken a month or thereabouts to reach me,
> which must mean of course that they aren't in this country,
> where at first they all came through in two or three days. Several times they send in little notes saying they expect to leave
> in a few days so they are hurrying up to send in several lessons
> at once.

The first course I taught was a basic high school traditional grammar one, and not very interesting. "In general, they don't show much personality because the material is so factual. But they have to write original sentences to illustrate this or that, and sometimes things flash through—as for example, 'Wives should be beaten regularly, like a rug.' 'What! Tim is in jail again!' 'God knows there are over 60,000,000 women in this country, but I can't get even one decent date.' 'Dear Teacher, You have been so kind and comforting I should like to buy you a drink.'" One student sent me a snapshot of three men, one in a GI in uniform and on either side of him a native, coal black and dressed in nothing above the waist. On the back the student had written, "I am the one in the middle."

> I had a very striking theme last week entitled "My First Visit
> to the City." When the boy was in sixth grade his mother
> promised him any present he chose if he got good grades,

---

308 Women's Army Corps (WAC), first created as an army auxiliary corps in 1942, was active from 1943–1978.

and he chose a trip to the city. So far, so good, and I read on expecting his reactions to Rockefeller Center, perhaps. I was brought up with a jerk when they started out, his mother, he, and a mule, on a twenty-mile walk, in the course of which he saw his *first* automobile. The thing in the city that impressed him most was turning on the electric lights. He had studied about electricity in school but had never seen a light bulb. I didn't think there was any place left in this country where a twelve-year-old boy hadn't seen a car. He writes now from a hospital, and I hate to think how much of life he has probably seen now.

This story, however, recalls an experience which happened after the war, when we were at the Island and I had taken Bill over to Dr. Gregory's clinic for a tetanus booster because he stuck a clam fork into his leg. There were two women in the waiting room, one with a girl whose little finger had grown, curled over, into her palm because after a bad burn her mother had not taken the trouble to have her follow the exercises the doctor prescribed. The son of the other woman was away at Army camp. The first expressed some doubt as to how he would like it after having lived in "rural Boothbay," as they call it nowadays. "Oh," said the mother, "he likes it *fine!*"

Eventually I was teaching on the college level, freshman composition and sophomore literature, which was much more interesting and also much more time-consuming. I got far fewer naïve papers than before, of course.

> Now if I get a man who is illiterate or a moron, instead of having to struggle with him it is really my duty to see that he doesn't waste his time by suggesting tactfully that a more elementary course would be more valuable to him now, and that I'll hope to meet him again when he has had the foundation work necessary for this more advanced course. Best wishes for speedy progress. It's nice to have it your *duty* to pass the buck. It's only with your children that you never can turn over responsibility to someone else.

It was good experience, and probably it helped me a good deal when I went back into the classroom. It furnished me with one story I told for years to my classes of prospective high school teachers to show that comments could be too long as well as too short. "Thank you very much for your comments. I sincerely hope I shall find time to read them." I purposely made the comments long, of course, since the students couldn't come up after class and ask questions about anything they didn't understand. I met only one student, and the meeting was not a success. The man was stationed at Truax, and I was delighted at the opportunity of actually seeing him. You and I picked him up on the Square after your Sunday school, and brought him out for Sunday dinner. I was even more delighted when I asked him his home town and he said "Boston." But unfortunately he lived on the other side of the tracks. When I said I came from Brookline and he sized me up as a proper Bostonian, no home atmosphere or my best efforts or your perfectly natural and friendly behavior could dent his antagonism. He was Irish, with political aspirations; it's too bad I can't remember his name (it certainly wasn't Kennedy) so we could know whether or not he realized them.

But a great many of my students wrote me very appreciative notes, far above and beyond the call of duty, thanking me for my interest, for my pains, for my constructive criticism, for the fact that I always pointed out the merits of their writing as well as its weaknesses. This is one of my basic principles of teaching composition anyway, but under these circumstances I naturally tried particularly hard to be as encouraging as I honestly could. The aim of the program, I am sure, was not only to provide servicemen with an opportunity to keep up with their education but also to help their morale. Particularly from the students who completed a course—a very small proportion of any correspondence work, even under ordinary conditions, you know—was I likely to receive appreciation, and this self-disciplined elite was representative of the veterans I was soon to meet in the classroom—as a group, the best students in the history of American education. Some of the men had been out of school before they went into service and found it hard to get back in the habit of studying. "I had no idea that it would be such a battle to make myself pick up the text and work on my own." "I took this composition course to see if I could concentrate and express my ideas, for time had passed and things had happened since I last studied and I was afraid I might have forgotten how. Your kindness in grading my papers as you did and your enthusiasm in my work gave me confidence in myself at a time when it was sorely needed." "By bolstering my confidence in my own efforts you removed a psychological block." "I want to express my thanks again for your valuable comments on my papers. They were what I needed to put me on a firm scholastic footing and have given me back my self-confidence." The men worked under heavy disadvantages, of course. The papers were censored and how many—if any—came from combat areas I don't know. But base life was busy, and they were constantly moving. "I regret that I am not able to send this lesson sooner but I have been commissioned, married and recieved (sic) a change of station." Sometimes they wrote from hospital. "I am anticipating another operation on my right arm in the near future. Will my work be acceptable if I dictate my written assignments during the time I am unable to use my arm?"

Some of the liveliest letters I got came from a broth of a boy with the true Irish wit and charm. It's too bad we couldn't have drawn him here instead of the Boston Irishman with a grudge against my forefathers.

> Dear Teacher,
> Thank you very much for your valuable comments on my completed units. I only hope that my work will continue to please you. As time passes my opportunities to study are becoming rare, but it is my firm intention to submit at least one unit every two weeks to the university.
> Your criticisms are very helpful and encouraging. Please try to continue them. Even though our contacts are remote, I can see that you are what some of the local GI would term "a right nice egg." English has always been a liking of mine. It's funny how we Irish foreigners have taken to the language. Shaw, O'Casey and O'Neill seem to be its best exponents, too. At any rate, the course has helped me greatly and cleared up many difficulties that troubled me.
> It is "lights out" time now, so I must quit my quilling. Thanks again for your kind assistance. May you be named with Socrates as a red-hot tutor, and as all teachers are underpaid, may you get a nice hoist in salary to pay for a post-war sable or mink. Don't spare the critic's cutlass.
> The Irishman

What I can't understand about the man who proposed to me was why he was ever accepted in the army to begin with. He had had polio, and I had written him to the effect that President Roosevelt was the most inspiring example possible of what a man could do to overcome handicap. He was honorably discharged from the Army a year before the end of the war, and wrote me then, "Please write and tell me if you are still living with your husband because if not I am interested, but if you and your husband are still man and wife, well I apologize."

As usual, I made a good story of it to Gwen. But put the arrival of his letter the day after the arrival of Wright's, and read between the lines for pathos (obviously this wasn't on the tragic level) as well as farce, and the whole thing would surely add up to a Hardy novel.

> I must say it took all this skill of mine you speak of in writing difficult letters to answer that one, but I really was proud of the little masterpiece I produced, saying I was afraid he thought of me as far younger than I really was, and that I had

two sons and a daughter and was old enough to be his mother and had had no picture taken for many years (he had asked for one), and wishing him success and happiness in his adjustment back to civilian life. It really was a wonderful letter, giving the impression I had one foot in the grave, and *final*, and I showed it to the Pooleys before I sent it, just for corroboration, and darned if the man didn't pop right back again.

"Mrs. Thomas when I wrote you the letter I had thought that mabby you were much older than I.

"But, Mrs. Thomas, when you like a woman, it doesn't make much difference how old or young she is.

"You see, Mrs. Thomas, not boasting, but, I am not the kind of man, that you run up on, every-day. In fact, when I pick a woman, I do not pick her only for her looks, but I do pick her by her personality, and charcter.

"If you do decided not to answer this letter, just remember regardless of how old you are, you are just as good, as any other woman.

"P.S. This letter is of only good intentions and it is only strickly business."

All these letters come through the Institute, of course, and are read there, and forwarded to me after they have had a field day with them. I suppose the people down there lead rather dull lives, and this man is certainly brightening them. This second letter came with a comment from the WAC lieutenant who is liaison officer between the Institute and the teachers. "We are all wondering down here to what you attribute your fatal charm!" She says they expect the man to turn up any day, which horrifies me. He is now in Virginia, and I devoutly hope he stays there. I'm going to try silence, since my letters keep on showing my personality and fascinate him more. He seemed to have an inkling of that himself when he said "if you decide not to answer," so I trust he will take the hint. If he writes again, the WAC lieutenant said they'd write something from there. The poor man is terribly pathetic, of course. I told the story at a dinner party at Ruth Wallerstein's, and Elizabeth Agard was entranced, as you can imagine, and thought he was probably a very simple soul (and that's no lie) and a wonderful shot with a rifle, like Sergeant York, I suppose. That suggestion sent the cold shivers running up and down my spine. At my time of life and with my looks it would be a pretty how-do-you-do to figure as the corpse in a crime passionel. But I really don't think it will come to that. I don't expect to get any more letters from him.

Nor did I. I hope—somehow—he had a happy life. And as I go over the evidence thirty years later, I think he was justified in saying he was not the kind of man that you run up on every day. His telling me that if I do decide not to encourage his hopes— "Just remember regardless of how old you are, you are just as good, as any other woman" —his consideration of *me* seems to show he was a gentleman in the best sense of the word.

On one other man, a very different type, I made such an impression that in June of 1971, when he was in Madison to attend his daughter's commencement, he telephoned me and we had a long talk. The girl had dropped in to see me in my office once, but I never got round to asking her out. He was born and lived his pre-war life in a small Southern village with a population of 1500, the only boy and the baby of the family, eleven years younger than his nearest sister, and his father had died when he was three. He went to a denominational junior college, got a job in Washington to get away from home, and was drafted shortly after our entrance into the war. He was lonely and wanted to discuss the eternal verities: "Suppose there's no God; is there such a thing as truth?" I served as a wailing wall to him; he wrote that his correspondence had dwindled to his mother and me, and he had to write cheerfully to his mother so he poured out his troubles to me. He served all through the war, first in Italy and then in the Pacific after peace had been made in Europe, and I'll quote some of his letters because they were written after the end of the war and show the restlessness the men understandably felt. He did have a happy life: went back to college on the GI Bill, married (he sent me a picture of himself and his bride and I sent him one of the four of us), and three children, is working in Washington (where he urged me to visit them) in something to do with the Bureau of Education, and seemed, when we talked in his relations with his children to be rolling with the punches and apparently doing very well in all aspects.

Manila Harbor

September 4, 1945

We have been here three days awaiting a pier to debark, after traveling approximately 1600 miles from Hollandia, New Guinea. Needless to say, I'm exhausted, a fact that is true of most every other soldier. The trip has been long (we have been on the ship nearly seven weeks), hot and tiresome, as only a troop transport can make a voyage; yet conditions could have been much worse.

On August 4th we were in Cristobal, Panama, Canal Zone, where for a mere three hours we were permitted ashore, restricted to the dock area. Incidentally this was the only time we have been off the ship. The three hours were the most enjoyable I've spent in a long time. The people—Americans mind you—combined with the USO and the Red Cross to provide us with a little taste of home. All the ice cream and hot dogs (with mustard, the first I've seen in three years) were served free of charge. Then the Army P X had established a store where we could buy souvenirs, cokes and other luxuries such as cakes, peanuts, candy and cigarettes, unrationed.

The next day we transited the canal, a marvelous engineering accomplishment.

. . . The next highlight was Aug. 14, the day President Truman announced the Japanese had accepted unconditional surrender. We were something like 1200 miles southeast of the Hawaiian Islands, and 3500 miles west of Panama. It had been rumored all day that it was over, although as you know on a boat it is very difficult to receive news—especially official news. At three we were alerted for abandon boat, and as we stood on the main deck by our life boats, the captain of the ship announced, "Attention, all hands, attention, all hands, President Truman has just announced that the Japanese government had accepted unconditional surrender." There was an uproar of joy. After the announcement the ship's chaplain led the entire boat in a prayer of thanksgiving.

Rice Field, Batangoa Vicinity

Luzon, Philippine Islands

September 8, 1945

"To hell with the Golden Gate by 48, I'll be home by Sept 8" is not a reality. Instead we are waiting patiently to go to Japan where we will be attached to the 11 Corps, 6 Army, a unit that is already there. Certainly I don't look forward to going, but in the army one is helplessly tied to his master, the government, who may take his individuality, his heart, his soul, and his life without regret.

We landed here day before yesterday. When I say "landed" it was just that. Our ship docked out in the harbor, and let us come to this obscure beach in combat landing craft. Fortunately, there were trucks waiting to carry us to this rice field some five miles from Batangoa [Batangas] and 95 miles south of Manila. We pitched camp—in a downpour of rain that soaked every piece of equipment and stitch of clothing we possessed, and left this field one complete mass of churched mud. One boy wrote home, "When we got off the ship we were put in a row boat, used our gun butt for a paddle, hit the beach with a bang, and threw out our barracks bag for an anchor."

As to when I shall get home or out of the army I know nothing. I have no confidence whatsoever in the army's point system until I see it put into action. If we could submit our new points as of Sept 2, I think I have the necessary 80; however, we have been told we must reach our destination before anything can be done. Whether that will be tomorrow or next year remains to be seen. In the meantime we will wait. I feel like an old worn out shoe that will be kicked aside when it is of no more use.

Now to the educational benefits mentioned in your letter of August 17. I haven't read the article in the *Saturday Evening Post* that you mentioned, but from what you wrote I believe it is true. About one out of 25 in our battalion plans on taking advantage of the educational benefits. This statistic was given to me by our information and educational officer. . . . Most of the boys with whom I am associated desire a job (with money) to knowledge. Our entire American system as well as our patriotism is based on the almighty dollar. I believe the home shares in the blame for such reaction. There seems to be little emphasis put on home life in the present-day world, in fact, marriage now is only for convenient adultery. It is alarming the number of men in my company alone who have divorced their wives, some with children.

I plan on continuing my education, although at times I don't know what is best. After all, I've spent a long time in the army, and it might be best to go to work. At one time I had a girl who was waiting patiently for my return, but after two years of overseas duty for me she decided to seek greener fields. She didn't bother to write, just sent an announcement of her marriage. This has caused me to doubt somewhat all girls under forty.

This morning I received a letter from mother. I told her that I was going directly to the Pacific, but poor mother she thought it was a bluff and that I was on my way home as a surprise. She had the house cleaned, and fixed things for me. You might know she was quite disappointed when I didn't arrive.

What do you think about peacetime military training? An article in February's *Reader's Digest* made a statement that hit me the wrong way: "More than two-thirds of the GIs, voting in secret polls, approve the idea, one year's military training." This I believe to be an untrue statement. Personally I'm very much against peace time training, and I believe most soldiers are. I agree with the *New Yorker* and Booth Tarkington who says it is a serious thing for all the Willies in America to start saluting. I realize we must be prepared, but believe me, Mrs. Thomas, the inefficiency of our modern army, and all too often the high casualties resulting from action, has not been due to a poorly trained soldier, but to incompetent leadership. I'm not speaking as an outsider, but as one who knows first hand. You can't pin bars on a senator's brother or a general's son and automatically make him a leader. The government should intensify ROTC in college, double the present enrollment of West Point; in other words, correct the incompetence of the higher bracket and the lower will take care of itself. In no case make it compulsory. Every time I see a picture of that clown Patton I feel like telling the American people to stop buying war bonds. If he's a general I should be commander-in-chief. Please do not think I'm too biased, but I'm so fed up with this medieval caste system called an army where "justice is the interest of the stranger," as says Plato's Republic, that the very thought of any boy becoming a slave to it meets me the wrong way. The overall picture is good to an outsider's eye, and I'm the first to admit that it has accomplished the immediate task. Now it is the time to correct mistakes. Concentrate on leadership by making it a prerequisite that men attend college.

I seem bitter; nevertheless I'm wise enough to see the good points. I've learned a lot.

Lemery, Luzon [Philippines]

Sept 17, 1945

We have moved from the rice paddy near Batangas to a cocoanut [sic] grove on a swimming beach near Lemery. It is better than our previous location, but it isn't satisfying us.

Mrs. Thomas, please do not think me a coward or a slacker if I say I'm completely at ropes' end with the Army. We have not even computed our score for V-J day, and that is bad. After scores are submitted to a higher headquarters it usually takes weeks for them to be acted on. We are camped out here without any books, any recreational equipment, any lights, any radios, any papers, in short without anything. Candles are rationed one per tent per night. (This letter won't be finished, if this candle goes out. I have no batteries for my flashlight.) *We live on rumors.* The men are ready for mutiny. I must tell you the enlisted men, one thousand strong, have called for a meeting tomorrow morning at nine, and to top it all we have already served notice on our colonel that he must be there to answer any questions we ask. This may seem outrageous, but if he knows nothing he should tell us instead of permitting us to live on rumors. And if we must live here give us something to pass the time with. The beach is marked DANGEROUS NO SWIMMING. I can assure you if the war was on we wouldn't be griping so much. It is over and we want to go home, as do eight million more. A large percentage of our battalion are ex-combat men, most of them with purple hearts, who were sent to a rear unit in Africa to replace other men who hadn't seen combat. But why bother you with our worries? In all the "bunk fatigue" I'm getting now I've had a chance to work out a few things for myself. There is a God, I've decided. Fortunately one question you asked some months ago, "Where did that idea come from?" the idea of something better than ourselves, did the trick . . . .

I wonder how the civilian attitude toward the different races in America is taking shape as a result of the war. One of the unfortunate aspects in the army is that soldiers have not been given enough, if any, education on race tolerance. The Jew is still the bastard Jew; the negro is still the Goddam negro. I grew up in the south where race prejudice is strong, but I never heard or harbored such thoughts as I've heard in the army by men who are supposedly half-way intelligent. Last night one boy remarked, "The war was caused by the Jews who desired more money." When I told him he was mad half the tent took his side. It is unfortunate that we have won a war, but have lost so much. I believe, however, we have made tremendous progress toward race tolerance, and that time with proper education will change factors; at least I hope so.

We had our meeting. The Colonel said that he was awaiting orders from higher headquarters to release men 35 years old and with 80 points. As yet the War Department has not notified this theatre that the points have been lowered or that we should even compute them as of V-J day. If the War Department is going to be slow, Congress should take matters in hand. Maybe by the time you get this letter things will be better.

P.S. Our theme song: "I have returned. Stick with Mac and you won't get back."

Manila, PH

Nov 5, 1945

While waiting in Manila for Congress and the War Department to wake up I've been attending the Tomoyuki Yamashita trial.[309] It is unbelievable the atrocities related. One Filipine actress said that a Japanese sailor bayoneted her nine times after shooting her once in the elbow and then murdered her 10-month-old daughter. Day before yesterday a girl who saw two Japanese soldiers bayonet her father and mother jumped from the stand and ran toward Yamashita, shouting, "I'd like to cut you in small pieces and feed you to the dogs." Old

---

309 Tomoyuki Yamashita (1885–1946), an Imperial Japanese Army general during World War II, was found guilty of war crimes in the Philippines and Singapore against civilians and prisoners of war and was executed in 1946.

Yamashita sits there, not moving once. I'm convinced he is guilty, but to be on the right side the American Commission, consisting of five generals, are bending over backwards to give him a fair trial.

Wake Forest College
Feb 10, 1946

I'm back in college, thanks mostly to your encouraging letters. I surreptitiously confess that it is difficult for me to study again, nevertheless I'm exerting a lot of effort toward that objective, even to burning midnight oil. Since I'm here I certainly want to make good. Strangely enough I'm majoring in Social Science, minoring in Music. My roommate, an ex-lieutenant of the Navy, is working on his M.A. in the same field. We have a lot of fun discussing our numerous experiences—some that were a bit too close to be funny. He was on a destroyer, doing convoy duty, both in the Atlantic and Pacific, as well as helping in two invasions.

You are doubtless wondering about my travels since last I wrote. Two weeks were spent in San Francisco awaiting train space east. I spent Christmas Day traveling across Arizona and Texas. To make a long story short I was discharged at 6:30 PM December 31. My mother and sister were to meet me at the main bus station in Fort Bragg, NC, but when I walked in neither of them recognized me, at least not for several moments. I had lost quite a bit of weight, hair, and had grown taller in three and a half years. Nevertheless it was one happy reunion. My mother remarked that if she lived to be a hundred years older she would never receive a bigger thrill than when I came over and said, "Hello, Mother."

I really don't know how to express how utterly wonderful it is being a civilian. I still feel it is all a dream. Two million dollars wouldn't buy my experiences in the last three years nor would 300 billion be temptation enough to go through them again . . . .

Now for a few civilian observations. At the college here there is a strong veterans organization, there being 1/3 of the present student body returnees who have entered for the most

> part this semester. We stick fairly close together in our club maybe because we are a little apprehensive right now. As to there being a great deal of adjusting I haven't found there to be too much. I don't believe I was as silly before as the group of "kids" going to school now. I can't comprehend how they scream at a ball game; yet I know I did the same thing only a few years back. An old man at twenty-four I guess. My roommate who is the same age says he feels the same way.
>
> Generally speaking, the U.S. hasn't changed any more than I have. Prices compared with 1942 level amaze me because everything is so high. I believe it will take everything the government gives us to make ends meet. But I'm not worried about that—I'm home and that is wonderful. I've had one date since I returned. She was too silly for me.
>
> P.S. the world for me is all too wonderful to comprehend.

The last letter I have, dated Feb 16, 1947, thanks me for the picture of the four of us I sent as a Christmas card, says "I wish words could express my joy and happiness during the past year and one-half. I have enjoyed every minute of college life to the fullest," gives a glowing account of the girl he is to marry when he graduates in June ("I believe I've found an almost perfect girl. She had maturity, a fact that is very refreshing to find these days. She is intelligent, pretty, sincere, understanding, and devoted. Could I ask for more?"), encloses her picture with his; and so we leave him. One reason I have quoted so fully from his letters is that I think him typical of the men who took advantage of the GI bill to come to college. The picture he gave me of himself, freer and more complete than that any of my actual students gave me of themselves, was very helpful to me in trying to understand them.

Back now to domestic scenes in Frost Woods as the war continued. Jack Maiken used my car on his last furlough before going into action and left me a little of his furlough gas, so I had enough for an extra trip in to see Mrs. Beatty. Hannah started Wisconsin High, and Bill first grade.

> October 2, 1944. Hannah likes Wisconsin High very much, I judge, and I certainly like it too. It's got all the latest wrinkles—they are studying nutrition by watching two white rats, to one of which they give a balanced diet (Hannah took in some Swiss chard from the garden for it), and to the other a bad diet of candy and white bread. When the malnourished

one has pined away enough, I suppose, they'll give it a shot of Swiss chard and bring it back. Individual attention is their long suit, and I think Hannah can do with it, after Nichols School, which is a bit on the underprivileged side, you know. There are twenty-two people in her class, eight girls and fourteen boys—pretty good ratio, these days. It seems to me she shouldn't grow up with an inferiority complex as I did, especially since she goes in to school every day with two boys. The eight girls seem to be having a very good time together, which is nice, since Hannah misses other girls here, you know. She has improved immensely in appearance, puts up her hair at night, wears sweaters and skirts, and altogether has taken one of those forward spurts in growing up that the children seem to take every so often.

I was now on all college-level Army Institute courses.

Much more interesting, but they take a good deal more time. Still, since Bill is in school all day now, I have a lot more time. I could spend it cleaning house—the place is so thick with cobwebs you can hardly see your way round—but for some reason or other that hasn't much appeal. It seems pretty lonesome without Bill coming home at noon. When your youngest child is in school for the whole day, you feel about ready to fall into your grave. Of course the break is worse for me since the children don't come home at noon, as most places they do.

October 30, 1944. It has been the loveliest October here I ever knew, one sunny day after another, cool nights but warm days, and I never saw the oaks brighter than they were this year. We are now engaged in raking up all those beautiful leaves. I could get quite poetic about it. We spent this weekend raking and burning, and will have to spend next too. The boys were supposed to help me yesterday afternoon—they did work a while Saturday morning—but they were engaged in a football game on the front lawn and I didn't have the heart to call them away. They then disappeared and came in at supper time glowing with exercise and saying what fun they had had helping Mr. Williams (Sally Marshall's tenant) rake his leaves. (I must have remembered how much I had enjoyed wiping dishes for Mrs. Case, our next door neighbor, Arvin's mother, when I was their age.)

I am having one of those spells now when I really am taking a great deal of pleasure in the children. Bill is in school all day so that I am fresher to cope with him when he is home and he is really learning to read so fast in school that I am quite impressed. Tommy is far more reliable and less forgetful than he used to be, and very sweet and thoughtful of me. And I told you how much Hannah has improved. The weather has been lovely and we've all been outdoors a lot, I've given up worrying about infantile paralysis and the winter colds have not started; everyone is looking and feeling very well.

Frost Woods is really noble. Alice Strang took the Nichols School kindergarten a couple of days this week because the teacher was sick and they couldn't get any substitute. She has the Brownies, I'm assisting with the Girls Scouts, Grace Maiken is a Den Mother, Setzie has the Health Clinic, Marie Ragsdale is secretary of the PTA and running a bakery sale.

A very pleasant intimacy developed among this group of women now, and we had begun to feel we could safely go out in the evening in the neighborhood sometimes after our children were in bed. Grace usually had coffee in the afternoons and the rest of us dropped in whenever we were not engaged in social service. We played contract [bridge] one night a week, Monday, to suit my convenience, because that was the day my papers were lightest.

A vignette of war time in December. "D. A. came home one evening last week to find all the lights in the house on and no doors locked. She thought it a bit strange, and stranger next morning when the maid was not downstairs getting breakfast, but in the effort to get the family off she had no time to investigate. When she did she found a note on the girl's pincushion saying she had eloped with a soldier from Truax. In addition to being sorry for herself, D. A. was sorry for the girl, because the man seems a bad lot and has been in trouble at Truax all the time he has been there." I had the carol party.

> It seemed very nice to get back to it again after last year's whooping cough. Most of the neighbors turned out, and there seemed a remarkable number of men; the women wore long dresses, so it seemed festive. I must say there never was a year when it was so hard to sing the Christmas carols, with

the horrible war news coming in (this was the month of the Battle of the Bulge; Germany's last desperate effort); but if you have children growing up and they have to cope with this world they can't have any too much peace and security in their childhood to prepare them for it.

I noted my constantly growing respect for Grace, who "takes the strain she is living under with consistent bravery." The January weather was good and crisp: 5 above one morning, 2 the next. "But as long as it is above zero the children say, 'Oh, this isn't cold.' They really seem very hardy." Early in March:

> The snow is beginning to melt. The mud is terrific, of course. Bill stands in the front yard and churns it up, and then comes in the house just after I have washed the kitchen floor. But after all I've lived here for thirteen years now, and you get hardened to misfortune. I'm thankful to see signs—not of spring yet, but say of the loosening of winter. There's been a mess of skis, ski poles, snow shovels and sleds outside my front door all winter forming a natural barricade that Von Rundstedt himself couldn't get through.[310] Bill and I took them all down to the garage this week. A few odd skis and poles were missing, but we took down everything we could find. One of the books I read aloud this winter was Sigrid Undset's account of childhood in Norway, and she described the mother going around in the spring as the snow melted, picking up scarves and mittens and so on at different layers.[311] She had nothing on us.

In these pre-TV days, parents worried about the debasing effect of too much radio on their children's minds, but "I have never had much radio trouble. Tom sometimes listens to *Jack Armstrong* and *Captain Midnight*, but he doesn't really care much about it. I limited him to those two. As a family, we listen to *Henry Aldrich*, whom I adore." As usual we put in our garden.

There was now a really frenzied demand for houses to rent because of Truax, and Grace decided to rent hers and spend the summer at Washington Island.

---

310 Karl Rudolf Gerd von Rundstedt (1875–1953), an officer in the German Empire and Nazi Germany, was charged but not tried for war crimes during World War II.
311 Sigrid Undset (1882–1949), a Norwegian novelist who received the Nobel Prize (1928), describes her childhood and flight from Nazi-occupied Norway in *Elleve aar* (*Eleven Years*), published in 1934. Her best-known work is the trilogy *Kristin Lavransdatter*, 1920–22.

the time she has had. First she rented the house for four months (May 1 to September 1) to an Army lieutenant with a wife and baby; the man came out, borrowed baby furniture from the Pooleys, and his wife and baby came up from South Carolina (he had an apartment they could stay in until Grace left). The day after they arrived, he was transferred to Amarillo, Texas. Grace then rented to a young doctor finishing up training at Wisconsin General, who goes into the navy in four months. He has two small children, one three months, one two years. Grace was endeavoring to clean house, as one would expect, and something essential burned out of the hot water heater. At first the man said it couldn't be fixed, then he said they'd send it to the factory and try. There was Grace, waiting along from day to day of course, for hot water. Then the part was shipped back, and expected, and didn't arrive, and finally was reported lost in the mail. At this point a letter arrived from Jack, saying the last port they had touched at they hadn't been able to take on any water, so he hadn't had a bath for six days. That was no shock for Grace; neither had she. The part was finally installed tonight, and the Maikens are now having hot water for the first time in ten days. They will just have a chance to get in baths all around and leave; but although all of us told Grace to be thankful she was going away and just to let the tenants struggle with the hot water, I think we all felt that it really would be nicer to leave your rented house with some system for heating water to a family that included a three-months-old baby. I shall miss her very much. She is very thoughtful of me.

In April Roosevelt died. None of you in these days without heroes (I wrote the first draft of this chapter during the Nixon-McGovern campaign, when it was a commonplace that our choice was between a knave and a fool, and I write the final one in the post-Watergate era) can realize the depth of the grief of the whole nation at the death of its President. In modern jargon, he was a father figure. "God—how he could take it for us all," said Lyndon Johnson, then a young Texas congressman, at his death (quoted in *Eleanor: The Years Alone*, by Lash). The similarity to the death of the martyred Lincoln—nearly the same time of year, the funeral train—added poignancy and solemnity. Like most other Americans, I sat later in front of the television set to look at the funeral pageantry of John F. Kennedy and agreed with the radio announcer who said the most poignant thing of all was the wooden cart and the riderless horse. At Roosevelt's death we listened, listened for two days, all the time the funeral train was coming north, to nothing but solemn music on the radio, and in bed I envisaged the train coming through the night. "Bill was so upset I had a terrible time getting him to sleep that night—he cried over and over, 'I wish President Roosevelt didn't die! I like President Roosevelt so much!' The next day he found a pole and went to a great deal of trouble, all by himself, fixing up a flag to hang half mast in his room, for the President. I was really deeply stirred all the time from the death to the burial. After that I began to recover a little; but while the train was traveling, it seemed more than I could bear, somehow, to think of that awful last journey." For those of us who lived through those days, no political analysis of weaknesses, no iconoclastic personal biographies, can alter the epitaph which Motley gave to William of Orange, and which we gave to Roosevelt: "As long as he lived, he was the guiding-star of a whole brave nation, and when he died, the little children cried in the streets."

Chores went on. "War-time living complicates things. Plain living like Robinson Crusoe's isn't simpler than civilized, but more complicated and time-consuming. I got the leader of Tom's Cub pack to get my storm windows off on the first floor, with the help of a friend, but I'm afraid to have him try to get the second floor ones off, so they're staying on. The man who has sharpened my lawn mower out here for some years isn't doing it any more because he has no motor, and so on and so forth." I went to Alice's commencement, and "was totally exhausted after sitting through the ceremony—for the first time since I've been in Madison. Thank heaven I see no prospect of going to another till Hannah's, which is just about time to rest up. At that, the old-timers say I'm a sissy; this was a war commencement, and there were only about half as many degrees given as usual.

"The Maikens' tenants are living in uncertainty as to whether they will be transferred somewhere else or not. So am I. If they move, I'll have to rent the house again, my favorite indoor sport. As a matter of fact, as I went out to the mailbox today, a woman driving a car stopped to ask if I knew of any houses to rent. The situation is desperate." The tenants were transferred, and I went through agony because so many people, all with good reasons, wanted the house. I chose a combat veteran pilot from the pacific, because with his record I thought he deserved a chance to be with his wife and baby. The runner-up was a warrant officer with a wife and two children who practically accused me of class favoritism because the other man was a commissioned officer. I was mowing the lawn (an old-fashioned man-power mower, of course) when the warrant officer came out and made his last desperate plea. I was within an inch of offering him our addition for his family of four. If it had occurred to him to say, "Here, let me finish the lawn for you," I certainly would have done it; but it didn't, and so I refrained, probably a good thing. He never knew what a trifle would have tipped the scale. Sally Owen's children came up from Texas to summer with their grandparents. "Fishing, riding the Owens' horses—David Ragsdale got bucked off yesterday as they put it—and baseball are the recreations of the younger set." The baseball diamond was here; a friend said, "I see you've chosen between your lawn and your children." "You'd be astounded at the number of fish the boys catch, and they clean their own. I saw in the A&P yesterday bullheads, cleaned, exactly like Tommy's only not so fresh, selling at fifty-nine cents a pound. . . . The beach has about twenty children each time, and it's a frightful job to lifeguard." I had three weeks vacation from Army Institute papers in August, and "naturally since the vacation began I have been doing more work than before, I canned twenty-one quarts of apple sauce and ten quarts of cherries this week, spent an all-day meeting with the Girl Scouts, did some fall cleaning, and continued to provide meals as usual. Alice is here now for her vacation, and Susie Ragsdale is spending the weekend while her parents have taken the boys north. One thing and another. . . . The great diversion this year has been swimming under Sally Marshall's instruction. Tommy is so good he really would be promising for college athletics, and Bill can dive just beautifully. It has been a very profitable summer from that viewpoint.

> We were speaking of children's letters at the Sewing Circle the other night, and I really though Johnny Hamel's was the best. "Dear Lairdy, I bit David and my tooth came out. I put it under my pillow and the fairies gave me five cents."

The end of the war was near.

> August 12, 1945. Life is moving very fast now. Who would have thought a week ago that the end was so near? Not I, not being in the secret of the atomic bomb. By the way, did you ever know anything like the number of people you know who have been working on the atomic bomb only you didn't know it until this week? Perhaps it is because I live in an academic community where I am likely to know a fairly large proportion of scientists; but all week this one and that and this one's brother-in-law and that one's cousin have been turning up until I could make a list as long as your arm of workers on the atomic bomb. I may say that I myself regard the bomb with horror, which is perhaps merely because I am middle-aged. I don't suppose our children will have any trouble adjusting

themselves to an atomic age—presuming that they live to do so—but our development has been so uneven we may well destroy ourselves. Along one line we have developed this tremendous power; but socially we are so backward we don't know how to use it safely. No doubt the Cro-Magnon man said the same thing—though possibly in a different vocabulary—at the invention of fire. Anyhow even I can see that we can't forget it, now that we know it, and it is certainly a cause for devout thankfulness that we thought it up first—from our point of view, that is.

No news on the radio about the final steps; but it can't be long now.

So we moved back to peace.

September 4, 1945. Frost Woods wind-up to the season, a pot-latch—an old Indian word, meaning gathering for the purpose of work or play, and it has been a cheery old Frost Woods custom usually inaugurated by the Owens, to gather the neighborhood together when some work was to be done. Yesterday it was taking in the diving board as the formal end of the summer, and then a pot-luck supper afterwards. The high point of the afternoon was surfboard riding. It was calm as a millpond, but the children thought it was loads of fun, and it was fun to see them. The surfboard belongs to the Pooleys, and Bob was towing it behind his boat with an outboard, so that it wasn't very fast; but it was fun and he had the patience of Job, towing them round and round in circles till each had had his turn and then each had had another turn. It was rather a chilly night, but they were so crazy about the surfboard they refused with chattering teeth to go home and get any clothes on until I positively had to knock them down and drag them home. The Owen children—that is Merle's, who have been here all summer—left last night after the festivities, and the Marshalls go home before the end of the week, there being no difficulty now about reservations. The native children, so to speak, all started in school today, so things are quiet. It seems a pity when the loveliest weather of the whole year is here now to have the children shut up in school.

Grace Maiken is back. You know I was keeping Raven, their big collie, for the summer. She is having a good deal of difficulty readjusting, like the soldiers, poor thing. Since Ray Owen threatened to shoot her (which I have carefully concealed from Grace because you might just as well avoid neighborhood feuds if possible) we kept her in the house all the time and she got a tremendous lot of attention from the children. Grace never did have her in the house and is particularly nervous now because Raven is jealous of Jeff if Grace gives him any attention and is likely to snap at him; so naturally Raven keeps coming back here. Last night she stood at the front door moaning to come in, and Hannah lay in her bed moaning for me to let her in and wailing that it was raining, and I felt like a cruel father in a melodrama with a child out in the snow.

The Reading Group met this week at D. A.'s at the Ela cottage across the lake. It was quite like old times to take a little expedition again. Betty Patterson drove us all out. I am going easy on driving still because my tires are pretty old naturally, and until tires are available to the general public I can't get any more. But it feels wonderful to be free of gas rationing and above all of fuel oil rationing. It will be such a comfort to be warm this winter—and a distinct change. It's such a release of tension as each restriction goes off. Grace Maiken said today that she called up to see if she could get some sand for the sandpile and when they said "We'll be right out," she nearly fell over. She observed, very truly, that we'll have to get over this habit of apologizing whenever we ask for anything.

And so the war ended. And the flood of returning veterans in the fall, in the post-war adjustment, got me my chance to start in again at the university. Classed as a teaching assistant, as I had been fifteen years before, I took humbly the first step on the path which led to a full, rich, and happy career.

The nearest published parallel to "my war," in which I was so much more spectator than participator, that I am aware of is in Arnold Bennett's *Old Wives Tale*: Sophia lives in Paris through the France-Prussian War quite untouched by any of it. To some extent this was true of me. The events were taking place thousands of miles away, at too great a remove to touch me. My own personal suffering, unconnected with the war, effectually blocked out my ability really to feel that of others. It is interesting, though, to see here how through the war I was following the personal experience that came to so many, many people on account of the war: learning to accept a loss which at first seemed totally crippling, and to re-make a life on the terms left us. Perhaps it was my characteristic lack of initiative; perhaps mere cowardice, like that of the ostrich hiding his head in the sand; perhaps something more justifiable, an effort to keep life as normal as possible for three small children; perhaps simply lack of opportunity for adult conversation beyond how well each other's tomatoes were ripening; perhaps so much hard physical work that it inhibited much mental occupation. ("I loved work—it has always been my favorite form of recreation," as Dr. Anna Howard Shaw says.)[312] Whatever the reasons, and whether they were creditable or discreditable, I was involved in "the ordinariness of life" throughout the war. I heard the news, and I heard the voices of the great men: Churchill, Roosevelt. But I think the only true keen pain which touched me personally (Sophia was altogether untouched) was at Roosevelt's death.

Unlike Sophia, also, I was supported by being involved in a great national effort. Of course it was in a humble way, but between the Army Institute papers and the Victory Garden, any waking hours not occupied with you were brim full. The experience of national involvement is an enriching one, though I think it is as dead as the dinosaur. All through this century, beginning with the World War I slogan, "The war to end war," men have recognized that war is not a good motive to bind a nation together. But the century has produced no substitute. If there is anything characteristic of our national scene today, it is that it is horrifyingly divided into splinter groups, countless, each crying in the wilderness for its own advantage and ignoring the claims of any other. No one I know questioned the justice of our cause, and I believe this was nationally true. Geoffrey Perrett, in *Days of Sadness, Years of Triumph: The American People, 1939–1945* (1973), says, "The country's participation in the war was accepted by almost everyone as a just and necessary act."[313] The restiveness of the soldiers my friend reported from Japan came after the war was over. As I look at the magazine clippings I kept from this period, there are countless sharp contrasts with the bitter civil strife that marked the late sixties. *Life* (April 5, 1943) showed a page of men back from North Africa: "Home from their first flight, U.S. soldiers smile with their medals at Army's Walter Reed Hospital." The smiles are *proud*. Perhaps you will remember the TV scenes when soldiers from Vietnam contemptuously hurled their medals into the White House grounds. Another picture from the same magazine is captioned, "Butchers besieging Port Green Market in Brooklyn

---

312 Anna Howard Shaw (1847–1919), a leader of women's suffrage in the US, a physician, and a female Methodist minister.
313 Geoffrey Perret, an English-born writer of American history, published this book with the University of Wisconsin Press. The quotation is on page 441.

started to riot when they found the wholesale houses had no meat to sell them." These were small retailers who claimed packers were giving preference to the large chain stores, hotels, and restaurants, and they were shouting "We want our fair share!" But as you look at the faces, they are laughing and as jolly as Santa Claus. I saw my share of real riots plenty of times on Bascom Hill twenty-five years after this. I am deeply aware of what "loss of innocence" means in American history between 1940 and 1970, and after reading these innocent pages perhaps you will be too. In the forties we were innocent and patriotic, and "patriotic" was not a dirty word, displaced from the language by "chauvinistic." We were united.

Above all, unlike Sophia, I was enfolded, and you were too, by personal warmth and friendship. The war in Frost Woods was to a very considerable extent women without men. All through history, I think, women have drawn together and comforted each other under these circumstances, always given the necessary requirement of physical propinquity. No neighborhood ever more happily lived up to the true neighborhood ideal than did Frost Woods during the war. We knew our responsibility to the nation, the community, the neighbors, everybody else's children and our own; and we got innocent pleasure fulfilling it. To quote Angela Thirkell, cheerfulness was always breaking in.[314]

---

[314] The quotation is actually attributed to Mr. Edwards, a fellow collegian of James Boswell (1740–1795) who, appearing in Boswell's biography of Samuel Johnson (1709–1784), says to Dr. Johnson, "I have tried too in my time to be a philosopher; but, I don't know how, cheerfulness was always breaking in."

TRANSITION: SEPTEMBER 1945 TO SEPTEMBER 1950

These two months delimit a significant passage in my life. On the former, I went back to university teaching, part-time, as a temporary stopgap for a Department of English so hard pressed for teachers they'd take anyone who spoke the language (as was said of a draftee during the war, he was in if he could stand on his feet, see lightning, and hear thunder), with classes only at 11 and 12 Monday Wednesday Friday, time which could be worked in with your demands. On the latter, Hannah left for Swarthmore. Never again did we four live together as a family, and in these five years I had become so committed to my work that your jibes of "career woman," "big shot," "big wheel" (a prophet is not without honor save with her own children) were in a fair way to become modestly true. This is the luckiest timing of my life. The return of the veterans came when you were all in school all day, with the further luck that Nichols served a hot lunch. Dick Quintana,[315] then acting chairman, made it clear, "and rightly so," I wrote Gwen, "that while I could teach if they couldn't get anyone else, it was only for the emergency. I know he's right. I'm middle-aged, and I haven't any illusions about what I might do professionally, having lost all this time and also having a main interest in life, the children, who would always have to come first."

Before I told Dick I'd do it, I discussed the matter carefully with you. Were you willing? Did you understand it would take time and I might not be able to do things for you I'd done before? Did you approve? Would you cooperate? Oh yes, Mother. But the only real accommodation I can remember your making was that you didn't mind at all using paper napkins instead of cloth ones, to cut down on the ironing. Otherwise you saw no reason why service should be curtailed, and the first weeks were hectic. In October I was positive I'd taken on an impossible load, and I'd tell Dick I couldn't go on next semester; but by November we were through the worst. It was like your first baby. At the beginning you haven't a minute to breathe in the twenty-four hours, but then you get used to handling the situation. Just the same it was a schizophrenic period, when I had both the professional responsibilities of a man and the domestic ones of a woman. But I like to work (I wrote Gwen I was temperamentally unsuited for life in the South Seas, so it was lucky I didn't live there), and I'm at my best when my capacities are taxed to the utmost. Two things pulled me through. First, the

---

315 Ricardo B. Quintana (1898–1987), a Harvard graduate, taught English at UW-Madison from 1927- 1969. His wife, Janet, graduated from UW-Madison in 1925.

nature of the work. I slipped into the classroom like a fish slipping back into water, and it was heaven to be in the element again. It can be said of me, as Dr. Johnson said of Pope, that I am "one of the few whose labor is their pleasure."[316] This can only be said when the labor is eminently congenial. Second, I was convinced that it was as much in your interest as my own that I should not lose a chance—even a slim one—of developing a life of my own to live as, one by one, you left me. When Wright[317] was gone, I knew that I must guard above all else against making unfair demands on you in the future. It would have been easier to take two or three more years before starting work, but the chance was now and I must take it now.

One thing which made the first weeks particularly hectic was that every piece of mechanical equipment in the house went out of order all at once—naturally enough, since they'd all been installed about the same time, and of course the war had prevented any earlier replacements.

> October 10, 1945. I had no heat until the last day of September, I had a week without hot water, and the radio is now out of order for the second time. Of course everything has reached the point of dying of old age, and I haven't been able to replace anything. I have a new pump and a new hot water heater on order, but it may be for years and it may be forever before they come. It was a great comfort to get the furnace fixed, I'll tell you. And of course you never appreciate running water until after it hasn't run for a while. We have reached such an age of specialization that sometimes it takes days before the householder can track down the particular service man who is supposed to remedy the trouble. If the furnace won't work, you'd think you'd call a furnace man. Not at all. It took a week before I could find out from one service or another what man to call. I wish I were a graduate of a good mechanics institute. Bill seems to show some aptitude that way, but it will be quite a while before he can take over, I'm afraid.

In spite of all this I was happy. A good deal of the USAFI work had been drudgery, and under any circumstances the percentage of students who finish a correspondence course is so appallingly low that the teacher cannot help feeling

---

316 From *Samuel Johnson: Selected Poetry and Prose* (1977), edited by Frank Brady and W. K. Wimsatt, p. 541.
317 Wright Thomas, Ednah's husband from 1927–1943.

that much of her effort is wasted.³¹⁸ It was wonderful to get back to live bodies right before me, and the stimulus of a class. Now, and always to the last class I met before retirement, I invariably had one sinking, disheartening moment. I'd get to class early, chat a bit before the bell rang, and when it did, go to shut the door and turn back to face the students. That less than minute of moving to the door and back was never less than dreadful. But once the hour started, my heart leaped up, and I forgot everything except how happy I was to be where I was. I wanted to plan for my classes all the time, and I had to force myself to stop thinking about them and plan your meals. These two strands have made this chapter very difficult to organize, but if it seems confused, so was the period.

Often, of course, the two strands came together, and I'll give one sample now.

> May 6, 1949. I brought out some new assistants I was conferring with to the house, to have dinner, as a gesture of hospitality, and since it was a business meeting I propositioned the children, Hannah to cook the meal and the boys to serve it. We started out with a bang, when Tommy summoned us to table, and he had a casserole dish and Bill followed with a vegetable dish, and we had no plates to put the food on. The ice being thus broken, we got on pretty well till the boys brought in coffee with dessert. I took one sip of mine and nearly fainted; it was practically stone cold and full of grounds. I looked around, and all the guests were drinking theirs. I didn't see how they could, but it seemed best not to call attention to it, so I said nothing. When I went out in the kitchen after dinner, Hannah said, "How did you like your coffee?" "Terrible," said I truthfully. "Well," said she, "there wasn't enough to go round and I thought it would look funny if you didn't have any, so I ran some water from the faucet through the grounds and gave it to you."

There was a lot of post-war confusion in every aspect of life, from worn-out furnaces to hospital services (Hannah Davis had a friend in charge of records in one of the big Boston hospitals whose father needed an operation, and there were 1500 people on the list before him waiting for admission), but I doubt if any anywhere was greater than in our Freshman English. I shall tell later the story of my first day and my meeting with Ed Lacy.³¹⁹ At the moment, Mark

---
318 In the World War II chapter, Thomas describes her involvement in teaching correspondence courses for the United states Armed Forces Institute (USAFI).
319 Edgar W. Lacy (1914–1981) earned his Ph.D. from the University of Illinois (1939) and

Eccles was titular chairman,[320] but he had no interest in the course whatever, and was leaving all the details to Charlotte Wood (my predecessor as course secretary). She had worked loyally under Warner Taylor,[321] chairman when I came as a teaching assistant, and had done an excellent job of scheduling all sorts of irregular sessions during the war, but she was near retirement and ready to let things go. Bob Pooley was supposed to take the course over, but in eighteen months he assumed chairmanship of Integrated Liberal Studies,[322] and handed the freshman work over to Ed. For the time being, those of us in the course were on our own, sink or swim.

I worried a little in these days over having to leave my newly attained Eden (a rather active paradise) but there was no need. Second semester, "the university is absolutely swamped under an unprecedented second semester enrollment, all veterans, and I have taken on a third section (this was the equivalent of full-time work)—ninety-five students in all, four of them women, and those ex-servicewomen. It's overpowering." The veterans were unquestionably the most admirable group of American students who ever came to college. It is mildly interesting that my teaching should have started with the best, the GI Bill veterans of the late forties, and ended with the worst, the trashing misfits of the late sixties. The veterans were the best kind of elite. They had deliberately taken advantage of the chance to come to college, choosing an education for future good rather than a job for immediate good, which involved always postponement and sometimes sacrifice. Few of them would have been able to go to college before the war. One

---

served in the US Army prior to being hired in 1946 as assistant professor in the UW-Madison English department. In 1948, he became director of Freshman English and invited Thomas to assist him (Fleming, 2011, p. 46). Lacy worked closely with Thomas for over twenty years.

320 Mark Eccles (1905–1998), studied at Harvard under George Lyman Kittredge, earned the Ph.D. in 1932, and taught at UW-Madison from 1934–1976. The term "chairman" here and in the next sentence means director of Freshman English.

321 Warner Taylor (1880–1958), earned BA and M.A. degrees from Columbia and taught there for six years before teaching at UW-Madison from 1911–1947, where, beginning in 1921, he directed the Freshman English program (Clark, 1966, pp. 5–6; Fleming, 2011, p. 38).

322 Robert C. Pooley (1898–1978) taught English and Education courses at UW from 1931-1968 and conducted pioneering research in English usage alongside fellow faculty member Sterling Andrus Leonard (1888–1931). Pooley was president of the National Council of Teachers of English (NCTE) and founder and past president of the Wisconsin Council of Teachers of English. In light of his education background, Pooley was asked to direct Freshman English after Warner Taylor's retirement in 1945. However, in 1948 Pooley was asked to direct the newly created Integrated Liberal Studies (ILS) program. This program grew out of the "Experimental College" established by philosopher and education reformer Alexander Meiklejohn (1872–1964) in 1927 as a residential college which emphasized an interdisciplinary, integrated approach to liberal education. Fleming (2011) describes the ILS program as "an attempt to retain something like a small liberal arts college in the context of [a] rapidly expanding, quickly fragmenting, and increasingly scientific-technical university" (p. 45)

able man told me he would never have dreamed of it, and added, "But I'm going to see that my kid brother gets here." They were mature. They were disciplined. They came prepared to work. Some, of course, hadn't the ability and dropped out. Almost all had a tough time the first weeks (like me). But they had will power, they didn't expect life to be easy, and most of them stuck it out. Nor, of course, were they all disciplined. In '48 a very able student of mine didn't come back after Christmas vacation. A friend told me they had both gone to a party, and he himself had left early. The other stayed, drinking more and more heavily, and when he finally drove home—luckily alone—at ninety miles an hour he ran his car into a telephone pole and broke every bone in his body. His father, a Milwaukee doctor, lined up a team of surgeons, but the boy died on the operating table. The rest of the semester I would look at that empty seat—it was always surrounded by empty seats; no one sat near it—and think of the man's mother. He had survived three years of combat flying without a scratch—what had she gone through then—and came home to pick up his life in his hands and throw it away. But as a group the veterans were the best students in the history of American education, and everyone I know who had experience agrees in ranking them as the best students he ever had.

The university coped as well as it could. The Legislature limited admission to state residents only. Fortunately, in view of their travels, we were in no danger of becoming provincial. "The campus is a terrific mess with Quonset huts all over the place."[323] I taught in one where the mall between the two libraries is now. The idea was mooted that a branch of the university should be set up in Baraboo, in the housing belonging to Badger Ordnance,[324] where production had now stopped, where the veterans and their wives could live, as could also the faculty to conduct classes. The classes came to nothing, I think because they couldn't get faculty willing to move out, but instead the veterans commuted the fifty miles in university buses twice a day. A young woman in our department who had been picked up like me in the emergency was married to a man who later became a professor in the Department of History here, and I got a good idea of contemporary housing by calling on them in every place where they lived: Badger Ordnance, the barracks at Truax, a trailer camp at Camp Randall.[325] The

---

323 Quonset huts were lightweight, prefabricated, semi-circular steel huts manufactured for temporary residence during wartime.
324 The Badger Ordnance Works, also known as The Badger Army Ammunition Plant, was the largest munitions factory in the world during World War II.
325 Randall Trailer Park, possibly the nation's first student veteran housing project, was created by relocating and installing surplus trailers used by war employees at Badger Ordnance Works to Camp Randall Memorial Park, east of the football stadium. Space was limited: the small trailers provided 600 cubic feet; the larger, 1,500 (Cronon & Jenkins, 1994, pp. 28, 31).

man, who was well over six feet, had no little trouble fitting himself into all those close quarters.

You will remember the inmates of our own house during this period.

> February 8, 1946. We've taken in a little German Jewish refugee who is an assistant in the zoology department, Mr. Levi. His family got out of Germany in 1938 and could take no money with them, and have been poor as Job's turkeys ever since. He is quite an odd little creature, singularly unattractive, with a strong accent, and when I looked at him I felt so sorry for him that I knew I must take him in for no one else would. I warned him about the children, and he clearly didn't want to come here, but he tried Mrs. Owen, who wouldn't take him—because he's a Jew—and the only other address he had was in Mazomanie! So he came, and really it works out pretty well. He is just as quiet as a little mouse and doesn't even smoke. He leaves at seven in the morning and comes back about seven at night, goes to bed very early, and of course the house is quiet at night because we do too. He gets his own breakfast. I didn't care much for that idea, but it will save him a lot of money and trouble, so I said he could get himself breakfast and Sunday night supper, which would save him a trip in town, if he'd clean up himself, which he does very neatly. He doesn't care much for children, I think, but he's not the type to appeal to them much, so they just don't pay much attention to him, and on the whole it's surprising that someone could live in the house and make so little impression on us. He likes the country. The driving bothers him now, but he looks forward to the spring. Mrs. Owen has rented rooms to three students, and the Pooleys have one too, a doctor who is taking a refresher course at the hospital. The Fulchers refuse to be troubled, desperate as the need is. I've heard of boys walking along the streets and going into houses at random and begging to be allowed just to sleep in a cot in the basement.
>
> March 10, 1946. We've had a really first class blizzard, just like the ones in *The Long Winter*.[326] I had a break that day, for I had taken Jack Maiken in town—he hasn't been able to buy

---

[326] *The Long Winter* (1940), from the *Little House on the Prairie* children's novel series, by Wisconsin-born American writer Laura Ingalls Wilder (1867–1957).

a car yet—and he drove me out and got the children from school. But Saturday I had to get Tommy in to a doctor's appointment at ten, and we shoveled for two hours to get out of your driveway. Then I got stuck again in town, parking, because just a strip was cleared down the middle of the street for traffic, and I had to borrow a shovel from a householder and shovel for forty-five minutes before I could get going home. Sunday I was so lame I felt like the sailor who was flogged in *Two Years Before the Mast*,[327] which I am reading aloud to Tommy. It was fun driving in town, though; we counted thirteen abandoned cars by the side of the road in three miles. Poor little Mr. Levi came home in a terrible state that night. He had had to leave his car by Hollywood, when he turned off the highway, and he was scared to death.

As a kindly gesture for that Easter, he brought home to the children three baby chicks, just out of the shell, which he had gotten at Birge [Hall] in the course of some experiment or other. "They are in a cardboard box and have to have an electric light bulb in with them to keep them warm, day and night, and messy! You wouldn't believe. Clearly we can't keep them when they once get to the point of climbing out of the box, which won't be long. Of course the boys are delighted, but Hannah seems to share my sanitary scruples. I can't say my standard of living is very high, but even I draw the line at chickens running around the house." We were keeping them in the dining room, where their eternal cheeping took away my appetite. She and I went to a movie that vacation, in which the Eastern schoolteacher arrives in a tough Texas town and says the men look "as if they would enjoy stepping on baby chicks." We felt we wouldn't mind it much ourselves. After Easter, I thanked him as tactfully as I could and he took them back to Birge. Later in the spring, he found a place in town which was more convenient for him, and he went out of our lives too.

But his successors, the Cowees, made a much greater impression on the family, and their stay was fortunate for us all, most of all for Bill, who found in John Cowee a very kind and helpful father-substitute.

> October 9, 1946. I've had a real stroke of luck—at least I think so—proving that virtue sometimes is its own reward. As the result of a terrific tear-jerker on the radio to rent room to students, I took in a veteran and his wife, John and Ann

---

327 *Two Years Before the Mast* (1840), a memoir of a two-year sea voyage, by American author Richard Henry Dana Jr. (1815–1882).

Cowee, from Sheboygan, and gave them the big room next to Hannah's in the addition. At first I told them they couldn't have kitchen privileges, but then I said they could, so now they get breakfasts, sometimes dinners and usually all meals over the weekend in my kitchen and eat in their room. It's a nuisance having to give them a shelf in the ice chest, for my ice chest is like Fibber McGee's closet anyhow;[328] but they are so considerate and quiet and thoughtful about keeping out of my way it's the least I can do. He has junior standing and plans to go into Law School. She has a job in town as a stenographer, so they are both gone all day. I have grown very fond of them both. He was a combat captain in the South Pacific for two years, and with the first division to enter Japan. I think he must have been a marvelous commanding officer. He certainly inspires confidence. He is quiet, but you feel he'd be a rock. She is very sweet and obviously well brought up. The other morning in the rush of trying to get off to Sunday school with the boys, at the last minute Bill insisted he ought to take a Bible; he didn't need one, but Tom had one so he wanted one. Like a flash Ann appeared at the door of their room saying, "He can have mine." Imagine putting your hand on a Bible like that. John will have a great help with the boys—just what Bill particularly needs. He will also put on the storm windows for me, and help with the driveway this winter. They have their own car, of course. He won't have much free time, and like all the veterans he is worried about his studying.

The arrangement lasted a little over two years, when the Cowees, in expectation of their baby, who arrived early in '49, moved to a small house in Monona, some distance beyond the Nichols School. Ann must have been glad to have her own house. While we were sharing the kitchen, I was impressed at her consideration, and realized that to some extent it was the result of the fact that she had had to share quarters with other women for some time. As we knew each other better, we ate Sunday dinners together, she getting the meal one week, I the next, and I can still remember some of John's war stories. Unlike Mr. Levi, he was fond of children and they were fond of him. He gave Hannah the nickname of "Brain" and they gave him that of "Cowee-bird." "He's very nice to

---

328 *Fibber McGee and Molly*, a popular American radio comedy series (1935–1959), featured a cluttered closet as one of the show's running gags.

Bill, and it's just what Bill has wanted all along—a man in the house, and what's more, a man of a mechanical turn of mind. He's always tinkering with his car or something or other to that effect, and Bill just loves to watch him." Surprisingly enough, he taught the boys (this was long before drip-dry) to iron their own shirts. He'd earned money doing that himself in college, where he had been for a couple of years before the war, and there was nothing effeminate if a war hero did it. The youngest man, the best athlete, and the veteran with the most combat experience, he considerably raised the boys' prestige in the neighborhood. It was a comfort to me, also, to have an able-bodied man in the house, particularly through the winter.

> February 2, 1947. The boys are out skiing. This is the first time the children have missed school, but there was none for two days, and even the university was closed Thursday and until ten o'clock Friday—something which had never happened before, I believe. (For the first time in its history, a great proportion of the staff and students were beyond walking distance, probably the reason.) I haven't had my car out since I managed to creep home Wednesday afternoon, for Friday I went in with the Cowees—John has chains on his car. The highways are clear now, but the streets in town are a terrible mess. It just depends on whether you want your winter spread out over five months or concentrated in one day. This time we got it in one day. This year we have all been well all the time, and the boys have been outdoors almost all the time, skating or skiing, and I haven't worried much about the driving because I knew I had John Cowee to fall back on in emergency. I've shoveled myself, of course, but he was shoveling too, and there's quite a difference between doing that driveway alone or with two reluctant small boys, and with one strong man. Also I am very pepped up after reading a whole batch of themes from returned veterans, who have been in the South Pacific and have had all the tropical islands they want in their lives, and are more than delighted to be back in a good old Wisconsin winter again.

John was kind enough to come back to help me with the storm windows after they moved, and he painted the upstairs bathroom so beautifully that I told Gwen it gave you a case of snow blindness to go into it. The snow motif continues later than you might think this year.

> June 3, 1947. On Decoration Day we had *snow*—that is, we
> saw it at the Dells. The Cowees took us up to the Dells for
> the holiday, which I must say was very noble of them. I ought
> to take the children out on trips oftener, but I'm timid. We
> had a lovely day—beautiful weather, and the country at its
> best—all the lilacs full out, and the leaves and the trees still
> small and with all the different spring colors in them instead
> of the heavy uniform later summer green. We took the boat
> trip to the Upper Dells, and to my great delight the guide on
> the boat was one of my former students and the captain the
> brother of another one. The children all behaved very well. I
> was quite proud of the boys, who were alert and interested all
> the time, and didn't get into any trouble or scuffling around.
> When we got home, I thanked the Cowees and said, in this
> fishing-for-compliment way that we mothers have, "I thought
> the boys did very well, didn't you?" "Frankly," said John, "I
> was amazed." Oh, well.

After John finished his graduate work (he went into the School of Commerce instead of Law) they went to California and we lost touch, though I believe they later came back to Wisconsin. But it was a fortunate interlude, especially for Bill; when he was upset because he thought he couldn't go to the Fathers-Sons banquet at the Nichols School, for example, John took him. (We mothers, in true Hitlerian fashion, were doing the cooking, serving, and washing up in the kitchen.) After that we had the house to ourselves.

The university was still struggling with the crowds.

> October 9, 1946. Overcrowded is right for the university. A
> boy came into my class in Bascom late because he had had
> to get there from a class in the First Congregational Church!
> I send you a newspaper picture of the line for books. About
> five students out of my English 1-a[329] class of thirty-seven
> have textbooks, and the rest just can't get them. This after
> three weeks of teaching. The classes are very large; I seem to
> be settled down now with 103 students in three classes. I had
> forty-six registered for one section and was supposed to send
> all but thirty-three to Mech Eng building—heaven knows
> where that is, nearly up to the Stadium. I did so and started
> class. About half through there was a timid little scratching at

---

329 English 1a, the precursor to English 101, emphasized grammar, usage, sentence-level composition, outlining, and use of library resources (Fleming, 2011, p. 48).

the door, like a mouse, and it opened, and a man whose face was faintly familiar sidled through in a timid and apologetic manner followed by others, and I realized that half of them were coming back. "What's the matter?" said I. "Couldn't you find it?" "Yes, we found it all right," said they, "but there were no more seats in the room so they sent us back here." So they'll be staying with me. At least it was a lovely fall day for them to have the walk up University Avenue and back. The classes are mostly veterans—that is, the freshman courses—and they are very good and responsive students. I've been very busy, but I am very happy in the teaching. It is going more easily than last year, because now of course I'm familiar with the material, having just gone through it.

That didn't, however, mean any timesaving on individual conference.

November 6, 1946. Sometimes I think it may not be exactly the function of a university English teacher to listen to what the conferences develop. It sort of depresses me to think about my children getting to the stage where they'll have love affairs, and don't think it isn't just around the corner. It seems to me I might as well be Dorothy Dix,[330] so many of my students come in and tell me their love troubles. I had a most brilliant and gifted young Jew in just yesterday, who explained he couldn't do any work because he was in love and the whole thing was so uncertain—he is nineteen and she eighteen! I said, as I always say, can't you talk it over with your parents, and he said, as they always say, no, no, no, certainly not, that's the last thing in the world I can do. It makes me worry—children are bound to fall in love with the wrong people and you're the last one they'll come to.

I understand better now than I did then the withdrawal of the child from the parents at a given age, however much love may exist between them. No one can help being conscious ad nauseam of the generation gap after all the psychiatric and psychological science and pseudo-science which has been poured out upon the helpless public in the past twenty-five years—some of it, I must admit, in spite of my prejudice against the social sciences, illuminating. I came on my own, partly as a result of my experience then, to feel that the parent

---

[330] Dorothy Dix was the pen name for Elizabeth M. Gilmer (1861–1951), a journalist who popularized the advice column.

must fully accept the withdrawal in the confidence that if there is love the child will return in due time. And I also came to feel that a very large element in the child's withdrawal—sometimes as large an element as rebellion—is the desire to protect the parent: protect the parent from knowing that the loved child is not in command of his situation. When he is, he will come back. In the meantime, the best help—it isn't much, since everyone must make his own decisions—is a trustworthy, sympathetic, and uninvolved listener. The conferences were after all on composition rather than love life, and I gave Gwen an account of a typical interview in "a stream of strong silent men gradually beating me down."

It was now understood that I was a permanent, if humble, member of the department, and I was given the most stimulating teaching I have ever done. Well in advance of Sputnik and the sudden rush of honors courses which in its wake broke out all over the easy-going adjustment-to-life don't-bother-to-use-your brain system of American education, Ruth Wallerstein[331] conceived the idea of an advanced Freshman English course which would allow superior students to complete the year's Freshman English requirement in one semester. It started with two sections only, she teaching one, I the other. "The students are terribly good and terribly keen, and I am afraid I may not be good enough to handle them, but they are very stimulating. They require a lot of extra work to try to keep up with them." English 11 (later 181) was the best course I ever taught, and it was with deep regret that I was forced to give it up later when I had my own advanced composition course, and the pressures of administrative work in Freshman English were too heavy to let me do any other teaching. It was the only course I ever had where you went into class tired and came out fresh, because the students gave so much to *you*.[332]

This is the time when the most successful work relationship of my life, that with Ed Lacy, started, and I'll take time now to give you an overall account of it. The greatest debt I owe to any man (always excepting Wright) is to him, and therefore yours too is great.

I have a vague recollection of having met him before the war, when I was married, but the picture of our meeting in Charlotte Wood's office is very clear. It was my first day back to teaching, and by coincidence Ed's too, in his case from the service, of course. The office was a scene of total confusion. Charlotte did give us our room numbers; but we had no idea what to do when we got there, how to explain the purpose of the course, anything at all. With his usual

---

331 Ruth Wallerstein (1893–1958), educated at Bryn Mawr and University of Pennsylvania, joined the English department in 1920 and taught English literature until her untimely death in an automobile accident in England while on research leave.

332 English 11, a one-semester, literature-intensive course, became the honors version of Freshman English at UW-Madison (Fleming, 2011, p. 47).

gallantry, Ed found me some bluebooks, and we set off to have our students write impromptus, making up subjects as we went. It is a pleasant irony that the two who met in complete confusion were to work devotedly together for years to manage a course as well organized as any in the country. When Ed was Director, no novice was ever at a loss; he always seen his duty, whether he done it or not.

As I have said, the course was first given to Bob Pooley. An excellent administrator, he began to get things under control and started a number of practices Ed continued, such as the "black book," a loose-leaf notebook for each semester in which were filed complete records—staff lists, calendars, teaching schedules, notices, and so on. But Bob didn't have time to do a great deal before he was offered the chairmanship of Integrated Liberal Studies,[333] a program just starting here as at many other places, and decided to take that. The position of Director of Freshman English was then offered to Ed. Some doubt was felt at the time as to whether this young man, with his gentle Southern manners, was strong enough to handle such a large and difficult assignment. There was no basis for the doubt. As Frank Sullivan says of Edna Ferber,[334] Ed has a whim of iron.

At this time, two senior department members asked me to assist them in their specific work: Merritt Hughes[335] in Chaucer; Ed Lacy in Freshman English. With the population explosion, teaching assistants had almost entirely replaced the full-time staff who had formerly taught in the class, and we would be called on for a thorough training program. My work with Ed would be primarily that, though I would also take over scheduling from Charlotte Wood as soon as she retired. I had had excellent Middle English training at Bryn Mawr under Carleton Brown, and I suppose I could have gotten the material up again; but that had been a long time before, and all the years between and all my experiences, including motherhood, had contributed to fit me for work with young teaching assistants in Freshman English rather than with Chaucerian scholarship. I told Merritt I was sorry and Ed I'd be glad, and this started the most

---

333 Integrated Liberal Studies (ILS), established in 1948 as an extension of philosopher and education reformer Alexander Meiklejohn's (1872–1964) Experimental College, was a residential college within the Madison campus that emphasized an interdisciplinary, integrated approach to liberal education.

334 Frank Sullivan (1892–1976), an American humorist and contributor to *The New Yorker*. Enda Ferber (1885–1968), the Pulitzer Prize-winning American novelist. As recounted in Sullivan's 1941 parody "A Garland of Ibids for Van Wyck Brooks," the phrase "She's got a whim of iron" originated in a conversation between Ferber and American writer and illustrator Oliver Herford (1863–1935), who used the phrase to characterize the impact of his wife's preferences on his choice of necktie, which Ferber had criticized.

335 Merritt Hughes (1893–1971), a Milton specialist trained at Harvard (1921), was hired as a full professor from the University of California. He taught at UW-Madison from 1936–1963.

absorbing and productive professional work of my life. I owe him more than twenty years of thoroughly congenial, thoroughly enjoyable work, to which could be applied Mr. Beatty's definition of ideal work as he gave it to Ham: "You should feel about your work that you would pay for the privilege of doing it."

That's quite a debt. But an even greater debt is that Ed Lacy made the main contribution in restoring my self-confidence. I owe gratitude to Dick Quintana, who as chairman asked me to come back to teaching; to Merritt Hughes, and very especially to Helen White and Ruth Wallerstein, who continually supported and encouraged me; and to Ray Agard,[336] who was on the Divisional Committee when the question of my tenure appointment came up, and who helped to get it through there. But all these people were personal friends of longstanding. I had enough confidence in and respect for them to believe that they would not recommend me for any work they did not think I could handle; and I had enough self-confidence and self-respect to believe that I would not abuse their trust. But just the same I couldn't help feeling they might be thinking poor-brave-little-woman-in-distress-how-can-we-help-her-out. Ed, whom I really hadn't known at all until the day we met in Charlotte's office, was free from any suspicion of this taint. By this time, I'd seen enough of him to know that he was an exceptionally exacting man, underneath his beautiful manners, and that he would never want me to work for and with him unless I could give, as the British say, very good value. He was in a unique position to help restore my self-confidence, and he took the action which did so.

Ed and I were a complementary pair. One of his most remarkable qualities is his unusual ability to see the ultimate implications and consequences of a small or casual action or decision. Personally, I have never come in contact with a mind more brilliant in abstractions. But I could be very useful to him in concrete detail. A lot of this was "busy work," perhaps, like schedules and notices, but it was congenial to me. Then he tends a bit to agoraphobia. He always worked in an inner office with the door closed, and that was where we did our conferring. No one ever dropped in on him uninvited; any visitor had to go through a protecting secretary. But I liked and invited contacts. I didn't go so far as Dorothy Parker, of whom the story is told that she secured a stream of visitors by posting the sign MEN on her door,[337] but whenever I was in my office, which opened directly on the corridor, my door was open, and I was in it a great deal of the time—early in the morning, well before 7:45 (since we scheduled a lot of 7:45's

---

336   Walter R. Agard (1894–1978), a Classics professor at UW-Madison from 1927–1946, taught in the Experimental College (1927–1932) and in the Integrated Liberal Studies (ILS) Program.

337   Dorothy Parker (1893–1967), American poet, critic, and satirist who published frequently in *The New Yorker*.

I thought someone in authority should be here to deal with emergencies), over the lunch hour, a very convenient time for people to drop in, and many others. Ed, remote and godlike, kept up his prestige; I was accessible and motherly. He worked without, I within the gates; that is, he ate lunch at the big table at the University Club[338] where the faculty big shots congregated, attended all faculty meetings, served on L&S and university committees, and I knew the problems, pleasures, and personalities of his staff and their wives.

Professionally, I was the more liberal of the two, which may surprise you. Politically the reverse is true, and I don't want you to think that his position (to use the words of a radio skit I heard the other day) was somewhat to the right of Louis XIV. But he was unquestionably authoritarian (though from behind the scenes) in his handling of the course, and I didn't get as far as I would have liked in my attempts to induce him to include the teaching assistants in more or less democratic participation. If I had been more successful it might not have made any difference when the world turned upside down and the TAA took over, for I never wanted to go that far.[339] One policy I did get him to institute which was very advanced for the time was to stop giving grades on individual themes, merely a tentative report twice a semester and the final grade. Wisconsin was twenty-five years at least in advance of other comparable institutions in this respect, and we had endless trouble trying to convince teaching assistants that the emphasis should be on the work, and on constructive comments about the writing itself, rather than on the grade—until all at once they threw out the baby with the bath and wouldn't use grades at all.

It must be unusual, I think, for two people as different as Ed and I to work together so well. The relationship was based on mutual respect, of course, but also on freedom from any possibility of rivalry. The ordinary person in my position would have had some personal ambition; I had none. I had never had a great deal, and even as a young wife, naturally ambitious for her husband, I felt I would be completely satisfied if Wright attained what—as it turns out—I have attained myself: a full professorship at the University of Wisconsin. When I came back to teaching, I knew I had no status to expect. I had lost the best fifteen years of anyone's professional life, those from twenty-five to forty. I had no degree but the M.A. I wanted—this motive was enormously strong—to find work which, as you grew up, would occupy me so that I would not make crip-

---

338 The University Club, which opened in 1908 and served social, residential, and university business purposes, became "a symbol of faculty unity and center of campus fellowship" (Cronon & Jenkins, 1994, p. 532).

339 The Teaching Assistants Association (TAA), organized in June 1966 by a small group of teaching assistants who sought to blend unionism and activism (Cronon & Jenkins, 1994, p. 494), is the oldest graduate student union in the US.

pling demands upon you and therefore compound the injury you had already received. You and I are all lucky that I found it. That the work was so congenial and done with so congenial a companion is a bonus.

Ed is a brilliant and stimulating man and a most courteous and agreeable companion. Since masculine attentions had disappeared from my life, I enjoyed the fact that he never let me carry my own brief case and that he was a perfect escort at the professional meetings to which we went pretty frequently. (Once when the National Council of Teachers of English met in Chicago we took the milk train down instead of going the night before, and I thought I'd telephone you from the station instead of waking you unnecessarily early before I left the house. After the telephone had rung seventeen times and none of you had answered, I called the Hamel boys, who very kindly came over with fife and drum and woke you up.) We met briefly every day, and had a long meeting at the end of each week: at first Friday night dinner at my house, and after Ed's marriage Friday noon lunch at the University Club, where we spread out our papers in the window nook of the lounge and became an expected part of the scenery. (I remember one Friday night when all the boys in the neighborhood went out camping and got caught in such a deluge that the mothers were worried sick. Ed and I were working on an exam, and as I was called away to the telephone or the door he kept on working, quite oblivious. I thought then he'd be wonderful to go through the Battle of Britain with, for he wouldn't notice a bomb unless it actually smashed the table in front of him.) It was balm to me to be important; the work was absolutely tailor-made to make use of all my abilities; and the difference in our minds brought out the best in both of us and made us accomplish in combination infinitely more than either could ever have done alone.

Ed saw that I got promoted as fast as possible. This was partly for the sake of the work—if I were to be in charge of the training program the assistants would have to respect my title and prestige—but largely, I am sure, because he felt he owed it to me. He needled me into working out the Master Teaching Assistant Program,[340] which got me my full professorship, though it was a casualty of the Zeitgeist. But more important was the more than twenty years of stimulating, congenial, valuable, absorbing work.

Tom started at Wisconsin High in the fall of '47. Since Bill Strang and Dave Ragsdale were still at Nichols, Bill wasn't lonely there. That fall I started advis-

---

340 The Master Teaching Assistants Program was a mentoring program in which experienced Freshman English teaching assistants were assigned to mentor 7–8 new teaching assistants in their first year. Master Teaching Assistants conducted class visits and portions of the weekly training meetings and sought to help new teaching assistants in any way possible (Fleming, 2011, pp. 52–53).

ing, which underlined my permanent status, but which in its general confusion shows university problems I was to have a lot of experience with in the next decade.

> October 5, 1947. We drive in in two cars now, because six children are going to Wisconsin High, too much for one car. Bob and I both leave at 8:10. It takes some doing to get up and get lunches made and everybody dressed and through breakfast and beds made and dishes washed by eight. Getting up early doesn't bother me, luckily.
>
> Heaven help my advisees. You have no idea of the screwballs I got. Most of them are on strict probation; one man was 292 in a high school class of 294; then in comes one junior who never got a grade here below A. One woman registered a week late because she has a five weeks old baby, and she and her husband are both veterans, living in a trailer camp; we had to fit all her work into early morning hours so her husband could take his afternoons. One girl comes from a town of 300 people, and she was so lonesome she came back two days later just to talk to the one person in the whole university she might possibly have an excuse for talking to. I hadn't the haziest idea what I was doing most of the time. I was supposed to advise freshmen, and I had a stack of stuff from the dean's office big enough to choke a horse, which I studied very carefully. I hoped I could grow up with the freshmen, so to speak, and by next semester know what they were moving on to. Then in came streams of upper classmen, transfers, English majors, everything you could think of. In the middle of it in came the department secretary to say she had forgotten to tell me I was supposed to have changed my office, and more advisees were looking for me in the new one. I wonder how many of the programs are going to bounce. However, the more I talk to people, the more I find that no advisers seem to know what they're doing anyway. It is also encouraging to find that sometimes the students seem to know something about it— sometimes, of course, not. But it must be a splendid way to develop self-reliance, which I suppose is the end of education.

The girl from the town of three hundred I remember well, and you'll be glad to know she had a happy and successful university career. She was one of three members of her high school graduating class, and no one from the town had ever come to the university before. She had a board-and-room job with a family on the east side, which meant she was too far away to make friends in any spare time she might have. But she was bright and she was spunky. She joined the International Club, an excellent choice as the most broadening activity she possibly could have found for her limited leisure, and she left college with a very good academic record. I remember she came in once to talk over something with me and was to come back the next day, because we hadn't reached a solution. When she did, everything was under control. "Some days you can cope," she said, "and some days you can't." I think of her as the spunkiest person I ever knew.

I was more clothes-conscious at this time than I ever had been before or was to be again after teaching. I felt I had to go into class looking as least well enough turned out so that the girls, who in those days were beautifully made up and dressed and very critical, wouldn't find anything to snigger at. When you think what they look like now!

> The campus is very odd looking this year. One woman told me she had thought it would take about a year before the new styles got enough of a foothold so that we all had to wear them. But we forgot that lots of girls buy totally new fall outfits to come to college in. The new look is so different from the old look, above all in those great big triangular coats, that the girls wearing the new styles look just like Martians compared to the rest of us.

All this time the cycle of the year was turning in Frost Woods.

> In '45 Grace Maiken and Alice Strang gave a joint Hallowe'en party for the neighborhood children, which was a noble deed and a boon to society. The children went around for tricks or treats, and produced a ghastly resulting mess, but not so bad as last year. Last year I had to go to a Girl Scout party, and so I did get home, the kitchen was a shambles, absolutely ankle deep with everything from potato chips to chocolate bars. This year I was home when they got back so that I was able to organize the food a little better. It ran heavily to salted peanuts, and Dick Fredrickson had eaten most of those up this weekend.

Dick had invited himself out for the weekend, and Tommy had looked at me "with those big brown eyes and said that Dick hadn't been here overnight for so long and of course I gave in. Hannah, who dislikes Dick heartily, made herself very unpleasant about the whole affair. He may make her appreciate her brothers better, and he did his share raking up leaves. I pointed out the moral that she should be nice to Tommy's guests and he would be nice to hers. But a mother gets it from both sides, doesn't she?" As a matter of fact, I noted later that the boys "always really try to make anyone who comes to the house feel at home," and they were very nice to Hannah's dates when they began to come. Once Tom answered the telephone and said, "Just a minute," and then yelled at the top of his lungs, "Sleeping Beauty! It's for you!" but that would hardly embarrass the *caller*.

> December 5, 1945. Ham will perhaps be interested to know that Mr. Morgan came out yesterday to install a new pump for me. What was the result? By evening was water gushing freely from the faucets and were we all reveling in hot baths? No, I know he knows Mr. Morgan too well to believe that. By evening we were processing across the snowy lawn to wash up and prepare for the night in Grace Maiken's bathroom, and she very obligingly left her door unlocked all night so that we could get in early in the morning, without waking her—my system of sleep having very little to do with hers. In fact, I have already been across at 5 A.M. (it is now 6). Quite invigorating, this walk under the stars, and yet it would be a convenience to have some water in the house.
>
> I have just prevented Tommy from using the bathroom— poor child, he thinks it is the natural thing to do. *He* can now start out across the snow. The sky is beginning to lighten in the east.

Ruth Wallerstein was a frequent visitor, but the next weekend gave me less pleasure than usual. She announced she was about to visit my class, which worried me, since I knew she was so high-minded she would be more critical of a friend that of a stranger; I had no idea how much of my own professional life would be spent visiting reluctant teachers. The oil gauge had stuck, so the furnace went off in the night. A fire in the fireplace roasts your front and freezes your back. Instead of driving her in, as I had planned, I had to stay home to deal with the oil man, so I got her a ride with Alice Strang, who ran her car off the snowy road into the ditch. Ruth rushed back into the house, lifted a shovelful of ashes from the fire with the result that it smoked so badly we had to take the logs out on the lawn, lost a valuable earring in the snow, and they finally got off. She didn't visit me Monday because she was down with flu, and as a matter of fact I never was visited. As I write it occurs to me that none of you have any pets (except the famous Squiggly): it may be just as well. On another occasion (in summer) the Agards and Ruth came out for dinner and contract [bridge]. Hannah was to help me by waiting on table, but developed a little temperature, so I put her to bed, shutting her door when I gave her her supper so the dog Dr. Weston had said we might try for her, Brandy, wouldn't get in and eat her chicken soup. Hannah opened the door and let the dog in while I was giving the boys a picnic lunch on the lawn, and Brandy was sick on her bed. I cleaned up the mess, re-made the bed, took sheets and blanket down to the laundry room, and Brandy was sick again—fortunately on the rug—and in the repulsive manner dogs have ate it all up before I could get the cleaning rag.

Christmas was always memorable. In 1945 we were all sick, and I commented that "the flu this year went straight to the children's disposition." In 1946 we were all well.

> December 10, 1946. It is so warm that it is a little difficult to work up any Christmas spirit. Last Saturday (after taking Brandy to the vet's to be wormed, incidentally), I took the children in town to do their Christmas shopping (which ranks very high among the list of things I'd rather not do). It was, as I say, very very warm indeed, unseasonably so, so that your tongue was hanging out and you were panting before you had gone to two stores. As a matter of fact, we did fairly well at first. Bill sees things he wants for himself, such as a squirt gun, instead of keeping his mind on getting presents for others, but we did go through most of the list. Finally everything went black—you know the feeling—and I thought we had enough so that we'd be able to produce something for everyone and we went away in comfortable time to keep the dentist's appointment. I stopped at the filling station, and there we discovered that Bill had lost his purse with five dollars in it. We rushed back and started going through stores where he thought he'd had it, without success, till I had to take the children to the dentist. I continued to chase the purse and get right into the Saturday noon traffic jam on the Square—and you know me and a car in traffic. Finally I did manage to get to Woolworth's, and found that—a great tribute to human honesty—the purse had been turned in. I then was able to get back to take the children away from Dr. Antonius' office just before they were swept out in the trash. Then we went home,

and the amount of Christmas spirit I had then could have been put in a thimble and you wouldn't feel it when you put the thimble on.

I gained a good deal, however, at the big tea the Pooleys gave at the College Club for the Freshman English staff (Bob was at this time chairman). He had wanted Setzie [Pooley] to have a series of supper parties, as I was later do for years myself, but she said it was too much work and she wanted to get it over at once.

> You have to bring your own centerpiece, and Setzie asked me if I had any ideas. All the ornaments I have are too small and delicate for that enormous dining room. But looking through the present drawer, I picked up a new gingerbread man cookie cutter which had never been used, nice and shiny, and it came to me (just like Newton and the apple, I may say modestly) that you could trim a tree with things you use to make cookies out of. It was more fun. So many of the kitchen things now are in red and green plastics, you see, just the right clear Christmas colors—measuring spoons and cups, and cookie cutters (a star one for the top of the tree), and packages of colored sugars, and little bottles of coloring liquid, and a lot of little doll cookie cutters that Alan Pooley and the Strang children had in all sorts of animal shapes, and then at the base, too heavy to hang on, a bottle of maraschino cherries and a wooden bowl of real eggs and Christmas tree balls. It made a very effective tree, which brightened up the College Club dining room marvelously, and made a good conversation piece, useful with so many people, lots of whom didn't know each other at all. The department is just full of new young assistants this year, people whom no one has ever set eyes on before, girls with husbands in Physics or Psychology or some other hinterland, and of course they brought those superfluous husbands along and confused everybody. Setzie put me in charge in the dining room for the whole three hours, rushing around and talking to people, which was quite a job although I really enjoyed it.

That year's carol party was the nicest we've had for a long time, the biggest turnout so far. The children are invited now when they're old enough to go in town to school, which meant this year Hannah, Robin, Dick Ragsdale, and Pete

Maiken. Then we had the Pooleys for dinner on Christmas Day, fell into bed with the usual exhaustion Christmas night, and are having the usual vacation. Up to today the children have spent practically every daylight moment skating, which is a good thing. I have one hundred thousand-word themes to correct during the vacation, by way of Christmas presents from my dear students, though I must do them the justice to say that they would have been delighted to avoid handing them in to me if they had been consulted in the matter." In 1947 Tom ran a temperature the whole two weeks. The neighborhood was having a succession of drinking parties, including "Picker Uppers, New Year's Day at noon," in which I was out of my element. In 1948, "I had 56 guests between December 23 and December 30, and enjoyed every one of them, and never got fussed or hurried." But I was ready at the end of vacation to go back to work. "One of my students handed in a theme on how to reduce, but no doubt that was just a coincidence."

The notation on the back reads "Ednah Shephard Thomas with her three children, Tommy, Bill, and Hannah, Christmas 1946." It is signed by Ruth Pochmann. Source: University of Wisconsin Archives.

The summers of '49 and '50, I worked—and hard—on the Freshman English textbook Ed Lacy and I did together.[341] Until then, summers remained entirely domestic. In 1946 we had the first post-war celebration of the Fourth of July,

---

341 *Guide for Good Writing: A Composition Text for College Students.* (1951)

and I complained that having had no noise and firecrackers for five years it was a pity to go back to it. "I got the children two firecrackers apiece that make a noise, and some sparklers; and I shall not be happy until the noisy ones are off and we all remain alive with our eyesight and limbs unimpaired." But the day turned out to be a great success.

> July 6, 1946. You will be pleased to know that the Fourth went off safely for everyone. It was really the first time in my life that the Fourth took on the status of a major holiday, something that you'd really call a red-letter day. The Frost Woods boys had challenged the Frost Woods men to a baseball game, which was played off in the field behind the Blaneys from four to six. The boys had been looking forward to it for weeks and I must say the men were marvelous sports. After an inning or two they decided they would bat left-handed, and in their magnanimity they overdid it a little so that the boys piled up a lead of 16 to 4, and the men had to shift back to right-handed batting in order to even things up a bit, the game ending triumphantly for the boys at 16 to 9. The boys were marvelous at stealing bases. Their heads were so close to the ground that the men never noticed them. A boy would get to first base, and the next thing you knew he had oozed around to third and then was trotting triumphantly over the home plate. I do admire the men. If you had seen Verne Hamel pitching in the seventh inning (it was good baseball weather and an excessively hot day); he looked as if he could hardly raise a finger and I thought he'd drop dead of apoplexy any second. As far as condition went, there was little comparison between the two teams, and I thought it was a miracle that all the men got off the field alive. Louis Schmitt was another good sport. He'd caught the ball and was racing for Bill to tag him, but Bill eluded him as easily as a butterfly, and poor Louis tripped and fell flat on his face while Bill galloped home at a canter. Jack Maiken much impressed the boys by catching a fly without moving a muscle for it; it just dropped into his hand as if he had a magnet. He is really the best athlete of the lot, and in pretty good condition; he played baseball a lot with the men on his ship; but he had to have a hernia operation before he got out of the Navy and isn't supposed to take any exercise at all, which is a source of great

Transition

> chagrin to him, poor man. Well, it was a great occasion; and when I tell you that Bill was the youngest on the team, and that Bill and Tommy between them accounted for eight of the sixteen runs, you will realize how agitating it was for me as a proud mother. I haven't had such a time since Tommy, without even telling me beforehand that he was going to do it, put in his masterly performance as MC at his Sunday School program. Then we all took a picnic supper over to the Owens and after that set off our firecrackers. I loathe the noisy ones, but I think the sparklers are lovely. There were about thirty-five children there—the child population far outweighs the adult here these days—including Owen grandchildren and a few visitors, and to see them all running about the lawn with their sparklers as it was growing dusk was one of the loveliest sights I have ever seen. It would make a beautiful ballet. Finally we went home and to bed, I in a complete state of exhaustion. Yesterday I felt just like the day after Christmas. However, I had to make currant jelly and do a few other little chores—you know how it is—so I gradually got back to normal.

But the second part of 1946 was a disaster. I had gotten up my courage to take you children to the Island[342] alone, after my long absence, and the boys—without our knowing it, of course—were exposed to mumps by the Ragsdales before we left, and came down with them our second day at the Island.

The next summers we stayed home, but all of you had some camp experience, as well as Frost Woods activities.

> July 7, 1947. This is Sunday afternoon and I am writing in the study, which is somewhat hot, considering that we are having a heat wave (the thermometer reached 96 yesterday) and that the storm windows haven't been taken off since the beginning of the war, but has the tremendous advantage of being a long way away from Tommy, Bill, two Ragsdales, Pete Maiken, a number of Owen grandchildren, Bill Strang, and others, who are all playing downstairs. Their play consists of exercising their lungs and yelling, "bang, bang, bang," with toy guns in their hands, and it palls on me after an infinitesimal space of time; but they can keep it up for hours.

---

342 A reference to Isle of Springs, an island community located in BoothBay Harbor, Maine, where the family spent summer vacations.

The Owens, incidentally, had a big family reunion this month:

> . . . including all generations and relatives spreading out to the utmost degree. They hadn't had any since the war, so the older generation were looking forward to it in a big way, Sally said. One cousin, who is a farmer, is butchering a cow or steer or beeve or whatever it is you butcher, and is bringing enough meat for roast beef for Sunday dinner and meat loaf for another meal, and ten pounds of butter. All are bringing their own sugar and cot beds. I admit it takes a lot of organization to feed ninety-two people.

Though now plenty of canned vegetables were in the stores, we still kept on gardening. "I'm not going to can any more string beans, because I cannot rid myself of a terrible phobia that home-canned string beans will kill you with botulism." The last straw was learning that the fatal symptoms sometimes don't develop for several days, so that the suspense is not over when you wake up in the pink next morning. Hannah, however, has always loyally insisted that my string beans were the best she ever tasted, due *to* the botulistic germs "I've never used frozen foods enough to know quite how to handle those, and I really should get used to them." Think of their part in our lives now. We celebrated Tommy's birthday this year with a treasure hunt, because he wanted something special, not the old baseball and wienies ("This keeping up with the Joneses is the curse of modern life") and also, for the family—it would have cost too much for the whole gang—our first flight. At the airport a mile away they were giving fifteen-minute tours of Madison, in a plane with pilot and two passengers. Bill and Tommy went up together first—they looked very small inside as the plane rose—and then Hannah and I. None of you had ever flown before (except Bill as a baby). My first flight was at the Island, in a hydroplane, just after World War I, and like that, the flight over Madison was excellent for the first because the view is varied and includes water. The pilot kindly flew low enough over our house so we could pick it out from the air.

Bill and Tommy went to camp at Lannon Fields Farm this summer, which was very successful. The Beattys came up to spend a month in Madison with Ham's aunt, and were out here a good deal, and Aunt Hannah and Uncle Jim made a visit. In 1948 Bill went back to Lannon, Tom (and Pete Maiken) to Boy Scout camp at Green Lake [Wisconsin], and Hannah did corn detasseling for some weeks and then took a trip up to see a friend in Chippewa Falls. In 1949 Hannah and Bill both went to Lannon, she as a junior counselor, and Tom to Green Lake again.

Transition

August 29, 1948. I have to drive up to Green Lake today with Grace and get the boys from Scout camp. They're been there a week—much too short a time. We just got rid of them and now we've got to go to the trouble of getting them. But I'll be glad when Tom gets back because it's so quiet without him. I think of Bill as a noisy child, but it isn't that; it's the combination. Bill alone is much quieter than just half of Tom and Bill, if you know what I mean. The noise and the squabbling when they are here drive me crazy, but the quiet without one of them is worse. How awful for a mother to get into such a state. Tom has been enjoying himself, I judge. Sample post card: Dear mother, I am fine and hope you are to. I am having a good time. We are just waking up. We are calling the next caban names. I swimming 4 times a day. Love, Tommy. Is the trouble in my children or in modern methods of education or what? In any case, a ghastly hot day for the trip.

I drove over to Lannon Fields Farm a week ago to get Bill, and took Mrs. Dodge, who was interesting because of her grandson in Chicago. She and I had a lovely time discussing bringing up children. What with one thing and another, there's quite a bit to it, isn't there? I went out to lunch the other day, and one of the women, a spinster, remarked she had observed over a period of years what a striking number of women there were in Madison who died in the nineties or so *unmarried*—childlessness being in her view the prerequisite for long life. She may very well be right, but personally I'd rather have a shorter life and have the children. It was a frightfully hot day. Incidentally I am going to stop sending my sons to camp if I can't find some place that runs buses. No sooner does the thermometer reach 97 than I find myself on the road driving to or from camp for one of the boys.

During this period Hannah and I got in a trip to see Eastern campuses. She had decided she would apply for a small coeducational college, and we went over to see the Swarthmore campus while we were staying with Aunt Hannah and Uncle Jim, and saw Oberlin when we stopped overnight with the Beattys in Cleveland on the way home.

The summer of '49 I worked hard, and the summer of '50 even harder, on the Freshman English textbook Ed Lacy and I did together. I've saved copies for you all. I'm not particularly proud of the book—I doubt very strongly if I knew enough to write one. Ed did the chapter on the dictionary, which in its depth of scholarship contrasts rather remarkably with the rest, and managed all the business part, applications for copyrights and so on, and I did the rest, using examples from a theme collection which was rapidly building up. Ed arranged for a publisher's advance to me so that I could get a new car in the summer of '49. "It's green and very nice looking and runs like a bird on the waves." This was a great relief, since for at least five years I'd been scared to death every time I took the car out for fear some essential organ would give up the ghost. It was a '39 model, and Wright had bought it used—a good policy if you have some mechanical knowledge, but not a good one for me. When I got my first new car, it was a milestone, and I have replaced each by another right off the assembly line. Since Ed and I were both far too busy through the year to get any work on the book done then, we had to concentrate in these two summers. As always, experience—any experience—is valuable.

> August 3, 1948. I had what you call a gruelling experience a week ago Friday night. The boys and the Ragsdale boys and Bill Strang and Don Schmitt had planned a camping overnight party across the lake at Turville's Point. I wasn't too crazy about it, but they'd all been on overnight trips, so I didn't want to be fussy and sissy and said OK. That night turned out to be the all-time record-breaking storm for the amount of water fallen in a given time, and the boys rowed home across the lake in the worst of it. The men were out scouring the land for them in cars, and got the police launch out on the water, and you can imagine my feelings. They were on the ten o'clock news, and in the paper next morning but not by name. They lost the Strang motor overboard, but luckily marked it and it went into a shallow place, and they retrieved it next morning. The thing that put the cake on was that Mr. Lacy, my boss, you know, had come out here that night to dinner and to work. As the storm raged on and the telephone began to ring with Eleanor Schmitt and Alice Strang and so on, I began to get a bit distracted, but he never noticed a thing. He is a young man, a bachelor, and of course there is no reason why he should enter into a mother's feelings. When I went back to work I could see very clearly that I had no right to do it if I asked for special consideration on account of the children; I'd have to work as a man does, and put the work first, and I always have done that; but boy, I

was under a test. I yield to no man in my admiration for Mr. Lacy and he certainly is single-minded; he'd be marvelous to go through the Battle of Britain with. As long as the house stood he wouldn't be conscious of the bombs; he was just like those clubmen in the *Punch* cartoons.[343] Each time I'd come back from the telephone he'd say, "Now about this passage on page 49 I'd suggest. . ." and so on and then the telephone would ring again and I'd say "Excuse me" and leap to it, and it would be Eleanor in hysterics and then I'd go back and he would have gotten to page 58 and have a suggestion on that, and so on. Even when the boys came in—separately—he still was barely conscious of any interruption. Well, they are born to be hanged, I can see that. They camped out again in the same place this last Friday night, but this time the weather was all right and the only trouble was that they didn't catch any fish and came home starving at 7 A.M. for breakfast.

I can give you a good account of the book's photo finish. You boys, luckily, had gone on an Adirondack fishing trip with Wright.

> September 3, 1950. The book is done, and on its way to the printer. You know the old comparison that writing a book is like having a baby, and there really is a great deal to it. I felt just exactly the way you do when you've had a baby—as if something which had been possessing you and absorbing you and fighting to get out was out, leaving you your own self and alone, so to speak. Also the final process was remarkably like childbirth in that it was long and sustained and full of unpleasant little details and you felt you just couldn't keep going and stand it any longer. The printer's deadline was September 1, but I never thought we could do it, and I don't think any man but Mr. Lacy would have done it. I never saw anyone like him for force of character, and he pulled the whole thing together at the end sheerly by an act of will. It was finished at exactly 11:55 P M on August 31, and what a three days we put in beforehand. It came out at 923 pages (typed), and three copies of each, one for the printer, one for him, and one for me, which is an awful lot of pages to keep straight. We had the stuff spread out all over the living and dining room,

---

343 *Punch*, or the *London Charivari*, was a British weekly satirical magazine established in 1841; its circulation peaked in the 1940s.

and two typewriters so we could both type pages that needed doing over, and we never picked anything up for the whole three days, which saved a lot of time. It was a break the boys weren't here. If they had been I would have had to stop and get meals but as it was we cleared off a corner of the dining room table and made a sandwich once in a while and he drank coffee until, as Hannah somewhat inelegantly observed, "I should think you'd be floating in it." She was very good and picked up a bit with us or by herself as things worked out; and she was in at the death because at the end when he was writing the cover letter to the printer and I was numbering the pages, I found I couldn't keep them straight and had to get her out of bed, where she was starting after getting home from a movie, to help me. It was a very interesting experience at the end seeing everything come together, but it takes quite a bit out of you.

Now for some pieces to make a rather un-chronological kaleidoscope. You boys led a very active life and had a fine Frost Woods gang to do it with. In the fall of '45 football resumed at the university after three years without it, and Marie Ragsdale used to take the neighborhood boys in town Saturday afternoons to a special section with sixty-cent seats for children. You started kicking the football around in my front yard—the most convenient place, since the Thomas house was located in the center of the neighborhood—as soon as you got out of school afternoons.

> March 14, 1948. The boys, especially Bill, have too darned much energy. We arranged for Bill to go to the City Y[MCA] every Saturday morning, and the idea was that he would work off his energy there. But unfortunately he just seems to generate more and wants to tumble (in the technical sense) on the beds all the time or play basketball all over the house with a ball he concocted out of knitting yarn—believe it or not.

Tom became a Second-Class Scout, and of course we attended the ceremony. But with the exception of Robin Pooley, who became an Eagle Scout, the neighborhood boys never really took seriously to Scouting, since they had so much scope for their own activities and hardly needed to seek out a sheltering organization.

> October 5, 1947. The Frost Woods gang is really grown up enough to startle you. Whenever I see them playing on the lawn, I notice that the group as a whole is taller by about a

> head than the group of boys I automatically looked for; and some of them—Robin and Pete Maiken particularly—have men's voices, not boys' any longer."
>
> May 9, 1949. They had a minstrel show at the Nichols School, in which both Bill Thomas and Bill Strang took part. Bill had to have a white shirt, white gloves, a red ribbon, dark pants, dark shoes, cold cream to remove the grease paint, and Kleenex, and a flashlight. He expressed himself as rather worried at dinner because, as he said, he thought "a Negro with red hair was unusual." I think he's quite right. It was hell getting the stuff off afterwards, though Hannah was a great help there. I gave him my own white gloves, which I had just gotten back in from Iowa (a trip to visit the English Department there), and when Hannah saw that, she said, "Mother love!" Bill Strang and Bill Thomas are very chummy, which is a great comfort to me. The Strangs are very nice to him, and are going to take him on a camping trip to fish this weekend. Bill Strang was very good in the show; he had one piece of dialog with the MC, David Ragsdale, also very good, and performed with lots of verve and spirit—almost surprising, because in general he seems quiet. My Bill was just in the chorus.

Perhaps the most exciting incident of the period is the historic time Bill Strang bit Bill Thomas.

> December 3, 1946. We had gone along without any illness or accident since September (although I must say we had our full share this summer before that) and I had a sneaking feeling that it was too good to last. How right I was. Bill went up to play with Bill Strang Sunday, and while they were playing war they collided (they must have hit like two little bulls), and Bill Strang's tooth (sheer accident, no malice at all) went way deep into Bill's eye socket, just under the curve of the eyebrow and just above the eyeball. Would you believe the things they'll do. It bled terribly, and of course a tooth wound is a bad kind, so I called Dr. Weston and then took Bill in to the good old accident ward of Wisconsin General. The car is now practically conditioned to finding its own way there, like the old-time horse returning to its own stable.) The intern on duty appeared to be a gloomy type. I explained the situation.

"Oh, dear, dear," said he, "oh, dear, dear, I don't like this at all." (Bill lying right there, of course, in full possession of his faculties of hearing.) "Oh, I don't like this at all. A tooth incision is very very serious. Infection practically always sets in and can be very very dangerous indeed." (You'd think poor Bill Strang was a cobra.) "Now I don't want to close this wound. I wouldn't dare do it. We'd be running a very serious risk of infection. I want to induce open drainage. Of course that will leave a scar." Wouldn't you think a doctor would have more sense? Who cares about a scar—especially in such an inconspicuous place? Heaven knows Bill has plenty already. You'd think the doctor would keep his big mouth shut. Well, he cleaned out the wound—and it was fantastic how deep it went—and shook in sulfa powder and gave him a tetanus booster shot (I certainly am thankful the children had the tetanus), and then we went home. I have to take Bill in to see Dr. Weston this afternoon, but as you know he is not one to look on the gloomy side, so I expect we shall come away from there leaping and skipping like spring lambs.

April 16, 1950. The great thing about a family is that it changes so rapidly. We started the day today with Bill pestering Tom who was trying to read the paper and only wanted to be let alone, which is the one thing Bill can't do because he is so gregarious, until—well, things mounted rapidly to a climax until Tom rushed upstairs and shut the bathroom door and Bill came after him with the hammer from the kitchen, ready either to pound Tom or the bathroom door to pieces with it, not that he cared which, and all of this when I had very carefully made it clear that I absolutely had to have enough quiet to work, just as any professional man had to; and now they are both outdoors, raking up the leaves they didn't rake up last fall and burning them, just as good as gold.

Some of the kaleidoscope pieces belong to the university.

May 7, 1947. I have had a very trying year on the Negro problem. I guess I wrote you that I had two Negroes in my class, for the first time. No one could behave better than they do, perfectly free and easy and unembarrassed and discussing everything that comes up with no sensitiveness at all; and fortunately one of them is the best student I have in the class.

> But I have been nervous all year for fear I'd hurt their feelings inadvertently, and since we studied first John Brown's Body[344] and then Othello and tomorrow, as the last straw to break the camel's back, Green Pastures,[345] we have never been able to forget the Negro problem for a minute, and I should think they'd be sick to death of it. I am. In connection with John Brown's Body for the long theme, practically every student chose "The History of the Negro Race in America," so I have been reading theme after theme on the same subject, and I shall be thankful when I'm through. However, "this is the last, this is the last," as they say in John Brown's Body when the Confederate soldiers go home on furlough and find the supplies of the South running out.

This was far to be the last of the Negro problem at the university, though as you know it has a new name now, Black. I remember those two men very well. They were both Milwaukee-born and bred, as opposed to Southern, which perhaps accounted for some of their poise, though innate courtesy, I think accounted for more. The excellent student, incidentally on the football team, went to New York and became a reporter on the sports staff of the *New York Times*. The other, less able but very persevering, finally got through Law School here, and established himself at Milwaukee, which at the time had only four Black lawyers and an enormously expanding Black population. Bill and I ran into him once in the cafeteria line while he was still in Law School, and had a pleasant chat.

> February 1, 1948. Quite a stretch of subzero weather. A Hawaiian in my class has never seen winter before, and is astounded at the time it takes him to bundle up to run down to the corner drugstore for cigarettes. On the 15-below days the Wisconsinites come glowing to class (and do you know that hardly more than one in ten men wears anything on his head at all, earmuffs or anything? Why their ears don't snap right off I can't think), and the poor creature wishes he were back in Hawaii. It's all in getting used to it. The children are very hardy, and Bill would *not* wear anything but a windbreaker to school on the coldest days, but he always seems to thrive.

---

344 *John Brown's Body* (1928), a Pulitzer Prize-winning epic poem about abolitionist John Brown by American writer Stephen Vincent Benet (1898–1943).

345 *The Green Pastures* (1930), a Pulitzer Prize-winning play by American playwright Marc Connelly (1890–1980).

> March 14, 1948. I met a student I had first semester and we exchanged a few cheerful words. He said, "Are you getting a cold, Mrs. Thomas?" I said I had lost my voice a few days before but it was wearing off. "I hope your students were not too delighted," said he. "I hope not indeed," said I. "Why should they be?" "Well," said he, "you know last semester some of the students used to tell me there were things they didn't like about your teaching. But as for me, I have decided not to be on the lookout to criticize but try to look on the bright side." "I think you're so wise," said I.

Student evaluation of faculty was an issue in the late sixties. For someone as thin-skinned as I, it was lucky it didn't arise until I was on the point of retiring. A number of times I asked for anonymous comments from my classes on the course and my teaching, but after a while I gave it up because they always seemed to cancel each other out. In general, I felt it was a blessing I *didn't* know what they thought about me; I could concentrate on doing what I believed sincerely was the best for them.

> December 13, 1949. For two or three days I entirely lost my voice and couldn't make a sound above a whisper, which is awkward in my profession. During this time, unfortunately, in addition to my classes, I had a very heavy conference schedule, so I just had to whisper to them. The odd thing was that everyone whispered back. It seems to take a lot more strength of mind than most people have to speak in an ordinary voice when someone is whispering to you. People would go by in the hall and see us talking away like mad and not be able to hear a sound, and of course thought we were planning to blow up the university. One of my students, whose experience of life seems markedly wider and more extensive than my own, told me that was the way to quiet a drunk—whisper to him, because then he'd whisper back. I don't know just when I shall need to do that, my life being pretty sheltered, but you never know when odd bits of information come in handy, so I have stored this away in my mind and am passing it on to you.

I began to make a few local trips and do a bit of public speaking, to a rather restricted public. In October, 1949, I spoke to the Richland Center Woman's Club, who had asked Helen White, our Department Chairman, to suggest someone. "I left the letter on Mr. Lacy's desk thinking he would take it as a joke, but to my surprise he said I was taking it too lightly and that it was my duty to go and build up good will for the university." The meetings started with a potluck supper, to which I was invited to bring a friend if I wished, so I took Alice Strang. (The food, mostly out of cans, was a considerable disillusionment of one's ideas of magnificent home country cooking). I gave a review of *The Mudlark*;[346] "at the end the program chairman leaped to her feet. 'Don't you wish you could get as much out of a book as that?' she said enthusiastically. 'It was as good as a sermon!'" But most of my talking was in connection with the Freshman English course. As the only universally required course at the university, and as the course in which the high school students of the state invariably turned in their poorest performances, it was the subject of considerable interest among high school faculties. In September 1949 when Ed was out of town he sent me up to Green Bay to give a talk to the junior and senior high school teachers there on desirable preparation for it. Very often we went together, since he liked to have me come along when he was asked to give such a talk. One time I remember we went to Baraboo at the invitation of a group of six high school principals in the region who met together monthly at their successive schools to discuss some matter of common interest.

In May 1949 I went by myself to The University of Iowa to visit the Freshman English course there, particularly a well-known writing laboratory for students who needed extra help, conducted by Miss Carrie Stanley.[347] I had never stayed by myself in a hotel in a strange town before, "but as you know I speak the language and everything worked out all right, and I made it there and back"— though I was so timid about going into a strange restaurant alone that I ate only one dinner in the three days I was gone (Sunday through Tuesday). This trip had the side effect of giving me as much ease as I ever attained in driving, proving a statement Ruth Wallerstein used to make about the learning process: that you learn to swim in the winter and skate in the summer, in other words, that a cessation of a practiced activity is necessary for mastery of it. It had required an effort of will up to this time whenever I drove the car; when I got back after this trip I got in and drove off with ease and comfort. (As of this writing, though, it's requiring more effort all the time for me to take the car out, and a pleasure to

---

346 *The Mudlark* (1949), a novel by American Theodore Bonnet (1908–1983), was also a film adaptation of the same name that was popular in Britain.

347 Carrie Ellen Stanley (1886–1962) earned BA and M.A. degrees from the University of Iowa and taught high school English before joining the English faculty at the State University of Iowa in 1920. In 1934, Stanley established a Writing Lab, which grew out of her use of the conference model employed in her literature classes to help students improve their writing. The Writing Lab was officially recognized in 1945, following the establishment of the Communications Skills Program. The Writing Lab, one of the first in the US, was influential on the development of writing centers nationwide.

walk to the Sentry [grocery store] to save gas. I'll try to keep on forcing myself, though, since driving is indispensable for independence.) This trip was only one detail in Ed's very thorough and exhaustive investigation of procedures and practices in the Freshman English courses all over the county. He was building up the largest course in a big university, already large and to become much larger, and one shamefully neglected before him. In the words of Ecclesiastes, there is a time for everything, a time to break down and a time to build up. I've gone through the whole cycle with Freshman English—and it is more fun to build up the British Empire than to preside over its dissolution. And after my powers, such as they were, had lain dormant for so long, I had a lot of fun.

There were considerable physical changes in the neighborhood during this time. There was a lot of building all through the open woods in which you had been able to roam free, since the protection afforded by the war was over. The Strangs built their house on the lake next to the Pooleys and sold the small one up in the woods to the new principal of Nichols School, Mr. Schwartz. The Maikens put on a considerable addition to theirs. The fall of 1948 was an exceptionally trying time.

> October 30, 1948. You know they were going to put the metropolitan sewer through our yard—is this Russia or is it a democracy?—and now they have done it. It was just like the scene in *The Grapes of Wrath* where the mechanized man runs the tractor right against the walls of the house and it falls down—bulldozers and cats and all sorts of engines in the yard and holes down to China and piles of dirt as high as the trees. What got me down was the pumping engine running all day and all night. Since they were so near lake level they had to keep it pumped out twenty-four hours a day. By the time they got to the Pooleys they didn't have any trouble with the water so they didn't have to run it at night—a break for Setzie. I couldn't sleep, and I was having the usual fall cold, which this year has been especially bad, a sort of grippe, and the office was being done over; so all in all I never had a worse time. For three weeks we were out of the office, which meant we didn't know where anything was and were sort of hanging like bats on the wall: there was no peace there, or obviously at home, or on the way to and fro, since Park Street is torn up and we have to take various detours. But now the office is finished, the men are through here, except for filling in the manhole, and Park Street is open, except a couple of blocks. Bill said the other

> day—you know how devastating children are—"Mother, you aren't fat anymore," so there's that to be thankful for anyway.

By December the sewer had moved beyond our houses, "and they are now sweating it out in the marsh at the entrance to Frost Woods. In the daytime the road there is such a snarl of workmen's cars that it is hard to get through, but at night I love to drive past because they have a long line of those little flare pots going around the curve, and it is like driving past a long line of camp fires glowing in the night. It makes an amazing difference for all of us along the lake—the trees are still standing but all the undergrowth has gone, so it's just one open space as far as you can see in either direction." It really was an improvement, after the seeding was done and the grass came up. One of the prettiest sights I ever saw was a few years later on a beautiful June afternoon with the sun getting low in the sky when I stood in my yard and looked across the unbroken expanse of green to the pastel colors of the girls' dresses at the Coketail party the Strangs gave for Bill's class the year he graduated from high school. You know Ray Agard has always compared us with the famous Backs at Cambridge.[348] This fall of '48 Ray Owen, the patriarch of Frost Woods, celebrated his seventieth birthday. "The neighborhood turned out en masse to honor him at a potluck supper. There was a great gathering, and they stayed for square dancing. Our newest neighbor, Mr. Schwartz, told me we had a wonderful design for living out here."

While you boys were growing up without particular psychological problems—of which I was aware, I should say—Hannah was taking adolescence very hard.

> May 4, 1947. I remember once hearing a lecturer say it was natural to have problems in adolescence; if a boy or girl doesn't, that is what should worry the parents. Fortunately I can dismiss all worry about Hannah. She doesn't speak to any of us without snapping our heads off, so probably she will come out all right—if *we* can live through it. The other day when I was bringing the children out from school, she got to the car first. I had noticed a couple of students snickering in class, and though it may not have been connected with me at all, you know that funny feeling you get, so I said to her, "Do you see anything wrong with me?" She looked at me and said "Yes." "What?" said I. "Everything," said she. And that is typical of our intercourse.

---

348 A picturesque area in England where several colleges back onto the River Cam.

But I never spoke of her with anyone outside her family, particularly her teachers, without their telling me from the bottom of their hearts "how marvelous and able and sweet and popular she is." Even with me she had her moments.

> March 31, 1946. The Elas have a new car. I don't know what black market they bought it at. I have a phobia because I expect a tire to pop every time I take my car in town, and now I have to go in every day. I have my name in for new tires, but nothing is happening. On the other hand, I have a pair of nylons and *Hannah* got them for me. My stockings had all reached the point where the feet were full of holes, and it seemed a long way to summer. Then Hannah came home and said she had been shopping at Baron's and the girl asked if she wanted hosiery. Hannah said no, she didn't wear them, and then she thought, "I have a mother." So she paid for them and they sent me out a pair of mesh nylons. It's the first time my children have really protected me, so to speak, and it is a wonderful feeling. However trying her adolescent development is, when I look at my legs I feel as if I could forgive her anything. If only Bill or Tommy would find me a tire or two.
>
> March 2, 1947. Hannah is going to her first formal this week. Dr. Nesbit's son, Mark, asked her. We went in and bought her dress Wednesday—very cute, green tulle, with a bustle. Ann Hastings' mother (who must be a saint in human form), has asked the eight couples going from the freshman class (this is the Wisconsin High Sophomore Shuffle) to dinner first, so it is quite an affair. You ought to see Hannah shop—much more business-like and determined than I am now. I noticed that whenever she put a dress over her head, she firmly pressed her lips together so as not to get lipstick on the dress—something that had never occurred to me at my age. Well, after all, I don't wear lipstick.
>
> June 3, 1947. Bill got his Bible at Children's Day service at church. The boys did look quite well that day. As a mother yourself, you will realize that it isn't boasting to say that, it's just that they look so much like tramps all the time you are so astounded you can hardly believe they are the same children. Anyhow they did look well, and I sat in the balcony in a pleasant sentimental reverie, only slightly broken in upon by the nasty cracks Hannah was making by my side—one

of those reveries so rare to a mother about what wonderful children she has after all.

There were two special times every week, exclusive of meals of course, during this period when the family was together: Saturday mornings, when we did the cleaning, and Sunday evenings, when we listened to "family programs" on the radio and I managed to get caught up on the family mending (of which there was much more with the fabrics we had then than there is now). We listened to *The Great Gildersleeve*,[349] but my favorite at least was *Henry Aldrich*.[350] One episode of Hannah's, with hardly a word of editing, could have gone on the air as a perfect program. Her Saturday night date had gotten stuck in our driveway when he brought her home, not surprisingly, and had taken our shovel to get out; but he had taken it home with him instead of bringing it back, and when I found that out Sunday morning, I said we needed it. Hannah was reluctant to call him, since in those days a girl never called a boy, but I said if she didn't I would, which would be even worse, so finally she did. He brought it back, got stuck again, and had to borrow it *again*—thereby providing the final punch line which always closed a *Henry Aldrich* episode after you thought the whole thing was finished up.

> March 14, 1948. Hannah and I bought her a formal last week, and she is heartbreaking in it, so young and pretty. When a girl lies around the house with her hair pinned up and in socks and pants all the time looking like death, then when she gets dressed up it takes your breath away. She has that freshness and it seems to hard to think that she can't keep it—that life will rub the bloom off. I thought that same thing when I first read *Kristin Lavransdatter*—the little girl going up the mountain so dewy and fresh, and so much happens to her, and it has to be that way.[351] I know you don't want a case of arrested development, and I know that you are ennobled by suffering, and I know that the end of life is development of character, and I know that an adolescent girl is very trying to live with and she will probably be much nicer when she is older. But there's that feeling just the same—she has the glow of youth and she's got to lose it.

---

349 *The Great Gildersleeve* (1941–1958), a radio situation comedy that was popular in the 1940s.
350 *The Aldrich Family* was a popular radio show in the 1930s-1950s;
351 *Kristin Lavransdatter* is a trilogy of historical novels about life in Scandanavia in the Middle Ages published in the early 1920s by Norwegian novelist and Nobel laureate Sigrid Undset (1882–1949).

April 19, 1948. Hannah is dating now, with boys who have just turned sixteen and are being allowed to handle the family car for the first time, which means some worry on my part, though I think really the chances of their driving carefully are better now that they will be in a year or two. Now that they know they're on trial they're not likely to take chances. A tragedy—I wonder if Ham and you knew the Wheelers, who live near D. A. Their son Gene, just sixteen, is in Hannah's class, and took her to the Sophomore Shuffle. He had just got his driver's license, and called for her with a car, the first time, and she was so proud and so was he. That was Saturday night; the next week she told me Gene had to go to the hospital for a few days for a leg operation, and we thought it would be something to do with the cartilage, like one another boy had had earlier (Gene was on the football team). The next Saturday afternoon, less than a week from the dance, another boy called Hannah and said Gene's leg had been amputated that morning. It was cancer and they took off the leg above the knee. Isn't that ghastly? He's still out of school and I don't know whether he'll get back or not this spring. It's so horrible for a boy that age. It was interesting to see the effect on all the teen-agers. They'd heard about things in the war and seen things happen to their parents—what you might call the senseless brutality of life—but nothing had hit one of their own age group before, and all that weekend different friends were calling Hannah and she was calling others, all trying to realize the shock and get used to it.

Observing this experience taught me a good deal about teen-agers. Gene's classmates were completely understanding, far more so than his teachers. When he came back to class, a teacher might suggest he sit when the others for some reason were standing; his friends never made that mistake. They kept him in the group as one of themselves with no allowances, demanding physical inconvenience or pain rather than the worse injury of treating him as if he were different. He lived a year. His parents bought him a sailboat, which he could manage, and he went out in it a good deal that summer. His funeral was the day of Polly Fulcher's, in March of 1949, the worst possible weather of a climate which can be horrible, a day of cold sleety rain. Never have I seen a day more fitted for the "Fear no more" song from *Cymbeline*.[352] Hannah and I went to our separate

---

352 The full title of the song from Shakespeare's play is "Fear no more the heat o' the sun."

services with our separate thoughts. I learned from this that the adolescent can be far more sensitive, far more understanding, than an adult. But the adolescent is not consistent. You observe the sensitivity and marvel at it; but if you count on it for another time, it won't be there, and you will feel as if you had put your foot on a non-existent stair. When I was conferring with teaching assistants who didn't seem to be getting on very well with their adolescent students, I used to tell them about this. Though the teaching assistant was far closer in age to his students than was I, that short gap was really much more of a barrier than the much greater one between me and my students. For I had the advantage of being in close daily contact with the age group—the only person in the course who was—and because there are six years between Hannah and Bill I kept that advantage for a considerable time. It may well have been my greatest contribution to my university work. Hannah's class dedicated their senior yearbook to Gene Wheeler.

It was a relief to me that Hannah "played the field and dated a different boy about every week."

> January 1, 1949. We all giggled together a lot this year. The children are past the dewy-eyed stage and there is a sort of loss in that; the bloom is off. But it is fun when they are a little older too. The boys have been fighting a lot, but I'm sure they really are fond of each other, in a quaint way. Hannah bought a new formal to go to a dance Thursday, and it was flame-color; and when I say flame I mean that it really did flame. The boy turned up with a lavender orchid. But youth takes these things in stride. She wore the orchid in her hair, and was so proud of it, it being her first, that she didn't mind at all any unusual color combination. She is still saving it in the ice chest to wear to school Monday.

She gave some parties herself, which did her and her friends the greatest credit.

> May 26, 1948. Hannah has blossomed like a rose. She had a party: fifteen couples of teen-agers. She explained firmly I shouldn't be seen at all—she would die of embarrassment if I were. I could provide the Coke and so on and then go to my room and lock the door. Of course they were noisy but nothing was broken or permanently harmed, and it was a great success. The next day people kept calling her up all day to tell her what a nice time they had, which of course was gratifying.

I suppose your children always present you with unexpected problems. I was all set for Hannah to do just what I did—get all A's, sit home shyly with a book all day, be so bright the boys wouldn't take her out, and develop an inferiority complex. Quite the contrary. She dates all the time. Well, *that* presents problems too.

October 11, 1949. Hannah had a party here the other night. She intended to have about thirty, but to hear her tell it the next day, not to mention the sounds I of course could not help hearing, about twice that number came. But not one thing was broken, not even a single glass, and though most of them smoke—she doesn't, but almost everybody else does—not a single cigarette was put down on anything but an ash tray—not a burn mark anywhere, which a similar group of adults might not have done. I was telling the Reading Group about it, and they were telling me about horrible parties where the teen-agers had started drinking, and finally things got so out of hand the parents had to call the police. I'm glad I didn't hear the stories before Hannah had this party. In one case, Virginia said she blamed the parents because they didn't lock up their liquor before the party started, and the kids found it: of course that problem wouldn't arise in my house. Anyway, I'm glad Hannah's crowd sticks to Cokes.

July 11, 1948. You and Ham are, I think, of just about everybody I know, that couple I feel no strain of any sort with, no having to put up a front. It seems to me—in my psychopathic moments no doubt—that with almost everybody, however, close I have to put on a front, even with the children, because with that generation barrier and your responsibility for them you can't be yourself as you are but what you wish you could be for their sake. (I refer you here to Margaret Mead's theory of the development of conscience in the child, a theory accepted by David Riesman also.[353] The parent who tries to appear better than he is is *not* a hypocrite, as he is often by youth accused of being; he is merely trying to build in his child a concept that good exists, and that all the rest of his life

---

353 Margaret Mead (1901–1978) was a prominent American cultural anthropologist who suggested that culture influences adolescent behavior as much as biology. David Riesman (1909–2002) was an American sociologist and popular commentator on American society.

he must strive to draw nearer to it; and the parent, according to Margaret Mead, is right in doing so—and reasonably successful.) With your friends you have to be merry and bright and with your students you have to be dignified, and there's almost no one but you two with whom I don't feel some sense of effort at having to try to pretend to be better than I am, which I suppose is the worst strain in the world. Hannah told me the other day she thought I should get very drunk and release my inhibitions. I tried to explain to her about sublimations instead. She says things that would distress me if I thought she meant them, but of course at that age a cynical pose is the natural thing. I do think this high school generation is old for its years. She and all her friends seem to accept it as perfectly natural that there is every possibility of a war within a few years. Personally I don't accept the likelihood—there is always a possibility of anything, of course. Helene Cassidy told me when I said goodbye to her before she went to France that she knew people thought she was foolish to go abroad when things were so unsettled, but that she had lived through the Post-World-War-I period in France and it was exactly like this—rumors and scares continually again. I hadn't thought if it before but now I believe I agree with her. The effect on the teen-agers, however, is an eat-drink-be-merry-for-tomorrow-we-die reaction which I don't think is a very good one. But I don't know what I can do about it, and as far as I am concerned personally I have perfect confidence in Hannah's ultimate fundamental good judgment and soundness.

June 20, 1949. Yes, I had a very pleasant birthday, thank you. Hannah of her own accord got the dinner including a cake, and after dinner we all went to Fred Astaire and Ginger Rogers in "The Barclays of Broadway," which was a great success. I am beginning to feel the children are really a comfort. Hannah is old enough to be understanding; Tom somewhat resents the fact that she keeps reminding *him* to help me with the dishes, but there are a good many things she does herself.

March 16, 1950. We had a really nice time Sunday. You know—I presume you know—how hard it is to get something to do as a family that everyone enjoys. In our case, I'd like us all to go to the movies occasionally together, though as Jack Maiken once said bitterly, "There is no such thing as a family movie," and having heard his family argue in the car on the way in about which one they wanted to go to, I could see his point. In our case Bill dislikes movies very much, because he's afraid he'll see something sad, having been taken once—not by me—to a Lassie picture. But someone told me that "Louisiana Story" was wonderful; have you seen it? It's the Flaherty documentary of the boy in the Louisiana bayou and it was back—it's an old film—at the Play Circle. So I talked Bill into going. The four of us went first to the cafeteria for dinner at 11:30, which was a treat for me and for them too, really, and then Hannah left us, but the boys and I went to the movie. Hannah had taken her College Boards the day before, and then in the evening to celebrate had gone to the movie with two or three other people taking them. They went to the Eastwood for a double feature and hit a sneak pre-view, so they sat through *three* movies, and Hannah felt she didn't want to see another one right away. That I could imagine, though I think the real reason was that she is afraid to be seen in public with her family for fear she may run across someone who knows her. The movie was wonderful; I enjoyed it more than anything I have seen for a long time, and the boys did too. So it was a great success, and I shall try it again. I always feel I don't take advantage of all the cultural opportunities in a university town to give my children, but between being rather busy and meeting less than no cooperation from them— they'd be glad to go to the university wrestling matches, but a French play? No—it has been too uphill a struggle. But I will make another effort. Basically, I really feel good about my children, because they seem to be pretty well adjusted and pretty popular in school and to have plenty of friends there, which I think is probably the main thing at their time of life.

Hannah graduated June 11. Wisconsin High held its commencements in the Union Theater, and it was the custom to wear pure white caps and gowns. "The boys all looked as if they felt like fools, dressed up in sheets for Hallowe'en, but the girls have more poise and looked lovely, most of them having started their suntans." As you know, she had been accepted by Swarthmore, her first choice, and in September she left for college. In family life there is no more poignant moment, it seems to me, than the one when the first child leaves home. It must come; it is, like death, a necessary end; but how it hurts. Hannah left by train. There is no other kind of transportation I have encountered in my life which has the solemnity and finality given by the great wheels of a train engine. They began to turn slowly, slowly, faster, faster, and I felt as if they were grinding over the heart in my body. We four would never live together as a family again.

You'll think I had great advantages in raising a family in days far simpler than today, and in a place which even then was a good deal of an anachronism in preserving values and virtues of days even simpler and earlier. I agree with you. I didn't even have a television problem. The first set in the neighborhood was the Owens, in August, 1949. "The Owens have a television set, which is a boon to humanity. That is, the evenings in all the other houses are peaceful and quiet, while the kids are seeing television at the Owens'. The children adore it, and since I doubt very strongly that I shall ever buy one myself, it is nice they can acquire their sophistication for free next door." The greater problems weren't even thought of; the terms "revolt" and "generation gap" hadn't come into the language. Of course everyone knew that at a certain stage children didn't see eye to eye with their parents, but, though trying, that was no more significant than the stage of childish diseases, and like that was sure to pass with no permanent ill effects. And though of course we knew there was such a thing as drug addiction, no one I knew would have dreamed for a moment that anyone in our way of life could ever have any contact with it. The controversial question of the time was whether or not to give children sex education in school. I attended several parents' meetings on this at Wisconsin High, where the parents on the whole were a pretty liberal bunch.

I wonder if this impression of these years which remains with me, as I have given it here, will be yours. For most of the rest of this autobiography, you won't be in a position to question my view. You weren't here at all, you were too young to remember, or you had left home. But you all must have a pretty clear memory of these years, and I wonder if you will think I have represented them fairly. I know you will remember many things I have forgotten or never knew.

As I was writing the first draft of this chapter, I read "Christmas Eve," a story by Maeve Brennan,[354] which appeared in the *New Yorker* for December 23, 1972. The New England tradition is not one of demonstrativeness, and I was struck by these sentences.

> [The hall] was a passageway—not to fame and not to fortune, but only to the common practices of family life, those

---

354 Maeve Brennan (1917–1993) was an Irish short story writer and journalist who contributed regularly to *The New Yorker*.

practices, habits, and ordinary customs that are the only true realities most of us ever know, and that in some of us form a memory strong enough to give us something to hold on to to the end of our days. It is a matter of love, and whether the love finds daily, hourly expression in warm embraces, and in the instinctive kind of attentiveness animals give to their young or whether it is largely unexpressed . . . does not matter very much in the very long run. It is the solid existence of love that gives life and strength to memory, and if, in some cases, childhood memories lack the soft and tender colors given by demonstrativeness, the child grown old and in the dark knows only that what is under his hand is a rock that will never give way.

To me, "grown old and in the dark," my mother gave this knowledge. Did I give it to you?

CONSTRUCTION: 1950–1966

This is the period of expansion, at first manageable, later completely out of control, not only at the University of Wisconsin but nationwide. In fact, one sound generalization for this period is that our campus was not unique, though later perhaps it became extreme. What was happening here, from calendar Freshman English changes in the teaching of grammar to increasing revolt against the Establishment all along the line, was not the result of local conditions. It was happening in all comparable institutions because it was the result of social and academic conditions which were national. The device by which the university met this expansion was the teaching assistant system, and I spent these years working hard to make it work in Freshman English, the largest course in the university. You can't beat the *Zeitgeist*, and by the time I retired I had come to feel the system was indefensible and was glad to take my thumb out of the dyke. But I do not regret these years, and I do not think they were wasted. Times change, but the system was a good one for its time. "Honesty and toil make in the end for happiness" (a quotation from the biography of Anthony Trollope, one of the lessons he learned at his mother's knee).[355] I worked very hard, I honestly believed in what I was doing, and I was very happy myself. And in general the assistants were happy too. The word used by these with whom I am still in touch, now teachers themselves all over the country, is "grateful." For the bulk of this period I was repeatedly called upon to defend the system in public, once before the Board of Visitors of the University, and did so sincerely.

The MEMO from the University of Wisconsin News Service, sent out monthly to all faculty, gave on November 1, 1958, "Some Pros and Cons of graduate assistant teaching, as reviewed by Prof Harvey Sorum (Chem) before University Regents October 18." Bill will remember him. Since his statement is highly pragmatic, it should be said that he himself had the reputation of being one of the best teachers on the campus and of being concerned about excellence in undergraduate instruction.

1. The System is Practically Inevitable
    a. Not enough fulltime teachers available
    b. Cost of teaching by fulltime staff would be prohibitive

---

[355] Anthony Trollope (1815–1882), a highly successful and prolific English novelist during the Victorian Era.

2. Pros
   a. Provides needed instruction at low cost
   b. Quality of teaching by assistants uniformly high
   c. Enables qualified scholars to do graduate work
   d. Training ground for future college teachers
   e. Provides senior staff with grad students to carry out research
3. Cons
   a. Frequent incidence of poor teaching
   b. High rate of turnover
   c. Requires great deal of supervision

It was George Bernard Shaw, if I remember correctly, who said that democracy was a bad system of government, but every other you could think of was a lot worse.[356] The alternative to the teaching assistant system (even assuming we could have afforded it, which Mr. Sorum did not believe) was a permanent corps of un-promotable instructors—which actually did exist in some places: men resigned to spending their lives in repetitive and elementary work, who both were, and were regarded as, second-class citizens. Simple from the standpoint of administration, this was bound on the whole to produce sterile, disappointed men and dull stagnant courses. In my defense of our system, I repeatedly quoted Jacques Barzun: "Young teachers are best: they are the most energetic, most intuitive, and the least resented."[357] I saw no reason to regret the fact that the system was inevitable. With safeguards and supervision, I thought it could work to the advantage of freshmen and graduates alike, and I think it did for many years. The eventual breakdown came when the assistants refused supervision. At the time when they were grateful for it, when we lived in a rosy atmosphere of mutual goodwill, I worked untiringly, in my motherly way (see Esther Summerson, *Bleak House, passim*) to provide it.[358] As a matter of fact, I would have liked to give more, for some of our staff always struck me as deficient themselves in writing skills. But Mr. Lacy[359] restrained me and was

---

356 Perhaps Thomas is referring to the following quotation attributed to British Prime Minister Sir Winston Churchill in 1947: "No one pretends that democracy is perfect or all-wise. Indeed, it has been said that democracy is the worst form of government except all those other forms that have been tried from time to time."
357 Jacques Martin Barzun (1907–2012) was a French-born American historian and philosopher of education. The quotation is from *Teacher in America* (1945).
358 Esther Summerson is a character in Charles Dickens's novel Bleak House (1853).
359 Edgar W. Lacy (1914–1981) earned his Ph.D. from the University of Illinois (1939) and

no doubt right; and as numbers increased we gave as much as was humanly possible.

One criticism sometimes made, that it required the person to divide his time between two unrelated activities, teaching and scholarship, both of which he would therefore do badly, to my mind has no validity at all. (By the way, we rarely used "teaching assistant" and never the derogatory abbreviation "TA." When *they* began calling themselves "TA's," it was the beginning of the end. We used "teacher" or "staff" or, in the generic sense, "instructor.") This is the condition which will ideally exist throughout his whole professional life. Each activity should enrich the other, and does. A good example from another field is Bill Sarles, who got a national award for excellence in teaching his last year, and the preceding year had been national president of the American Association of Biochemists.[360] (This involved two interesting experiences Marion related to Reading Group: her entertaining in a posh penthouse in New York at the national convention over which he presided, and the trip to Moscow where he took the American delegation to an international convention.) A man who professes himself dedicated "only to teaching" is going to get very stale and have little to teach without continual outside stimulus. This can come from professional meetings and journals, but the main source is scholarship. But I must admit that the system was susceptible of abuse (like any system, for that matter), and Mr. Sorum's summary obviously suggests possibilities. One main abuse—which actually did exist in some places—was that the graduate student, in his desire to get through, would overload himself. If he did, with his Ph.D. prelims hanging over him, his teaching would suffer. We guarded against this by strictly limiting the amount of teaching a person could do in proportion to the amount of graduate work he could carry, and by allowing no one to do more than half-time teaching. But this was a department, not a university, regulation. Departments varied greatly in their requirements for the teaching assistantship and in the amount of supervision given. That the university policy was not uniform is, I must in fairness admit, an argument for the teaching assistants union—undreamed of in this golden age.

The Department of English had the most stringent requirements. We granted the appointment only to Ph.D. candidates who already held the Master's (with the exception of "emergency" appointments, given for first semester only, when

---

served in the U.S. Army prior to being hired in 1946 as assistant professor in the UW-Madison English department. In 1948, he became director of Freshman English and invited Thomas to assist him (Fleming, 2011, p. 46). Lacy worked closely with Thomas for over twenty years.

360 William B. Sarles, a professor in the bacteriology department, was president of the American Society for Microbiology (ASM) in 1967. His wife, Marion, was a member of Thomas's weekly reading group.

enrollment exceeded predictions). We also had the most extensive training program. But we needed to. We alone gave the teacher complete contact with his class in composition courses. A teaching assistant in physics would have charge in the lab only; in history, he would meet once a week for discussion a small group who had been part of the large lecture addressed by the professor the other two days of the course meeting. In both cases, he would work directly with and under the professor in reading the final examinations and giving the grade. But our freshmen (unless they came in to gripe to me, naturally a small proportion) had no course contact with any department member ranking above graduate assistant. That was the one who met them three times a week, read their themes, held their conferences, assigned their grades. We were therefore obliged to exercise a good deal of supervision and build into the course a number of safeguards.

The department had a particular advantage first in Mr. Lacy. He is a brilliant administrator (though I thought with a trend toward over-complexity), very hard-working, conscientious, dedicated, and gifted with a theoretical mind whose scope I never ceased to admire. He was always much more conscious than I of all possible future implications of a given immediate concrete detail. But I think it is fair to say our combination was another advantage. My mind is limited and concrete (typically feminine?), no doubt with a trend toward over-simplicity. It requires unusual circumstances, like ours, for two such different but complementary minds to cooperate so well. We had a typical joke about the bluebooks in room 314. I reported to him once that a lot of old exams which should have been destroyed were lying on the desks in 314 where anyone could pick them up. "Theoretically," he said, "there are no bluebooks in 314." "Walk down the hall," said I, "and look at them." Again, though there is no better or more genial host than Ed Lacy, he would not have found as congenial as I did the repeated personal contacts with graduate students, let alone their wives, which I honestly enjoyed. He had an inner office, and his door was always shut. Mine opened on the corridor, and my door was always open. After all, he could hardly have the background to understand a mother's feelings, like David Copperfield's landlady, but, thanks to you, I did. And my experience as an unwelcome guest at Mrs. Tucker Brooke's had sunk very deep in giving me sympathy with young wives.[361] For years I called on each new one, and I knitted booties for every department baby, once racing the stork for unexpected twins. Housing was very poor before the university put up Eagle Heights, especially for couples with children.[362] I called on wives all over Greater Madison and beyond, many so far

---

361 In the New Haven chapter, Thomas recounts an unpleasant experience with Mrs. Brooke.
362 Eagle Heights, a high promontory on the south shore of Lake Mendota, is part of UW-Madison's Lakeshore Nature Preserve. The name now refers to a student apartment complex, built in the 1960s and surrounded by Preserve lands, which houses a culturally diverse

away they'd have no chance of making friends. One particularly far-flung visit, to a couple living in a converted cheese factory out beyond Belleville, gave me one of my best Christmas memories: real cows in the front yard of a farmhouse, in true proportion for the cardboard figures of the Nativity scene near them. The graduate students themselves had plenty of company; the working wives did too; but the others, especially those tied down with babies, were lonely, and I gave all sorts of parties trying to get everyone out to the house even once so she'd have some slim chance of establishing contacts. I'll come later to details of my role as the Perle Mesta of the Department of English of the University of Wisconsin, but my point here is that I really liked all these contacts.[363] I had domestic experiences in common with the women (for that matter with the men who were fathers) as well as pedagogical experiences in common with everybody. And the timing was right. As time went on there were far fewer demands on me at home, and once Bill moved into his fraternity house, none. I could use my time as I chose. I was therefore well equipped to operate intramurally within the family, and enjoyed it. Mr. Lacy was equally well equipped to operate intermurally within the university community. Before he married he lived at the University Club,[364] and he continued to eat lunch there, usually at the big table where people sat who had no special engagement. This was frequented by the most important men in the community, such as Dean Ingraham,[365] and a variety of professors and administrators from different departments and colleges. He was greatly and deservedly respected and well known in the university as a whole. He always attended faculty meetings, and had the type of mind to deal with parliamentary procedures, and his participation in university affairs gave our course status. Through this period he and I regularly ate lunch at the Club Fridays, and were landmarks in a window niche of the lobby going over everything necessary to keep Freshman English running for the next week. You all know what TGIF means. This was a pleasant ending to the week for me, with themes to do over

---

group of international and American students and their families.
363 Perle Reid Mesta (1889–1975), an American socialite, political hostess, and U.S. Ambassador to Luxembourg (1949–53).
364 The University Club, which opened in 1908 and served social, residential, and university business purposes, became "a symbol of faculty unity and center of campus fellowship" (Cronon & Jenkins, 1994, p. 532).
365 Mark H. Ingraham earned an MA (1922) at UW-Madison and a Ph.D. (1924) at the University of Chicago, both in mathematics. He taught as an instructor (1919–1922) and as an assistant professor (1924–1926) at UW-Madison. He returned to UW-Madison in 1927, where he spent the remainder of his career. He chaired the mathematics department (1932–1942) and was dean of the College of Letters and Science (1942–1948), in addition to serving on or chairing university committees. He became one of the most highly respected and experienced faculty members on campus (Cronon & Jenkins, 1994, p. 354).

the weekend but two clear days intervening before any new strain. We worked Fridays at the Club instead of in Mr. Lacy's office (where we did confer for a period on the other mornings) because on third floor Bascom we were liable to interruptions, from which we were protected at the Club.

But there was one great disadvantage, which comes from the peculiar nature of the subject loosely called "English." In most places, it includes three rather ill-assorted parts: composition, literature, and language, the "tripod" on which, for example, the Commission on English based its summer institutes.[366] When you look at it, the skill of writing clear, expository, utilitarian prose, the aim of Freshman English and the reason why the course was required of all freshmen in all colleges, has little in common with aesthetic appreciation of *King Lear* or "To a Skylark."[367] The third division, language, developed during these very years from traditional grammar, through structural, through transformational, into a highly specialized and difficult new science, linguistics. The dichotomy between the other two has always existed, on the high school as well as the college level. In 309,[368] many a student said at the first conference, "I dreaded this course. I don't like writing and never did. I want to be an English teacher because I love literature." At Mount Holyoke in my day there were two separate departments, English Composition, my major (and the fact that I had been that almost unheard-of thing, a composition major, was one of the main reasons for my getting the work I had at Wisconsin), and English Literature, my minor; but this, I'm afraid, was due to the incapacity of Miss Marks, chairman of English Literature, to get along with anybody else and was so unusual as to be almost unique. Almost without exception our teaching assistants had come to get the Ph.D. so they could teach literature. As I went through the application forms in these years, I would sigh to read that the heart's desire of the candidate was to teach metaphysical poetry in a small liberal arts college, with particular emphasis on the years 1620 to 1630, and then visualized his prospective Freshman English class, which would contain engineers, dance majors in Women's Physical Education, and future farmers as well as possible majors in any department in Letters and Science. You yourselves can easily visualize by far the most sophisti-

---

366 The Commission on English was a national committee appointed by the College Entrance Examination Board in 1959 to improve English instruction, curriculum, and training in high schools and colleges nationwide, resulting in the publication of *Freedom and Discipline in English: Report of the Commission on English* (1965). Later in this chapter, Thomas describes her involvement in the commission, including directing one of its summer institutes at UW-Madison in 1962.

367 The poem "To a Skylark" was written by British Romantic poet Percy Bysshe Shelley (1792–1822) in 1820.

368 English 309, Composition for English Teachers, was the advanced composition course for English education students at UW-Madison.

cated and cultured members of his class if you think back to Whiskey High.[369] After the first year, if a teaching assistant were re-appointed (most were), he could express his preference for other than composition teaching, and almost everybody before leaving had experience in teaching literature, the best of them in advanced work in their own fields. But they all started in Freshman English, where the university, and the department, needed them. We thus had the advantage of being able to give everyone a consistent and intensive training program. But again in fairness I must admit it is a weakness in a system to require many of its members to do work they don't care to do and will not be doing in the future. But again this is perhaps extreme. In no other way could they have had actual classroom experience. During the Christmas season of 1973 a man new at Wausau[370] came to give me the book on Dickens he is trying to get a university press to publish. "The teaching assistants now haven't any idea what they have lost," he said. "When the TAA told me I was being exploited, I laughed in their face. I learned more about teaching in my four years here than I could ever have learned by myself in four years, and if I'd have to do it my students would have suffered." I think we taught them lessons of value to any teacher: don't treat your class as a captive audience, but let them have the fun of participation; learn everyone's name at once (the course was never popular, but many freshmen, lost in the big lectures, did enjoy the fact that they were individually known); above all, respect your student, the lesson I had learned from Rukstela.[371] Many learned these lessons and profited by them, I know, and are putting them into practice today from Maine to Idaho, from Wisconsin to Texas.

This dichotomy, discrepancy, weakness, whatever you want to call it, complicated the attitude of the department itself to our work. In the big universities, typically the Departments of English had an ambivalent attitude to Freshman English. Without it the professors would have few or no graduate students, so they knew they had to have it but they didn't like to think about it. In our own case, there was a long gap when the course was bandied around from one indifferent member to another, between Warner Taylor,[372] director when I was a graduate student, and Edgar Lacy, two men who took the position seriously. This gap is evidence of how little the department cared, and how rare people are

---

369 The nickname for Wisconsin High School.
370 A reference to a junior college (UW-Marathon County) in the University of Wisconsin Colleges, a unit in the University of Wisconsin System.
371 In the Danielson chapter, Thomas describes a formative learning experience while teaching high school English that involved this student.
372 Warner Taylor (1880–1958), earned BA and MA degrees from Columbia and taught there for six years before teaching at UW-Madison from 1911–1947, where, beginning in 1921, he directed the Freshman English program (Clark, 1966, pp. 5–6; Fleming, 2011, p. 38).

who are willing to devote themselves to the subject. We were somewhat better off here than at many other places. There was a tradition that senior members visited new teaching assistants, and I always made a point of telling new teaching assistants this at the first staff meeting to show that the department "cared." Re-appointments were voted by the whole department, also, on the basis of the recommendations Mr. Lacy presented to them, so thorough and complete that his judgment was generally automatically accepted.

But we had our troubles. A petted graduate student, brilliant in literature, might be quite incompetent in composition (though in the specific case I am thinking of I believe the lack was in effort rather than in ability). Nor were the senior staff always good visitors. Some might be too easy-going to give the teacher any useful comment; and later, as our assistant professors came to be thorns in the flesh, they might judge on political coloration rather than pedagogy. Limited by the actual teaching hours (I always had trouble getting anyone to visit at 7:45 and sometimes had to ask it as a personal favor, which was hard on my friends), I had a good deal of power, since I made out the visiting schedule. To weed out an incompetent, Paul Fulcher was our best hatchet man as long as he was well enough to visit. It's a pity his reports were confidential, because they were good reading: "She looked like Helen Traubel, but she did not sing."[373] On the other hand, I would protect a shy but competent teacher from a brusque and intimidating professor; or, if I thought we might be recommending a particularly promising staff member for one of the university awards for good teaching, which were introduced in this period, I would assign a visitor likely to carry a lot of weight. Most of the visits, of course, were just a matter of fitting schedules. The closest relationship in graduate work is that between the Ph.D. and his thesis advisor. Since this did not develop for several years after our own contacts, it might seem our work had no connection with it. But I have always cherished a compliment from Henry Pochmann,[374] no man to throw them around lightly, that we taught the graduate students to read. I think he was right. I worked very hard in staff meetings and individual conferences to get them to read their freshman themes so that they saw on the page not what they thought was there or wanted to see there or would have put there themselves, but what actually *was* there. This ability certainly would contribute to intelligent reading of literature. Surprisingly enough, few supposedly educated people can read.

What Ed considered my greatest contribution, I think, and the reason he asked me in the first place to work with him, was the fact that I was genuinely

---

373 Helen Francesca Traubel (1899–1972), an American opera and concert singer.
374 Henry A. Pochmann (1901–1973), an American literary scholar , taught at UW-Madison from 1938 to 1971.

interested in freshman composition and genuinely enthusiastic about it. He hoped the staff would catch it from me. To some extent, perhaps this happened. Not to a very great extent, I am afraid; the whole system, as you see, was against it. But they were surely better off with someone who genuinely cared about the work than with someone who didn't. Very very few people care about teaching utilitarian prose, though some are interested in "creative writing." I say this on the basis of my years at Wisconsin, when every year at job interviews at Modern Language Association Ed was always on the lookout for men or women who did, and never found any (though some, to get a foothold, occasionally pretended to, dragged their feet for a few years, and then disappeared). To my mind, expository prose is teachable (and "creative" not, though you can perhaps furnish a favorable climate) and worthwhile.

And I felt working with freshmen was worthwhile. I often quoted at the first staff meeting Charles Schlichter's statement, one of the great men of Wisconsin in its greatest days, who had himself taught freshmen. "Actually I did not teach freshmen. I taught attorneys, bankers, big businessmen, physicians, surgeons, judges, congressmen, governors, writers, editors, poets, inventors, great engineers, corporation presidents, railroad presidents, scientists, professors, deans, regents, and university presidents. For that is what these freshmen are now, and of course they were the same persons then."[375] I have always felt the first semester of college, like the first year of life, which none of us remember, is one of our most important learning times. Often the Freshman English instructor would be the only personal faculty contact a student would have; his influence could be decisive, for good or bad.

The dates of this chapter are significant for my own career. I might have used 1967 and Helen White's death for the end of an era.[376] But 1966 was my own high point. In 1951, on my fiftieth birthday, the regents made me assistant professor. Janet [Quintana], as chairman's wife, very sweetly made Dick let her call me up to call me "Professor Thomas." This was the giant step you would have thought impossible, in view of my lack of the union card, the Ph.D. I owed something to my friends, of course. Mr. Lacy is a shrewd strategist, and

---

375 Charles Sumner Slichter (1864–1946), professor of applied mathematics at UW-Madison and dean of the graduate school. The excerpt is from his book *Science in a Tavern; Essays and Diversions on Science in the Making*, published by the University of Wisconsin Press (1940).

376 Helen Constance White (1896–1967) earned a Ph.D. in English from UW-Madison in 1924 and remained there throughout her distinguished career as a specialist in British literature. She became the first female full professor in the university's history in 1936 and served as chair of the English department between 1955–1958 and 1961–1965. She was also active professionally, serving as president of the University of Wisconsin Teachers Union, the national president of the American Association of University Women, and as a U.S. delegate to UNESCO meetings (Hoeveler).

Construction

[Walter] Ray Agard[377] was on the Divisional Committee, which had to approve the recommendation after the department made it, on the way to the Dean, and then the Regents. But I also owed something to my position not as scapegoat but perhaps sacrificial lamb. During this period of graduate expansion, the gap between professors and undergraduates was widening, and the universities were under criticism for it. A department with a member who was working hard to improve undergraduate instruction was like a company today employing a black, a woman or a black woman, and could well give her some recognition. Also, I needed status to impress the assistants (the little snobs). Incidentally I have spent my life being incorrectly addressed as Doctor Thomas. The custom at Wisconsin, as at all top-flight places (said she possibly with a little inverted snobbery of her own) was to use Mr., Miss, or Mrs., so I had no embarrassment at home. But at meetings like those of the Wisconsin Council of Teachers of English, where most people attending were School of Education products, they were so scrupulous in the use of "Doctor" you'd think it was a bunch of veterinarians, and I got fed up trying to explain and generally let it go.

Ednah Shepard Thomas teaches an English class at the edge of Bascom Woods, ca. Fall 1950. Source: University of Wisconsin Archives.

---

377 Walter R. Agard (1894–1978), a Classics professor at UW-Madison from 1927–1946, taught in the Experimental College (1927–1932) and in the Integrated Liberal Studies (ILS) program.

However, it was to the credit of the department that they did promote me. I would never have left my home in Frost Woods, so I would never have offered a horse trade, which they knew. And I wouldn't have thought myself exploited, or anything but unbelievably lucky in having such enjoyable work. My motive was to make a life for myself independent of you, and it still seems almost a miracle that the opportunity so perfectly suited me. The work was the substance; the title the shadow. Still, we never object to a little recognition or a little more money, do we? In incongruous moments, such as scrubbing the bathroom floor, I've often had a childish pleasure in thinking, "I'm a real professor." I don't remember the intermediate step to associate professor, which carried with it membership in the Executive Committee and insight (sometimes disillusioning) into department inner workings. All that ever crossed my mind was that since the department had promoted Charlotte Wood to full professor her last year, as a gesture of recognition of past services when it was too late for her to be involved in anything important, they might do the same for me. But I was promoted in 1966, due to Mr. Lacy, who "needled me" (his word) into coming up with the Master Teaching Assistant Program,[378] enough of a contribution to undergraduate teaching not only to justify the promotion but special action on the part of the regents, since university regulations forbid promotion after the sixty-fifth birthday without such special action. After that, the roof fell in. The Master Teaching Assistant Program failed, undergraduate teaching—and all teaching, sank lower and lower, and education slid rapidly down the chute into the pit where it wallows today. Sam Blount,[379] no mean judge, ascribes this descent to permissiveness and lack of commitment, two qualities my worst enemy couldn't accuse *me* of. But like the gods, the Regents of the University of Wisconsin cannot recall their gifts. So every time I pick up my handbag I pick up the official card from the University Registrar which identifies me as "Professor Emeritus."

My predecessor, Charlotte Wood, and I overlapped by a couple of years. During this time she continued to do the scheduling. But she had never been interested in the teaching of composition—Warner Taylor had conducted his own training meetings—and had filled out her schedule by literature quizzing, so that the staff training part of my work began at once.

---

378 The Master Teaching Assistants Program was a mentoring program in which experienced Freshman English TAs were assigned to mentor 7–8 new TAs in their first year. Master TAs conducted class visits and portions of the weekly training meetings and sought to help new TAs in any way possible (Fleming, 2011, pp. 52–53).

379 Nathan Sam Blount (1929–1989) taught high school in Miami before earning his doctorate in education at Florida State in 1963, after which he was hired by the UW-Madison English department. He held a joint appointment in English and in Education.

Construction

Charlotte was different from me in every possible way. Above all, she was a personage. Self-confidence, I think, is an innate quality; but it doesn't hurt either if all your life you have money and position. A wealthy woman and a member of an old Wisconsin family (the position doesn't have to be in the international jet set, just in your own milieu), she played a large part in Madison society, and had a great many interests outside of the university. She was not only a member but also an officer of the famous Mad Lit,[380] and this was only one of many activities. She was not at all domestic; I don't think she ever boiled an egg in her life. She lived in an apartment in Sterling Court, one of the picturesque Madison quarters ruthlessly bulldozed during Harrington's regime for the erection of what the *New Yorker* calls the New Brutality,[381] and ate her meals at the University Club around the corner. She was authoritarian; enjoyed, and was good at, telling people to do things, whereas I have always had the bad administrative weakness of preferring to do something myself rather than ask someone else to. She was born with the worst pair of crossed eyes I have ever seen. Today I am sure it could be corrected by an operation in infancy, but in her youth medical science had not advanced to this point and she lived out her life as God had seen fit to make her. But this near-deformity did not prevent her from spending a great deal of time and money on her appearance. She had beautiful white hair, impeccably dressed from frequent visits to the hairdresser, and her clothes were expensive. I think of her as invariably dressed in black velvet, but perhaps this is not wholly accurate. The comment of a janitor at the time she retired, however, I am sure is: "She looks grandly."

Charlotte had the nicest retirement part I ever had any contact with, and for years I used to fantasize that I might have one like it. It was a dinner at the Union, then a very pleasant place, with all department members, senior and junior, invited, and everybody turned out. I decorated the tables with Maypoles and pastel-colored crepe paper streams and spring flowers. After the dinner everyone waited in line to shake hands and do her honor. But the main reason the party was so pleasant was that Paul Fulcher, who was very fond of her, was master of ceremonies, and it was his finest hour.[382] He had the light touch; he avoided sentimentality and lugubriousness alike, and it was the most skillful per-

---

380 The Madison Literary Society, originally Club, was founded in 1877 to promote literary discussion and social interaction among individuals "'of acknowledged literary taste'" (Thwaites, 1904, p. 27). Thomas mentions this club in the Wisconsin chapter.

381 A reference to Brutalist architecture, or brutalism, an outgrowth of early twentieth-century modernist architecture, which flourished in the 1950s-1970s and is characterized by massive concrete structures. The term derives from Swiss-French architect Le Crobusier's (1887–1965) description of the material: *béton brut* (raw concrete).

382 Paul Fulcher (1895–1958) joined the English department in 1925 and taught literature and creative writing.

formance he ever turned in, even more skillful than his brilliant birthday lecture on George Bernard Shaw. I like to think of it now.

She lived just over a year after her retirement, and died alone in her apartment the next summer; she was not found for several days. I took Paul to the funeral on a hot muggy night, and he was then beginning to be so ill I was a little worried at the responsibility. Paul regretted her death, because he thought she might have had more good years of life. I never regret the death of anyone over seventy; there is no question that many people do have many good and happy and productive years after that, but the dice are loaded against us, and the quick stroke is much more merciful than slow dying. Five horrible years of living death lay, ironically, before Paul himself. He became an appalling, repulsive changeling. He died of combined emphysema and alcoholism, a hair's breadth at a time, a source of cruel suffering to himself and embarrassment to his friends. He lived out that travesty of life in squalor—companioned (after Jim Dodd's move to Michigan) by a series of callous, careless students and a dog so bad tempered that Jim's first action at Paul's death was to have him destroyed—tied to an oxygen tank (the company garnished his university salary). He was a shameless parasite, making no return for the university's charity. In the days before teachers' unions, the university stood unflinchingly *in loco parentis* to more than its students—even to such a bitter disappointment as the once promising Professor Fulcher had turned out to be. Worst of all, that last version of himself was so deeply bitten into his friends' minds that even now it is very hard for me to overlay it with the picture of him at his best, with charm, humor, wit, kindness, at Charlotte's retirement dinner.

The year started with a bang: registration and first class week. For many people the new year may be Times Square on New Year's Eve with popping champagne corks, whistles, sirens, and the singing of Auld Lang Syne. But for me it was always a quieter though not undramatic moment on a Monday September morning in Ed Lacy's office, when, after our infinitely meticulous planning, preparations, checking, and counter-checking, he would say, "here we go again," and stand aside to let me precede him into the big lecture-room at the end of the hall where we held our staff meetings, and where a group of strangers would be waiting, strangers immediately to occupy much of my time, energy, and thoughts. Registration both semesters was complicated, hectic and exhausting; but the first semester was much the worse, since orientation of the new staff was added to the assigning and scheduling common to both.

As I have said, we required the Master's degree for our regular appointments, and accordingly the staff had the maturity gained from at least one year's experience beyond the four undergraduate years—sometimes a good deal more. Some of them had gotten the Master's degree from us and knew their way around. Most of them had had some teaching experience, though this was not a requirement; but it varied widely from Sunday school or high school or small liberal arts colleges with conditions very different form ours to a few other Big Tens. The maturity in itself was an asset; its lack was very noticeable in our emergency appointments, which we had to make in the years of swollen enrollments, and which were always unfair to both teacher and student. In 1953, for instance, we expected 2650 entering freshmen, "and by the end of next week I will have had to place them all in classes; an awful thought. Also our staff have been dropping like flies. In the last three days we have lost one who had an auto smash on the Penn turnpike (not permanently, fortunately, but for an indefinite time), one who was picked up by his draft board, one from Canada who was having visa trouble, and one who reached Madison and was immediately carted to the hospital with a ruptured appendix. Since we had no people to spare anyway, the prospect is grim." (The wife of the man with the ruptured appendix, who had stayed East at her own job, flew out and stayed with me a few days before she found a place closer to the hospital; and when he was discharged, both of them spent some time in our addition while he was convalescing. These are the people who owned the big house in Peacham, Vermont, where I spent the night on my way over to see Hannah the year she had the summer job in Vermont.) When we had these last-minute drops, or when enrollment was unexpectedly large, the M.A. graduate advisers would send likely candidates down to Ed to be added to staff. They almost never performed well, though I do think the girl I told Reading Group about was exceptionally lacking in know-how. "She walked up the Hill with me the other day, and told me she was going to have a baby. Oh, how splendid, said I. When? Oh, twelve months or so, I suppose, said she. I think, said I, usually it only takes nine. All right, nine then, said she agreeable. Virginia thought the poor girl might have been reading about elephants." While they had more need of training than the others, they of necessity got less, since they hadn't received the welcome letter, the course calendar, and the texts we sent out in the spring, and they missed the staff meetings in registration week itself—meetings designed to build confidence in every teacher, experienced or not, that he could handle the first week. I gave them what meetings and individual conferences I could, but the time wasn't there. This was a bad fault in the system—blamable on the university for keeping the welcome mat out far too long. Not until late in the fifties was there an attempt to discourage late registration by an extra fee. Nor was pre-registration introduced till 1957, when "it certainly was bungled."

> There are always so many people involved in anything as big as this place now that if something goes wrong it's like the Army,

they pass the buck from one to the other and you never can pin it down. I expected things to be hectic and took my lunch with me, and Ed brought me some coffee when he went out at noon; and it was 6 p.m. before I had one moment's break in the stream of students to even drink the coffee, let alone eat the lunch.

"Assignment committee" courses were printed in bold face on the time table. They meant the student must present himself in person so enrollment numbers would be known before classes started. We never published the times and places of Freshman English at all, we had so much trouble with advisers on their own putting a student into a section convenient to him—and a thousand others—where we only had twenty-five spaces. As time went on, Ed included practically all the department courses in this category, since he had to know numbers for staffing purposes. We had a rotating chairmanship, a man or woman (Dick Quintana, Merritt Hughes,[383] Helen White) serving for three years at a time. But though it was some years before Ed was officially designated Associate Chairman, he always provided continuity and did by far the lion's share of the work. I thought romantically the first year I saw it from the inside that he and Dick were like two generals directing a battlefield. The execution of their plans came to be like an overloaded traffic system at rush hour on a badly designed highway—within a hair's breadth of breaking down, maintained only by a miracle: an impossible amount of work for Ed and me. Bascom [Hall] was actually unsafe for the streams of people flooding through it (Hannah will remember feeling the stairs shake when she brought Robert up to my office during a change of classes only), and we moved the big courses to other buildings—without telephone communication. That the maintenance department did over the floors in Bascom one year in registration week, however, was unusually bad luck for a place whose policy was never to let the right hand know what the left was doing. For every half-day, Ed kept careful figures for next year's predictions; but it took all my lunch hour to pick up the sheets, give him the figures, and give the sheets back with new directions when committees re-opened at one. I kept my own notes, too, of over- or under-staffing or trouble spots of any kind.

The actual recording was done by teaching assistants. In Charlotte's day, when numbers were small, or at any time in small departments like Classics with a few people directly under the supervisor's eye, this was workable. Wright and I, incidentally, met in this situation. But with our numbers now it became a killer. Charlotte, with great simplicity, expected all assistants to be on duty all

---

383 Merritt Hughes (1893–1971), a Milton specialist trained at Harvard (1921), was hired as a full professor from the University of California. He taught at UW-Madison from 1936–1963. He served as department chair for a total of ten years; his first term began in 1937.

week—which meant the conscientious people worked all the time and the lazy ones never. We instituted a policy of share-the-load-equally, which meant a lot of time making out work schedules keyed to the alphabetically rotating university distribution of registration materials. The first time the assistants were so grateful for time to do their own registering and free time of their own that my popularity went up like an Apollo rocket. After that, of course, they took it as their due. But gratitude is scarcer than hen's teeth anyway, and I knew of no one on record but Disraeli who showed any.[384] We hectographed and distributed foolproof directions, and if I could I tried to have a little continuity from semester to semester. But I was limited by the changing alphabetical distribution; the staff itself had a big turnover; we had a high proportion of newcomers, and I would have no way of knowing ahead of time, for instance, that man's handwriting was so illegible we couldn't read his class list. In itself the situation was always bewildering. The kind of ability needed here is not a quality that necessarily goes—or should be expected to go—with scholarship or pedagogy. What we needed was a permanent corps of workers to come in for a week or so twice a year, say, faculty wives. They could have been thoroughly trained at leisure, not during the worst confusion, and would soon be experienced enough to do a much better job than the assistants with far fewer numbers. But we never got it, because registration work was budgeted into the teaching assistant system and there was no other financial provision for it. The first year I had any real help was the fall of 1960, when we had 64 *new* teaching assistants, and registered 4200 students in Freshman English courses alone. "We had a young man to help us this year, who couldn't have been more willing or more competent." He had had experience with the type of work at the University of Illinois. "Friday night of registration week he went home at six, lay down to rest, and woke up just twelve hours later still in his clothes." (Incidentally he left the groves of Academia and is now an Episcopalian priest.) "Sunday we worked in Bascom reading placement papers till 1 a.m., and I was up at 3:30 to get my figures ready for the next day. Yesterday I had the staff meeting for the emergency appointments, and we are in routine from now on." While clearly we desperately needed extra help during registration, if we appointed a teaching assistant to do it as part of his work, he would have nothing to do for his money the rest of the semester. We did eventually make a series of such appointments, but I always felt they were dishonest, because the young men just rode the gravy train all the other weeks. I got no help from them myself anyway, since they were put onto the sophomore literature courses. But by this time Bill Lenehan had joined us, and he carried the brunt of assignment and changes from then on.[385]

---

384 Benjamin Disraeli (189401881), a British politician and writer who served as Prime Minister and helped create the modern Conservative Party.
385 William (Bill) Lenehan (1930–1993), trained in American literature at the University of

Things got progressively worse through the week, as we got progressively more tired, as the popular courses were filled and closed, as students who had been in the late groups getting their material and therefore had trouble all the way came in to complain. The big push, freshman registration, came Friday. Freshman English could never be closed, since it was required of all freshmen in all colleges and was a prerequisite for all other work. So while Ed hunted emergency appointments, I dealt with the sob stories of people who couldn't take early morning or late afternoon classes or anything Saturday. From my experience, I am convinced that if you have plenty of time to talk with a student, he will invariably be reasonable, appreciate your point of view, and make the best of the situation. But I didn't have plenty of time. The staff had an infallible way of getting rid of trouble: "See Mrs. Thomas." While I tried to deal with one student, ten or twenty more were lining up in the corridor. It seemed as if the day would never end, but finally the sullen footsteps of the last aggrieved student echoed through the empty halls, I dictated the last figures for Ed to record on the adding machine (we were really thankful for the machine age when the department bought that; you can imagine how accurate we were when we had to do the adding on our own), and we thanked God it was Friday and we were still alive—in spite of what was coming up. Registrations were ordeals to the very end. I wrote Gwen in January, 1966.

> As usual, registration was worse than usual, but we've all lived through it. We're in a very uncomfortable transition period between man and the machine, but life must go on and students must be placed somewhere. The only episode of comic relief this time was the (low) student who wrote in his final examination that he was concerned about the superhighways in California which were threatening the Deadwood trees. Unless you count the teaching assistant who blithely went off to New Orleans for a vacation instead of doing her own graduate registration so that I didn't have her schedule for the teaching schedule, and who happily telephoned me at 11:00 p.m. (you can guess where I was then) one day when I had gotten up at 4 a.m. and worked steadily in Bascom for twelve hours. This seems a little funnier to me now that it did at the moment, but not much.

Oklahoma, began teaching at UW-Madison in 1962, was made assistant professor in 1964, and began directing Freshman English in 1968. Thomas wrote a tribute to him that is included at the end of the memoir.

Construction

Let me go back now to the beginning of the week, to the orientation for the new teaching assistants, who reported Monday so our first meeting at least could be held in due leisure without assignment committee pressures (which started Tuesday). They had had welcome letters the preceding spring, the Freshman English calendar, and the textbooks for the course. The first meeting was called for the luxurious hour of 9:30. The current Department Chairman welcomed them briefly and left. Mr. Lacy introduced himself and me and gave some necessary information, and then asked each person to identify himself, his college, and his field. I watched carefully as each one spoke; I had already spent a lot of time studying the photographs which, until it became illegal to ask for them, were enclosed in applications, and when, after a break, I took over the meeting alone, I went round the group calling each person by name. (I've always done this stunt at the second meeting with my own classes, too.) Then I explained the principles of the course, and we had a discussion meeting on the basis of various themes I had hectographed for distribution—the composition discussion hour being the heart of our work. Then it was lunchtime, and we separated until next morning promptly at 8:00. Monday afternoon the experienced staff came back, and checked in at the office to get their assignment committee schedule and leave their addresses and telephone numbers. One invariable rule of registration week, I know you will not be surprised to hear, was that any assistant Ed needed to get hold of to ask him about new work never had a telephone, which added some driving around the city to both Ed's and my duties. The second new staff meeting covered the teaching of an essay; the third teaching the use of the dictionary, with exercises I had prepared keyed to the essay read, which the inexperienced staff could take if they wanted. The first day the teacher met his class they had to write an impromptu (on material we prepared for all the different hours) so that the greenest man need only sit behind his desk, and then greet the students next time with the poise of having already conducted his first class. A far cry from the total confusion the day Ed from the war and I from domestic life went back to teaching. Remember that the careful organization was warranted by the fact that many new staff members had no experience at all, nor had experience in our special circumstances, and all were graduate students half of whose time, energy, and creativity had to be protected for their graduate work. In addition, there was a good deal of inevitable shifting of students from class to class during the first week, and they needed to be protected by a common content.

My main job during registration week was making out the teaching schedule, which had to be ready for distribution at the total staff meeting Saturday afternoon. Here I took over the individual-attention method Charlotte had used with far fewer teachers, and I gallantly stuck to it to the end. The department was obligated not to let the teaching assignment conflict with a graduate course, and I had to work with the schedule the adviser had okayed. This was the only real obligation, and the only one honored at many comparable places. But in my motherly way, it seemed to me it was to the advantage of the teaching assistant, his students, and the department if I could do not merely this, but give him as convenient a schedule as possible in accordance with his own wishes. This meant individual conference; when teachers left their preferences, they generally asked for combinations of hours which didn't exist. They looked at our range of hours, which were Monday Wednesday Friday from 7:45 through 4:35 inclusive; Tuesday Thursday Saturday (at first) 7:45 through 11:00 inclusive, and later early morning Tuesday and Thursday with the third hour Friday afternoon; still later Tuesday, Thursday, Friday 12:05, 1:20, and 2:25, which sounded difficult to fit in but as a matter of fact worked out very well. I asked each for three preferences in order, which since most people taught two sections meant generally three combinations: 7:45 and 8:50, 11:00 and 1:20, or whatever. These I wrote down on the back of his schedule card. One rule which I never broke was to give an 8:50 with anything but a 7:45, since the early morning hour was the greatest problem, and though every year plenty of people tried, they accepted the fact that the rule was fair. Otherwise I put down what the teacher wanted, though we had to discuss places as well as times. These were the years of greatest campus crowding, and Freshman English, as an elementary course serviced after all the advanced courses were taken care of, got a heavy proportion of rooms on the Ag and Engineering courses in the hinterlands. It was simply not possible in the fifteen minutes between classes for someone to cover the ground between many of these and Bascom, where most of the English graduate courses were held, even less the Library, where most of the seminars met. During this time a member of the Women's Physical Education faculty reported in faculty meeting that she had walked from one end of the campus to the other in fifteen minutes. But it wasn't a fair test, for she had done it in the middle of a class period and was not slowed down by the rush of people leaving or entering a building. I trained myself to leave the assistant big blocks of time; a cut-up schedule, with a class, a free hour, another class, and so on, is the big time-waster, unless the free hour fits in for an office hour, which our assistant were required to offer their students, of course. The variety of tastes in so large a group was a help. A few—too few—always did want 7:45 and 8:50, which as a matter of fact was a good schedule because the teaching was over so early in the day. Luckily also there were always two or three who requested 3:30 and 4:35 as their first choice; these were students who had finished their course work and were working on their dissertations, and it gave them nearly the whole day free for that. I was always glad for this, since to me this would have been the most punishing schedule, and we ran only two or three 4:35's anyway; nor would we have run those if we had not been requested to

Construction

by the College of Engineering. (They had an annoying habit of requesting these and then not filling them.) It took most of the night Friday to get the schedule finished, for although I could do some tentative preliminary work as schedules came in, I could make no permanent decisions till I had the last card. Latecomers never fitted into holes, and I learned early that it was impossible to make a single change; you had to throw the whole thing away and start all over. I got the same kind of satisfaction from doing it that I get now from crossword puzzles, and I was proud that there were very few requests for changes a the total staff meeting Saturday afternoon, whereas in Charlotte's day there had been a good many. I never gave what I thought was a really bad schedule, though of course it was impossible to honor all the first choices and in order to give very few third choices I often gave more seconds. The understanding when the assistant left the office was that he would be given one of the three choices we had agreed on; which one he wouldn't know until Saturday afternoon. The conferences were helpful in getting to know the new people at once, and in sizing them up too; and though it's useless and childish to expect gratitude, it must have contributed to morale for them to know that a senior department member cared enough to put time and effort into suiting their wishes as far as possible.

It came to be quite an experience to go into [room] 312 Saturday afternoon and face the whole staff. The room has a seating capacity of 150, and in many years people were standing in the aisles. It was Bob Pooley,[386] in his brief tenure, who instituted the meeting, I think, because he wanted to make sure everyone would turn up as expected in the right place Monday. The ostensible reason was that it gave a chance, since the whole staff was there, for anyone who disliked his assignment to try to swap it for someone else's. I prided myself on the fact that there were few or even no requests for changes; of these requests few were made, since place as well as time had to be considered, but of course some were.

I began by brief thanks on behalf of the whole department, which I tried to make individual and not absolutely repetitious year after year. A note on my staff meeting outline one year gives me the chance to quote the old chestnut about Robert Browning when asked for explanation of "The Ring and the Book"; "originally God and Robert Browning knew, but now only God knows." It is "unique and similar to others: wait Henry Higgins." The "unique, and very similar to others" is a quotation from T. S. Eliot's *The Cocktail Party*,

---

386 Robert C. Pooley (1898–1978) taught English and Education courses at UW-Madison from 1931- 1968, conducted pioneering research in English usage, was president of the National Council of Teachers of English (NCTE), and founder and past president of the Wisconsin Council of Teachers of English. Pooley began directing Freshman English in 1945, but in 1948 he was asked to direct the newly created Integrated Liberal Studies (ILS) program.

which I often used to emphasize the necessity of considering each student as an individual, but the application of Henry Higgins now escapes me. A couple of weeks later, when I sent out the file cards to be made out in class for the stabilized course, the final step, I formally repeated the department thanks. "Your services (to use a Churchillian pattern) were marked by smoothness, by efficiency, by courtesy, by cheerfulness, and by good will for which we are most sincerely grateful." "We hear by the grapevine that the students are pleased and surprised at the speed and efficiency (though not always at the hour) of their English assignment. The efficiency is yours, and the credit and our thanks are also yours." "We extend special thanks to those who fought with us upon St Crispin's Day" (one time when there was an especially bad rush owing to a registrar's mistake). "When the machines take over, they may or may not be as efficient; they will *not* be as enjoyable to work with as you." It was a blessing the thanks were given on Saturday, when I could give them sincerely in the relief of the respite. If it had been Monday, when the first class day was showing up all the mistakes the staff had made, the words would have died in my throat. Then, again as briefly as possible, I went over the procedures by which during the first class week we kept sections equal and provided for late registration. (Mr. Lacy was a wonderful administrator, but his fault was a tendency to over-complexity, and I worked hard for simplicity.) I worked out a very simple Pavlovian scheme: pink sheet, green sheet, yellow sheet, each mimeographed with essential information, and minimum essential. The pink sheet was to be returned to my office with the number of students attending and the names of those assigned who were not. The green sheet meant student coming: you mustn't take any student not on your class list unless he hands you one. This caught on so well that it was not unusual for students wanting to get into another Economics or Spanish class to come to me and ask me for a green sheet so they could do it. The yellow sheet meant student going; you will find it in your box with the name of the instructor to whom he has gone, and you cross his name off your list and send his written work on. After this I distributed the schedules, finished up the horse-trading, and then the staff made out the temporary course file.

This also was my own invention, worked out in consultation with some of the assistants. Under Charlotte, the Freshman English office had no record whatever of where any student was until the end of the first class week, when it got from the Registrar the list made on the basis of the processed cards the student himself had turned in there. The only record we had was the original class list filled out in registration, which had been handed to the instructor taking the section. It seemed to me absurd that we couldn't tell a dean who wanted John Doe, registered in [English] 1-a or 1-b,[387] where he was; or that if John Doe himself had lost his program and came in, we couldn't tell him where he was supposed to go. So we instituted the system Saturday afternoon of making duplicate lists, an alphabetized one for the instructor, the original one left with us (again and again these settled questions of mistakes in registration), and making a file card for each student, alphabetized by the efforts of the whole staff, so that before we left we had a big wooden tray with a card in it for every student properly registered in the course. In the early days, after this everyone adjourned to Frost Woods (for several years Ed provided a bus), for a picnic supper and a junior-senior faculty baseball game. I felt very proud in contributing Tom and Bill to the senior faculty; they were the unquestioned stars of the team. But after Ed's marriage Margaret very sensibly decided both Ed and I were too exhausted for hospitality at then end of such a week, and the gathering developed into an all-department Sunday afternoon reception here a week or two later, hosted by the current chairman and his wife, the Lacys, and me. This system spread a good deal of good will, and lasted until our disaster chairman, Tim Heninger,[388] moving with the times, along with the not very happy Lacys, invited senior staff only to a cash bar in a big public room at the Hilldale Shopping Center.

Monday was first class day, when our file allowed us to send to their permanent places countless students who had lost their programs or were the victims of staff mistakes. The office was open from well before 7:45 to well after 4:35, including all the lunch hour, and there was a flurry of activity at the beginning of each period. I tried hard to impress on the staff that if they had an unauthorized student in their class they must send him *at once* to the office, where we could find out his proper place and see he got to it *at once*. But there were generally a few sentimentalists (who might well have had trouble finding the right place themselves) who would say, "You look tired. Sit down and write here, and I'll see about it later." Then the student would remain lost the rest of this week.

---

387 English 1a and 1b were the names for the courses that comprised the two-semester sequence of Freshman English that the majority of entering students were required to take (Fleming, 2011, p. 47).

388 Simeon K. (Tim) Heninger (1922–2008), a renaissance scholar educated at Oxford (1952) and Johns Hopkins (1955) and Guggenheim Fellow (1962), taught at Duke University prior to joining the UW-Madison English department in 1967. In 1968, following a split vote for department chair, the dean selected Heninger, a presumably neutral faculty member, to become chair. By 1970, after leading the department in its most turbulent years, Heninger resigned as chair and left UW-Madison for UNC-Chapel Hill, where he finished his career. While Thomas was very critical of Heninger, others in the department, including Walter Rideout and Charles Scott, viewed him with more sympathy, given the challenge of leading a highly polarized faculty with an increasingly aggressive teaching assistant.

This was also the day when in addition to late registration we had requests for changes. A class conflict whether from our fault or from the fault of another department was always a valid reason; so also were three classes in a row, over the lunch hour, 11:00, 12:05, and 1:20, again whether from our fault or another's. This was forbidden by university regulations for health reasons. Otherwise we dragged our feet as hard as we could. Monday was a hard day, since the bulk of the classes met then, and by now we'd usually gotten to the silly stage. As I wrote Gwen, though, "one of the secretaries says you have to be punchy or the humor doesn't strike you. A boy came in Monday to know where his English class was. Barbara, our secretary, looked him up in the big English l-a file and couldn't find him, so she called me. I asked if he had his official program with him. He said no. 'It's late,' I said, 'and we're all tired. Suppose you bring it in tomorrow morning, and we'll see if we can figure it out.' 'I'm not tired,' said the boy. 'I feel fine.' Then it occurred to us to look in the English l-b file (the second semester course, which is repeated first) and there he was." No student ever knew the number of his course; he always came to see about his "English course," of which we were handling half a dozen. "Barbara said she couldn't stop laughing about that 'I'm not tired, I feel fine' all the way down the Hill when she went home, and everyone looked at her as if she were crazy. Well, I can see it doesn't sound very funny now. The only thing that still does is a theme in low placement reading, about the house the writer would like to own, which had a breakfast snook." But Tuesday, with fewer classes, was easier, and after that the whole class cycle had been run so there were only a few stragglers, though late registration lasted for two more weeks.

Another difference between first and second semester registration was that first semester meant a heavy burden of reading placement papers, very much reduced second when the entering group was comparatively very small. First semester there was a great deal. At the beginning it was for rejection from the credit course to the no-credit English 0. Later it was at the other end of the class, for admissions to the honors course. At first every student in the class wrote two papers to be read—an unnecessary as well as very soon an impossible burden. We gave an objectively scored test to the whole class in registration week, which I made out myself after consultation with experts here and a seminar in Chicago under Paul Diederich of Educational Testing Service, and then renewed for each college generation.[389]

---

389 Paul Diederich (1906–1997), trained in classics at Harvard (BA, 1928; M.A., 1930), earned a Ph.D. from Columbia's Teachers College, taught at Ohio State (1932–1935), worked with I.A. Richards on Basic English (1940–1941), as a reader of English exams at the University of Chicago, and as a research in English for Educational Testing Service (ETS) for nearly three decades (1949–1976). His landmark study, *Measuring Growth in Writing* (1974), published by the National Council of Teachers of English, addresses large-scale writing assessment.

Construction

This we validated by trying it on all staff members who wanted to take it—practically everyone. As you know, objective testing is more reliable at top and bottom than in the middle. We needed to test only to pick out the top and bottom groups, and then those students did further writing, which it was for a number of years possible for us to read. The upper group wrote Saturday afternoon, a two-hour paper testing ability to organize as well as to write. The papers were distributed for preliminary reading to instructors and assistant professors, and returned Sunday afternoon to an inner group: George Rodman,[390] John Enck,[391] Alvin Whitley,[392] Ed and I. We broke to go to the Lacys' for Margaret's steak dinner, but otherwise worked from Sunday noon until all decisions were made in the small hours of Monday morning, more than once arousing the suspicion of the Bascom night watchman. Students then got their English 11 assignment Monday.[393] Lower placement reading took place during the first class week. Every student in the course wrote an impromptu at the first class meeting (used for material for composition discussion at the second), and in addition the students picked out in the low group wrote Wednesday or Thursday night, as the case might be. Here the preliminary reading was done by experienced assistants, chosen because we trusted their judgment, and Ed and I made final decisions. This chore provided some comic relief: "This semester he is our house treasure." "To make a long story short I am very happy to say that my plan to overcome being nervous in large crowds was overcame." "Meeting people from the lowest class to the highest, and trying to sell them something which doesn't suit them, is another interesting phase of salesmanship." "The ability to speak is a trait which I think stands a person out from other people. They act the same and are of no more intelligent, but can express ideas in a much better manner than I can." "My mother love, encouragement and advice help me to decide on a teaching profession."

---

390 George B. Rodman, an English professor at UW-Madison, directed divisions of English 1a in the 1930s, published an anthology with Robert Doremus and Ed Lacy called *Patterns in Writing* in 1950, served on the Freshman English faculty committee with Ed Lacy, Robert Doremus, Robert Pooley, and Ednah Thomas from 1948–1968 (Fleming, pp. 45, 48, 51).

391 John J. Enck, a scholar of Elizabethan literature trained at Harvard (M.A. in 1947, Ph.D. in 1951) with an interest in modern American poetry, joined the UW-Madison English department in 1951. He was a Guggenheim Fellow in 1957.

392 Alvin L. Whitley, Jr (1926–1987), English professor at UW-Madison from 1950–1984, specializing in Romantic-era poetry. Whitley chaired a committee that created the Honors Program in the College of Letters and Sciences which commenced in 1960, and directed the program until 1963.

393 English 11 (later 181) was the one-semester, literature-intensive honors version of Freshman English.

Monday afternoon came the test given to all transfer students who were to be held to any composition requirement. Ed and I read these Monday night, so they could get their placement by Tuesday noon. It was I who made out all these tests, but of course that was done well in advance. We worked against time once the reading started. You will note that all of this was dependent on the principle of multiple reading. If the first two readers agreed, the case was quickly settled. If they differed, more readers were called in and we all discussed cases, pointing out this or that concrete detail, until we all agreed.

For many years we also were responsible for testing foreign students. It was some time before much work was done on the teaching of English as a foreign language (Michigan pioneered in this field), and department members were added who were specialists and took it over. In the meantime we had to struggle as we could, untrained and incompetent as we were. Theoretically foreign students were not accepted by the university unless their proficiency in English was certified; but, as with the bluebooks in [room] 314, there was a wide gap between theory and practice. In many cases the certification, especially in some of the South American countries, was meaningless, a mere matter of pull in the home state department. It is pleasantly ironic that the group which gives me my greatest pleasure in retirement (Bill and Kathy particularly will know how much I enjoy the Japanese girls)[394] should have given me the greatest trouble in my early working years.

A letter to Gwen in '52 shows I rather agreed with Jimmy, when he told me this past Christmas season, as the Japanese families were coming across the lawn, "I don't like people I don't know." Sally Reynolds was bringing weekly to the Reading Group the wife of a visiting professor the Reynolds had known in Brussels, and I rather resented the intrusion on our privacy.

> She speaks very little English. If you don't talk to her you feel rude, and if you do it breaks the intimacy of the group. I guess I am very provincial and anti-foreign at the moment because we have such a hard time with foreign students at the beginning of the semester. They've always been a problem because they are in a special category, and the university never has determined a definite policy as to whether they are or are not to be held to the standards we expect of native speakers in FE. If they get a degree, they will go out as our representatives,

---

[394] As an extension of her memoir, Thomas wrote about her extensive involvement in retirement with English tutoring for spouses of international graduate and post-doctoral science students who were living in university student housing. In addition to meeting these women in their homes, Thomas regularly hosted Sunday dinners in her home, and she maintained written correspondence with many long after they had left the university.

> of course. Some write very well, but others know almost nothing, and in an ordinary FE section demand special tutoring. This isn't fair to the instructor, who first hasn't the specialized knowledge to give it, and also needs protection for his own time for graduate work. We're finally getting a special course set up and a special testing procedure, and next go round should be easier. But this year in registration week every time I turned around another foreign student came crawling out of the woodwork grinning at me, climaxing in one—I know you won't believe this, but it's true—who was not only foreign but totally deaf and dumb.

As a matter of fact, he was no problem at all. When he filled out a form and I saw he had been at Gallaudet College in Washington [D.C.], a famous institution for the deaf and dumb, I asked him to sit down and write a theme on the spot, which he did so well that I took it in to Ed and we exempted him from the course in ten seconds flat. The Eastern prince who came without a word of English and with his own interpreter was a little more difficult. And though things were better with a specially trained staff taking over the work, by 1964 there was still trouble.

> We have 1400 foreign students this year, and the man in our department who handles the Foreign Student English work, by a triumph of university planning, was moved out of Bascom into the basement of a private apartment three blocks away on North Charter Street with no sign. It took all my knowledge to find it, and I've lived here nearly forty years. You could hardly expect a foreigner to. Finally, I had to take time off to escort an African and two Asians over myself, so I could come back and draw and hectograph a map; after that every time I looked up and found myself confronted by frustrated foreigners I had something helpful to give them.

Second semester registration, while still an ordeal, was easier. It was different in many respects, which was confusing, particularly as time went on and they put in pre-registration in the summer, which affected first, but not second, semester. But at least all the staff now had some idea of what they were doing, and we dropped emergency appointments, always our weakest point. The entering freshmen were a comparatively small group, which meant very little placement reading. We did have to notify staff of all students getting A in English 1-a, which exempted them from English 1-b, and students getting F. We tactfully headed the latter list "Students Ineligible for English 1-b," and those who had gone ahead and signed for it were found when we made the course file and notified by their instructors. The special hazard of the second semester was bad weather—an ice storm or a blizzard. Once Margaret [Lacy] very thoughtfully asked me to spend the night there when I had been reading papers with Ed late Thursday night, to spare me the drive home. But I had to get to Bascom earlier than he in the morning, so I left my car in the street; the thermometer dropped to 14 below, the car wouldn't start, and when the AAA man arrived after I had waited an hour, he had to push me about three miles in the morning traffic down Monroe Street, all the cars around me wrapped in clouds of steam, like dragons, before my engine caught.

Looking back, I admire my own resilience in settling down each time to the semester's work after these two weeks. It's wonderful how quickly you forget, as I would tell unhappy students with bad programs; and I hope it encouraged them to see that I could go through it year after year and shake it off like a bad dream when you wake up in the morning.

Now I'll pick up the staff training part of my work. Staff meetings were held at first every Tuesday afternoon at 3:30, an hour at which no department seminars were ever set, so that it might be free for this purpose. Each assistant was visited with in his classroom and conferred with afterwards, but we didn't start these visits until after the six weeks period so that he would have time to get to feel at home with his class. No one was very anxious to be visited, and it was really hard work physically going all over the campus to fit the visits in. I always got to the room early and sat down in the back, looking invisible. We notified the assistant ahead of time, and assured him we would be as inconspicuous as possible, and when I first discussed the matter in staff meeting I always told them the story I've told you, of being visited by Warner Taylor, who came ten minutes late, stayed about twenty, and then got up and walked out.[395] I believe the visit was a real service to the teacher, quite apart from its necessity from the standpoint of the department. If we found a good hour we had no hesitation in saying so, and then we had firsthand evidence to justify our recommending the person for a University Teaching Award, or for giving him especially stimulating work. If a teacher was inept or inexperienced, you could give him a good many practical pointers. The main problem for most of them was involving the whole class in discussion, and I had a simple solution: ask a question and have the whole class write down the answer on a piece of scratch paper. Then ask half a dozen to read their answers, and you had a general discussion started right there. Everyone was thinking about the question and therefore might contribute, whereas asking

---

395 Thomas recounts this experience in the Wisconsin chapter.

one person leaves a good many untouched. The most valuable service perhaps was to someone who had annoying mannerisms of which he might be quite unconscious. (I'd check off the number of times a man said "er" and tell him in conference he'd done it twenty-five times in fifteen minutes, which would shock him out of it; this was before the creeping paralysis of "you know" between every alternate word had been invented—one of the most annoying features of our culture.) Sitting in the back of the room, I was in a position to tell a man his hour was fine but no one beyond the first two rows could here a thing he said. As with written theme comments, I always tried to give any honest compliment I could, of course. This was a real service; I've encountered many men established in their profession who would have profited by it. Once at Mad Lit the paper was delivered by a very able young history professor. Apparently he had never had the luck to be visited in the classroom by someone who could tell him that his writings and posturings made it almost impossible for an audience to pay attention to what he was saying. (As Miss Trotwood said to Uriah Heap, we didn't want to be corkscrewed out of our senses.[396]) Some of our own assistant professors, who came to us recommended as good teachers, obviously never had been visited. I had to visit those in English 11, and I remember one man who gave in fifty minutes a bare ten minutes worth of instruction because he spent the other forty writing sentences on the board and erasing them: the use of the department hectograph machine had never occurred to him. I did my own teaching in a good-sized room with a back door, so that staff could visit me inconspicuously if they wanted to come, or if Ed sent them. The classroom visiting was a time-honored custom of the department, which had a much better record in this respect than most others.

The substantial amount of training on theme reading was our addition. I might mention here the young man who told me he was trying to get his students to use concrete detail. Of course I commended him. "Yes," he said. "I had a theme where the student wrote about falling in the lake and getting his pants wet, and I told him that *pants* was an abstract word and he should be more specific and concrete." We gave all staff copies of my pamphlet *Evaluating Student Themes*, which, you may be surprised to know (and not merely because of staff copies) is the all-time best seller of the University of Wisconsin Press.[397]

---

396 Characters in Dickens's *David Copperfield*.

397 *Evaluating Student Themes* is a forty-page pamphlet of fourteen student themes, arranged according to three levels (unsatisfactory, middle, superior), each with an accompanying terminal comment. The foreword highlights an "ideal process" for commenting on student writing, based on the conviction that a teacher must aim not to edit but to (1) promote the lifelong development of students' writing skills, (2) balance criticism and encouragement, and, above all, (3) show both interest in and respect for students' work as a whole (Thomas, 1955, pp. iv-v). Fleming (2011) notes that the pamphlet anticipates features of the writing process (p. 50).

I'm proud of the fact that I introduced a minimum grade policy—no grades on individual themes, and only two tentative reports to the students, at six and twelve weeks, before the final grade—many years before the idea became at all common. Ed backed me in the teeth of a good deal of opposition; not only did we adhere firmly to the policy but it was adopted by the other composition courses. Among its merits perhaps the greatest was that it forced the instructor to make a comment on the work.

As Director of the course and head of a largely inexperienced staff, Ed was conscious of the necessity of policing the course so that unqualified students would not pass it and go on out into the university community to discredit the department and to suffer themselves. His solution was an objectively scored test given to all students early in December. This I made out each year with a committee of teaching assistants, our final meeting a dinner one here. It was given on a Saturday afternoon, with a Friday cut to compensate. And to compensate the staff, I gave a Christmas party in 361 Bascom, the old "tea room," lugging up coffee pots, Christmas bread, cookies, decorations. I still carry, just above my right knee, a scar about the size of a half dollar from the time boiling water dripped on me while I was pouring. Any student absent from the test, or ranking in the lowest 5%, received his grade not from his own instructor, but from a committee primarily consisting of Ed and me, though we called in others in doubtful cases. The instructor turned in a form with grades already given, and the final exams and the student's last impromptu (true to our policy of never judging on a single piece of written work alone), and his recommendation for the final grade. If there was much discrepancy between that and the grade we assigned, I went over the work with the instructor later to show him why. Like lower placement reading, this was on the whole a disheartening chore, but not without comic relief: "The temptations at college are many. You have no mother to wake you up in the morning." "By the way, my high school teacher wasn't too young. In fact was, and still is fairly old." "The person who never socializes may become a professor, but I doubt if he will have many friends." "I like to study, but sometimes I wonder if anything is registering upstairs. This has bothered me for a long time."

Personally, I never was completely happy about the grading in the course— and I imagine Bill knew a good many students who weren't either. It tended to be a C course; this may be expected from any universally required, but a contributing factor, I'm afraid, is that some of our staff felt they'd keep out of trouble from either side if they gave C's. Ed's solution to the problem of the poor students was, I think, a good one. But I was concerned that the better students were not getting enough recognition. In my considerable experience with high school English teachers, I have concluded that experienced teachers differ little in coming to a sound judgment about a poor student, but differ widely in coming to a discriminating judgment about a good one. The reason, I think, is that the good student shows individuality; and his may clash with the instructor's, unless the latter is very careful to be objective. We have evidence that Mark Twain did not appreciate Jane Austen, and I guess the reverse would have been true, though fortunately neither tried to teach the other. In an attempt to cope with this problem, we asked the assistants to bring in what they thought were superior themes in the required conferences; and many were undiscriminating in admiring work they shouldn't as well as in failing to admire work they should. Fortunately, owing to Ruth Wallerstein,[398] we early introduced an honors course. About half the students picked by our test to write for this didn't make it; and I placed them in special sections within the ordinary course, handled by our best teaching assistants who had a good deal of freedom in constructing their own calendars. These were experienced, offered the opportunity in the spring, and therefore had time to plan in the summer. I held regular staff meetings with these teachers and enjoyed them very much.

I also enjoyed very much my staff meetings with the full-time department instructors who taught the honors course [English 11]. The course itself was the great joy of my professional life, and I hated to give it up. I've never had anything to touch it. My own advanced composition course [English 309] had juniors, seniors, and some graduates, all English majors; but the group was never so good, never so stimulating, as English 11 freshmen. The latter had, of course, the advantage of variety. They were the pick of the university. They were the equal, I will maintain, of the best students in any college or university in the country, bar none. (There is however a difference between Harvard, say, and Wisconsin; we had a considerably wider range between our best and worst than I think exists there.) When Ruth Wallerstein's wisdom started the course, the fashion was to decry excellence as conducive to snobbery, and many of the students had tried in high school to hide the fact they had brains, and were delighted to be able to be themselves. My own theory is that the true test of superiority is humility, and these students bore it out again and again. The conceited person, I found again and again, is the mediocre one, so limited he cannot conceive of anything better than what he does himself. In English 11, no matter how superb the paper was a student turned in, he was humbled about it because he himself could conceive of the reach beyond what he had grasped. After I had to give up teaching, I continued in charge of the course, which meant that I visited, their first semester, most of the young men who came to

---

[398] Ruth Wallerstein (1893–1958), educated at Bryn Mawr and University of Pennsylvania, joined the English department in 1920 and taught English literature until her untimely death in an automobile accident in England while on research leave.

us as instructors or later assistant professors. This gave me the first contact with younger men whom I am now fortunate to count as friends: Alvin Whitley, Tom Tanselle,[399] Jim Nelson,[400] Bill Lenehan.

I guess this is the time for my profile of Bill, with whom I had a work relationship second only to that with Ed Lacy. He didn't make much of a splash in the department when he came. He is physically unimpressive, and though not shy not particularly assertive. His wife is so gorgeous that the first time I met them at a department party she stood out from the rest of the academic wives like Liz Burton[401] or Sophia Loren[402] and I hardly saw him standing beside her (he is shorter than she). Also, academically he was rather under a cloud. He came from the University of Oklahoma, hardly a prestigious institution, to a department which has always preferred Harvard men and been pretty snobbish even about Big Ten doctorates. (Ed Lacy got his bachelor's at Vanderbilt and his doctor's at Illinois.) Worse still, Bill's doctorate hadn't actually been conferred. When a man, eight or ten months before, is offered the position of assistant professor here to begin in September, he is usually finishing up his dissertation, which it is assumed he can do before fall. If he doesn't, he must do it as soon as possible, which naturally shortchanges the institution to which he comes. In Bill's case, the fault was not his, but the negligence of his Oklahoma committee; but it was still a mark against him. So when I visited classes in the fall of 1962, I went to his without any particular expectation.

From his class, I went straight to Ed and said, "I've found the man who can take over from you in Freshman English." We'd been looking for such a man for a long time, for it was obviously unfair, as the department grew and Ed's administrative work there consumed all his time, for so important a course to be headed by someone who was giving it not much more than his name. I could keep it going as it was going, but I was approaching retirement myself, and any institution needs to change to keep healthy. We had never seen anyone we thought had the necessary ability with even the possibility of interest. Bill was not primarily interested in composition; he is an American Literature man. But he had turned in a good composition hour, and I thought he was worth sounding out. My main reason was a character judgment. With complete good humor

---

399 G. Thomas Tanselle (b. 1934), a Melville scholar, taught at UW-Madison from 1960–1978 and served as vice president of the Guggenheim Memorial Foundation (1978–2006).
400 James G. Nelson (1929–2015), a graduate of Columbia (1961) and a Guggenheim Fellow (1965), taught in the UW-Madison English department from 1961–1995 and was Thomas's bridge partner.
401 Elizabeth Rosemond Taylor (married name, Burton) (1932–2011) was an Academy Award-winning British American actress.
402 Sophia Loren (b. 1934) is an Academy Award-winning Italian film actress.

and courtesy, with complete consideration for the individuality of his students, he had the guts not to be dominated by them but to point out reasonably where he differed from them. Ed approached him, and he decided, after some consideration (which no doubt included likelihood of promotion in a department where the top positions in American literature were very solidly filled by men with national reputations), that he was interested. At first he was a third in our conferrings, but he took over more and more work and responsibility until Ed handed over to him the title of Director. He is very good with people, perhaps suggestive of Kissinger[403] in patience and ability to get on with anyone not actually certifiable, and to do it without apparent strain, and obviously this quality was of great value in the nature of the work.

In many respects, my relationship with Bill is the opposite of that with Ed. While Ed discovered me and involved me in Freshman English, I did the same for Bill. While Ed managed my promotion, I, departing from my usual passivity, initiated and urged Bill's. I brought him up first because I was furious at Heninger's unpardonable treatment of him in trying to impose on him a ridiculous teaching assistant's demand without even consulting with him first. (Heninger was our disaster chairman, who plays a heavy role in the next chapter.) In spite of what some of my colleagues kindly called my eloquence, the promotion did not go through that year, and I didn't really expect it to, since the department budget was thin; but I repeated my urging the next year, and succeeded—which was really lucky for Bill, since my rhetoric was based on the enormous pains and difficulties of the job of Director of Freshman English (by now probably second only to that of Chancellor in view of our teaching assistants, the most aggressive on the campus) and Bill's almost superhuman good nature, equanimity, and success in handling it. In another year the course had been discontinued. Finally, as Ed and I had been joined in the building up Freshman English, Bill and I were joined in destroying it. It's more fun to plant than to pluck up that which is planted, but when the plant has become rotten it must be destroyed, and I was glad to be working with a good man to do it. This, however, belongs to the next chapter. I might say that contrast never extended to my dominating Bill as Ed dominated me. As both older and more experienced, I suppose I had some influence, but I would never have urged him on Ed for the position if I hadn't been sure he would be his own man, as he was. Since retirement and the institution of a monthly contract [bridge] four—the Lenehans, Jim Nelson,[404] and me—I have grown to

---

403 Henry A. Kissinger (b. 1923), an American diplomat and politician who served as National Security Advisor (1969–1975) and U.S. Secretary of State (1973–1977). He received the 1973 Nobel Peace prize for helping arrange a ceasefire in Vietnam.

404 James G. Nelson (1929–2015), a graduate of Columbia (1961) and a Guggenheim Fellow (1965), taught in the UW-Madison English department from 1961–1995.

know Angelina very well also. In spite of her gorgeousness and my plain-Janeness, we have a good deal in common: interest in gardening, interest in detective stories, interest in foreign students, among others. It took her a while to get over calling me "Mrs. Thomas" and use "Ednah," as Bill had done for a long time, in view of the difference in age, but she finally made it.

To go back to the period of this chapter. During it I acquired my own course, handed over by Bob Pooley, English 128, or in the new numbering system, 309. This was an advanced course in composition for prospective high school teachers, open to minors and required of majors in English. I kept it to the end of my work, usually teaching two sections. It was given me because I was the only member of the department beside Bob Pooley who had ever had any actual high school teaching experience. Would you have thought that Danielson, at the time apparently such a tangent, would have rewarded me like this? Over the years, the course changed and developed, and I think I can feel justified pride in its growth. I started out with an essay collection, usually a contemporary one, which offered models of writing for analysis and a variety of fields for theme assignment, and I changed this every year for the sake of variety, since I never had any break from teaching the course. This wasn't a particularly functional organization, though, and I was delighted when I finally came upon a perfect text: Connolly and Levin, *The Art of Rhetoric*,[405] with content material ranging from Aristotle and Plato to Kenneth Burke, really good challenging stuff for college students, and examples in essays by Steele, E. B. White, Samuel Johnson, Saul Bellow, Edmund Burke, Abraham Lincoln, J. F. Kennedy, John Henry Newman, Howard Mumford Jones, Walter Pater, and E. M. Forster among others. It was a good tough unified course. I always did a lot of individual conferences, of course, and the students wrote a theme a week. It seems reasonable to include one substantial source paper in an advanced composition course, and I tailored this to fit the student, a prospective teacher. All through these years, the research paper was a problem in Freshman English and in high schools, with us and all across the country, mainly because it was generally nothing but an invitation to plagiarism, a cut-and-paste job of no profit to anyone but the typist. We solved it ourselves in Freshman English by limiting the student to one novel on which a variety of critical papers could be written, so that his instructor was thoroughly familiar with the source and therefore could judge his handling of it. In 128, I started with the view that I had to be thoroughly familiar with any sources my students used, which meant limiting their choice. But I gave them some. Each

---

405   *The Art of Rhetoric* (1968) by Francis X. Connolly and Gerald Levin, was a college composition textbook that introduced students to classical and modern rhetorical theory and included a collection of classic and modern essays for analysis, organized by modes (description and narration, exposition, argument and persuasion, expository narrative, and expository argument).

must choose two novels written by one of the three great Victorians, Dickens, Thackeray, and Eliot (it certainly would do no high school teacher any harm to read two such novels) for I myself knew all these works well. Then I paired together students who had made the same choices—which sometimes required a little juggling, but generally worked out, after I explained the reason. Miss A and Miss B both read *David Copperfield* and *Great Expectations* independently, and wrote their papers independently, on any literary or critical points which occurred to them—a small point in depth, a larger point in breadth. I called the papers in before a vacation, which gave me plenty of time to go over them carefully, typing all my comments, marginal and terminal, on separate pieces of paper. I then returned Miss A's paper to Miss B, and Miss B's to Miss A. The two signed up together for a conference with me, at which each would criticize the other's paper and I would contribute my own comments. All through this period in gatherings of high school teachers ways were continually sought of lightening the composition teacher's reading load, and it was often proposed that students could correct each other's papers. This in my view is altogether unsound. As I found repeatedly in this work, where the pairing was done on the basis of common sources, a mediocre student would be too mediocre to appreciate excellent work, just as she was too mediocre to do it. Nonetheless, it was good practice for prospective teachers, surely, and an excellent lesson in backing up what you say. No one was going to make a hasty and unsupported criticism to the girl sitting across the desk from her who was about to criticize her own paper. And of course I was there not only to guide the conference but to give the final word all on my own (this was not told to the other student): the grade. With occasional exceptions, of course, the conferences generally went very well; most of the students took the project very seriously and conscientiously and behaved with real courtesy and consideration. (I have used the feminine pronoun in this paragraph in my examples, because although I did have some men in the course, generally they were pretty much in the minority.)

This was an advanced composition course, not a course of moral instruction or a sensitivity session. But its basic aim was to contribute to clear thinking, which in my view is essential to good writing, and I hope it contributed in some degree to the awareness that others have feelings. It is remarkable how obtuse many people are as to the effect produced on others by what they say or write. For example, recently Christine Foster Long (from the Island[406]), who is facing a cataract operation, wrote me a friend had "scared her to death" by describing in detail the horrors the friend's husband had gone through with his, for a solid

---

406 A reference to Isle of Springs, an island community located in BoothBay Harbor, Maine, where the family spent summer vacations.

year both before and after it. The basis of 309 was the Aristotelian theory of rhetoric: three elements are always involved, the speaker (or writer), the audience, the situation; and good writing depends on harmonious balance among the three. You must consider not only what you want to say but how it will affect the person to whom you say it in order to bring about the desired result. This does not mean deceit or sophistry; it is based on respect for your audience as well as yourself. Each semester, well in advance, I would announce a persuasion theme. The student might write on any subject he chose, to any audience he chose, in any persona he chose, his own or another. It was surprising how often students failed to consider the audience. One girl wrote in the persona of a high school guidance counselor explaining the parents why she had not informed them or anybody that she knew a number of students were smoking pot. To begin with, she was muddled in her purpose between personal justification and an argument for the legalization of marijuana. The latter, of course, could be a possible point of view. But what her paper did was to tell the parents that a strong argument for legalization was that smokers often become hooked on hard drugs if marijuana is illegal, whereas if it were legal they would be satisfied with it. In other words, she told parents that their children might already be hooked on hard drugs, that she had known all about it, and had not lifted a finger to prevent it. Another student, this time a man, had obviously given his paper real pains and thought. He wanted to persuade his parents to let him have the second family car for his use in Madison, and he brought up the right kind of arguments to appeal to parents: it would be easier for him to spend more time at the library studying if he had a car, since he lived some distance out and bus service was poor. But he left one glaring omission, which occurred neither to him not to any of the class until I guided them to it by some leading questions. The second car must have been the one used by his mother, and she must have built her habits of life around it. It never occurred to him that to ask her to give it up would mean readjustment and inconvenience, and that he should have raised this point, with possible solutions, in his persuasion.

I might say here that clear thinking was the aim of the freshman course as well as of mine. And my considered opinion here is that this requires *omission* of controversial topics. And my teacher's first reaction, including my own, is that the student will write best on something controversial. He doesn't. Such themes are always a recapitulation of the last article the writer has seen in a newsmagazine or local paper. They generate heat but no light. The student's emotion disqualifies him from free thought. In Freshman English we warned the inexperienced staff about this, and when they disregarded the warning and had to bring me the resulting themes for discussion, they always confessed the results were disappointing. The habit of objective dispassionate analysis and thought needs

Construction

to built up gradually, and of course it is to be hoped that all college courses contribute to it. Ruth Wallerstein originated the source paper in Freshman English (my own in 309 is indebted to her): it was based on a novel, in connection with which a variety of literary and critical topics could be suggested, which would give the student intellectual practice in coming to a conclusion he must support by evidence. This had the further advantage that the instructor was familiar with the only source used by the student, and therefore in a position to judge intelligently how well he had used it. Ideally, if the staff understood my careful preparation and followed our policy, this paper should have been valuable in developing the students' power of thought. I'm afraid, however, this was another case of discrepancy between theory and practice like the bluebooks in room 314, and the discrepancy grew more and more glaring as time went on and the staff became less and less concerned with teaching writing and more and more involved in social propaganda.

When the Wisconsin Council of Teachers of English was formed (as time went on, of course, I would meet more and more former students there), Ed and I both joined, and we both went to the annual meetings for some years and served on various committees. This was all good experience. I met a number of people I would not have otherwise, and it was a chance for me to know the state better.

To Gwen, who was in Paris, I gave a vignette of Ham's home state.

> When I got to my hotel room and started to dress for the evening meeting, I heard band music and down the street right under my window came the Legionnaires' Band and fifteen automobiles, each containing a contender for the title of Miss Wausau, each girl wearing white gloves and waving graciously, in the manner of Queen Elizabeth II, to the populace, who lined the streets—and among whom, with a perfect view from above, I did not see the one soul who moved a muscle of the face or responded in any way. After the parade they held a style show in Penny's, right across the street. You may feel you are seeing life in Paris, but I tell you you haven't lived until you have seen Wausau, Wisconsin, on a Friday night in spring.

On the whole, however, the WCTE is a good illustration of the old adage, Never wish for anything because you may get it. Before it was formed, we used to wish we had some means of communication with the English teachers in the state in addition to the various individual letters and visits we received. But the organization has not had a very fortunate career. One great difficulty is that the other people in higher education (the bulk of membership was among high school teachers) all tended to be jealous of the University at Madison, and were therefore rather prickly to work with. The Executive Secretary, for a good many years, who shall remain unnamed, was a very aggressive man, long on ambition but short on judgment or intellect. Since he forgot to register WCTE as a non-profit organization, Bob Pooley got into trouble with the income tax people on contributions he had made and claimed deductions for. This, as a matter of fact, was rough justice, for Bob once told me he himself had persuaded the man to leave business (I think he was really cut out for the kind of salesman described earlier in this chapter) and go into teaching. He undertook stupidly unjustified publishing ventures, and the whole organization for some time has been tottering on the verge of bankruptcy. For all I know it may have taken place. I'm glad to say I've lost touch, though Joyce Steward, I think, continues to attend the meetings.[407] From my membership, however, I did get some valuable experiences, and contacts with a group very prominent in the organization with which otherwise I would have had little or nothing to do, the teaching Sisters in a number of Catholic colleges in the state.

Membership in a university committee provided me with more experience along the same line: the University High School Relations committee, on which I served for a number of years. Our main function was to visit private schools (usually though not always Catholic) which wanted university accreditation: that is, permission for their students to enter the university, as graduates of the public high schools did, without taking special entrance examinations. A team of five people or so would visit the school in question, attend classes, talk with the staff, make their recommendation (generally favorable in my experience, though once with a new school we have only a tentative approval subject to a re-visit by the same team the next year to check progress), and write up a very full report, of which a copy was sent to the school in question, and which was probably the most valuable part of the work. The schools varied greatly. One, in a tiny town over on the Mississippi, was so small the visiting team outnumbered the staff, and when Miss Emily Chervenik, who fortunately was along (I was usually the only woman: Miss Chervenik was head of University Placement, a very able woman I always enjoyed contacts with), inquired pleasantly, "Sister, where is the powder

---

407 Joyce Stribling Steward (1917–2004) completed doctoral studies in English at the University of Iowa and Yale University and taught English at two high schools in Madison—West (1951–1963) and La Follette (1963–1966). She was recruited by the UW-Madison English department to assist Thomas in composition instruction, first in the NDEA institute (1965), then in the department (1966), where she taught English 309 and literature courses. In 1969, Steward became the founding director of the University Writing Lab, which she directed until her retirement in 1982. She published one of the first books on writing centers: *The Writing Laboratory: Organization, Management, and Methods* (1982).

room?" the nun after a little pause indicated across a couple of open fields the little wooden shack you may see in state parks. At the other extreme was St. Francis Seminary in Milwaukee, obviously very well endowed, with so large a complex of buildings that each one of us was given a student to take us around all day to guide us wherever we wanted to go. I felt like a nurse in the South Pacific, being obviously the only creature of feminine gender around for miles. The Monsignor in charge, a man whom I have never seen surpassed and rarely equaled, in poise, courteously indicated to me on arrival that a certain bathroom near his office would be at my disposal throughout the day. Since Bill was a friend of Dean Zillman,[408] who was along on the trip, he will appreciate this story. Ted Zillman, out of his usual genial goodness of heart, inquired of the Monsignor if they ever had any social events, like dances, where girls came in for the evening. Without turning a hair, the Monsignor replied that since the boys were in training for a life of celibacy, it was thought they couldn't begin too soon. Poor man; he was not young then, and I could hope he is not around now to see what has happened to his church. For the most part, the other members of the visiting teams were School of Education faculty, with whom I'd had some contact when they were your teachers at Whisky High, and we were usually mildly glad to see other again. I forget now the name of the man who turned to me once in a music lesson, when the Sister told the girls she was going to play selections from *Peer Gynt*:[409] "You'll like that, won't you, girls?" and they all chorused joyfully, "Yes, Sister!" and said, "If the kids at Wisconsin High answered like that, I'd think they were sick," but I'm sure you all knew him. It was all interesting experience. One class I visited was the best I've ever seen anywhere in all my life, from the standpoint of student involvement. It was a class in advanced Latin, and the Sister was drilling on various verb forms. She would ask a question and get an answer, which might be right or might be wrong; she never gave away which. She would ask the same question over again of two or three other students, who might agree or disagree with the answer. And only then did she end the point. Every student in the room was thinking just as hard as he or she could every minute of the time. But you note that this was factual instruction, where there is a right or wrong answer to the proper form of the pluperfect. The instruction was always weak in history or social science, where the questions tended to be leading questions which could only be answered yes or no—the yes or no so clearly established by the form of the question that the student couldn't mistake it—or by one key word, and only one, which had to be inserted in a furnished sentence. The students rarely formed any sentences at all themselves. This was the sort of thing we used to deal with

---

408 Theodore W. Zillman was UW-Madison's Dean of Men (later Students) from 1944–1975 and president of the Phi Kappa Phi Honor Society (1971–1972).
409 *Peer Gynt* (1878) is a play by Norwegian dramatist Henrik Ibsen (1828–1906).

tactfully, in our reports. I doubt if any of the students we saw ever came to the university anyway. We generally took these trips in the early spring, as soon as the roads were clear; they were pleasant outings, and I enjoyed them.

Many of these years I taught in summer school, usually a workshop for high school teachers—work related, as you see, to my own course and very helpful for it. The group in 1956 was "very varied and interesting—from Main, Saskatchewan, Missouri, Louisiana, New York, Illinois (to name a few) and of course Wisconsin, and just as varied in the work they do, some with superior students wanting to get ideas for a program which will warrant exemption from college Freshman English from their graduates (private school) and another who teaches at the Oregon School for Girls, which, as you may remember, is a reformatory. Some of them have no experience at all and would believe anything you tell them, and others have had so much you can't tell them anything at all." In 1958 the workshop had 45 registrants, instead of the former 20. "Since I feel there should be plenty of individual conferences, that's the way I'm still doing it, but it takes more out of you to confer with 45 than with 20. I have a good variety, mostly Wisconsin with quite a few from Illinois and Ohio, but at least one apiece from Maine, New York, Connecticut, Arkansas, Ontario, Mississippi, Alabama, Montana, and California. I enjoy the work, and it is interesting to get in touch with what high schools are doing." These summers also I would often be in charge of a three-day conference on the teaching of English, and would involve a fairly big-name speaker and planning for a number of small workshops.

This work and experience made me the natural person to serve as director of one of the twenty Commission on English summer institutes in 1962. The Educational Testing Service began its program to improve the quality of high school English teaching by creating the Commission on English, under the direction of Floyd Rinker, who visited Wisconsin in the fall of 1960 to invite us to join. This movement mushroomed in the sixties, and through my involvement in it I met the national leaders in the field and had a modest amount of experience in travel and meetings. The first was a planning session of all directions at the Drake in Chicago that same fall. In the summer of 1961 all directors and teachers met for three weeks at the University of Michigan to establish a common curriculum to be offered on the twenty respective campuses in the summer of 1963. Three teachers came from each of the twenty institutions, for composition, literature, and language respectively (Tom Tanselle and Fred Cassidy[410] were Wisconsin's other representatives); and each group of twenty

---

410 Frederic G. Cassidy (1907–2000) earned the Ph.D. from the University of Michigan and began teaching at UW-Madison in 1939. In 1962, he became chief editor for the *Dictionary of American Regional English*.

was chaired by a nationally known expert: Albert Kitzhaber[411] for composition, Nelson Francis[412] for language, our own Helen White for literature.

I found the three weeks fatiguing, in spite of the fact that Bill, who was then stationed in Detroit, had time off my second Saturday, and came over to drive me around Detroit and have dinner with the Dodds. We lived and ate in the Michigan Union, and I was glad of the chance to get to know another Big Ten campus. (Ours, of course, is much better; we've got the lake.) "There were some interesting things about the session, but it was really too long and too confining and too exhausting. We had meetings morning, afternoon, and evening, and ate with each other in between times, and I got sick to death of the sight of everyone else, and most of all of myself. The only time I got out was for an hour or so before breakfast, when I would walk around the campus and the town alone to try to escape cabin fever.

We had speakers in the field, including both the then and now executive secretaries of the National Council of Teachers of English, but I regret to say that few of them struck me as having first class minds. An exception was Hal Martin[413] of Harvard, not only a brilliant man but a most impressive one physically, needing only an embroidered robe to walk straight on stage and play Tamberlane. He was an odd contrast to Floyd Rinker, almost a dwarf. I wish Martin had been in the composition group, where I'm sure Kitzhaber did his best but, I think, was deficient in leadership. Each group was expected to come up with a unanimous report, and it was thought there would be no difficulty in composition or literature but there might be trouble in language, since at this time the new linguistics was just developing. As it turned out, this was not the

---

411 Albert R. Kitzhaber (1915–2006) received his Ph.D. from the University of Washington (1953) and taught at the University of Oregon from 1962–1980. Kitzhaber conducted foundational research on the history and practices of teaching writing that contributed to the emergence of composition studies as an academic discipline, in particular his 1953 dissertation, *Rhetoric in American Colleges, 1850–1900*. In 1959, Kitzhaber chaired the Conference on College Composition and Communication (CCCC); in 1964, he was president of the National Council of Teachers of English (NCTE).

412 W. Nelson Francis (1910–2002), an American linguist specializing in corpus linguistics, received his Ph.D. from the University of Pennsylvania (1937) and taught at Brown University, where he co-compiled the Brown Corpus (1964), a one-million-word computerized cross section of American English.

413 Harold C. Martin (1917–2005), chair of the Commission on English, taught high school English and served as a principal before earning his Ph.D. from Harvard (1954). Martin directed Harvard's expository freshman English program, titled General Education A (later Gen Ed Ahf), from 1952–1964, then served as president of Union College (NY) from 1965–1974. His more popular publications included *The Logic and Rhetoric of Exposition* (1958) and *Inquiry and Expression: A College Reader* (1963), co-authored with English professor and former College English editor (1966–1978) Richard M. Ohmann (b. 1931).

case. Only the composition group could reach no common agreement and split right down the middle, ten to ten, and accordingly had to present two differing calendars, between which next summer each director could choose. Gossip said Hal Martin had been put with Helen because it was thought that, while her national reputation was unequalled, she was past her prime and might need help in handling her people. They underestimated her (Tom Tanselle told me stories about her skill) and overestimated Kitzhaber. Perhaps the fault was not his. The difference was a bed-rock one.

The split was between Aristotelians and Platonists. Coleridge says every man is one or the other.[414] I'm an Aristotelian, and told my Institute students so when they came in 1963. Here are some notes from my opening talk.

> The main need in the schools, the main need for the college preparatory student, and therefore our main need here is rhetoric rather than poetic, expository rather than creative pose. . . . The distinction is fundamental. Aristotle was the first to make it, and with differing turns of phrase, it has been repeated again and again. Read[415] says in *English Prose Style:* "Poetry is creative expression; prose is constructive expression. By creative I mean *original.* In poetry the words are born or re-born in the act of thinking. There is no time interval between the words and the thought. Constructive implies ready-made materials; words stacked round the builder, ready for use." According to Baldwin, "rhetoric is primarily intellectual, a progress from idea to idea determined logically: poetic is primarily imaginative, a progress from image to image determined emotionally."[416] For our work, the most fruitful approach is Aristotelian, and we will take for its basis his definition of rhetoric: "the art of discovering all the possible means of persuasion on any subject whatsoever." Our approach is intellectual, not intuitive. We will consider writing an affair in which the writer will consciously consider a great many possibilities—techniques if you like—and choose the best for his purpose.

This is the only kind of writing, I have always thought, though from this experience I learned more about my reasons, which can legitimately be taught.

---

414 The full quotation, from British Romantic Poet Samuel Taylor Colridge (1772–1834) as recorded in *Table Talk,* is, "Every man is born an Aristotelian, or a Platonist. I do not think it possible that any one born an Aristotelian can become a Platonist; and I am sure no born Platonist can ever change into an Aristotelian" (2 July 1830).
415 From English literary critic Herbert Edward Read's (1893–1968) *English Prose Style* (1928).
416 Charles Sears Baldwin (1867–1935), American professor of rhetoric. The quotation is from *Ancient Rhetoric and Poetic* (1924).

Construction

For creative writing, self-expression, you may establish a congenial atmosphere, as Hannah did with her fifth graders, but you can't teach it. It has, of course, its values, among them therapy. The man here who said his students wrote about "their love life and how they hate their parents" indicated this rather unkindly. But the poet is born, not made. However, you can make a good expository writer, with surprisingly few and simple principles and plenty of practice. (There are two places of greatest emphasis in any unit of writing, beginning and end; and of three, the end is the greater. What do you think is most important? Put it at the beginning or, preferably, the end, never in the emphatic middle. Do you want to show similarity of ideas? Cast them in similar form, which will emphasize both similarity and difference (see quotation from Baldwin). And so on. The acquisition of a skill is a consciously intellectual matter. This was always the basic approach in Freshman English, and the reason why all colleges of the university required the course of their students. Until I went to Michigan and did some of the reading, I had not realized how pervasive Aristotle's influence was. Porter Perrin, whose *Writer's Guide and Index to English* we used for many years, through four different editions, was an unabashed Aristotelian, in his basic writer-audience-situation organization.[417] The greatest benefit of the work to me, then, was a great deal of reading, largely though not solely in classical rhetoric, which, to be qualified for the work I was doing, I should have done years ago. This reading, and my attempts to get it under control so I could give the Institute members what of it was relevant—and astonishingly relevant! *everything* was there—freshened and stimulated my teaching for so many years that I was only beginning to run dry when I was rescued by retirement.

I learned something else from this experience. In the sense that I came into close personal contact with a considerable number of national leaders in my field, it was an initiation. And I think that one thing you learn from initiation is generally disillusionment. "Is this all? Are these the people I've been looking up to? Why, I can do as well as this myself."

A common such first experience, perhaps, is when a high school (or a college) senior holds a position (class president, editor-in-chief, whatever) which seemed the pinnacle of earthly achievement when he was a freshman. It happened to me there. It happened to me at my first Annual Meeting at the Island, where I was the youngest member of the Association because Uncle James had left me the cottage. Although more slowly, it happened to me as I moved up into the department.

---

[417] Porter G. Perrin (1896–1962) earned his Ph.D. from the University of Chicago (1936), where he was trained in rhetoric, and was president of the National Council of Teachers of English (NCTE) in 1947. During the late 1940s and early 1950s, Perrin taught graduate courses in rhetoric in the English department at the University of Washington, where he trained Albert R. Kitzhaber (1915–2006), a pioneering scholar in composition and rhetoric.

Partly because of my essential naiveté, partly because of my lack of the Ph.D., I had been humble and silent when I attended department committee meetings as instructor, Executive Committee meetings as tenured professor, finally the Council of Full Professors. Not until the late sixties, when the juniors in the department were crazy and many of the seniors cowed if not crazy themselves, did I begin to stand up and talk myself. The Michigan experience fits well into the pattern. I met and talked with a variety of national leaders in the field, and thereafter repeatedly encountered in my professional reading articles written by people I could say I knew. And for many—not all—I felt "Is this all?" I never lost so much touch with reality that I didn't retain a deep respect and admiration for many undoubtedly by far my intellectual superiors: Helen White, Ruth Wallerstein, Madeleine Doren (to name only women) at Wisconsin; Hal Martin at Michigan.[418] I don't mean to over-simplify. Not only the quality of mind but also temperament has to be taken into effect in making a judgment. To be really effective you need patience and understanding, which I think would lead me to rank Helen White above Ruth Wallerstein, with all her greater brilliance and keenness. The people I met at Michigan had had a good deal of experience working with others and had developed attributes not to be despised. But there were fewer than I expected at whose feet, shall we say, I would have thought it a privilege to sit.

This raises a question for which I have no answer. But I'm sure it is a contemporary problem which applies today in many fields besides teaching: loss of contact between the influential men at the top of a profession and the actual person for whose benefit the profession exists. It occurs outside professions: the rental car is an example from my own experience. I commented to Hannah on the fact that the girl at the Philly airport couldn't have cared less what happened to me and hardly saw I was there, while the publicity for the concern presented their girls as breathlessly dedicated to the welfare and happiness of each customer. "The trouble is," said she, "that the good people go right on up the line in the organization, and the ones that the public has the contact with are the ones who don't give a damn." This has been much spoken of in the profession of medicine, where the patient, even to diagnosis, is increasingly handled by machine. My point is that the doctor and the nurse are lessened as their firsthand contact with the patient lessens. Many of the people I met at Michigan spent more and more time in meetings and conferences from O'Hare to Washington, from Boston to Hawaii, and less and less in the classroom with students. I have a feeling—there is no basis for this beyond just that, "a feeling"—that the born

---

418 Harold C. Martin received an A.M. degree from the University of Michigan in 1942, but, as noted earlier in this chapter, he taught at Harvard (1951–1964). Thomas must be referring to the location of the Commission on English institute, which was held at the University of Michigan and which Martin chaired.

teacher, the true teacher, the real teacher just wants to be with students. And yet, on the other hand, the days of Mr. Chips and Miss Dove are long gone. I doubt if in the whole country today there are living more than twenty, perhaps, of the old battle-ax type (to which I humbly aspire to belong) who made her students work and cared that they should learn something, and didn't care whether they liked her or not, and on whom the big-city executive always calls when, once in ten or fifteen years or so, he comes back to the home town. Another manifestation of the basic problem of our times: size.

My disillusionment was just a normal part of growing up. The only remarkable thing is that I should have had it so late. It continually strikes me, as I write these pages, how often I am years off in having an ordinary experience. But it would not be right to denigrate the work of the Commission and its successors. On the whole, it must have broadened and improved the teaching of many persons, as, for that matter, it did mine. A number of publications sponsored by the Commission are basically sound and valuable. At least they took a stand for some discipline and against permissiveness, and when the pendulum swings back, as inevitably it will do, they may be revived. Their best-known work was *Freedom and Discipline in the Teaching of English*. After all, everyone agrees you must have both. The difference is between those who think that freedom leads you to discipline, and those who think that discipline leads you to freedom, I'm one of the second group—i.e., an Aristotelian.

Tom Tanselle and Fred Cassidy and I worked hard the next spring making our selections from the applications. Forty-five students were to be taken. Each institute was supposed to service local needs; roughly speaking, you were confined to applicants within a radius of fifty miles. This was not to be taken literally. Milwaukee was considered within our radius, for instance, while with some New England districts very thickly studded with colleges, the distance was much less than fifty, and with some Far Western districts very thinly settled, it was a great deal more. The attempt was to cover the nation; the participating institutions were Cornell, Duke, Harvard, Indiana, New York, Ohio State, Pennsylvania State, Rutgers, St. Louis, Southern Illinois, Stanford, State University of New York—College of Education, Albany, Tulane, and the Universities of California, Michigan, Nevada, Pittsburgh, Texas, Washington, and Wisconsin. We were confined to the state (and for this reason I found the institute itself less stimulating than the NDEA[419] one I directed in 1965, where there was no geographical limitation on applications, and where therefore we had much more variety.) "I

---

419 The National Defense Education Act (NDEA) was passed by U.S. Congress in 1958 in the wake of Sputnik to direct funds to educational areas deemed significant for national security. Initially directed towards science and math, the Act was amended in 1964 to include a broader range of subjects, including the humanities.

never worked harder in my life than I am doing on this Institute, mainly because I started having individual conferences with the 45 teachers on their writing and found they needed the conferences so much that I don't do anything else, except of course conduct the classes. I am putting in about an 80-hour week, and this is exhausting. It is a very odd sensation; I sleep in my own bed every night, but really it is like nothing so much as being on an ocean liner with that forced and sudden intimacy that you have with a group of perfect strangers; I can't think about anything else. Obviously I have little waking time to do so." (Incidentally, this was the year when Katherine Anne Porter's *Ship of Fools* was the national best-seller.) Tom Tanselle, who was the literature teacher and the staff member who during the fall semester visited every institute member in the latter's own classroom—an important provision in the Commission's original plan to see how the influence was spreading—was a never-failing support. He was also a great help when visiting firemen from the Commission itself or from the Office of Education turned up and had to be entertained. One of the latter was a personal friend of Bob Pooley's, Donald Tuttle. Fred Cassidy flew to Africa in the middle of the Institute to attend a conference on the linguistic problems confronting the emerging nations. Should they deny their heritage by establishing an official language, presumably English, entirely alien to them but understandable to the world at large; or should they choose one tribal dialect from among many for patriotic reasons, which no one outside the country, and few in it, would comprehend? He gave a talk to us all when he got back which must have broadened the students' scope, even if they had to have a substitute for him for a few days in their own curriculum.

There were some sticky problems about these institutes. First was the question of graduate credit. The Commission was anxious that this should be granted all institute members for prestige reasons, but many institutions, Wisconsin among them, were reluctant to give it—and rightly so, I think, for the work we were giving them was not the kind that would be accepted for the Master's, which here as in most graduate schools is simply the first station on the road to the Doctorate. There might well be another kind of road for teachers to take who mean to stay in high school and not go into college work, as far as that goes. This was a serious difficulty, in any case; I don't know just what kind of compromise Ed Lacy worked out, but he did work out some. Among my students both in '62 and '65, some took this first opportunity to do graduate work as the entering wedge to do more, and therefore cut themselves off from high school teaching, for whose betterment the program was designed. To that extent high school teaching was weakened rather than strengthened. But I'm not sure the numbers were significant. The only participant in this category from whom I still hear at Christmas went on and got his doctorate at Illinois. He was an excellent student and probably would have done well in the college field from the beginning.

Another problem was that of the workshop: should the institute include one, who should handle it, what should be demanded of its products. This had been much discussed at Michigan, but no solution had been reached. I solicited criticisms of our institute at the end, signed or anonymous as participants chose, and there is remarkable unanimity among those I received. Our main strength, according to them, was the excellence of instruction. "The teachers have handled their subjects with skill, often with brilliance. While the composition class seems to me to be the one most immediately rewarding, the content and experience gained in the others cannot help but be beneficial to me. I am grateful to all three teachers for a valuable learning experience. "It was a privilege to see three master teachers sing three different approaches yet at the same time effectively coordinating their efforts." "Our instructors were outstanding. We were fortunate in having people so interested in *our* understanding." "I have had excellent teachers, have enjoyed my work (hard though it was), and appreciated the opportunities to meet with them socially. I appreciate the great amount of effort that each member of the faculty has put forth." "I sincerely feel that we were fortunate to have had such outstanding teachers; each of them was always interesting; and I learned a great deal about the process of teaching itself, as well as about language, literature and composition." There was also general agreement that the planning and organization of the institute were excellent. There was also general agreement that the workshops were completely unsatisfactory. In 1962 everyone did come up with some sort of project—many of them pretty feeble—and everyone went home with a copy of all of them. As the clerk in the Circumlocution Office says in reference to Arthur Clennam, "Give him a lot of forms."[420] (I was reminded of the comment of one of our very intelligent teaching assistants, when I asked her how a certain project was going in her class. "The good ones are doing it well, and the poor ones are doing it badly," she answered.) In 1965 I left out the whole thing, and I really think this was the answer. In a limited time, and, everybody felt, under mounting pressure, it was not possible to combine satisfactorily the substance of the courses and workshop work. There's always been some divergence (not only here but in other contacts I've had, such as WCTE) between the high school teacher who says "I want you tell me exactly what to do in my classroom at such-and-such a time on such-and-such a day," and the university teacher who says, "I won't plan your curriculum for you but if you will attend to the work and theory I'm giving you, you will improve your own power to do it for yourself." We did not get enough direction

---

420   A reference to characters in Charles Dickens's novel *Little Dorrit* (1857).

on this point at Michigan, surely. Perhaps the solution would have been a week or two of workshop after the original institute for such as wanted it; but this would have brought up a whole host of problems, especially financial ones.

The Commission on English movement mushroomed. In 1964 the NDEA Act was extended to a number of new fields, including English. Applications were invited on a very general scale, not to be confined to this stock tripod curriculum but tailored to a variety of needs and situations. The department wanted to apply again, did so, and was successful. "We have had to make out the application, which is *very* complicated, in a tremendous rush to meet the deadline, which is December 30; naturally everyone wants to be doing something else on the 25th at least, and this has to be signed by practically every official in the university except the Bascom janitor, and why they left him out I don't know." This meant another trip for me—going to Washington in March for a big meeting of all directors; I'm sure well over a hundred institutes were awarded. "The trip was rather wasted one, I'm afraid. I'll bet you a small sum that when I turned in thirty cents for lunch (a cup of coffee out of the coffee machine, a cup of chocolate, and a package of rye crackers, each ten cents) instead of going out on the Office of Education to a restaurant, I turned in the smallest sum for a meal ever turned in on a federal expense account." Though as usual I get little out of the public meetings, I did enjoy seeing some of our former teaching assistants, now scattered over the country from California to Maine, who had also been successful in their applications, and talking with them.

The Institute duly took place the next summer, and was, I think, more successful than the first one, since I was more on my own and had learned something from the previous experience. I had a new staff, which included Joyce Steward, added as liaison officer between high school and college, as well as to share the composition work. I was doubling as director and composition instructor, of which the authorities took a rather dim view, since each was presumably a full-time job, so she was to assist me in both capacities. I had had some contacts with her before, when we were both involved in a project for superior high school Madison students who might by special work be able to by-pass Freshman English, but this summer was the beginning of a close relationship, and led, incidentally, to her being appointed a department member who has taken over my place. Personally, it was luck for me as I grew older to make a new, younger friend.

One excellent provision of the NDEA, which had not been in effect in the Commission on English, was that not only was the actual participant subsidized but also his dependents. This allowed a man with a family to apply who could not have afforded to do so if only his own expenses had been available. We had, for instance, a man from Sheboygan with four children. The summer before he had run an ice-cream wagon; I think his work with us made a more relevant contribution to his teaching. Perhaps because of this provision, and perhaps because of growing public interest, we had a much greater number of applicants this time, ten for every place, and as a result a better group. We were not limited to our own state as we had been before, so participants came from California, Florida, Illinois, Indiana, Massachusetts, Minnesota, Missouri, New York and Tennessee as well as Wisconsin. We had 23 men, 16 women; 24 married, 15 single; 27 with the Master's, though only 10 of these had it in English, the others being in Philosophy, Theology (the best member of the group was a Jesuit priest from a private boys' school in Massachusetts), Education, Physical Education, Political Science, Library Science, School Administration, etc.); 35 from public schools, 4 from private; 2 from schools with enrollment 100–499; 4, 500–999; 16, 1000–1499; 8, 1500–1999; 9, 2000–3999; 5 in the age range 25–29; 10, 30–34; 13, 35–39; 7, 40–44; 1, 45–49; 3, 50–54; 6 had teaching experience of 4–5 years; 13, 6–10; 20 more than 10. Thirty-five worked for academic credit, and 4 wanted none. Since NDEA Institute credit at Wisconsin was not applicable to UW-Madison advanced degrees (this must have been the compromise Ed worked out), none of them were working for advanced degrees here. We had two Blacks—though that statistic did not appear in my formal report. This added up to a varied and stimulating group. I still exchange Christmas cards with a number of them.

In 1962 we had recommended but not required that participants live on campus. In 1965 we required it. This was another advantage, since it fostered group solidarity. Some of the women, including our three nuns, lived in Chadborne; but most of the group lived in the dormitories by the lake shore, where there was a common dining room for men and women. In order to prevent the kind of claustrophobia I had felt at Michigan, I worked out an Extra-Curricular and Recreational Calendar as well as an academic one for each discipline, in which Frost Woods, of course, figured heavily. So many of the members had their own cars that there was no transportation problem. We began with a "get-acquainted picnic supper" here and ended with a farewell picnic lunch, at which certificates of completion were presented, and every Friday afternoon at 4 we had a "weekly social hour" here. The Residence Halls scheduled tours to Wisconsin Dells, Blue Mounds, and the like, and boat trips on Lake Mendota, which usually occurred Saturdays. Every Monday we all had dinner together in the Hall where I shamelessly exploited my friends (Helen White, Fred Cassidy, Bob Pooley) so the Institute members could meet socially some of Wisconsin's VIP's and talk informally with them afterwards. At the get-acquainted meeting we were all happily eating and chatting in the backyard when a Monona policeman appeared, to my surprise, to inform me that he had seen a boy take a purse out of one of the cars parked in the park strip. It belonged to one of the nuns, and had in it her entire stipend money. She had cashed her check that afternoon and brought it along with her, the sheltered innocent. The Jesuit priest appeared in his regimentals at the farewell picnic: he had been wearing shorts and a sport shirt all summer, and when he turned up to get his registration material I blurted out, "*Father Kelly?*" in astonishment. I provided a huge bowl of shrimp for the Catholics, and it looked so good that the Protestants nearly emptied it before the Catholics could get to it.

> It ended on August 6 and ended very well in a general glow of warm feelings. It was a lot of work, but I feel it was worth it, and everyone else seemed to too. The participants gave all the staff very sweetly chosen presents, and then dispersed. I had keyed every nerve for so long to getting through August 6 that when it was over I felt like those people who believe the end of the world is coming and sell their houses and all their possessions and go up into the mountain to meet Judgment Day; and then Judgment Day doesn't come and they have to come down again and take up their lives. I had a lot of work to do, which I'm still doing, annotating the final papers which were turned in on the last day and are to be sent back by mail, writing up my report for the Office of Education, getting things ready for the fall.

In September I was required to attend a meeting of all NDEA English directors at the University of Colorado.

> Colorado was the first of *four* successive weekends in which I was attending a conference on the teaching of English, at two of which I spoke—and a lot easier to speak yourself than to hear other people, I must say. Colorado was the only one out of the state, but what with modern air travel it didn't take so much longer to go there than it did to drive to some of the places in the state. Colorado was beautiful, and I wish I had had time to stay a little longer and see more of the scenery. But I had a real stroke of luck Saturday night. The conference ended at 4 p.m., and since it was impossible for me to get back to Madison that night, I had to stay over. One of our former teaching assistances is now on the Colorado faculty, so he and his wife very kindly took me out for a drive in the mountains and then gave me dinner at their house, which is

right on a canyon. From the kitchen window she looks out on the face of the cliff about six feet away, with mountain plants growing in the crevices, and they have a mountain stream, complete with trout, in their front yard. They have no problem about cutting grass, because they have no grass.

This was my last national meeting, and my last encounter with people I'd first met through the Commission: James Squire,[421] Robert Hogan (former and current NCTE Executive Secretaries),[422] Donald Tuttle (Office of Education), Albert Kitzhaber and many others. I knew I wasn't going to do any more summer work. The fact that I was at Colorado points up the problem of conflicting interests between federal grants and institutes and basic university work. Ed Lacy, a very busy man, had had to give hours and hours to the details of these projects. The department had not been particularly happy about releasing a third of Tom Tanselle's time the first semester after the 1962 Institute for him to visit all participants in their classrooms. The Colorado conference started Thursday of our registration week. I did as much as I could before I left and handed over to Bill Lenehan; even now it warms my heart to think of the relief and joy with which his face lighted up when he saw me back on Monday. This work was rather a sideline with the department anyway. They wanted to pick up a grant or two if any was lying around, and felt an obligation to be involved in a significant movement. But honor was now satisfied. I myself felt I would need Island summers to generate energy for regular work, and no one wanted to take my place. Federal money obviously meant a lot of time and effort on the part of some members of your faculty whom you might need more for their own homework. So I withdrew from the national scene (nor was I missed) and confined myself thereafter to the campus.

Two jobs outside the department were good experience for me in this period. The first was membership for a number of years on the Residence Halls Faculty Committee. The whole committee, a large body chaired by Dean Luberg,[423] met seldom, but my subcommittee, Men's Residence Halls, met frequently, most of the time to interview prospective house fellows.[424] (Wright had held

---

421 James R. Squire was executive secretary of the National Council of Teachers of English from 1960–1967.
422 Robert F. Hogan was executive secretary (1968–1977) and executive director (1977–1981) of NCTE.
423 Leroy E. Luberg (1908–1982) was an assistant to the president and Dean of Students at UW-Madison (1946–1973).
424 A house fellow was a graduate student who lived in an undergraduate residence hall and was part of the staff.

this position the first year the dormitories were occupied.) We consisted of half a dozen men and one woman, and we met for lunch in the Schlichter cafeteria before we started business. I gained great respect for Newell Smith, Residence Halls director, who met with us, and I bracket him with Ed Lacy as the two of all the servants of the university I have known here as most useful and best adapted to their positions. I gained great respect also for Paul Ginsberg,[425] now a dean, then in charge of house fellows. At the interviews I didn't ask many questions myself, but I found them an interesting chance to study human nature (as Rebecca of Sunnybrook Farm[426] found the train), and I saw so much of my own department it was always a relief to have some contacts outside it. Ex officio, we were invited to the orientation banquet for new house fellows every fall, and to the banquet given to honor out-going house officers every spring, where we had steak ("and the University of Wisconsin can give you as good steak as anywhere in the world"). In fact, when a student once asked me why I liked serving on the committee, I told him it was because I got so much free food. I'd meet and talk with people like Dean Ruedisili,[427] who very sportingly congratulated me on Bill's having defeated his son Lon (whom Chet had spent a lot of time coaching) for city tennis champion. The Residence Halls staff were all dedicated to making dormitory life more than board and room; valuable character-building experience. Other times, other customs. With the exception of a few places reserved by state legislative action for foreign students, the dormitories were primarily for Wisconsin residents, who had priority. Since through Bill I saw something of Greek life on Langdon, it gave me a better-balanced overall view of the university to have a chance to see this other segment of the population. One statement often made of Wisconsin during this time was that it was unusually fortunate in that the student body divided into three approximately equal groups: Greeks, dormitories, independents. That no group dominated and that everyone had a chance to find a congenial place meant a healthy atmosphere.

The other job was secretary of Alpha of Wisconsin of Phi Beta Kappa, which I held for about ten years. This also involved some travel, since the secretary is always sent to the triennial convention. Unfortunately, the first year I was

---

425 Paul Ginsberg (1925–2015) earned undergraduate and graduate degrees from UW-Madison and worked in student life for nearly 40 years, including as Dean of Students (1970–1987).

426 *Rebecca of Sunnybrook Farm* (1903) is a children's novel by American educator and writer Kate Douglas Wiggin (1856–1923).

427 Chester H. Ruedisili (1910–2002) received his Ph.D. from UW-Madison (1941) and worked there for nearly forty-five years (1936–1980), serving as assistant and associate dean of students and teaching part-time in the psychology department.

committed to the Commission on English planning session; and I was the more disappointed because the convention was held in Salt Lake City, an exotic place for me which I would have liked to see and now never shall. The next meeting was at Burlington, Vermont, a part of the country I already knew, though I had the fun of flying back to Madison with Helen White, for many years a Phi Beta Kappa senator, which was rather like traveling with Queen Elizabeth; and the next at Duke, a new part of the country to me, where I saw not only the Duke campus but also Chapel Hill and went to the planetarium there. At home, as is usually the case in this kind of thing, the secretary provided continuity and did all the work. The presidency was an honorific office, changing each year. It gave me contact with friends like Gaines Post,[428] whose wife was a member of Reading Group, as well as with men known nationally and internationally, such as David Fellman[429] and Farrington Daniels,[430] the distinguished expert on solar energy, who incidentally was always in the Galapagos Islands or some such place when I needed to have him sign a letter. The work was really confined to a few weeks in the spring, when we held the annual elections and have the annual banquet to honor the new members. The speakers were often distinguished, like Howard Mumford Jones.[431] One pleasure for a number of years was coming in contact with former English 11 students. And each time I loved to take my place behind the table on the stage in the Play Circle, where the initiation took place, with the certificates of membership ready to hand out, see the initiates files in and take their places, and then look down the rows of keen-eyed young men and women.

All this time I counted high among my blessings—and I think among my services to the department—the fact that Ham had built a distinctive house in a beautiful setting. I had an ideal place to entertain large or small groups, and a remarkably flexible one, which seemed automatically to expand or contract to suit the guests. It was off the beaten university track, which did mean some problems about transportation; but when people got out the novelty made them feel as if they had taken a refreshing trip to the country. You could feel many

---

428 Gaines Post (1902–1987) received his Ph.D. at Harvard (1931) and taught in the UW-Madison history department (1935–1964). He finished his career at Princeton University (1964–1970).

429 David Fellman (1907–2003), a political scientist and constitutional scholar, received his Ph.D. from Yale University (1934) and taught at UW-Madison for the majority of his career (1947–1979).

430 Farrington Daniels (1889–1972), a pioneer in solar energy research, was a professor of chemistry at UW-Madison (1920–1959) and directed the university's Solar Energy Laboratory.

431 Howard Mumford Jones (1892–1980), a Pulitzer Prize-Winning American intellectual historian and English professor at Harvard, graduated from UW-Madison in 1914.

more miles away from the university than you actually were. No one else in the department ever had a house or grounds large enough to accommodate senior and junior staff together; I did so for many years. At first, we had a baseball game and picnic supper. But as the wives of the men on the Freshman English policy committee,[432] who helped with the food, began to get a little restive at the work, as numbers grew, and as Margaret quite rightly felt Ed was too tired for entertaining so soon, we changed to a reception for everyone Sunday afternoon a week or two later.

> Helen [White], in her big way, thought how nice it would be to include the members of the English Department at Milwaukee now that they are officially part of the university; and there is no doubt that she was absolutely right and they were very pleased—so pleased that carload after carload of them kept coming. I had laid in 180 paper cups and plates, and there were only two left. That doesn't mean 178 people came, though, since many people told me happily that they had both coffee etc. (served in the dining room) and cider etc. (served in the rumpus room). (The etc. always included my orange bread, for which twenty years later I'm still getting compliments on Christmas cards.) But I'm pretty sure there were more than 150. It was a beautiful day, and we had the receiving line out on the front lawn, and then they went in the house either by the front door or the back and then they wandered down by the lake and then they came back and went in the house either by the back door or the front and then they went home. I want you to tell Ham how wonderfully he planned the house (when I doubt if he had functions of this sort in mind). There must be few places where you can handle so many so comfortably and yet don't seem at all big or empty when there are only two people in it. The secret is using the back door for access to the rumpus room. The room is such fun to decorate—it responds wonderfully to very little work. All I have to do is go outdoors and pick branches or shrubs at random and put them around, and the result is a beautiful bower.

---

432 Members of the Freshman English Policy Committee were Ed Lacy (chair), Thomas, Robert Doremus, Robert Pooley, and George Rodman. Fleming (2011) notes that this committee, under Thomas and Lacy's direction, managed a curriculum that "literally did not change for more than two decades" (pp. 51–52).

Construction

Even without the Milwaukee people, we would generally have a couple of hundred guests from our own campus. We worried about the weather, but on the only occasion I remember out of twenty years or so that we had a bad day,

> it turned out not to be so bad when it actually happened. I solved the main problem when I realized people could hang their coats in the garage and leave their umbrellas there. To have 200 people trying to put coats in my bedrooms, blocking the stairs, would have been impossible, but those overhead garage doors have a frame which runs across the ceiling, so I just spread hangers along that. Then we had the receiving line in the rumpus room, and people went upstairs for coffee. I really think they saw more of each other than they generally do outdoors. When they go out in small groups to look around the yard, they sort of melt away to their cars; but when they stayed in, there was more chance to visit. They stayed and stayed; in fact, many were still happily talking when a couple of my friends began to move the furniture back from the addition, where it had been moved for the afternoon, and with that delicate hint they did begin to get the idea that it was time to leave. I had a note of thanks in which the girl said my house was "amazingly expansive," and I think indeed it is.

A basic reason for the success of these big department parties was that the senior members cooperated gallantly in welcoming new assistants. Margaret got the wives to take stints not only in pouring but also in "mingling." Often in this kind of thing, especially after the summer when people haven't seen each other, old friends fall into each other's arms and newcomers stand in isolation looking out the window. But these mixers really mixed, and the teaching assistants would go away feeling they had joined one big happy family. Once we ran out of cider, into which we had put dry ice, which steams in a fascinating Halloween effect, and Ed picked up some grape juice at the nearest grocery to finish up the afternoon. Due to a chemical reaction which is still a mystery to us, the grape juice when poured over the dry ice not only foamed up but crawled out of the punch bowl over the table cloth and the floor. What more typically family style than such a mishap?

One department party which did not include the assistants I gave in honor of the Lacys in January, 1957, when they were to spend the second semester in England. Cocktail parties have never been in my line, and I took advantage of their destination to have the novelty of a real English tea.

Construction

The food went very well: bread and butter, with different kinds of jams for people to choose from; cucumber, tomato, anchovy sandwiches; gooseberry tarts; fruitcake; hot buttered scones; chocolates; and of course the tea. I used my grandmother's tea set and my white and gold china, and not a thing was chipped or broken. The feature was all the pictures from your *Punches*[433] which I had collected through Christmas vacation—cartoons, poems and parodies, political pieces, ads, all sorts of things for local color. I put them on the walls all over the living room and the rumpus room where people put their things. Bill opened the door and told them where to go and was very helpful. Everyone went around and looked at the *Punch* pictures and laughed and talked about them; and I'm sure they had a good time because they stayed and stayed. Practically everyone spoke to me in Bascom the next day about what a nice party it was. The prize remark, however (reported but not made to me, so I'm not sure by whom) was "Isn't it nice to be at Ednah's without the assistants."

But I wanted the assistants. And I wanted to have them all—though of course not necessarily all at once. But I didn't want to have favorites, as Charlotte [Wood] had had. It was legitimate to have Elizabeth Brinkman convalesce here for a couple of weeks where she came back from the Mayo Clinic; it was legitimate to have the members of the Achievement Test committee come to dinner for our last meeting. But my aim was to give every teaching assistant, and also every wife, an opportunity once during the year to come out on a purely social friendly occasion. This was quite a problem. On what basis should I invite whom, and when, and with whom? And how about transportation, which many people didn't have? I never got the real solution until it turned out to be built into the Master Teaching Assistant Program. But I kept working on it. I had different kinds of parties—everything that occurred to me. When I spent the summer here, there were comparatively so few teaching assistants on the staff that two or three picnics took care of them all. Once I had a party for mothers to bring their babies to show each other (which Bob Pooley, a shameless punster, told me he was sure would be a howling success). Christmas, of course, is a very good time for parties. Most of the staff went out of town during the vacation itself, so I could easily handle a supper party for the ones who were here. The

---

433 *Punch*, or the *London Charivari*, was a British weekly satirical magazine established in 1841; its circulation peaked in the 1940s.

year Bill was abroad and I had been East for Tom and Diane's wedding, Twelfth Night came at the end of the vacation, which is very unusual, and I gave a Twelfth Night party—a festivity few have attended. "I got home feeling that quite a bit had happened in the vacation and rather sorry I had committed myself to fifty or sixty people for tonight. But luckily I found Bill's package, which had not arrived before I left, and he sent me such lovely Christmas things, a beautiful molded Bavarian candle and little copper candle holders and so on, that my Christmas spirit blazed up again brightly, and I was delighted to be able to show them off." If I wanted to include the whole staff at Christmas, though, I had to start so early in December that my Christmas spirit had to burn for a solid month—too long. Our ancestors knew what they were doing when they set the twelve days. The house really won't hold more than eighty for singing, say, so I had to have a series. Ed Lacy, I think, viewed my hospitality with some reservations; he thought the assistants might feel coerced into coming in order not to offend the Establishment. But the invitations were pure social invitations; anyone was free to refuse or accept. One man certainly did not feel coerced: "Dear Mrs. Thomas: Thank you for your invitation to the Christmas party, but to tell you the truth I never go to parties. I haven't been to a party for twenty years. Sincerely yours." But the majority did come and enjoyed themselves. Those strong young voices produced the best singing the house has ever known. One wife had a perfectly beautiful voice, really professional (she went over to Minneapolis for the Met try-outs) and she took us all with her. I particularly like to remember a Jewish girl smiling into my eyes as I sat at the piano and she stood on the upper stair at the back of the group engaged in a spirited rendering of "It Came Upon the Midnight Clear." (She was the one who wrote Ed Lacy after she left, "I've griped a lot about your program while I was here but I'm damned if I can see now any way it could be improved and I'm glad I had it." He wrote back, "Thank you for your gentle letter.")

In the last years before the guns began to roar, I was entertaining twenty-five or thirty people every Sunday evening, usually teaching assistants, but as a carry-over from Holyoke I always to the end of my teaching asked my own students to my home for a social occasion once during the semester. "One good thing: I used to think having twenty-five students was a little work, but it is nothing by comparison with the assistants. I give the students a picnic meal that is finger food—hamburger on buns and so on, and the assistants have to have trays and forks and real meals. The students will sit on the floor but the assistants have to have chairs. It is like the woman who had eight children starting with twins, which were so much work that all the rest of the family was like rolling off a log." I got quite proficient at catering for thirty, knew my quantities, and the easiest way to do everything. I specialized in mince tarts, bite-size, pastry made the day before, slipped into the oven on a cookie tray when I took out the casserole, so they were warm when I carried them around. "Every Sunday afternoon I feel, as I always do before any party, that I must have been out of my mind to get trapped into this, and I am sick of filling huge bowls of food. But it's either all or none, of course, and I'm not willing to have it none. Then they come and they laugh and talk and have a good time, and I enjoy myself too, and when they leave I feel good about the whole thing." These amenities ended in the era of tear gas and National Guard and riots to be described in the next chapter. But for many years young men and women in a junior capacity in the department came into the home of a senior member who wanted and enjoyed them; and if I look back on these years with some nostalgia, so, I know, do they.

Hannah had gone to college before I really got into the swing of what the Madison Friends of International Students[434] call "home hospitality." But as long as they were at home, the boys supported me nobly, with my own students and with the assistants, and they helped to make it seem like a visit to a real family. I know they are part of the nostalgic memories of many of our guests—Bill more than Tom, of course, simply because he was around so much longer, not only while he was in high school but also in college or even after. I think I had a unique advantage, as a single-woman university professor, in having not only the house fronting the lake but also two attractive sons growing from boyhood to manhood, who played baseball, passed food, and made guests welcome.

As is true with any teacher, the recipients of my efforts flowed in an ever-changing stream. I never taught any but semester classes; the summer institutes lasted six weeks only; and while I saw something of teaching assistants after their first year, always at least in registration week, many in special course or committee work, the period of greatest contact was their first two semesters. I have described the moment that began each new year. The close, I think, though I was observing and not participating, was Commencement Day. I've only been to two Commencements here, Alice Ream's and Bill's so it wasn't, for me, the ceremony. It was standing in the window of my office in Bascom, where I generally had work to do that day, locking out on the Lincoln Terrace after the ceremony, watching the little groups lined up to get the photograph for the family album of the son or daughter in cap and gown with the parents in front of the statue. This always seemed poignant to me; it was the definitive break with home.

And for every class I had, there was a beginning and an end. In the beginning I went into the classroom to introduce myself and the course to a group

---

[434] This organization, now a non-profit, aims to connect international college students in the Madison area with local residents to promote cultural exchange and global friendships.

of strangers, neither friendly nor hostile but reserving judgment, giving nothing away. I loved to see that guarded look give way to confidence and ease after I had done my stunt of calling everyone by name and we had talked together for a meeting or two. And the ending was the last few minutes of the final examination, when each student, one by one, came up to put the bluebook on the desk before me—often without speaking, sometimes with a word of thanks or goodbye. As each walked out of the room, I knew I might never see him or her again, and I felt I was losing a little part of myself. Dean Ingraham's son was a student of mind in English all his freshman year. The year of his graduation I ran across his father at a social affair and asked for him. "Edward spoke of you when we were talking about his college experience," Mr. Ingraham said. "He said you would always be a little part of him."

This is what it is to be a teacher. And the teaching assistants were my students as much as, if not more than, those actually enrolled in my courses. It is for this reason, perhaps, that my grandchildren have not occupied the place in my life that apparently they do in the lives of many. I love, admire, and respect my grandchildren, look forward to knowing them better and better as they grow older and older, and I cannot conceive of any more promising and attractive group. But I do not depend upon them alone for my immortality.

During these years, the lives of the four of us diverged but of course were not severed. There is no pang like that when the first child leaves home; it is an end. It was not so painful for me with you boys. Tom—let's face it—was a late bloomer, and I hoped a new place would furnish him with the stimulus he hadn't found at Wisconsin High. And nothing could be gentler than Bill's transition. Though ostensibly living at home his first year, he spent so much time at the Chi Phi house that there was not much difference the next year, particularly since the house didn't serve Sunday meals, and he was always home then to eat dinner, do his laundry, and bring back my car, which he had used for weekend dating.

And when a child comes home again to visit, this is a beginning—the beginning of infinitely varied experiences including your visits to your children as well as theirs to you. Hannah came home for the first time at Christmas, and I was glad because it made that Christmas special, and I could happily write a whole book just about my Christmases. In fact, I think I'll take advantage of the chance to devote this part of the chapter to them.

Many of my friends were sharing the experience of having the first home-coming of son or daughter away at college.

> Everybody had a terrific time getting home—I mean all the kids away at college—because it was just when Chicago was so jammed with the storm. I met only two trains before Hannah got here, but the station was like Old Home Week, with parents coming for one train, and coming again the next, and so on, all reuning together until their children arrived. I had a very nice visit with Grace Frautschi, whom I hadn't seen for years. Stephen had been sick in the Harvard Infirmary, and they were doubtful about letting him travel, so I felt especially sorry for her; she had to meet four trains before he got in, but he is all right now. Robin Pooley was going to fly, but the flight was canceled, so he had to sit up two nights on the train and got in at 4 a.m. thirty-six hours after he was expected.

Robin, you may remember, went to William and Mary for a couple of years. I can hear Paul Fulcher now when I told him where Robin was going. "I wonder why he chose that," said Paul. "Why not?" said I. "Well," said Paul, "it's very old." He made the kind of pause that Mark Twain believes is the essence of humor, and then added, "And it isn't very good." This year I did have to face the fact that we could no longer do our family mass-production Christmas cards. We had faked the picture on this year's by photographing Hannah before she left, as if she were carrying her suitcase home to her welcoming family, and I faked her signature, but obviously this couldn't go on. I have made my own Christmas cards ever since and enjoy the activity very much; but if I were asked to name the single item in my child-rearing I thought most successful, it would be the mass-production cards, and I was sorry the time had come to give them up.

Tom's first Christmas home from college was 1953. "Bill and I have been so quiet here together that I had forgotten what our family life was like at its normal strength." ("Gay" was the word Janet used after they had been out to dinner and she told me Dickey blamed them because he was an only child.) "Last night was typical: all three children going out to different parties (I admit it was New Year's Eve) and coming in at different times, all before it was light, I must admit, but not much—and it gets light pretty late this time of year."

> We all went to the midnight service Christmas Eve, and I enjoyed it very much. While we were gone we left Caffy in the living room, where we had put our stocking presents for each other on the fireplace bench, because I had mislaid our stockings (among other things, including the stand for the tree.) When we got back, Caffy was in the middle of the rug

> absolutely surrounded by tiny scraps of paper. She had unwrapped just about every present and chewed up the wrapping, and she looked *so* pleased with herself, waggling her whole rear-half to express her thanks to us for being so considerate as to leave her something to entertain herself with while we were gone. She had done surprisingly little damage, though—mainly eating out the end of a packet of cigarettes and then deciding she didn't care for the flavor of tobacco after all.

This was the year Hannah and I went together to Elspeth Hughes' marriage "after the fashion of Friends."

> Quite an experience. The Friends Meeting here includes Negroes, Hindu, and Chinese. I was to meet Hannah at the church, and of course got there early, so I was waiting for her in the hall as most of the guests came in. I felt alternately like a character from Tobacco Road[435] and someone dressed up like Mrs. Astor's horse[436] as—I won't say enemies, shall we say wordlings, like Elizabeth Agard, entered, and the Friends, whose minds were evidently on higher things than dress. The ceremony was very touching and sincere. Then everything was still for five more minutes. Then a Friend was moved to speak on the constant presence of God. Then everything was still for twenty-five minutes, actual count by my watch. I sat there crawling with sin; I never felt so black and loathsome and corrupt in my life, because I couldn't keep my mind on communing with God, which obviously everyone else was doing. I don't know whether Helen White beside me was reciting a Hail Mary or meditating that the rest of us would all be sent to Hell for being so far away from the True Church, or what. But I do know that when the elders rose to end the meeting and everyone shook hands with the person next to him, I shook hands with her, which I found out afterwards meant I had made her participate in an alien service, which her confessor wouldn't like at all. Paul Fulcher had been invited, and I was supposed to take him, but he decided he didn't feel well enough to go, and I was just as glad because he doesn't like

---

435 The novel *Tobacco Road* (1932), about Georgia sharecroppers, was written by American writer Erskine Caldwell (1903–1987).

436 Caroline Webster "Lina" Schermerhorn Astor (1830–1908), a prominent American socialite, was referred to as Mrs. Astor. Her husband was a racehorse owner and breeder.

> Merritt, and I think sitting next to him would have been even
> more trying than sitting next to Hannah, who, dear child,
> kept looking at me to see how I was holding out.

I'll digress to say my letters here often refer to Paul[Fulcher], who was causing his friends and the department increasing worry. He still had flashes of wit. "I told Paul about your low water pressure thinking it might cheer him up to hear of other people's troubles; but he said he had troubles of his own; when he came in the house the other day his ice chest began to sing in a high soprano voice." Merritt [Hughes], now chairman, was tirelessly kind, and drove out often. As a neighbor it was easy for me to drop in almost daily, but the slow death gave me a horror of my own old age. But back to our happy Christmases.

In 1954 Hannah and Tom, who were both at Tufts, drove out with a couple going on to Minneapolis, and I expected them in the afternoon. I got up at my usual hour of 4:30 a.m., put on the water for coffee, and looked out the window to see the lights of a car coming down the driveway. At how many houses can you arrive unexpected at 4:30 a.m. and find the hostess up and dressed and making coffee? It was a quiet vacation for Hannah because by now most of her friends had left Madison; a good one for me because I had such a good chance to visit with her.

> And a beautiful season. Thirty-six hours of snow. There has
> been a lot of building around here, the little matchbox houses
> which are not very impressive; but they all have picture win-
> dows, which are the perfect setting for a Christmas tree, and
> they all have Christmas trees; so every time you go out you
> feel as if you were going down streets of Christmas cards, with
> the lights of the trees shining out on the pure snow.

As you know, Hannah and Tom both had Christmas weddings, Hannah at home in 1955. Tom had been the first of us to meet Peter; his opinion was that "he seemed to 'like Hannah a lot, but that's only natural,' that he was not athletic but a very good guy and would make a good brother-in-law." Peter made an equally favorable impression on our friends here.

> Elizabeth Agard told me how witty Peter was, and I said,
> "What did he say?" and she said, "He didn't say anything,
> but he looks witty." Dick Quintana told Janet that Hannah
> couldn't have met so attractive a man in the middlewest—a
> nice broad-minded thing to say, isn't it? Dick and Peter are
> both Harvard men, of course, and as we all know, you can
> always tell a Harvard man but you can't tell him much.

Christmas is a lovely time for a wedding, and the house lent itself well. The guests came in through the garage and left their coats in the rumpus room, decorated for Christmas with a big tree and as many bright colors as I could get. Then they came upstairs to bridal white and green: white candles, no cut flowers but bowls everywhere of the living sweet-smelling paperwhites, some little white-painted branches hung with tiny pale Christmas balls, to which our beautiful new while (almost all) Persian kitten Charis kept putting out a delicate paw to make them swing, white ribbons and green swatches. "There is no trick about decorating for a wedding; as fast as a present comes into the house, you take off the beautiful while bow and put it somewhere." Hannah of course wore white. The matron of honor, Hannah's college roommate for whom she had been maid of honor, wore a red velvet dress for which the wedding was perfectly timed, since she expected her second baby in July. I can remember that the strongest impulse in my whole life, early in the afternoon, was to go down, get in the car, and drive away—drive away *anywhere*; but of course I didn't yield to it. I played Christmas carols for Hannah to come down the stairs, including Peter's favorite, "Greensleeves." Dr Swan officiated; Wright gave Hannah away. It never even occurred to me to shed a tear; nor did it occur to me until Tom, with his infallible presence of mind, gently suggested I ought to be in the receiving line. The couple left to the prettiest of winter sights; a fine, gentle snow just beginning to fall, glinting in the light. The guests left. Wright took you boys out to dinner. Hannah [Davis] and Jim and I were left alone. The house was quiet. All at once there was a terrific crash in the basement. Since even then they were pretty deaf, they didn't notice anything, fortunately. When I could excuse myself and went down, I found Charis had knocked over the big Christmas tree, which lay prone on the floor with most of the balls shattered around it. I've always toyed with the idea of Hannah's wedding as a little musical fantasia: the delicate tinkle of the tiny Christmas balls under Charis's paw, the swelling of the carols, and then, after the ceremony, the crash. Charis, like the devoted young officers in India throwing their glasses over their shoulders when they had drunk their toast to the young Queen Victoria so they could never be out to any meaner use, decided that the tree had served its purpose.

Hannah and Peter spent their bridal night at a Madison motel, and dropped in next day, which is an extremely nice custom. I shall never forget how considerate Tom and Bill both were to me the rest of vacation. We took down the bridal parts of decorations but left what belonged to Christmas up till the end of the week. The wedding, I wrote Gwen, was "more work than I thought it would be, but I am very happy and thankful that I did it. Everyone was so good and so kind and so helpful that it gives me a very warm happy feeling to think about it now."

Christmas of 1957 was "the happiest I ever remember," with all the children home, including Peter. Tom was on leave from Newport, where he had been accepted for the intensive Naval Officers' Training Program. He bought champagne to celebrate the wedding anniversary. "He expects to be commissioned on January 23rd, has applied to be a supply officer, and will be sent to a special school in Athens, Georgia. He brought his uniform home so I could see it, and he put it on for the celebration and looks very handsome. I have managed the housekeeping smoothly by one single policy with the merit of all great inventions: simplicity. I don't pay any attention to breakfast. Other years everyone was getting up at different time, eating at different times, and I was in the kitchen cooking and washing up all day long, like a waitress in a twenty-four hour restaurant. So this time I ignored breakfast altogether, though of course anyone is at liberty to eat anything he can find himself, and serve two good meals, lunch and dinner, at stated times, in decorum. It works fine. The happiest Christmas I can remember, it is also the one which receded most rapidly into the past with roughly the speed of a supersonic jet. In twenty-four hours beginning at noon of New Year's Day, I was notified of two ruptured appendixes and a premature baby in the FE staff. By the time I had substitute arrangements made, which took all day Friday, Christmas might as well have been in 1857."

In 1958 Bill and I were alone and Tom in the Mediterranean.

> Do you know about the Red Cross "talking letters" to servicemen? Bill and I went down to the building a week ago to make one for Tom, and I must say they did it very nicely. They had a Christmas-decorated table, and a silver coffee service, and gave us coffee and Christmas cookies, and there were four or five women around, all as pleasant and helpful as could be. I got upset, of course, and cried, but luckily not until after I had finished doing my part of the record, which I had written out ahead of time. The woman wanted to play it back to us, but I said heaven's sake no. That I couldn't have borne. Then they put the record in the envelope, with cardboard, all stamped already with a postage meter, so that all I had to do was put on the address and drop it in a mail box.

Christmas started rather discouragingly, when Bill and I came out from the midnight service and found the lights on the car wouldn't go on. Bill consulted a policeman we met on Park Street—nothing was open that hour—who said he wouldn't stop us from driving home, and it was a moonlight night with snow to mark the sides of the road. The Pooleys came to dinner, including not only Robin and Janet but their three-week old daughter—the first of the coming grandchildren generation. Bill's friend Lee Prentice, Executive Director of the Madison Boy Scouts, rented my addition for a couple of years in here, though he had gone home for Christmas. This year he contributed to the décor.

> Did I tell you about Lee-the-lodger's canoe? On Monday, December 15 when I arrived home I was mildly surprised to see a blue (and very beat-up) canoe in the snow at the top of my driveway. It seems he had stored his canoe with a friend, who had suddenly moved, and had brought it out and dumped it. I was giving a party the 22nd for the teaching assistants staying in Madison, and I thought the canoe didn't strike quite the seasonable note, so I suggested he and Bill might carry it down in the back yard; but he said he was trying to sell it and the prospective purchaser was expected any minute. In the meantime the neighborhood was making somewhat ribald suggestions that I should turn it over and plant a Christmas tree in it, or fill it with packages, like a sleigh, as is sometimes done. This was to be a party like the old days, with white candles and paperwhites and carols. I had begun to be afraid no one would turn up, for I had had all sorts of notes and cards from people saying what a lovely idea and how thoughtful, but they expected to be in Tallahassee or Brooklyn or Tucson. But about twenty-five came, just a nice size, and we had a good time. The canoe disappeared just half an hour before the first guests arrived.

Christmas of 1960 is the only one in my life I have spent alone without some member of my family. But it was by no means unpleasant, in its way. I had thought of going down to Orlando to see Tom, who was finishing up his Navy service. But he was coming home in February, and said there wasn't much to see anyway, so I've still never been to Florida. (The memory did cross my mind of the time Bill was a counselor at Lannon, and wrote, in answer to my question of whether he wanted me to come over on Parents' Day or not, "I think it would be wise for you not to come, because it would be a lot of trouble for you and also for me.") So I planned that every day I would do something—go out myself or have someone in, which included a Dickensian Christmas party for Reading Group, and I turned to Dickens, where time is always well spent, and went through the whole canon of the fourteen novels in chronological order during the time. I cooked the Christmas turkey dinner for not only the Pooleys but also the Searleses; and all of us, our children all occupied elsewhere, had a very pleasant quiet companionable time. Bill flew in from Detroit for forty-eight hours the night of December 31, and I cooked another turkey for him, for Dick Christiansen, of whom I have always been very fond, and for Dick's parents. ("It knocked me out to have him go. I don't mind being alone, but when the children come and go, it shatters me.") However, the next day I went back to work, my eternal comfort.

As Charis contributed to Christmas of 1955, so Mewa contributed to this. The day I had Reading Group for luncheon and needed extra chairs, I brought some out from the addition, which I had had closed off from the furnace for the winter, and took them back rather in a hurry when my friends left, since I had a dinner engagement. The temperature dropped very suddenly while I was gone, and it was so cold I had trouble starting my car; and when I got home I was surprised not to see Mewa. I was sure I'd left her in. She didn't turn up, and I spent a restless night, getting up and going downstairs to look for her. I thought someone might have taken her in for the night, since it had grown so cold, but she didn't turn up in the morning, and the Humane Society had no news of her. This went on for three days. Of all sad times of the year to have a family member lost! From time to time, I fancied I heard spirit mewings, and I would rush outdoors and go round the house, calling and looking under the evergreens, with no result. Finally the mewing got so loud I realized the poor cat had been under my roof all the time, shut up in the addition, where she had gone without my noticing when I put back the chairs. There was a blanket in a partly-open drawer where she had been sleeping; but of course she was hungry and thirsty. Mewa hadn't been as affectionate a kitten as I had hoped she would be when I got her. But she was so pleased to be let out, and I was so pleased she bore me no grudge for having kept her shut up, that we fell into each other's arms, and as she grows older and older—she is by far the longest-lived of any of my cats—she is increasingly demonstrative.

Christmas of 1962 was a very exciting one.

> Tom got out here the evening of the 22nd, and in the most depressing and unglamorous setting of the Greyhound bus station he said, "I'm getting married next Saturday." I was overcome that with all the details to arrange in such a hurry he still took the time and trouble to come out to Wisconsin so that I would not be alone on Christmas, and that Diane agreed. Wasn't it wonderfully considerate? We had a lovely Christmas, and this was true of the weather as well as of the home. I have never known a more beautiful one. The ground was bare up to the 22nd, and then it snowed. Sunday it

Construction

cleared, and was sunny and cold. Christmas Eve it began to snow again. Tom took me to the midnight service, and as we came out the snow was falling with that lovely light glinting. It snowed all day Christmas (we had dinner at the Pooleys), which is a pleasant feeling when everyone is home and doesn't have to go anywhere, and then the next day it dropped to 22 below, clear and cloudless, day and night. We left the morning of the 27th. By then more snow was predicted, and Tom was getting nervous. We arrived at the airport to find the planes about to take off for the Rose Bowl—a howling mob, as you can imagine.[437] It wasn't till we got to O'Hare, the sun shining, a cloudless sky, and every available meteorological convenience for flying, that Tom really believed he was going to get to Boston and could relax.

The wedding was in the Harvard Chapel, Saturday morning at eleven, a simple, lovely service. Each had one attendant, and there were only about fifteen or twenty people there, all young (including the minister) except Wright, who came on from Cortland, and me. Diane's parents didn't come; they live in West Virginia, and Tom and Diane are going down there for a couple of days this week. I have never seen a wedding where the bride and groom, instead of expecting attention, did so much for everyone else. Tom sent me a gardenia, he arranged for someone to drive his father to the airport after the reception, and he thought of everything. After the service we went to the apartment Diane has been sharing with two other girls, which was quite near, and had champagne, and then lunch. I had a chance to talk with her the night before when she and Tom and I could see her face; and she looked beautiful. I shall be glad all my life to remember her eyes as she looked at him. Tom was exuberant on his wedding day—and you know Tom, so you know what that means with him. I spent a pleasant weekend talking things over with Hannah and Peter and seeing Robert and Anne. The weather was cruel, five below zero with gale winds, which I think meant a

---

437 The 1963 Rose Bowl (college football bowl game), played in Pasadena, CA, featured the USC Trojans and the Wisconsin Badgers. At Thomas notes later in this chapter, this was the first time Wisconsin played in the Rose Bowl. It is considered one of the greatest bowl games of all time.

chill factor of fifty below or so, and I am delighted to get back to an easy winter in Wisconsin.

The Christmas of 1964 was also memorable, since Tom brought Diane and David home, taking advantage of a long weekend. By great good luck they had good weather and flights on time both ways. I remember while Tom was checking in at the airport and Bill and David were sitting with Diane and me, everyone looking at the two handsome redheads. I wish all of Tom's children, now they're old enough to remember it, might sometimes see Frost Woods as well as the Island, as Robert and Anne have done. Of course I gave a reception for Diane, and all the old friends and neighbors turned out. Another new member of the Frost Woods family was Robie Fleming, whose engagement to Alan Pooley had just been announced, and who arrived in Madison just in time for the party; so she and Diane kept each other in countenance. "I had a very good Christmas," I wrote Gwen, "and it is still echoing. Diane's letter this week had a sweet tribute, I must say; she said she understood now why Hannah did so many things with her children, it was because I must have done so many things with mine, and it was nice having been there Christmas because now she knew how Tom had grown up." Certainly no mother ever did more things with her children than Diane herself.

Well, life is not all Christmas. I can't resist reminding you of some other experiences, most family ones, though I'm exercising rigid will power in not making this section three times as long as it is. In the summer of 1951 I ventured back to the Island, the first time since the mumps fiasco.

> I really enjoyed the trip home, which I never would have expected, mostly owing to the fact that Bill turned out to be such a good traveler. One of our graduate students here, Stella Clifford, lives in Boothbay, and she was also in summer school; so she went with us both ways. On the way out, it was she and Hannah and I; the boys had flown east to visit Wright, and came over later from there. On the way back, it was the boys and she and I; Hannah stayed east and went on down to college. Travel suits Bill; he is so interested in everything new that he is at his best and you share his enthusiasm. We played "Horse" (do you know the game?) and roadside cribbage and various other things, all across New York and Ontario and Michigan, and I never laughed so much in my life. I didn't have a bit of trouble with the car, and the whole trip was much easier than I expected.

Construction

In December I had a bad case of flu, but "Bill is really a marvelous nurse. If you are sick he is quiet and gentle and sympathetic and very obliging and he brought me hot water bottles and fruit juice and all sorts of things all day." Sometime in here he and Tom and I went to "Rhubarb," a real family movie about a cat who owned a baseball team.

> Rhubarb looked *exactly* like Pronoun—just the same go-to-hell expression in their eyes. I saw Pronoun on the lawn two days before Thanksgiving just ready to spring at a pheasant walking innocently across the grass. Wasn't she sweet? She knew Thanksgiving was coming and wanted to contribute.

The summer of 1952 we were all home, and successfully carried out the project of painting the house with rubber base paint; I had had some professional plastering done in the spring. Each person did his own room, and we all worked together on the living room.

> Bill took three days on his room and it looks absolutely professional. Once in a while I heard him saying a naughty word to himself, but he never once blew up or stopped work, and he painted his ceiling too. I had no idea he had so much control and patience, and I am pleased as can be. I found him some splendid curtain material, just right. Tom had a day or two off from the peas, and he did the part of the ceiling that is so terribly hard to reach, coming down the stairs; once that is done, anything can be done. My study was hardest of all, because it took a day to get the books out and a day to get the books back, let alone the painting. Now like the Little Engine we know we can do it, and we will have a tremendous surge of increased self-respect. For a long time its looked like a stage set for *Tobacco Road*.

In the fall the Strangs took me to the first Wisconsin High football game of the season.

> I was thrilled to the core to see Tom, who played almost all the game. He—and the other members of the team who happened to be on the field at the same time—won 27 to 6, which was nice for everybody concerned expect the opponents, Fort Atkinson, and what do I care about them. I was really impressed; for someone as casual as he is, and at his age, I think it must be valuable to feel yourself a part of a close

unit like that with prestige, and you could see he was a part. Also this raises his prestige with Bill.

November 23, 1952. I think I haven't written you about the last game, which they made a Parents' Day with all the mothers wearing big white chrysanthemums presented by their sons. And Tom caught a pass and ran for a touchdown! It was just like the movies, not like real life. Of course it was kid stuff, but it was thrilling moment for me. All fall, and it has kept on now that he's out for basketball, Tom has been on the sports page every other day. Every time someone clicks a camera, there he is in front of it. He ought to go into politics. D.A. is a saint. She went with me to the game and behaved like an angel through all my maternal effusions, and her son has not gone out for anything.

I started all this because I was going to tell you about last Friday. It was the afternoon of the annual tea at which parents and teachers are supposed to confer, and she and I agreed to go together. Especially since Tom has late practices, life beyond the bus line with one car has gotten more and more complicated. This day he was suppose to take some Frost Woods kids home in my car at 1:30 and bring himself back after they'd eaten, to get the school bus to the out-of-town game, and then leave the car for me to get home in. I was working late so I didn't get to the tea till late—D.A. picked me up. When I got there I looked out in the hall and was surprised to see Tom. I went out, and he said he had lost his car key. (We each had a set.) I wasn't upset because I thought he had left it at home in his other coat, which indeed turned out to be the case, so I gave him mine and told him to leave it for me in the glove compartment. Five minutes later I looked out in the hall and there he was again. "He's probably lost yours now," said D.A. "Oh no," said I confidently, "he can't have. I just gave it to him five minutes ago." My Lord, he had. And to this minute we have no idea how or where it could have gone. It just vanished into thin air. And then I was upset. We called the AAA and they made some new keys, and the timing worked out all right, and then my sense of humor—too bad it is always a delayed reaction—began to function.

This was the first year Wisconsin went to the Rose Bowl.

Construction

> The excitement is terrific. It was announced yesterday morning and the students went wild, rushed out of classes as if the building were on fire, and celebrated all day long—a nasty day with a mixture of snow and rain falling, enough to chill the marrow in your bones. The Union had loudspeakers blaring "California, here we come" and served free coffee. Youth, youth. But to be honest, Tom's career is making me more understanding of the appeal of athletics than I used to be. I seem to have spent my life in a stage of arrested development, always getting to a normal reaction about forty years late.

The next year after Tom went off to college, Bill and I settled down very comfortably. Tom and Bill seemed to me at that time very different in temperament—though as they grow older they seem to be growing more and more alike—and it was easier to suit one taste than two. Tom, for example, never wanted to start anywhere until half an hour after Bill and I, both early birds, thought we should be on our way. "Bill likes to tell me about his day and likes to hear about mine; and if he isn't backward at saying he doesn't care for my cooking, he isn't backward at saying that he does, either. Also he has taken over a lot of responsibility very nicely. When two boys are home, they try to fob off work on each other; but with only one here, he faces up." Since Bill had a healthy social life and was too young to get a driver's license, however, I had my share of a typical American parent problem.

> There was a class party at Maple Bluff, and Bill was double dating with a boy whose father took them and I was supposed to bring them home. The boy's girl lived only a block or two away from the party, so that was easy. I found the place, way out beyond the old LaFollette farm (I hadn't been over there for twenty years and it was 11:30 pm) and we got rid of that girl; but Davy Hamel, about whom I had not heard a thing, joined himself and his girl to our party, and she lived out in Middleton. So yoicks and away, off across the state. We got rid of her, and left Bill's girl in Midvale, where the roads have been put through with a bulldozer and left that way. "Be careful," said the girl brightly, as we turned off the highway. "Go slow or you'll break an axle." She was so right. I hoped to get out an easier way, and the boys thought they could get me to the beltline. We ended up in the Arboretum and finally got out, left the third boy in South Madison, and as the sun was rising, got back to Frost Woods. What a night.

Construction

Hannah's graduation, like so many other experiences I had as a parent, increased my sense of community with all other parents, and never after that did I see the cars on the campus driving away after Commencement, so heavily loaded the exhaust pipes were dragging on the ground, without feeling a stab of kinship with the unseen occupants.

> June 9, 1954. I flew to Philadelphia Saturday, went to the Commencement doings Sunday and the graduation itself Monday morning, and Hannah and I flew back Monday night. Monday I was on my feet for 20 hours. There is two hours difference in time, you know, and when I am in a strange place I wake up fantastically early. The graduation itself was the nicest I have ever seen. The campus is very beautiful, with great stretches of green, and huge trees, and beautiful shrubs. Rhododendrons were still in bloom and roses at their height; and I had forgotten how lovely that section of the country is. Swarthmore has a natural amphitheater which is where the ceremonies were held, and the class is so small that each person gets his own diploma and the president shakes hands with each. But my Lord, getting away in the afternoon. My sister and her husband drove up from Delaware for the day, and we had that car to transport packages to the post office. Dear little Hannah hadn't packed till after lunch, and when I tell you she spent eight dollars on postage you will realize there were quite a few. (Modern readers must allow for about a tenfold increase in postage rates since those days.) The dormitory was about half a block from the nearest place you could leave a car, and there was a constant stream of parents and graduates carrying things out. One father said these were indeed graduation exercises; another likened it to a Chinese coolie [laborer] line; a third said things were multiplying in his daughter's room faster than they could carry them out. I was reminded myself of an ant heap where you turn over the sheltering stone and all the ants go off for safety, each carrying something in his mouth. All this time I was foaming at the mouth for fear we'd miss the plane, which of course we didn't do. But how we looked! My sister, by sheer good luck, had in her car quite a nice cloth shopping bag (Hannah said, "The Lord will provide"), which she lent us, and we put in that everything left over. No one by that time had any idea of what

> was in it, expect for Hannah's diploma, a pair of old sneakers, a box of candy, and some artificial flowers. It must have been like Christmas for her when she unpacked it next day. I know it weighed a ton because I was carrying it, but I was carrying it in preference to what she was carrying, which was all her pictures, framed and glassed, which she took off the wall the last minute and tied up in brown paper. She also carried two large handbags and two coats, and all our pockets were stuffed with objects, mostly breakable. We looked like refugees from Paris at the German invasion. When I got to Chicago I saw on the wall of the TWA lobby (by which we were traveling), a nice account of what you could carry on a plane: a lady's handbag, an umbrella, food for a baby during the flight; and what you must check: a brief case and practically everything else. They hadn't bothered to specify that you couldn't carry half a dozen framed pictures any more than they had bothered to specify that you couldn't carry a hydrogen bomb, for I suppose it never occurred to them anyone would want to carry either. But Hannah certainly fooled them.

Incidentally, I think my decision not to go back to any college reunion, even my fiftieth, was a byproduct of this trip. As we arrived on campus rather late Sunday evening, we passed a lighted building from which sounds of jollity issued forth. "What's that?" said I to Hannah. "That's the alumni," said she with the completest, coolest contempt in her voice I have ever heard.

Though an incident in September of 1954 had no connection with any of you, I can't refrain from putting it in because I have never forgotten it and because it surely shows the fond and happy mutual relations that in these days existed between the teaching assistants and me.

> One of our assistants was marrying another, Saturday of Labor Day weekend, at her parents' home in a Chicago suburb, and I had promised her I would come and bring some of her friends down. The wedding was at four, and I thought traffic would have thinned out (silly girl). I also picked up some extra driving, since one of my passengers, who was going on to Utah after teaching in a summer institute for foreign students, had optimistically counted on getting into Chicago by a commuters' train and found out after the ceremony that on Saturday commuters trains don't run. As a matter of fact, he was informally attired in a Hawaiian sports shirt, and had

not planned to go to the wedding at all; but we all told him how fond Lois and her husband-to-be were of him, and how they wouldn't mind his clothes a bit. So he did, and I spent most of the reception time driving into Chicago and back again. No one knew the way, we got lost on some of those superhighways, and saw no human being for miles, expect a foreigner selling vegetables who unfortunately spoke neither English nor any of the languages our man had any experience in. When I finally got back, I felt as if the couple must at least be celebrating their silver wedding anniversary and was rather surprised not to see their children and grandchildren playing about their knees. When we started back to Madison, I was feeling rather tired—it had turned into a very hot day—and I thought it would be nice if I could get a little driving relief. Guess what I had in my car: two pregnant women and two men who'd never learned to drive. These academic men—if you want to know anything about psychosomatic influences in the critical essays of Virginia Woolf, they are right on the ball, but if it is something a little more practical—of the women one hadn't driven for three years, and the other had just gotten her license and her husband had made her go with me because he didn't think she was up to the trip. So I kept on through the dark and the night. My passengers started singing, and their fresh young voices were lovely as we drove on though the dark; but when we finally reached Madison and I let them out, I was literally shaking.

The joke of the whole thing was that the man who let me in for the extra driving into Chicago and out is a chivalrous Southerner, who had very carefully arranged the trip for me, explaining that he would be going down with me and not coming back, but that a man who was ushering at the wedding and had gone down the day before would be coming back in his place so that I would always have a man along to take care of me. This return passenger, of course, was one of the two who'd never learned to drive. I had omitted a lot of fascinating details about the trip. The personnel, so to speak, kept changing up to the last minute. Two people scheduled to go had changed their minds and told me they wouldn't be coming, so when two more people had asked if they could come I said yes, of course, I had two free places. One of them was a man who had bought a 1940 car in Boston for $40 and driven out in it. He had arrived safely, but he hadn't had a chance to get it checked over, and he had come back early on purpose to go to the wedding, so could he drive with me. When we reached the meeting place, two others turned up who hadn't bothered to ask if they could come, but had simply assumed, hearing that two people had dropped out, that they could take their places. So the man with the 1940 car had to drive after all. The car went perfectly; the only trouble was that the brakes gave out altogether the last twenty-five miles and it couldn't stop. You remember this was Labor Day weekend and all roads stiff with state police. He told me it was quite a strange feeling to press down as hard as you could on the brake and have absolutely nothing happen. I had not felt too inelegant when I left Madison, but we were all a little taken aback to find the bride's family obviously much more wealthy than we had thought from her unassuming and democratic behavior among us. Her parents' estate—which was what it was—filled with their guests, apparently wealthy Chicago bankers looking down their noses at our Bohemian contingent—particularly the Hawaiian shirt—headed by the brakeless car which rolled to a stop against the garden wall. However, fortunately the ushers were all teaching assistants and therefore on our side, so they let us in.

Bill, like Tom, was a mainstay on all the Whisky High teams, and usually I went to see him play with Mr. and Mrs. Christiansen, parents of his best friend Dick. In the fall of 1954 he chipped a piece off his shoulder at a football game and had to wear a brace which held the arm out from his shoulder. "It was just like a suit of armor with steel plates around the body and supporting the arm, and I felt like a squire in a Scott novel when I helped him put it on. One of the saddest sights I have ever seen was Bill lying flat on the couch (it didn't hurt so much when he was standing or lying as when he was sitting) holding up his good hand the only book in the house he felt he could get any pleasure from: *Tennis, A Manual of Self-Instruction*." Fortunately his shoulder healed completely, and in time for that year's basketball season. This accident led to an experience I have always remembered as illustrating the tremendous range of students comprised under the egis of the university. We had to get two boys to put on the storm windows, and they could not have been greater contrasts. One was here for a short-term course in the College of Agriculture, and I'm sure he could not have handled ordinary academic work. Though very strong and willing, he put the ladder up with the spikes protruding outward, and Bill had to tell him to reverse it before he started carrying the windows up it. He came from an Italian family, of whom the original founder had been the first man to introduce Italian cheese making into Wisconsin. They lived in a small town upstate and were very successful; the big chains handled their products. Cheese making, he said, is something which can't be taught; you have to have the feel for handling it and knowing when is the right time. He was one of a large family, all of whom were involved in the business, and all of whom lived in almost medieval domination under the father and the priest. "Always do what your mother says," he said to Bill, when at lunch it came up that Bill wanted to go to the university here and I wanted him to go away to college somewhere. "If you do you'll always be all right and you'll never be worry!" The other man was a brilliant graduate student working for his Master's in Political Economy, though when I heard how much he'd moved around already I doubted whether he'd stay here long enough to get it. He was a Jew, originally from New York, who had completely cut himself off from his family, and who had traveled a good deal both in this country and in Europe. Though he knew for what purpose he had come and was conscientiously ready to fulfill it, he was obviously physically timid and afraid to climb a ladder. Among other things, he had taken part in the kind of act in movie theaters where someone purports to read the minds of the audience; and I've never seen anyone quicker. He would know what we were going to say long before we finished our sentences, almost before we started them. Both of these were part of the University of Wisconsin. When I took them back in town and left them, they were making a date to meet again—both of them, for completely different reasons, being lonely.

As I've just said, I would have preferred to have Bill go away to college somewhere, as Tom and Hannah had, but he preferred to stay here; and I'm glad now. It gave me a lot of pleasant and enriching experiences while he was here, and since after all I did devote my whole professional life to the University of Wisconsin, I'm glad one of my children is an alumnus of it. I had thought it would be hard for him to be the son of someone associated with the most unpopular course on the campus, but apparently he took it in stride, and, if his fraternity brothers criticized it, told them very sensibly, "It's nothing to do with *me*." I was forewarned by the very intelligent attitude Sally Reynolds had taken when her three children all went to the university. "She said to herself that if they had gone away to college she wouldn't be knowing a thing about it, and she wasn't going to know anything about it here. I've done my best to take the same attitude, and really it hasn't been difficult, since Bill is very level-headed and conscientious and an excellent organizer." A popular Wisconsin High boy and star athlete, he knew and was known on he campus already, and he and Dick Christiansen pledged Chi Phi, of which Bill Strang was a member already. Chi Phi was right in the center of things and right where most of the water fights started; but on one particular occasion when the paddy wagon swept plenty of students off to jail (including a graduate student in psychology who had gone out to observe mass reactions and found himself an unwilling participant instead of a spectator), "Bill was studying for chemistry exam with a friend at the friend's house in South Madison and didn't know a thing about it till the paper came next morning." I was a guest at the house on several occasions; I remember once driving down Langdon with the car full of pails of lilacs for decorating, completely helpless in the traffic. But Dave Hamel saw me, got in, and, it seems to me now, must have lifted the car into the air like a helicopter and out it down again, for the next thing I knew we were safely in the Chi Phi parking lot. My last appearance on Langdon Street in the football season as a parent was when Bill was president his senior year. "Yesterday was Dads' Day, the parents turned out in force, the team redeemed itself, and everybody got drunk last night (I assume from little human interest notes in the morning paper—not from first hand knowledge). I went to Bill's house for lunch. It was really touching to my maternal pride to see him, so neatly dressed, so polite and cordial to all the mothers and fathers, so encouraging and fatherly to the other brothers in getting them to be polite and cordial too. Dear Bill." He was in Naval ROTC, and it was a thrill for me to see him in the uniform. It was a pleasure when he would drop in at my office Saturday afternoons, where I usually worked so I could use the department hectograph machine, on his way to or from the football games. And all through the four years if I looked out my window and saw a red-gold head in the stream of students going up or down the Hill, I knew it was my son. No one else in the university had one like it.

Tom graduated from Tufts in 1957 and spent the summer at home, working at a filling station while he waited to hear if he was accepted at Newport. "It is nice for me to have him home. I feel as if we were getting acquainted all over again. He doesn't write much (like most men) and he hasn't been home for more than a week or two at a time since he went away to college. It is nice for Bill to have him here too." Bill was a counselor at the Y camp across the lake that summer, and he was away when Tom left for Newport, providing me with an experience I rank with Hannah's graduation.

> On August 30 I walked over for the mail (Tom was asleep, since he was working nights at the station) and I said to myself that if I had three wishes for what I'd find in the box I

Construction

would use them all on wishing that he would be accepted, not save any of them for anything else at all; and there in the box was a big envelope from the Navy. He was to be in Boston to be sworn in on Friday, September 6, at 8 a.m. Well, he had to work that night again, since the man couldn't be let down the Labor Day weekend, and he decided to leave Saturday night. He was scheduled to play in a softball team, and so many people were away he made the ninth man and without him they would forfeit, so he decided to start out after the game (6:30–8:30) Labor Day weekend. I would have thought it would be a good idea for him to start some packing in the afternoon, but he thought it would be a good idea for him to lie on our little beach in the sun with a cool bottle of beer so that is what he did. This I vowed he was a man of twenty-two and I'd let him live his own life. And I am glad to say I kept my word all summer. He didn't want to eat before the game, of course. I went to watch him, since I couldn't see sitting at home alone. Then Tom said would I get dinner in five minutes and by one of those miracles a man ignores I did. One reason he wanted the old car he bought—he had never had one before—was that he was tired of borrowing from his roommate, and another was that when he had traveled before he had always had to pack suitcases and now he just wanted to throw things in the car. And believe you me, that was exactly what he did in the five minutes I was putting the meal on the table. Then he ate, and then he drove out of the driveway. The house was a shambles—the kitchen and his room. I did the dishes because I couldn't bear the thought of seeing them when I came down next morning, shut the door on his room, and went to bed; but I kept jerking awake every half hour all night dreaming of sirens rushing up to accidents on the road. I forgot to say he was spending the night, whatever of it was left, with a friend in Chicago; he had the address but no idea what part of the city it was in, and I'm told Chicago is a good-sized place. The next morning, I cleaned up his room, and I thought life has always been like this for women, since the days of the Trojan War and before. The men go off somewhere, leaving utter chaos behind. The women clean it up, and when they have done so, what do they have? Nothing. It is neat, it is tidy, it is empty. Of course I recovered in a day or two, and I am very very happy he has the appointment. The car sprung a bolt on the way east and had to have the crankcase rebuilt or something, but he got there in time.

When Bill graduated, his Commencement, in addition to my personal pride in him, deepened my understanding and appreciation of the university. I hadn't gotten very much out of Alice's, the only other one I ever went to here, partly because I wasn't so personally involved as I was with my own son, but partly also because in the intervening years I had worked so hard and intimately, seen the seamy side, seen the mass of detail, and therefore could appreciate the splendid apotheosis. I dropped in after Bill's to visit with Alden White, Secretary of the Faculty, who was always in charge. (You remember his son Ray drove east with the four of us one year when he was going to the Audubon camp at Damariscotta [Maine], and we still have in the cottage the sketch he drew.) Alden told me Commencement was really for the parents; that is, for the state; and I could understand. It was a beautiful day, and from the stands you could look down on the impressive massing of the groups at a time; not till the doctorates were individual candidates escorted across the platforms. However cheapened academic dress has been in our day by its adaptation to high school or even below, the real thing is not only picturesque and colorful but surely must give all but the most insensitive with the sense of history. After the awarding of the academic degrees at Bill's came the swearing in of the officers in the services. The men withdrew to take off their academic robes and came back in their uniforms, the Navy's, of course, being far the handsomest. When the men uncovered, the sun shone on Bill's bright head, and I felt every person in the stadium must see him and admire him.

Tom, I think, was especially lucky in his Navy assignment and Bill correspondingly unlucky. But I had a memorable Thanksgiving with him in 1961.

> Thanksgiving was very nice, but unique, not traditional. I had plane reservations for 8 pm Wednesday to go over to Detroit. Madison and the whole region were closed in by as thick a fog as ever London boasted of, and after a day of considerable uncertainty, at almost exactly the time I was due in Detroit, 5:45 pm, I was leaving Madison by train, with the prospect of a fourteen-hour trip ahead of me. It brought back the days of my youth to be traveling in the college crowds; I should say roughly 15,000 of the 20,000 students supposed to be on campus this year were on the train to Chicago. I had to cross the city and change stations and leave the second one at what is to me the grim hour of midnight. But by good

Construction

luck I got a roomette in Chicago, so that I was able to get on board at 10:30 and could rest if not sleep most of the night. I was surprised to find that the cost of train travel, first class I admit, from Chicago to Detroit was just exactly twice the cost of flying.

We were to go to Bill's ship for Thanksgiving dinner, which was why I felt I had to travel all night. There was quite a jolly family atmosphere. All the crew who had wives in Detroit (I mean of course one wife apiece) were allowed to have them aboard for Thanksgiving dinner, and they were all eating somewhere I didn't see. Of course we ate in the officers' quarters, Bill being the officer on duty. We were served by a Negro steward, and the service was not quite up to Ritz-Carlton standards. He'd come in with a dozen little paper cartons of milk held in one big hand and deal them around the table as if he were dealing cards. But he was very nice, especially with the Dodd's little girl, Elizabeth, not quite two. He brought in all sorts of things and put them down for us to help ourselves, as Bill graciously allowed him to do so he could go and eat his own dinner: turkey, ham, gravy, sweet potato, white potato, corn, peas, pickles, olives, cranberry, nuts, candy, pumpkin pie, milk, coffee, so on and so forth. After dinner I said with my most gracious manner, developed on the model of Queen Elizabeth this summer when I did summer advance registration work, that it had been a very good dinner and we had enjoyed it. With true Southern hospitality he responded, "You all hurry back." Friday Bill came over to the Dodds in the afternoon, after captain's inspection, and then we had dinner and he drove me to the airport. I got back to Madison, putting my key in the door and hearing Mewa mewing anxiously on the inside (I had asked Janey Ragsdale to come in and feed her on Thursday), almost before I knew I was off the ground in Detroit compared with the trip over. Air travel is wonderful if you can get it.

At least the Detroit assignment made possible Bill's months abroad. When he came back from Europe, he entered the house "Sunday morning at eleven after an absence of sixteen months with the practical question, 'Is there anything to eat?'"

Construction

☙ ❦ ❧

March of 1959 was a milestone: my first grandchild.

> I have a grandson: Robert Stewart, born March 13, weight 6 lbs 10 oz. I'm having quite a time getting used to the idea because Hannah's doctor told her it was going to be a girl and all along she was joking about naming the baby for its father and had (humorously) said they were debating between Peterina and Peterella, but had decided on Peterella. There is something very catchy about the name, don't you think? The child took on real personality in my mind. Well, Peterella has now vanished into the eternal shades of the unborn, just like Betsy Trotwood Copperfield.

And the real baby, like David Copperfield, now has plenty of personality in real life. He was born so near our spring vacation that I was able to go East only a few days after Hannah brought him home from the hospital. He looked very small to my out-of-practice eye, and Hannah took all the care of him while I did some housework. He gained nine ounces while I was there, which was very satisfactory. "I very much like the demand feeding system. It takes strain out of things." In October of 1960 Hannah and Peter and Robert were here for two weeks, and I have a very pleasant picture of Robert playing in the leaves which Peter kindly raked for me, a nice companion to a later picture of Robert and Anne running in and out among my little rose-bushes on the front lawn as if they were doing ladies' chain.

> In a way I was sorry Hannah and Peter and Robert were here while I was working because I was gone all day and saw comparatively little of them, especially of Robert; but I felt in one way I was making a real contribution to the child's idea of femininity. He kept making advances to me and coming out in the kitchen to hold on to my skirt. Hannah wears slacks all the time (I think she had two skirts with her for a three weeks vacation) and it seems to me if it hadn't been for his grandmother he really wouldn't have known the difference between a man and a woman.

Two months after Robert's birth I picked up a companion of my own "so there'd be something glad to see me when I get home from a hard day at the office." After the sad day I found Charis dead under the yews by the house, where she had just had strength to get after being struck by a car, I didn't intend to have another cat. But the Rodmans are the soul of generosity, and when their cat had kittens Betty called me to say they wanted me to have my pick of the litter. The next day George came into my office to say they wanted me to have *all* the litter. Overcome, I agreed to come out and just look at the kitten, and you know what happened. Mewa, only a few weeks short of her fifteenth birthday at this writing, is the longest-lived of all my cats. I have already told the story of her getting lost under my roof, which was the Christmas after the Morehouse visit.

I started this section with Christmas, and perhaps I could end it with one Easter picture, the Easter of 1964. In general, possibly because of my Unitarian upbringing, Easter, though pleasant, has never meant to me nearly as much as Thanksgiving or Christmas.

> We have had more snow the last week before Easter than all the winter before it. This included one of those days you get once a winter when the storm strikes at late-afternoon traffic hour; it took me a solid hour to get home from the university, for at every little rise cars with poor winter drivers or no snow tires were skewed across blocking both traffic lanes, while traffic behind piled up for miles. In my foolhardiness I had asked two young families in the department with small children to come for Easter dinner, counting on the nice big back yard for the children to hunt eggs in. As soon as I could see out Easter morning I saw the sky was full of snow—one of those featherbed storms. When I went to church for the nine o'clock service, it sounded pleasant, but a bit odd, to hear the chimes ringing the Easter music through the snow. Everything went all right. We hid the hard-boiled colored eggs down in the rumpus room and small foil-wrapped chocolate eggs upstairs in Bill's room; so the children had two hunts. It is more time-consuming to hunt eggs outdoors, of course, since you have more space to cover; but I am glad to say they found all the hard-boiled ones—glad for obvious reasons. Hard-boiled eggs outdoors don't matter. But did I ever tell you about my student theme describing an Easter egg hunt at her former small college? The hiders didn't count the eggs, and all the rest of the spring eggs were being found—by nose—in classrooms all over the campus. My young guests didn't find all the little chocolate ones, but that was all for the best. I had thought they would take the chocolate ones home for their mothers to

dole out one at a time, but the children with great presence of mind ate them on the spot; so I'm sure they found as many as their mothers wanted them to. The snow stopped, and some of us went out to walk in it after dinner. One family was from Oklahoma (the Lenehans); the wife said she had never seen a white Christmas. Isn't she underprivileged? I felt so *sorry* for her. She has seen a white Easter, but it isn't the same thing, is it? By the way, on Sunday I saw three lovely snow Easter bunnies in someone's yard, a big one and two little ones. We can now define Wisconsin as the place where winters last so long that the Easter rabbit is a snowman.

To end this chapter, I should come back to the university, for in this period I was giving it almost all my time and thought. And this is probably a good place to give an account of my friendship with President Emeritus E. B. Fred[438]—with the expectation of Helen White the most famous person nationally I can count as a personal friend. I was lucky in my timing here, for until he retired, he would have been much too occupied for our contact to develop. It started because we are both early risers. He walked across campus from 10 Babcock Drive at 6:30, and I got into the habit of walking with him.

At first, we were both going to Bascom, where he had a basement office under the then President's office (Harrington[439]). Here we often exchanged greetings with the third member of a rather oddly assorted trio, Rodney, the Bascom janitor, a character in his own right, also of course an early riser. Mr. Fred had of course knew him for years, and told me that once Rodney had come to him to complain of a faculty member, who had taken Rodney by the arm to suggest he leave the classroom, where Rodney was still sweeping or something of the sort. "If he does that again," said Rodney, "I'll punch him right in the kisser!" When Central Administration moved to the top floors of the new Van Hise, Mr. Fred was given an office on the sixteenth floor there, and I would have little visits separately with my two friends. Rodney often came in to my office early, to tell me about the trip abroad he had taken or (like LBJ) to show me the scar from his operation.[440] When he said goodbye before my retirement, he

---

438 Edwin Broun Fred (1887–1981), American bacteriologist, dean of UW-Madison Graduate School (1934–1943) and College of Agriculture (1943–1945) and fifteenth president of UW-Madison (1945–1958), was highly regarded by students and faculty alike.

439 Fred Harvey Harrington (1912–1995) earned his Ph.D. from New York University and joined the UW-Madison history department in 1937. He held several administrative positions prior to his tenure as president (1962–1970).

440 In 1965, U.S. President Lyndon B. Johnson was photographed lifting his shirt to reveal a surgical scar from an operation to remove his gall bladder.

observed solemnly, "I'll always think of you as Mrs. Thomas." From his manner I am sure he meant a compliment, though its exact nature escapes me. And about once a week I would drop in on (rather, up to) Mr. Fred for an early visit. While Kathy[441] was Dean Luberg's secretary,[442] she saw a great deal of both Mr. and Mrs. Fred, and was very fond of both. I have seen much more of Mrs. Fred since my retirement than I did before, and have become equally fond of her. Both of them have the best gift your fairy godmother can give you at your christening, the gift I admire and envy above all others: zest for life.

Mr. Fred has a sense of humor. The expression I've heard him use almost every time I've seen him, in a wide variety of contexts, is "I had to laugh." Harrington, I'm afraid, is deficient in it, and the two are hardly congenial. Mr. Fred always scrupulously called him "the President," and invariably says when he is mentioned, "He's been very nice to me" and "He's gotten a fine physical plant for the university." So many of the Van Hise secretaries had babies that Mr. Fred professed to believe it must be something in the water, and once suggested to Harrington that one floor should be turned into a nursery. "He looked at me so funny." Mr. Fred was brought up on a farm in Virginia, and often quotes Uncle Sol Smith, a "colored fellow" there. When John Weaver,[443] the incumbent All-University President, was appointed, Mr. Fred said, "As Uncle Sol Smith used to say, he'll be all right if he can spit tobacco with the boys." He had said this to Harrington, and Harrington had said, "What do you mean?"

Mr. Fred is a man of wisdom and has a good memory. He compiled *A University Remembers*, a beautifully gotten up book perpetuating gifts to the university, and has spent a lot of time since retirement saving memorials of historic value which without him would have disappeared in rubble under the bulldozers. When these gifts were accepted, he says, the university promised to care for them; it should keep a promise. He has seen to the erection on top of Observatory Hill of a marble seat given by "someone who has looked into the eyes and shaken hand of everyone in the graduating class," an early President's wife. Size disturbs him. His solution for many past problems was to split big departments into smaller ones, and I think the English Department might well have operated better if this had been done to us. He looks back with relish to

---

441 Kathy Thomas, wife of Bill Thomas (Ednah's son).
442 Leroy E. Luberg (1908–1982) earned his Ph.D. from UW-Madison in the late 1930s, served in World War II, then returned to UW-Madison (1946–1973), where he was assistant vice president for academic affairs, then assistant to the president, then dean of students.
443 John Weaver (1915–1995), a professor of geography and university administrator, was hired as president of UW-Madison in 1971, the year in which the University of Wisconsin System (the merger of the University of Wisconsin and the Wisconsin State Universities) was created. Weaver was president from 1971–1977.

the days of John Bascom, the last President qualified to teach every one of the fifty courses his university offered (over two thousand today). Bascom was also the man who kept the grade records himself because he didn't trust the faculty. When he learned a pretty girl had gone to see her professor and gotten her grade raised, "the old man said he'd take care of it himself." Mr. Fred remembers when at the fall faculty meeting the dean of each college personally introduced each new member of his faculty. Dr. Waters, a nationally famous anesthetist, who incidentally presided over Hannah's birth, was presented as particularly distinguished in a capacity often illustrated by faculty members, the power of putting persons to sleep. Mr. Fred can tell story after story of the now vanished individualists who, in such contrast to our anxiety-ridden age, were afraid of nothing on earth. One, annoyed at a student's stupid question, said, "Well now, Bill, I'll tell you; wait after class and ask the janitor." This professor was the man who thanked God before his class that the student making stupid mistakes on the board was not *his* son. The boy turned out to be the son of a regent, and the Board summoned the professor to apologize. "All I can say is that it's truth," said he cheerfully. "Good morning, gentlemen." Another had a prejudice against women. When he saw one seated in his class at its first meeting, he politely offered her his arm, escorted her to the hall, shut the door on her, came back in, and started the lecture.

Mr. Fred is very shrewd. Schlichter, he told me, said that when a college president was appointed there should be an arrangement to take him out and shoot him at the end of ten years, because by then he would have given his institution everything he had to give. (In the recent years it would hardly have been necessary to make any special arrangement; Swarthmore's president, for instance, dropped dead of a heart attack in his office while it was under siege by Black Power sympathizers.) When [John] Weaver was appointed here after [Robert] Clodius had been acting president,[444] Mr. Fred said no man should ever be appointed acting president unless he has one foot in the grave; for when the actual president is appointed this tells the other man he has been a failure. Mr. Fred defines academic freedom as "the right of any professor to say anything he pleases on any subject he doesn't know a damn about," a definition which would not please the AAUP.[445] He also believes a university president should concern himself with selecting good faculty, since members of a big department don't seem able to do it themselves, and I am afraid our own department could

---

444 Robert LeRoy Clodius (1921–1990), a professor of agricultural economics, was the first provost (president) of the Madison campus after President Harrington created separate administrations for the university campuses. He was acting provost from 1963–1964.

445 The American Association of University Professors (AAUP) is a non-profit membership association that advocates for fair standards, quality working conditions, and academic freedom.

be cited in support of his view. He never, of course, criticized our department to me.

Mr. Fred is a man of integrity, and has lived with men of integrity. While Mark Ingraham was Dean of the College of Letters and Science, he never gave the administrator a higher salary than some of his professors, and a number of L&S professors were more highly paid than he. Mr. Ingraham also returns to the university the fee he is paid whenever he goes to a conference at Washington, instead of putting it into his own pocket, since he is receiving his university salary and does not feel entitled to the other. Merle Curti refused to accept an increase in salary unless a similar one was given to Paul Knaplund and several other colleagues. I think times have changed. Mr. Fred once said to me, "Did I ever tell you that I gave my resignation to the Board of Regents the day I took office as President? They wanted to tear it up, but I said 'No, you may want to make a change, and if you do I'll come round and shake hands with every one of you and smile at you and go back to Bacteriology.'" At Weaver's appointment he told me, "I hope this man will go out and go around the state. The one thing you can't delegate is that the President must impress the state with his honesty; that's the one important thing."

Above all, Mr. Fred is a man of sanity. In the bad years to be described in the next chapter this was a very rare commodity on this campus. It seemed to me I spent most of my time in the company of the insane, both students and colleagues. My early morning visits to Mr. Fred were a support. I never came away without feeling that for a few minutes, in an age of creeping pollution of the physical and mental atmosphere, I had breathed pure air.

Another great advantage to me was that through this contact, and the scope of Mr. Fred's own contacts (he had been a Dean of the College of Agriculture before he was President), I learned a great deal more about the university and its history than I ever would have otherwise. And how it was changing. This period was one not just of expansion but of explosion. Trees fell; roads were laid out; buildings were put up. The sixties called it construction; the seventies, looked back, tend to call it destruction. I was continually harping on the theme in my letters to Gwen.

> They are widening the belt line where I have to drive every day in and out of town, which provides me with a traumatic experience every day. The trees stand there marked for felling; the trees are felled; and the results are as painful to me as a battlefield of dismembered corpses would be; about two months later they take away the corpses; and about two years later, you have a concrete desert, and as the New Yorker says, concrete is eternal.

Construction

> The whole campus is torn up; they are cutting down the trees by the Historical Library and planning to extend that monstrosity right straight up to the street, and they are erecting a new eighteen-story language building at the bottom of Bascom Hill in back.
>
> The whole block from Park to Murray and State to University is rubble.

I used to think that visually there was no difference between Madison during this time and London during the war bombing. I would drive in town up Park Street in the morning and see a house standing; when I would drive home the same night it would be dust. I remember meeting a woman at the back of the Hill one day, looking about her wonderingly. "What is that building?" she asked me. "Social Science," I told her. "What is that?" "Van Vleck." "When I was here," she said, "these were all green slopes." "Modern architecture and I, you and Ham will be sorry to know," I wrote to Gwen, "are growing further and further apart. If you could see that math building you night understand why. It is a particularly nasty-looking example of the egg-crate style." The general rule was that each new building was uglier than the one before it, but the consensus was that the McArdle Laboratory for cancer research, on which the architect had unfortunately spread some irregular stone facing suggestive of leprosy, held its own against all competitors. "The campus is going to be skyscrapers with canyons between them, and my own feeling is that the people responsible should be boiled in oil, but no one pays any attention to me, though I am not alone in my feeling." There was some faculty opposition to building, and at one faculty meeting Einar Haugen[446] led a gallant fight, opposing the extension of Social Science into the woods behind it. His motion was narrowly defeated. I congratulated him after the meeting on his courage and effectiveness. "We lost," he said. The Dean of the College of Engineering was appointed head of the Campus Planning Committee, and most opposition was feeble and futile and expressed verbally. "I understand now how the Indians felt when the white men came." Ray Agard invited people to join his Penelope Club, whose members were to take away at night the stones erected during the day—erected, of course, on a solid concrete base going down to China.

There was, it must be admitted, reason for building. The campus population was going up by thousands. I hated to get caught out of the building in the change between classes. "The crush is like a big-city downtown rush hour." "And half the students are beatniks. The appearance of the student body has certainly

---

446 Einar Ingvald Haugen (1906–1994), an American linguist of Norwegian descent and a pioneer in sociolinguistics, taught at UW-Madison (1931–1962) and Harvard (1964–1975).

changed since I first came here and so much admired the Scandinavian gods and goddesses walking up and down the Hill." Nor were there many familiar faces left among the faculty, which was swelling in proportion to the student body with hordes of anti-Establishment assistant professors. "The university reminds me of something Ham said once about a country which has had a revolution; you look around and you don't see a face you ever saw before." In 1965 there were 29,000 students on campus. "Lincoln remains unchanged, but nothing else does."

Lincoln still remains unchanged. Once during these years when life was fun I came up the Hill on February 12 to find him holding a placard inscribed "Happy birthday, Abie baby." His face did not change then, or later when the guerrilla theater acted their plays before him, or a mob poured kerosene on the effigy of the Chancellor and burned it across his knees, leaving ineradicable stains on the marble of the exedra. All these years I was glad every day that my office looked out on Lincoln sitting so quietly in his chair. He sits there still, looking out into the sky.

DEMOLITION: SEPT 1966 TO AUGUST 1970

In the chapter on World War II, I said apologetically that my material was lacking in sensation, since I merely sat out the war in Frost Woods.[447] Luckily we can now make up for the lack. In this five-year period now to be covered, the ivory tower of academe was a dead ringer for a Saturday night free-for-all in an early Western saloon. There were disturbances, greater or less, on most campuses; the killing of four people at Kent State, though an isolated incident, gave that institution an unenviable immortality; but by common consent Berkeley, Harvard and Wisconsin were tied for the place where the action was. And Art Buchwald put us first.

> "You'd better get over to the Diamonds' right away," my wife said when I came home the other night.
>
> "What's the trouble?"
>
> "I don't know, but they sounded terribly upset."
>
> I dashed over to the Diamond House and found Larry and Janet in the living room looking as if the world had fallen apart. "What is it?" I asked.
>
> "Billy got his notice," Janet said.
>
> "He's been drafted?"
>
> "It's worse," Larry said. "He's just been accepted for college."
>
> "That couldn't be so bad."
>
> "He's been accepted at the University of Wisconsin," Janet cried.
>
> I didn't know what to say.[448]

The explosion hit me at the high point of my career, happier in my work than I had ever been, and in a euphoric honeymoon with teaching assistants in general and the Masters[449] in particular. The official statement of the program

---

447 A community in Monona, WI, where Thomas lived and regularly hosted neighborhood and department gatherings.
448 Art Buchwald (1925–2007), an American humorist and Pulitzer Prize winning columnist. The quoted excerpt is from "He Got His Notice," syndicated in 1969.
449 A reference to experienced teaching assistants who mentored new teaching assistants through the Master Teaching Assistant Program, which Thomas created.

Demolition

is at the end of the chapter.[450] There were plenty of such groupings all over the country, as increasing numbers at megaversities made some delegation of guidance inevitable, but ours was unique in that the Master made no evaluation of or report about his group to the authorities. To combine the office of judge with that of friend and guide seemed to me to make full confidence impossible, and my contribution was to separate them. Not once during the program was any specific name mentioned in our meetings, though a Master might raise a type of problem for anonymous discussion. This is the truth; and it did not prevail; in the climate of the times no one believed it.

The first year of the program, 1965–66, I was living in a fool's paradise, but it was a paradise. The year began with the all-department party in Frost Woods, the biggest turnout ever, since the Masters saw that all their charges had transportation. I admit Jean Rideout,[451] by now the chairman's wife, had some justification for saying my house was over-crowded. Like Tennyson's good custom which would corrupt the world, its success was its downfall. Do you remember the apple tree on the border between the Beatty's land and ours? One year it blessed heavily and produced such bushels and bushels of apples I worked frantically making them into applesauce, which filled the freezer and lasted us till the next summer. In the spring the tree was dead and had to be cut down. This was the last time the whole department, junior and senior staff, ever met. There has never been another attempt since.

The year was apparently a great success and a blissful one for me. By a program slip, Bill Lenehan,[452] now Director of Freshman English, who should have shared the Masters' weekly meetings with me, had a class himself at the hour set, and I had them all to myself. We achieved a perfect relationship, open and honest on both sides, possible, of course, only because of good will and intelligent realism on both sides. The new teaching assistants were happy, and responded splendidly to the TLC they received. At Christmas the Masters took me out to dinner and gave me a corsage of white orchids and a handsome coffee-table art book, for which, of course, I wrote nine charming thank-you notes, each different from all the rest. At the end of the year I reciprocated with a party here for them and their wives, with a few departmental VIP's to honor them because

---

450 This statement was, unfortunately, not included in the typescript of the memoir.
451 Walter Rideout (1914–2006) earned his Ph.D. in English literature at Harvard (1950) and taught at Northwestern University (1949–1962) and UW-Madison (1962–1986), where he was department chair from 1965–1968.
452 William (Bill) Lenehan (1930–1993), trained in American literature at the University of Oklahoma, began teaching at UW-Madison in 1962, was made assistant professor in 1964, and began directing Freshman English in 1968. Thomas wrote a tribute to him that is included at the end of the memoir.

they had done so well in the experimental program. ("Bill was a great help," I wrote Hannah, "and the wives all thought he was marvelous. One said he was 'so all-American.'") In June the Regents, somewhat prematurely convinced I had made a great contribution to undergraduate teaching, made me full professor by special action, required since I had passed my sixty-fifth birthday.

Now let me use a flashback to May, a month marked by two special events. The first weekend of that month was the dedication of the big new university complex, the Southeast unit, which contained Arthur Beatty[453] House and Paul Fulcher[454] House. Ham and Gwen,[455] and Jim Dodd, were here as houseguests, and in addition to the official university banquet and events we had a Frost Woods reunion. I had a wonderful time reliving my youth, for all my associations that week-end were those of thirty or thirty-five years earlier when I really was young; but after it I had to come back to reality. The second event was a grim reality, a curtain raiser for the five-year drama to come. I reported it to Gwen as follows:

> May 24, 1966. I don't know how much national coverage the activity at Ham's Alma Mater has gotten, since sit-ins protesting the draft seem to be the fashion at all the universities these days, but camera men are popping in and out all over the place, and the sit-in is at the moment taking place downstairs in Bascom. (I'm catching up on my letters after my last class.) It started down in the new Administration Building on Murray Street, right next to poor Helen White—singing going on till 3 am, I hear.[456] Fortunately she and Olive are moving tomorrow to an apartment on Pinckney, and high time too. A special faculty meeting was called yesterday afternoon, and the

---

453 Arthur Beatty (1869–1943), a graduate of Columbia University who specialized in Wordsworth, taught in the English department from 1897–1939

454 Paul Fulcher (1895–1958) joined the English department in 1925 and taught literature and creative writing. During World War I, he volunteered as an ambulance driver with the American Field Service in France.

455 Hamilton (Ham) Beatty, son of English faculty member Arthur Beatty (1869–1943), studied English at UW-Madison and architecture at London's Bartlett School of Architecture. Ham and his wife, Gwen, were neighbors and lifelong friends of the Thomas family. After the Beattys moved, Thomas and Gwen corresponded regularly for over thirty years. Thomas later borrowed and used her letters to Gwen as source material for portions of the memoir.

456 This anti-draft sit-in was organized by the Madison chapter of Students for a Democratic Society (SDS), an influential student activist movement in the US (1960–1969). The sit-in, which spanned several days (May 16–20), was organized in response to a draft qualification test being offered on campus; the sit-in in the administration building was "[d]isciplined, orderly, and peaceful" and protestors "did not interfere with the employees or offices of the building" (Cronon & Jenkins, 1999, pp. 454–455).

Demolition

off-stage effects were almost too dramatic. A series of thundershowers had begun, so that in moving from Social Science, because it was too small for the turnout, to Music Hall, which still was—people were standing—some of us got drenched and rolls of thunder punctuated all the speeches. Fleming,[457] who presided—we never see Harrington[458] any more—said that we were the only university of our size that had been able to discuss the controversy with free expression of all opinions and without disorder. I hope we'll able to keep up.

Three students spoke, one representing an ad hoc committee of Students for Free Choice, who took the point of view that a student who wanted his grades sent to his draft board should be able to do so, and a student who didn't needn't (with which I am in complete agreement); one representing the protestors, who went over the time he was allowed and had to be cut off, asking that the university should refuse to give any information to draft boards at all and should not allow a building to be used for the Selective Service test; one representing the Wisconsin Student Association; then a faculty member representing two hundred teaching assistants, in sympathy with the protestors; then the chairman of the university committee, faculty elected; then two other professors, supporting the protestors. All of these people had mimeographed resolutions or whatnot which were handed out. At the beginning the faculty voted to cut off discussion at 5:30 and vote then on whatever motions were on the floor. There was comparatively little discussion from the floor, since all possible points of view were already presented, and in writing. By a very large majority, the faculty voted for the resolution of the university committee: we should continue to furnish information at the student's request; to refuse to allow a

---

457 Robben W. Fleming (1916–2010) received a law degree from UW-Madison (1941) and worked in administrative and academic positions outside of Wisconsin until his appointment as provost of the UW-Madison campus (1964–1967).

458 Fred Harvey Harrington (1912–1995) earned his Ph.D. from New York University and joined the UW-Madison history department in 1937. He held several administrative positions prior to his tenure as president (1962–1970). During his tenure as president, Harrington reorganized the university in 1963–1964 to have a central administration and separate administrations for individual campuses. He also prepared the university for its merger with the Wisconsin State Universities in 1971.

university building to be used for the purpose of the Selective Service exam would be a complete violation of our historic tradition, which had never meant that use of the building implied approval of activity or speaker; and a faculty-student committee (4 faculty, 3 students—the students asked for the other way round) should be formed to investigate the whole subject. I then drove home in such a downpour that I saw two cars stalled on the highway just before my turn-off, and I was thankful to get home alive.

This morning, a beautiful rain-washed day, I came in to my office to find the demonstrators had moved into Bascom in the night, and they haven't been washed at all. They really do look like the Paris mob during the Terror. The halls are strewn with trash and blankets and whatnot. I came quietly up the back stairs and it is peaceful as a desert island on the third floor; but it is surprising how disruptive the feeling is that they are downstairs.

My friend Rodney, the cleaning women, and I, good Middle Americans all, were all disturbed, Rodney and the cleaning women particularly, since their whole lives were focused on establishing order. One of the women was particularly shocked at the girls "laying there like pigs. What would their mothers say?" The last classes had met, so there was little more of the semester to go—the reading period and final exams only.

The second year of the program, 66–67, started out well enough. The Frost Woods party had to be given up. The Rideouts and Lacys gave a party for full-time staff only (the snobs) at the Wisconsin Center; but since the department now numbered 69 full-time staff, most of them married, and 191 teaching assistants, at least two-thirds of them married, it had really outgrown any private home. I had begun to worry about my retirement, four years away, particularly since Esther Piper had just retired, and was finding it, I wrote Hannah,

> "a great adjustment"—which means very hard. I don't wonder. She told me on the telephone you feel no use any longer, which I can easily see is true. Through registration I kept priding myself every day on the messes I was straightening out. It is true that most of the time I was telling students how to get to 375 Bascom, a room you can reach only by the stairs at the back of the building, and a recording could have done it as well as I; but still they were confused and I helped. She is taking a course at the Vocational School in Charm and Per-

sonality. I have a feeling myself that at sixty you've got about as much personality as you're likely to have, let alone charm, but of course one can only admire her open-mindedness. She said it was something to do.

I myself still had plenty to do. Bill Lenehan and Joyce Steward[459] were coming to the Masters' meeting this year, but we all worked well together. Of course I had my own teaching. And with the exception of one weekend in Milwaukee on a workshop on Advanced Placement (an activity of the Wisconsin Council of Teachers of English), I had a supper party every Sunday night for thirty people or so; a Master and his wife, his current teaching assistants with their wives, his last year's people with theirs, the Lenehans or Joyce, and perhaps another senior department couple, like the Rodmans.[460] These affairs, it seemed to our naïve minds, were bringing the junior staff into pleasant contact with each other as well as with us. That the tiny bonds thus formed were to snap like rotten threads when the Teaching Assistants Association forged a true bond, stronger than steel, hatred of us, we were happily ignorant.[461]

But as the year went on the general situation steadily grew worse. I wrote Hannah in February:

> Any national news about our demonstration here? Protest against Dow Chemical interviewing for jobs because they make napalm? (Incidentally, one of my students, an easy-going black exchange student from somewhere in the south, wrote in a theme that she didn't see why people were getting so excited over napalm. "Somebody has to make it. Why not Dow?") This was an ugly one, and seventeen students were

---

459 Joyce Stribling Steward (1917–2004) completed doctoral studies in English at the University of Iowa and Yale University and taught English at two high schools in Madison—West (1951–1963) and La Follette (1963–1966). She was recruited by the UW-Madison English department to assist Thomas in composition instruction, first in the NDEA institute (1965), then in the department (1966), where she taught English 309 and literature courses. In 1969, Steward became the founding director of the University Writing Lab, which she directed until her retirement in 1982. She published one of the first books on writing centers: *The Writing Laboratory: Organization, Management, and Methods* (1982).
460 George B. Rodman, an English professor at UW, directed divisions of English 1a in the 1930s, published an anthology with Robert Doremus and Ed Lacy called Patterns in Writing in 1950, and served on the Freshman English faculty committee with Ed Lacy, Robert Doremus, Robert Pooley, and Ednah Thomas from 1948–1968 (Fleming, 2011, pp. 45, 48, 51).
461 The Teaching Assistants Association (TAA), organized in June 1966 by a small group of TAs who sought to blend unionism and activism (Cronon & Jenkins, 1999, p. 494), is the oldest graduate student union in the US.

arrested, all but three of them out of state.[462] The faculty is fed up and the Chancellor has said he will call in the city police to keep order if he is forced to—what of course he tried to avoid before. One nice thing about the pictures was that the university police, who did the arresting, didn't look brutal at all, but like nice good-natured boys—a good deal nicer-looking than the protestors, who run pretty true to type. I've really come to believe now that we have troublemakers for the sake of trouble making, and I have no respect for their principles. (I did them less than justice. Revolution is principle.) At any meeting where free speech is supposed to be the order of the day, the professional protestors yell and scream so that no one else can be heard, and they barricaded the Chancellor in his office and used force to prevent him from leaving—hence the arrests. The trial comes up next month.

One of the men arrested was David Thompson, son of Dr. Kenneth and Helen Thompson, who, as Virginia's friend, was in our Reading Group. He had recently eloped with a firebrand Leftist girl, under whose influence he was deeply at odds with his parents, staunch Rightists. (Incidentally, the couple are now—1973—in process of divorce.) The Sunday following this hoo-hah the Thompsons had asked Reading Group, and husbands, out to dinner to see some Antarctica slides David had taken (he was working for a Ph.D.). But Ken had "blown his top" when he found David had been arrested, Mary, the wife, was "being difficult," both young people refused to appear and Bill Sarles[463] brought some of his beautiful color slides of wild flowers. The next Thursday Helen passed around the group a long letter David had written his parents: "their reaction had been worse than he had expected, they were concerned about what he had done for the sake of the family name and not for his own (I think there

---

462 Thomas is referring to the first of two student protests against the company Dow Chemical: the first, in February 1967, which Thomas describes later in this chapter, was confrontational but non-violent, extending several days and in several locations and leading to the arrests as Thomas describes; the second, in October 1967, which Thomas describes later in the chapter, is the Dow sit-in, where a "more numerous and more militant" crowd of demonstrators blocked access to interview rooms and disrupted classes (Cronon & Jenkins Vol. 3 p. 462). When University police were unable to intervene, Madison police were called in, and the ensuing confrontation led to clubbing and tear gas. For many students, both participants and observers, the experience marked a turning point in the antiwar movement. For a detailed account of the riot, see Marnass (2003), pp. 348–399.
463 William B. Sarles was hired by the Bacteriology department in 1932. In 1966, Sales was editor of the *Journal of Microbiology*, and in 1967, he was president of the American Society for Microbiology (ASM). His wife, Marion, was a member of Thomas's weekly reading group.

Demolition

was truth in this thrust, and would have been for me if I'd been in his parents' shoes), they hadn't worried about whether he was hurt or not, though he was roughly handled by the police, and they ought to realize that a demonstrator is engaged in a risky business and is really brave even if he is a "pacifist" and so on. Fine example of generation gap. This adolescent was chronologically twenty-five. Julian Bond, the radical Negro lawyer,[464] altruistically (it was thought at first) assumed the defense of the people arrested, and sent Dr. Thompson his bill. You can imagine what happened then.

That most of the ringleaders were from out of state contributed heavily to rapidly deteriorating relations between the university and the state, which to me seemed one of the most distressing aspects of the situation.

> The demonstrators are known as SDS,[465] a regular student group organized according to university regulation, with a charter granted by Student Senate. I think most of our people are bona fide students, though there is one townswoman, on relief, who was the leading disturber at the [Bobby] Kennedy Lecture and has received a lot of very unfavorable publicity. Student Senate has just revoked the charter of SDS, and they have appealed according to university procedure. What worries me is the reaction to the Chancellor—we never see Harrington any more because he is the All-University President. Our Madison Chancellor is Robben Fleming, and it was he whom the students tried to confine in his office by force. After they were arrested, he paid their bail money out of his own pocket, which I thought a magnanimous and admirable thing to do. He said he didn't like to deal with people in jail under restraint, and he didn't want the women to spend the night in jail, so he wrote out his own check.[466] It was not he who called in the police, but a man in Engineering, who was in charge of scheduling the interviews with Dow Chemical which set off the furor, and that was the man who made the charge of disorderly conduct.

---

464 The attorney was Percy L. Julian, Jr. (1940–2008), who graduated from UW-Madison's law school (1966) and soon thereafter became "the lawyer for student demonstrators, one of the few attorneys in town who would take up their cause" (Maraniss, 2003, p. 175). He later established a law firm, Julian & Associates, in Madison, and continued representing civil rights cases.

465 Students for a Democratic Society (SDS) was an influential student activist movement in the US (1960–1969). The Madison chapter was launched in 1962 (Cronon & Jenkin, 1999, p. 451).

466 Cronon and Jenkins (1999) note that Fleming "personally provided $1,155 in bail money for eleven of the arrested students who lacked funds to secure their release from jail" (p. 459).

The liberal paper defended Fleming, but the conservative one attacked him violently and I heard among my own friends' bitter criticism, which I couldn't quite understand. He was only furnishing bail, which would be returned. He wasn't paying fines or anything like that. But many people were violently against him for the action.

> I am concerned about the great resentment which seems to be building up against that vague entity "the University" because such awful things are taking place here. And as Bill, who does travel in the state, says, if I feel that even in Madison, what do I think it is elsewhere. Well, there's another special faculty meeting Wednesday afternoon. I was on the faculty for years and never went to meetings, and now I'm going twice a week. It makes life interesting.

I wrote Gwen in March, "Never a dull moment in Bascom with demonstrations: 'on the brink of Berkeley,' as the Chancellor puts it. Special faculty meeting Wednesday. My instinct is always to keep out of trouble, so when I saw crowds in the front hall I went quietly out the back and home. This makes my memoirs (if I live to write them) less exciting than they might be, but it makes life quieter now." I was mistaken in thinking I could keep out of trouble, but not so mistaken as Clark Kerr, quoted in *Time* in April: "Student demonstration is on the way out, and will disappear like the coonskin coat." I hated to think education had turned into two embattled camps, but it had. In May, "The university has been somewhat more trying than usual. I am fed to the teeth with demonstrations, and now completely against any cause anyone demonstrates for even if I was for it to begin with. Did you see us in the national news about the bus strike brought on by student demonstration?" That was a student protest against the city's instituting a one-way bus lane on University Avenue.[467] Hundreds of students turned out to cross and re-cross the street, while the long-suffering Madison police directed traffic, and I got caught in the jam when I was taking flowers and membership certificates in to the Phi Beta Kappa initiation banquet. We got through the semester, with much much worse to come, but before the fall I had the personal interlude of Bill and Kathy's wedding and a summer at the Island.[468]

The wedding was lovely, and though I didn't think they did it with this aim in mind, it rounded out very nicely my maternal experience with children's weddings. At Tom's, when Bill was in Europe, I remember Hannah saying, "Bill will

---
467 This "mass blocking" of traffic, in response to an accident involving a UW-Madison student, is mentioned in Cronon & Jenkins, 1999, p. 461.
468 A reference to Isle of Springs, an island community located in BoothBay Harbor, Maine, where the family spent summer vacations.

probably get married on the Fourth of July," since hers and Tom's were both Christmas-time weddings and both small. He did get married, as you all remember, in June, and had a big affair. When he and Kathy told me at Christmas they were planning a June wedding, I said in the carefree way you do about something in the future that may never come, "Would you like to have the reception here?" As spring came on with every weekend a rainy one, I began to worry more and more about the prospect of feeding three hundred people in my house, where the only possible place, the basement, was just about big enough for the caterer to put out his things. But it was a perfect day. I felt Nature had in one generous gesture paid me everything she could owe me all my life, and I'd never have the right to complain about weather again. I'm glad we were brave enough to take the risk (the Strangs weren't when Betsy was married), for a wedding reception at home, if you have the place for it, is so much more intimate and memorable than one in a public place where others have preceded and will follow you. The weather was clear and lovely all week, and the rehearsal dinner the night before, which Kathy to my pleasure had chosen to have outdoor in the back yard too instead of in a restaurant, was as pleasant for the small group as was the reception for the big one the next day. Everyone looked beautiful (or handsome) particularly the bride; the bridesmaids' dresses were charming; the church (conveniently in Monona) a new and handsome building. I was happy that Tom was best man and Hannah a bridesmaid, that the ushers included the children of old neighbors, and that the priest was Father Brown, whom I knew and admired for his great kindness to Helen and Olive White. Most of my big parties have been indoors, according to the season, and I'm glad you can remember a June one with lilacs and crabs still in late blossom, everything fresh and green, the sun sifting through the trees on all the pretty pastel dresses, the air fresh and soft and cool.

After any interlude, the world immediately comes back. I drove East three days after the wedding, leaving the house for Bill and Kathy to come back to, and while I was on the road the Arab-Israeli six-day war broke out and Helen White died.[469] At Hannah's I found Ed Lacy had called her rather than trying to reach me on the way, and Walter Rideout had telegraphed to ask me to represent the department officially. (This was the second time in three years I got East barely in time to attend the funeral of a close friend; before it was Marie Sharp, to whose service I taxied from the airport, leaving Hannah to collect my bags.) Again, Hannah coped, though she had heavy school commitments at exactly the time, and she took me that night to the funeral home. The next day Peter left me at the church in Roxbury, where I had arranged to meet a former teaching assistant, now a professor at Boston College. I sat with him,

---

469 These events occurred June 5 and June 7, respectively, in 1967.

and with some other old friends, including the official representative of the university, John Solon, now of UW-M[ilwaukee] but someone I had known well here in the old days. My knowledge of Catholic ceremonial was considerably enlarged with Bill's nuptial mass and Helen's requiem within one week. I was glad to stand with them at the cemetery. We were all united by our love and admiration and respect for a great and good woman. John Solon said, "It is the end of an era," and we knew he was right, and we were glad Helen would be spared what we saw before us.[470]

I got to the Island early enough to see all the spring flowers I usually miss, and to revel in the masses of white and light and dark purple lilacs blooming in every yard all over the Boothbay Harbor region. I sweetened the cottage with bunches of them from the old farmhouse bushes. The end of the summer for me came early too, since I went in August to the Phi Beta Kappa triennial convention at Duke. Here I first heard of Tim Heninger, who surprisingly within a year was to be our Department Chairman.[471] Bob Sharp[472] had a friend from Harvard days on the Duke faculty, whom I had met at the Island with his wife. They politely asked me to lunch, and mentioned that a friend of theirs was going to Wisconsin. The Heningers had recently been divorced, to everyone's regret. On the strength of this contact, I asked Tim (with Sam Blount[473]) out to have supper in the back yard when I got home, before registration. He seemed pleasant enough, though some of his ideas struck me as rather half-baked. He had lived the past year, he told us, in a Duke dormitory set up for faculty-student contact, a suite for a faculty member in a wing with about thirty students. Night after night he had sat up talking with the young men, whom he admired tremendously on the grounds that they knew what they wanted and wouldn't put up with anything they didn't like. If they take a job and don't like it, he said,

---

470 John J. Solon worked at the University of Wisconsin-Milwaukee (UWM) from 1965–1981, first as Assistant Chancellor and Director of Summer Sessions and later as UWM Secretary of the University.

471 Simeon K. (Tim) Heninger (1922–2008), a renaissance scholar educated at Oxford (1952) and Johns Hopkins (1955) and Guggenheim Fellow (1962), taught at Duke University prior to joining the UW English department in 1967. In 1968, following a split vote for department chair, the dean selected Heninger, a presumably neutral faculty member, to become chair. By 1970, after leading the department in its most turbulent years, Heninger resigned as chair and left UW for UNC-Chapel Hill, where he finished his career.

472 In the Settling Down chapter, Thomas introduces Marie and Robert (Bob) Sharp, who moved to Madison in 1927 when Bob was hired to teach in the English department while completing his Ph.D. at Harvard. Marie had an assistantship in the history department. The Sharps became lifelong friends of Thomas.

473 Nathan Sam Blount (1929–1989) taught high school in Miami before earning his doctorate in education at Florida State in 1963, after which he was hired by the UW-Madison English department. He held a joint appointment in English and in Education.

Demolition

they'll just drop it. "Do you think they will always be able to do just exactly as they like?" said I, remembering the Great Depression. "Oh, yes," said he. "There'll be no trouble about that." I saw nothing much of him through this year, but in 68–69 and 69–70 I thought he was playing the role of Lord George Gordon and was ideally cast for it.[474] In our alarums and excursions we had our little devices for keeping sane, and one was re-reading *Barnaby Rudge,* and noting with fascinated awe at Dickens's prescience that we could supply the whole cast of characters right in our own department.

From October 18, 1967 to August 24, 1970 is a period marked by a series of dates, each one a black blotch on a white calendar, a discord like a fingernail scraping a blackboard, a physical shock like a branch hitting you in the face or a stumble on the last step that isn't there; and after each, with the invincible reaching for the normal which keeps the world turning, we got up and went on. The first, and perhaps the worst of all, was the riot caused by the presence here of Dow Chemical recruiters on October 18, 1967. Never before in my sheltered life had I seen, bare naked, such vicious hate.

Fleming had left to become Chancellor at the University of Michigan, and one of our own faculty, William Sewell, Vilas Professor of Sociology, had been appointed to succeed him. It was a very unfortunate choice. A professed liberal, he was presumably appointed with the idea that he might have some influence with the campus liberals, who, it was thought, genuinely anxious for reform, were conducting the opposition.[475] This was not the case. It was the Far Left, real revolutionaries, who were in charge. It has never been settled how many bona fide students were involved, here or elsewhere. But there is general agreement that the ringleaders were nomads, who operated with remarkable efficiency and success on various campuses at various times. The San Francisco Mime Troop, its woman leader just released from jail on a drug-possession sentence, led the parade which stormed up the center of the Hill.[476] The kindest word for Sewell is

---

474   Lord George Gordon (1751–1793), a British politician after whom the anti-Catholic "Gordon Riots" of 1780 are named.

475   William H. Sewell (1909–2001) earned his Ph.D. in sociology from the University of Minnesota (1939) and taught at Michigan State and Oklahoma State before joining the sociology department at UW-Madison (1946–1980), where he was chancellor from October 1967 to June 1968. For a detailed examination of the dilemmas faced by Sewell during his short-lived tenure as chancellor of UW-Madison, see Maraniss (2003), and Cronon & Jenkins (1999, pp. 461–469). Sewell resigned because he was unable to "restore order to an increasingly fractured and tumultuous campus" (Cronon & Jenkins, 1999, p. 462).

476   The San Francisco Mime Troupe was a political satire troupe, established in 1959 to showcase alternative theatrical concepts, which became increasingly involved in the 1960s protest movement. The "woman leader" is likely radical activist Vicki Gabriner (b. 1942), who became involved in the civil rights and anti-war movement as a student at Cornell University. Gabriner was associated with the San Francisco Mime Troupe because she was dressed as a whiteface mime

inept. The interviews had been scheduled in Commerce [Building], in the most crowded area of the campus, where between periods some thousands of students, going legitimately about their business from one class to another, were bound to be innocently involved in any trouble. The *Cardinal*, unabashedly revolutionary from the beginning (a *Cardinal* editor was one of the four arsonists who blew up the Physics Building on August 24, 1970, the *terminus ad quem*[477] of our period), had announced the intention to disrupt the interviews. Sewell took that to mean that protestors would be present, but would "go limp" and allow themselves to be lifted unresisting into the paddy wagon. That stage had gone by. The demonstrators came carrying book bags full of bricks, and they used them. Harrington was in Milwaukee; Sewell and whatever others he called in to be with him were shut up in his office on the first floor of Bascom, growing more and more appalled at the disorder which built up until he called in the Madison police, a step he had been anxious to avoid since it would inevitably swing large numbers of students over to the side of the demonstrators. When they arrived, in riot gear, the protestors had already so filled the halls of Commerce that no one could move in or out, and the parking lot behind Bascom was filled with a yelling, screaming mob. I looked down on it from the Bascom third-floor fire escape and saw the whole thing clearly from above. There was much talk afterwards of "police brutality." Bill Strang, whose office was right in the center of the interviewing area in Commerce, was one of twelve Commerce faculty members who signed a statement distributed at the faculty meeting two days later saying the police had behaved with restraint. They were of course badly handicapped by arriving late and by having to operate in cramped quarters. Before you have actually seen a riot, you think men in riot garb carrying nightsticks could control a mob; but the problem is to get at them. Twenty policemen were hemmed in by hundreds of students, and they couldn't move. As I watched them trying to use the nightsticks, I thought, "Why don't they use the tear gas? It would be humane! It would disperse the mob!" But when they did, it was throwing a lighted match into a keg of gasoline. The mob scattered, mainly through Bascom, like a herd of wild elephants (this is Kathy's simile; Luberg's office was then on Bascom first floor), making a shambles of the ground floor, breaking the glass on John Bascom's portrait, disrupting any classes still going on, setting wastebaskets on fire, setting off fire alarms. The gas was floating all through Bascom, I could smell smoke besides the tear gas, and like everyone else I ran, crying, out onto the front of the Lincoln Terrace, where I met one of the associate deans, a kindly man but like all his sort given to jargon, who advised

---

and arrested during the Dow riot, but she was actually a UW-Madison graduate student in the School of Education (Maraniss, 2003, p. 451).

477   Latin for "limit to which," indicating the latest possible date of an era or period.

Demolition

me we were "about to have a riot situation" and I'd better go home. I was only too anxious to do so, but I was afraid to try to get through the mob to my car, which was parked up on Observatory Hill, facing east, which would mean driving down through the melee—obviously impossible. I had promised to give Bill Lenehan a ride home that day, since he didn't have his car and there was a bus strike on, so when the gas began to clear a little I ventured up to the fourth floor, where his office was, and ran into demonstrators coming down from the roof where they had cut down the American flag. Luckily I finally did find him, and by going down the hill away from the melee, then up University Avenue by the hospital, and from there up the hill again, we got to my car. Bill turned it neatly in the teeth of oncoming traffic, and we drove west to Shorewood, where he and I could recover from the tear gas, and whence I could go home.[478]

Next day I went in early, while everything was quiet. All through this period my established habits, which I never changed, were greatly to my advantage, since the rioters habitually carried out their raids by night, got a little sleep in the early morning, and then resumed activities towards noon. The janitor showed me the marks of burning rags pushed under the door of the dean of students so that it was charred on both sides. There had been four arson attempts in Bascom. Some of the teaching assistants went on strike, and all day demonstrators on Lincoln Terrace were urging students not to go to class. I had no Thursday classes myself. A girl appeared at Mr. Lacy's lecture, but the students booed her and she left. On Friday I had normal attendance, "though yells of 'Strike, strike, strike' outside the window hardly produced an ideal academic atmosphere." Throughout I had a ringside seat. Someone like Bill Sarles, in Biochemisty on the Ag campus, would hardly know anything was going on, but Lincoln Terrace was, as always, the heart of the campus, and it was always occupied with guerilla theatre, mass meetings, anything. Not only my office but also my 11:00 o'clock classroom overlooked it.

I enquired pathetically of Hannah in a letter dated October 21 why I hadn't been getting frantic telephone calls from her. "Aren't you in touch with modern communication media? Don't you know that we now have beaten Berkeley and have the distinction of having the worst student riots on record? Don't you remember that my office looks directly out on Lincoln Terrace?" I went on to give her an account of the faculty meeting the Chancellor called in the Union Theatre Thursday afternoon.

> No one was admitted without his faculty ID card, and it was
> so packed they had to take down the backdrop and put a cou-

---

478 For a more descriptive account of the Dow riot, including an alternative perspective on the behavior of the Madison police, see Maraniss (2003, pp. 348–399).

ple of hundred seats on the stage. It started at 3:30, recessed at 5:30, reconvened at 7:30, and went on till early midnight. Bill Lenehan and I went up to eat at Tripp in the recess instead of going home. Going through the first floor of the Union was like going through Skid Row or the worst ghetto you can imagine. And everybody hates you. When we took our trays to the corner of a table, the students looked at us with hate. The faculty wrangled endlessly, but finally did pass a resolution supporting the Chancellor in calling the city police. I was so tired I left early, and missed the most unnerving thing of all. When the meeting broke up, students had formed solid lines from all doors, in all directions, leaving just space for a single person to pass through and extending for blocks. They didn't say a word—just stood there in the dark hating and hating, while each faculty person walked and walked and walked. On the way to my car, which I had left at the afar parking space for fear of trouble, I met a student I had never seen, going down no doubt to take his place in the line, and as we passed he spoke. Neither of us stopped, and I didn't hear the words; but the tone was unmistakable: insult.[479]

The faculty is split wide open, about two-thirds conservative to one-third radical. Someone must have done a lot of work between Thursday and Monday, because at the second meeting Monday afternoon we almost unanimously passed a resolution to appoint an ad hoc committee consisting of equal number of faculty and students to bring back recommendations. (To appoint a committee is not, of course, a very controversial measure.) The legislature appointed an investigating committee, and the bitterness in the state against the students was up to Joe McCarthy pitch.[480]

---

[479] Meeting minutes indicate that 1,350 of 1,800 faculty attended and hundreds of students in the surrounding lobby, hallway, and terrace. Following an opening statement and a motion to support Chancellor Sewell's actions in response to the Dow riot, faculty engaged in heated debate. When faculty reconvened after the recess, many more students were present, and a countermotion was proposed to acknowledge Sewell's efforts to protect the university and to condemn the police's violent response. The countermotion failed (562 to 495) and the initial motion passed (681 to 378). Many students left the meeting disillusioned and upset that faculty were unwilling to condemn police violence, so they lined exits and chanted "Shame" as faculty left the Union (Maraniss, 2003, pp. 432–440).

[480] According to Maraniss (2003), the Senate investigation led to "no major findings" but increased legislators' and antiwar students' dislike for Chancellor Sewell (pp. 499–500).

Demolition

Of course now the publicity began, and reports spread out over the country like ripples in a pond. Many were very inaccurate. Much play was made of the statement that seventy students were injured. At the Thursday meeting we heard the official report: seventy students were taken to the University Hospitals, of whom sixty-nine were treated for hysteria and immediately released, the seventieth kept overnight for observation and released the next day. In contrast, three police were hospitalized for severe injuries; the only one of them at Wisconsin General (and therefore the only one reported at the meeting) had been hit in the throat by a thrown brick and could neither speak nor swallow. Unofficial statements I heard were from Helen Thompson, who had talked to a doctor in the emergency ward where the students were brought in, and who told her, "They were like worms that just crawled out of the woodwork and never saw the sun before," and Dottie Searles, who before coming to Madison had lived on a street where there was a Holy Roller[481] church, and had seen the congregation in their frenzies and said the students were just like them. Bill Strang reported seeing a girl dishevel her own hair and clothes and then have her picture taken by a friend, to use for publicity purposes.[482]

> Yesterday we had what Ed Lacy called "a million-dollar rain." It was not only raining hard but blowing hard, and even the Jacquerie would have called off the storming off the Bastille on such a day. This comparison keeps coming to mind mainly because the students look *just* like the descriptions we've read of the French mobs—dirty, long-haired, dressed in rags, all the rest. It seems to me the French aristocracy is now primarily remembered for what the modern generation would call their cool in going to the guillotine, and I'm resolved to identify myself with them.

To be specific, I continued throughout the period to wear heels (which I kept in my office) every time I went to class. The flat shoes I used in the car would have been easier if I'd had to get out of the building in a hurry, but noblesse oblige. The extremists demanded that all six weeks exams should be put off for a week, but no one I know did so, and no one had any trouble.

I learned a very profound lesson.

> I think it's good to continue to have new experiences as you grow older, and though I didn't expect to get my first taste

---

481 A reference, typically pejorative, to Pentecostal Christians.
482 Maraniss (2003) confirms accounts of some protesters exaggerating their injuries, but many were legitimately injured, some seriously (p. 383).

of tear gas in my sixty-seventh year I'm sure it's broadening. What I really learned from this past week—and it is still going on—is a very terrible lesson, though I suppose it's good for me to learn it since many people in our culture must have had it. I have been looked at with hate—hate—not because I was a person but because I represented something the hater would like to destroy. This is a terrible thing, because if you are disliked, or even hated, as a person, it is still possible, think, to do something about it and to establish communication. But if you are hated as a representative there is nothing you can do. I think this is what Negroes have experienced for a long time—not perhaps hatred, but contempt. "Whitey" looked at them as he looked at a dog or a cat, even with affection, but they knew he was looking at them as representatives of something which could never be changed, which it was unthinkable they could ever do anything about, not as individuals with varying human potentials. (I was later to be looked at with hate by Blacks, too, but that does come later.) I would not know go into the student cafeteria because I might be insulted. The Union, of course, is the hangout for the protestors—hardly a cross-section of the student body.

In my own class, of 26 students, I had two girls who were not in class the day the strike was called. They were both back now, and one is very pleasant and cooperative. The other hates me so much she couldn't sit in the room with me (she came to my office with two other students this morning for obligatory grammar session). I think she's sick—she certainly looks in bad shape, and I don't suppose she's had much sleep lately. For all I know she may be on pot. But after barely answering any question I asked her—I was continuing business as usual—she finally refused to answer, on which I asked one of the others, and five minutes afterwards she got up and rushed out. She came to class afterwards, and sat there looking ill and I didn't call on her.

It's an interesting example of what I've called the innate tendency to normality—or escapism, or forgetting anything unpleasant, or whatever term you like—that now I don't remember a thing about this poor girl, though in almost everything else the letters bring back to me a full sense of the times with a wealth of detail, and I relive them vividly—so vividly that if the telephone rings while I'm typing I can hardly bring myself back to the present. The news had reached my Island friends, and Phyl Webster wrote sweetly, "Are you involved in conferences and so on or is that taken care of by the male members of the faculty?' The vistas that that opens up on the protected, cherished, Victorian female—in 1967—really overpower me." The invitations had already been sent out for the usual Sunday night supper party for the teaching assistants. "I was somewhat apprehensive, but it went very nicely and everyone was very cordial indeed. I strongly suspect one of the girls there had been out on strike, but she was particularly helpful about pouring coffee. This is all for the best. If she wants to indicate that we can maintain civilized social relations while differing ideologically, I am all for it, and I feel I perform a valuable service in providing the opportunity."

Janet said, "You could quarrel with your best friend."[483] The Dow riots marked for me not exactly a quarrel but a difference with Ed Lacy which was a fundamental one. It is a truism that we have the defects of our qualities. I had always thought of him as a peacemaker; I came now to think of him as an appeaser. And through this period I was increasingly critical of and impatient with those who were old enough to have learned nothing from having seen where appeasement got Hitler's adversaries.

A disturbing incident had occurred earlier in the fall, when a student in my [English 309] class[484] refused to make any of my indicated revisions on her theme because she was completely satisfied with it as she had written it. Knowing she was a prickly case, I had used great pains and tact in annotating her theme, and I was all set to pick up her challenge. I relied very much on Ed's judgment and as a matter of course showed him the paper. He advised me not to make an issue of it, but allow her to do as she chose. This was against my principles. To me it was not only silly but morally indefensible to have in my class a student who refused to learn anything from the instructor, and I called up one of the counselors in the office of the Dean of Education, and told her so. The next day the girl came into my office to say she was withdrawing from the program (for which mine was a required course) and dropping the course. I signed the drop card, wished her good luck, and she went out of my life forever. I had solved the problem easily, and I think, since she obviously wasn't a very receptive student, that the School of Education were grateful to me for bringing the issue to a head. But the episode left me feeling that if something larger came up, something I

---

483 Janet Quintana, a graduate of UW-Madison in 1925, was the wife of faculty member Ricardo B. Quintana (1898–1987), a Harvard graduate who taught English at UW-Madison from 1927–1969.

484 English 309, Composition for English Teachers, was the advanced composition course for English education students at UW-Madison.

couldn't handle by myself and would need help on, I couldn't count on getting it from Ed.

The day of the Dow riots, he stayed shut up in his office, and when I told him I was going out on the fire escape to look at them, he said nothing would happen if the rioters had no audience to play to. I felt things had gone beyond that stage. A basic difference came in the next day or two, when some of our teaching assistants had gone out on strike, and others came to see me to offer their services to keep classes going. I was delighted, and went at once to Ed, who was not only Director of Freshman English but Associate Chairman of the Department and therefore in the absence of Walter Rideout, the Chairman, off recruiting, in absolute charge. Ed was appalled. We must do nothing at all, he said, and so that was what I had to do, since I could hardly on my own responsibility deliberately act in opposition to my superior in authority. From now on the breach widened until I went as far as telling him to his face that I thought him like the Jewish rabbis who had made things as easy as possible for the Nazis by leading their congregations straight into the concentration camps, as the Judas steer led the animals into the Chicago stockyards. He is not a hot-tempered man, and he showed me no more sign of being affronted by my accusation than of being influenced by it; but complete confidence between us was over. Fortunately, we were no longer working together; Bill Lenehan had taken over all the Freshman English work, though Ed still kept the title of Director.

It was much easier for me than for him to settle any ethical problem, of course. In any case, I had only two or three more years to teach, while he does not retire until 1984 (we used to laugh about that date).[485] He had a wife and three young children, and I had no dependents. Therefore, my New England conscience and I were perfectly free to hold hands and do as we chose. He was in a very difficult position, caught between pressures, and in the next two years, with our disaster chairman, Tim Heninger, was to be in a worse. Few choices in life are between good and bad; they are between one good and another, between conflicts of loyalties. Ed was genuinely dedicated to holding the English Department together, and he acted consistently with that aim, according to his lights. It seems to me now, when to my mind the department has greatly lost in permanent stature, that he was wrong. But I'm not an impartial judge. The times certainly tried everyone's souls to the utmost, and it is useless and futile to speculate on what might have happened. I'm open to the charge of rigidity, of lack of realism, of youthful naiveté (despite my chronological age). Margaret Lacy is now my best friend, and when I meet Ed—which is not often, but at

---

485 Ed Lacy died of a heart attack in 1981, which his wife, Margaret, attributed partially to the stresses of decades of administration coupled with dealing with teaching assistant student radicalism.

such occasions as my going there every Christmas time for a family dinner and to play for their carols—I do so with pleasure. At a crucial stage in my life he performed one of the most valuable services anyone ever performed for me—and therefore for you—in giving me back my self-respect. For many years we had a most successful working relationship with giving and taking on both sides (the phrase I was to use later before the Department Committee, describing the relationship between the department and the teaching assistants up to these few late unhappy years). I was very useful to him; but I was deeply indebted to him, and when all accounts are in, still am. And therefore so are you.

Janet had followed her statement that you could quarrel with your best friend by saying how well she thought Chancellor Sewell had done in his appearance before the legislative investigating committee. "I had taken a really violent dislike to him on the same occasion because I thought he was just giving aid and comfort to the enemy, so I could see how right she was and changed the subject at once. I began to understand, as I had never done before, what we must have been like in the French Revolution or the American Civil War or any such period." "The worst is that you feel surrounded by enemies and you don't know who they are." "Your hope for bad weather," I wrote Gwen, "is not likely to be fulfilled. Of course the demonstrators would be put off by six feet of snow or thirty below zero, but we haven't much chance of getting anything like that for another couple of months. Chairman Mao will send them some pennies to buy nice red mittens, and they'll be perfectly comfortable at thirty or so." The Legislature had appointed a committee to investigate, and WHA was broadcasting the sessions live evenings.[486] I couldn't tear myself away.

> Last night (this has been going on for three weeks) was the first appearance of a student. They have had the President of the Board of Regents, Harrington, Sewell, Cameron (Chairman of the University Committee), Hanson (Head of University Protection and Security), and so on. The student came with two attorneys and refused to answer any question, even "Do you reside in this state?" without first consulting with them. They had in the morning filed a suit in a federal court charging that the committee was unlawful because it interfered with his right of privacy (if I understood the point correctly), and there were hours of hassle before he even got as far as responding to every question, like a stuck record, "Since you gentlemen have denied my request, and on the advice of

---

486 WHA, a non-commercial AM band radio station, now the flagship for Wisconsin Public Radio, was started at UW-Madison in 1922.

my attorneys, I respectfully decline to answer." The assistant district attorney, who is conducting the questioning, was too old a hand to lose his temper, and I admired him. I may be a little carried away, and I admit it is going too far to look under the bed to see if one of the teaching assistants at my Sunday night supper parties has left a Molotov cocktail[487] there. As a matter of fact, the man I had in mind, supposed to be a ringleader, was not in the department himself but a husband, and no one could have been pleasanter. He complimented me as he left not once on my cooking but twice.

I certainly was carried away all through this period, and felt considerable sympathy with the citizen (this letter was read before the investigating committee) who complained his daughter's education was being interfered with. She had gone to class for the education they were paying for, and her teaching assistant wasn't there. "Why don't you fire them first, and then go into the legality afterwards?" Since the revolutionaries were clearly following the policy of committing the illegal act first and then relying on the protection "due process" would afford them in presenting legal delays until everyone concerned died of old age, it was not surprising this idea should have occurred to him. The feeling in the state—and from my first arrival this campus the strength of the university seemed to me to lie primarily in its close relationship with the state—was increasingly bitter, and the Legislature was at least as frustrated and helpless feeling as any student could be. They held the simple view that the state was supporting a university where bona fide students should be going for an education, instead of being tear-gassed out of their classrooms, and there seemed little they could do about it. They introduced a bill to limit out-of-state enrollment to 15 percent of the total, since in every disturbance the great majority of ringleaders were out of state students. (This wouldn't of course necessarily eliminate the right—from their point of view—out-of-state students.) They signed into law a bill establishing two years in jail and a fine (I don't remember how much) for resisting a police officer; and establishing one year in jail for failure to leave unlawful assembly. But obviously the enforcement of these laws would present serious problems. It was during this time that Diane wrote that her sister (I'm not sure where she was) said she was the only teaching assistant who wasn't leading a revolution at her institution and the only one who wasn't actually insane. We were not fortunate in our leadership here. Sewell, as I have said, was certainly

---

487 Molotov cocktail, a generic term for a bottle-based improvised incendiary device. Cronon and Jenkins (1999) note that it was "regarded by white student leftists as a cheap and easy manufactured weapon of the proletarian revolution" (p. 467).

inept and, in my judgment, an extremely weak man. "At the University Club[488] the other day, the manager, Miss Lindquist, came over just after Sewell had gone out. She said he had been lunching with some of the university's attorneys, and they all had to have special orders because they all had stomach trouble."

> Harrington said Cohen (the leader of the mob, and a teaching assistant in History, I think it was)[489] should be relieved of his teaching duties (this is different from being fired, because your check would go on) on the grounds that the strong suspicions under which he rested would interfere with his effectiveness; Sewell said he should not until "after due process of law." There is much speculation as to why they don't present a united front, and the theory is that Harrington is trying to appeal to the conservative legislature and Sewell to the liberals. I'm sick to death of all this strategy—if that's what it is. Cohen, as a matter of fact, had been legally convicted of and sentenced for disorderly conduct the preceding February, but had not served his sentence because his lawyers were appealing.

Obviously this sort of thing could go on forever, and plain down-to-earth citizens like the father whose daughter wasn't getting her money's worth and me were becoming impatient.

> On December 4 the ringleaders appeared before a university committee, which was to decide whether or not they should be dismissed from the university. They were accompanied by about a hundred students with cowbells, whistles, and other noise-making apparatus. Since it was impossible to hear anything at all, the hearing was postponed, and reconvened the next day in a more carefully selected spot in the center of a building, where access was controlled. The three turned up with their attorneys, stayed a little while, and then walked out in the middle of the proceedings to the surprise of everyone— including their attorneys—on the grounds that the hearing was unauthorized and unfair because it wasn't public. The commit-

---

488 The University Club, which opened in 1908 and served social, residential, and university business purposes, became "a symbol of faculty unity and center of campus fellowship" (Cronon & Jenkins, 1994, p. 532).

489 Robert Cohen, a teaching assistant in philosophy, was eventually dropped as a teaching assistant and student (Cronon & Jenkins, 1999, pp. 463–65).

tee then expelled them from the university. This was Thursday. Friday was a miserable day—freezing rain—and since everyone was taken by surprise, the opposition hadn't gotten organized. They had a rally on Lincoln Terrace, but it was a feeble affair and petered out, as did an attempt to sit-in in the Administration Building Thursday night. More significant, a sympathizers' meeting to protest the expulsion called for the Stock Pavilion, with an attendance of 2,500 expected, drew 200. But the ringleaders appealed their expulsion to a state judge, who denied the university's right to act (note that this was an intramural action only), which stated a new legal wrangle.

The burnt child dreads fire. The first week in December, as I was listening to a hearing—they were held in the Capitol—I heard sounds of singing or chanting or something, obviously made by a lot of people, and I thought, oh dear, here are the protestors coming to break up the hearings again, as they did the ones on campus. Then the presiding officer inquired what the noise in the rotunda was, and someone explained it was Madison high school students practicing for the Christmas pageant. When I took the car up to the grocery on a -12 day, I felt it was so over-privileged to have a heated garage to live in that I expected the other cars to form a demonstration to protest me in it. The Wisconsin climate (unlike that of California) doesn't lend itself well to winter demonstrations, the ringleaders left the state, and vacation was restful. This incidentally was the month Bill and Kathy went to Linda Bird Johnson's wedding in the White House.

The new semester got off to a pretty good start. "I haven't yet felt any real hostility on the part of any one of my students—such a relief after last semester, where one girl showed it so strongly the first day I couldn't miss it. I don't blame my students for disliking me once they get to know me, of course, but I do feel they needn't pre-judge the case." But, as you know, 1968 would see LBJ's withdrawal from political life as a result of student antagonism; the assassination of Martin Luther King; the assassination of Bobby Kennedy; and the horrors of the Democratic National Convention in Chicago in August.

Hannah was working for Gene McCarthy[490] in Massachusetts. I wrote her:

> McCarthy has a lot of supporters on this campus, to judge by the buttons. But there's none of that Be-neat-and-clean-

---

490 Eugene McCarthy (1916–2005) was an American politician and U.S. presidential candidate in 1968. At the Democratic National Convention that year, which was marred by fighting on the convention floor and rioting on the streets outside the convention meeting, McCarthy lost the nomination to Hubert H. Humphrey, who would lose the general election to Richard M. Nixon.

> for-Gene jazz here. I haven't seen anyone wearing his button who has had a bath for six weeks or a shave or haircut for six months, and the women are just as bad . . . One unpleasant incident here concerns the Acting Dean of women students, a very pleasant sensible person who you wouldn't think was the type to antagonize anyone. She was subjected to one of those persecutions where they send you all sorts of things you didn't order, but with a particularly nasty tone: a hearse twice, an ambulance once, a twenty-five dollar funeral wreath, and so on. She finally went to stay with a friend for a while, and as far as I know no one knew why she was attacked.

There was a lot on ingenuity and excellent organization on the other side of the war. Once someone spurted cement into the locks all along the corridor of third floor Bascom (they didn't get down to mine) so people couldn't get into their offices when they came in. Once the demonstrators rigged up a bell, like a church bell or the one on a big bell buoy, by the Lincoln statue, right under my window, and tolled it all day long, knelling the death of freedom; one stroke per minute. Another time they put white crosses all across the two top sections of the grass just below the Lincoln Statue, with a sign: "Bascom Memorial Cemetery: Class of 1968," and then went through the building and down the hill chanting, "Pray for the dead and the dead will pray for you." The administration made no attempt to interfere with this use of university property, even when (as the weather grew milder) a band poured kerosene on the effigy of the Chancellor and burned it across the knees of the patient Lincoln. What tried me most personally was a man whose trousers were made out of an American flag, who was in the habit of sitting on a bench in the hall outside my office a good deal of the time. The Chancellor continued to play the ostrich. But I must admit now, fiercely as I resented his spinelessness, that the strong support given the rebels by practically all his younger faculty put him in a difficult position. The students could never have gotten anywhere, of course, here or elsewhere, without this strong support, indeed incitement, from a section of the faculty which had become numerically very strong during the swelling of enrollments.

We had another arson attempt in Bascom, which fortunately was discovered in time by Dick Quintana, who was in the habit of going up to his office Sunday mornings.

> It has gotten now so that the day is hardly normal without something which in happier days might have been viewed as an infraction of the law. The Dow interviews passed off smoothly last Saturday. They were scheduled for the Saturday

before the primary, the first sign on the part of the Administration of what my mother, in her brisk New England way, used to call almost human intelligence. There were so early in the morning that not many people were up, but two demonstrators were arrested (provoking arrest), one of them, of course, an English TA. He is now meeting his classes and sleeping in jail under the Huber Law, a provision of this state, at least, which allows someone who is jailed to carry on his occupation as usual. On the grounds that he is suffering a civil penalty for a civic crime or misdemeanor or whatever they call it, the department is pretending that nothing happened.

On the national political scene, Bobby Kennedy—with only a few months more to live—declared his candidacy. *Punch* wrote, "Nice to see that Bobby Kennedy finally got the courage of Eugene McCarthy's convictions." "The people I know think Bobby was a heel to muscle in on McCarthy, and that, the facts of life being what they are, it won't do him a bit of harm to be a heel."[491]

Within the department we had our meeting to nominate next year's Chairman. The Dean of the College of Letters and Science makes the appointment, but generally on the basis of department nomination. This was transmitted to him in the form of a signed ballot from every department member. The whole procedure was a gentlemen's agreement. The chairman rotated, an incumbent serving three years and then handing over someone else willing to take it on. That person tactfully absented himself from the meeting, and the vote was usually unanimous. The only attempt in my memory to break this pattern was an abortive revolution in the 30's, under the leadership of Ethel Thornbury. The Young Turks were defeated, drifted away from the university, and disappeared into academic oblivion. Ethel's rivals, Ruth Wallerstein, Helen White, and Madeline Doran,[492] remained here and went on to national prominence, including specific recognition in PMLA as "the distinguished triumfeminate of Wisconsin."[493] In 1968 the person expected in the ordinary course of things to take on the chairmanship was Mark Eccles, not only a distinguished Shakespearian scholar but thoroughly familiar with technical detail since he had spent many years in graduate advising; he would have carried on department traditions. His rival was a much younger man whom I never saw much of: Ed

---

491 *Punch*, or the *London Charivari*, was a British weekly satirical magazine established in 1841; its circulation peaked in the 1940s.
492 Madeleine K. Doran (1905–1996) was an American literary critic and poet who earned her Ph.D. at Stanford (1927) and taught at UW-Madison for four decades (1935–1975).
493 The source for this quotation has not been identified.

Lacy distrusted and disliked him. The vote was an even split, 30 to 30, which obviously called for a compromise candidate. Tim Heninger, who had been here only a year and was accordingly not very well known to anybody, was suggested to the Dean and appointed.[494] But before this solution was reached for our own problem, Martin Luther King was assassinated.

This whole period was marked by Black militancy, as you know. I'm sure there were as many differing points of view among Blacks, much more deeply involved, as there were among us in all our problems. I had made a note on this the year before.

> We spent four hours Friday afternoon with three representatives of North Carolina State, a Negro institution to which UW is playing Big Brother. Two men and a woman came up for the weekend, particularly to meet with us to talk about their problems in Freshman English. It was quite interesting (for the first three and a half hours). They were all very fluent talkers and sounded just like anyone I ever heard in the Commission on English or similar gathering.[495] They were having a lot of trouble with Black Power. Their students test very badly on national norms, but at least up to now they were willing to try to learn, even if not very able. But not the Black Power people, who are able, form a good-sized group and they don't want to learn standard English, or accept, as the jargon goes, middle-class mores. I can see that the Black Power problem would be at it most troublesome for the Negroes who have accepted middle-class mores and are trying to educate others to do so too.

At King's assassination this campus, almost all other campuses, and almost all Negro ghettos in the country flared up like the old wharf house at the Island with its gasoline-soaked floor when a lighted match was dropped on it. "When I think of how things have worsened since our riot last October it's as if the pit of hell had opened under my feet," I wrote. "Have you seen Johnson? I saw him

---

494 According to Fleming (2011), Mark Eccles received 28 votes, and Karl Kroeber, the candidate preferred by most junior faculty, received 29, with one faculty abstention (p. 65)

495 The Commission on English was a national committee appointed by the College Entrance Examination Board in 1959 to improve English instruction, curriculum, and training in high schools and colleges nationwide, resulting in the publication of *Freedom and Discipline in English: Report of the Commission on English* (1965). In the Construction chapter, Thomas describes her involvement in the commission, including directing one of its summer institutes at UW-Madison in 1962.

Sunday, then Thursday, then Saturday, and he's aged ten years in that week. I doubt if he lives out his term."

The university held a memorial service, the Chancellor presiding, on the Lincoln Terrace Friday, April 5, starting at noon followed by a march of "concerned Black students" led by Sewell up State Street to the Capitol. Classes were called off that afternoon. Sewell came into the University Club after the march, looking tired to death. I had gone out on the fringe of the crowd to hear the speakers, Blacks whom I never identified. A nice-looking Negro woman in front of me made her way out of the crowd as the speakers became more and more hysterical and abusive, saying as she passed, "I'm ashamed of my race." I thought that show of respect sufficient (we had had a similar one the first class day after John Kennedy's assassination), and I angrily accused Sewell of cowardice when he also called off all classes the day of King's funeral, the next Tuesday, and urged the faculty to allow make-ups for exams missed the rest of the week.[496] Since spring vacation started Friday, it seemed to me a clear invitation to drop the week down the drain.

> I wonder what it would be like to have a good night's sleep—between the department and the nation, it's been quite a while since I had one. I get some sleep the first part of the night and have found a New Orleans station which gives the news on the hour all night, and where I check in at 3 a.m. Last night I stayed up until I had seen Johnson and Humphrey, and then went to bed. I came down at 3 to hear "violence had erupted" in Memphis, Harlem, and elsewhere. I cannot believe Johnson is younger—chronologically—than I am. He looks like an old man, and I was stunned to realize there were only five years between him and Nixon: 1908 and 1913 birthdates. I feel so sorry for him. His "Mrs. Johnson and I have sent our sympathy to Mrs. King" appeals to me with my Victorian background, but I doubt if it does to our young hard-core friends.
>
> At 9 last night the telephone rang, one of my two Negro students. He is very quiet in class but unquestionably my best writer. On a comparison theme once he compared Saturday and Sunday, and said on Sunday he always spent at least five hours in church, sometimes all day, "where I feel peace while

---

[496] Cronon and Jenkins (1999) suggest that Sewell's decision to suspend classes, along with a host of other proactive decisions, prevented rioting that was happening nationwide (pp. 466–467).

listening to the story of a quiet man who brought a message of love and mercy to a doomed and doubting world." Since he lived in Racine, he could go home weekends. He asked me the assignment for the theme due today; I remembered he had been a little late to class the day I gave it, and such a call isn't unusual. But it did seem strange he was sitting down to write as if he'd never heard of King. I was tempted to say "What a tragedy!" but I thought it best to keep the talk professional. It's so difficult. If it had been a white student calling, it would have been natural to speak of King; but as it was a Negro, I didn't. It may be, of course, that his Saturday-Sunday theme was not really autobiographical. There is not reason to assume that something written in the first person singular necessarily is so. However, what I have learned from my training here is not to say everything I think, and what I drew in with my mother's milk is to act in accordance with what we Victorians call our duty, if we are able to so see it; and according to that concept I shall go to class in an hour and conduct a discussion of literary style.

April 10. I stayed home yesterday morning, as I had planned to do in any case, since I have no classes Tuesday morning, and watched the King funeral, and I was quite moved—until it got too long and I got restless, which was at the point where the one representative of our race spoke. I thought Mrs. King looked beautiful, like a Byzantine Madonna—there was something about the band of her hat and the band on the veil that suggested that. Most of the hymns sounded very familiar to me, from the old days at the Island, when we used to sing a great many of them. I thought the whole thing was Christian—a quality we could use a good deal more of these days. I can't get "Sinner, come home" out of my head now. I watched until twelve, when I had to come in to be here in the afternoon for the Phi Beta Kappa people, and saw a good deal of the march. At least the day seemed to go off without any new trouble, which is something, and Abernathy[497] does seem to be taking a strong non-violence stand, which is good deal. The thought has crossed my mind that the assassin (and

---

497 Ralph David Abernathy, Sr. (1926–1990), a civil rights movement leader and close friend of Martin Luther King, Jr.

isn't it interesting that no one seems to feel any interest in him at all?) may have done for King what Booth did for Lincoln: preserved him for posterity at his highest. King lost control of his followers last week and might well not have been able to maintain it in the future. Anyhow, I thought the service was moving and sincere and simple and Christian.

A national student strike was scheduled for Friday of the week we resumed classes after vacation, but it couldn't have been important here, at least, for I don't refer to it in my letters. I do refer to a "Sleep-in" in honor of Martin Luther King on Bascom Hill the night before that Friday, but when I got to my office at 7 the only sign I saw of it was two people in sleeping bags still there, and I doubt if it had much impact.

A disquieting event, and a mystery unsolved to this day, was the discovery one Sunday near the end of May of the body of a murdered girl in the bushes in front of Sterling Hall, just below Bascom. She had been beaten, stabbed, and strangled, and death had occurred between 10 and 12 a.m., though the body was not found till evening. She was not a drug-taker herself, but she was known to consort with people who were, and she might have met a friend on a trip. There was talk of students' disrupting Commencement in protest, which illustrates the lack of connection and reason which gave these years so much of their nightmare quality. I felt a little nervous myself, since I was in the habit of going in to Bascom Sunday mornings—when the place was completely deserted—to get my materials ready for class next day, when no one else was using the department hectograph machine. Like the murder of Valerie Percy,[498] this is an unsolved mystery. By coincidence one of our department teaching assistants, who had impressed me as a rather moody young man, had been a friend of the Percys and had had dinner with Valerie the night before her death. He had a key to Bascom. Of course I knew this was nothing but coincidence, but in the temper of the times irrational feelings come to you. This incident, of course, was simply local and isolated, without ideological significance.

Then the assassination of Bobby Kennedy struck everyone in the nation.

> June 9. I've had the TV on for the better part of two days—not all, because I gave an exam late Friday afternoon. I was too worn out to read my papers intelligently Friday night, but I started on them early Saturday morning and got them done

---

498 Twenty-two-year-old Valerie Percy, daughter of U.S. Senator Charles H. Percy (1967–1985), was murdered in her bed in Chicago on September 18, 1966. The case remains unsolved. In *Sympathy Vote: A Reinvestigation of the Valerie Percy Murder* (2013), Glenn Wall revisited the case and posited a culprit.

before I turned on the TV, knowing of course that once I did I'd never be able to leave it. So I missed Teddy's eulogy—I turned on just at the beginning of the mass. But the eulogy was repeated that last thing at the night so I did hear it again. The modern media certainly increase national participation in tragedy. I think there has never been a day, not even after John Kennedy's funeral, when so many Americans finally went to bed so physically and emotionally exhausted as last night. Those Kennedys! There can hardly be a person in the United States who doesn't feel empathy with them—either because they represent the log-cabin-to-White-House mystique in a more subtle form than Abraham Lincoln, since they represent it from the immigrant more-than-one-generation standpoint, or because we hope we could act as heroically as both the men and women do in the face of tragedy. It is interesting to see the springing up of the noblesse oblige—Ethel Kennedy's going through the funeral train to shake hands with everyone, and the oldest son's doing so also. There's a better Crown Prince for you than little Charles. Did you hear the Irishman reading poetry? "My sons were forceful / And they fought."

Never was there so violent a spring in American history, and I was glad of a beautiful summer at the Island to rest. But August brought the worst violence yet, that of the Democratic convention in Chicago, which as one result cut down all the leaders of the party.[499] I didn't watch much of it. I've always been escapist at the Island. It seems more fitting to watch the tide come in and the tide go out, immemorially, than to go over to Marion's [Sarles] for the events of the day. But of course I did see a little, and I thought we were like Rome "just before the fall." I got back to Madison to find 33,796 students enrolling, and crowds like New York's all over the campus. On one of the first days, I noted the sound of a power saw cutting down trees to get space for enlarging the Historical Library, and it seems to me now that that, to me the most intolerable of all sounds, is a fitting accompaniment to these years, generally in connection with the spreading Dutch elm disease all over the city.

I found everyone very jittery about disruption. *Newsweek* predicted that Wisconsin was to be the prime target for that this year. There was never any

---

499 The 1968 Democratic National Convention, held August 26–29 in Chicago, was marred by fighting on the convention floor and excessive police force in response to protests outside the convention meeting, which triggered rioting.

let-up from strain, and of course you'll realize it's simpler, easier, and more dramatic to involve yourself in overthrowing an institution than it is to try to keep it going, while you must recognize it has many faults.

> If I were middle-aged, I think it would be an ethical problem for me as to whether I should stay here. As it is (no doubt rationalizing) I think I'll just stick it out. But life is wearing. The students as yet are not as destructive or belligerent as at Columbia, but there is a serious effort of the teaching assistants to take over any courses in which they are teaching, and this is bound to lead to trouble. It is unpleasant to be surrounded by hostility, since anyone over thirty but Dr Spock is ipso facto a member of the Establishment, especially when you don't know who is hostile, and have to wear a false face to everyone. I'm not important enough to be singled out for attack, but these are not good working conditions. All these years I operated under the assumption of good will on both sides; on the other side, this no longer holds true.

Our first department meeting with the new chairman "lasted for two hours when the business could easily have been completed in less than one, simply because several of last year's first-year assistant professors continued their trying habit of talking at length with nothing to say, and they have some strong recruits this year." But there was an unusual note of humor. One man announced that "Peter Pan" was being performed in the Union Play Circle, that it contained a dance of girls in the nude, and that this was forbidden by state law in a state-owned building.[500] A sample performance was to be given for the Chancellor, and we were cordially invited so we could go to court later to defend it. (I missed a good chance to appear in public to say I'd seen Maude Adams as Peter Pan and saw no reason to improve on her performance with these new-fangled ideas.) Dick Quintana came into my office next morning to tell me "No nudes is good nudes," and Bob Presson commented after the meeting that the department, like the university, was obviously following the policy of hiring the handicapped. These Peter Pan nudes made such a stir they even reached *Punch*, and were referred to in its New Year's issue for 1969. The performance was closed down,

---

[500] This 1968 production was staged by Stuart Gordon (b. 1947), a student at UW-Madison majoring in theatre, and is described on Gordon's Internet Movie Database (IMDB) biography page as "a psychedelic adaptation of Peter Pan as a political satire." The production is mentioned in Bates (1992, p. 106).

> and the district attorney of the state is trying to find the girls and no one will tell him. No one seems to be paying any attention to the dope ring—that's just an ordinary concomitant of college life today. The Madison police are complaining of lack of cooperation on the part of the university, and the legislators are whetting their knives for the university budget. It's a pity when you sympathize with people you don't sympathize with, if you know what I mean. I won't vote for the anti-university Republican candidate for governor, but I agree with the Wisconsin man-in-the-street who wants the university to clean out the out-of-state rabble rousers and dope peddlers.

The Masters' program was rather an empty shell, and I had Sunday night suppers only for the new teaching assistants and my own students. The woman who was supposed to share my course had left, so I had more to do there than expected. Since it took a little while for newcomers to get corrupted, their suppers were quite pleasant, and I had the sure-fire Squiggley story.

> I must quote Hannah's last letter. I wrote you they had a pet snake, Squiggley, a little boa constrictor, because Robert has allergies and can't have anything with fur or feathers? And that Squiggley was playing around on the dining room table during meals when I was there last June? Here's her last letter. "I forgot to put Squiggley back in his cage last night. We left him peacefully curled around a flowerpot and he had disappeared this morning. I got a good deal of fall cleaning done looking for him (in fact, it's probably all that will get done and it's more than I usually do)—furniture pulled back from the wall, and while it was out I vacuumed behind it, books pulled from the shelves and dusted, and the couch in the sunroom pulled apart and aired. Finally around noon, when he had to be there because he wasn't anywhere else, I took off the front panel of the dishwasher and there he was, curled around the motor. There is some question about if we had started the motor whether it would have killed Squiggley or Squiggley would have killed it. I called Peter to tell him the snake had been found and had to leave a message. Tonight he said the girl had written a straightforward message in ink and then in pencil had added, 'Your house sounds like a nice place to visit but I wouldn't want to live there!'"

I've never yet been in a social situation where this didn't work, and if Ho Chi Minh, Bobby Seale,[501] Golda Maier,[502] any Arab sheik, Richard Nixon and Sam Dash[503] dropped in together for a cup of tea this afternoon I'd trot it out with perfect confidence. But comic relief or no, the times were bad. "The best lack all conviction while the worst / Are full of passionate intensity."[504] Dick Quintana, who either is, or enjoys posing as if he were, extremely pessimistic, said people fell into two camps, and personally he didn't know which was the worse. One was dominated by Marx and the other by Freud, and neither had anything admirable to offer. I've gone through various historical approaches in my life. First, I thought all times are pretty much alike. The problem of the past—"The Critical Period in American History" or the Civil War or the Crusades or anything—presented as many difficulties to their contemporaries as do problems of the present, and just look simpler because, in one way or another, they have been solved. Then I thought we were living in particularly difficult times. In the past people had been sure they were right, whether they were or not, in a way no modern product of Freud and the social sciences could ever find comfort in. But now I think I have come back to the first view. There always have been fanatics, double-dealers, heroes, cowards, self-seekers, altruists, milquetoasts, self-deceivers, and there always will be. The human condition will always be a rose bush with thorns—but at some periods there'll be more roses than thorns and at others more thorns than roses.

> October 10, 1968. When I turned on WHA tonight I found myself in the non-stop hearing of the Legislative investigation into the drug situation at the university, which went on for four hours straight. The point was made, valid, I know, that this is a national, not a local, condition, and that most university students have had drug experience before they come here, but nonetheless there is a great deal of hostility in the Legislature, and I think, not without reason. They brought up the nude performance of Peter Pan, not strictly relevant, but as long as they had the acting dean of students there they gave him a

---

501 Robert George Seale (b. 1936), an American political activist, co-founded the Black Panther Party in 1966.
502 Golda Meir (1898–1978) served as the fourth Prime Minister of Israel (1969–1974) and garnered a reputation as the "Iron Lady" of Israeli politics. She graduated from Milwaukee State Normal School (now UW-Milwaukee) in 1917.
503 Samuel Dash (1925–2004), an American lawyer, was chief counsel for the Senate Watergate Committee during the Watergate scandal.
504 An excerpt from Irish poet William Butler Yeats's "The Second Coming" (1920), a modernist poem about post-war Europe.

rough time. (The real dean left last year to go to Rhode Island, which was smart; when someone asked me why we didn't have a real dean instead of an acting one, I said I thought anyone bright enough to be considered for the position was too bright to take it.) "Was there action on the part of the university officials forbidding the performance of Peter Pan?" "Yes." "Was the performance nonetheless presented?" "Yes." "Has any action been taken?" "No." "Well, then, what the hell goes on?" (The last sentence, unlike the others, is a paraphrase and not an exact quotation.) A woman asked the acting dean if he and his wife had ever been to the Union in the evening and seen the clothes and conduct. He answered rather lamely that there was a supervisor on duty. "What's the matter with him?" said the woman. Harrington appeared very briefly at the end of the hearing, mainly to introduce Edwin Young, and Young spoke briefly and well, and was not heckled. (Sewell had resigned, and Young was brought back to assume the Chancellorship from University of Maine, where he had gone a few years before to take the Presidency. He had formerly been Dean of Letters and Science here.) Since he's just come, I suppose they thought he had a right to catch his breath. He gave the impression, I'm sure intentionally, that the university would do some cleaning up, though he didn't put it in very specific words. The legislators pressed the acting dean hard because he kept saying the university was "very concerned" about the drug problem. He was in a weak position anyway, because when the drug thing first broke he said it wasn't much of a problem as far as he knew, which means either that he was lying or that he didn't know as much as he ought. "What is the point of saying over and over that you're 'very concerned' when you don't do anything? What does that mean to any student who takes or pushes drugs? Why aren't you explicit?" I felt sorry for him because you (or at least I) always feel sorry for someone who is being publicly pilloried, but I didn't think he was very impressive (nor have I thought so when I have heard him before), and I didn't think he went over very well either. Dow Chemical is coming back on November 8. If the university can't keep order then, I think we've had it.

We did get through the Dow interviewing and the national election without any riots, "the prevalent idea, borne out by several student themes I've just read, being that SDS lacks discipline and leadership, unlike the Communists, and therefore is ineffective." But the English Students' Association, a Far Left student group, issued a "demand" that all English classes Monday and Tuesday be devoted to student-led discussion of the election.[505] Of course I paid no attention, and I was not challenged, though some people were. Madeleine Doran allowed her class to vote, and since half voted for political discussion, she lectured half the time and then turned class over to the students, upon which the half that had voted against political discussion walked out. Neither then nor now do I see how a conscientious teacher could feel justified in giving class time to students who had twenty-three other hours in every day to talk about politics as much as they chose. Wednesday, when I though the whole thing was over, a student in my own class did challenge me and I expressed myself to that effect. I was supported by a big guy in the back of the room, about Tom's height and fifty pounds heavier, who said he had already wasted two class hours that day where discussion got nowhere and he thought we should tend to business. I then took the gamble of calling for a class vote (I hadn't intended to invoke democracy, which has its place but is hardly a practical method of conducting a classroom, any more than it would be if you consulted the first ten people you met on the street about the terrible pain in your abdomen). I got an overwhelming majority for the big guy, so I said the three or four who constituted a minority could leave if they wanted to talk politics, and we would devote the class hour to the purpose of the course. Everyone stayed, and we did. But this sort of thing rather takes it out of you.

A serious crisis now arose in the Department which widened our divisions and produced great bitterness. The fall is always the time for tenure discussions, "up or out," and everyone always dreaded them. Some decisions were bound to be painful, when the interests of the Department might force you to vote against someone you liked personally. But the atmosphere had not formerly been vitriolic. Two young men had to be considered, according to AAUP[506] rules: Barton Friedman[507] (the man who had invited us to see the nudes in Peter Pan) and

---

505 The English Students Association (ESA) was one of several student associations formed by SDS in 1968, mostly in the College of Letters and Science and the School of Education. These associations supported antiwar activities and issued "sweeping demands for curricular change in their respective departments"; however, Cronon and Jenkins (1999) suggest that the motivation behind such demands was primarily to "build. . . a revolutionary undergraduate base" (p. 471).
506 The American Association of University Professors (AAUP) is a non-profit membership association that advocates for fair standards, quality working conditions, and academic freedom.
507 Barton Friedman (1935–2009) earned his Ph.D. from Cornell University (1964) and taught at UW-Madison from 1963–1978, during which time he won the William Kiekhofer Teaching Excellence award (1967). He left UW-Madison for Cleveland State University (1978–1997), where he was chair of the English department (1978–1987).

John Conder. Friedman was Far Left and had a strong following among Far Left students who publicly threatened demonstrations and violence if he were not promoted. Conder tended right, though he did not intrude politics on any occasion, and had forbidden his students to try to give him any support in what was an Executive Committee, not a student matter. Both men had written books. At such a point in your career to have a book published by a reputable University Press was generally considered about 90% of the battle. Friedman's had been repeatedly sent out and repeatedly turned down. Conder's had been accepted by the University of Wisconsin Press, and was at the printer's. Friedman was strongly backed by our new chairman.

> November 27, 1968. A week ago yesterday we had the first of the two Executive Committee meetings to discuss tenure promotions. The Department, now it is so large, has set up a procedure of Area Committees, which will recommend, or refuse to recommend, a person in a given field as those best able to evaluate his work and those who would work with him if he were promoted. It is impossible any longer for a man to be known by everyone . . . .[508]

I felt bitterly ashamed of the Department, and still do. It can be said that many were confronted with a conflict of loyalties, and that many felt a new chairman deserved support, even if they questioned his judgment. Still, I see no way out of concluding that many people yielded to intimidation and voted against their consciences. Since I had no Ph.D., which is like being a bastard on the throne of England in an academic community, I had always had an inferiority complex at Executive Committee meetings. I now at one blow lost respect for most of my colleagues. I simply couldn't see how people old enough to remember Neville Chamberlain[509]—as they all were—could feel that to

---

508 In the remainder of this excerpt, Thomas describes the details of the Executive Committee's two meetings. According to her recollections, at the first meeting, the Area Committees over Friedman refused to recommend his promotion; however, the meeting was adjourned without a vote. At the second "much reduced meeting," most Area Committee members reversed their initial positions and supported his promotion. Thomas was one of only a handful to vote against. She describes the subsequent discussion about Conder's promotion as "sniping," after which his promotion was denied. The conclusion of Thomas's entry reads: "These meetings are supposed to be top secret. The very next morning the Cardinal headlined: 'Tenure Controversy Avoided: English Department OK's Friedman.'" This section has been omitted, since it involves details of confidential personnel deliberations.

509 Arthur Neville Chamberlain (1869–1940), British conservative politician who served as Prime Minister of the United Kingdom from 1937–1940, is known for appeasement foreign policy in order to avoid war with Germany.

yield to the student New Left pressure was the way to keep peace. It seemed to me there was little to choose between the violent New Left and the decadent Old Guard. I was ashamed to go to class that day, but I was supported by the fact that even if my students didn't know it, my conscience was clear of yielding to intimidation and blackmail. The idea of retiring early had of course crossed my mind in these bad days. Now, out of stubbornness, I resolved to stay every minute of my time and speak up in the Executive Committee meetings where I had previously been modestly silent. New England guts might be worth more than the Ph.D.

Just after this I flew to Delaware for Thanksgiving, and in the airport ran into a Classics professor I knew slightly, who told me he was resigning from ILS because he could no longer stand the student "ignorance and arrogance."[510] His Shakespeare class had just been disrupted, because it was the first room they came to, by Blacks protesting the expulsion of Black rioters from the University of Wisconsin at Oshkosh.[511] One of the strong elements of unreason through this period was the lack of connection throughout, as if you knocked a pedestrian down because a passing car had splashed you. It was true that there was a basic connection—to hit out at random at anything near you, like a child in a temper tantrum; but this wasn't very high-level in the academic community dedicated to sweet reasonableness. I made Christmas cards and sent them to all the teaching assistants, but without the true Christmas glow. I wouldn't have dared now to invite them to a Christmas carol party.

It was now clear to all that our chairman had an abnormal bias for youth and against age. It is proper, of course, for a chairman to be concerned about all his department members, and to look to the future. One reason we were now in such bad straits was that earlier chairmen had not sufficiently done so. But it is proper for him to be at least as concerned about the views of his permanent members, who have made the department and on whom it depends, as about the views of the members who in many, perhaps most, cases will be temporary. Tim didn't see it that way. He had to spend a good deal of time with Ed, in Ed's capacity as Associate Chairman (and Ed suffered deeply). Otherwise the stream of visitors to the Chairman's office were the young Far Left assistant professors, the young Far Left teaching assistants, and the young Far Left English

---

510 Inspired by philosopher and education reformer Alexander Meiklejohn's (1872–1964) Experimental College, a residence-based liberal arts college that operated at UW-Madison from 1927–1932 and enrolled a select number of students, Integrated Liberal Studies (ILS) was established in 1948 to emphasize an interdisciplinary, integrated approach to liberal education. It is one of the oldest continuous interdisciplinary programs in the United States.

511 For an account of black student activists striking on campus, which Thomas describes below, see Cronon & Jenkins, 1999, pp. 478–486. The "Black rioters" were three black students who were expelled from the Wisconsin State University at Oshkosh for violent conduct (p. 482).

Student Association members, graduate and undergraduate. Tim gave the ESA permission to put a table in the hall next our assignment committee rooms in registration week of the second semester, where they came snooping around giving advice of a subversive nature to any student who hadn't yet thought of a grievance on his own. For the first time, Joyce Steward took over the job of liaison officer between assignment committees and Ed Lacy. This was a killing job, which I had heretofore had to handle as well as interviewing teaching assistants for schedule preferences, involving continuous running up and down the hall dealing with complaints, while Ed remained protected behind two closed doors. The ESA made it really hell for Joyce. "What bothered her most is what she calls 'those wormy dogs,' since it is the fad now to have a dog, and everyone brought one along. Do you suppose they are training a K-nine corps to bite us?" Relieved of this, I was not only able to eat the lunch I brought with me but to finish the schedule Friday afternoon, instead of having to start work on it dead tired Friday night.

By accident during this week I ran across a passage in *The Other End of the Leash*, by Berkeley Rice.[512]

> An ancient Chinese fable tells about a time before the rise of man when the dominant creatures on earth were cats. After ages of trying to cope with famines, plagues, wars, injustice, greed and folly—in short, the normal anguish of mortality—they convened a congress of the wisest cat philosophers to see if anything could be done to improve the conditions of life. After long deliberation these feline sages concluded that the dilemma was insoluble . . . and they should abdicate. They decided to select from among the lesser creatures on earth a species optimistic enough to believe that something could be done about the mortal predicament, and ignorant enough never to learn better. This is why cats live with us today, completely dependent on us for their food and shelter, but independent of our affection and unwilling to lift a paw to help us. It is why they look at us the way they do.

I cannot make up my mind even now to what extent Tim was sincere, to what extent dishonest, to what extent mentally disturbed. During this period, I wrote I was sure he should be institutionalized, but whether in a place for the mentally retarded or the criminally insane I didn't know. As I have gone over this material, his duplicity seems more and more evident, and perhaps he was

---

512 The full title is *The Other End of the Leash: The American Way with Pets* (1968).

Demolition

Gashford[513] rather than Lord George Gordon. It doesn't matter now. At the time I thought he was the perfect embodiment of the "optimistic and ignorant" and I could hardly look at him without laughing. I preserved my sanity through department meetings by sitting on the aisle, very near the front, where he had to see me, and staring steadily at him with the best imitation of Mewa's expression I was capable of. I may not have gotten the point across to him, but it was a big help to me.

One of our deepest grievances was his habit of holding interminable meetings, lasting literally hours. In general, they started at 4:30, since some people had classes up to then, and at six, at seven, at eight the department wives would call up Margaret Lacy to ask if she knew what their husbands could possibly be doing. The wives accused Tim (you remember he was divorced) of making sure, since he had no life of his own, that no one else could have any either. Tim operated on the principle that if people differ, the more they talk together the better they will agree. Once a certain point is reached, of course—and we had long since reached it—the exact opposite is true. The Old Guard felt also he was favoring the young, who were resilient enough not to be physically exhausted after a four-hour meeting, while people of my age were not only worn out that night but also in poor shape to meet classes the next day. Of course we felt our first obligation was to our classes: the young, theirs to the cause, which could be discussed impromptu at any bull session-class.

And through this period I, who had been too shy to speak, fought tooth and nail against politicizing the department—not single-handed, of course, or even with four just men, for a good many moderates did see the danger. Once you abandon dispassionateness and take a weapon for however good a cause, the sword turns in your hand for the next cause, which may not be a good one. The building up of pacifist propaganda before World War I provided all handy war propaganda machinery once war was declared.

> Daily life was not made easier by the fact that this was by far the worst driving winter since I've been living alone. This week most of the time it has been freezing rain and fog. I really gave up on the driveway and I'm not home enough to keep it clear. I'm leaving the car at the top (which means warming it up in the morning) and going into the house across a path I shoveled on the lawn, since the driveway is too slippery even to walk down. You have no idea what it is like all over town—main roads pretty good but all secondary streets and parking lots a mess. Yesterday morning I had gotten the car about six

---

513 Lord George Gordon's secretary in Charles Dickens' *Barnaby Rudge* (1841).

Demolition

inches too far down the driveway—you know that slope—
and even my stud tires couldn't get me out. By the grace of
God, the village sanding truck came by while I was struggling,
and the men came nobly to the rescue. They brought sand,
and then both of them got in front and pushed. I wonder
when the car will get in its warm little bed again.

Not for some time. But this was only a little wave in the sea of troubles.

It was suddenly revealed that the state was suffering from a bad financial deficit, and it occurred to some of the bitterly anti-university legislators that remission of tuition for teaching assistants, most of whom were out-of-state, would be a good economy measure. This was merely raised for discussion, and even if it passed would not apply to the current year, since the university was legally committed for that, of course. But naturally this roused great antagonism, and provided a legitimate grievance to the Far Left Teaching Assistants Association, which had been losing influence.[514] They immediately raised the cry of "Strike." And we were embroiled in a strike for about a month, though the grounds were those of Black demands, a cause very much in evidence now not only here but all across the country.

We had one particular local issue. UW-Oshkosh, jumping on the bandwagon, had by great efforts recruited a considerable number of Black students, and it hadn't worked out well. A number,[515] with all due process, had been expelled for rioting, and they aroused much sympathy here. There were demands that UW-Madison should reverse the action taken by UW-Oshkosh (which was like saying that the legislature of the state of New York should reverse an action taken by the legislature of the state of Texas), and when those were recognized as obviously impossible, there were demands that the expelled students should be accepted here. This was only one aspect of the Black Power movement, however. They presented thirteen non-negotiable demands, some of them unconstitutional by state law. Not only here but also on many other campuses demands for the establishment of Black Centers and Black Programs to which whites could have no access ran counter to state anti-discrimination laws, and were impossible on those grounds alone. But such a reason had no validity to people like a

---

514 The Teaching Assistants Association (TAA), organized in June 1966 by a small group of TAs who sought to blend unionism and activism (Cronon & Jenkins, 1999, p. 494), is the oldest graduate student union in the US. Cronon and Jenkins (1999) note that this proposed legislation dramatically increased student membership in and support for the TAA (p. 494).
515 Three students were expelled for participating in a violent demonstration.

Demolition

student of mine, who wrote she yearned to teach "in a rat invested getto." Her emotions were too easily stirred by the current fashion to allow her reason to tell her 1) she'd be a more useful teacher if she could spell and 2) she was highly unlikely to be persona grata in any ghetto. She was typical, I think, of many of the supporting students. And there was certainly to be observed in some an almost psychopathic masochism in actually welcoming abuse. I remember one theme in which a girl dwelt almost lovingly on an experience she had had in the cafeteria where a completely strange Black had sat down at her table and attacked her violently and at length for the sins of her race. When we were considering the tone a speaker should take to his audience—I was presenting the relationship as one of mutual respect—another girl refuted me with the overwhelming applause a Black speaker had received for a lecture which was highly abusive. But it would be entirely wrong to give the impression that many, or indeed most, students were not completely sincere. One girl who had the problem very much in mind and made continued attempts to develop natural and friendly contacts with Blacks and really to understand them used to come into my office to talk to me not merely the semester she was in my class but all the time she was in the university—I think because I had once quoted her Thomas Jefferson's prescient statement: "I tremble for my country when I think of the Negro and remember that God is just."

Our Black Revolution started Friday afternoon, February 7. I was typing busily in my office, getting material ready for class Monday, when I vaguely noticed a stir in the corridor. I looked up and saw in my door way a tall Black who said "in the most amiable way in the world, 'Too much noise in the hall,' and shut my door staying outside. I was really too absorbed in my work to pay attention, but I heard him giving directions: 'Twenty people to 312, the rest to the Library Mall.'" 312 was Alvin Whitley's lecture room.[516] As I heard later, the twenty went into it to recruit, Alvin asked the class if they wanted the lecture to continue, they voted they did, the protestors shouted him down, and he left, thereby avoiding being carried out forcibly, which was happening elsewhere on campus. That night WHA reported that Chancellor Young, whom the rebels wanted to confront, "'had not been available.' Do you think this means he was hiding in the cellar? I wouldn't particularly want to confront them myself, I admit, but I had hoped better things of him since he comes from Maine."

Of course Friday afternoon is not a good time to start a revolt on any university campus, but the wheels began to roll vigorously on Monday. A mass meeting

---

516 Alvin L. Whitley, Jr (1926–1987), English professor at UW-Madison from 1950–1984, specializing in Romantic-era poetry. Whitley chaired a committee that created the Honors Program in the College of Letters and Sciences which commenced in 1960, and directed the program until 1963.

425

Demolition

of strikers was called at the Union at 9:30, and at 10:15 "I saw masses and masses of students coming up the Hill. There is something very formidable and frightening about seeing masses advancing towards you." At the top they split up to cover the main campus buildings, a batch remained on Lincoln Terrace. When I went at 11:00 to my class in 215 Bascom, which overlooks the Terrace, my students were looking out the window, as well they might, "but as soon as I came in they took their seats and behaved admirably. Outside there were rhythmic cries of 'On Strike! Shut it down!' varied occasionally by the beating of drums and a leader asking 'What do we want?' and 'When do we want it?' with the answers 'Freedom!' and 'Now!' but we continued to discuss rhetoric as if there wasn't a Black nearer than Africa."

Tuesday afternoon I went in to Bascom to hold conferences, and to attend a department meeting scheduled for 4:30.

> The atmosphere was getting increasingly uncomfortable with crowds shouting on the second floor (they didn't actually come up to the third) and sounds of people scampering all around overhead on the fourth, dragging things that were heavy. The word came that they were blocking the exits so that no one could get out. I would certainly have liked to go home, but I felt honor required I stay for the meeting. But at four the police came through, clearing everyone out of the building. Joyce Steward and I, with Linda and June [the two Freshman English secretaries], June very much upset, went out the back way, toward Commerce. June started to go out through 272, the big lecture room which leads to the back stairs, but one of the policemen called her back and sent her down the main stairs—a good thing because when I came in the next morning I found a woolen scarf tied so tightly across the handles of the exit doors of 272 that Rodney had to cut it with a knife; in other words, she would have been trapped. Kathy called in the evening, and considered the police action, which I had viewed as protection, a defeat. The strikers had succeeded in getting the police to do their work for them—that is, shut down classes. At home, watched some news, and so, as Pepys[517] says, to bed. First I telephoned Hannah for the comfort of talking to her. She said they were snowed in, but the electricity was not cut off so it was a pleasant adven-

---

517 Samuel Pepys (1633–1703), an English naval administrator and Member of Parliament known for his decade-long diary.

ture, I suggested they all watch the *Today Show* next morning because they might all have the fun of seeing Nana carried out of Bascom.

Wednesday morning (February 13) I came in at the usual time and all was quiet. "I stopped to see Mr. Fred, hoping for some moral support. But he is too old. He's living in the past—not that I blame him; after eighty it's the best thing you can do. It was cheerful to have him explain he was a little later than usual because he had been looking for the cat, who generally spends the night in the heated garage and hadn't come in. But, as the students say, is this really relevant?" The strikers' rally was set for 11:00, and it wasn't until nearly the end of the period that they came up the Hill again. I went home after class, Bill Lenehan having promised to call me if the postponed department meeting were to be held. I always parked now facing west, in front of Liz Waters,[518] so I could get out, but the students were now blocking all university buses, so poor Joyce Steward had to walk a mile and a half to Lot 60. Two busloads of riot-equipped police, she told me that night, had driven into the Bascom parking lot, on which her classroom looked, and then she hadn't been able to hold her students.

For Hannah's information, there was no need for me to write her these long letters which are my sources now, since Cronkite was reporting every night from Madison as a matter of course, just as he did from the national capital.

> Cronkite had a splendid coverage with a sequence of people struggling on the steps of the Social Science Building which would have done credit to any filming of *A Tale of Two Cities* or *Barnaby Rudge*. However, any childish pleasure I got from that shouldn't be grudged me in view of the evening. We had our meeting at the University Club, since both Bascom and the Union were impossible. I drove to Joyce's and Bill Lenehan picked us both up there. A demonstration of strikers was scheduled in the Library Mall for 6:30, and another of counter-strikers (a strong movement is developing which uses H for Hayakawa) there for 8:30, but at no time did we see or hear anything. Bill parked in the lot across from the Club, where there were only a few cars, and when we came out at 11:00 it was as peaceful as the Island. One of our assistant professors referred dramatically to "the crisis," saying that if we listened we could hear noises outside the room; but that was just hooey. The only noise I heard, or anyone else either,

---

518 A reference to a residential hall, one of the few on UW-Madison campus named after a woman.

was the washing up of dishes in the University Club kitchen, for the first half hour.

It was an uncomfortable meeting in an uncomfortable setting, the back half of the dining room, rather dimly lit, crowded, with what seemed like a preponderance of almost strange faces, the new young members. Word had come that Governor Knowles had called out the National Guard to restore order on the campus.[519] The policemen we have been having are members of the Madison Police Force, called in in their off time, and since they have their regular duties they'll be getting no sleep at all if this goes on. According to the news, Knowles took the action in response to the request of Mayor Otto Festge and the city police authorities, and it seems reasonable to me. But what seems reasonable to me seems tyranny to a good many department members.

I've never been at my best at this kind of meeting, since I don't have the parliamentary type of mind and can't follow hidden motives in this or that motion or substitute or amendment. I used to have a simple procedure; there were a couple of people I trusted, so I voted the way they did, and a couple people I didn't, so I voted the way they didn't. This worked well for many years. Unfortunately, it's too simplistic now. I have lost respect for some people and gained it for others. But while the revolutionaries are very thick, there is dissension in the rapidly thinning conservative ranks, and we have no real leadership.

The main reason I went to this meeting was that I intended to move a resolution in support of the Chancellor's keeping the university going, if no one else did. Someone did—and the action was tabled, which was to me the worst thing that happened during the whole strike. I wrote a personal letter of support to Young next morning—not much but all I could do. A resolution supporting the strike was also introduced, and also tabled—a little comfort but not much. After much wrangling and emending we did pass a resolution (I abstained because by then I was too confused to understand its tenor) which supported two of the thirteen Black demands: that a Black Studies program administered by Blacks

---

519 The governor's decision to call in the National Guard, on February 12, 1969, was made in response to requests made by President Harrington, Chancellor Young, and Madison Mayor Otto Festge. The initial 900 guardsmen were later joined by an additional 1,000, some of whom remained on campus until February 21 (Cronon & Jenkins, 1999, pp. 479, 481).

should be established, and that action should be taken promptly. There was a good deal of emotional discussion that night, and appeals to conscience. My conscience told me to meet my classes and maintain the business of the university. The consciences of the assistant professors and some others told them not to meet their classes and show their sympathy with our black brothers. These two points of view are irreconcilable. The comparison now was frequently made between the New Left and the Nazis. I had heard it a week or so before when I had seen Bruno Bettelheim[520] on TV, a pathetic figure, afraid of going through again in his country of refuge what he had gone through in his country of birth, and I heard it increasingly now on campus where, the counter-strikers said, anyone else had as much chance of expressing his opinion as a Jew would at a Hitler Youth meeting. Before we adjourned, we also passed a motion, pushed by the chairman, that a department meeting open to the public, to which students should be encouraged to come, should be held Saturday morning, a sort of Town Hall meeting for free expression of opinions.

The National Guard arrived Thursday morning, a bunch of good-natured looking boys, though I must admit it gave you a queer feeling to walk down the hall and see them standing there with rifles at the ready—like a concentration camp, as I heard a student say. The TAA called a three-day strike: Thursday, Friday and Monday. Dean Epstein issued a directive saying classes must be met, and asking students to complain to their respective department chairmen if they found theirs were not.

> I went to Reading Group in a state of near-collapse, having left at noon just in time while the students were blocking buses down below the hospital. As I went off campus by the exit halfway between the hospital and the Congregational Church, I looked back down University Avenue and saw it solid with people as far as I could see, with two or three islands of trapped City buses that the students were beginning to rock. Marion was very kind; she gave me aspirin and let me lie down a little while to recover myself before the others came. She says Bill hasn't seen any trouble at all on the Ag campus. It's focused on and right around Bascom and Lincoln Terrace, and the worst departments are English and Philosophy and History.

Friday was a rather trying day. June came in in tears saying she couldn't stand the strain, and the husband of the head department secretary called up to say

---

520 Bruno Bettelheim (1903–1990), Austrian-born child psychologist and writer.

he wouldn't allow his wife to come on campus at all. As usual, the 11:00 o'clock class was in competition with the demonstrators outside, but whereas while we were having discussion I could forget what was going on, today the students were writing a test, and it was harder for me to ignore it though I hoped they were able to. I had, however, no trouble getting down the Hill to the University Club to a luncheon meeting of the Phi Beta Kappa Executive Committee. One of the men had a sinister little contribution. Ten years before, he had spent a year at the University of San Marcos in Peru, establishing a heart research unit at the medical school. The university there is an old monastery, surrounded by a wall, and when the students wanted to strike they simply locked all the doors in the wall and the faculty couldn't get in. The year, he said, had impressed him deeply with the stability of the American higher education system; he didn't then realize that the Peruvians were merely ten years ahead of us. From the Club I saw a rather informal parade down State Street at noon. The car of one of the strike directors pulled up to the curb to park, and at once other strikers, including a Black girl, began to call, "No, no, don't park there—there's a hydrant!" The Blacks were undoubtedly being used by the SDS. Tom Hayden[521] was here, and I may have seen him, but without recognizing him.

In the afternoon I heard the announcement that the strike was decelerating and the National Guard were to be withdrawn—to my personal regret. "I felt a lot more comfortable with them around. They looked very young; in fact, they seemed to be growing younger and younger every time I saw them, and they have the most beautiful manners. I admit that they would like to be at home with their own families and occupations, and at the cost to the taxpayer of $22,000 a day they shouldn't be kept longer than necessary. I also admit that the atmosphere Friday seemed much pleasanter, indeed even cosy. While I went out to the back door of Bascom to go home, the girls were taking pictures of the Guardsmen, reminding me for all the world of when I was in Washington in cherry blossom time and saw tourists taking pictures of the mounted policemen in the Basin, handsome young men on handsome horses." My approving view of the National Guard, of course, was not shared by many of my colleagues. I am thinking of one man in particular—not one of the new Young Turks either though clearly their soul brother—who refused to meet any class while the Guard was on campus because he felt he would be teaching under duress. In my naïveté, I felt that a Black threatening to carry me out of my classroom was much nearer to duress than a nice-looking young National Guardsman politely opening the door for me.

---

521 Tom Hayden (b. 1939), an American social and political activist, was one of the founders of the Students for a Democratic Society (SDS).

Saturday I felt it my duty to go to the open department meeting. I didn't think anything would come of it, but it's hard to fault an opportunity for free speech.

> We moved into a Committee of the Whole and talked (not me, of course) for two hours and a half. This gave our young men a chance to show off and pose as sympathetic heroes, but I was prepared for that; it was interesting to hear the students, some of whom were simply lunatic fringe and merely abusive; but others were quite intelligent, many of them motivated by genuine idealism. One of our TA's, for instance, who is supposed to be very far-out, spoke (to my mind) very well, saying there were things we could do to provide the things the Blacks are asking for, which will take a lot of money; he was prepared to donate one-tenth of his salary to such a fund. I was not prepared for the attempt, after we moved back from the Committee of the Whole, to have the Departmental Committee take action. If I had understood this was on the agenda, I would certainly have protested Wednesday night. It is intimidation in the highest degree to take action in the presence of the Far Left among students and TA's. Madeline Doran gave a little historical perspective (she came here in 1935) about other times when the legislature had been at odds with the university, and how our freedom has always been preserved; but the audience felt little interest in any history unrelated to Blacks. Bob Doremus spoke, and well in his dry-as-dust way, on the practical consequences of action.[522] He said the Legislature controls the budget, that they can and will cut it if they wish, and that the chances of obtaining money from the Legislature for the purposes of the strikers proclaim—which would require a lot of money—are much poorer today than they were before the strike. All this is very true, but made, I fear, little impression on his audience, many of whom care more about showing off than accomplishing anything anyway. Otherwise the speakers were our department rabble-rousers currying favor with the militants.
>
> I had taken Joyce Steward to the meeting, and when we got back to the car she was in tears, wanting to get out. I went

---

522 Robert B. Doremus (1915–1982) taught at UW-Madison from 1940 until his death. He published an anthology, *Patterns in Writing*, with Ed Lacy and George Rodman in 1950, and *Writing College Themes* (1960), and was an associate dean in the College of Letters and Science.

home with her and stayed for a pick-up lunch, because she was in a bad way and needed an audience. I hope I convinced her that she should do just what she wanted regardless of me, because it wouldn't make much difference to me what happened in the next two years. All this is striking at the concepts of discipline, loyalty, impartiality, which is what distresses her—and me. The academic community should stand for the humanities, for reason, for the continuation of education, which is its business, not for any single cause. You strike for one cause, and the next thing you know your propaganda is turned against you. This is the AAUP stand, and mine, and hers. I feel sorry for her because she must have at least fifteen professional years ahead of her. I'm also sorry for Bill Lenehan. I'm responsible for his promotion and position here, but now I'm not sure he owes me gratitude for it.

Sunday morning Bascom was delightfully quiet with some very pleasant young MP's [military police] sitting around in the basement. I offered them my faculty ID card, but since I had just let myself in with the key, they said there was no need to bother. I must not *look* like a rioter. Monday was quiet as usual early, but in the 9:55 period the rioters charged up the Hill from their 9:30 strategy meeting. A howling mob (this cliché is quite literal) came into Bascom rampaging up and down the halls, setting off fire alarms, and yelling "Support the Black Demands!" at the top of their lungs. The National Guard, who had been kept near enough to get back quickly, had arrived by 11:00 and again were as thick in the halls as dandelions on my lawn in spring. My 11:00 o'clock class, for once, was so peaceful you wouldn't know anything odd was going on at all. This is one of the surprising things about such an experience—how quickly you can forget when you have the ghost of a chance to do so. A man turned up in class whom I hadn't seen since the first week and hardly recognized, and made himself at home in the most agreeable manner possible. In my office afterwards, he said there was no use lying, he had been out supporting the strike, but mine was a required course and he wanted to come back and would take any grade penalty I imposed. (Since I don't believe in disciplinary grades, I never could take the easy way out here.) If his conscience required him to strike, I said, did it justify his returning? You have to be realistic, he said, and the strike was over anyway.

I had an interview with our chairman Monday—I guess we could use the fashionable term "confrontation"—to enter a formal protest about his calling for department action at the meeting Saturday morning, which I had thought was for expression of opinion only. I must do him the justice to say that he saw me as soon as he arrived (when I got in I called his secretary to ask for an appointment at any time during the day except for my two classes, and she called me down at 8:15); and that when I had to leave for my 8:50 he offered to see me again later for as long as I liked. I admitted that my misunderstanding might owe something to my stupidity in parliamentary matters. He admitted that he must take some responsibility for the misunderstanding—an honest mistake on his part, he said. He himself had felt very pleased with the meeting Saturday because it kept open the lines of communication. I said I thought the English Students Association was not representative, nor the TAA, and he said, "They will be." I said the NAACP was not sponsoring violence, and he said it was not representative. You could hardly call it a meeting of minds. He sees himself as a leader: "We must listen to these people so we can guide them"; I see him as a dupe, being used and laughed at. So I left, politely refusing his polite offer of another appointment. I hadn't expected to accomplish anything, and I didn't, except that "at least I can have the comfort of having been brave enough to go and try to say to his face what I'm repeatedly saying behind his back." Also in fairness I must say that a girl in my class, both nice and intelligent, the only one of my students I saw at the meeting, used exactly his phrase about "open lines of communication." She wanted me to comment on the meeting, and I did, not in class, but after it in private with her. I believed, I said, that the business of the university should be carried on, that I was opposed to force instead of reason, and that I had hoped to show my views by my action in conducting the class rather than by talking. She said yes, she did understand that, and she and I parted, I hope, on terms of mutual respect. She thought it a pity the English Department was divided: "This is a great university and department." At the same time one of our teaching assistants was regretting it was his fate to be present when a great university was cut down—as Columbia had been no more than a hundred students. After my confrontation with Tim, I considered retiring again, "but Bill Lenehan really looked shaken when I told him so, and I won't leave him in the lurch if he thinks I am any help—though it seems to me I may just be making things worse for him."

This girl who approved of the Saturday meeting perhaps had not many to agree with her. As I was privately accusing Tim in his office of bad faith, the English Student Association came out publicly with the first number of their *Newsletter*, making exactly the same accusation.

> The chairman's bad faith with the students was demonstrated at Saturday's in the following ways:
>
> (1) He assured students that the meeting would not be a Committee of the Whole, but "a regularly constituted

> Departmental Committee meeting with students invited and taking party equally in a town-hall atmosphere of free discussion between all parties."
>
> (2) He assured students that the first item on the agenda would be consideration of the faculty resolution dealing with Black demands. (This was taken at the Wednesday evening meeting at the University Club. This *Newsletter* described it as a "token resolution. The department apparently is willing to allow its public seal of approval on black-related activities *only* as long as those activities preclude action to help the blacks.")
>
> (3) He assured students that adequate copies of the resolution would be available for the meeting.
>
> There were no copies of the resolution provided at the meeting. We never did get to substantive discussion of the resolution. We met in a Committee of the Whole. The chairman seems to have told students one thing and faculty something else.

No more than anyone else ever does did poor Tim find it easy to run with the hare and hunt with the hounds, and naturally his difficulties were increasing every day.

During this time, I thought my course had real "relevance."[523] Our text was *The Art of Rhetoric,* and we considered everything we read and everything we wrote from the standpoint of Aristotle's thesis: communication (rhetoric) is a matter of appropriateness and balance among three elements: writer or speaker, audience, situation.[524]

> One boy wrote an impromptu on the basis of the text title, describing the interruption into his classroom of Blacks, who would not let the professor either leave or go on with his lecture, so that all remained in turmoil. He concluded that

---

[523] As Fleming (2011) notes, relevance became a key term in debates between students and faculty about curricular reform. For TAs, relevance meant making course content pertinent to students' lives and to current events; for senior faculty, it meant "lack of standards and loss of control" (p. 103).

[524] *The Art of Rhetoric* (1968) by Francis X. Connolly and Gerald Levin, was a college composition textbook that introduced students to classical and modern rhetorical theory and included a collection of classic and modern essays for analysis, organized by modes (description and narration, exposition, argument and persuasion, expository narrative, and expository argument).

rhetoric was of the greatest practical value these days, and it was a pity some couldn't have been used which would have brought everyone together. He was obviously disappointed in his professor because the poor man hadn't worked a miracle. I used the theme for class discussion. We agreed that after all rhetoric has to be heard. Mark Antony over the body of Caesar persuaded an audience of the opposite of their conviction; but they lent him their ears. To expect the professor to deal with shouting rioters meant no test of his rhetorical ability but of the strength of his lungs, and one voice will always be shouted down by thirty.

All this made stimulating class discussion. But the situation was beyond rhetorical skill, useful though it may be in ordinary life. People had made up their minds, and neither rhetoric nor force would change them. Racking failed to persuade Anne Askew.[525] At the first Annual Meeting I ever attended at the Island, the main business was whether or not to introduce electricity. Some wanted it, some didn't. After a couple of hours of argument, everyone voted as he would have done if the vote had been called as he entered the room. Nothing would make me believe the university should take a political stand. Nothing would make the revolutionaries believe it shouldn't.

At the next university faculty meeting, a motion was presented that some of the Blacks expelled from Oshkosh for rioting should be admitted here. It lost, 524 to 518.[526] This is one time in my life I felt my vote really counted. I rather expected new riots to flare up, but none did. A bill was introduced into the State Legislature to put teeth into disciplinary measures against the university, and it provided for more teeth than a bulldog has, and would have reduced us to a cow college. It began with the abolition of the tenure system, provided for dismissal of faculty members if they should "honor, aid, or abet" students in strikes, demonstrations and riots, and authorized the governor to take over disrupted campuses by proclaiming a state of emergency. It was of course far too extreme to have any chance of passing, but it indicated the extent of anti-university bitterness in the Legislature.

The national media of course were giving us a lot of attention. *Newsweek* published a lead article with so many errors I canceled my subscription. One was the picture of a beaten-up student allegedly beaten up by the National Guard.

---

525 Anne Askew (1520–1546), the English poet and Protestant who was condemned as a heretic, tortured, and burned at the stake.
526 Technically, the motion was to call on the administration to reverse its decision not to admit the three black students (Cronon & Jenkins, 1999, p. 482).

Demolition

In fact, the beating had been done by other students before the Guard arrived. Another was the statement that the disorders were decelerating, not accelerating, before the Guard was called in. This I was in a position to contradict from my own firsthand experience in Bascom the day the rioters tried to block all exits. Governor Knowles wrote a long letter to *Newsweek* carefully pointing out the factual errors. The Madison newspapers published it in full, but *Newsweek* only in part, and under "Letters," not in the body of the magazine. The original erroneous account remains in libraries everywhere waiting for historians.

The last, and most spectacular, episode I missed myself. On March 3 I wrote Tom and Diane:

> I guess I know how our ancestors must have felt during the Indian attacks. They kept working in the fields and stirring mush in the cabin without paying much attention to when the savages would come rushing out of the woods. We had a terrible flare-up Thursday afternoon, the most destructive yet, but I missed it because that's the one time in the week I'm not on campus. This really was like an Indian attack because small bands of whooping and hollering savages rushed through half a dozen of the buildings, throwing rocks through windows and any office doors with glass panels (there are a lot of those), scaring the stenographers to death, naturally, setting off fire alarms, tearing down pictures, including those of the Nobel Prize winners in the Physics Lab, which terribly upset the present Physics students, wrenching the hands off electric clocks, overturning vending machines, and so on. Worst of all, they threw stink bombs into some of the lecture halls. When I came in Friday morning, you could still smell the one in Bascom. Things were much worse in Social Science and Van Vleck, the janitor told me. He said a whole truckload of broken glass had been carried away.

My friend John Conder called me Thursday evening to tell me about this. As a lecturer in a big course, he had suffered a number of times from disruption (the reason I never did was that I had only small classes) and had been bitterly resentful of the fact that he got no protection from the administration (which he rather naively considered responsible for allowing him to carry out the duties they were paying him for) or from the department. He had been lecturing in a building where stink bombs were thrown, and he wanted to know what I thought would happen the next day—in which respect, of course, I could be just as helpful to him as Mewa could. The *Cardinal* announced a rally for 10:30, so I went to my 11:00 o'clock expecting shoutings on the Lincoln Terrace as usual. Not a sound. Four students were absent at the beginning of the hour; one by one they came in, rather out of breath. It turned out that no leader had turned up to conduct the rally, so seventy-five students waited around for half an hour and then gave up and went to their classes. So now I know which of mine are involved, as I told Bill and Kathy later. "How do you know?" said Bill, who has evidently profited by his study of due process. Well, I couldn't take it to court—nor is there any need to, luckily—but circumstantial evidence was enough for me, as Thoreau said when he found a trout in the milk. "The report is that this time pictures were taken of rioters in the act of destruction, which would be admissible evidence in a court of law, and arrests were made. The state Legislature is holding budget hearings, and naturally if they have any legal grounds for prosecution the university authorities will go along with them as far as they can." The strike was now over, but we were having at least three meetings a week, between department and university faculty, lasting three or four hours apiece, say 3:30 to 7:30, and these really made a long hard day at the office.

In March I gave a theme assignment leaving the choice of topic to the student; the method I did assign, keyed to our text, treating something involving a group of people. They wrote, I told Hannah, on a variety of topics:

> These include a stay at a mental institution, a prize fight, an appearance of the Beatles, the beating up of a factory owner in a small town by strikers, an epileptic attack, the celebration of Israel's 20th anniversary of freedom, a tornado, a child's drawing of a beach, a student rift which ended forever Sheboygan's traditional Bratwurst festival, lion hunting the Maasai way, gate crashing a leper doctors' convention party in Mexico, an avalanche in Utah, a kidnapping, and worst of all the account of a student-playwright's production in the Play Circle here which roughed up the audience. I trust you're not thinking of sending Anne to college here. Only two people wrote anything about our own riots, which rather surprised me, but I guess most students are sick of the whole business.

One of these two described a torchlight parade of reputedly 10,000 students around the Square to show sympathy for the Black demands. This had received a good deal of national publicity, and Hannah had referred to it. Since it took place at night, when I wasn't in town, I had no contact with it except through this theme. Anything with torches at night is always fascinating, and this girl was thrilled when the leader dismissed them back at the Library Mall with "Keep the

Demolition

faith." (He may possibly have been the Black who so agreeably closed my office door the day the whole thing began). I don't know whether the number was accurate or not, but it was said a good many marchers were not university students, but Madison high school kids, who always like to get in on any fun going.[527]

It was a long hard winter in more ways than one, but it finally wore itself out. "The loveliest time of year here (May 10), with the trees leafing out and the lilacs almost in bloom, and trouble has broken out again, just when I was over-optimistically hoping we could get through the rest of the semester—only two more weeks before exams. The way-outs down on Mifflin held a block party[528] without asking for permission, the police were called, poor Hannah called up from Boston to know if I was still alive, and the presentation on Walter Cronkite looked like a major battle of World War II." As a matter of fact, though this naturally did nothing to improve relations between the university and the city, of the university and the legislature, when the action was so far away from campus I felt comparatively untouched by it. A large number of the young people living in Mifland, as the section just off the Square came to be called, were not registered students at the university anyway, though whatever they did reflected on the university. There were some personal milestones in this month. In May Bill and Kathy moved in here to stay until their house was ready, and Jimmy was born in June. Setzie Pooley suddenly died. I hope never again to go through a day like the one that held her funeral service at Grace Episcopal and Dick Quintana's retirement dinner almost immediately after it. That was held at a restaurant in Middleton, and I drove the Quintanas out. But I can end this semester of turbulence and violence on a pastoral note.

> May 25. There was such a pleasant, peaceful sight on the campus Friday it brought tears to my eyes: a woodwind quintet, which apparently thought it would be agreeable to practice outdoors and set up their chairs right in front of Lincoln, where they proceeded to play Vivaldi in the most soothing manner. Various students and dogs gathered around, lying on the grass, and it was almost like Orpheus taming the wild beasts. When I think of the scenes I've watched on that terrace before!

---

527 The number of demonstrators and supporters involved was estimated at times to be 8,000 to 10,000 (Cronon & Jenkins, 1999, p. 479).
528 This was the first of what is now an annual event, called the Mifflin Street Block Party, held on the first Saturday of May. It began in 1969 as part street dance, part protest against the Vietnam War; the ensuing violent clashes between police and students led to a three-day riot, footage of which was captured in the 1979 documentary *The War at Home*.

The first significant event of the fall semester was the October Moratorium, staged in Washington by anti-war forces all over the country, an attempt to disrupt all normal activities and bring the Federal government to its knees.[529] Since the most dedicated protestors converged on the national capital, things were comparatively quiet on campuses.

> October 18. The only demonstration I saw was a little ballet skit on the Lincoln Terrace, involving perhaps a dozen students and carefully restricted to a fifteen-minute between-class period, so they couldn't be accused of disruption. A number of students stayed away from classes (more than half my class was present, but this was far more than most people had) and went to a big evening rally and a torchlight parade around the Capitol. I am sure many were sincere; I believe others went for kicks—they thought the faculty would do nothing important that day anyway. Joyce Steward, who went down to the Madison Library in the early afternoon, reported seeing large numbers who had come to shop or go into bars. The TAA voted not to strike; they just stayed away; if they had come out officially as not meeting classes the authorities might have been able to penalize them by salary cuts. This morning's paper quotes the Chancellor as telling the Regents that to his knowledge no classes failed to meet. From firsthand experience in Bascom, I knew many failed to meet. So either this was a deliberate lie or he purposely kept himself in the dark so as not to know what was going on. I'm not so childish as to think you can manage public business without compromise. But you don't have to lie. Moreover, there's a difference between compromise and sell-out, which, in my view, has been happening on this campus since the first Dow Chemical riot.

The view that there had been an academic Munich was beginning to appear in various places. Joseph Wood Krutch published an article in the *American Scholar*,[530] which had quite the flavor of the Old Testament prophetic writings,

---

529 This nationwide event, called the Moratorium to End the War in Vietnam or the Vietnam Moratorium, took place on October 15 and culminated with a march on Washington on November 15. "More than fifty meetings took place on campus on Moratorium day, and some faculty and teaching assistants devoted their class to a discussion of war. The event culminated with the largest campus rally yet, a packed Field House crowd estimated at 15,000;" but this was largely peaceful, and there was "declining campus interest in the November Washington march" (Cronon and Jenkins, 1999, p. 488).
530 The quarterly magazine published by the Phi Beta Kappa Society.

accusing the academic world of completely rejecting reason. He ended with a quotation from Pope: "And universal darkness covers all." A similar article, written by a professor of History at Smith, appeared in both the Smith and Holyoke *Alumnae Quarterlies*. This accused the academic world of having destroyed democracy, since it was the influence of college faculties which led their students to act as they were now doing. During the Cambodian crisis to come in May, Henry Kissinger[531] took the blame for the riots on his own shoulders and those of his colleagues, who had spent the past years analyzing everything wrong with our system but never giving any attention to anything right or any way to make it better. He still refused to believe, he said, that deep problems could be solved by emotional spasms instead of reason. Even some members of the antiwar factions expressed regret (an article in *Newsweek*) that the moratorium had amounted to academic communities taking a political stand. Well they might regret it, I thought; I had been feeling and saying all along "if the colleges begin to take sides, they'll reflect the fashionable view, whatever it is, every time there is any pressure, and real truth and freedom will go right down the drain."

On our own campus, the disturbances of the preceding year had been caused by Black demands; those of this by trouble with teaching assistants. The question of labor unions and strikes is controversial and complicated, and it would be unwise for me to try to go into it here. I'm writing for a future audience, and what will be the generally accepted attitude when you read this if far beyond the powers of my crystal ball. Wisconsin is historically a liberal university, and its greatest days were the days of John R. Commons.[532] His successors in general held the view that the system of conflict between labor and management is the best possible, and accounts for the very large American productivity. Labor does not want concessions given by a benevolent management, but rights won by their own fighting, and this is the ideal attitude psychologically. I have heard Jack Barbash,[533] one of our experts, express this view on a number of occasions, and I thought him convincing. Past history seems to show that capital is as benevolent as it's forced to be, and naturally is as benevolent as Scrooge before his conversion. On the other hand, contemporary history seems to show that labor unions are supremely indifferent to public welfare if they get what they want

---

531 Henry A. Kissinger (b. 1923), an American diplomat and politician who served as National Security Advisor (1969–1975) and U.S. Secretary of State (1973–1977). He received the 1973 Nobel Peace prize for helping arrange a ceasefire in Vietnam.

532 John R. Commons (1862–1945), an influential economist and reformer, taught at UW-Madison from 1904–1933 and drafted progressive social welfare, economic, and labor legislation that was implemented in Wisconsin. He is considered the "spiritual father" of Social Security.

533 Jack Barbash (1911–1994), professor of economics and industrial relations at UW-Madison from 1957–1981.

themselves, and England today (February 1974) may be a case in point. I think rather longingly of what I believe obtains in one of the Scandinavian countries: three representatives at every dispute, the third representing the public. Edwin Young's field is Labor. He knew the university ran well with the janitors having a union, and probably thought it would run better if the teaching assistants had one. They did, of course, already have one (1966) though it did not contain a majority of them, and this summer he acknowledged it as bargaining agent for all teaching assistants. It was the first such recognition in the country, and he may have felt it would bring him prestige. To the best of my knowledge (I checked recently with Ed Lacy on this, who would be in a better position to know about it than I), not many institutions have followed his example.

In my judgment, which I still see no reason to change, it was a disastrous mistake.[534] By a stroke of his pen, he turned our co-workers into antagonists. To begin with, I think the analogy between a commercial plant and a university is false. A commercial plant is run for profit; the university is run for the benefit of its students in particular and society as a whole. A commercial plant has permanent employees; the university teaching assistants are always both temporary and part-time. A commercial plant has jobs; the university gives the teaching assistant an "award," the term used on every appointment letter that ever went out of the English Department office. A commercial plant has a time clock, and management knows whether employees are on duty or not. The university relies on the honor of its teaching assistants to meet their classes, and has neither the wish nor the power to check up. In Freshman English we had over two hundred classes, meeting every academic period from 7:45 through 4:35, in every part of the campus from way out on the Ag and Engineering campuses to Science Hall on Part Street. Most fundamental difference of all, management and labor are two separate entities. Labor will not turn into management. But the teaching assistants (caterpillars to butterflies) will be faculty themselves in a year or two, and will be faculty thereafter all the rest of their lives. I had spent all my professional life very happily working with assistants. Young set up the situation in which they worked against us.

It's still surprising to me that the university through all this period was so badly served by its Public Relations Office. It unquestionably had, and spent, the money to secure the highest degree of professional skill; but throughout the publicity was handled as ineptly as Sewell handled the Dow riot. This may have

---

534 Many faculty criticized Young's decision, especially because he made the decision without faculty senate approval, but his specialization in labor relations influenced his decision to address labor disputes through established negotiation processes. Years later, he expressed regret for recognizing and bargaining with the TAA; he felt the university "'gave in too much'" (Cronon & Jenkins, 1999, p. 495).

Demolition

been due to inconsistency and weakness in the leadership the Public Relations people were representing—I have no way of knowing. On the other hand, the TAA, which had little money, presented itself to the public—TV appearances, newspaper articles—with great skill and success. They were lucky in their president, one of our own teaching assistants, Robert Muehlenkamp.[535] Attractively boyish and clean-cut (the bearded ones lurked in the background and didn't go on TV), he would appeal to the maternal instincts of any Middle American Madison housewife. When he and I ran across each other, which was not often, since my close contacts with assistants were confined to their first year, we always exchanged cordial notes, owing to the coincidence of his wife's having had her first baby only a couple of days after Kathy had Jimmy (not at the same hospital). The Muehlenkamp baby cut his first tooth a little before Jimmy, and I congratulated the proud father warmly, keeping to myself the knowledge that Jimmy, in the 100th percentile both in height and weight, would easily be able to knock it out if the babies came into conflict.

If you remember my earlier explanation of what "English" is, you'll know we had two special disadvantages. The first was size. In a department like Classics, say, where close personal contact was inevitable, problems would hardly arise. Second, and far more serious, was the controversial nature of the work. In the sciences, teaching assistants supervised lab periods, and lab techniques are not very debatable. Similarly, in the languages, assistants must without question give a good deal of rote material in beginning courses. But English composition? So many men, so many minds. What's more, other approaches in other places might be very successful—there. Our assistants must respect a professor's knowledge in a given field: Merritt Hughes on Milton,[536] Madeleine Doran on Shakespeare, Dick Quintana on Swift, were recognized authorities nation-wide. But the assistants wouldn't necessarily accept or respect my views on Freshman English, which were far from universally held, and which I had never claimed should be. We only felt they were appropriate under our conditions here—which included, of course, the reasons the deans and faculties of all university colleges required our course for their students.

For many years, I had honestly defended the teaching assistant program. Now I couldn't. I thought we should get rid of it, even if it meant going to television, and I had said so in department meeting several years before, though

---

535 Robert Muehlenkamp, an English teaching assistant and, at one point, TAA president at UW-Madison, is a social justice activist and trade union organizer. He holds a BA from Marquette and an M.A. from the University of Chicago.

536 Merritt Hughes (1893–1971), a Milton specialist trained at Harvard (1921), was hired as a full professor from the University of California. He taught at UW-Madison from 1936–1963. During ten of those years, he served as department chair.

nobody paid any attention. Bill Lenehan took the sensible view that if the assistants thought they were exploited and abused, we should stop using them. There were, however, two problems. First, the assistants wanted the money the university paid them even if they weren't willing to do for what they accredited university representatives thought they should. Here again they were very skillful in their publicity, and I'm sure many were sincere. One poster showed an appealing girl pathetically demanding "Why should I lose my job just because I am trying to make it better?" They were unable to realize that—on their own merits—they never would have had a class in Freshman English at all; they had it only because of general belief that they were under the direction of responsible senior English department members. A recent letter of Hannah's makes this same point in connection with one of her practice teachers. Second, the professors were unwilling to take any action which would reduce the numbers of their graduate students. So we had an indefensible system, with two vested interests entrenched in it.

Through these uneasy years there were, of course, all kinds of attempts to increase student and staff participation in our course planning. My own experience with these (once the good days of the "company men," the Masters, were over) was not happy. I believe students can be helpful in an advisory capacity, and that variety of ways of getting such advice should exist. But I think safeguards are needed. I don't think a student on entering college knows as much about what he should learn in his field as do men who had spent their life in it, for instance; nor do I think he is in a sound position to evaluate a course until he has finished it and can see it as a whole. And I believe decisions should be made *only* by permanent staff members who will be right on hand to take the consequences of the decisions. Two extended experiences I had here, one in 67–68, one in 68–69, will show you why I came to these conclusions.

The Wisconsin Student Association decided to investigate Freshman English, and appointed a committee consisting of one graduate, one senior, one junior, one sophomore, and one freshman, to meet with Bill Lenehan, Joyce Steward, and me. The only time we could all get together was 4:30 Friday, a particularly hard time for Joyce and me since for us the weekends were not breaks but two days of intensive work on our themes, so we could return them at the next class meeting after they were handed in. The graduate had transferred here as a junior from Lawrence, and had no experience with our course at all. She contributed some interesting ideas, workable in a small place, with full-time experienced staff, but not workable here. The senior had had Freshman English here, and had several changes to suggest, all of which, it happened, we had already made. The junior was the only man among the students. He appeared about one time in four, and never opened his mouth when he came. The sophomore was the moving spirit in getting the investigation going; she was an extremely able girl with political aspirations and of course quick to see that Freshman English, as the only required course on campus, was a highly popular target. She herself had been in 181, the Honors course, which throughout this whole period was almost totally free from criticism, so she had had herself no experience with the regular course, which was the committee's topic of investigation. The freshmen, of course, was currently enrolled, so in October, November or even December not in a position to judge of it as a whole. We did our best to be pleasant and patient and answered all questions fully and freely, with the happy result that by March the students had decided Freshman English was an excellent course. People were unjustifiably prejudiced against it before they even started it, they decided, and this was a great pity. The committee members could think of no particular improvements, but they thought it would be a really good idea to send out a questionnaire to all enrolled freshmen, which would have the desirable effect of making them see how really good Freshman English was. We spent a number of meetings working on the questionnaire, and then Miss Jordan, the sophomore, bethought herself of checking with WSA to see if any funds were available for it. No, she was told; there wasn't a cent. We then adjourned for the summer. Early next fall Miss Jordan came in to see me and say she had been admitted to the Nursing School, that she was fascinated by her work and spending a lot of extra time on it, and the committee would not re-convene.

The next year the committee in which I was involved was a department one, four faculty (one man added to even numbers who had little or nothing to do with Freshman English) and four teaching assistants; we were charged to determine textbooks and program for next year's Freshman English. The four assistants were all experienced. For one, I had great admiration and respect. A very able man, after his initial year we gave him a section in the Honors course, which was taught by our new assistant professors and our best teaching assistants. He handled it well, but asked for the next year to be assigned to 101. This was a small course for the small portion of the entering class (determined by testing) who needed elementary instruction. A good many of these were Blacks who had been recruited by a very energetic university program, of course not at all well prepared for university work. All the preceding year I had met weekly with the 101 staff, all dedicated volunteers, all confronted by difficult and delicate problems, and I had been impressed with this man's moderation and practical good sense as well as by his idealism. He and his wife had adopted a Black child in addition to their own little boy. There may be some doubts as to the wisdom of this action, for I'm told an adopted Black in a white family is subject to special strains (the little girl was a darling but very black-skinned and very kinky-haired), but there is no doubt about his sincerity.

Our meetings were agreeable—Bill Lenehan, who chaired them, is good at creating an easy atmosphere—and I cannot remember a single loss of temper or courtesy (how unlike the English Department). Bill made a great point in his report to the department of fact that on not a single vote was the division four to four, as might have been expected. The assistants urged upon us some texts and programs to which all the senior members—that is, all the most experienced members—saw serious objections on practical grounds. We presented our objections, and everything was very thoroughly thrashed out. They held to their position, and finally, against our better judgment, we accepted it. In the fall, the program met with very strong and general objection from the teaching assistants in the course—on exactly the grounds Bill and Joyce and I had presented meeting after meeting. And where were the four teaching assistant committee members? Three of them, including the man I respected, had left the campus. The fourth (whom I also knew well and did not particularly respect) took an early opportunity of dissociating himself publicly from the unpopular program just as seen as he saw it was unpopular.[537]

The teaching assistant, you should remember, was playing a double role, that of a scholar and teacher (which as a matter of fact he would continue to do throughout his professional life). Our department was very scrupulous in protecting enough time and creativity for him to do good graduate work and advance steadily toward the degree he needed to become a full-time teacher. Our department—and Ed Lacy deserves the credit—was truly admirable in this respect, but I must admit that all departments were not so—one justification, I confess, for the TAA. You will remember that in English alone the assistant had full charge of his class and did not merely meet lab or quiz sections. We felt the assistant, with the demands his graduate work made on him—and this might well determine his future success—would have neither time nor energy to spare to create a new course, which, as anyone who has done it knows, takes an enormous amount of both. We wanted to provide an experience according to principles which must be recognized as just: respect for the student, objectivity, individual attention, full class involvement, reasonable planning, and so on, on which, when the assistant became a full time teacher, he could draw as much or as little as he chose.

---

537 Fleming (2011) summarizes Lenehan's memo, which concludes by endorsing the shared faculty-student governance model constituted by the Freshman English 102 policy committee (p. 88). Fleming also summarizes a report prepared by Thomas and five TAs on the revised English 101 course, which Fleming notes is admirable for its flexibility and student-centeredness but problematic in remedializing composition along racial lines; nonetheless, the report and course were praised by the department and even the college dean (p. 90), which suggests that the TA resistance Thomas mentions was more likely in response to curriculum changes proposed by the English 102 policy committee.

Demolition

Naturally, the abler the doctoral candidate the better he could handle the double role. Ten years before we had had brilliant classroom teachers whom we successfully recommended for the Kiekhofer teaching award (some of these were specified for assistants, some for assistant professors) whose graduate grades were uniformly A's. But in the rush for bigness we had collected a considerable number of weak people who couldn't hold the balance well. Some of them took time they owed their students for their graduate work; these, when asked to suggest books for inclusion in the course, would turn in highly unsuitable works for undergraduates because it would help them review for their prelims. Others marked time in graduate work, losing interest in the degree, resented the solid work of teaching composition, and rationalized by turning their teaching into propaganda for one or another cause. Of course, the condition was not merely local, but national. Many places were giving up on any attempt at uniformity and control, and letting every assistant do what he chose. The result was chaos. We still fought that, though the battle was growing harder all the time, because we refused to give up the basic principle that we were obligated to provide a valuable course for our freshmen. Though we had also a responsibility to the teaching assistants in the way of training (a responsibility they were increasing unwilling to let us fulfill), we had a fundamental responsibility to the university for the protection and education of its freshmen.

Tom Tanselle[538] was on leave this semester, and on October 23 I gave him a rather wordy account of the home front.

> Thank you for your card, and the sympathy, which is well-deserved. Things have come to a head with the refusal of one of the TA's (Carr)[539] to use the texts adopted in the course by the faculty-TA committee, Tim held a TA meeting which Bill Lenehan describes as Sherman described war, at which they ganged up on him (of course we all knew he'd been asking for it) and passed a resolution demanding that the Departmental Committee turn [English] 102 over to a committee of seven TA's and one faculty advisor.[540] This is coming up for action

---

538 G. Thomas Tanselle (b. 1934), an American literary critic, taught at UW-Madison from 1960–1978, during which time he held many prestigious national fellowships. He left Wisconsin to become vice president of the John Simon Guggenheim Foundation (1978–2006).

539 Joseph Carr, a second-year teaching assistant, whose resistance to the established textbooks and meetings with Bill Lenehan and Tim Heninger marked the beginning of the faculty-teaching assistant impasse that resulted in the department's eventual abolishment of Freshman English (Fleming, 2011, pp. 133–149).

540 Fleming describes this meeting, held on October 13, as "perhaps the key event in the story" of the abolition of Freshman English because it marks the moment when English faculty

next Tuesday. Bill is going to present a substitute motion calling for the abolition of 102 and 181, something I've been urging for three years. The TAA is carrying on an "informational" picketing on Lincoln Terrace this week, probably preliminary to a strike, which I wish would come. I'm all for confrontation. There has been too much appeasement.

When I think of the happy years I worked *with* the TA's—all those baby booties and Christmas carol parties! I don't think I can even bear to send them Christmas cards this year. In 1965 I'd walk down the hall on third floor Bascom and be greeted by as many cheerful smiles—"Hi, Mrs. Thomas!" "Hi, Mrs. Thomas!" "Hi, Mrs. Thomas!"—as John F. Kennedy got at the Democratic convention which nominated him for the Presidency. In fact, the comparison occurs to me because once when one of my students was walking with me he said, "You ought to run for office." Now in the same corridor I meet the cut direct, the baleful glare from shadowed eyes that Madame Defarge cast upon little Lucie Darnay, or merely the look of disgust one would give to a caterpillar in the salad or (to use a contemporary figure from one of my student themes) an electric hair in the soup. An electric hair, as no doubt you know, comes out of an Afro hair-do on a non-African. Did you know Jean Turner?[541] She's very active in the TAA. When she passes my office, she looks in and smiles at me the way the wolf smiled at Red Riding Hood.

Since Bill and Kathy and Jimmy are with me now, I felt the house was a little crowded to have my usual Sunday night supper parties. Joyce Steward has moved to a new apartment complex which has a clubroom a tenant can rent for entertaining. I went out to look at it with her and we made plans, but over the weekend she changed her mind and said she just didn't feel she *wanted* to ask the assistants out. Bill Lenehan said he didn't blame her at all: if he had just moved into a new neighborhood, he wouldn't want that crew coming out to see him either.

Have you seen "Oliver!"? I enjoyed it very much, except the ending, which was foolish. Didn't Fagin remind you of Tim

---

felt that the teaching assistant had sought to take over English 102 (pp. 135, 137)
541 Jean Turner, an activist teaching assistant in the English department.

[Heninger]? Have you read the book on the Peter Principle? Like Parkinson's Law (how well that is illustrated in both Executive and Department Committee meetings, where a possible five minutes worth of business swells to an hour and forty-five minutes invariably), the Peter Principle is clearly illustrated right here. A man gets promoted up to the position in which he can do the most harm, and then gets stuck—which explains why everything in our culture is the way it is. Tim is a perfect case in point.

Tim was now, as had been predictable from the beginning, at odds with everyone. He had begun by alienating the senior members, and now, which it was obvious he couldn't fulfill the expectations he had aroused in the junior ones, the teaching assistants, and the English Student Association, he hasn't a friend in the world. A series of comic strips, run off on our hectograph machine (at least *a* hectograph machine, presumably ours), labeled "Sayings of Chairman Miaow," began to appear overnight on all the hall department bulletin boards: for example, "I believe in democracy! That's what keeps our country strong. I believe in fair and objective processes of Law! That's what keeps Justice strong. I believe in Parliamentary Procedure as an extension of these. *That's what keeps ME strong!*" These were unkindly illustrated by someone who had a very clever pen. Tim was easy to caricature; he wore glasses and had a thin pathetic little beard.

This issue referred to in this strip was whether or not department meetings were private. The point was being raised in many departments, including History, where graduate students had attended uninvited, expressed approval or disapproval of members' observation by whistling or booing or hissing, and had on some occasions forced adjournment.[542] The State of Wisconsin has an Anti-Secrecy law, which requires that all meetings of the Legislature be open to the public. The question was whether this applied to State employees such as university faculty, although of course, unlike legislators, they were not publicly elected. The matter had not yet been tested in a court case. The university was asking the Attorney General for a legal ruling, but it had not yet been given.

The abolition of Freshman English, of course, was a matter which would affect teaching assistants, and therefore there were grounds for their being informed of it. Before the matter could be brought up in the department at all, it was necessary to provide in some way for teaching assistants currently on the

---

542 Cronon and Jenkins corroborate this, noting the presence of an SDS-informed History Students Association, but also note the formation of an alternative organization, History Students for Reform (HRS), a "more moderate" group who outnumbered the HSA and rejected "SDS-style confrontation" in interactions with faculty at meetings (1999, pp. 473–475).

staff, who had come in good faith expecting to be subsidized for four years, the average time in which a graduate student completed his course work for the doctorate. Legally, we were bound only a year at a time; this was always the term of the "award" of the teaching assistantship. And it had never been intended as a job on which a man[543] could bring up a family; only to make it possible for him to manage temporarily on his way to the degree. But it was generally understood that if duties were satisfactorily performed a man could count on four years. This was usually the case; the handful of hopeless teachers each year had decided themselves they'd prefer another occupation and did not re-apply (until the TAA harassed the Department by getting hold of a complete incompetent whose entire class had complained of him and presenting him as a martyr). But re-appointment was the general rule. So Ed Lacy and Tim went to the Dean and the Chancellor and got assurance that funds would be available to provide for the current staff who would not be absorbed in other courses. This settled, we could go on.

The last week of October Tim called a Department meeting, to which all teaching assistants were invited, in B-10 Commerce, one of the biggest lecture halls on campus. Bill Lenehan was to present his motion of abolition and give reasons, and I was to support him, as the only senior staff member with twenty continuous years of experience in the course. Tim of course presided. The room was packed. The meeting was a debacle. I needn't describe it here, since the appended letter will give you a good idea.[544] I never sent the letter, but I wrote it as therapy to relieve my own feelings—which were, and even after four years continue to be, bitter. I think now I do accuse Tim of lack of sincerity, though I can't fathom his motive. But I think he must have been acting with duplicity, since it seems impossible that anyone could be that stupid. I had a great store of good will on the part of teaching assistants to draw on, handed down from experienced to new over many years, and our dissidents were still numerically inferior, though extremely conspicuous. Did he cut off my access to the group because he thought I had too much influence with it? At the end of the meeting a vote was taken as to whether we should have another public one. Ed, Bill, and I all voted yes; it could have been impossible for Tim to spin out his nonsense and keep us off the podium again. But the motion lost, because too many department members saw no sense in sitting through such another fiasco. Bill and I did

---

543 Although nearly half of teaching assistants were women, Thomas employs—here and throughout the memoir—the use of the male pronoun to refer to both sexes, as was customary at the time.

544 This letter was not included in the memoir. Fleming (2011) provides a detailed account of this meeting, held on October 28, 1969 (see pp. 138–142). Charles Scott recalls the atmosphere as very tense (interview with the editor, June 2016).

Demolition

speak before the department, and effectively. But it was the teaching assistants we wanted to reach, and I cannot forgive Tim for this injury.[545]

Whatever his motives, his action was extremely ill-advised, since it laid us open to the charge of secrecy on a matter affecting the assistants; and the matter on which the Department made up its mind in November was not finally settled until the middle of February. Moreover, this was the occasion for a lot of unpleasant publicity through these months, of which the *Cardinal* took full advantage.[546] On the occasion of the next Department meeting, November 18, half a dozen TAA members appeared and sat down. Tim checked with the Dean and called the head of the University Police, Hanson; we moved from [room] 350 to 312, where Hanson stood outside the door for two hours while we carried on our business, which at first was punctuated by flashbulbs taking pictures of him.[547]

> After the most uncertain and agonizing two hours I ever spent, the vote was overwhelming for abolition of 102 and 181: 28 for, 4 against, 6 abstentions. Most of the assistant professors had left before the vote was taken, several of them stamping out in temper tantrums.[548]

> It is time for the system to end. One man said he had worked in composition for fifteen years, part as a teaching assistant, part as an assistant professor (he didn't do it here), and it was like cutting fifteen years out of his life, but he felt it was necessary. I think that's silly. I feel no more regret over having spent twenty years working in the system than I do over having spent twenty years bringing up my children. The work in both cases was necessary and useful while I was doing it, and when things change so it is no longer necessary and useful you accept the change.

---

545 Thomas is referring to Heninger's decision that the following department committee meeting, scheduled for November 4, 1969, would be held without the teaching assistants present (Fleming, 2011, p. 142)

546 Thomas does not mention the November 4, 1969 meeting in which she voiced support for the proposal to abolish Freshman English in the absence of feasible alternatives (Fleming, 2011, pp. 143–144). Nor does she mention the November 11, 1969, meeting in which Lacy formally moved that the department abolish English 201 and 181, which was rejected by faculty by a vote of 12 to 34 (Fleming, 2011, pp. 145–146).

547 Fleming reports that the front page of the student-run newspaper, the *Daily Cardinal*, ran a front-page article on the meeting, and included a photo of campus police chief Ralph Hanson blocking the door, looking like a Nazi stormtrooper (p. 162).

548 According to Fleming (2011), the vote was 27 yeas, 8 nays, 4 abstentions, and several junior faculty members, including Frank Battaglia and David Siff, were boycotting the meeting to show support for the teaching assistants, who were prohibited from attending (pp. 148, 146).

We no longer have any control over the assistants. They won't, or can't, teach composition. They use their students as a captive audience for politicizing. There is no attempt of objectivity of analysis, and certainly no freedom of expression for anyone who doesn't agree—or pretend to agree—with his TA. Nor will they cooperate in mechanisms which seem to me indispensable if the degree from Wisconsin is going to have any more value than a Confederate dollar. One young woman doesn't believe in grades. She doesn't want to hand in an all-A grade list, because that would attract the attention of the Dean, so she has each student choose a card at random from a deck on her desk and whatever grade is on it will be his. Altogether the Department is in a very painful situation, with people talking together conspiratorially in corners or cutting each other dead.

It is to the everlasting credit of the Department, I think, that two responsibilities were fairly met before any action was taken, and most of the discussion time was consumed in assurances that this would be the case. The first was that money would be available to fulfill the expectations of the assistants currently on staff. The second was that some provision would be made to meet the needs of students who really required help in writing. This took the form of a Writing Laboratory, to which students might be referred by other department faculty, or to which they could come on their own. Joyce Steward and I set this up the following spring (including a trip or two to institutions where we thought we could get ideas), and she is now running it with conspicuous success. Ed and Bill and I were to spend a good deal of time second semester meeting with faculty of other colleges—Agriculture, Engineering, Business, Education—and representatives of other L&S departments, explaining how this institution could serve their students.

The Department had acted decisively. But the TAA announced in the *Cardinal* that the action was secret and therefore illegal and accordingly they intended to take the case to court with the request that it be rescinded. They won their case, and it was not until the next February that we had rescinded it and then retook it, and the matter was settled.

I have already spoken of our annual fall tenure review, an invariably painful time, more or less drawn out according to the number of people who had to be considered. Always after I was once a member of the Executive Committee (tenured professors), I had felt the meetings were conducted with true objectivity and honest soul-searching. I don't think the decisions were always right; but I do think they were conscientiously reached. AAUP rules bound us to notify a man a year before his termination date as to our decision; that is, if the initial contract with which the assistant professor came terminated in June, 1971, he must be notified of department action by June, 1970. This gave him one full year to look for another job. The best opportunity by far was Modern Language Association, which met annually just after Christmas, since everybody was there; without leaving his hotel, a candidate could interview six or eight department chairmen. We took our action in November, a great advantage to a man who was not to be retained, since it gave him two opportunities, not one, at MLA. But our considerateness had an unfortunate result for ourselves. If action had been taken in June, when everyone was leaving, including the man himself, for the summer, he would have had three months to get over any disappointment and might well have rubbed along fairly pleasantly through the next year. But since it was taken in November, he had all of second semester as well as all the next year, and if he were aggrieved had an excellent opportunity to show it and to spread his discontent around.

One of our assistant professors, David Siff,[549] was an unabashed revolutionary and a good counterpart to Hugh in *Barnaby Rudge*: big, dark, charismatic, violent. He came up new because his original contract expired a year from the next June. He had come, as all assistant professors came, with a three-year contract, and that, of course, was legally binding. It was the usual practice in such cases to vote a one-year extension, which gave a four-year probationary period. But Siff "has been thoroughly political, and nothing else from the start. He has not met classes, not appeared at examinations, and so on, and finally demanded that the typists in one of the offices take time and departmental supplies to run off political material for him with no connection with his course. Even our chairman had to veto that."

I digress to say that the university was very vulnerable on this point, which caused great bitterness in the Legislature and the state: the shameless use of university facilities and postage for propaganda for such things as the Black Panthers. One of the first acts of Tim's successor as chairman was to require all outgoing mail to clear through his office. One of my own students told me her father had received a letter "from the English Department" soliciting funds for Black Panthers defense. He had thrown the letter away, she said, when I asked who had signed it; it might well have been Siff. The girl, not the "rat infested

---

549 David Siff, an assistant professor of English at UW-Madison whose antiwar activism influenced the departments decision not to renew his contract (see Fleming, 2011, p. 141). Cronon and Jenkins note that Siff and Frank Battaglia were "[t]wo of the more militant campus protest leaders" (p. 476). Siff was listed as a co-author of a 20-page pamphlet, distributed by the Madison SDS chapter, entitled "The Case Against the Army Math Research Center." After his dismissal from UW-Madison, Siff taught at Brooklyn College (CUNY) and, in the mid 1970s, published on freshman composition in *English Journal*, *College English*, and *College Composition and Communication*.

getto" one but equally unbalanced between head and heart, had gotten herself into almost unbelievable trouble. She was sharing an apartment with a friend, who invited a Black from Chicago to join them; the Black was picked up by the police for shoplifting and suspected her of giving them information; she narrowly escaped a court charge herself (the Black used the apartment for storage of his loot), and the police advised her to move out of the student district so he couldn't find her when he came out on parole. The father, a good old-fashioned Middle American in Green Bay, was frantic with worry and swore no child of his ever again would come within a hundred miles of the university. He was not a good subject for Siff's solicitation, if the letter did come from Siff.

And now back to Siff. "So we voted not to give him the extra year—not of course on the grounds of his revolutionary view, which as a private person he is at liberty to hold, but on grounds of failing to fulfill his professional responsibilities." There is a clear legal distinction between "firing" and "not renewing a contract which has expired," but the *Cardinal* never bothered with such niceties. Siff had a considerable following in SDS, which was running the *Cardinal*, and got a lot of martyr's publicity. SDS published their intention to disrupt English classes for three days, because the English Department was "the enemy of the people." They gave two reasons: we had voted not to renew Siff's contract, and two Black Panthers had been killed in Chicago. They announced they would pay particular attention to people who had been leaders in getting 102 abolished, and I was one of those, though not important in the whole picture. But my classes were small, and disrupters liked to go for the big lectures, so I wasn't much worried. The threat came to nothing anyhow.

> Tuesday morning the university administration asked one of the judges to issue an injunction, and the judge refused because he had to have evidence of "clear and present danger." That was furnished during the day, when a History professor, a student in his lecture, and a campus policeman who had arrested the disrupters of the lecture on grounds of trespass, all gave evidence; so he issued the injunction and nothing much happened after that. They had a rally of a couple of hundred students on Lincoln Terrace in the afternoon, and then marched to the Capitol looking for the Attorney-General, who, smart man, had gone out to lunch; so they disbanded—no violence and practically no publicity. I think the media are now paying a little attention to Agnew;[550] I

---

550 Spiro Theodore Agnew (1918–1996) was U.S. Vice President (1969–1973) under Richard Nixon.

certainly have observed myself cases here where there were almost more camera men around than rioters and Agnew had some justification.

Also, the national SDS applied for the Dane County Coliseum for their national meeting, and were turned down, on grounds that the organization is financially untrustworthy, not having paid money it owes already, and that the county couldn't afford the expense of having all their police force on call, which they'd have to do to keep the peace.

I don't know where they went, and I am sorry to say my devotion to free speech was not burning enough for me to care either. This was the first time the university had taken any steps to protect the faculty and maintain order in the classroom. I thought it was long overdue, but I was glad to see it at last.

Bill Lenehan thought the teaming up of the TAA with the SDS was the first bad tactical mistake they had made. The TAA was accusing the university administration of stalling, and now set January 8 as the deadline on which their demands must be met. The eighth of the month is payday here; therefore, the assistants could get their checks, and still have time before the end of the month to disrupt examinations if they wanted to. SDS, Bill said, is regarded as a lunatic fringe, so any target of theirs is to be congratulated. If the Regents didn't like our giving up 102,[551] the fact that the SDS didn't either would swing them at once to our side. Bill Strang sent me a message that the teaching assistants in the School of Business—as opposed to ours, they of course were very conservative—"were feeling so ashamed that they don't like to admit anywhere that they are teaching assistants at the University of Wisconsin." The polarization was pretty complete.

An early December snowfall, lovely and clinging, everything softened and blurred and beautiful, put me in the Christmas mood. I drove home from Reading Group about sunset, through Nakoma where people were beginning to put up their decorations and lights shone in uncurtained windows, and through the unspoiled snow of the Arboretum. I was well ahead on my Christmas cards, and of course ready to send them to all the assistants as usual—I couldn't bear not to. But before vacation we had both expected and unexpected trouble. As

---

551 Whether the Regents approved of the English department's move to abolish Freshman English, the campus community was shocked and, in many cases, angered. The Curriculum Review Committee salvaged the situation by gaining college faculty approval to have the English composition requirement reduced to one semester with the possibility of exemption but condemned the department's unilateral action (Cronon & Jenkins, 1999, pp. 290–294). Fleming (2011) indicates that the abolition of Freshman English elicited "a barrage of complaints" from students, TAs, and faculty across campus (p. 162).

expected, the TAA and six specific grad students filed a court case naming Tim as defendant, on the grounds that a department meeting was closed to them at which matters of concern to them were discussed. As we heard the news on the radio, our Bill said kindly of Tim, "Poor guy." I felt he had brought his trouble on himself.

> The unexpected trouble was that sixteen of our assistant professors wrote a letter of complaint to the Dean of L&S[552] asking him to appoint some sort of outside commission to investigate the Executive Committee, and saying if he did not do so they would make the matter public—presumably in the Madison newspapers. The Dean came to an Executive committee meeting on December 15—a completely unprecedented action, and completely unexpected by us—to read us their letter and his answer, which was that he didn't think calling in outside investigation was a good idea but the "fierce chasm" in the department referred to in the letter must certainly be bridged. They have given him the deadline of December 15, but he had received the letter Thursday, been in Milwaukee Friday, and his office had been closed for repairs Saturday and Sunday because the SDS had heaved a rock through the window late Friday, so he had not been able to act before. He is a man with a strong resemblance to the Great Stone Face, and one could hardly feel he was very sympathetic; but he did announce before he left that he would be glad to see any of us individually. When he came out of the meeting, which continued after that for three jolly hours, there was a plastic dinosaur in the center of the halls, about three by five feet, hung with Christmas balls and holding a placard: "Merry Christmas from the English Department. Progress is our most important power." And I do not think the intent was genial. Of course I thought myself getting rid of Freshman English was progress, but apparently these people didn't agree.

I did go down to see the Dean, more because I thought I ought to than because I expected to accomplish anything. This was his first year of incum-

---

552 Stephen C. Kleene (1909–1994) was a distinguished American mathematician. He received his Ph.D. from Princeton University (1934) and began working at UW-Madison in 1935. After serving in the US Navy during World War II, Kleene returned to Wisconsin and spend the rest of his career there, retiring in 1979. He was Dean of the College of Letters and Science from 1969–1974.

bency (all top administrative positions had heavy turnover in these years), and he was a mathematician, whose mind doesn't work much like ours. He is a forbidding man personally, and didn't know any of us; he started by taking me for Madeleine Doran. I showed him the article in the *AAUP Bulletin* protesting against the politicizing of the academic world, and told him our department division was largely due to our attempts to resist this on the part of the assistant professors. He hadn't seen the article, but promised to look it up, and said he agreed with its point of view as I gave it. One of the assistant professors' complaints, he told me, was that none of the senior staff paid any attention to them. So as a gesture—however futile—I spent the afternoon I might have been at Reading Group making forty more cards for all the assistant professors, and addressed them at 4 a.m. the next day (which sounds like the supreme sacrifice, but of course I'm up then anyway.) I'm sure it did no good, but having thought of it I would have regretted not doing it, just as I would have regretted not making the effort to go to see the Dean. Madeleine made a nice gesture which achieved the light touch. She is in the habit of making a good-sized Christmas-card collage to post in the main English office as a general greeting. This year she signed it "Merry Christmas from an old dinosaur."

Now came Christmas vacation, and private life. This was the last Christmas in the long series of Pooley-Thomas celebrations. Alan and Robie and Nathan flew over from England, young Bob and his family drove up from Florida, and it was the last time the Pooleys were to be together in the house that Ham had built. There was some sadness, but no occasion can be really sad with so many small children around; Bill and Kathy and Jimmy were living here, of course. Our house was full of paperwhites, and everyone came here for supper and carols Christmas Eve. Christmas Day Janet and Robie cooked the turkey, I brought over dessert, and we all had dinner there and sat most of the afternoon talking pleasantly about old times. After the Pooleys dispersed, Bob stayed on getting packed for his move to Jacksonville, which he made in January with some confusion since the movers didn't appear when they said they would, so he had a few extra meals here. On the last night he read aloud to us from *The Peterkin Papers*,[553] which I had happened to mention and which he likes, the sketch where that family moves.

On January 1, 1970, I started a five-year Line-a-Day (I wish I'd done it a year or two earlier) so from now on my chronology is accurate. The new semester, the last and the worst of the campus disorders, was to be a good example of the cliché that it's always darkest before daylight.

---

553 *The Peterkin Papers* (1867), a book-length collection of humorous stories, was written by American author Lucretia Peabody Hale (1820–1900).

Demolition

The Armory[554] was fire-bombed on January 3, where the firemen fought for seven hours with the thermometer never getting up to 10 above, and the Navy Center on January 25. Registration was more trying than usual. "The mass of the TA's seem to be suffering not from the morbid fear of Saki's Mrs. Packletide's[555] companion of giving an atom more service than she was paid for, but from the even worse one of giving anything like as much. What distresses me is the thought of all the students signed up for courses with TA's this semester." And I prophesied more truly than I could know, for in all the history of American education in the twentieth century, more students had infinitely less instruction in this period than in any other. The TAA did not call their strike on January 8, but we knew one was coming.

> The Chancellor, who is responsible for the whole thing by his recognition of the TAA as a bargaining agent last fall, sent out a statement wishing "to share his concern" with the faculty. That's a lot of help, I must say. The heating employees, we hear, are going to go on a sympathy strike. The Regents want to fire Harrington, who is unpopular, even with his own faculty. Bill Lenehan says that if the TAA succeeds in shutting down the university even for a day—and this they may very well do—he thinks the Legislature will step in, take over the university, abolish the TA system, and get rid of Harrington. I can see justice on their side, but it would not be a reform of the evils of the present system; it would be a swing to the extreme right, and between the extreme left and the extreme right I'm really at a loss to choose—or, as regards methods, even distinguish.

Now in my late sixties, when most people are reclining by the fire with a faithful dog bringing them their pipe and slippers, I found myself involved "in the most heated political atmosphere you can imagine."

> I feel as if I had lived through every war in history, and I understand much more how wars are conducted than I ever did from history books, with everything neatly analyzed by

---

554 The University of Wisconsin Armory and Gymnasium, referred to as the Red Gym, was built in 1894 and resembles a red brick castle. It was designated a National Historic Landmark in 1993. Karl Armstrong, one of four student radicals who bombed Sterling Hall, was responsible for firebombing the Red Gym, which at the time housed the campus ROTC offices, which were not damaged by the fire (Cronon & Jenkins, 1999, p. 491).

555 Saki is the pen name for British short story writer and satirist Hector Hugh Munro (1870–1916). The name of the story is "Mrs. Packletide's Tiger."

> hindsight. The reality is not two neat sides, but positions sliding all the way from extreme right to extreme left, people shifting back and forth, traitors on your own side, no one you can trust, lies and rumors and fantasies everywhere.

The strike was declared on March 16.[556]

> Ideal strike weather—perfectly clear and sunny, cool (20 at sunrise) but not cold. Drove through the Arboretum and saw two does; ah Eden. Buses drawn up at the end of Lot 60, presumably for the duration. The University Employees Union voted not to honor the strike, but the bus drivers, who belong to the teamsters' union, are doing so, and creating a good deal of inconvenience, since Lot 60 is a mile and a half from Bascom. Pickets out by Natatorium, none on center of campus. When I was working Saturday, people were putting up big orange strike signs on all the trees on the Hill: "Strike for a better education. Honor the TAA picket lines." The trees are bare this morning—someone took the signs down over the weekend. Red armbands being distributed. A big pile of strike signs under my window for pickets to get, and many old friends among our assistants arriving to do so.

Dick Quintana this year was a visiting professor at University of Delaware, and I wrote Janet on the 28th to describe our department meeting.

> The Dean has directed chairmen to certify the payroll so that striking TA's will not be paid for performing duties when they're not doing so. Heninger told us he had sent a form to every TA to be returned; if it were, signed, he would certify that person for the payroll. The form read "My name should be on the payroll" and not another word. Bob Doremus promptly pointed out that the wording was ambiguous and would not provide evidence, and he was supported by Walter Rideout. Tim said the statements were already mailed; he wasn't asking us, he was telling us.
>
> He has long lost any resemblance to a presiding officer. He generally acts as a witness in his own behalf, and is greeted steadily by opposition from the floor, sometimes courteous

---

556 For an account of this TAA strike, which was generally "orderly and non-violent" (p. 502), see Cronon & Jenkins, 1999. pp. 494–506.

and restrained (like Bob's yesterday), sometimes heated and rude (like Friedman's often, biting the hand that promoted him). There is no unanimity of opinion in the department on any subject, except that we all thank God these are Tim's last month as chairman. (As a matter of fact, they were his last months at Wisconsin. On his own initiative he had applied for leave the next year, and he never came back.) We are no longer a body. We are a shambles. Even if the university can pull through, which I don't believe in spite of your quoting Lighty that the university can survive anything, I don't think the department can.

The picnic atmosphere of the strike continued for the first few days. There were big pots of "coffee for strikers" in front of Van Hise, and dogs running round with placards on their backs, though they didn't stand still long enough to let you read what the placards had to say. I crossed the picket lines myself without harassment, though some of my students reported they had suffered it. Young appeared on TV, but according to Alice Strang "seemed incoherent confused, answer questions badly, and altogether let the side down. He probably hasn't had much sleep lately (and who has) and he's old enough to lack the resilience of youth." I kept thinking of a story in Gibbon.[557] When the barbarians sacked Rome, a vandal brought his ax down on a very beautiful mosaic swan and Leda, the product of infinite patience and art, because he thought the swan was real, and shattered it to bits. And then he sat down and cried. I was tempted to tell the story to the pickets some time when I crossed the line, but wisely resisted temptation. John Conder neatly summed up the attitude to our chairman. As he and Joyce and I were walking down the hall together, he was complaining that his class had been disrupted, and he said so to Ed, who was coming in the other direction. "Report it to Mr. Heninger," said Ed, going on. "The hell I will," said John. Every student I had showed up at least once during the week. Four people were absent Monday and Wednesday, but they came back Friday—under duress, since I had announced I would take attendance and report three successive absences to the dean. This, I should explain, was published university policy, pretty largely honored in the breach rather than in the observance. In a beginning course like Freshman English, it was very useful, and I always emphasized it at early meetings, on the grounds, which I genuinely believed, that a student who is not coming to class is heading for trouble, and if his dean knows it he will be helped to avoid the trouble before it becomes too

---

557 A reference to historian Edward Gibbon's (1737–1794) multi-volume publication *The History of the Decline and Fall of the Roman Empire*.

Demolition

serious. The precaution saved countless messes and mix-ups at the end of every semester. A dean has the right to know if his student is not appearing in a course for which he is registered. If this policy had been followed in the fall of 1971 it would have protected our department and the university from a rather nasty scandal which resulted when one of our teaching assistants turned in a passing grade for a student who had been killed in an automobile accident in October. Her father, pardonably outraged, made the incident public. But of course most people didn't bother with this, and I was not typical. Very few people had anything like as good attendance as mine. Having concluded that all was lost, I was operating peacefully in the calm of despair.

Nathan P. Feinsinger,[558] nationally known as a very successful mediator in a variety of labor-management disputes, was meeting with the TAA and the administration, but making no progress. In an interim report he stated: "I am especially interested in the question whether mediation techniques proved successful in one area of conflict resolution or dispute settlement in the private sector of the economy, such as labor management relations, can be transferred successfully to the other areas such as disputes in the public sector, racial disputes, community disputes, student-faculty-administration disputes and international disputes." This episode then may be considered as an item in a social development which is not yet resolved, but may perhaps be in the lives of my grandchildren. From my own standpoint, which I have not altered, the analogy between labor-management on the one hand and the assistants-administration on the other is unsound. The point at issue in the talks was the claim of the TAA to "decision-making power over the educational planning." The Administration was willing to concede only "meaningful participation in educational planning." Mechanisms were to be a matter of negotiation on the departmental level in each case, which meant endless hours of quibbling. You might remember that a given professor had no large supporting staff of aides as does Henry Kissinger, but was supposed to find the time for these negotiations from time which was already presumably totally consumed in scholarship and teaching. The university also took the point of view that the strike was illegal in any case, since the assistants had accepted a contract which did not expire until September 1971. Neither side would yield. The Administration, according to the grapevine, couldn't because they would be fired by the Regents if they did. As you probably know, unlike faculty, administrators have no tenure.

The place was swarming with Trojan horses, our own chairman, of course, at the head of the list. The department played the ostrich. George Rodman was

---

558 Nathan Paul Feinsinger (1902–1983) was a professor in UW-Madison's law school (1929–1973) and a prominent labor mediator.

Demolition

in charge of sophomore composition, largely staffed by teaching assistants and I offered him my services, but he thanked me politely and let it go at that. The policy of pleasant persuasion was getting them nowhere, and the pickets grew ugly. I felt very sorry for the civil servants, mostly older women, who came into Bascom under my window. One of our own teaching assistants, a divorcee with a small child, to whom the department had been particularly considerate in the line of scholarships and convenient programs, was on duty there a good deal of the time, and I've never seen anyone nastier. The last I heard of her, a couple of years later, she was driving a taxi.

It was now spring vacation, and I went to Delaware to plan for the golden wedding anniversary, under some difficulties because of airline controllers' strikes. "It takes as much stamina to travel these days as it did in the days of the covered wagon," I wrote Marion. "By all accounts [Chicago] O'Hare is like the lion's den in Aesop: 'I see the footprints going to the door but none returning.'" Kathy got my ticket down changed so I wouldn't have to go that way, and Bill and Tom cooperated to get me back on an airline not on strike. The plane sat on the runway at Philly for two hours while we wondered what was going to happen, but it was finally airborne, and Kathy and Jimmy drove over to Milwaukee to meet me there. In the meantime, the university had applied for an injunction against the strikers: according to Feinsinger's interim report, it was first refused because the picketing had not interfered with freedom of access to classes; but when things grew worse it was granted. The TAA refused to honor it, and the pickets were still out, now staking jobs and arrest.

> Speaking of strikes, Bill's house is indefinitely postponed.
> A carpenter's strike was scheduled for April 1, and the men
> wanted to get the carpeting down before then; but on account
> of the wildcat teamsters strike it didn't come, so now when
> the time, the place, and the loved one, as it were, will all get
> together, nobody know. Never a dull moment.

In addition to the injunction, which might erode somewhat the support of the less zealous, student support of the strike fell off. The students had enjoyed a little fun in the nice early spring weather—and who goes to classes the week before spring vacation anyway?—but now they began to think they had better buckle down if they wanted any credit for the semester's work. A university faculty meeting was held in the Union—or rather two, Monday, April 6, 4:30 to 6:45, when we had to vacate the Theater; Tuesday, 3:30 until we finally finished up. Between the two, an anonymous sheet headed THE EDGE OF CHAOS, Part 1, appeared in our mailboxes. It wasn't very well done, and I'll quote from it

461

only two details: Young's statement, "The strike has occurred in part not because the faculty oversupervised their TAs but because they neglected them," which strikes me as one of the rare utterances in which he justified his Maine tradition: and the chairman's ruling Heninger out of order when he inquired "How can students and TAs participate meaningfully in educational planning without infringing on the 'ultimate responsibility of the faculty'?" —also a rare example of a time when Tim made a valid point. At both meetings we went through groups of strikers yelling, "Power corrupts, gives us some of yours," and "Support educational planning," which of course we were spending our lives doing anyway. (Whose planning? My whole professional life has been spent endeavoring to foster precision of language as a reflection of precision of thought. You know the epitaph Keats wrote for himself.[559]) Policemen stood inside the Union doors with university representatives checking our faculty identification cards, which had pictures on them.

After voting down one Far Right resolution and then one Far Left one, the faculty passed the resolution submitted by the Council of Ten, the elected faculty committee (Ed Lacy was a member), which had been serving as the university bargaining team. (Some of these men had the windows of their homes broken, but Ed was not among them.) The resolution read: "It is in the interest of the university community to insure that there are mechanisms in each department that give students and teaching assistants an opportunity to participate in a meaningful way in educational planning. Such departmental mechanisms shall be developed by the faculty of each department on the Madison campus in collaboration with the students and teaching assistants involved in the courses offered by that department." Like many compromise statements, this was so vague as to be very antithesis of meaningful itself, and I was much disturbed when I first saw it. It would lead, I felt sure, to endless wrangling and quibbling, and then to inevitable trouble. Fortunately, Theodore Hamerow of History (one of the Phi Beta Kappa Executive Committee) offered an amendment: "Such mechanisms, however, shall not infringe upon the ultimate responsibility of the faculty for curriculum and course content." It was in this connection that Heninger had raised his question, and he was out of order because he raised it after the amendment had passed. I was glad to vote for the "Council of Ten Resolution as amended," and so were an overwhelming majority of my colleagues; it passed 4 to 1, and the faculty stand was crystal-clear. Nineteen teaching assistants had been arrested and taken to court, the TAA voted to end the strike, and the Regents "reluctantly" approved the settlement. This was the end. For the time being.

---

559 "Here lies One whose Name was writ in Water."

Demolition

April saw an expensive trashing which developed from Peace March, permission to march around the Square properly obtained. Three splinter groups broke off and rioted all over the city, doing an estimated $100,000 worth of damage, most of it in smashed windows up and down State Street and West Washington Avenue, IBM first of all. The University Avenue Branch Bank had never uncovered their boarded-up windows since the last trashing. I was working in my office that Saturday afternoon, and saw the sinister sight of groups coming up the Hill, strips of cloth tied over their faces below their eyes to make identification difficult, but they didn't come into the building. A former teaching assistant wrote me he would never come back to Madison to see the boarded-up windows: he wanted to remember it as it used to be. Eventually, many of them were replaced with narrow slits in solid walls, on the order of the block house at Wiscasset [Maine]. A speech therapist in the bank building told me the children were frightened to come into the boarded-up place for their appointments with her.

The significant department event in April was the meeting to nominate next year's chairman, a particularly shameful affair though the outcome was fortunate. Even under Wisconsin Anti-Secrecy law, personal matters could be discussed in private, so there was no reason but Tim's general insanity for his having invited the English Student Association, all our graduate students and teaching assistants, Uncle Tom Cobbley[560] and all. We met in 312 and the room was packed. It had always been department policy for the recording secretary to preside at this meeting, and to appoint an assistant professor as recording secretary; the incumbent was particularly far out, and aided and abetted his colleagues to behave as rudely and ridiculously and childishly as possible. "It shows only what everyone knows, that we have a bunch of young men, most of them selected by Walter Rideout, I'm afraid, who are without taste or courtesy or ability." The usual procedure was to start with a straw vote: if it showed division, others were taken until the consensus became apparent, and then someone would move the final vote. The secretary read aloud with relish the results of each straw vote, which included scattering singles for Nathan Feinsinger, Porky Pig, Abbie Hoffman, Susan Friedman (one of our most revolutionary teaching assistants), and the like, with a fair block of Siff, and another for a man who had been so misguided as to campaign tirelessly and ineffectually for himself. The Executive Committee's choice, who had a clear majority on the first ballot, was Charles Scott. The worst lapse of taste fortunately misfired. A telegram was sent to our presiding officer but since the delivery boy didn't want to interrupt the meeting he gave it to June Stone in our office, and of course she had sense enough not to

---

560 A phrase used in British English as a humorous way to say et al.

bring it in. It read "We nominate Ruth Wallerstein Helen White." On the final ballet the office-seeker had 12 votes, Siff 16, and Scott 31. This was enough to enable the Dean to appoint Scott without hesitation, and Charles is now serving his fourth term.[561]

Historically, the worst time of the whole era came in May, when Nixon went into Cambodia and every campus in the country exploded. The most publicized episode occurred at Kent State, where the National Guard killed four people.[562] There were no deaths on our campus—here, at least, after the news of Kent State came, the forces of law and order carried no guns. The University Police, the windshields of their cars crisscrossed with tapes against stones, and the National Guardsmen played "at cat and mouse" with the rioters, as the news put it, through night after night. The weather was beautiful. I would walk across the campus at 6:30, the tree buds turning into leaves and glistening in the sun, the birds singing, the whole atmosphere that of Eden before the fall—and I would see the marks of the night in rows and rows of broken windows in one building after another, and in the twenty-feet concrete pillars holding lamps on Observatory Drive knocked over at the base. Mornings were quiet, afternoons bad, and nights horrible, not only on campus but all up Langdon and the adjacent streets. John Condor, who lived in an apartment there, brought out his notes to me for safe-keeping (I felt like a Confederate lady burying the neighbors' silver in her garden) because so many street barricades were being set on fire. His furniture, he said, was insured, but his notes were irreplaceable. It was wittily said that we should be drawing combat pay. Parents of students summoned their children home, or drove down to Madison to get them. The students who stuck it out were getting almost no sleep and were being scared silly. One resident of a university dormitory told me the rioters had spent the night prying up the pavement in front of the building and smashing it to get rocks to throw. Almost everyone ran into tear gas—either caught in a mob, or studying in the library, where the rioters ran into the building, the police followed with tear gas to flush them out, and the tear gas stayed. The rioters gave special attention to the library, one in a quick dash overturning the main catalog and ripping out most of the cards, so that it took days of work for the staff to get them back. Near the hospital was another favorite rioting site. Kathy got caught there once, and so did Helene Thompson. Once university employee was struck in the eye there by a thrown brick and reported in danger of losing the eye.

---

561 Thomas likely means the fourth year of Scott's four-year term, which concluded in 1974.
562 The Kent State shootings, which killed four students and wounded nine, occurred on May 4, 1970. Two of the four students killed, and some of those wounded, were not protesters.

To me, as to many, the nadir was the night firebombing of 10 Babcock Drive, the residence of President Emeritus Fred and his wife.[563] They are both the salt of the earth. They were octogenarians, they were very deaf, they lived alone in a house on campus opposite Slichter Hall, into which they had first moved when Mr. Fred was appointed Dean of the College of Agriculture. When he was appointed President of the university, they preferred to stay there, since it was on campus among students and the official Presidents' residence was two or three miles away on University Heights. I have spoken of Mr. Fred in another chapter. During this time, I was keeping up my weekly early morning visits to him to try to maintain my own sanity by contact with his. The day he told me of the firebombing is the only time I remember seeing him when, in one connection or another, he didn't use his characteristic phrase: "I had to laugh." This time he said, "Rosa woke up and there were five men in her room!" What's more they were police in crash helmets and riot gear, who had had to break into the house when the flames—fortunately before they had done damage to anything but rugs and furniture—were seen.

This attack was so senseless—Mr. Fred had been retired for fifteen years—that it came to be believed, I think rightly, that a mistake had been made, and the real target was the house of the incumbent president, Fred Harvey Harrington. The coincidence of the names and the fact that it was the Emeritus President, not the incumbent as might have been thought, who was living on campus are enough, I think, to account for a mistake made by people from away. This is perhaps support for what came to be very generally believed, that most of the disruption throughout the country was the work not primarily of registered students in a given institution but of peripatetics who went from one place to another. This attack was also an example of ineptness, as was the final event in this sequence, the bombing of Sterling Hall, the Physics Building, which killed a completely uninvolved graduate student, Fassknecht,[564] instead of its neighbor, the Army Research Mathematics Center, the intended target. A week or so after the Freds' firebombing, Mrs. Fred showed me a letter without address, signed by a name which did not appear in either University or City Directory. It was written in beautiful handwriting on beautiful note paper with a leaf designs, and read in part: "We hope you will forgive us for damaging your house. We are young, idealistic. We are frightened, so very frightened . . . Pray that we may find the truth." "It's a whiny letter," said Mrs. Fred.

---

563 In addition to the Freds' residence, five other faculty homes were firebombed (Cronon & Jenkins, 1999, p. 509).

564 The victim was Robert Fassnacht, a 33-year-old postdoctoral researcher in the UW-Madison physics department. For a detailed account of the bombing, see Bates (1992).

Demolition

All day long the cry was sounding "Shut it down! Shut it down! Shut it down!" Bill drove me in town, let me off on Johnson Street, and picked me up again when he went home. I was afraid to leave my car on campus. I'd take my chances in a mob on foot against those in a car, though when a student of mind who was on Canadian [forearm] crutches stopped coming to class I could see why. I met every class. Of course I was very fortunate that they were morning ones, and generally they were quiet, though the 11:00 o'clock, as I shall relate, had adventures. But in general instruction, which had already suffered heavily during the TAA strike, was in a very bad way. Art Buchwald published a pungent account of students who graduated this semester building bridges that fell down at a touch and letting clients go to the electric chair because they had missed basic parts of their Engineering or Law curriculum. While I was working on this chapter, one of the students from this time, returned from the Peace Corps, asked me to recommend him for graduate work in Journalism. We had a cozy chat about old times. "Yes, I never missed your class," he said. "It was the only one I came to. The rest of the time I was out supporting the strike, but I came to yours because you seemed to have a sense of purpose in your work that most others didn't." At the time one student told me her seminar had met only five times during the semester. Another was taking a philosophy course which required five papers. The teaching assistant said he would pretend they had handed in #2 and #3, and if the strike went on he would pretend they had handed in #4. It hurt her that the students were so cynical they were willing to take credit for a no-course. A week or so after the strike my students were laughing before class, first incredulously and then bitterly, because the thousand dollar Kiekhofer award for the distinguished teacher (which I've referred to before) had gone to an assistant professor in Education who hadn't met his class more than six weeks during the whole semester; some corrected that to three. Hannah called up and said the media couldn't really give many details about Wisconsin because by the time they'd listed the colleges and universities shut down or in trouble there was no time left. Newton High Schools (North and South) were out on strike, she said, the junior high was considering going out, but the kindergarten was still placid.

The faculty, many and indeed most, were swept by hysteria. Friday afternoon an all-university faculty meeting was held in the Stock Pavilion, life and limb being comparatively safe out there. (Before I went over, I had looked out the window on the National Guard patrolling the Lincoln Terrace, and seen a truck drive up. What were they bringing, I wondered. Tear gas? Bombs? Live ammunition? It was supper. The driver let down the tail-piece, spread out the meal, the men picked up plates and cups and utensils, helped themselves, and had a nice picnic.) Neither Harrington nor Young appeared at the meeting.

McShain, Young's second-in-command, for a reason I couldn't fathom then and can't now, allowed students to be present. Our own firebrand Siff spoke with great effectiveness (if you like that sort of thing), so strongly supported by student yelling and screaming and applause that it was just like Hitler supported by his bully boys in Edward Murrow's "I Can Hear It Now." In my Line-a-Day I called the meeting three and a half hours of hell and said the faculty were all crazy.[565] I had a dinner engagement that night, at Blackhawk Country Club with the Strangs and Gwen and Ham, who were here with them; Ham had come out at Allen's request to address the architects' convention in Rockford. I was very late, but they understood, and looked with great interest at the day's *Cardinal*, which I brought along. "It's a handbook for revolution," said Ham; and so it was: directions on how to prepare for tear gas; where first aid stations would be so you could avoid the hospital, where you'd have to give your name; how to behave on being arrested; numbers of defense attorneys to call; and so on. At this point Harrington announced his resignation. Since it was not to take effect until October 1, it is hard to see any motive for the announcement just at this time except self-protection. This was not just a rat leaving a sinking ship; it was a rat gnawing through the few planks in the bottom first to make sure his successors would go down more quickly.

We never officially shut down, but Young announced that the following Monday and Tuesday classes should be canceled, and the week would be one of "concern and involvement." I was furious at his backing down. On Friday I had written him a letter of support at keeping the university open, which later when all the shouting was over he politely acknowledged. I had comparatively little trouble myself practically, since I had already announced an impromptu and handed out preliminary material; so I merely gave my students the option of writing on that or on how they felt the present situation affected them as teachers. All over the campus classes were beginning to resume, and all my students were back. I still think he had no need to wobble, but he was under a lot of conflicting pressures, poor man.

On Wednesday, when we were looking forward to a little peace and quiet, a student tossed a pepper gas bomb into the Bascom Hall ventilation system during at the 11:00 o'clock hour. My class and I were lucky, being on second floor only and right at the stairs above the side door, so we all rushed out onto the Lincoln Terrace. Most people had much more trouble getting out, particularly those who got in the elevators, and some had to be rescued by firemen on ladders. I must confess at once that I was completely taken by surprise and

---

565 Cronon and Jenkins (1999) note that both groups of participants at this lengthy, emotional meeting—the estimated 1,200 faculty and 1,000 students—"agreed that it was not the faculty's finest hour" (p. 511).

instinctively obeyed the law of self-preservation by rushing down the stairs as fast as I was able with my students behind me, instead of waiting nobly to be the last man off the ship. On the terrace we caught our breath and wiped our eyes, a couple of the girls exclaiming so hysterically, "I'll never go into that building again! I'll never go into that building again!" that I invited them on the spot to come out to Frost Woods to meet Friday, and we settled the transportation then and there since we were all together. We had a very pleasant meeting Friday, and an even pleasanter informal lunch to which all stayed who had the 12:05 period free as well as the 11:00. It's easy to develop rapport under such circumstances. When I wondered where the student got the pepper gas bomb he had thrown into the ventilator, one man said there would be plenty lying around. A friend of his was using as a paperweight one thrown at him which hadn't gone off. No one minded going back to Bascom Monday, when peace was thoroughly established, but the unlucky 11:00 o'clock got routed out again by the fire alarm, set off by someone who also released the sprinkling system and sent tons of water crashing down into a lecture room. Without undue haste we moved out on the lawn—it was a beautiful spring day—and carried on, ignoring the fire engines rushing up the hill behind us.

Every little sheep was back in class by May 20. And I worked with everyone, individually or by twos and threes, until I was completely satisfied that they had done all the work of the course. There's no way of knowing how many faculty handed out grades for no work. I felt bitterly we were producing an illiterate citizenry all right. Unquestionably, it was true that grading presented a difficult problem. "Young has issued a statement saying that academic standards must be maintained, and that no punitive measures must be taken against striking students. It is obvious to a three-year-old that the two statements are mutually exclusive." The same afternoon as this last fire alarm we had an L&S faculty meeting, where many members were honestly and legitimately concerned about students who had been forcibly prevented from coming to class or from studying in the library. The final vote allowed every student in the college who wished to do so, to take advantage of the Pass/Fail option (hitherto restricted) in any or all courses. I would have had no compunction in voting this for graduating seniors, all others who wished to be allowed incompletes which they could remove the next semester. I did feel it an academic sell-out to extend it to everyone. As a matter of fact, I felt—and feel—Pass/Fail is a sell-out anyway. I don't know what the current opinion will be when you read this. My own experience was limited, since my course was required, and Pass/Fail generally did not apply, but my work on the Phi Beta Kappa election committee and my personal interview with every initiate did give me some wider contact, and I never encountered a student I respected who wanted to avail himself of it.

I said goodbye to my students on May 25. All through the years I saved the last few minutes to say something special. Usually, of course, I didn't write it out, and I was surprised when among my papers I found that I had done so this year. But it was a special year, and apparently I had made a special effort to make the strongest attack I was capable of on the parrot-cry of "relevance." Another interesting comment from the man I spoke of earlier was that he had found, after he left college, there was "relevance" in a lot of things he hadn't seen it in while he was there.

> In this course I always save the last few minutes to say goodbye—and to say something unfashionable which I think needs to be said. Over the years what was unfashionable became fashionable, and then I say something else.
>
> Today I want to say first with what great reluctance I say goodbye. You will not know how great until you are teachers yourselves and see your class walk out of the room for the last time. Today I feel more reluctance than ever before; perhaps it is my age, since I shall not meet many more classes; but I think mainly because this has been the most painful semester I ever knew, and we went through it together. There are obvious differences in ideologies among us. The first time we met I said we shared many things, above all the same professional choice. I hope among what we share is respect for those with whom disagree. If we do not share this, you will not live long under a democracy, so I hope we share it, and I believe we do.
>
> One thing we do not share is youth, and I speak to you as an old woman. I do not address you as "the younger generation"; obsolescence sets in very quickly these days, and you will soon be in touch with a generation younger than you. There have always been differences between youth and age, as Aristotle well pointed out. But youth and age share much: humanity. Emphasis in the past has generally been on the sharing, while today there is dangerous emphasis on the difference. I want to tell you what I see as the advantage of age, an advantage you will increasingly share: experience. When you are old you see over and over again how quickly the future becomes the past, and you learn to think of the future as well as you can before you take present action, and to think of what the past shows you of the future.

I ask you for your own sake and for that of your students to think of time as a continuum. It is true the dead hand of the past can crush the future; this has often happened. But today I think the danger is the opposite one. Those who will live longest with the future are forgetting the past and thereby cutting themselves off from humanity, which binds the dead to the living and living to the unborn, in Conrad's words. Our present is full of turmoil; future historians may well spend a lot of time on it. This semester I have looked very carefully at our present—through the events here you have shared, through TV, newspapers, newsmagazines, and I have been fortunate that friends in other parts of the country have sent me much material I would not have seen. But two books I read by accident have thrown the greatest light for me on the present: one, the autobiography of the director of the Tate Gallery in London, on an incident that occurred there in the 40's; and the other, a new examination of the Salem Witchcraft trials. These two, much better than anything contemporary, helped me to understand what those around me were doing and saying and thinking.

When I went to the University of Colorado for a conference a few years ago, I was impressed by the legend carved over the library door: "He who knows only his own time remains forever a child." But Auden puts it even more strongly: "Though the great artists of the past could not change the course of history, it is only through their work that we are able to break bread with the dead, and without communion with the dead a fully human life is impossible."

Our last department meeting this year, the last time I ever saw Tim Heninger, was one in which he ran very true to form. He called a special meeting when we had thought we were through, because he had turned in the department budget to the Dean with a raise for Siff, whom we had voted not to retain. The dean had refused the raise and he wanted us to protest the Dean's refusal. The week before, Siff (according to the grapevine with Tim's blessing if not indeed at his instigation) had filed a suit against the Regents, the President, the Chancellor, and the members of the Executive Committee of the English Department, asking $50,000 damages because we had not renewed his terminated contract. We were all served with processes, no doubt the easiest job the server had ever had, because we were all assembled in one place and he could simply hand them out.

With all these dignitaries on the list before me, I didn't feel there was anything to worry about, nor was there. Eventually the suit was simply dropped. It seemed to me a racket, like the first breach-of-promise suits. But it certainly showed that times had changed. In our gentlemanly way, we had always assumed that if the Executive Committee decides, for whatever reason, that a man has no future in its department, it is to his advantage to find somewhere else as soon as he can with as little publicity as possible thrown on his deficiencies. It had never entered our innocent heads that we'd have to get chapter and verse like a private eye for the days a man cut classes or failed to give his examinations or misused university stationery or led a mob up Bascom.

A letter from Alice Ream about now in her forthright way represents a widespread attitude.

> What is absolutely incredible to me about these riots is that if you had a 7 year old throwing bricks through windows or lighting fires in houses you'd bang his bottom until he knew better. But anonymous gangs of young adults seem able to do these things with impunity and then shout "brutality" if the police arrive and someone gets hurt. Also, I am fed up with adults who agree it's all their fault. That's bunkum. These rioting punks have never produced anything in their lives, never held a responsible job & are still being nurtured by the establishment they proclaim so loudly is rotten. Well by heaven I'm for the establishment because I don't want to live in anarchy & chaos which is all the loud-mouths have to offer.

Her opinion is echoed in different language by Professor Norman Risjord of the History Department here. For four successive semesters his lectures on American History from colonial days to the present were broadcast on WHA to my very great enjoyment. And I should say he is no old fuddy-duddy, but a young man who didn't care what icons he smashed and who, delivering an elementary course to freshman and sophomores, struck dear old Merle Curti as playing a bit overmuch to the gallery.[566] His concluding lecture gave his opinion merely—too soon for anything else since no thorough research has yet been done—on this Far Left movement. It was ineffective, Risjord said, and one reason was that there was no joining with Labor. Labor rather disliked and despised the students, who had no knowledge of grim reality themselves and exploited the parents they professed to despise. (A current *New Yorker* cartoon showed a father playing a guitar to his son and singing "My son says I'm square and funny/

---

566 Merle Curti (1897–1997), a Pulitzer Prize-winning American historian, taught at Wisconsin from 1942–1968.

Demolition

But he drives my car and he spends my money.") More importantly, Risjord said, the movement was undisciplined. No real revolution has ever succeeded that was not marked by iron discipline. These people had none. They did their own thing when they felt like it, and that was that. Another professor later said, interestingly enough, that no one knows why the student riots started or why they stopped.

This June was the occasion of the golden wedding anniversary for Aunt Hannah and Uncle Jim, and since you all remember it I needn't describe it. It was a great success. I spent the summer at the Island. On August 25 as I was walking down to the post office, Mary Jane Reed called over that there had been a bombing at Wisconsin.

Sam Blount wrote he thought the university would not open, but he was unduly pessimistic. Joyce Steward flew out to drive home with me, and I got details from her. People living blocks away had been thrown out of bed by the force of the blast. All windows were broken in the University Hospitals across the street. Sterling Hall was three-fourths rubble. A brilliant graduate student in Physics, Fassnacht, had been spending the night there watching the progress of an experiment, and had been instantly killed. He left three very young children, two of them twins. The arsonists had disappeared, after having been picked up by the police and let go again. When I got back and went on campus, there was a hand-lettered sign on what was left of the building: "The Physics Department calls upon students and staff of the University of Wisconsin to reject and resist violence in our community." The appeal was honored.

Through this time, I thought continually of the metaphor of a man in high fever, acting in delirium. Often I believe he would never recover. I was wrong. It was as if this bombing was the crisis of the disease, and the patient woke up the next morning weak but sane. I think this act ended the era not only here but all over the country. There had been a great deal of passive support for the revolutionaries: the tie of youth, the instinct to dislike any authority, a too-permissive upbringing which left its victims quite unable to deal with the situation when they said "Gimme" and the answer was "No"—none of these applied any longer after this death of the innocent bystander in the wrong building. Karleton Armstrong was found in Canada, extradited to Madison, tried in the fall of 1973, found guilty of arson and manslaughter, and sentenced to twenty-three years in prison—nearly the maximum sentence the judge was able to give.[567] There was apprehension that the trial might revive rioting; it did not. After conviction, before sentencing, the judge listened to nearly three weeks of hearings at

---

[567] For a detailed account of Karl Armstrong's radicalizing experience at UW-Madison and his role in the Sterling Hall bombing, including his trial, sentencing, and release from prison, see Bates (1992).

which those who felt Armstrong was a hero said so. It made no difference. Times have changed. Of course a lunatic fringe is still in existence, here as elsewhere, and there were to be one or two outbursts in 70–71. But to all intents and purposes this was the end.

My last year was comparatively so quiet as to be dull, and I really didn't have enough to do. The only connection I had with staff now was to make out the teaching schedule for a literature course offered instead of 102. I had little respect for it from what I heard of it, and glad I had no connection with the course itself. I enjoyed my own students—but more first semester than second. I don't know whether I was just losing my effectiveness and my power to "relate" (a girl had told me a few years before, "I never saw any other teacher relate to her students the way you do!"), whether the group happened not to be very good, or what. But I had no pangs about its being my last semester, and I was quite ready to go.

Young had announced at the end of the preceding semester that arrangements would be made for students to participate in the fall political campaign and had appointed a committee to work them out. This annoyed me very much at the time. It seemed a problem to make out a calendar when you didn't know whether, or how many, students would be on campus for two weeks of it. Worse yet, to nominate something as more important than the work you came to college for was to belittle that work. If the students could go off campus for two weeks without missing anything, why not four, eight, sixteen? We could then be a correspondence school, which would be cheaper and simpler for everyone. This idea was named after Goheen of Princeton, its initiator.[568] Young, however, put an escape clause in his statement. "Each faculty member should announce early in the semester if a student who misses classes for campaign work will be able to make up his course studies. If the course of studies is too intense, the student should be urged to drop the course and take it later." Rather reluctantly, because I was just establishing rapport and didn't want to spoil it, and resentfully, because I felt the Administration had put me in a false position, I did announce that my course was an "intense" one, where each day's work depended on that of the day before and led to that of the day after and none could be missed, and that if anyone wanted to go campaigning, he should drop the course. I needn't have worried. There wasn't a flicked of interest on anyone's face, and Young announced on TV that week that there was "an amazing lack of interest in politics on the part of all the students he had talked to." This state of affairs was national; I heard the figure recently from a Political Science professor

---

[568] Robert F. Goheen (1919–2008), a professor of classics at Princeton who, at age 37, was appointed the sixteenth president of that university (1957–1972).

that student participation in campaigns that semester was less than 1% more than it had been two years or four years before.

This fall I remember one false alarm. A girl came in for conference, looking apprehensively out the window, and told me Humanities Building had been evacuated on a bomb scare. "It's frightening to see a crowd," she said. It seemed a student, unprepared for a test, had cleared the building and sent a thousand students into the street by calling in an alarm. But the Telephone Company had just put us on a special arrangement by which a call cannot be terminated until the party called hangs up. The man was immediately identified, and the police arrested him as he was trying to destroy his telephone.

One real flare-up in May I described to Janet, who this year with Dick was at Tallahassee.

> When they held the first rally on the Lincoln Terrace Monday noon, with the Viet Cong flag presiding (at least I think it's the Viet Cong flag), there was very little general interest and everyone kept basking in the sun. As the hard core carried the flag down the Hill chanting "Ho Ho Ho Chi Minh!" there weren't more than thirty or forty of them, and passers-by didn't even bother to look. But it has built up now and reminds you of last year. Tuesday night they were rampaging all over the university district, holding their rallies in front of the dormitories so that when the police threw tear gas to disperse them the tear gas went into the dormitories where it stayed. It's a pity the bad guys have the brain and the good guys are feeble-minded.
>
> Yesterday when I was having a conference at 12:30 the shouting got so loud I had to shut the window. Then I saw the police come out and spread out in a long line in front of the building. They are really frightening in their riot clothes; they need them all right, but they don't look human. Then a wave of rioters came up the Hill, the tear gas bombs went off, everybody ran, and things settled down again.
>
> This morning I drove around the university district and Langdon Street at 6:15 a.m., the ideal time for sight-seeing, with hard-working rioters and police all catching up on their sleep. The streets were hosed down and littered with trash, some obviously the remains of bonfires, as well as rocks along the gutters. In places where the concrete is set in small blocks

instead of big squares, the blocks had been pried up. I hear it was a bad time in the Library yesterday, not from tear gas but from stink bombs, which the rioters had planted all over the building. Some were found in time, but not all, and some staff members were sick or even fainted from the ones that weren't.

But this was all. Even this was highly localized. While on that afternoon you couldn't get through the mob and the tear-gas to get in the front door of Bascom, if you came in the back from the other side of campus you wouldn't have known anything at all was happening out of the ordinary. No longer was there any support for the Revolution. A new conservative student paper, the *Badger Herald* (Bill Strang was faculty advisor) was making money, and the *Cardinal* was losing it.

As for the department, our new chairman, Charles Scott, was a blessing. The word went round early that he intended to have as few meetings as possible, and he carried out that resolve. When he hold meetings, we tended to our knitting and got out at 5:15 or 5:30, greatly helped, of course, because such rebels as were still around knew they were beaten and didn't bother coming. In person, Charles is impressive: tall, solid, ugly, Lincolnesque; in temperament, he is deliberate, and he has a calming effect. He is a man you must respect; he is a man of integrity.

I am proud to remember November 16, 1970, which made amends for a good deal of previous suffering at Executive Committee meetings. Among those coming up for the regular tenure review, four assistant professors had requested, as it was their legal right to do, a public hearing. At this, no one not a member of the Executive Committee might speak but anyone might attend. One of the men had such a following among the revolutionaries left on campus that we had to leave the usual meeting room, 350, which holds about a hundred and fifty, and move downstairs to 165, which holds over five hundred. Even there, many people were standing, "Bastille types with snake's eyes," I wrote, and they had come on purpose to create disorder. Charles was superb. He stood like a rock, and for three hours by sheer force of character kept the room quiet while the discussion went on. It ended in a 2 to 1 vote against promotion, just as it would have done in private session. Perhaps this was the department's finest hour. After the last few years, what a deep-down comfort it was to me to be able to feel pride in it again.

My last year, to my relief, I lived out in Bascom. The department moved to Helen White Hall the subsequent summer. Originally, the move was planned for the proceeding summer, but there is no recorded case in history where a campus building was ready for occupancy on schedule, so I knew I needn't worry. Like everyone else, I am glad and proud that such an impressive building should be named for Helen, and I appreciate the courtesy of a small office of my own in it now. But I felt closer to Helen in the shabby old Bascom where I had known her, and I always loved my view down the Hill over the Lincoln Terrace. When Bill was in college, I'd see him go up or down and know my own son out of all the thousands. I had a front seat at the combat scenes, and in the peaceful years I had loved to stand at the window for a few moments between classes, watching the panorama of the ascending and descending students all through the cycle of the year.

Henry Pochmann[569] and I both retired this year. Henry appropriately had a big reception at the University Club one Sunday in May, with a number of guests from out of the city. I had a small party at the Lacys' home a couple of weeks later. It was a beautiful golden day and a lovely party—small and intimate so that I could feel everyone there cared about me personally. Kathy and Bill represented the family, and there were a few close out-of-department friends like the Curtises and the Freds. Janet and Dick were in Florida, but sent me my corsage. As I arrived, department wives were bringing in flower arrangements and cookies, very sweet and neighborly. The Lenehans took me to dinner at the Edgewater[570] afterwards, with Joyce and Tom Tanselle and Alvin Whitley (who picked up the check), and we ate overlooking the lake while the golden sun sank in the sky and turned the water golden. A golden day.

But to tell you what no one else must ever know, least of all the friends who wanted too much to make the occasion just what I would like, the golden memory is tarnished with a tinge of disappointment. In Browning's poem, Andrea del Sarto, looking back ever an unhappy life, says, "I regret little, I would change still less";[571] and looking back over a happy one I echo him. But there are a few things—trivia—that I could wish had been different. I wish I'd started Greek when I went to Holyoke instead of going on with Latin. I wish I'd been able to do a lot more square dancing. I wish I had gotten started young on birdwatching—there must have been some kind of nature walks in the spring at Holyoke, you'd think, wouldn't you? But if there were I never knew about them. And I wish I could have had a retirement party like Charlotte Wood's. You will remember I described it: a big dinner party at the Union, with all the senior department members and all the teaching assistants there, Paul Fulcher presiding with the light touch in his finest hour, complimentary speeches from Dick Quintana, then our chairman, and two or three others, on what she had done

---

569 Henry A. Pochmann (1901–1973), an American literary scholar, taught at UW-Madison from 1938–1971.

570 A historic hotel on the south side of Lake Mendota, built in 1948 and renovated in 2014.

571 Robert Browning (1812–1889), the Victorian poet, published the poem "Andrea del Sarto," translated as "The Faultless Painter," in 1855. Andrea del Sarto (1465–1530), an Italian painter, was a contemporary of Leonardo da Vinci, Michelangelo, and Raphael.

for the department and the university, and then every senior member and teaching assistant coming up afterwards, in a long long line, personally to shake hands with her and thank her and wish her well. After I once realized my place in the department was permanent, for many years in odd moments I used to fantasy that someday I would have a retirement party like that; I even used to compose the few well-chosen words in which I would return thanks and bestow upon the young folks a priceless and inspiring bit of wisdom. Only, unlike Charlotte, I would have you three children all there too, which would show that I had had the best of both worlds.

Well, if I had retired in 1966, when the world was not so innocent as it was in 1914, or when Charlotte retired, but more innocent than it is today, perhaps I might have had such a function.[572] And I might very well have retired at sixty-five, for Wisconsin is unusual among comparable institutions in having seventy as mandatory retirement age; in most it is sixty-five. If I had done so I would have missed five painful years. But I would also have missed five exciting years, the most dramatic and exciting of my life, and years in which I learned a lot about myself and my world. I say "a lot"; I don't want to use the superlative and say "the most of all my life." In point of fact, I have learned a great deal from this process of going over my life for you here. One thing stands out; as long as you live you never have to stop learning. But it may be—it may be—that the lessons you learn in old age are the hardest lessons you learn in all your life, and it may take more bravery than most of us possess to keep on with the learning.

---

572 Charles Scott had offered to host a retirement party for Thomas on behalf of the department, but she refused. He eventually convinced her to attend the small gathering at the Lacy's (interview with the editor, June 2016).

WILLIAM LENEHAN: A REMINISCENCE

Bill Lenehan joined the English Department on this campus in 1962. A word or two on the situation is in order. Freshman English was the largest course in the university since it was required of all entering students in all colleges. On the basis of testing during registration week, a small proportion of the entering class was assigned to the Honors course, English II; the bulk of students took English 1a followed by English 1b. Edgar Lacy chaired the course. The students in the big group were taught by teaching assistants; those in English II by full-time department members who came with the rank of Instructor. Bill Lenehan was one of these.

I met him at the party always given for new members, but got no particular impression of him. It was my business however to visit all new instructors in their classrooms so before long I went to an hour when he was conducting composition discussion. The aim of the instructor was two fold, to allow the students to express their own ideas and to conduct a useful discussion on a topic suggested by their own themes. This required not only competence but also character. I had been in Bill's class less than five minutes before I knew that his teaching was of a superlatively high nature, and when the bell rang I slipped off leaving students crowding round his desk to make points they must bring out and went in to Edgar Lacy's office to tell him I had found the man who could take over Freshman English when he went on to something else. And so it turned out; Edgar took the important position of Associate Chairman and Bill chaired Freshman English as long as the course was offered. And I worked out very closely with him during that time.

Bill was completely reliable. This period included the time when teaching here was more exciting than any other before or since. Half the people on campus were working tooth and nail to force the university to close, and the rest of us were trying to keep it open. One rather melodramatic day the Dean put in a hasty call to say a riot situation was developing and we should go home at once. We could hear the riot all right for a mob was coming up the hill like the stormers of the Bastille in *A Tale of Two Cities* except that they were yelling in English instead of French: SHUT IT DOWN; SHUT IT DOWN. Bill got me out by the back door of Bascom and over to my car, parked in front of the Observatory, turned it on a dime, and we escaped by the peaceful Ag campus.

Of course it wasn't always that exciting. But it was never simple or easy. We were dealing with large numbers. The students disliked the course because it was required and they had to write a theme a week. It did have, however, a side which meant a good deal to many students; they were known by face and name to the instructor almost from the first day they went to class, unlike the situation in the big lecture courses. The staff didn't like it because they all wanted to teach literature instead of composition. We always had a large proportion on the staff of people new to teaching here and many new to teaching altogether. This meant giving much time and attention to staff training, including class visitation and staff meetings, and many individual conferences on theme annotation and other things. Whatever the situation, Bill was always in command and met routine or emergency with intelligence and composure.

He was a stimulating teacher. Perhaps my account of my visit to his class has already suggested that, but I want to add a personal experience which occurred some years later. The Lenehan family were having Sunday night supper at my house, and my grandson James who had just returned from a year of study abroad in Germany was of the party. I hadn't been very successful in hearing about his experiences and what they meant to an American undergraduate but that night, sitting across the table from Bill, he talked freely and fully. It was not in the slightest a dialogue; Bill slipped in a word or question or transition from time to time which kept James talking. After the Lenehans had left I asked him why he had talked so well for Dr. Lenehan when he hadn't for me, and he said "I guess he knew the right questions to ask"—a good definition, I submit of a composition teacher in the kind of writing we were dealing with.

Above all I admired Bill's breadth of vision and understanding. He knew what the course meant to the department, the different colleges, the university, the staff, the student. Above all, he cared about the students; he had a sensitivity to their needs and opportunities and experiences. He and they were in it together. There's an old American definition of education as the student on one end of a log and the teacher on the other.[573] With Bill learning was a shared experience. I once heard a student say of the teacher he was leaving "He will always be a little part of me." No teacher was ever more generous to his students of this gift than Bill Lenehan.

---

573 This phrase is attributed to U.S. President James A. Garfield (1831–1881), a graduate of Williams College, who at an alumni dinner in 1871 paid tribute to college president Mark Hopkins by describing the ideal college as Hopkins and a student together in a log cabin; as the phrase circulated, the log cabin was replaced with a log.

LUNCH AT THE MADISON CLUB: MAY 12, 1986, OR THE KING AND I

The Chancellor was hosting a luncheon in Daniel Travanti's[574] honor at the Madison Club, to which, to my surprise, pleasure, and trepidation in equal parts, I was invited.[575] According to my custom, I arrived early—also because I thought faintly that the guest of honor might possibly be early too, which might give me a chance to speak to him; otherwise, I feared I'd be as unnoticeable among the university VIP's as a Babe in the Wood buried by robins under the leaves. No one else of the party had arrived at all, but after consulting various Club staff members I penetrated to a basement dining room giving on a small one which could be cut off by folding doors, containing a single long table seating five or six on each side and one at top and bottom respectively. Not a soul was in sight but a waitress distributing glasses, to whom I was obviously invisible; so I sat down in a convenient chair to rest from the trek up to Monona Drive to get the bus. Then it struck me the others were probably assembling upstairs and I'd be missed when noses were counted and should go up again; but in the corridor I met the Chancellor's secretary, who had given me my invitation over the telephone and was now coming down to check the table and distribute place cards.

She put the host, Vice Chancellor Cohen since Shain is out of town, at the head;[576] Arlie Mucks, Alumni Association Director, who has been masterminding Mr. Travanti's coming and goings for four days, at the foot; the guest of honor in the center of one of the long sides; and me at his right. I sat down in my chair to be out of the way. For several of the men I had some slight points of contact. Dean Cronin's son has written *Changing the Landscape (*ecology in New England),[577] which Merle Curti has recommended to me, and which I

---

574   Daniel Travanti (b. 1940), a Wisconsin-born American actor known for his role in the 1980s television drama *Hill Street Blues*.

575   The lunch, sponsored by the Wisconsin Alumni Association, was also an awards ceremony, where Travanti was one of five recipients of the Alumni Association's Distinguished Service Awards (Wolff). In 1995, Travanti again honored Thomas at a Gala Tribute to Teaching, held at UW-Milwaukee.

576   Bernard C. Cohen (b. 1926), a political scientist trained at Yale, taught at Princeton before joining the faculty at UW-Madison (1959–1989). He became acting chancellor in 1987. Irving Shain (b. 1926), a chemist trained at the University of Washington, taught at UW-Madison (1952–1977) and was Chancellor from 1977 until his retirement in 1986.

577   A reference to the book *Changes in the Land: Indians, Colonists, and the Ecology of New England* (1983), by distinguished environmental historian William Cronon (b. 1954), who taught at Yale University before joining the history department at UW-Madison in 1992.

had bought, read, liked, and given to Anne. Bob Rennebohm is head of the Wisconsin Foundation, which annually entertains the Emeriti at breakfast; I'd gone various times, but, more to the point, he and his wife Jean are intimates of the Youngs, and Dot Smart is fond of Jean and has often talked about her. Haberman (Speech) on my right and next to the Vice Chancellor, remembered Bill as an athlete at Whisky High. The other two men were placed directly across from Mr. Travanti and me.

The guests began to arrive. Cohen, whom I'd never met, introduced himself and several others. I was talking to one of them and never even saw Daniel Travanti come in. But I heard a voice say, "That's my lady," and I looked up, saw him, and rose to greet him. He came around the table to my side and we both sat down.

Travanti was looking very handsome with a nice tan which I took to be Californian, but he said no, it was Wisconsin, from a canoe trip he had just taken with his niece. He spent four days in Kenosha with his family before he came over to Madison. His newspaper picture had looked unfamiliar and unlike him to me, and I said he was much handsomer in real life than in it. He agreed it was a bad picture and said he was sorry they had used it, and then told me more about the Kenosha visit. He had spoken at a lot of schools, beginning with very young children and going up through high school, and had loved it all; if he were not an actor, a teacher is the only other things he could conceive of being.

By now the party was getting settled and going through the business of ordering, and thereafter there were only a few scattered times when Mr. Travanti and I got in a few words with each other edgewise. Of course he was the focus of attention, and the talk was mainly a monologue on his part, with a prompting question or two from one quest or another. He talked about leaving *Hill Street Blues*, which he will do when his contract expires in 1987, and the producer's efforts to induce him to stay one, and his agents; about acting in *Hill Street Blues* (the working day is never less than twelve hours and fourteen is by no means unusual); about *Murrow*, which had appeared on HBO in January; and about *A Case of Libel*, which was to air on Channel 21 Monday evening. He didn't, I'm afraid, get much to eat in spite of the tender loving care of the waitress, who was obviously out of her mind with ecstasy at waiting on Daniel Travanti. She served him always before the host or anyone else and when she brought in the dessert wagon and collected orders skipped over me altogether. Fortunately, his order was apple pie, which is sustaining, and he did get a chance to eat a good deal of it. In addition to doing by far the lion's share of the talking, he had to autograph sheet after sheet of paper the guests had brought for souvenirs to take home to friends and family. Of course I didn't need one and the Alumni Association bunch had had four days to get their needs filled, but everyone else

Lunch at the Madison Club

lined up. Dean Cronin's son, the ecology writer, is a great Furillo[578] fan, his father said.

Once in a while Mr. Travanti and I did have a little exchange. I distinctly remember his saying to me "You're sweet," and I think that was elicited by a compliment I paid him on his strength and energy, which had been stressed in the feature story. "What nature project do you have on hand?" he asked me once. At the time I had no notion how he knew anything about my interest in nature, but two days later it suddenly came to me that Will Mackenzie[579] must have told him all about the nature walks at the Island. I said I didn't have any on hand just now but was having a wonderful time with a group of Japanese and Korean wives of graduate students and research faculty, and he seemed quite taken with that, for later I overheard him telling someone else about what I was doing.

I did tell him one story from last winter. Hiroko's six-month-old baby wasn't as sleepy as usual one morning when we arrived, so his mother put him down on the floor for a few minutes before she took him up to bed. He wanted to turn over and struggled hard to do it but couldn't; his muscles weren't yet quite at the command of his will. When I left later that morning, I struggled hard to get my snow boots on; my muscles are increasingly less and less responsive to my will. I said it was funny to think of the baby so near the beginning of his life and of me so near the end of mine together in the same room sharing the same frustration. Mr. Travanti said, "It's poetry."

Except for the Vice-Chancellor, the university men had engagements and were beginning to excuse themselves and leave. The Alumni group moved up from their end of the table to the side across from us, the conversation grew general, and I was drawn into it. Arlie Mucks sat down opposite Travanti and said to me, "Well, you did a good job with Daniel." As was always true and as I always say, I said that at the end of each semester when I looked at my class lists for the last time, I always felt I had done nothing; I hadn't been able to be of much use to the weaker students, and the good ones had done it all themselves. I quoted "The days to come are the wisest witnesses," and said I'd lately been impressed by Time's revenges. In 1958, Mr. Travanti had been in a class of the best freshmen in the university, and they all were not only very able but very hard working. He and all of them, I knew, had worked hard on their weekly themes to hand in to me. In 1986, after I had seen *Murrow* and wrote about it to the star, I had worked very hard so he wouldn't think my letter was too dumb. They laughed, and he said he had worked hard on his themes—and when they

---

578 Captain Furillo, the main character in *Hill Street Blues* played by Travanti.
579 Will Mackenzie (b. 1938), an American television director and actor.

483

were returned my comments took up more space than the original theme. And he hadn't wanted to have to read them; he just wanted me to put "It's OK" or words to that effect. I felt I owed Ed Lacy and Freshman English a tribute, so I said course policy was always to tell the student his good points and then go on to show how he could write even better next time; I'd always practice that policy myself and always stressed it in staff training. And I said I had worked with every age level at college, including graduates as indeed I was doing now, and the age I enjoyed most was the freshman. I've always felt that to be the definitive year.

Mr. Travanti brought up things he remembered which I had completely forgotten, including coming to my office in Bascom to order his Phi Beta Kappa key and my asking him to deliver the response for the seniors at his initiation banquet. (He said he had lost his key, and Arlie Mucks at once undertook to see about getting it replaced for him. Mr. Travanti is used to being waited on, like a surgeon at an operation.) Probably I was Phi Beta Kappa secretary here for ten or fifteen years, and one of my jobs was to select the students to respond for the juniors and seniors respectively, since I saw them all and was the only officer who did so. I must have asked twenty or thirty students to speak at the banquets, and I had entirely forgotten Daniel Travanti was one of them, though he must have been the obvious choice his year because of his stage experience. In his six semesters here he starred in five plays (by university policy he was not allowed outside activity his first semester) and he remembered all the plays and their directors. But of course only one person in his life had ever asked him to speak at a Phi Beta Kappa banquet, and I was the one.

Finally, the party broke up. I thanked my host and looked around for Mr. Travanti to say good-bye. He was standing behind me, waiting, and he took me into the big dining room now empty except for a staff member or so clearing up, and over to a private corner. But the privacy lasted only a moment, for the head waiter came over to ask if the star would pose with our waitress, who wanted the picture to take home to her husband, and he went over at once to do so.

Upstairs there was a bit of confusion—have you got a ride, which way are you going, whatever. I meant to take the bus home, which I could get only a couple of blocks away, but Arlie Mucks overheard me and was as horrified as if I were going on a motorcycle or by ox-cart. He insisted he would see I got home, so he, his assistant Gayle Someone-or-other, Mr. Travanti, and I got into his van. We went first to leave Travanti at his motel, the Howard Johnson on Johnson Street.

Driving over, Travanti told us stories, which I think I started because I made some reference to the throngs of people all over the country and the world into whose homes he comes weekly and who look for him as if he were an idolized member of the family. Once in London a cabby had refused to take a fare from him because the man his wife had had so much pleasure from *Hill Street Blues*. And once in Portugal walking down a street at night he heard on man calling to another, "Furillo! Furillo!" and the two came running over to talk to him. Once at the Dickens Fellowship, I put in, a member back from Yugoslavia had spent the night in a little village where everyone turned up weekly at the pub, the only place in town with TV, to his show. It seems that abroad everyone is always surprised to find him so tall; apparently his height doesn't come across on the film. He must be about Tom's height, an inch or two over six feet, a bit taller than Bill. His weight had come up at lunch when one of the men who had been at the gym with him in the morning challenged the others to guess it. Bob Rennebohm was close with 190 lbs; it's 193.

When we got to the motel Arlie and Gayle went in with him and came out laughing. In the lobby a student had said, "You look familiar. Who are you?" He answered, "I'll tell you my name if you'll tell me yours." When she did and he said, "Daniel J. Travanti," she nearly went through the roof. He had signed over twenty autographs for everyone on the motel staff. Then Arlie took us back to the Alumni Office singing Travanti's praises all the way as the nicest, the most obligating, the most cooperative guest they've ever had (Bob Hope has been there three times). Before the visit Mucks had written Mr. Travanti to ask whom he wanted to see and what he wanted to do when he came. He wrote back he wanted to see Mrs. Ednah S. Thomas—head of the list—and two or three people from Speech and Drama, and then he'd be glad to do anything and everything they'd like him to. From the Youngs the next day I learned that he had gone to the hospital to see Ronald Mitchell, his old major professor, who is very seriously ill. Then we arrived at the Alumni Office, Aries and Gayle went in, Arlie brought out a young staff member, and she drove me home to Monona. The clock struck twelve and the coach turned back into a pumpkin.

When Will Mackenzie years ago told me about Daniel Travanti's meteoric rise to fame, he said, "It couldn't have happened to a nicer guy." He may be a blazing Hollywood star earning enough money to pay off the national deficit, but he's the nicest guy I ever met.

REFERENCES

Bates, T. (1992.) *Rads: the 1970 bombing of the Army Math Research Center at the University of Wisconsin and its aftermath.* New York: HarperCollins.

Brereton, J. C. (1995). *The origins of composition studies in the American college, 1875–1925: A documentary history.* Pittsburgh, PA: University of Pittsburgh Press.

Clark, H. H. (1966). Influential teachers of literature at the University of Wisconsin. *Wisconsin Academy of Sciences, Arts, and Letters, 55,* pp. 1–9.

Connolly, F. X. & G. H. Levin. (1968.) *The art of rhetoric.* New York: Harcourt, Brace & World.

Cooke, B. W. (1979). The historical denial of lesbianism. *Radical History Review, 20,* pp. 60–65. doi: 10.1215/01636545-1979-20-60.

Cronon, E. D. & Jenkins, J. W. (1994.) *The University of Wisconsin: A history.* Vol. 3, *Politics, depression, and war, 1925–1945.* Madison, WI: University of Wisconsin Press.

Cronon, E. D. & Jenkins, J. W. (1999.) *The University of Wisconsin: A history.* Vol. 4, *Renewal to revolution, 1945–1971.* Madison, WI: University of Wisconsin Press.

Fleming, D. (2011). *From form to meaning: Freshman composition and the long sixties, 1957–1974.* Pittsburgh, PA: University of Pittsburgh Press.

Gold, D. (2015.) "Whose hair is it, anyway?" Bobbed hair and the rhetorical fashioning of the modern American woman. *Peitho, 17*(2), pp. 172–199.

Hollis, K. (2004). *Liberating voices: Writing at the Bryn Mawr summer school for workers.* Carbondale, IL: Southern Illinois University Press.

Lacy, E. & Thomas, E. S. (1951). *Guide to good writing: A composition text for college students.* Harrisburg, PA: Stackpole and Heck.

Maraniss, D. (2003.) *They marched into sunlight: War and peace, Vietnam and America, October 1967.* New York: Simon and Schuster.

Mastrangelo, L. (2012). *Writing a progressive past: Women teaching and writing in the Progressive Era.* Anderson, SC: Parlor Press.

Mastrangelo, L. & L'Eplattenier, B. (2004). "Is it the pleasure of this conference to have another?": Women's colleges meeting and talking about writing in the Progressive Era. In B. L'Eplattenier & L. Mastrangelo (Eds.), *Historical studies of writing program administration: Individuals, communities, and the formation of a discipline.* West Lafayette, IN: Parlor Press.

Palmer, M. R. (1955). The United States Armed Forces Institute. *Public Administration Review, 15*(4), pp. 272–274. Retrieved from http://www.jstor.org/stable/972982.

Thwaites, R. G. (1904). A brief history of the club. In W. H. Hobbs, *The Madison Literary Club 25th Anniversary, 1877–1902.* Madison, WI: Parson Printing.

Vasiliev, A. A. (1952). *History of the Byzantine Empire, 324–1453.* Vol 1. Madison, WI: University of Wisconsin Press.

Wolff, B. (July 1986). Back to the hill from Hill Street. *Wisconsin Alumnus, 87*(5) p. 11.

AFTERWORD

David Fleming
University of Massachusetts Amherst

When Susan McLeod first approached me about participating in this project, I was a little apprehensive, as I think any historian would be when a previously unknown source turns up regarding a research project he or she has already put to bed. On the one hand, I was curious to see what Ednah Thomas had to say about a topic I thought I knew a lot about—the abolition of the University of Wisconsin (UW-Madison) Freshman English (FE) program in the late 1960s—especially when I heard from David Stock that her memoir dealt at length with the topic. In fact, as I soon discovered, she regarded it as the single most important event of her professional career. In the final paragraph of the memoir, she even writes that, although the last five years of her time at UW-Madison (1966–1971) were painful, they were "the most dramatic and exciting" of her life; and, in her Foreword, she suggests that sharing her experiences of that period, negative though they were, was one of the main reasons she wrote the book. Given the time and effort I put into those years, researching and writing *From Form to Meaning: Freshman Composition and the Long Sixties, 1957–1974*, Ednah Thomas' declaration of their importance was affirming.

On the other hand, I couldn't help but wonder: what if her account exposes errors in my own? What if she provides information that upsets my version of the events? I had a momentary "house of cards" feeling: to put so much work into one's edifice and then to see it all come crashing down when a single piece is pulled out. . . . Fortunately, in my opinion, the two accounts are broadly compatible; they often coincide closely, and, when they don't, they're more often than not complementary, each adding information or perspective the other lacks. On one fundamental point, to be discussed below, they differ starkly; but it's the same difference that my account—based as it is on original interviews with graduate Teaching Assistants from the time—has with all previous faculty accounts of the events in question. (On all this, I'm grateful to David Stock who, in his excellent introduction, carefully analyzes where Thomas' account and my own overlap, where they diverge, and where, both books now published, there are still unanswered questions.)

However the two versions align or misalign, I would certainly have benefited from reading this memoir long ago. Thomas' account of the history of FE at UW-Madison from 1945 to 1971 is vivid, insightful, and invaluable. She provides useful background on the UW-Madison English Department, going back literally to the 1920s. She shares important memories and insights about the early years of her work in FE with Edgar Lacy, about whom Thomas is unusually informative and even eloquent. And she supplies rich information about the daily administration of the course, from enrollment, scheduling, and placement to staff training, supervision, and support, perhaps unique in our records of a FE program during the golden age of U.S. higher education—especially valuable because it concerns what was arguably the best-organized and most thoughtfully designed and managed FE program in the country.

In their Foreword and Introduction, Susan McLeod and David Stock identify several admirable, even innovative, features of the program that can be attributed to Ednah Thomas: for example, the care with which teaching assistants were taught to respond to student themes and the use of minimal grading in the course. Having managed a large freshman composition program myself, I was especially struck by the combination of efficiency and humanity in Thomas' work. She was clearly a skillful manager: impressively detail-oriented, unfailingly reliable, extraordinarily hard-working, morally scrupulous. But she was also deeply *human* in her treatment of students and teachers alike. To give one example that I would like to have known about earlier: throughout my book (and even in this Afterword), I refer to the graduate instructors at UW-Madison as "teaching assistants" or "TAs," as most of us still do today; but Ednah Thomas writes in her memoir that she and Ed Lacy considered the term, and especially the acronym, belittling and that they always called their staff members, simply, "teachers" or "instructors" (185). It's a small but telling detail.

Academic readers today will probably most be struck by the generous *social* life with which Ednah Thomas surrounded her colleagues, students, and teaching staff (to say nothing of her friends and family). The memoir is *replete* with descriptions of the dinners, parties, teas, picnics, receptions, baseball games, and other events she hosted, mostly at her home in the Frost Woods neighborhood outside Madison; it is a picture of academic life that contemporary academics will simply not recognize. In the composition programs that I have been associated with, we pride ourselves on providing snacks and occasionally drinks once or twice a year at staff meetings; Ednah Thomas entertained literally dozens of teaching assistants in her home *every Sunday evening*, had the whole English Department over *every fall* (with numbers approaching 200 some years), invited *every new professor* to her house when they arrived in Madison, went out of her way to meet and welcome the spouses of *every teaching assistant on her staff*, knit booties for *every baby born in the program*, sent Christmas cards every year to her *entire staff*, had *all* of her students over at least once per semester, etc. It is no wonder that, at the end of her career, when she glimpsed academic life on the other side of the "hinge" of the late 1960s (on that word, see my book, 215n79), Ednah Thomas didn't like what she saw. (By the way, I loved finding out that one of her greatest regrets in life was not having done more square dancing!)

I also learned things about Ednah Thomas here that directly contradicted statements I made in my book. In his "Introduction," David Stock mentions one, my claim in a 2009 essay that the FE program at UW-Madison was "innocent" of rhetorical theory during the 1950s and 1960s, precisely when it was being revived in English Departments across the country. In fact, it turns out that Thomas' teaching was deeply informed by classical rhetorical theory—though the influence seems to have been felt primarily in English 309, Composition for English Teachers, not in Freshman English, and more towards the end of her career than at the beginning—note, e.g., the Aristotelianism of the ETS and NDEA workshops she planned and conducted in the early 1960s.

All this—her unfailing attention to details, her deep respect for students and staff, her abiding hospitality, her thoughtfulness about course design and teacher training—speaks to Ednah Thomas' extraordinary devotion to FE during these years. If others in the department didn't care about the course—lowly and universally disliked—she did. "Very, very few people care about teaching utilitarian prose," she writes; and most faculty look down on freshmen: "I have always felt the first semester of college, like the first year of life . . . is one of our most important learning times." The fact is, as Lacy and the rest of his faculty colleagues quickly discovered, presumably to their great relief, Ednah Thomas was, in her own words, "genuinely interested in freshman composition and genuinely enthusiastic about it," and she found working in the program "the most absorbing and productive professional work" of her life.

Unsurprisingly, we get a darker picture of FE as the memoir proceeds. Thomas divides her history of the course into two long chapters, one titled "Construction," treating the years 1951–1966, a generally happy time; the other, "Demolition," recounting the painful last five years, 1966–1971. Together, the two chapters comprise over half the memoir. The latter chapter, which touches most directly on the narrative I lay out in my book, provides a first-hand account of the dramatic events at UW-Madison during the late 1960s, which made Madison one of the two or three most important sites of student protest during the period: there's the anti-draft sit-in of 1966, the Dow riot of 1967, the Black strike of 1968, the Mifflin Street riot of 1969, the TAA strike of 1970, to say nothing of the endless faculty meetings, the tumultuous student protests, the constant classroom disruptions. We have other accounts of all these events; what Thomas adds is the response of a thoughtful observer who was neither a direct participant nor a random onlooker. It's the response of a relatively conservative white woman in her late sixties, an English professor, who, without the Ph.D., was identified primarily as a teacher and a teacher of teachers but who gradually worked her way up the administrative levels of her own department. By the end, she was, in a sense, at the center of UW-Madison undergraduate *and* graduate life, perhaps the key authority figure in the largest undergraduate course, and the largest employer of teaching assistants, on campus, who nonetheless refrained, as a woman in a male-dominated culture, from playing a determinative role in the most dramatic confrontations. The image of her standing on the fire escape in the back of Bascom Hall, watching the Dow riot of 1967, while Ed Lacy and others stayed in their offices working, is memorable. We often see her here sneaking into and out of buildings by the back stairs or sitting in on decisive meetings but not actually taking part. Yet we know from her memoir that she was *intensely* involved, intellectually and emotionally, in all this turmoil, even if she seems in the end not to have played a direct role in any of the most important decisions.

(In the memoir, Thomas frequently talks about the view from her office on the third floor of Bascom Hall, looking east towards the center of UW-Madison's campus, a view that gave her a front row seat onto Lincoln Terrace below, where so many of the most dramatic marches, protests, and demonstrations of the late 1960s took place. As it happens, the editors at the University of Pittsburgh Press placed on the cover of my book a black and white photograph of an immense sea of people on Lincoln Terrace during this period, identified inside as "Crowd gathered on University of Wisconsin-Madison campus for Martin Luther King Jr. memorial march, April 5, 1968," courtesy of the UW-Madison Archives. The photographer looks down on the scene from a height—as if from a third floor window in Bascom Hall. I can't help but think that Ednah Thomas witnessed the exact same scene from a nearly identical vantage.)

Regarding the final years of FE at UW-Madison, there is much here of interest. Thomas provides valuable information about the Master Teaching Assistant Program, which she designed and implemented (and which earned her promotion to full professor in 1966), an ultimately unsuccessful attempt to adapt FE to the dramatically increasing size of the University in the 1960s. She writes about the gradual replacement of Ed Lacy by Bill Lenehan as the decade wore on. She describes experiments in power sharing on the joint faculty/teaching assistant FE Policy Committee during those last years. And she confirms the largely negative account in my book of the leadership provided during this turbulent time by English Department chair Tim Heninger.

There are also intriguing tidbits that left me wanting more information. Previously unknown to me, for example, was the intra-faculty discord surrounding the fiery October 28, 1969, English Department meeting with teaching assistants, during that fateful abolition semester, when, apparently, Thomas was promised a speaking role by Heninger but never actually allowed to speak. She mentions a letter she wrote in protest but never sent, though it is not provided in the memoir itself. One wonders if events might have developed differently had Heninger given her the floor at that meeting.

As for the central question itself: were the UW-Madison English faculty justified in abolishing Freshman English in 1969, and could that decision have been avoided or handled better, Thomas provides, as I read her here, three interrelated answers. The first and perhaps main one is predictable and coincides with other accounts from faculty at the time: Freshman English at UW-Madison was abolished in 1969 because of teaching assistant insubordination. Clearly, the very size of the program had become unmanageable or nearly so—the number of students and teaching assistants associated with FE was simply too large, a problem compounded by the drastic changes that had taken place in manners, dress, and politics, changes that made personal interactions on a campus like UW-Madison increasingly fraught. Thomas vividly describes the disrespect, even hate, she felt from students and teaching assistants alike during this period for no other reason than her age and institutional position. She repeats the charge that protest ringleaders were mostly out-of-state students. And she makes a case, one still made in some quarters today, against the very idea of a teaching assistant union, the organization she blames for exacerbating the rift between FE faculty leaders and graduate teaching staff at UW-Madison.

But, as I discuss in my book, the actual evidence provided here of *widespread* teaching assistant insubordination in UW-Madison's FE program is sparse. What we get instead are exasperation and complaint, often with one or two egregious examples offered in support. She repeats, for example, the same tired anecdote I heard again and again in my research, about the Freshman English teaching assistant giving out grades by having students draw cards from a deck. But, as I ask in my book, in a program this large, with teaching assistants so diverse, in a state still largely rural, with most students and teaching assistants still mostly just wanting to do their work and finish their degrees, did the faculty in 1968–69 exaggerate the problem? Did the disruptive radicalism of a few teaching assistants, admittedly distracting, justify the drastic steps taken?

What I didn't quite expect was the hostility Thomas directs toward other *faculty* here, especially ones she thought insufficiently confrontational during this time of student protests and teaching assistant demands. She expresses vehement anger at many of her own colleagues—including Lacy—who are referred to here as "appeasers," with explicit comparisons to the enablers of Hitler in the 1930s. One must forgive Ednah Thomas for these moments: most of us weren't there, we don't know how we would have responded, we would not likely have done better, we may well have done worse. But when she writes about insufficient faculty confrontation against the excesses of the protestors, did "confrontation" have to mean abolishing the very course to which she had devoted the deepest professional commitments of her life? Was there not a way of resisting, or at least containing, the worst excesses of the most "revolutionary" teaching assistants in a way that would have saved the course itself? Couldn't the faculty have waited for the protest movement to die down, as it did, as all eventually do, and then pick up the pieces and go on, perhaps prepared to change for the better?

In two places in the memoir, in fact, Ednah Thomas hints at the kind of personal philosophy that would have counseled such an approach: early on, in talking about a childhood fear of fire, she wishes her parents had talked to her more not just about how fire destroys but about how one survives a fire, how one repairs one's house or builds a new one: "No one can know what misfortune, great or small, will come to him, but human nature fortunately possesses a very deep-rooted characteristic, the instinct to meet the emergency, to rise to the occasion, to deal with the misfortune, to clean up and go one. I've observed this in history, in literature, and in life, and I ask my descendants to trust to it, believing that they may do so safely." Similarly, later in the book, and speaking specifically now about the disruptive tendencies of students in the 1960s, Thomas writes, "[O]f course you'll realize it's simpler, easier, and more dramatic to involve yourself in overthrowing an institution than it is to try to keep it going, while you must recognize it has many faults." Doesn't this apply as much to the faculty who allowed FE at UW-Madison to die as it does to the protestors who tried to overthrow it?

We should remember, of course, how much Ednah Thomas had put into Freshman English by 1969, how hard and for how long she had worked to build it up, and how distressed she must have felt by the carelessness of those around her, students, teaching assistants, and faculty alike. In fact, it's hard at times not to suspect that her own impending retirement may have made her susceptible at the end to simply giving up on FE and letting the program self-destruct rather than trying to see it *through* the crisis. She was by then in her late 60s; retirement at age 70, in 1971, would happen whether she wanted it to or not, and so the long term future of FE at UW-Madison was becoming less and less her concern. But where were the freshmen at this point in her thinking? Where was her eloquent defense of the teaching of "utilitarian prose," the project she was so "genuinely interested in and enthusiastic about," the great, absorbing task of her professional life? Had she by 1969 fallen into the trap of the *manager*, for whom, in the end, it's the bureaucracy one is most committed to, the institutional order that has become one's primary devotion?

There's a third explanation available here. Perhaps the crisis of Freshman English at UW-Madison in 1969 was less about any particular people—trouble-making teaching assistants, weak-willed faculty, a deflated administrator on the verge of retirement—and more about the system itself, one that was, in its very form, unsustainable. I tried to get at this explanation in my book, when I looked at the over-extension of the teaching assistant system at UW-Madison—too many unsupervised graduate student teachers in charge of too many important undergraduate general education courses and filling too many graduate seminars for too many research-focused faculty. Thomas herself addresses this contradiction in her memoir: "First, the assistants wanted the money the university paid them even if they weren't willing to do what the accredited university representatives thought they should. . . . Second, the professors were unwilling to take any action which would reduce the numbers of their graduate students. So we had an indefensible system, with two vested interests entrenched in it." The specific problem of Freshman English itself, that course so open, so susceptible to being used by others for their own purposes, only further complicated the situation. And when you add to all this the simple fact that FE at UW-Madison at this time was just too big, with too few faculty involved in it, it's easy to imagine an embattled and lonely administrator, without much power in her department, feeling that the whole thing was unsustainable.

Still, I continue to think that one lesson of this memoir—for compositionists, for writing program administrators, for educators in general—is to *never* voluntarily give up curricular space if you can avoid doing so. If others take the space from you, after fighting the good fight against them, so be it. But don't do it to yourself. Because the end result is clear: it will be very hard, perhaps impossible, to ever get that space back again. Yes, allow the project to change, to evolve, experiment with new mechanisms for organizing it, certainly try as hard as you can to keep it relevant. But don't surrender the space itself. Of course, surviving UW-Madison English faculty from that time will counter: this was precisely what intransigent and irresponsible teaching assistants prevented them from doing.

From Ednah Thomas' point of view, meanwhile, the single most important lesson of her life, at least professionally, was that she had been witness to the decline of U.S. higher education. After all, she had taught the returning veterans of the late 1940s and found them to be "the best students in the history of American education." From that perspective, it's easy to understand her disillusionment with the students of the late 1960s, whom she refers to as the "worst" in the history of American education: "trashing misfits" she calls them. It must have been truly disappointing, and the disappointment must account for perhaps the most notable feature of this memoir: its lack of any attempt at a happy ending. Yes, there are two cheerful addenda, written much later, one about William Lenehan for his retirement, the other about a 1986 party in honor of former student Daniel Travianti. But the memoir itself ends when Thomas retires in 1971, at the height of that era of riots and turmoil, the period she says most revealed to her the awful late twentieth century decline of U.S. higher education. In that sense, it's a sad story, but one that Thomas rather boldly prepared us for in her foreword.

But was Ednah Thomas being true to *herself* in this bleak assessment of U.S. higher education at the end of her career, this picture of "trashing misfits" occupying the seats that the "greatest generation" had filled a quarter century before? Either out of bitterness over what happened to her own program, or from a rhetorical effort to heighten the main claim of the memoir itself, did she overstate her own disappointment with the students and teaching assistants of the late 1960s?

Those questions are perhaps impossible to answer, but I believe a second contribution of this book, outside of its value as evidence for understanding a critical chapter in the history of freshman composition in this country, is its portrayal of a deeply devoted secondary and postsecondary English teacher in the mid-twentieth-century United States. In fact, some of the most moving passages of the book for me were Ednah Thomas' accounts of her life as a teacher during this half-century period.

And the best of those, in my opinion, is chapter six, about her year teaching high school English and history in Danielson, Connecticut, in 1924–25. If some of the chapters of this book could probably still use editing—no one, I think, will wish the chapter on World War II to be longer than it is—the chapter on Danielson is, to my mind, nearly perfect: self-contained, lovingly composed, completely original, and, for me at least, deeply moving. It is the story of a sheltered young woman, academically gifted but socially untested, unprepared to teach public school of any kind, let alone in a challenging situation, and simply being thrown into it—and, to her own and perhaps the reader's surprise, *thriving*, finding a dedication, an energy, a talent that she must have had no inkling of and which must have done much to direct the rest of her life and give that life meaning. The chapter stands, in my opinion, with the best examples of writing about teaching: Sylvia Ashton Warner's *Teacher*, Mike Rose's *Lives on the Boundary*, Tracy Kidder's *Among Schoolchildren*. The vivid portrayal, never self-congratulatory—in fact, deeply and touchingly modest—of a young female teacher in a small working-class mill town in the 1920s, completely alone, out of her depth, searching for her own path in life, not only trying to figure out how to teach and what to teach but also becoming deeply, memorably, devoted to her students, is among the best and most inspiring stories of a young teacher in her first job that I have ever read.

Afterword

That dedication to her students, that sense of purpose, which must have surprised Ednah Thomas as much as it surprises us nearly a century later, would carry her through her two years teaching English at UW-Madison in the mid-1920s, then, after more than a decade of keeping house and raising children, in correspondence courses with servicemen during World War II, then in the late 1940s in UW-Madison's Freshman English Program itself, including gratifying work in English 11, the Honors version of freshman composition. After 1950, her work in FE would be primarily administrative, including training and supervising teaching assistants, which would take up much of her time in those two decades; but she would show some of the old classroom spark in her highly important and innovative English 309, Composition for English Teachers.

Perhaps one of the tragedies of this book, and of the events Ednah Thomas relates here, is that this dedicated, tireless teacher, who was so skilled at both teaching students and teaching other teachers, and who was so adept as a day-to-day administrator, was probably ill equipped for the political wrangling involved in running a large, controversial program like FE during highly turbulent times. By the same token, it is to her credit that Ednah Thomas' greatest professional gifts seem to have been the most personal ones: classroom teaching, one-on-one tutoring, mentoring, advising, supervising. That's not to say she was a softie: if the Danielson chapter shows flashes of warmth, compassion, and humor, at UW-Madison in the 1950s and 1960s, one can see why teaching assistants were afraid of Ednah Thomas. Dedicated, purposeful, organized, hard-working, and strict—she made no attempt to hide her high standards and uncompromising demands.

The final thing I want to say about this memoir concerns Ednah Thomas as a writer. I have dealt here mainly with her role in a controversial set of historical events, commenting also on the way she writes about her own growth as a teacher. I haven't yet mentioned how much pleasure I derived from this book as a *reader*. As I hinted above, the manuscript could probably have used some additional editing to make it shorter and more palatable for a wide audience. Susan, David, and the family no doubt took a light touch to preserve the memoir as Ednah Thomas wrote it. I understand that.

But even with its flaws, this memoir was clearly not written by someone mechanically recounting her life. It is the work of a genuine *writer*. And, although Ednah Thomas didn't really see *herself* as a writer (see, e.g., the first page of the memoir), she clearly had a writer's sensibilities and a writer's skills. The Danielson chapter is one example of those sensibilities and skills, but there are others. They reveal her talents of pacing and organization, her feel for telling details, her ability to capture the drama that surrounded her work at UW-Madison, especially at the end of her career, as well as the day to day pains and pleasures of an ordinary life in twentieth century middle America.

And there were passages that I thought simply exquisite: the image of Yale Professor C. F. Tucker Brooke, the great Shakespeare scholar, in his office before a lecture in the 1920s, his hands shaking nervously; Ednah sitting with Wright Thomas by Lake Mendota, "in the sunshine, while, from time to time, a falling leaf struck the water with a sound like a note of music;" a woodwind quintet playing Vivaldi on Lincoln Terrace in the same place where students had noisily protested just days before.

I mention all this not just in praise of the memoir, and in admiration of Ednah Thomas, but because drawing on one's own experience as a writer when teaching writing to others is an important point of principle in my field. Janet Emig complained in the late 1960s of high school English teachers who were themselves not writers and who therefore often misrepresented writing to their students and probably thereby thwarted their writing development (see my book, 78). I worry about that to this day, even at the college level. I don't expect writing teachers to be novelists and poets; I do think it helps if they themselves *write* and see themselves as writers *of some kind*—with the attendant love of language, desire for readers, and ambition to create. The lack of such traits is hard to compensate for in the teaching of writing, whether with kindergartners or adults. Without that experience, that identity, that love, the activity we stage for our students can easily become just busy work in the perpetuation of school itself.

Fortunately—for her students and for us, her readers—Ednah Thomas was a writer. If this book shows her to be much else besides—a mother, daughter, friend, colleague, teacher, administrator—it is definitely testament to *that*.

– October 25, 2016

www.ingramcontent.com/pod-product-compliance
Lightning Source LLC
Chambersburg PA
CBHW070123080526
44586CB00015B/1530